D1605601

Date: 1/26/17

796.510976 WIS
Wise, Kenneth, 1950-
Hiking trails of the Great Smoky
Mountains /

Hiking Trails of the Great Smoky Mountains

HIKING TRAILS OF THE GREAT SMOKY MOUNTAINS

◆ SECOND EDITION ◆

Ken Wise

THE UNIVERSITY OF TENNESSEE PRESS / KNOXVILLE

Library of Congress Cataloging-in-Publication Data

Wise, Kenneth, 1950–
Hiking trails of the Great Smoky Mountains / Ken Wise. — 2nd edition.
    pages cm
ISBN 978-1-62190-054-2 (pbk.)

  1. Hiking—Great Smoky Mountains (N.C. and Tenn.)—Guidebooks.
  2. Great Smoky Mountains (N.C. and Tenn.)—Guidebooks.
  I. Title.

GV199.42.G73W57 2014
796.5109768'89—dc20
2014004155

For Jamie

Away from Fools I'll turn my Eyes,
Nor with the Scoffers go;
I would be walking with the Wise
That wiser I may grow.

—Isaac Watts

Contents

Acknowledgments

Things change. This is no less true in the isolated wilderness of the Great Smoky Mountain backcountry than of any other sphere of nature or human activity. Change has overtaken the first draft of *Hiking Trails of the Great Smoky Mountains* published in 1996; and this current draft represents nearly twenty years of additional research as well as a reflection of the changes that have taken place on the Smoky Mountain trails over this span.

I will be eternally grateful to Bob Lochbaum who not only supplied the distances for each of the trails in this book, but carefully reviewed the manuscript in its entirety to verify accuracy. A detailed explanation of Bob's protocol in measuring the Smoky Mountain trails is outlined in the introduction.

To Don Casada I owe a debt of gratitude for his careful reading of the North Carolina half of the book, offering sage advice on the context of the storylines, and pointing me to sources of which I was unaware.

Tim Robbins, a retired ranger with the Great Smoky Mountains Park Service, reviewed the entire manuscript, directing my attention to errors in the historical context as well as offering additional vignettes that would be of interest to the reader.

Over the past twenty years, Annette Hardigan, librarian at the Great Smoky Mountains National Park, has been unfailingly helpful in chasing down the most obscure publication or document that might contain some slice of Smoky Mountain lore that made for a better storyline. I am greatly indebted to Annette for sharing her knowledge of the sources of Smoky Mountain history.

A long-forgotten philosopher once advised that people should strive to maintain close contact with childhood friends and siblings because "they know what a doofus you really are." Accordingly, I asked my brother, Steve, to read the manuscript. I got back about what I had expected. His lengthy comments and criticism were the only ones I received that were delivered with great peals of laughter and accompanied by exaggerated allusions; nevertheless, the derision forced me to sharpen the style, inject movement into the narrative, and focus on the reader perspective.

This book was a long and arduous project. Often, when the trail was steep and the pack heavy, or when progress on the research seemed hopeless, I just wanted to quit. Encouragement and cheer came from my wife, Deborah, who is the most understanding friend and companion I could ever possibly imagine.

Introduction

Twenty years after a daring escape from a Confederate prison in North Carolina, General J. Madison Drake recounted the dangers he and his fellow soldiers confronted while fleeing north through an unfamiliar country. General Drake understood the Great Smoky Mountains to be something of a safe haven, inhabited by a fierce race of Union loyalist willing to aid those fighting against the Confederacy. He had also been made aware that the Smoky Mountains were the haunts of guerillas, outlaw soldiers hiding from the war in the remote recesses of the mountains and conducting indiscriminate depravations on any they encountered. Traveling through this country, Drake wrote,

> was bad and exceedingly fatiguing. We had now reached the chain of the great Smoky Mountain Range—the very place of all others we had been particularly cautioned against visiting just before we left Charleston, owing to the presence there of Indians, most of whom, an East Tennessee captain had assured us, were acting in the interest of the Confederacy. The mountains here rose to a height of between five and six thousand feet, and seen from a distance they seemed bathed in a mellow haze, like that distinguishing the atmosphere of Indian summer. We passed through a gap which had a great elevation; beneath us were vast canyons, from which came up the roar of the creeks, greatly swollen by recent rains. We looked down upon the tops of mighty forests, never tiring of their grandeur. The path-ways grew rockier as we clambered along, but the air was pure and refreshing, and had I been comfortably clad and in "good condition," I should have reveled in the beauty of the scenes, which like a panorama, constantly presented new beauties. As far as the eye could see, on every hand, stood long lines of towering crags, from which there seemed no outlet. Once I turned on the crest of a prodigious mountain, and, looking Carolinaward, I saw our old friend of the Blue Ridge and Allegheny ranges, scattered for miles in friendly groups among the dark and forbidding-looking forests. Before us and behind us were deep ravines, and beyond all, uncounted peaks.

In his inauspicious flight into the towering mountains of "dark and forbidding-looking forests," Drake glimpsed wilderness of indescribable beauty yet tinged with mystery and foreboding. Ten years earlier and under different circumstances, James M. Safford had made a comparable observation. Safford, the recently appointed geologist for the State of Tennessee, was conducting fieldwork in the Great Smokies in pursuit of a scientific understanding of the geology of the mountains. Tucked unobtrusively within the rigid prose of his scientific report, Safford comments that the mountain's "bald summits, its semi-arctic plants and balsam peaks, the magnificent scenery it affords; its roaring rapids and wild cascades; its game and the trout of its cold streams, altogether make it an elysium."

It would be well into the twentieth century before Safford's "eylsium" would become widely known to the outside world. Even as late as 1875, while preparing for a trip to Qualla, a Cherokee village hidden deep in the recesses of the mountains, Rebecca Harding Davis could muster only a few useless scraps of contradicting information about the places she intended to visit. Davis was told

> the Indians were half starving; somebody had gobbled up their appropriation from Congress years ago; they never had an appropriation; Colonial Thomas was a white man who had governed them autocratically for twenty years. The nation was Christian, and in a condition of peace and prosperity, with him at its head: the nation was heathen, living in polygamy and unbridled revolt, and Colonial Thomas was a maniac chained to the floor. The road to Qualla was a safe and good one; the road was utterly impracticable even for the mountain-mules. But nobody had ever seen Qualla itself, and nobody had ever wanted to see it. On that one point all were agreed.

Similarly, in planning for his sojourn into the Smokies in 1904, Horace Kephart would later confess that "the most diligent search failed to discover so much as a magazine article, written within this generation that described the land and its people. Nay, there was not even a novel or story that showed intimate local knowledge. Had I been going to Teneriffe or Timbuctu, the libraries would have furnished information a-plenty; but about this housetop of eastern America they were strangely silent; it was *terra incognita*." In 1926, when members of the Great Smoky Mountains Conservation Association began exploring the mountains in anticipation of a proposed national park, they discovered disjunct pockets of eighteenth-century pioneer culture hidden away in isolated areas. How such anachronisms survived well into the twentieth century is not only a sociological phenomenon, but also a subject for the history of the Smoky Mountains in light of its peculiar geography.

It was at least 15,000 years ago that the first human beings—small nomadic bands of aboriginal hunters venturing into the wilderness in search of game—began encroaching on the Great Smoky Mountains. The Cherokee followed, building villages along the larger streams in the lower elevations. Although historians credit the Spanish conquistadors Hernando De Soto (1540), Juan Pardo (1566), and their followers with being the first Europeans to see the Smokies, white men likely did not reach the mountains until 1673 when two traders, James Needham and Gabriel Arthur, attempted without success to barter with the Cherokee. Needham was killed. There is no record of pioneers again attempting to reach the highlands for the next hundred years.

Around 1769 small groups of Scotch-Irish, German, French Huguenot, and English immigrants began settling in the northeast corner of Tennessee along the

Watauga River, but a strong presence of the Cherokee checked any advance into the highlands. The areas immediately to the north and west of the Smokies were opened for settlement in 1789 when the federal government formed the Territory South of the River Ohio, which extended to "the Painted Rock on French Broad River; thence along the highest ridge of said mountain to the place where it is called the Great Iron or Smoky Mountain." An official declaration by the federal government supposedly prohibited settlers from entering the Smoky highlands until the land could be acquired through a treaty with the Cherokee.

With the Treaty of the Holston, 1791, the Cherokee ceded the northeast corner of the Smokies and with the Treaty of Tellico, 1798, the southern portion. The Cherokee relinquished their claim to the remainder of the mountains with the Calhoun Treaty of 1819, after which the Smokies were officially open for settlement. Despite the treaties, massive numbers of settlers did not begin moving into the mountains until the Cherokee were forced out along the Trail of Tears in 1838.

White settlers ventured into the Smokies primarily from the north and west rather than from the south and east. Because of the complex geography of the region, it was easier to enter from the wide valleys on the Tennessee side than to traverse the row upon row of high, rugged, densely forested ranges that flank the Smokies to the south. Many of the settlers were descendants of Scotch-Irish immigrants who forsook the old country to escape religious and political suppression for the promise of better economic conditions in the New World. Some of the immigrant ancestors landed in the old Swedish settlement at New Castle, Delaware, which, in an odd twist of historical fate, was to be of great significance for the future settlers of the Smokies. It was the Swedes who introduced the log cabin to America. This architectural type was adopted by the settlers and brought into the mountains where it continued to persist well into the twentieth century, long after it had been abandoned by the rest of the country.

In the old countries of Scotland and Ireland, the general population was divided against itself by an intense belief in clan brotherhood, often manifested in inter-clan hatred and blood revenge. Despite the close contact with settlers of other European descent and the severe conditions of the new environment, these Scots and Irish settlers managed to retain something of their clannishness, transferring it to their new homes in the Smokies. The strong isolation of the mountain coves and the relative difficulty of travel fostered this tendency, as the settlers cut themselves off from the outside world. Early travelers to the Smokies commented on having met mountaineers who had never ventured more than a few miles from the cabins in which they had been born.

On encountering Smoky Mountaineers for the first time, Rebecca Harding Davis depicted them as having "clear-cut Huguenot faces and incredibly dirty clothes" and living in "unlighted log huts, split into halves by an open passage-way, and swarming with children, who lived on hominy and corn-bread, with a chance opossum now and then as a relish. They were not cumbered with dishes, knives, forks, beds or any other impedimenta of civilization; they slept in hollow logs or in a hole filled with straw under loose boards of the floor." Moreover, Davis sensed, they were shiftless. On passing a road in great disrepair, she concluded that the men were "too lazy to even lay a log toward the mending of this road. They'd rather run the risk of rolling down into the river, wagon, steers and all, as some of them do every winter."

After becoming acquainted with perhaps the same mountaineers encountered by Davis, Horace Kephart in *Our Southern Highlanders* submits a telling conclusion to his essay on the native mountaineer when he attempts to "remind the reader again that full three-fourths of our mountaineers still live in the eighteenth century, and that in their far-flung wilderness, away from large rivers and railways, the habits, customs and morals of these people have changed but little from those of our old colonial frontier."

Life in the more remote reaches of the Smokies was harsh, barren, and changeless. There were few roads into the higher elevations. The only one crossing the main Smoky divide was the old Oconaluftee Turnpike, upgraded by the Thomas Legion of the Confederacy during the Civil War, and, at its best, no more than a "difficult mule path." There were but few churches and schools prior to the twentieth century. The practice of medicine was essentially non-existent. A cursory examination of the badly worn headstones in the mountain cemeteries gives the impression that few mountaineers reached adulthood, and, on occasion, whole families perished at once, being carried away by influenza, typhoid fever, rheumatic fever, and hookworm.

The primitive hovel of the poorer mountaineer was often a crudely constructed one-room cabin with neither loft nor cellar and having no windows and only dirt for a floor. The lower elevations of the Smokies, however, were populated by higher-quality homes, frame houses floored with hand-hewn puncheons and shingled with shakes of white oak. In addition to a loft and a cellar, the house would be trimmed with wide porches and accoutered with a huge fireplace built of rocks, mortared with clay, and finished off with a half-log mantle. It would likely have been surrounded by a split-rail fence enclosing a compound that might include a large cantilevered barn, a springhouse, corncrib, blacksmith shop, gear shed, and a variety of other outbuildings. Running water and electric lights were not uncommon in the more prosperous mountain homes.

Except in the wider bottomlands and the more fertile expanses like Cataloochee and Cades Cove, mountain farming in the higher elevations was subsistence agriculture consisting primarily of vegetable gardens and corn patches. Corn was the chief staple of the poorer mountaineer's diet as well as the fodder of choice for moonshine stills. Farmers living near the more populated areas had access to grist mills for having their corn stone-ground to meal while the isolated mountaineer relied on the tub mill, a rickety homemade device that could barely grind a quart of corn over the course of an hour. Apples from the orchard, chestnuts from the woods, and vegetables from the garden were stored for winter use in underground cellars. Honey was collected from bee-gums, and sorghum was squeezed through horse-driven presses and cooked into molasses in huge open kettles. In summer, blackberries, blueberries, and huckleberries were gathered and eaten fresh.

It is of more than passing significance that many of the first settlers in the Great Smoky Mountains were Scots and Scots-Irish. As Frederick Taylor points out, the national origin of the settlers is "a fact worth remarking on since Scotland and Ireland were notorious in the Old World for the primitive rapaciousness of their land ethics. Raised in cultures with almost no tradition of wise usufruct, the Scots and Scots/Irish immigrants and their descendants helplessly recapitulated in the Southern Appalachians what they knew of land abuse." As the settlers advanced into the higher elevations, their most expedient means of clearing farmland was to cut only enough trees for a small patch, then girdle the peripheral ones so that neither shade nor encroaching roots would stunt the crop. After a few years the trees would rot and fall, only to be gathered into heaps and burned. The patches, planted in corn, were quickly worked into exhaustion and then abandoned as worthless, after which the settler would move elsewhere to repeat this same ruinous practice. When asked if he did not despair of these endless shiftings, one mountaineer replied to Horace Kephart, "Huk-uh; when I move, all I haffta do is put out the fire and call the dog."

Wherever settlements advanced, the wildlife was quickly thinned out with many species being hunted to extinction. The eastern woods buffalo and the elk were the first to go, sometime in the early nineteenth century. The disappearance of these large animals, accompanied by a drastic reduction in the Virginia white-tailed deer population, drove the larger predators, the wolf and the mountain lion, into an increasingly desperate reliance on farmers' livestock. The farmers, predictably, took revenge on these hapless predators. The mountain lion was gone from the Smokies by the middle of the nineteenth century and, fifty years later, so was the wolf. The Carolina beaver and eastern otter also disappeared from the Smokies. They, like the wild turkey and ruffed grouse, were deprived of suitable habitat. Other smaller animals also suffered losses, particularly those creatures that caused inconvenience to the farmer—the raccoons and turkeys in the corn patches and the weasels, foxes, and skunks that raided the chicken coops.

Nothing, however, matched the level of destruction visited upon the Great Smoky Mountains as that wrought in the war waged against the wilderness by the lumber companies. Timber had always been harvested from the slopes by the native mountaineers, owners of small tracts culling a select few species for their own use or for delivery to the local sawmill operator. By the early 1880s, the first wave of logging operations reached the Smoky Mountains. These early operations were characterized by what historian Robert Lambert refers to as peripheral logging, selective cutting in areas most easily reached by the loggers. The companies were interested only in certain species of lumber and thrived on the ready supply rather than on the economies of an integrated operation from stump to mill. Black walnut, cherry, and ash were the trees most widely sought, but before long yellow poplar and oak were in great demand.

These early operators, according to Lambert, relied heavily upon the natural flow of streams to provide transportation for a steady supply of logs to the mill. Teams of horses and oxen dragged logs to the summits of ridges from which loggers simply rolled or "ball-hooted" them down cleared lanes into the streams. In the rivers and wider streams, logs were retained in booms, then released to flow downstream to the mill when the water reached a favorable level. On the upper tributaries, splash dams were built, forming large pools upstream of a supply of cut timber. When the hatch to the dam was opened or exploded with dynamite, the released water flushed the timber down to a larger stream.

This dependence on water for transport proved economically inexpedient. During the dry seasons, low water levels in the streams disrupted the supply to the mills. Worse, perhaps, unexpected thunderstorms unleashing raging torrents down the mountain would burst the booms and scatter the timber for miles along the riverbanks. A downturn in the late-nineteenth-century economy eventually spelled the end of this less-than-efficient means of logging. By the turn of the twentieth century, most of the early lumber companies cutting in the Smokies had either failed or ceased operating and moved elsewhere.

But this was a mere and minor prelude to the destruction that would be wrought by the twentieth-century industrial behemoths that soon descended on the mountains with their arsenal of logging equipment, taking up great tracts of woodlands with the intent to clear-cut and exploit the forests for all they were worth. Their arrival in the Smokies coincided with an upturn in the economy, stimulating a strong demand for lumber at a time when the old hardwood properties in southern Appalachia were showing the effects of sustained cutting. The most revolutionary change introduced by this second wave of loggers was the adaption of steam-powered mechanization to the rugged conditions of the Great Smoky Mountains. The railroad locomotive and the machine-driven skidder brought the birch, beech, oak, chestnut, and other higher-elevation species into reach. Eastern hemlock and red spruce, also now within reach, were procured both for pulpwood and lumber.

Machine logging marked the end of selective cutting in most of the Smoky Mountains. Now lumbermen tended to harvest any timber that was "merchantable," which, according to Lambert, usually included any tree larger than twelve inches in diameter four feet from the ground. The economies of "clear-cutting," as the new practice was called, introduced a new set of outside elements into the heretofore undisturbed isolation of the mountains.

Hundreds of men, armed with saws and axes, were unleashed on the mountains. Others followed, sent to skid the logs, handle the animals, lay the railways, and build the trestles, bridges, and flumes needed to move the timber down to the mills. The lumber companies employed many of the locals. Some still owned small tracts in the Smokies; others had sold their land, but were permitted to stay in their homes though they were now company property. Hired hands brought in from the outside were housed with their families in portable shanties near the worksites or in one of the mushrooming lumber towns, places like Elkmont on Little River, Smokemont on Oconaluftee River, Proctor on Hazel Creek, and Crestmont on Big Creek.

Hotels, lumber camps, stringtowns, commissaries, and company stores sprung up to meet the influx of loggers. This new economy provided a booming cash market for homegrown produce. Garden vegetables, butter, eggs, honey, apples, peaches, grapes, chestnuts, pork, and venison were exchanged for money. The money, in turn, was used to purchase tools, farm implements, household goods, and other items the mountaineers could not make for themselves. With the growth of the cash economy, soon came the roads, schools, health clinics, and other amenities of modern society.

Within twenty years, the lumber companies had clear-cut slopes in virtually every sector of the Smokies, hauling out billions of board feet in timber. One lumberman bluntly outlined his company's objectives to Kephart. "All we want here is to get the most we can out of this county, as quick as we can, and then get out." Like the white mountaineer before them, when the lumber companies departed, they just "put out the fire and called the dog," leaving behind a mountain desert of stumps and tangled debris that Kephart later described as "wrecked, ruined, desecrated, turned into a thousand rubbish heaps, utterly vile and mean."

Ironically, it was the coming of the lumbering industry that stimulated the initial demand for the preservation of the Smokies as a national park. Reverend Canario Drayton Smith of Franklin, North Carolina is generally given credit for being the first to suggest federal protection of the mountains, a proposition he submitted as an editorial to a Waynesville newspaper. However, it was Chase P. Ambler, a retired physician from Ohio, who in 1899 fomented the first organized agitation to establish a national park in the Great Smoky Mountains. Ambler's idea was slow in gaining traction. Some factions insisted the Smokies become a wilderness reserve, and others contended it should be maintained as a national forest. On May 22, 1926, the U.S. Senate agreed in principle to the idea by approving "An Act to provide for the establishment of the Shenandoah National Park in the State of Virginia and the Great Smoky Mountain National Park in the States of North Carolina and Tennessee, and for other purposes." The act identifies the size and location of the proposed park and stipulates that it "shall be known as the Great Smoky Mountains National Park." The act further stipulates that the lands for the park would not be purchased with "public moneys," but "only by public or private donations."

With the 1926 act, the political and bureaucratic wheels were set to grind on their appointed missions. Suddenly, a way of life that had for generations been marked by constancy was now to undergo drastic change. Much of the area proposed for the new park consisted of no less than 6,600 separate tracts, many still owned by the small farmers whose families had controlled the land since the departure of the Cherokee. Within the next few years, nearly all human inhabitants were forced to leave, allowing the Smokies to return to wilderness. By 1934, the Great Smoky Mountains National Park was officially established.

As with the arrival of the lumber companies, the establishment of the national park introduced another wave of economic expansion. In the early years, the Civil Conservation Corps enlisted hundreds of young men to build infrastructure—roads and bridges, upgraded trails, campsites and campgrounds, and other amenities for future visitors to the new park. From among the local mountaineers, the Park Service itself recruited rangers to protect the wilderness and serve the tourists. What began as a mere trickle of visitors soon burgeoned into an influx of ten million tourists by the end of the twentieth century. The growth in numbers inevitably attracted what Edward Abbey once called "Industrial Tourism," a blatant and vulgar commercialism with its consequent degradation of the Cherokee and the Smoky Mountaineer to the rank of curiosities. This was not the intention of the founders of the park.

Both the history and future of the Great Smoky Mountains can be reconciled within the story of the Sibylline Books, prophecies kept by the Cumaean Sibyl and containing knowledge necessary to avert extraordinary calamities and expiate ominous prodigies. The Sibyl offered to Tarquinius, last of the Roman kings, nine of the books. King Tarquinius rejected her offer, recoiling from the exorbitant price she demanded. The Sibyl burned three and offered the remaining six to Tarquinius at the same price. The king again refused, whereupon she burned three more and repeated her offer. Coming to his senses, Tarquinius eventually relented and purchased the last three at the full original price, yet saving but a fragment.

HIKING IN THE SMOKIES

The trails crisscrossing the Great Smoky Mountains are like etchings on a rune stone, mysterious tracings left by ages of man's comings and goings. They once linked cabin to cabin, community to community, and, ultimately, generation to generation. They trace the significant courses, the main strains of the history of this insolated enclave of the southern highlands. These are paths of friendship, love, and devotion, of misery and joy, of exile and homecoming, of life and death, and each with its own story to tell.

Like the stories they represent, each trail has its own setting, purpose, style, and theme, and even a different beginning and end. Just as one must hear a story to appreciate the fullness of its meaning, so one must hike the trails to gain a true sense of the adventures they hold in store.

This book is a guide to the trails of the Great Smoky Mountains, intended to offer the bare outlines of their courses, something about where they begin and where they end, perhaps a cursory note on surviving place-names, and maybe a few disconnected facts about some event in their history. All of the trails outlined in this book are official trails, part of the accepted canon and enjoying the imprimatur of the Park Service. Each trail is accompanied by a schedule of distances and a descriptive narrative. When the narrative is strictly describing the course of the trail, the print on the page is in a light type. Whenever the narrative diverges into some adjunct discourse, the text appears in shaded boxes, alerting the reader that the trail description has been momentarily suspended.

Trail narratives are organized by sections roughly corresponding to the major watersheds in the Smokies. The sections are presented sequentially from east to west with those on the Tennessee side of the mountain followed by those on the North Carolina side. Because it traverses several watersheds in North Carolina, the Lakeshore Trail is treated as a section unto itself. Similarly, the Appalachian Trail is treated independently and placed between the larger division of the Tennessee and North Carolina trails. Except in the few instances where a trail's upper terminus lies along a road, the narrative begins with the trail's lower terminus.

Two trails not mentioned in this book are the Benton MacKaye Trail and Mountains-to-Sea Trail. Both are long-distance courses that incorporate all or parts of several trails in the Great Smoky Mountains. The Benton MacKaye Trail, nearly three hundred miles long, runs from Springer Mountain, Georgia, to Big Creek in the Smokies. Within the Smokies, the trail remains on the North Carolina side of the mountains, traversing no less than fifteen trails, mostly along the lower elevations. The Mountains-to-Sea Trail runs across North Carolina from the Outer Banks to Clingmans Dome at the Appalachian Trail and incorporates seven trails within the Smokies. The courses of both trails are indicated on park trail maps and marked at appropriate signposts; however, since they are both interconnected trail systems rather than stand-alone trails, they are not treated here as Smoky Mountain trails.

Most sources cited in this book are also cited in *Terra Incognita: An Annotated Bibliography of the Great Smoky Mountains, 1544-1934*, edited by Anne Bridges, Russell Clement, and Ken Wise and published by the University of Tennessee Press, 2013. Those not in *Terra Incognita* are included in Database of the Smokies (DOTS), an online bibliographic resource supported by the University of Tennessee Libraries. DOTS can be found at dots.lib.utk.edu.

The distances cited for all the trails are measurements completed by Bob Lochbaum, an experienced Smoky Mountain hiker and retired engineer with a penchant for detail. Over a course of several years, Lochbaum has measured and re-measured the distances of each trail with a wheel, which he carefully checks and calibrates at both the beginning and end of each hiking day. His measurements are made according to a well-defined protocol insuring standardization across all trails and precision in determining the placement of trailheads and intersections. In the latter years, Lochbaum corroborated his distance measurements with data points collected from Global Positioning

System equipment which he carried along the trails. Bob Lochbaum further refined his results through repeated measurements that reduced the degree of variance to less than 0.5 percent.

In the detail summaries accompanying the trail narratives, Lochbaum's measurements are rounded to the nearest tenth of a mile, and as a result inconsistencies may occur in the distance intervals. These instances are very few and of minor consequence. As a stylistic convention, distances cited in the descriptive narrative are rounded to the nearest five yards.

U.S. Geological Survey quadrangle maps are cited for the area covered by each of the trails. The maps offer a good two-dimensional image of the mountain, especially for the experienced hiker wishing to explore more of the terrain. Not all of the trails, however, are marked on the quadrangle maps.

Hikers and backpackers in the Smokies are required to follow the park's backcountry rules and regulations:

1. You must possess a backcountry permit while camping in the backcountry.
2. Camping is permitted only at designated sites and shelters.
3. Use of reserved sites and shelters must be confirmed through the Backcountry Reservation Office (865-436-1231) or online at https://smokiespermits.nps.gov/.
4. You may stay up to three consecutive nights at a site. You may not stay two nights in a row at a shelter.
5. Maximum camping-party size is eight persons.
6. Open fires are prohibited except at designated sites. Use only wood that is dead and on the ground. Use only established fire rings.
7. Use of tents at shelters is prohibited.
8. Food storage: When not being consumed or transported, all food and trash must be suspended at least ten feet off the ground and four feet from the nearest limb or trunk.
9. Toilet use must be at least one hundred feet from a campsite or water source and out of site of the trail. Human feces must be buried in a six-inch-deep hole.
10. All trash must be carried out.
11. All plants, wildlife, and natural and historic features are protected by law. Do not carve, deface, or cut any trees or shrubs.
12. Polluting park waters is prohibited; do not wash dishes or bathe with soap in a stream.
13. Pets, motorized vehicles, and bicycles are not permitted in the backcountry.

14. Firearms and hunting are prohibited.
15. Feeding or harassing any wildlife is prohibited.

Backpackers staying in any of the shelters or rationed backcountry sites must make reservations with the Backcountry Reservation Office. Reservations can be made online at https://smokiespermits.nps.gov/, by calling the Backcountry Office at (423) 436-1297 or 436-1231 between 8 a.m. and 5 p.m., or in person at the Sugarlands Visitor Center two miles south of Gatlinburg on US441 (Newfound Gap Road). Reservations may be made up to one month prior to the first day of the trip.

The fee for shelters and backcountry campsites is $4.00 per night for each camper up to a maximum of $20.00 per person. Campers may not stay consecutive nights at any shelter or at campsite 113 and may not stay in any other backcountry campsite for more than 3 consecutive nights. The maximum group size is 8, except at the following campsites where a party of 12 is permitted by reservation only: 17, 20, 46, 60, 86, and 90.

As an additional rule, practice common sense and courtesy. Never forget that the Smokies are home to a great diversity of wildlife. As a visitor, treat the mountains with no less respect than that deserved by a gracious host.

Backcountry Campsites and Shelters

Site numbers correspond to the Great Smoky Mountains Trail Map.

COSBY
29 Otter Creek
34 Sugar Cove
35 Gilliland Fork

GREENBRIER
31 Porters Flat
32 Injun Creek
33 Settlers Camp

MOUNT LE CONTE
Mount Le Conte Shelter

SUGARLANDS
21 Mile 53

ELKMONT
19 Upper Henderson
20 King Branch
23 Camp Rock
24 Rough Creek
26 Dripping Spring Mountain
27 Lower Jakes Gap
30 Three Forks

TREMONT
18 West Prong
28 Marks Cove

WHITEOAK SINK
6 Turkeypen Ridge

CADES COVE
1 Cooper Road
2 Cane Creek
3 Hesse Creek

5 Rich Mountain
9 Anthony Creek
10 Leadbetter Ridge
11 Beard Cane
12 Forge Creek
13 Sheep Pen Gap
14 Flint Gap
15 Rabbit Creek
16 Scott Gap
17 Little Bottoms

APPALACHIAN TRAIL
113 Birch Spring Gap
Shelters
      Mollies Ridge
      Russell Field
      Spence Field
      Derrick Knob
      Silers Bald
      Double Spring Gap
      Mount Collins
      Icewater Spring
      Pecks Corner
      Tricorner Knob
      Cosby Knob
      Davenport Gap

BIG CREEK
36 Upper Walnut Bottom
37 Lower Walnut Bottom
38 Mount Sterling

CATALOOCHEE
39 Pretty Hollow
40 Big Hemlock
41 Caldwell Fork

RAVEN FORK
Laurel Gap Shelter
Pecks Corner Shelter
42 Spruce Mountain
44 McGee Spring
47 Enloe Creek

OCONALUFTEE
Kephart Prong Shelter
48 Upper Chasteen
49 Cabin Flats
50 Lower Chasteen
52 Newton Bald

DEEP CREEK
46 Estes Branch
51 Georges Branch
53 Poke Patch
54 Nettle Creek
55 Pole Road
56 Burnt Spruce
57 Bryson Place
58 Nicks Nest Branch
59 McCracken Branch
60 Bumgardner Branch

NOLAND AND FORNEY CREEKS
61 Bald Creek
62 Upper Ripshin
63 Jerry Flats
64 Mill Creek
65 Bearpen Branch
66 Lower Noland Creek
67 Goldmine Branch
68 Steeltrap Branch
69 Huggins
70 Jonas Creek
71 CCC
74 Lower Forney Creek
75 Poplar Flats

LAKESHORE TRAIL
74 Lower Forney Creek
76 Kirkland Branch
77 Pilkey Creek
81 North Shore
86 Proctor
88 Possum Hollow
90 Lost Cove
98 Chambers Creek

HAZEL CREEK
82 Calhoun
83 Bone Valley
84 Sugar Fork
85 Sawdust Pile
86 Proctor

EAGLE CREEK AND TWENTYMILE
89 Lower Ekaneetlee
90 Lost Cove
91 Upper Lost Cove
92 Upper Flats
93 Twentymile Creek
95 Dalton Branch
96 Eagle Creek Island
97 Big Walnut

◆ COSBY ◆

Once known locally as "the moonshine capital of the world," the Cosby section of the Great Smoky Mountains is confined to a small semicircular basin tucked in the curvature of the main Smoky divide in the northeastern corner of the park. The higher slopes of Cosby are furrowed with inaccessible hollows, which were once a bane to the logging industry but a boon to moonshiners.

The Cosby section boasts two outstanding features, Albright Grove and the Mount Cammerer Lookout Tower. Albright Grove harbors an exceptional enclave of virgin cove hardwood forest, an undisturbed remnant of a primeval forest type that once covered much of eastern North America. The Mount Cammerer Lookout Tower occupies a prominent pinnacle on the eastern end of the main divide and affords one of the Smokies' truly surpassing vantage points. The tower is just off the Appalachian Trail, but easily within reach from two trails that originate in the Cosby section, the Low Gap Trail and the Lower Mount Cammerer Trail.

The Cosby section contains only six trails, and all but two originate from the vicinity of the Cosby Picnic Area and Campground. The Lower Mount Cammerer Trail is a lateral course that proceeds east to reach the Appalachian Trail where the main divide descends to Davenport Gap and the Pigeon River. The Low Gap Trail and Snake Den Trail also reach the Appalachian Trail, but both entail steep climbs. The Gabes Mountain Trail is a lateral connector proceeding west to a crossroads intersection with the Maddron Bald Trail and Old Settlers Trail.

The Maddron Bald Trail, one of the finest in the Smokies, follows the western perimeter of the Cosby section and traverses an exceptional range of mountain terrain through forest types that range from old-field yellow poplar and eastern hemlocks stands, to old-growth cove hardwoods, and on into the balsam zone. Access to Albright Grove is off the Maddron Bald Trail.

The Cosby section harbors three backcountry campsites—the Gilliland Fork Camp (#35) on the Lower Mount Cammerer Trail, the Sugar Cove Camp (#34) on the Gabes Mountain Trail, and the Otter Creek Camp (#29) on the Maddron Bald Trail. The Otter Creek Camp is one of the higher-elevation backcountry camps in the park.

To reach the Cosby section, drive from Gatlinburg east on US321 to a dead-end intersection with TN32. Turn right on TN32, and drive 1.2 miles to Cosby Road, which immediately enters the park and continues 2.0 miles to the Cosby Picnic Area and Campground. From I-40, take exit 440 onto US321, and continue to the junction with TN32.

GABES MOUNTAIN TRAIL

Cosby Road at the Cosby Picnic Area to the Maddron Bald Trail and Old
Settlers Trail—6.6 miles.

POINT OF DEPARTURE: From Gatlinburg, drive east on US321 to TN32, turn
right onto TN32, and proceed 1.2 miles to the Cosby entrance to the park.
From I-40, drive west to Cosby, Tennessee; then turn south onto TN32.
From the park entrance, follow Cosby Road 2.0 miles to the Cosby Picnic
Area and park in the adjacent lot. The Gabes Mountain Trail begins across
the road from the picnic area.

QUAD MAPS: Hartford 173-SW
Luftee Knob 174-NW
Mount Guyot 165-NE
Jones Cove 164-SE

0.0—Cosby Road.
0.3—Alternate access enters left 450 yards from Cosby Campground.
0.4—Rock Creek. Footlog.
0.6—Crying Creek. Footlog.
0.7—Crying Creek. Footlog.
1.0—Road turnaround.
2.1—Access path exits right 280 yards to Henwallow Falls.
2.3—Switchback.
2.6—Lower Falling Creek.
2.9—Lower Falling Creek.
4.8—Greenbrier Creek. Sugar Cove Backcountry Campsite (#34).
5.4—Buckeye Creek.
5.9—Cole Creek.
6.2—Maddron Creek.
6.6—Maddron Bald Trail exits left 1.7 miles to Albright Grove and right 1.2
miles to Laurel Spring Road. Old Settlers Trail exits straight 15.8 miles to
Greenbrier.

The east end of the Gabes Mountain Trail has two alternate beginning points. The
first is along Cosby Road just opposite the Cosby Picnic Area. The second is up-road
along the lower west side of Cosby Campground. The access that begins opposite
the picnic area proceeds 550 yards before being joined by the one that begins from
the campground. The access from the campground to this point is 450 yards. Along
both access trails, the flanking terrain is heavily encumbered with rocks, reflecting
the ruggedness and shallow depth of soil that characterizes much of the Cosby area.
Beyond the junction, the Gabes Mountain Trail remains a single course.

Sixty yards beyond the point where the two trails join, the Gabes Mountain Trail clears Rock Creek on a short footlog. It then continues winding through the rock-studded terrain for 500 yards before dropping to a footlog over a tributary of Crying Creek. A hundred and fifteen yards farther, it negotiates another footlog over the main stream.

A quarter-mile beyond the Crying Creek crossing, the trail engages what appears to be a turnaround marking the end of an old roadbed. The road, once an automobile access to Henwallow Falls, leads back down on the right a mile to Cosby Road. The trail exits the upper end of the turnaround and climbs for about a half-mile to clear a small gap at the back of Bearneck Cove. Ten feet to the right of the gap is the lone grave of Sallie Sutton. According to legend, Sallie Sutton had hoed corn on this slope all of her life and wished to be buried here.

From the Sutton gravesite, the Gabes Mountain Trail climbs about 600 yards to pass through Bearneck Gap and then begins descending on a wide smooth track lined with rhododendron and well cushioned with layers of deciduous leaves. Soon, the flanking terrain becomes more rugged; cliffs and outcroppings form up on either side. Slightly less than a half-mile beyond Bearneck Gap, the trail intersects an access that exits to the right 280 yards to the base of Henwallow Falls.

The descent to Henwallow Falls is exceedingly steep and near the bottom approaches a jumbled talus at the base of a bare cliff over which Lower Falling Creek descends in a long picturesque waterslide. The falls begin as a narrow stream cascading down a striated surface, then fans out across the bottom of the cliff before plunging onto the talus.

 Henwallow was once the name of a mountain farming community of about a dozen houses and known for growing apples and grapes. According to a story preserved by Carson Brewer in *Hiking in the Great Smokies*, the origin of the name is the result of an act of spite on the part of one community toward another. One spring, a man in a nearby community purchased a hundred baby chickens from a hatchery with the intent of raising the chicks to egg-laying hens and then selling their eggs. When the chicks became old enough for their gender to be obvious, the man counted ninety-five roosters and five pullets. People living in the community below the waterfall thought the chicken episode to be rather amusing and started referring to their neighboring community as "Roostertown." The folks in Roostertown, not being the appreciative sort, responded by calling their neighbor community "Henwallow." There was no basis for the name Henwallow. It was strictly an act of revenge. The exact locations of neither Henwallow nor Roostertown are known. Both survive in Smoky Mountain nomenclature, although Roostertown occurs as the name of a road off US321 just outside the park boundary.

Two hundred and thirty-five yards above the point where the access to Henwallow Falls exits the trail, Lower Falling Creek flows through a culvert under the trail. Just prior to reaching the stream, a remnant of the original access to Henwallow Falls can be seen below to the right. This older access is steep, treacherous, and not recommended.

A hundred and twenty yards beyond the crossing of Lower Falling Creek, the trail enters a sharp switchback to the left that affords a fine vantage point. Threetop Mountain (3,017 feet) and Round Mountain (3,062 feet) appear as cone-shaped peaks in the intermediate distance. Below is Cosby and in the distance Douglas Lake. Far to the right is Mount Cammerer (4,928 feet), the high peak evident where the main Smoky divide drops off sharply to Davenport Gap.

From the switchback, the trail climbs a quarter-mile to enter a narrow flat-bottomed cove heavily infested with rhododendron and drained by the slow-moving Lower Falling Creek. The trail winds among the rhododendron, crossing the stream twice within an interval of 515 yards. Just above the second crossing, the trail passes through a slight gap to leave the Lower Falling Creek watershed and begin circum-navigating the base of Gabes Mountain. A short interval of level grade precedes a one-mile winding descent to Greenbrier Creek. Over this interval, the trail probes into a succession of cooler recesses and engages a few headwater streams of Gabes Creek, a couple of which may not necessarily be easy to cross.

Greenbrier Creek is a difficult crossing. Immediately beyond is the Sugar Cove Backcountry Campsite (#34).

The Sugar Cove Camp is composed of three distinct sites spaced out along the stream. Two are below the trail and one above. The two lower sites, about fifty yards apart, are large plats of gritty surface liberally interspersed with boulders. Each enjoys proximity to the stream and each has a food-storage cable suspended nearby. The campsite above the trail affords the best tent sites of the three, but is much smaller, considerably farther from the stream, and does not have its own food-storage cable. Collectively, the sites in the Sugar Cove Camp are not the most accommodating in terms of quality tent placement, but they do occupy one of the nicer wilderness settings of the backcountry campsites in the park.

Upon leaving the Sugar Cove Camp, the Gabes Mountain Trail climbs out of the Greenbrier Creek drainage and then into a long steady descent that does not abate until trail's end. Except for the occasional retreat into and out of the recesses separating intervening finger ridges, the descent precedes at a brisk pace.

First, the trail crosses Buckeye Creek. Cole Creek is crossed and then crossed again eighty yards downstream. By the time the trail has dropped alongside the stream, it has entered the upper edges of old mountain farm fields. Tall slender yellow poplars occupy the fields, and thickets of rhododendron crowd the stream banks.

Five hundred and fifty-five yards downstream of the second crossing of Cole Creek, the trail crosses Maddron Creek, then eases onto a moderate grade for a half-mile approach to its terminus in a wide crossroads intersection with the Maddron Bald Trail and Old Settlers Trail. The Maddron Bald Trail climbs from Laurel Spring Road in the lower bottoms of Cole Creek to Albright Grove, and then on to Maddron Bald to reach the crest of Snake Den Mountain. The Old Settlers Trail is a long lower-elevation course that leads 15.8 miles to Ramsey Prong Road in Greenbrier Cove.

LOW GAP TRAIL (TENNESSEE)

Cosby Picnic Area to the Appalachian Trail at Low Gap—2.9 miles.

POINT OF DEPARTURE: Follow the directions to the Gabes Mountain Trail. Park at the upper end of the lot adjacent to the picnic area. The Low Gap Trail begins at the upper end of the parking lot.

QUAD MAPS: Hartford 173-SW

Luftee Knob 174-NW

0.0—Upper end of the Cosby Picnic Area parking lot.

0.2—Footlog. Cosby Nature Trail exits left.

0.3—Footlog.

0.3—Cosby Creek. Footlog.

0.4—Lower Mount Cammerer Trail exits right 0.1 mile to Cosby Campground and left 7.4 miles to the Appalachian Trail.

0.9—Alternate course of the Low Gap Trail merges in from the right.

2.5—Headwaters of Cosby Creek.

2.9—Low Gap. Appalachian Trail. Low Gap Trail (North Carolina) continues 2.5 miles to Walnut Bottom on the Big Creek Trail.

When white settlers first began moving into the Oconaluftee River Valley, they found an abandoned Indian trace that proceeded up Raven Fork and then along Straight Fork to the flank of Balsam Mountain. The old Indian trace then crossed over Balsam Mountain and descended along Gunter Fork to Walnut Bottom on Big Creek. After crossing to the north side of Walnut Bottom, it climbed to the spine of the main Smoky divide, passing through Low Gap and descending into Tennessee. That part of the Indian trace between Walnut Bottom and Cosby was claimed by the settlers as an access between the settlements on Big Creek and those in Cosby, Tennessee. With the advent of the park, the settlers' trace was upgraded to Park Service specifications and officially designated as the Low Gap Trail.

Under the current Park Service configuration, the Low Gap Trail climbs 2.9 miles from Cosby Picnic Area to the main Smoky divide and then descends 2.5 miles to Walnut Bottom on the Big Creek Trail. It is the only trail in the park that crosses the main divide between Tennessee and North Carolina without changing names. For the sake of consistency in grouping trails according to geographical sections, the Tennessee part of the Low Gap Trail is treated in the Cosby section while that in North Carolina is found in the Big Creek Section.

On its Tennessee side, the Low Gap Trail has two alternate beginning points. The first is along the upper end of the Cosby Picnic Area parking lot. The second is at the southeast corner of Cosby Campground adjacent to campsite B90. The two trails merge a half-mile up-trail from the course that begins at the campground.

From the trailhead at the parking lot, the Low Gap Trail eases out on a level course following Cosby Creek upstream, first skirting the lower end of the campground's outdoor amphitheater, and then, at 400 yards, crossing a footlog spanning a small feeder stream. Fifteen yards farther, the Cosby Nature Trail exits on the left. After another 120 yards up Cosby Creek, the trail crosses a footlog over another feeder stream, then turns and proceeds seventy-five yards to a longer footlog that spans Cosby Creek. The upper end of the Cosby Nature Trail merges in on the left where the Low Gap Trail leaves the stream and begins winding through a hummocky terrain shaded by large eastern hemlocks. A hundred and five yards beyond the stream crossing, the Low Gap Trail intersects the Lower Mount Cammerer Trail, a wide light-gravel track whose trailhead is along the southeast corner of the campground 220 yards to the right. Here, the Low Gap Trail turns left and follows the Lower Mount Cammerer Trail for twenty-five yards, turns right, exits, and then proceeds on a narrower track into a rough boulder-strewn terrain.

The boulder fields along the Low Gap Trail are a result of the latest episode in the geological history of the Great Smoky Mountains that ended perhaps 20,000 years ago when the ice age retreated for the final time. The Smokies were well south of the leading edge of the ice sheets and were never visited by glaciers, although the mountains did experience a more rigorous climate than now. The rocky exposures high along the main Smoky divide above Cosby, riven by the intense cold and frost action, broke free and tumbled, forming the bolder fields on the lower slopes. Over time, rain and water have worn the frost-fractured rocks into the smooth boulders and glen stones that flank the Low Gap Trail.

The rocky ruggedness of this section of the Smokies was a hindrance to large commercial lumbering operations, and consequently these slopes were not logged beyond limited selective cutting by local mountaineers. Large trees, mostly yellow poplar, yellow buckeye, and eastern hemlock are common at this elevation.

Slightly less than a half-mile above the Lower Mount Cammerer Trail junction, the Low Gap Trail merges with the alternate course that originates at the upper end of the campground. The alternate beginning at the campground follows an old fire road that climbs 170 yards to a concrete reservoir that once supplied water to the campground. It then passes a low stone wall on the edge of a bench up to the right. Until late into the twentieth century, a log crib built by local mountaineers stood near the stone wall. Two hundred and eighty yards above the reservoir, the trail intersects on the right a horse trail that connects the Low Gap Trail with the Snake Den Ridge Trail. The horse trail is 445 yards long.

Two hundred and twenty yards above the intersection with the horse trail, the fire road ends in a turnaround. From here, the Low Gap Trail continues as a narrow graded track 120 yards to a footlog spanning Cosby Creek. Thirty-five yards beyond the stream, the trail joins its counterpart from the picnic area.

From where the two alternate courses of the Low Gap Trail join, the trail follows closely along Cosby Creek. It remains along the stream for only a short distance before easing away and resuming a winding course among the boulders where the steepness is somewhat mitigated by a series of switchbacks. About a mile above this point, the cove hardwoods yield abruptly to a closed oak association of pignut hickory, red maple, sourwood, black gum, and yellow birch in addition to a mix of chestnut, northern, and white oak.

A half-mile into the oak association, the trail enters a small cove where it passes a spring that forms the headwaters of Cosby Creek. The trail then angles obliquely across the face of the mountain, climbing almost a half-mile before easing into Low Gap, a deep V-shaped notch in the main Smoky divide. Here, the Low Gap Trail intersects the Appalachian Trail before beginning a 2.5-mile descent into Walnut Bottom on Big Creek. Three-quarters of a mile west along the Appalachian Trail is the Cosby Knob Shelter. Two miles east is the Mount Cammerer Trail, leading a half-mile to the Mount Cammerer Lookout Tower.

LOWER MOUNT CAMMERER TRAIL

Cosby Campground to the Appalachian Trail—7.5 miles.
POINT OF DEPARTURE: Follow directions to the Low Gap Trail. Either hike the Low Gap Trail 0.4 mile until it intersects the Lower Mount Cammerer Trail, or walk along the road to the southeast corner of Cosby Campground. The Lower Mount Cammerer Trail begins across the road from campsite B93.
QUAD MAP: Hartford 173-SW

0.0—Southeast corner of Cosby Campground near campsite B93.
0.1—Cosby Creek. Footlog.
0.1—Low Gap Trail exits left 0.4 mile to Cosby Picnic Area and right 2.5 miles to the Appalachian Trail at Low Gap.
0.7—Road turnaround.
1.0—Toms Branch. Footlog.

1.4—Sutton Overlook.
3.3—Gilliland Fork Backcountry Campsite (#35), lower site.
3.4—Gilliland Fork Backcountry Campsite (#35), upper site.
7.5—Appalachian Trail.

The Lower Mount Cammerer Trail is a long easy course that traces the low-elevation contours along the base of the main Smoky divide between Cosby Campground and a point along the Appalachian Trail just east of Mount Cammerer. The trail begins from the upper southeast corner of the campground (across the road from campsite B93) and follows a wide light-gravel track 140 yards to a long footlog spanning Cosby Creek. Fifty yards beyond the stream, the Low Gap Trail intersects from the left, leading up from the parking area near the Cosby Picnic Area. The Low Gap Trail does not cross immediately over the Lower Mount Cammerer Trail, but follows it up-trail for twenty-five yards before exiting on the right.

From here, the Lower Mount Cammerer Trail winds through former hardscrabble farm fields, into a hemlock grove, and to a spring along the right that is walled up in a quaint square corner of stone. The elevation here is such that the trail remains in the transition zone where the steeper slopes of the mountain yield to the more moderate terrain of the bottomlands. Chestnut oak, yellow poplar, sweet gum, and red maple are prevalent.

Almost two-thirds of a mile beyond the campground, the gravel track ends in a turnaround, the trail continuing as a narrower graded course dropping to a footlog over Toms Branch. From Toms Branch, the trail leaves the cove hardwoods for a 600-yard climb into a dry-ridge pine-heath mix. The climb ends in a sharp turn where an access path exits to the right, leading to Sutton Overlook.

Access to Sutton Overlook is a steep 175-yard climb through pine stands culminating in an opening astride a ridge point. The immediate view is across Cosby to English Mountain and Green Mountain, appearing as two long ridges in the distance. Round Mountain (3,062 feet) is the distinctive cone-shaped peak across the Cosby Creek drainage, and farther to the left are Maddron Bald and Snake Den Ridge. Above Snake Den Ridge, the main Smoky divide is visible between Inadu Knob (5,918 feet) and Cosby Knob (5,180 feet).

Beyond the access to Sutton Overlook, the slopes adjacent to the Lower Mount Cammerer Trail become markedly steeper, but the trail itself maintains a moderate grade. The first stream crossing is Riding Fork, a narrow slither of such declivity that it more resembles a cascade than a stream course. The flow of water has washed away the surrounding layers of soil, exposing the strata of the underlying rock formations and the thinness of the turf on which the forest cover must gain purchase. Below the trail, the stream drains a narrow hollow which, in spring, is home to several species of wildflowers, particularly spring beauties, halberd-leaf yellow violets, bloodroots, wild irises, hepatica, sweet white violets, and several varieties of trilliums.

From here, the trail continues patiently plying the contours of Lower Mount Cammerer, encountering no streams and little variation in grade. When it reaches a pine heath, Snake Den Ridge and Maddron Bald come into view. Two miles beyond Sutton Overlook, a crossing of Gilliland Fork marks the entrance into a narrow draw that harbors the lower part of the Gilliland Fork Backcountry Campsite (#35). The lower campsite consists of three separate plats arrayed in descending order along the stream. All three are level and rigidly defined by logs arranged in closed perimeters. The upmost of the three is a large tract of bare ground while the two lower sites are smaller plots of grassy turf. A food-storage cable is suspended between the two lower sites.

On a grassy knoll a hundred yards up the Lower Mount Cammerer Trail, an access path exits right into the upper part of the Gilliland Fork Camp. A food-storage cable is suspended immediately to the right of the entrance, and on the left is the first of two campsites on the knoll. Though well secluded by thickets of rhodo-dendron, the ground on the left is a bit rough and a little too steeply pitched for an ideal campsite. The food-storage cable is convenient, but the closest water source is the stream at the entrance to the lower camp.

Fifty yards farther up-slope is a second, larger campsite that occupies the crest of the knoll. An open weedy field extends below the campsite, bordered on the back by a hedge of laurel and rhododendron. The more level places are along the hedge. Everywhere below the hedge the ground is a turf of tall grass. Neither water nor the food-storage cable are convenient; nevertheless, this upper site on the grassy knoll is among the nicer backcountry camping places in the Smokies.

Beyond the Gilliland Fork Camp, the trail returns to its previous routine of trac-ing the contours of the mountain, working in and out, negotiating the hollows sepa-rating the intervening finger ridges. The iterative pattern becomes more exaggerated as the finger ridges become wider and farther extended from the base of the moun-tain. The first is Leadmine Ridge, followed by Rowdy Ridge, and then Groundhog Ridge. At Groundhog Ridge, an unmaintained manway exits to the right and up the ridgeline to the Mount Cammerer Lookout Tower. During the wetter seasons, water may be found flowing in Robinson Creek, Rowdy Creek, and the headwater prongs of Groundhog Creek, streams that drain the hollows separating the ridges.

Once the trail clears Groundhog Ridge, the flanking slopes become noticeably steeper and the frequency of the cycle from ridge point to hollow to ridge point accelerates as the spur ridges become smaller and more closely spaced. The grade remains level. The track is frequently dry and weedy. Two prongs of Tobes Creek and two of Carolina Creek may be encountered during the wetter seasons.

The trail eventually rises into a low swag in Cammerer Ridge and terminates into the Appalachian Trail 2.8 miles west of Davenpoint Gap at the park bound-ary. Along the Appalachian Trail 2.3 miles west of its intersection with the Lower Mount Cammerer Trail, the Mount Cammerer Trail leads out 0.6 mile to the Mount Cammerer Lookout Tower.

SNAKE DEN RIDGE TRAIL

Cosby Campground to the Appalachian Trail at Inadu Knob—5.3 miles.

POINT OF DEPARTURE: Follow directions to the Low Gap Trail. Walk up the road to the southwest corner of Cosby Campground. The Snake Den Ridge Trail begins near campsite B51.

QUAD MAPS: Hartford 173-SW

Luftee Knob 174-NW

0.0—Southwest corner of Cosby Campground near campsite B51.

0.2—Horse trail exits left 445 yards to the Low Gap Trail.

0.6—Campbell Cemetery.

0.7—Road turnaround.

0.8—Rock Creek. Footlog.

1.8—Inadu Creek.

2.4—Switchback. Overlook.

4.2—Clearing.

4.6—Maddron Bald Trail exits right 7.3 miles to Laurel Spring Road.

5.3—Inadu Knob. Appalachian Trail.

The Snake Den Ridge Trail is a demanding climb into one of the more beautiful deciduous forests in the park. All of the great trees of the Smokies are here—yellow poplar, American beech, red maple, eastern hemlock, yellow buckeye, Fraser magnolia, black locust, Carolina silverbell, and several varieties of oaks. Higher up, in the boreal zone, red spruce, Fraser fir, fire cherry, yellow birch, mountain ash, and mountain maple are prevalent.

The Snake Den Ridge Trail begins from the upper corner of Cosby Campground near campsite B51 and follows a light-gravel fire road leading up the mountain away from the campground. A quarter-mile up the road, an access from the Low Gap Trail enters on the left. The access, 445 yards long, allows horse traffic to reach the Snake Den Ridge Trail by circumnavigating the campground by way of the Low Gap Trail.

The Snake Den Ridge Trail continues on the light-gravel track another 530 yards to the Campbell Cemetery, a level quarter of land harboring several worn field-stones and an unusual marker bearing the name Ella V. Costner. The marker identifies Costner as "the Poet Laureate of the Smokies." Ella Costner was born and raised on Crying Creek near the Gabes Mountain Trail and is best remembered as the author of *Lamp in the Cabin* and *Song of Life in the Smokies,* collections of poems and stories of the lore, legends, and mountain life in Cosby.

In her tale of "Old Man Macy's Pot of Gold," Costner describes Dan Macy as a hardworking, thrifty mountaineer who kept his earnings in gold coins, which he stored in a jar he kept buried in a mountainside above Cosby. One day when Dan Macy was getting up in years, he told his wife, "I want to show you where the gold is buried."

Macy's wife replied, "Just a minit 'til I run to the spring," and off she went to fetch the butter and milk for breakfast. She was perhaps thinking that she had waited all these years to find out about the gold, so what difference would another minute make? But that minute made all the difference. When she returned, she found her husband dead. His soul had passed to eternity. If the story is true, buried somewhere in the mountains of Cosby, perhaps even along the Snake Den Ridge Trail, there is a jar of gold waiting to be discovered.

Two hundred and thirty yards beyond the cemetery, the gravel road terminates in a turnaround, but the trail continues as a graded track traversing old farm fields to reach a footlog crossing of Rock Creek 250 yards above the turnaround. The grade remains fairly moderate as the trail clears a low intervale that separates Rock Creek from Inadu Creek. At Inadu Creek the grade stiffens. The trail follows upstream for about 200 yards and then turns away and onto a jumbled slope of rocky talus that bears little undergrowth other than low browse and a luxuriant mat of mossy covering. Trees of enormous proportions rise up out of the talus and ascend seventy feet or more before breaking out into a shading canopy of interlocking limbs.

A switchback to the right directs the course back across the talus for a half-mile return to Inadu Creek, where the crossing may not be easy after rain. Over the next half-mile, the steepness of the climb is ameliorated somewhat by three switchbacks. Over this interval, the trail eases out of the cove hardwoods and into dry-ridge conditions where pines and mountain laurel are prevalent with galax, trailing arbutus, and wintergreen the primary groundcover.

At the third switchback, the trail reaches an exposure that affords fine views across Cosby to the cone-shaped Round Mountain (3,062 feet) in the foreground. To the right are the low ranges of Sutton Ridge and Gilliland Ridge. South, much of the main Smoky divide between Cosby Knob (5,180 feet) and Mount Cammerer (4,928 feet) is visible. Ranging to the east is Camel Hump Mountain.

By the time the trail completes the third switchback, it has reached the flank of Snake Den Ridge. With the assistance of additional switchbacks, it scales the side of the mountain to the spine of Snake Den Ridge where, in places, the ridgeline is no more than a few feet wide. A light corridor of mountain laurel and rhododendron ushers the trail along the ridge, where occasional openings in the thicket permit views of Inadu Mountain ranging close along the left.

The trail remains in the corridor for about a half-mile before passing through a band of large red spruce trees and resuming the steep climb up the mountain. Eventually the grade lessens, leveling out momentarily as the trail passes through a small grassy clearing shaded by a large yellow buckeye.

Immediately beyond the grassy clearing, the trail deteriorates noticeably, becoming rough and rocky in addition to returning steepness. The course is mostly a bed of loosely shifting rocks frequently saturated with water. Red spruce and yellow birch are the predominant species with Fraser firs beginning to make tentative appearances. Spring beauty, Clinton's lily, and rosy twisted-stalk abound in mid-spring. Occasional openings in the forest cover permit glimpses across Cosby and out to Douglas Lake.

A little less than a half-mile above the grassy clearing, the Maddron Bald Trail intersects from the right. On the right above the intersection is the former site of the Maddron Bald Backcountry Campsite. The campsite is now abandoned, but in its day it was served by a picnic table and a fine spring.

At this juncture, the grade moderates slightly as the trail engages a long transition between Snake Den Ridge and the main Smoky divide. Shifting permutations of red spruce, yellow birch, Fraser fir, and mountain maple accompany the course. A half-mile above the Maddron Bald Trail junction, in a conspicuous opening on the left, are the remains of an airplane wreck.

According to research compiled by Jeff Wadley and Dwight McCarter, on January 4, 1984, an Air Force F-4 Phantom II traveling 450 miles per hour slammed into Inadu Knob. The jet made initial impact with treetops about 150 feet below the summit and hit the ground eight feet below. Debris was scattered in all directions from the point of impact, creating a crash site of almost twenty acres. Some of the wreckage can be seen along the Appalachian Trail on the far side of Inadu Knob.

A noticeable moderation in the grade heralds the approach to the main Smoky divide and the Appalachian Trail. The Snake Den Ridge Trail terminates into the Appalachian Trail just below the summit of Inadu Knob. The intersection is marked by a large boulder often commandeered by hikers as a convenient place to sit and enjoy a well-earned rest.

MADDRON BALD TRAIL

Laurel Spring Road to the Snake Den Ridge Trail—7.3 miles.

POINT OF DEPARTURE: From Gatlinburg, drive east on US321 about 15 miles to Baxter Road just east of the Yogi Bear Jellystone Park Camp Resort.
Turn right on Baxter Road and proceed 0.4 mile to a right turn onto the unmarked Laurel Spring Road. The Maddron Bald Trail begins about 200 yards down Laurel Spring Road.

QUAD MAPS: Jones Cove 164-SE

Mount Guyot 165-NE
Luftee Knob 174-NW

0.0—Laurel Spring Road.
0.7—Willis Baxter Cabin.
1.2—Gabes Mountain Trail exits left 6.6 miles to Cosby Road. Old Settlers
Trail exits right 15.8 miles to Greenbrier.
2.3—Road turnaround.
2.8—Indian Camp Creek. Footlog.
2.9—Albright Grove Loop Trail.
3.2—Albright Grove Loop Trail.
3.4—Indian Camp Creek.
3.8—Copperhead Branch.
3.9—Indian Camp Creek.
4.3—Indian Camp Creek.
4.7—Copperhead Branch.
5.7—Otter Creek. Otter Creek Backcountry Campsite (#29).
6.8—Maddron Bald.
7.3—Snake Den Ridge Trail exits right 0.7 mile to the Appalachian Trail at
Inadu Knob and left 4.6 miles to Cosby Campground.

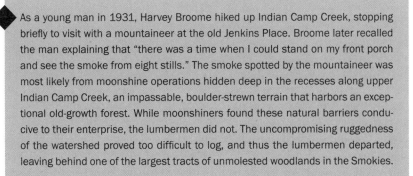

As a young man in 1931, Harvey Broome hiked up Indian Camp Creek, stopping briefly to visit with a mountaineer at the old Jenkins Place. Broome later recalled the man explaining that "there was a time when I could stand on my front porch and see the smoke from eight stills." The smoke spotted by the mountaineer was most likely from moonshine operations hidden deep in the recesses along upper Indian Camp Creek, an impassable, boulder-strewn terrain that harbors an exceptional old-growth forest. While moonshiners found these natural barriers conducive to their enterprise, the lumbermen did not. The uncompromising ruggedness of the watershed proved too difficult to log, and thus the lumbermen departed, leaving behind one of the largest tracts of unmolested woodlands in the Smokies.

The most difficult part of the Maddron Bald Trail is finding the trailhead. It leaves from an obscure junction along equally obscure Laurel Spring Road. The trail then follows an old light-gravel fire road into low mountain country once heavily settled by farming mountaineers and cultivated in cornfields and apple orchards.

Three-quarters of a mile above Laurel Spring Road, the trail enters a small grassy dell harboring the Willis Baxter Cabin, an eighteen-by-sixteen-foot one-room log house build around 1889. The cabin has two doors and no windows, a wooden floor, and a ceiling that is only slightly more than six feet high. Wide spaces between the chestnut log walls of the cabin correspond aptly with Horace Kephart's observation that "no mountain cabin needs a window to ventilate it: there are cracks and catholes everywhere, . . . the doors are always open except at night."

Beyond the Willis Baxter Cabin, the trail continues on the light-gravel track, following a leisurely course winding through farm fields now recovering in tall slender yellow poplars. A half-mile above the cabin, the trail enters a wide crossroads intersection. Exiting on the right, the Old Settlers Trail leads 15.8 miles into Greenbrier. On the left, the Gabes Mountain Trail leads 6.6 miles to the Cosby Picnic Area on Cosby Road.

Continuing through the intersection, the Maddron Bald Trail remains on the light-gravel track, sometime engaging a slight steepness and at others encountering virtually no grade. The course stays mainly to the edge of the farm fields, where they begin yielding to the steeper terrain of the adjacent slopes. A mile above the intersection, the gravel track ends in what appears to be a fork or turnaround in the road. The left fork is a mountaineers' trace that is now abandoned. To the right is the continuation of the Maddron Bald Trail.

In the fork of the junction stands a fine example of a birch tree growing up off the ground and supported only by its roots. As a seed, the birch tree germinated on a stump, sending its roots into the rotting host. In the early stages of colonization, the birch would appear to be perched on the top of the stump itself. As the tree grew, its roots extended down along the stump until finally reaching the ground. As the nurse stump decays, the birch is left with its roots like curved stilts, propping the trunk well off the ground and nothing but a cavity where the stump once stood. Here, the stump is not yet fully decayed, but sufficiently so to demonstrate how the birch will soon be standing on its own.

Above this junction, the grade becomes noticeably steeper, and the forest cover changes abruptly to stands of larger trees, mostly eastern hemlock, Fraser magnolia, red maple, Carolina silverbell, and yellow poplar. The trail continues into these old-growth stands for a half-mile before crossing Indian Camp Creek on a footlog. Two hundred and twenty-five yards beyond the footlog, the trail enters a sharp switchback and intersects the lower terminus of the Albright Grove Loop Trail exiting to the right.

From the switchback, the Maddron Bald Trail climbs 550 yards to intersect the upper terminus of the Albright Grove Loop Trail and then proceeds another 315 yards to a difficult crossing of Indian Camp Creek. Here, the trail turns up into a rugged draw where Ollie Creek is heard rushing madly down to the left. Four hundred yards beyond the Indian Creek crossing, the trail turns and leaves the Ollie Creek drainage, dropping quickly to a difficult crossing of Copperhead Branch.

Sixty yards beyond the Copperhead Branch crossing, the trail completes another difficult crossing of Indian Camp Creek. After another half-mile of climbing through old-growth stands, the trail crosses Indian Camp Creek for the final time.

Over the next half-mile, the trail leaves the Indian Camp Creek drainage to traverse a boulder field where the footing is extremely uneven, reaching Copperhead Branch for the final time. After crossing, the trail begins negotiating a steep angling course across the face of a ridgeline slope, continuing for slightly more than a quarter-mile to reach a ridge point sporting a small heath bald. At the apex of the ridge point, an access path on the left leads out twenty-five yards to a rocky exposure that affords a splendid view down over Snag Mountain and across Cosby. On a clear day, Douglas Lake can be seen in the distance. Visible on the left is Pinnacle Lead with its upper end anchored to the main Smoky divide at Old Black. On the right is the long ridge of Maddron Bald.

After circling the ridge point, the trail traverses another boulder field of such ruggedness that the birch trees growing here have but few places to root except on the bare surfaces of the boulders themselves. At this elevation, the old-growth cove-hardwoods stands yield to a transition zone separating the hardwoods from the boreal forests. Shortly beyond the boulder field, the trail clears Otter Creek and immediately enters the Otter Creek Backcountry Campsite (#29).

The Otter Creek Camp is perched on a long slender rocky exposure high over the stream in a campsite setting rarely matched in the Smokies for rugged beauty. During the 1930s, this site was used as a high-elevation sub-camp by the Civilian Conservation Corps. It is pitched a bit steeply, and even the best of the few suitable camping places are gritty surfaces tucked in along a rocky ledge. Food-storage cables are suspended at each end of the camp and water is available from the stream immediately below.

From the campsite, the trail angles up the flank of Maddron Bald and into a drier environment. At the top of the climb, the trail switches back right and into a pocket of red spruce and sand myrtle that heralds the approach to the narrow ridgeline of Maddron Bald. The trail proceeds along the ridgeline through a corridor of rhododendron and balsams, then emerges onto a south-facing heath bald bearing galax and tussocks of sand myrtle in the understory. On the left, an access path leads to a higher vantage point from which Inadu Knob (5,918 feet) can be seen as the high peak southeast along the main Smoky divide. Old Black (6,370 feet) is south with Mount Guyot (6,621 feet) visible just beyond. The powerful ridge on the right is Pinnacle Lead. From here, the trail enjoys a level run which ends near a boulder on the right that affords a vantage point for looking northwest back across the Tennessee Valley. Dupont Springs at the end of Chilhowee Mountain is seen presiding over the city of Sevierville.

Maddron Bald is named for Rev. Lawson Maddron, a veteran of the Union Army who was born in 1808 in Trade, Tennessee, and lived near Maddron Bald until he died in 1896. In 1866 Maddron founded the Raven's Branch Church of Christ, which he served for several years. There is a story that Maddron once gave a circuit preacher named Dr. Ashley Johnson a mule to use in his ministry. Johnson founded in 1893 the School of Evangelists in nearby Knox County. The school's name was changed in 1909 to Johnson Bible College and changed again in 2011 to Johnson University.

At this juncture, the trail rolls off the ridgeline of Maddron Bald and through a band of tall stately red spruce trees. Soon Fraser firs begin sharing space in the understory with the rhododendron. The appearance of seepages and heavy runnels saturating the course heralds the approach to the crest of Snake Den Ridge, where the Maddron Bald Trail terminates into the Snake Den Ridge Trail.

ALBRIGHT GROVE LOOP TRAIL

Maddron Bald Trail looping back to the Maddron Bald Trail—0.7 mile.
POINT OF DEPARTURE: Hike 2.9 miles up the Maddron Bald Trail. The Albright Grove Loop Trail begins at a switchback.
QUAD MAP: Mount Guyot 165-NE

0.0—Maddron Bald Trail.
0.3—Access path to big poplar.
0.4—Switchback.
0.7—Maddron Bald Trail.

The Albright Grove Loop Trail is a three-quarter-mile circular route through one of the outstanding remnants of virgin cove-hardwood forest in the Smokies. The grove was once owned by the Champion Lumber Company but was sold to the Park Service before the loggers had the opportunity to harvest the timber.

The grove is named from Horace M. Albright, a Californian who was instrumental in shaping the framework of the National Park Service after it was formed by the Organic Act of 1916. Later, as director of the National Park Service, Albright adroitly garnered the financial and political support necessary for bringing to fruition the Great Smoky Mountains National Park. Perhaps of equal importance, he was responsible for thwarting Tennessee Senator Kenneth McKellar's proposal for building a skyline road following the Appalachian Trail along the main Smoky divide.

The Albright Grove Loop Trail begins three miles up the Maddron Bald Trail, where the latter executes a sharp switchback left. The Albright Grove Loop Trail is a steep rugged course that winds around between Dunn Creek and Indian Camp Creek in a land of giant yellow poplar, eastern hemlock, sugar maple, and Fraser magnolia trees. At this elevation, the two streams are only a few hundred yards apart, yet by the time they reach the park boundary they are separated by several miles. Dunn Creek flows into the East Prong of the Little Pigeon while the waters of Indian Camp Creek reach the Pigeon River by way of Cosby Creek.

Five hundred and ninety yards up-trail, an access path exits left to the base of a yellow poplar considered to be the largest in the Smokies. The tree is twenty-five feet, three inches, in circumference and once stood 135 feet high. The tree's crown has been reduced to a snag, probably the result of lightning, leaving it with just a few lower branches.

A hundred and fifty yards beyond the access to the big poplar, the trail reaches a slight knob, where it executes a switchback and enters a stand of large American beech and Carolina silverbell trees. Many of the trees in Albright Grove are of such gigantic proportion that they have developed a miscellany of buttressing roots to help stabilize them more securely to the ground. Roots of the beech trees are particularly noticeable, appearing as taut sinews grappling the earth.

A mix of hemlocks and silverbells heralds the loop's return to the Maddron Bald Trail. The distance up the Maddron Bald Trail from the point where the Albright Grove Loop Trail begins is 550 yards.

◆ GREENBRIER ◆

The Greenbrier section encompasses a considerable quarter of Smoky Mountain wilderness stretching from the western perimeter of Cosby to the north face of Mount Le Conte along the Roaring Fork Motor Nature Trail above Gatlinburg. It includes an ordering of low-elevation bottomlands that widen out from the northern flanks of Pinnacle Lead and Mount Winnesoka as well as a vast basin defined by the encirclement of Pinnacle Lead, the main Smoky divide, and Mount Le Conte. Within the basin are the distinct geographies of Greenbrier Cove and Porters Flat. The lower elevations in the Greenbrier section were once occupied by settlement farms and still retain a considerable number of relics from the area's pioneer past. Conversely, the higher elevations contain some of the most remote and rugged terrain found anywhere within the Great Smoky Mountains.

The Greenbrier section is visited by only five trails. Two are low-elevation courses that follow old wagon roads traversing the hollows and bottomlands through the former settlement farms. The 15.8-mile Old Settlers Trail links Greenbrier Cove to Cosby. Similarly, the 7.6-mile Grapeyard Ridge Trail links Greenbrier with the Roaring Fork Motor Nature Trail above Gatlinburg.

The Bushy Mountain Trail traverses Porters Flat to climb to the summit of Brushy Mountain, a prominent outlier on the north flank of Mount Le Conte. Only the Ramsey Cascades Trail and the Porters Creek Trail probe into the inner sanctums of the Greenbrier fastness. One follows Ramsey Prong, remaining in the shadows of Pinnacle Lead until terminating at Ramsey Cascade, one of the most spectacular displays of water anywhere in the Smokies. The other follows Porters Creek to terminate at the Porters Flat Backcountry Campsite (#31) under the lee of the main Smoky divide below Charlies Bunion.

The Porters Flat Camp is the only backcountry campsite in the higher elevations of the Greenbrier section. The Settlers Camp Backcountry Campsite (#33) and the Injun Creek Backcountry Campsite (#32), along the Old Settlers Trail and Grapeyard Ridge Trail respectively, occupy former homesites.

From Gatlinburg (at the intersection of US321 and US441), the Greenbrier section is reached by driving 5.9 miles east on US321 to Greenbrier Cove Road. A right turn onto Greenbrier Cove Road leads immediately into the park and along the Middle Prong of the Little Pigeon River. Three miles along Greenbrier Cove Road, a bridge over the river leads to Ramsey Prong Road. Greenbrier Cove Road continues another mile beyond the bridge to a turnaround at the head of the Porters Creek Trail. The Old Settlers Trail and Ramsey Cascades Trail are reached from Ramsey Prong Road. The Grapeyard Ridge Trail begins on Greenbrier Cove Road at the bridge intersection. The Brushy Mountain Trail begins one mile up the Porters Creek Trail.

OLD SETTLERS TRAIL

Ramsey Prong Road to the Maddron Bald Trail—15.8 miles.

POINT OF DEPARTURE: From Gatlinburg (at the junction of US441 and US321) drive east 5.9 miles on US321 to the Greenbrier entrance to the park. Follow Greenbrier Cove Road into the park 3.2 miles to Ramsey Prong Road, which immediately crosses the Middle Prong of the Little Pigeon River on a wooden bridge. Cross on the bridge and proceed 250 yards to another bridge. The Old Settlers Trail begins on the left of Ramsey Prong Road at the far end of the second bridge.

QUAD MAPS: Jones Cove 164-SE
Mount Guyot 165-NE
Mount Le Conte 165-NW

0.0—Ramsey Prong Road.
0.3—Bird Branch.
3.6—Snakefeeder Branch.
3.8—Snakefeeder Branch.
3.9—Chimney ruin. Snakefeeder Branch.
4.2—Chimney ruin.
4.4—Access path exits left to Lindsey Cemetery.
4.7—Tributary of Soak Ash Creek. Access path exits right to Green Cemetery.
4.7—Soak Ash Creek.
4.9—Evans Creek.
5.0—Manway exits left to Steiner-Bell resort.
5.9—Timothy Creek.
6.3—Darky Branch.
6.6—Settlers Camp Backcountry Campsite (#33). Redwine Creek.
7.8—First crossing of Ramsey Creek.
8.9—Manway exits left to Noisy Creek and US321.
9.2—First crossing of Noisy Creek.
9.9—Tumbling Branch.
10.7—Texas Creek.
11.7—Manway exits left to Texas Creek.
12.6—Webb Creek. Access path exits straight to the Tyson McCarter Barn.
12.8—Stone wall.
14.9—Dunn Creek.
15.2—Indian Camp Creek. Footlog.

15.4—Maddron Creek.

15.5—Access path exits left to Maddron Cemetery.

15.8—Maddron Bald Trail exits right 1.7 mile to Albright Grove and left 1.2 miles to Laurel Spring Road. Gabes Mountain Trail exits straight 6.6 miles to Cosby Road.

High on the north flank of Greenbrier Pinnacle tiny rills collect in narrow defiles, forming small streams that hasten down the mountain. By the time these streams have reached the lower elevations, they have merged into larger streams with the names Bird Branch, Snakefeeder, Soak Ash, Timothy, Redwine, Ramsey, Noisy, Texas, Webb, Dunn, and Indian Camp. In the mid-1880s, pioneers moving south into the Pinnacle lowlands advanced up these streams, settling in the bottoms flanking the drainages. Here they built cabins and barns, planted crops and orchards, raised cattle, and endeavored with an indomitable spirit to wrest a living from the stony soil.

Along with their homes and farms, the settlers built roads, rudimentary dirt byways that meandered up the hollows, usually stopping at the last cabin up the creek. Though there were a few exceptions, the settlement roads adhered closely to the streams, rarely crossing over ridges into the adjacent hollows. In the 1970s, the Park Service began rehabilitating portions of the old settlement roads and connecting them with new graded trails that crossed the dividing ridges. This configuration of old roads and new trails eventually completed a long course extending from Greenbrier Cove to the Indian Camp Creek perimeter of Cosby. This new trail was originally known as the Lower Elevation Trail. The name was later changed to the Old Settlers Trail to reflect the area's rich heritage of pioneer settlements.

The Old Settlers Trail affords more visible remains of early Smoky Mountain community life than any other trail in the park. Standing chimneys, stone walls, remnants of log outbuildings, and non-native plants such as boxwoods, Spanish sword, daffodils, and privet hedges reveal the places once busy with cornfields and orchards, barns and tub-mills, corncribs and smokehouses, schools and churches, log cabins and frame houses.

The Greenbrier, or western, end of the Old Settlers Trail begins at the far end of the second bridge along the gravel road leading to Ramsey Cascades. The trail leaves on a smooth level course that winds through a hummocky bottomland flanking the confluence of Bird Branch and the Middle Prong of the Little Pigeon River. Five hundred and sixty yards below the road, the trail makes an easy crossing of Bird Branch and then climbs quickly to a ridge immediately above Middle Prong. Although the river is directly below the trail, it remains obscured by intervening rhododendron. The trail continues above the river for only a short distance before turning and dropping into the Little Bird Branch drainage.

Little Bird Branch is confined to a narrow hollow, yet it is wide enough to have once supported a small farm. Two sections of stone wall on the right separate the mountain slope from a farm field on the left. The trail proceeds upstream for a quarter-mile, then crosses and starts up the flank of Copeland Divide.

The crest of Copeland Divide is marked by a level stretch of 200 yards. From here, the trail begins a long descent to Snakefeeder Branch, passing first through open hardwood woodlands, then pine stands, and then onto a dry exposure of laurel and rhododendron to clear the headwaters of Copeland Creek. Slightly more than a mile beyond the Copeland Creek crossing, the trail reaches a tributary of Snakefeeder Branch, crosses, and sets a course downstream.

Snakefeeder Branch, a slow-moving stream flanked by small tracts of bottomland bounded on either side by steep slopes, is the archetypical setting for the remote Smoky Mountain cabin by the creek. The trail adheres closely to the stream, never venturing more than a few feet away and crossing it four times. Noticeable on the left eighty yards below the third crossing are the crumbling remains of a stone chimney. The cabin that once accompanied the chimney stood only a few feet from the stream and attended a plot of land no larger than a quarter-acre. The space was perhaps large enough for a garden and a small outbuilding or two, but little else.

Five yards below the chimney, the trail crosses Snakefeeder Branch for the fourth and final time. Noticeable in the stream are sections of stone retaining wall built by the mountaineers to firm up the bank against erosion. At this elevation, streams on the north flank of Greenbrier Pinnacle are more characteristic of meandering cut-bank creeks than that of the fast-moving torrents of the higher elevations.

Six hundred yards below the last crossing of Snakefeeder Branch, the hollow widens sufficiently to accommodate a one-acre farm plot. A chimney stands along the stream with a field immediately behind. In wintertime, when weeds have abated, it is possible to identify the locations of outbuildings that once stood in the back part of the field.

Within 400 yards of the chimney ruin, the hollow narrows again, forcing the trail into closer proximity to the stream. On the left, a path drops to the stream, crosses, and then leads about 300 yards to the Lindsey Cemetery. The cut-bank character of the stream requires a difficult climb down to the water's edge. The crossing is easy, but the climb up the opposite bank is difficult. The path to the cemetery emerges from the forest cover into a well-kept grassy plot that marks the end of a road. The entrance to the cemetery is forty yards to the right. The cemetery resides on a slight knoll and harbors a mix of about sixty fieldstones and modern headstones.

A few yards beyond the access to the cemetery, the hollow widens again, opening out onto a gently sloped woodland tract flanked by a wide weedy intervale between Snakefeeder and Soak Ash Creek. The Old Settlers Trail leaves Snakefeeder Branch and crosses the intervale to an easy crossing of a tributary of Soak Ash Creek. On the right, ten yards beyond the crossing, a faint path leads 200 yards to the S. S. "Dock"

Green Cemetery on the crest of a small wooded knoll. The cemetery bears only a few graves, and all but a couple are marked with well-worn fieldstones.

Sixty-five yards beyond the tributary, the trail enters a field, then completes a wide shallow crossing of the main channel of Soak Ash Creek. After 310 yards through another soggy intervale, the trail crosses a tributary of Evans Creek, and then fifty-five yards farther, crosses Evans Creek itself. At this point, the trail turns away from the stream and continues 185 yards to an intersection with a well-maintained manway leading north to the Steiner-Bell resort on US321. At the manway, the Old Settlers Trail bears right and begins climbing upstream along Evans Creek.

The hollow drained by Evans Creek is narrow and thoroughly clogged with rhododendron. The trail remains up on the slope out of the undergrowth, climbing a quarter-mile to a low ridge that separates Evans Creek from Timothy Creek. After climbing another quarter-mile, the trail levels out and begins following an old settler's road that runs for a considerable distance between two stone walls. Forty yards beyond the end of the wall, the trail drops to clear Timothy Creek in a wide shallow crossing. It then climbs eighty yards to another stone wall lying athwart the trail. As the trail approaches the wall, a dug road can be seen on the right parallel to the wall. About fifty yards down the road, the remains of a fifteen-by-seven-foot log crib stands on the right. One corner of the crib is well preserved, showing hand-hewn timbers notched and fitted in the customary log-cabin fashion. Two walls of the crib are in fair shape, and a third, though intact, has collapsed into the middle of the crib.

When the Old Settlers Trail rises from Timothy Creek and crosses the dug road, it passes through an opening in the stone wall and climbs immediately into the yard of another homesite marked by a fine chimney. Unlike the nearby wall, which is made of smooth rounded glen-stones, the chimney is constructed with flat thin sandstones stacked square and plumb. More noticeable is the lintel above the hearth which is in the shape of an inverted "V." This embellishment is common to several chimneys along the Old Settlers Trail and is likely the informal trademark of a local Smoky Mountain stonemason.

Four hundred yards beyond the chimney ruin, the trail falls in with an old roadbed running alongside a massive stone wall that is five feet high and over a hundred yards long. Other, shorter sections of stone walls spring up farther along the trail. The trail soon crosses Darky Branch, then reaches a low ridgeline where it intersects an unmaintained manway leading left to US321. From the manway junction, the Old Settlers Trail turns right and drops fifty yards to cross a large feeder stream. Seventy-five yards beyond the stream, the trail enters the Settlers Camp Backcountry Campsite (#33). The camp is 6.6 miles from the trailhead in Greenbrier.

Settlers Camp is composed of three distinct campsites dispersed along the trail. The first, on the left, is situated on a small, but attractive, knoll that is crowded with boulders, leaving little room for actual camping. The space is level and convenient to a food-storage cable suspended on the opposite side of the trail.

The second campsite is twenty-five yards up-trail on the right and located on a level, grassy plot that was once occupied by a cabin. The cabin's chimney commands one end of the camp. The camping area is restricted to the confines of the former cabin, whose perimeter is clearly discernable. This campsite is a bit more secluded than the first but is large enough for only a single tent.

A path leading out the upper side of the cabin site continues thirty yards to the largest of the three campsites. This camp is heavily shaded by hemlocks but is quite level and remarkably free of rocks. Settlers likely built the cabin on the rockier ground and then cleared this parcel for a farm field or barnyard. The absence of turf and undergrowth suggest that it was once heavily used.

The Settlers Camp Backcountry Campsite is equidistant between Darky Branch and Redwine Creek. Redwine is the larger of the two and a more convenient source of water for the two campsites on the right side of the trail.

When the trail leaves Settlers Camp and approaches Redwine Creek, it passes on the left an unusual U-shaped wall-like stone structure that is set in the ground just at the trail's edge. The top of the structure is flush with the ground, and its open end is exposed to the stream. Its appearance is similar to that of the rock-work in a spring-house, utilizing an inlet of Redwine Creek to provide the coolness for refrigerating milk, eggs, butter, and vegetables.

After a wide easy crossing of Redwine Creek, the trail climbs out of the drainage and onto a dry open exposure of laurel and pines shading an undergrowth of rough woody growth. The terrain along here is composed of sandy sedimentary rock which stonemasons in this area found versatile for building tightly stacked chimneys.

When the trail ceases climbing, it turns and begins descending steeply through a hemlock grove into the Ramsey Creek watershed. A ten-foot chimney of neatly layered flat sandstones stands on a level tract to the right of the trail. There is no evidence of any other building in the area, but it is clear from the scarcity of under-growth that this was once a heavily farmed gradient.

Two hundred and fifty yards below the chimney site, the Old Settlers Trail enters a hollow and crosses Ramsey Creek, a shallow slow-moving stream that was named for the dozens of Ramsey families that lived in the vicinity. Proceeding down-stream, the trail crosses Ramsey Creek four more times over an interval of 635 yards. Between the first and second crossings, another homesite appears on the left, marked by a seven-foot chimney just ten feet off the trail. Foundation stones betray the perimeter of the cabin that once accompanied the chimney, and two rusty pots lie on the chimney's hearth. Between the third and fourth crossings, a fallen chimney twenty feet to the right marks yet another cabin site. After the fourth crossing, the course becomes noticeably rough and rocky.

After the last crossing of Ramsey Creek, the trail continues downstream for the better part of a quarter-mile before turning right and leaving the stream to ascend the ridge that separates Ramsey Creek from the Noisy Creek drainage. Here, the trail follows an old dug road fenced on both sides by stone walls. In an open field on the right stands an impressive thirty-foot chimney with a hearth on two sides. The fireplaces in both hearths are accoutered with an inverted V-shaped lintel, though one has partially fallen out. Given the size of the chimney, it was likely once the center of a two-story frame house. The fireplaces are higher above the ground than other chimneys along the trail, suggesting that the house may have been built up off the ground with steps leading to a high porch.

Beyond the chimney ruin, the trail stays to the dug road, passing through an opening in one stone wall and following another that is five feet high and a hundred yards long. Other stone walls appear, varying in length and quality. The terrain flanking the walls is fairly level, although the roadbed remains rough and rocky.

Sound from the rushing of Noisy Creek heralds the approach to an unmaintained manway leading left down to Noisy Creek and then out to the park boundary along US321. Here, the trail turns right and proceeds upstream through the wide hollow drained by the fast-moving Noisy Creek, following a fine roadbed well above the stream. A stone wall soon forms up on the right. Almost 600 yards above the junction at the manway, the trail converges with the stone wall at the edge of Noisy Creek. Up to the right and beyond the stone wall is another standing chimney with an inverted V-shaped lintel. Foundations stones on the ground clearly outline the outside walls of the former cabin.

After a difficult crossing of Noisy Creek, the trail continues on the dug road following the stream. Heavy undergrowth encumbers the bank of Noisy Creek, and stone walls form up on the left. Unlike other walls along the Old Settlers Trail, these are embedded in the adjacent slope as a bulwark supporting a terraced tract above the trail. Four hundred and twenty yards upstream and just prior to reaching the second crossing of Noisy Creek, a standing chimney can be seen beyond the stone wall in the middle of the terraced ground. A few feet directly in front of the chimney is a low, well-preserved stone entrance to the house that once accompanied the chimney. On all sides of the cabin site are large vigorous clumps of Spanish sword.

The second crossing of Noisy Creek is also not necessarily easy. Beyond, the trail continues climbing, following the roadbed along the stream for another 700 yards before crossing Noisy Creek the third time. The trail continues climbing. Stone walls form up on the left. After about three-quarters of a mile, the trail passes one last wall, then turns away and enters a steep 250-yard climb to the top of the adjacent ridge.

From the ridgeline, the trail drops steeply to Tumbling Branch, then executes an equally steep climb to a ridgeline on the far side. The whole exercise from ridgetop to the stream and up to the next ridge occurs over an interval of less than a quarter-mile. The terrain is rough. Weeds and woody growth encroach. The mountain here was once known by the settlers as Chestnut Ridge, so called because of the abundance of American chestnut trees that once thrived here. After the chestnuts were killed by a blight early in the twentieth century, eastern hemlocks, yellow poplars, and a variety of oaks and maples have claimed the territory.

At 2,700 feet, Chestnut Ridge is the highest point of elevation reached by the Old Settlers Trail. When the trail begins descending, it falls in along another stone wall, following it to Texas Creek.

According to an old Smoky Mountain legend, sometime in the early nineteenth century a newly married mountaineer moved to Texas to seek his fortune, taking his bride with him. The young bride became homesick for the mountains and persuaded her husband to bring her back. They settled on this creek in the shadow of Pinnacle Lead. The young man later named the stream on which they lived Texas Creek so that he could reckon to have attained some measure of his dream.

After crossing Texas Creek, the trail turns downstream through the hollow and soon crosses two feeder streams. A stone wall forms up on the far side of the second feeder. In the bottom between the trail and the wall stands a tall structure of squarely stacked rock that resembles a chimney. It has no fireplace and no flue, yet situated in a clearing that appears to be suitable for a cabin site. Otherwise, there are no clues as to the function of the stone structure.

Three hundred and eighty-five yards downstream of the chimney-like structure, the trail passes on the right two real chimneys standing adjacent to one another. One is broken down. The better of the two bears the distinctive inverted V-shaped lintel. The two are in such proximity that they may have been affixed to adjacent sides of the same cabin. A couple of decaying logs lying on the foundation stones look uncannily like the cabin's original timbers.

Along here, the trail is quite pleasant. The grade is gentle, the track smooth, and the edges of the trail are carpeted in wintergreen. Two hundred and sixty-five yards below the adjacent chimneys, the trail intersects a manway leading left down to Texas Creek and out to US321. From this junction, the trail eases away from the stream for a course into the Webb Creek drainage. Over this interval, four feeder streams intervene. A mile beyond the adjacent chimneys, an impressive stone wall forms up on the right. It is six feet high and well over two hundred feet long. After a short interval, a second wall forms up, leading down to Webb Creek.

Immediately upon crossing Webb Creek, the Old Settlers Trail turns right onto a narrow track up along the stream. More noticeable, however, is a wide outlet road leading away from the stream to the Tyson McCarter Barn. The outlet road intersects a large gravel track 110 yards beyond the Webb Creek crossing. A left turn onto the gravel track engages a dogleg back to the right that leads another hundred yards to a large wooden barn.

Built around 1876, the dirt-floored Tyson McCarter Barn is a haphazard assemblage of enclosures clustered around two pole cribs covered with a double-cantilevered roof. The front of the barn is open, and the back closed in by a wall of rough-hewn boards. A lean-to hitching rack and a long, narrow, floored corncrib are affixed along one end of the barn. Across one side of the open end of the barn is a gabled-roof smokehouse.

Fifty yards below the barn, two ten-foot chimneys about thirty feet apart mark the site of the McCarter cabin. Photographs of the house indicate that it had a steeply pitched roof overhanging a porch across the entire front of the cabin. A nearby springhouse, which served as a cool storage for perishable foods, still stands in what was the front yard of the cabin.

When the Old Settlers Trail turns and proceeds up Webb Creek, it begins passing an array of stone walls, some at right angles to the trail, others following along on the far side of the stream. In places, the occasional chestnut fence post can be spotted in the fields to the left. Three hundred and fifty yards above the outlet road to the McCarter Barn, the trail climbs through a gap in an intervening stone wall. Here the grade stiffens noticeably. A half-mile farther, the trail crosses a feeder stream and then continues 275 yards to intersect an access path that exits straight on, leading a half-mile to a chimney ruin that marks a former homesite. At the intersection, the Old Settlers Trail turns sharply left and leaves Webb Creek for a half-mile climb along Snag Mountain, crossing the feeder stream a second time. Going up Snag Mountain, Greenbrier Pinnacle (4,597 feet) is visible to the right. On the way down, Gabes Mountain comes into view.

When the trail leaves Snag Mountain, it descends through an exceptionally dense thicket of rhododendron to a switchback that directs the course down through a hollow drained by Snag Branch. Two small feeder streams intervene. A hundred yards beyond the second crossing, another chimney-like stack of rocks is noticeable in the bottom to the left. Like the first, this structure also stands in the middle of a clearing, is built remarkably in the shape and size of a chimney, yet has no flue or fireplace.

Here, the hollow widens appreciably, and the trail eases away from Snag Branch to cross a bottomland flanking Dunn Creek. A stone wall forms up, heralding the approach to Dunn Creek. At the end of the wall, the trail completes a crossing of Dunn Creek, which can be difficult if the stream is up.

Five hundred and fifty yards beyond Dunn Creek, the trail crosses Indian Camp Creek on a footlog. Three hundred yards farther, it crosses Maddron Creek. These watersheds, like the others traversed by the Old Settlers Trail, were blessed with an over-abundance of rocks. Many found their way into chimneys and foundations for cabins and barns; others were used in the stone walls that line the old roadbeds; and yet others were stacked in miscellaneous piles that can be seen in the old farm fields between Indian Camp Creek and Maddron Creek.

A hundred and fifty yards beyond the Maddron Creek crossing, the trail intersects an access path on the left leading sixty yards to the Maddron Cemetery. The access passes through the yard of a house that once stood facing the trail. A crumbling double-chimney marks the location. Directly behind the house is the Maddron Cemetery, which bears eleven fieldstones. Only a few are readable.

The Old Settlers Trail terminates 525 yards beyond the access to the cemetery in a crossroads intersection with the Maddron Bald Trail and the Gabes Mountain Trail. To the left, the Maddron Bald Trail leads to the Willis Baxter Cabin and then out to the park boundary just off Laurel Spring Road. To the right, it climbs 1.7 miles to the Albright Grove Loop Trail. The Gabes Mountain Trail exits east from the intersection and leads 6.6 miles to Cosby Road at the Cosby Picnic Area.

RAMSEY CASCADES TRAIL

Ramsey Prong Road to Ramsey Cascades—4.0 miles.

POINT OF DEPARTURE: Follow directions to the Old Settlers Trail, then continue to the end of Ramsey Prong Road. The Ramsey Cascades Trail begins at the end of the road.

QUAD MAP: Mount Guyot 165-NE

0.0—Ramsey Prong Road.
0.1—Middle Prong of Little Pigeon River. Bridge.
1.5—Old road turnaround. Manway to Greenbrier Pinnacle on left.
2.2—Ramsey Prong. Footlog.
2.6—Big poplars.
2.9—Ramsey Prong. Footlog.
3.6—The Cherry Orchard.
4.0—Ramsey Cascades.

The trail to Ramsey Cascades begins at the end of Ramsey Prong Road, a well-maintained gavel track that follows the Middle Prong of the Little Pigeon River upstream to a parking area. The trail exits the parking lot on a wide gravel track that proceeds an easy eighty-five yards to a sturdy bridge spanning the Middle Prong, a stream which Harvey Broome once aptly described as the yellow-white surging "of a great stream beating against solid boulders in a roaring violence of sight and sound."

Upon crossing the stream, the trail diminishes noticeably, becoming a rough road that maintains a respectable distance from the stream as it courses through second-growth farm fields. Until sometime in the late 1970s this part of the trail was open to automobile traffic, allowing vehicles to proceed an additional one-

and-a-half miles to a turnaround near the confluence of Ramsey Prong and Middle Prong.

As the trail approaches the turnaround, it enters an old farm clearing now occupied by a copse of struggling saplings. Early hikers following this route to Mount Guyot noted having seen a cabin or lean-to in the field, most likely an outbuilding used by whoever farmed the slope. Noticeable along the left side of the turnaround is the lower terminus of what was once an access road to a fire tower on Greenbrier Pinnacle. For many years this access road served as the Greenbrier Pinnacle Trail until its status as an official trail was rescinded by the Park Service. The fire tower was dismantled several years ago when it became obsolete. All that now remains is an unmaintained manway leading to the foundation ruins of the tower and warden's cabin.

The Ramsey Cascades Trail exits from the far end of the turnaround and immediately narrows to a rocky root-infested track hedged with masses of rhododendron. It passes just above the mouth of Ramsey Prong, then climbs up and away, leaving the Middle Prong for a course along Ramsey Prong and into a transition from old-field second growth to a cove-hardwood mix of red maple, yellow poplar, eastern hemlock, yellow buckeye, sweet gum, and several species of oak. The terrain along Ramsey Prong is more rugged than that of the Middle Prong, making the course more strenuous to travel. After a half-mile, the grade levels briefly where a feeder stream crosses and drops sharply to a deep pool in the nearby stream. Within the next fifty yards, the trail descends to a long slender footlog suspended immediately over the pool.

A near-vertical scarp defines the back edge of the pool, whose bottom is lost in the gloom. The stream, cascading over a short ledge beneath the footlog, replenishes the water that escapes over the outer lip of the pool. Masses of rhododendron filter out what little direct sunlight reaches the stream gorge, casting the pool in a perpetual twilight.

The trail climbs up and away from the pool in a rocky winding course for about two hundred yards before being forced by intervening cliffs into a close tangent encounter with Ramsey Prong. The cliffs soon subside, permitting the trail to inch away from the stream and eventually into a clearing where it passes between two colossal poplars. The understory fades to little more than a carpet of partridge-berry, and the grade moderates to a fairly level course. Twenty-five yards beyond the twin giants stands another larger poplar. Early hikers into the area remarked on having seen a small pole cabin that stood within the clearing.

The distance across the clearing is short, and the trail soon returns to its rocky course, entering a terrain that is marked on the right by steep slopes of large boulders and on the left by a wide creek bottom completely submerged in dense arbors of rhododendron. A rock stairway of twenty-five steps ushers the trail up through a particularly rugged stretch. A small cave is noticeable immediately to the right, halfway up the steps. Seventy-five yards beyond the cave, a footlog leads across Ramsey Prong.

At this juncture the trail begins moving decidedly away from the stream and into a forest of large yellow buckeye trees. Within the next quarter-mile, it crosses a feeder stream then completes a wide horseshoe bend to cross the feeder a second time farther up-trail. Along here, the understory thins considerably, the woody growth giving way to scattered clusters of crested dwarf irises, foamflowers, wild golden-glows, Queen Anne's lace, and crimson bee-balms. Buckeyes, red maples, hemlocks, poplars, and white basswoods are interspersed throughout one of the finest stands of wild black cherry trees in the Smokies. The cherry trees, distinguished by their small, thick, dark reddish-brown scales, are so prevalent along here that early travelers to Ramsey Cascades often referred to the place by the picturesque name "Cherry Orchard."

 On one of his early hikes to Ramsey Cascades, Harvey Broome remarked on seeing a barbed-wire fence that enclosed a half-acre or so of ground where the understory thins out. There was no shelter within the confines of the fence. Back down the trail, where it enters the horseshoe bend, there was, Broome recalled, a small lean-to that stood at trail's edge. Were the lean-to and the fence partners in some common venture? One can only speculate as to what enterprise involving a fenced enclosure in such a high, remote, and rugged place would have been profitable.

The "great aisle of the Cherry Orchard," as Broome described it, extends for only a hundred yards or so, terminating where the understory reappears and the trail, returning to the stream, becomes noticeably rocky and steeper. Soon, great boulders increasingly straiten the course, pressing it into a tentative winding passage along what little ground is suitable for hiking. Surface soil is so exiguous here that the occasional American beech tree is compelled to germinate on bare rock and seek sustenance from detritus that collects in crevices. As the trees grow larger, their roots reach around the boulders, gripping tightly for support. After a steep climb through the beeches, the trail crosses a feeder stream then leads quickly over enormous boulders and out onto a wide ledge to at the base of Ramsey Cascades. The Ramsey Cascades Trail terminates at the falls.

Ramsey Cascades is the most spectacular display of water anywhere in the Smokies. Its forceful stream plunges over a sharp precipice and drops eighty-five feet to a flat, seventy-foot-wide, bare-rock apron that separates the upper cascades from the stream below. The falling water pools momentarily on the shelf, gathering composure before rushing off in a display of dazzling whiteness as it cascades violently down a rocky thirty-foot staircase. This whole amphitheater is sequestered among great yellow birches, red spruces, and rhododendron massing in walls of green.

PORTERS CREEK TRAIL

Greenbrier Cove Road to Porters Flat Backcountry Campsite (#31)—3.6 miles.

POINT OF DEPARTURE: From Gatlinburg (at the junction of US441 and US321) drive east 5.9 miles on US321 to the Greenbrier entrance to the park. Turn right, and follow Greenbrier Cove Road into the park 4.0 miles until it terminates in a large turnaround. The Porters Creek Trail begins at the end of the turnaround.

QUAD MAPS: Mount Le Conte 165-NW
Mount Guyot 165-NE

0.0—Turnaround at end of Greenbrier Cove Road.
0.7—Long Branch. Bridge.
0.8—Access path exits right to the Ownby Cemetery.
1.0—Road turnaround. Brushy Mountain Trail exits right 4.9 miles to the summit of Brushy Mountain. Access path exits right to the Messer Barn and Smoky Mountains Hiking Club Cabin.
1.5—Porters Creek. Footlog.
1.8—Access path exits left to Fern Falls.
3.6—Porters Flat Backcountry Campsite (#31).

Prior to the arrival of white settlers in the Great Smoky Mountains, a contingent of Cherokee inhabited a small community known as Indian Nation in the Porters Flat section of Greenbrier Cove. Cherokee living there crossed the mountain to the larger Indian towns on the Oconaluftee and Tuckasegee rivers along the only significant path that traversed the Smoky divide east of Indian Gap, an ancient trace that followed out of Porters Flat along Porters Creek and crested the divide at Dry Sluice Gap. Early white settlers entering Greenbrier Cove followed the Indian trace through Porters Flat as they crossed over the mountain to escape the crowded conditions of the older settlements on the Oconaluftee. Later, the route through Dry Sluice Gap would serve as the primary artery between the growing settlements in Greenbrier and those in North Carolina. The current Porters Creek Trail follows roughly a remnant of the old Cherokee trace between Porters Flat and the main Smoky divide.

The Porters Creek Trail begins along the upper end of a long turnaround at the end of Greenbrier Cove Road. For the first three-quarters of a mile, the trail follows a wide gravel road, a former settlement trace that is now maintained as a jeep track. Porters Creek runs closely on the left, and on the right are abandoned farm fields now shaded by uniformly tall, slender, second-growth poplars. Networks of stone walls testify to the presence of former homesites and barnyards. One of the more noticeable of these is about a half-mile up-trail and marked by steps on the right leading up to the remains of a house chimney.

A sturdy wooden bridge ushers the trail over Long Branch and into a sharp bend. Just around the bend and to the right, a set of stone steps leads up the bank to a gently sloped moss-covered tract that harbors the Ownby Cemetery. A few yards beyond the entrance to the cemetery, an automobile chassis lies rusting in the middle of an abandoned barnyard ranging along the right of the trail. The gravel road proceeds around another bend and then terminates in a turnaround along the lower eastern edge of Porters Flat.

Three trails exit from the end of the turnaround. From the west side, an access trail proceeds a hundred yards to the John Messer barn, a double cantilevered structure built in 1875. Beyond the barn are a springhouse and the old Smoky Mountains Hiking Club Cabin. At the far end of the turnaround is the lower terminus of the Brushy Mountain Trail, which traverses Porter Flats before climbing to Trillium Gap and Brushy Mountain. A few yards to the left of the Brushy Mountain trailhead, the Porters Creek Trail exits the turnaround, narrows considerably, and begins following a streamside course circling along the east edge of Porters Flat.

 In the late 1920s, hikers from the Smoky Mountains Hiking Club noted a cabin of immense poplar logs that stood along Porters Creek Trail just beyond the turnaround. The cabin was part of the Champion Fibre Company's Camp Number One and stood not only within the boundaries of the Champion property, but marked the lower extension of the virgin timber.

The Porters Creek Trail drops to the stream, crosses on a long footlog, and then enters the soothing gloom of a moist cove-hardwood forest of gigantic yellow buckeye, red maple, and yellow poplar trees where the stream is banked on both sides by verdant arbors of rhododendron which bloom profusely in late June and early July. On the left, the boulder-infested lower slopes of Porters Mountain encroach on the trail, providing shade and moisture for the spring-beauties, bloodroots, trilliums, blue cohoshes, creeping phloxes, bishop's caps, toothworts, foamflowers, speckled wood lilies, Indian-pinks, Dutchman's-pipes, Jack-in-the pulpits, prostrate bluets, and carpets of white fringed phacelia that thrive there.

About six hundred yards above the footlog, the forty-foot Fern Falls graces the slope fifty yards to the left of the trail. Harvey Broome once described Fern Falls as "a slithering veil . . . delicate and unexpected." The cascade is set back in a wooded diorama, framed attractively by heavy vegetation arching in on both sides. It can be approached by a faint trace that winds through boulders and nettles to the base of the falls. It is near Fern Falls that the Champion Fibre Company maintained its Camp Number Two. Early passersby noted that the camp was nestled in an exceptionally beautiful setting, but served by a poor shelter.

Beyond the access to Fern Falls, the grade moderates, the trail edges closer to the stream, and the understory subsides to a carpet of partridge-berry and ferns. The stream remains buried under massive arbors of rhododendron out of which rise huge boles of yellow poplar reaching seventy or eighty feet before branching out at the first limb.

Within the next half-mile, the trail begins climbing again on a rough uneven course. Eastern hemlocks, Fraser magnolias, and yellow buckeyes enter the mix with the large poplars. The trail edges closer to the stream and quickly enters a wide flat cove that harbors the Porters Flat Backcountry Campsite (#31). The Porters Creek Trail terminates at the campsite.

Near the entrance to the campsite, a stream crossing the trail is the most convenient source of water for the camp. The stream is not reliable; however, a noticeable path at the entrance to the camp circles wide around the campsite and eventually drops to Porters Creek where the water is plentiful. Though the camp is situated on a level bench immediately above Porters Creek, intervening tangles of rhododendron and an exceedingly steep slope make direct access to the stream difficult.

The Porters Flat Camp is one of the most remote in the park and enjoys an uncommonly attractive setting. It is divided into an upper and lower site, both engulfed in rhododendron and shaded by large widely spaced hemlocks. The upper site is a bare slight gradient with space for three or four tents. It is more distant from the trail than its lower counterpart, and thus affords an element of seclusion. The lower site is considerably smaller and endowed with a bit of grassy turf. The two campsites are about fifty yards apart, and each is supplied with its own food-storage cable.

The campsite marks the extreme upper reaches of Porters Flat. Immediately above the camp, the land formation changes abruptly as the cove gives way to the jagged escarpments of the Sawteeth and the cove-hardwood giants yield to the smaller hardy species that can gain purchase on the rocky exposures. For the early settlers crossing from Greenbrier Cove into North Carolina, the level plot at the Porters Flat Camp marked the last respite before the difficult climb over the Smoky divide.

BRUSHY MOUNTAIN TRAIL

Porters Creek Trail to Brushy Mountain—4.9 miles.
POINT OF DEPARTURE: Hike along the Porters Creek Trail 1.0 mile to the road turnaround. The Brushy Mountain Trail begins at the end of the turnaround.
QUAD MAP: Mount Le Conte 165-NW

0.0—Turnaround on Porters Creek Trail.
0.3—Upper access to the Smoky Mountains Hiking Club Cabin.

1.0—Fittified Spring.
2.7—Trillium Branch.
3.3—Switchback.
4.5—Trillium Gap. Trillium Gap Trail exits left 3.6 miles to the summit of
  Mount Le Conte and straight 5.3 miles to the Old Sugarlands Trail near
  Cherokee Orchard Road.
4.9—Summit of Brushy Mountain.

The Porters Creek Trail starts along a wide gravel road that, after the first mile, loops back upon itself in a turnaround. The trail then exits the turnaround along its lower side and continues as a narrow track. At about the midpoint of the turnaround, the Brushy Mountain Trail exits, veering south and entering the sub-cove, Porters Flat. Farther along the turnaround, about forty yards from the Brushy Mountain trailhead, an access path leads about a hundred yards to the Messer Barn and the Smoky Mountains Hiking Club Cabin.

The Messer Barn, built by Pinkney Whaley around 1875, is a large two-crib double-cantilever structure that is open on both sides. Like all well-sited barns, it is situated on a slight rise in the landscape so that rainwater drains away from the building. The corner timbering is V-notched as opposed to the half-dovetail notching found in most barns and cabins in the Smokies. Cantilever barns are common in the Smoky Mountains, but as a building type it is unique to the mountain regions of Tennessee and North Carolina. The architectural origin of the cantilever-type barn is uncertain. It has been speculated that they were common in the mountains because of the availability of suitably large trees and the natural protection they afford from termites.

Just beyond the barn, the access path passes a log-cabin style springhouse that straddles a small stream. Above the springhouse is the Smoky Mountains Hiking Club Cabin. Sometime in the middle of the nineteenth century, Pinkney Whaley bought and cleared this patch of mountain land. He built the barn and a fine frame house that stood where the cabin now stands. Just prior to the twentieth century, Whaley sold his house and farm to John Messer, and it then became known as the Messer place. Messer lived there until the property was bought by the Tennessee Park Commission. The house was subsequently torn down by the Park Service, leaving only a standing chimney.

After securing permission from the Park Service, the Smoky Mountains Hiking Club began in 1934 to build a new cabin on the site of the old Whaley house, using timbers taken from abandoned cabins throughout Porter Flat. The club cabin is actually two cabins which have been reassembled, one on each side of the chimney. The left half is built of hewn poplar logs and the right of chestnut. The roof is split-oak shingles, and the doors and door-jams are chestnut. The cabin has puncheon floors and two lofts. It was once furnished with corded beds, corner cupboards, benches, tables, and dog irons in the fireplaces. When finished in 1936, the club named it affectionately "Th' Cabin in th' Brier."

Two millstones lie near the slate porch in front of the cabin. Most likely they were hewn of stones from nearby Long Branch. Long Branch stones were especially hard and composed of a conglomerate material which chipped just right when the stones ground against one another, almost in a self-sharpening manner. Smoky Mountain tradition contends that many of the stones used in the grist mills on Mill Creek (now Le Conte Creek) above Gatlinburg were taken from Long Branch.

The yard around the cabin still bears testimonies to its former role as a homesite. Daffodils still bloom in spring; daylilies crowd the space between the cabin and springhouse; and an old-fashioned snowball bush still yields its clusters of milky blossoms in early May. Placed strategically around the yard are traditional boxwoods, an ornamental species popular with the settlers who came to these mountains.

Behind the cabin is a two-seater outhouse. The outhouse is a later addition, built sometime in the late 1990s. A manway exits along the upper side of the cabin yard, affording a 100-yard shortcut to the Brushy Mountain Trail.

From the road turnaround, the Brushy Mountain Trail follows an easy course along the lower perimeter of Porters Flat. Until forced to leave when the park was established, several families lived in Porters Flat, having cleared the land and built farms. The rocky fields these families once cultivated are now grown up in tangles of vines and thickets of young spindly trees. Cairns of rocks here and there mark the boundaries of fields, probably corn patches, which now harbor yellow poplar and black locust.

About a mile above the turnaround, the Brushy Mountain Trail veers away from Long Branch and soon encounters a faint path on the left that leads fifty feet to the old Mark Whaley homeplace and a fine spring that was once curiously known as the Fittified Spring.

 When Harvey Broome passed this way in 1966, he noticed that "the double barn which stood 50 feet off the trail below the Fittyfied Spring had collapsed and was engulfed in vegetation. The cabin at the spring had fallen in." The term "fittified" which Broome applied to the spring is usually reserved for a spring that flows "in fits," that is, with determined periodicity rather than constancy. Such springs often occur as the result of a natural siphon. The stream feeding the spring flows underground and into a small cavern. The exit to the cavern is near the top, and when the cavern is full, the flow of water drains the whole cavern, much like a siphon. When the cavern is empty, the stream refills it again, during which time the spring does not flow, thus the appearance of "fits."

Like many natural features in the Smokies, the Fittified Spring has a lore of its own. On February 12, 1916, the mountains around Porters Flat were shaken by an earthquake felt as far away as Asheville and Knoxville. Before the earthquake, according to some who knew, the spring flowed evenly, but from then on the flow was markedly altered, with the period of time between high-output points being about eighteen minutes. Evolena Ownby, whose sister lived in the old log house by the spring, once commented that the locals referred to it as "Spasmodic Spring." "The water ran out of the hill for about eight minutes and then would stop and be dry for the same length of time. It would run from seventy to eighty gallons each time." Ownby often observed her sister's cow going down to the spring branch for a drink. If the spring was dry, the cow would stand there until it started running again.

Theories have been advanced to explain the unusual ebb and flow of the Fittified Spring, but the spring defies easy explanation. One of the more logical attempts to explain the change in behavior attributes it to dynamite blasts by the Civil Conservation Corps crews working on the trail in 1936. However, geologists first noticed the absence of fits in 1935. The latest reported activity occurred in 1984 when two hikers placed a bottle in the spring and observed the water level slowly rising and falling around it, attesting to the fact that the spring is still slightly fittified.

Porters Flat was first cleared and occupied by a contingent of Cherokee from the larger Indian villages on the Oconaluftee River. Whether this outpost was a permanent village or a summer hunting retreat is not known. When white settlers moving into the flat discovered evidence of previous occupancy, they named it Indian Nation.

A mile above the Fittified Spring, the Brushy Mountain Trail eases out of Porters Flat and into the Trillium Branch drainage, climbing steeply along a drier south-facing exposure where the hemlock-hardwood association yields to pine stands. The high point directly across Porters Flat is Greenbrier Pinnacle (4,597 feet), punctuating the lower end of Pinnacle Lead. The lower range farther to the right is Porters Mountain, and on the horizon behind Porters Mountain are the main Smoky divide and Mount Guyot (6,621 feet). A little farther up-trail, Mount Le Conte (6,593), Trillium Gap, and Brushy Mountain (4,911 feet) come into view. The latter is far to the right, almost out of sight, and the gap is the low point directly along the line of the trail. A rounded knob in the foreground hides all the peaks of Mount Le Conte except Myrtle Point, visible just to the left of the knob. The Boulevard peaks out through a saddle in the ridge extending from Myrtle Point.

Pine stands, such as the ones here, generally occur in small patches, usually of only a few acres, and each patch dominated by a single species, in this case Table Mountain pine. Whatever the size of the pines in any one place, the trees are all about the same age. The explanation accords that pine trees seed abundantly after fire, but it is a matter of chance whether one species or another is able to seed at any one spot.

Once, when Harvey Broome stood in this south-facing pine forest with its laurel and xerophytic groundcover of galax, wintergreen, and ground pine, he looked across Trillium Branch to the north-facing slope, which he described as one of the superb forests in the world. "The two slopes," Broome noticed, "represent two worlds. The one lived richly upon its abundant moisture. The other was marginal, supporting a poverty-line of have-nots."

To reach the north-facing slope and Broome's "superb forests," the trail crosses Trillium Branch on slippery moss-covered rocks and climbs through an old-growth stand of eastern hemlocks. A half-mile above Trillium Branch, the trail executes a sharp switchback onto a boulder-strewn slope where the shallow-rooted hemlocks cannot compete well with the deep-rooted deciduous trees. Of these, the yellow buckeye with its opposite leaves of palmate leaflets and white basswood with it alternate heart-shaped leaves and basal sprouts, are dominant with small sugar maples and black cherries as associates. In late April, spring beauties blanket the slopes with squirrel corn, toothwort, Dutchman's-breeches, and crimson bee-balm interspersed in various niches.

More noticeable, however, is the massive flat dome of Brushy Mountain with its striking, light-green, heath bald. Because of their appearance from a distance, mountaineers referred to heath balds as "laurel slicks." But Brushy Mountain is neither bald nor slick. It bears some of the most impenetrable vegetation in the Smokies. While describing a Smoky Mountain heath bald, one mountaineer once commented, "We call 'em 'slicks' when we stand off and look at 'em and 'roughs' when we're crawling through 'em."

A little more than a mile above the switchback, the trail levels out into a spacious park-like setting astride the ridge between Mount Le Conte and Brushy Mountain. Originally known by the mountaineers as both Grassy Gap and Beech Gap, the name was later officially changed to Trillium Gap, an unfortunate choice as trilliums are conspicuously scarce here. However, a fine display of painted trilliums can be found along the trail to the summit of Brushy Mountain just north of the gap. Trillium Gap is forested with gnarled wind-agonized beech trees, and, except where paths have been worn, the ground in the gap is covered in lush grass.

In describing beech stands like this in Trillium Gap, botanist Stanley Cain pointed out that beech gaps in the Smokies are restricted to small areas in saddles and gaps, an occurrence that is determined by climate factors and soil conditions. Air currents circulate through the gaps where everywhere else the air is still. In early spring, beech trees in the gaps are frequently covered with hoarfrost when the adjacent spruce woods are relatively free. Throughout all seasons, moisture-laden clouds drift back and forth through these gaps. Wintertime sleet storms are frequently severe. The soil in beech gaps, as Cain points out, is relatively deep, friable, rich, and well drained. It is only slightly acidic and has no accumulation of peat, conditions that are ideal for beech trees. A short distance away, in both the spruce forest and the heath bald, all these conditions are reversed, and the soil may have a hundred times the active acidity.

In Trillium Gap, the Brushy Mountain Trail intersects its western counterpart, the Trillium Gap Trail, rising in from the opposite side. Here, the Trillium Gap Trail turns south and climbs 3.6 miles to the summit of Mount Le Conte. The Brushy Mountain Trail turns right and continues 675 yards to terminate on the dome-like summit of Brushy Mountain.

The trail to the summit of Brushy Mountain threads a rocky trough between solid walls of laurel and rhododendron that are at first tall but which become progressively shorter as the trail approaches the peak. The mountain was burned in 1925 and probably once or twice before then. The fire destroyed all of the trees on Brushy but failed to eradicate the hardy broad-leaf evergreens. Such burning inhibits slow-growing plants, especially trees, and so, subsequent to the fire, the absence of the shading deciduous species encouraged the growth of the faster-growing shrubs to the extent that Brushy Mountain was transformed entirely into a heath bald. In addition, when these heath species lose their leaves and twigs to the soil's surface, the debris tends to make the soil more acidic, thus inhibiting further growth of plants not already tolerant of such conditions.

Because the trail to the summit is so deeply eroded, it affords a convenient place to observe some important principles of soil composition in this unique plant community. The soil surface over much of the mountain is covered with a rather hard crust of gray-green lichens. Seeds germinate on this crust only with great difficulty. Water penetrates the layer, but the surface soon dries out, leaving the crust hard to pierce. Just under this surface crust lies a dark spongy layer of decayed leaves, moss, and other plant debris commonly called peat. The peat layer is very acidic, from ten to one hundred times that of the surface soil in a deciduous forest. Any seed that succeeds in sending its roots through the tough lichen crust must then contend with this hostile subsurface layer.

The next layer below is likely to be gray, very granular or sandy, and perhaps more eroded than the peaty layer above. In heath balds, all the nutrients are leached from this layer by the percolation of water, so it tends to be rather sterile. If roots are able to penetrate the peat layer, they must pass quickly through this layer of malnutrition to reach a thin layer of life-sustaining loam. Beneath the loam is bedrock. The trail itself is rocky because it has eroded through to this bedrock.

When the trail reaches the summit of Brushy Mountain, it breaks out into an opening of low-growing heath, affording a superb view of the imposing north face of Mount Le Conte. All it its peaks—Cliff Top (6,555 feet), High Top (6,593 feet), and Myrtle Point (6,200 feet)—are clearly distinguishable against the skyline. Farther to the east is Mount Kephart (6,217 feet). East of Mount Kephart and visible just over the rim of the aptly named Horseshoe Mountain (5,288 feet) is Charlies Bunion, a barren rampart that juts out from the face of the main Smoky divide. On the main divide beyond the Bunion stand the Sawteeth, steeply tilted strata of rock that have been eroded into a jagged sawteeth formation. Visible farther along the divide are Laurel Top (5,907 feet), Mount Chapman (6,417 feet), and Mount Guyot (6,621 feet).

Looking north, Brushy Mountain is seen falling away to the wrinkled plain of the Tennessee Valley. Cove Mountain looms immediately over the city of Gatlinburg on the left, and anvil-shaped English Mountain is low on the right. To the right of English Mountain are Douglas Lake and the city of Newport. The large rounded peak directly below Brushy Mountain is Mount Winnesoka, "the place of the grapes."

GRAPEYARD RIDGE TRAIL

Greenbrier Cove Road to the Roaring Fork Motor Nature Trail at the Jim Bales Place—7.6 miles.

POINT OF DEPARTURE: From Gatlinburg (at the junction of US441 and US321), drive east 5.9 miles on US321 to the Greenbrier entrance to the park. Turn and follow Greenbrier Cove Road into the park 3.2 miles to Ramsey Prong Road, which crosses the Middle Prong of the Little Pigeon River on a wooden bridge. The Grapeyard Ridge Trail begins along Greenbrier Cove Road opposite the bridge.

QUAD MAP: Mount Le Conte 165-NW

0.0—Greenbrier Cove Road.

0.1—Access path exits right to the Friendship Missionary Baptist Church Cemetery.

0.8—Rhododendron Creek.
1.3—Rhododendron Creek.
1.5—Rhododendron Creek.
1.7—Rhododendron Creek.
1.8—Access path exits left to the Dodgen-Rayfield Cemetery.
2.8—James Gap.
2.9—Injun Creek.
3.2—Access path exits right to Injun Creek Backcountry Campsite (#32).
4.8—Dudley Creek.
4.9—Horse trail.
7.4—Roaring Fork.
7.5—Jim Bales Place.
7.6—Roaring Fork Motor Nature Trail.

> One of the few Cherokee place-names to have survived in Smoky Mountain nomenclature is Winnesoka, meaning "place of the grapes." The name refers specifically to Mount Winnesoka, a high rounded peak below the north face of Mount Le Conte. White settlers did not adopt the name Winnesoka, preferring to call the peak Round Top. They did, however, recognize the prevalence of grape-vines in the area and thus attached the name Grapeyard to the ridge extending north from Mount Winnesoka.

The Grapeyard Ridge Trail is a long course that winds through old farm fields along Rhododendron Creek in Greenbrier, then around the base of Mount Winnesoka and over to the Jim Bales homesite on the Roaring Fork Motor Nature Trail. The trail begins on the west side of Greenbrier Cove Road just a few yards below its intersection with Ramsey Prong Road. It climbs away from the road steeply for eighty-five yards to intersect an old roadbed on the right that leads to the Friendship Missionary Baptist Church Cemetery. Above the trail, as it approaches the roadbed, a stone retaining wall forms up on the left. The wall is part of a terrace that was once the church's property.

The old roadbed circles 600 yards around a knoll and returns to the Grapeyard Ridge Trail. Halfway around, it passes on the left a grassy clearing that harbors a graveyard of about two dozen graves. The graveyard is referred to both as the Friendship Baptist Church Cemetery and the Whaley Cemetery.

Beyond its first intersection with the roadbed, the trail climbs another 290 yards to meet the road again where the trail now follows the roadbed for a quarter-mile to the top of a low ridge. A quarter-mile down the far side of the ridge, the trail crosses a feeder stream and then enters a bottomland flanking Rhododendron Creek.

Prior to the park, Rhododendron Creek was known as Laurel Creek. The name was changed by the Smoky Mountain Nomenclature Committee to reduce the number of streams in the Smokies known as Laurel Creek. Though there is rhododendron along the stream, the name nevertheless is an unfortunate choice in that rhododendron was not a word commonly used by the Smoky Mountaineers.

Within the next mile, the Grapeyard Ridge Trail crosses Rhododendron Creek five times. The bottomland is wide and level and once occupied by farms. Rhododendron Creek itself is quite shallow and runs only a few inches below the plain of the bottomland. The trail stays to the roadbed close along the stream.

The first crossing of Rhododendron Creek is easy. A half-mile up-trail, a second crossing angles sharply upstream. Three hundred and fifty-five yards farther, the trail crosses a third time where the stream is wide and the crossing is not necessarily easy. About thirty yards prior to the third crossing, a standing fieldstone is noticeable beside the trail on the left. The stone most likely does not mark a grave as it appears to have been propped up along the trail as a prank.

Two hundred and forty-five yards beyond the third crossing, the trail clears a large tributary and then, ninety-five yards farther, crosses back over the main stream. The last crossing places the trail on the right side of Rhododendron Creek.

About 200 yards above the last crossing at a point marked only by a large rock in the middle of the trail, a faint access path crosses the stream to the left and proceeds 500 yards to the Dodgen-Rayfield Cemetery. The access passes through a lowland of feeder streams, then follows a dug road to the crest of a slight ridge. Here, it turns left and climbs through dense forest cover to a grassy opening perched on a high knoll. At the entrance, chestnut posts mark what may have once been a tiny enclosure within the cemetery.

A quarter-mile beyond the fifth and last crossing of Rhododendron Creek, the trail clears a headwater stream and soon passes a low stone wall to reach a hollow that once harbored Backcountry Campsite #33. The campsite is now abandoned. The trail turns abruptly away from the stream and winds gently up the flank of James Ridge, reaching the ridgeline at James Gap. Prior to the park, the gap was known as Bear Pen Gap.

In 1920, one of Ike Huskey's boys was returning a self-propelled steam engine tractor to Webb Creek from Big Laurel (on Rhododendron Creek), where it had been used to power a sawmill cutting boards to build the new Greenbrier Cove School. The young Huskey had intended to drive out of Big Laurel through James Gap and then down the road along Indian Creek. As he started down from James

Gap, he lost control of the tractor, turning it over in Indian Creek 125 yards below. Huskey managed to jump to safety.

The workhorse tractor was manufactured by the Nichols & Shephard Company of Battle Creek, Michigan, in 1915. It was a side-mounted double-cylinder tractor that burned wood and generated about thirty-five horsepower. This model was among the earliest self-propelled steam units built in the United States.

The wrecked tractor quickly became the main topic of conversation in this part of the Smokies. Those who came to see it later remarked that it was "a sight to behold." Art Shultz and Johnny Manning were retained to collect the parts of the steam engine that could be salvaged and transport them to Hartford. The men hauled a wagonload apiece.

Pieces of the wrecked engine that Shultz and Manning did not collect remain in Indian Creek today. They include the main boiler, the large iron wheels, a spider gear, and parts of the piston drive. Stamped on the boiler are three numbers: 4246, 1726, and 4379.

At the time, the stream in which Huskey overturned the steam engine was known as Indian Creek. After the wreck, it came to be called Engine Creek. When inventorying place-names for the new park, the Smoky Mountain Nomenclature Committee thought that "Engine" was the result of the local mountaineers not being able to properly pronounce the word "Indian," leading them to officially fix the name as "Injun Creek."

As an aside, the new Greenbrier Cove School was built in 1920 with the lumber from the sawmill powered by the steam-engine tractor in Injun Creek. The next year the schoolhouse burned down and the students were sent for the remainder of the year to schools in church houses.

A hundred and twenty-five yards below James Gap, the Grapeyard Ridge Trail crosses Injun Creek at the site of the wreck and then follows a settler's road downstream through the hollow between James Ridge and Grapeyard Ridge. About a half-mile downstream, it intersects an access path on the right that leads a hundred yards to the Injun Creek Backcountry Campsite (#32).

The access path is an old road that first passes through the Tom Rayfield farm and then descends along Injun Creek to the Greenbrier Ranger Station on Greenbrier Cove Road. The campsite is a hundred yards down the road on what was once the Rayfield homeplace. It is situated above the road on a grassy gradient that remains open and lightly shaded as though it were still a farmyard. The old farmyard is spacious and affords several nice tenting spots.

A food-storage cable is suspended above the upper corner of the camp. Beyond the cable a well-worn path leads thirty yards to a small feeder stream that is sufficient for water. A few yards downhill, there is a small annex campsite situated on a level bench above the stream. The annex site is heavily shaded and completely free of grassy turf, but it enjoys seclusion from the access path and the main campsite. In the event the feeder stream is dry, water can be found in nearby Injun Creek, which is on the far side of the road and down a very steep bank.

At its intersection with the access path to the Injun Creek Camp, the Grapeyard Ridge Trail turns left, crosses a spring branch, then begins an easy climb up Grapeyard Ridge. Dog-hobble, galax, and stripped pipsissewa are the more noticeable flowering species along the trail and are shaded by tall eastern hemlocks, cucumber trees, and red oaks, many of which are heavily draped with thick grapevines. After a mile of climbing, the trail descends to Grapeyard Branch near the foundations of a tub mill which once stood by the stream.

Stone walls along the trail signal the approach to Dudley Creek and the former Levi Ogle farm which occupied a 100-acre tract on the slopes flanking the stream. Though the surrounding bottomland may not be the most suitable farmland in the Smokies, the Ogle farm was purchased for the park in 1929 for only $1,900.

Upon crossing Dudley Creek, the trail passes more stone walls, continuing 140 yards to intersect the Dudley Creek Horse Trail. Here, the Grapeyard Ridge Trail turns sharply left and begins a long circumnavigating climb along the base of Mount Winnesoka on a narrow hard-packed clay track that is surprisingly slick in places. Here, the cove-hardwood forests yield to the dry-ridge species that thrive in the more open and sunny exposures.

A mile and a quarter above the junction with the horse trail at Dudley Creek, the Grapeyard Ridge Trail passes an old signpost marked "Roaring Fork 1.5 miles." At the sign, an overgrown manway leads away from the trail to the right. Here, the trail leaves the Dudley Creek watershed and begins descending into the Roaring Fork drainage, where a hardwood mix of oak, maple, and yellow poplar constitutes the primary forest cover. In the springtime, Vasey's trillium, wild geranium, bellwort, and trout-lily are conspicuous.

Soon after crossing the headwaters of Indian Camp Branch, the trail clears a low ridge and then descends to Roaring Fork, a fast-moving stream that forms up at Basin Spring on the summit of Mount Le Conte. When it reaches Roaring Fork, the trail switches back sharply to the right and follows a rocky course downstream. Though Roaring Fork is nearby, intervening rhododendron hide the stream in all but a few places.

A quarter-mile below the switchback, the trail passes through an opening in a stone wall and emerges into a large clearing of close-cropped grass that is known as the Jim Bales Place. Three log structures occupy the clearing. The first is a small four-crib pole barn with V-notching at the corners. The barn has a passway through the middle just wide enough for a wagon. Above the cribs are lofts for storing hay. In one of the cribs is a dugout log trough for feeding livestock. Below the barn stands a corncrib with puncheon floor in each of the two crib beds. Entrance into the cribs is through small square doors that are hinged at the top.

At the lower end of the clearing is a large one-room cabin with doors on three sides and a fireplace along the fourth wall. The cabin is constructed of thick poplar logs fastened at the corners with dove-tail notching. The cabin has a puncheon floor, one window, and a low loft that is entered through a small opening near the door opposite the fireplace, but has no porches. The cabin was built by Alex Cole and originally stood in the upper end of the Sugarlands. It was dismantled, moved here, and reassembled as part of the Park Service's effort to preserve historic structures of the Smokies.

Near the lower end of the clearing, the Grapeyard Ridge Trail terminates into the Roaring Fork Motor Nature Trail. Sixty yards up the road, a parking area marks the head of the Baskins Creek Trail.

◆ MOUNT LE CONTE ◆

The Mount Le Conte section harbors the greatest concentration of notable geological features of any section of the Smokies. The Jumpoff, Myrtle Point, Cliff Top, Rainbow Falls, Rocky Spur, Arch Rock, Duckhawk Peak, and Alum Cave Bluff are among the most surpassing mountain landmarks in eastern North America. At the center of this panoply of waterfalls, vantage points, and incongruous rock formations is Mount Le Conte, the crown jewel of the Great Smoky Mountains.

Originally known as Bull Head, the mountain received its current name when Samuel Botsford Buckley, an itinerant botanist from New York, named one of the peaks on Mount Le Conte in honor of John Le Conte, a scientist from South Carolina College (now the University of South Carolina) who in 1859 had assisted Buckley and Thomas Lanier Clingman in measuring the highest point on the main Smoky divide by monitoring a stationary barometer in Waynesville and then making the necessary calculations to determine the peak's elevation. Later, the name Mount Le Conte came to designate the entire massif with individual peaks being known as Cliff Top, High Top, and Myrtle Point.

A massive outlier standing apart from the main Smoky divide, Mount Le Conte rises a mile from base to summit, a respectable declivity even by Rocky Mountain standards. The north face of Mount Le Conte acts as a barrier to the moisture-laden air moving in from the Gulf of Mexico, chilling it and precipitating the heavy rains that make Le Conte one of the wettest places in North America. The abundance of moisture contributes to the riot and diversity of plant life for which the mountain is noted.

Mount Le Conte is literally covered with trails. The Boulevard Trail approaches from the east, Alum Cave Trail from the south, the Bull Head Trail from the west, and the Trillium Gap Trail and Rainbow Falls Trail from the north. The Brushy Mountain Trail visits the northeastern flank of Mount Le Conte; however, it is treated in the Greenbrier section. Two other trails, the Baskins Creek Trail and the Twin Creeks Trail, are lower-elevation courses that visit the northern flank of Le Conte where it grades into the large cove that now harbors Gatlinburg.

There are no backcountry campsites in the Mount Le Conte section. Camping is limited to Le Conte Lodge and the Mount Le Conte Shelter, both on the summit of the mountain. Le Conte Lodge, a commercial operation, is available only by reservation at 865-492-5704. The shelter may be reserved through the Park Service at 865-436-1231 or online at https://smokiespermits.nps.gov/.

Of the seven trails in this section, all but the Alum Cave Trail and Boulevard Trail can be reached from either Cherokee Orchard Road or its extension, the Roaring Fork

Motor Nature Trail. The Alum Cave Trail is along Newfound Gap Road (US441) about nine miles above the Sugarlands Visitor Center and the Boulevard Trail is most easily reached by hiking the Appalachian Trail 2.8 miles east from Newfound Gap.

THE BOULEVARD TRAIL

The Appalachian Trail at Mount Kephart to the summit of Mount Le Conte—5.4 miles.

POINT OF DEPARTURE: From the Sugarlands Visitor Center, drive on Newfound Gap Road (US441) 12.9 miles to Newfound Gap. From the Oconaluftee Visitor Center drive north on US441 15.5 miles to the gap. From Newfound Gap, hike the Appalachian Trail east 2.8 miles. The Boulevard Trail exits left from the Appalachian Trail.

QUAD MAP: Mount Le Conte 165-NW

0.0—Appalachian Trail.
0.1—Access path exits right 0.4 mile to The Jumpoff.
1.6—Overlook.
2.5—Anakeesta Knob.
4.4—Slide scar.
4.9—Access path exits left 360 yards to Myrtle Point.
5.0—High Top.
5.2—Mount Le Conte Shelter.
5.3—Access path exits left 0.3 mile to Cliff Top.
5.4—Rainbow Falls Trail. Trillium Gap Trail.

The Boulevard, one of the most tortuous and precipitous of all the longer divides in the Smokies, is a thin ridge that connects the main Smoky divide to its prominent outlier, Mount Le Conte, four miles to the northwest. The trail that traces the spine of the Boulevard shares the same name and, by providing access to The Jumpoff, Myrtle Point, and a few lesser-known overlooks, affords more vantage points than any other trail in the Smokies except the Appalachian Trail.

The Boulevard Trail begins along the Appalachian Trail about three miles north of Newfound Gap, exiting left and angling up and along the Tennessee side of Mount Kephart.

 Mount Kephart has not always been known by this name. In a published report of his surveys of the Smoky Mountains during the mid-nineteenth century, the pioneering Swiss explorer Arnold Guyot named this mountain Pecks Peak in recognition of Judge Jacob Peck, an amateur geologist who had conducted surveys of the mountain region in the 1830s. At that time, the Smokies were a vast uncharted wilderness, and Guyot's notes were difficult, if not impossible, to interpret. Consequently, the name Pecks Peak never became popularly identified with the present Mount Kephart. Instead, Mount Alexander was adopted, a name Guyot had originally applied to the circus-tent-shaped peak now known as Mount Chapman. By the turn of the twentieth century, other names, particularly Laurel Top and Fodderstack Mountain, had crept into the local vernacular and were being applied to the mountain.

In 1921 the U.S. Geological Survey added to the confusion by issuing maps which labeled the peak Mount Collins, the name of another peak located three miles northeast of Clingmans Dome. This situation persisted until 1932 when it was proposed that the mountain be named for Horace Kephart, the librarian whose book *Our Southern Highlanders* did much to foster widespread appreciation of the Smoky Mountain region. The honoring of Horace Kephart returned the name Collins to its former location and erased Alexander permanently from official Smoky Mountain nomenclature.

Three hundred and twenty-five yards above the trailhead, a manway exits right from the Boulevard Trail, ascends a half-mile to the summit of Mount Kephart, and then leads out along a short path to The Jumpoff, a precipitous point at the end of a razor-thin rib. The first half of the manway entails a tortuous climb up a deeply rutted path obstructed with roots and closely confined on either side by thickets of Fraser fir. The summit of Mount Kephart is marked by a tiny level clearing that affords a fine view along the spine of the Boulevard to the eastern end of Mount Le Conte. Beyond the clearing, the manway completes a short, rugged, near-vertical descent and then levels for the final approach to The Jumpoff. Here, the ridge narrows to a single ledge projecting out over an enormous basin. From The Jumpoff, the mountain falls away precipitously a thousand feet. In all of the Smokies, only the Chimney Tops and a cliff ledge on Greenbrier Lead compare with The Jumpoff in affording the spine-tingling sensation of being perilously close to a dangerous edge.

The south wall of the basin is formed by the main Smoky divide meandering to the east. In the intermediate distance the Sawteeth appear as a jagged row of closely aligned, sharp-edged peaks. Prominent farther along the divide are Laurel Top (5,907 feet), Mount Chapman (6,417 feet), and Mount Guyot (6,621 feet).

The far side of the basin is defined by Greenbrier Lead, a massive ridge that extends north from the base of Old Black (6,370 feet), ending abruptly at a cliff formation known as the Cat Stairs. Beyond the end of Greenbrier Lead is the distinctive anvil-shaped English Mountain. To the left, rising from the bottom of the basin is the aptly named Horseshoe Mountain. Down and to the right, a grotesque rock formation known as Charlies Bunion can be seen projecting like a flying buttress from the main Smoky divide.

From its intersection with the manway to The Jumpoff, the Boulevard Trail climbs briefly before settling into a long, gradual, half-mile descent that ends in a slight swag. Even at this elevation, the trail is in the balsam zone, sometimes confined within a narrow corridor of red spruce and densely growing Fraser fir. In places, the trail is impeded by protruding roots and upturned strata of rock. In others, it is smooth and soft underfoot. At the swag, the trail mounts the main ridgeline of the Boulevard where a flat open area affords the first of several vantage points.

Once the trail reaches the crest of the Boulevard, it continues either on or just slightly off the spine of the ridge. This portion of the trail is easy, alternating between beech gaps and stands of balsam interspersed with pin cherries, mountain maples, and yellow birches. To the south is Anakeesta Ridge, a long rugged knife-edge that abuts the Boulevard at Anakeesta Knob. Anakeesta Knob appears as a high point to the left of the trail, covered in densely growing spruce and fir. Anakeesta, meaning "balsam place," is one of a relatively few Cherokee place-names that have survived in the Smokies.

After a switchback at Anakeesta Knob, the trail dips into Alum Gap and then enters another climb along the narrowest section of the Boulevard. In several places the mountain drops precipitously from the edge of the trail into the Tennessee Valley, affording extensive vistas. On a clear day, the great sweep of the Smoky Mountains is visible out to Douglas Lake and beyond to the distant Cherokee Lake.

When it reaches higher elevation, the trail curls off the ridgeline onto a course that proceeds beneath the cliffs that form the eastern summit of Mount Le Conte. Here, the balsam stands are densely growing and the slopes heavily saturated with water. Yellow bead lilies, wild golden-glows, closed gentians, monkshoods, filmy angelicas, and pink turtleheads are prevalent as well as the bright-yellow blossoming mountain St. John's-wort and the beautiful grass of parnassus with its white fluted petals. On the faces of the cliffs are tussocks of sand myrtle which in early summer bear star-shaped blossoms ranging from white to pale pink. In late summer the most noticeable flora may well be the mountain ash trees with their striking bright red-orange clusters of fruit. The mountain St. John's-wort, grass of parnassus, sand myrtle, and mountain ash all thrive in the Smokies only at the highest elevations.

Before returning to the ridgeline, the trail proceeds along an outlying spur, passing through a massive scar in the face of the mountain caused by an earth slide.

 As is common on the steeper mountain slopes, the soil and roots are confined to a shallow depth, usually less than eighteen inches. During heavy rains, the water reaches bedrock quickly and, having nowhere to seep, it runs along the bedrock. Like a lubricant, the flowing water loosens the soil-root mass, separating it from the bedrock, and sends it sliding down the slope, taking everything it its path.

Such slides often begin with one or two large trees. These take a few others with them, starting a domino effect, with the slide widening quickly as it descends. Eventually the marginal trees begin to resist and the slide narrows again, finally dumping its consignment of soil and vegetation down the slope. The result is often a diamond- or lens-shaped scar, such as the one through which the Boulevard Trail passes.

Hostile climate conditions, short growing seasons, and a paucity of remaining soil deter a quick re-vegetation of the scar. In the twenty years since the slide, very little new growth has encroached. In another fifty years, grass and blackberry brambles are likely to be the only cover, with a few trees gaining purchase on the perimeter. It may well be two hundred years before the scar is totally forested again. The slide scar fortuitously affords a fine vantage point for surveying the whole of the Greenbrier basin, as well as much of the meander of the Boulevard.

Beyond the slide scar, the Boulevard Trail executes a set of climbing switchbacks before returning to the main ridgeline at the point where a manway exits left 360 yards to Myrtle Point, the eastern vanguard of Le Conte.

The manway to Myrtle Point adheres to the spine of the ridge that marks the eastern extension of Mount Le Conte and is confined to a narrow single-file track bounded by rhododendron, bands of fir trees, and rock ledges. It soon reaches a bald headland of rock and low-growing sand myrtle, affording one of the most spectacular vantage points in all of the Smokies. On a clear day, one can see the meander of the Boulevard to Mount Kephart, and east along the main Smoky divide to the Sawteeth, Laurel Top, Mount Chapman, Mount Guyot, and, in the far distance, Mount Cammerer (4,928 feet). Visible along the western half of the divide are Clingmans Dome (6,643 feet), Silers Bald (5,607 feet), and Thunderhead (5,527 feet). Beyond the divide, layers upon layers of mountains extend into North Carolina as far as the eye can see.

Below and in the intermediate distance is the rugged maw of Huggins Hell. When Myrtle Point is heavily shrouded in clouds, Huggins Hell takes on an unearthly aura where, as Harvey Broome noted, "the mists dissolve and re-form, . . . vague shapes of mountains appear and vanish, and one is aware of stupendous, formless depth all around."

From its junction with the manway to Myrtle Point, the Boulevard Trail turns sharply right and follows the ridgeline 275 yards to High Top which, at 6,593 feet, is the highest point of elevation on Mount Le Conte. A pile of stones alongside the trail reflects the efforts of generations of hikers attempting to build High Top to an elevation higher than Clingmans Dome at 6,643 feet.

From High Top, the trail begins a gentle descent into a shallow basin that harbors a compound of rustic cabins known as Le Conte Lodge. Just as it enters the basin, the trail passes the Mount Le Conte Shelter on the left in an open field that slopes away from High Top. The shelter enjoys a fine setting and affords proximity to both Myrtle Point and Cliff Top, the western vanguard of Le Conte. The closest water source to the shelter is at Basin Spring 300 yards down-trail at Le Conte Lodge.

Halfway between the shelter and the lodge, the Boulevard Trail intersects a manway that exits left and traces the upper rim of the basin along its south-facing cliffs to terminate on Cliff Top, a superb vantage point. From Cliff Top, a second manway leads back down to the entrance to Le Conte Lodge.

Within forty yards of reaching the entrance to the lodge, the Boulevard Trail terminates in a three-way intersection with the Rainbow Falls Trail and Trillium Gap Trail. Entering in along the upper side of the lodge compound, the Rainbow Falls Trail intersects straight on the end of the Boulevard Trail. The Trillium Gap Trail leads up from the right along the eastern perimeter of the compound. All three trails terminate at the intersection.

ALUM CAVE TRAIL

Newfound Gap Road at the Grassy Patch to the Rainbow Falls Trail—5.0 miles.

POINT OF DEPARTURE: From the Sugarlands Visitor Center, drive Newfound Gap Road (US441) 8.6 miles to the parking lot on the left. From Newfound Gap, drive 4.3 miles into Tennessee. The Alum Cave Trail begins at the back of the parking lot.

QUAD MAP: Mount Le Conte 165-NW

0.0—The Grassy Patch. Walker Camp Prong. Footbridge.
0.1—Alum Cave Creek. Footbridge.
1.1—Styx Branch. Footlog.
1.2—Styx Branch. Footlog.
1.4—Styx Branch. Footlog. Arch Rock.
1.4—Styx Branch. Footlog.
1.5—Gully washout.
2.0—Inspiration Point.
2.3—Alum Cave Bluff.
2.6—The Pulpit.
3.8—Switchback at steps.
4.2—Slide scar.
5.0—Rainbow Falls Trail exits right 200 yards to Le Conte Lodge.

Given the richness of its history and the number of outstanding natural landmarks along the way, the Alum Cave Trail is arguably the signature trail of the Great

Smoky Mountains National Park. Arch Rock, Inspiration Point, the Duckhawk Peaks, Alum Cave Bluff, the Pulpit, and Huggins Hell are notable Smoky Mountain landmarks encountered en route to the summit of Mount Le Conte, which itself affords Cliff Top and Myrtle Point, two of the finest vantage points east of the Mississippi. The trail begins along Newfound Gap Road at the lower corner of a parking lot situated just above the confluence of Walker Camp Prong and Alum Cave Creek.

Prior to the road, the space now occupied by the parking lot was a one-acre clearing known as the Grassy Patch. The clearing was enclosed by a rail fence and occupied by a possession cabin built in 1918 by local mountaineer Davis Bracken to mark ownership of the mountain by the Champion Fibre Company.

Until the arrival of the park, the Bracken Cabin, or the Grassy Patch Cabin as it was sometimes called, was a remote outpost frequented only by the occasional hunting party, timber rangers, or outdoorsmen venturing to explore Alum Cave. As a teenager, Harvey Broome visited the Grassy Patch and recalled seeing a tiny log cabin which had been erected in a rough clearing above the stream. The gaps between the logs were closed by clean, hand-split shingles that had been nailed horizontally on the inside. The work was crude and the air circulation remained excellent. The cabin had a puncheon floor and a roof of spot shingles.

A small iron stove with a flat working surface was propped on billets in one corner of the cabin. Pole bedsteads with corn husk mattresses occupied two corners, and a pile of firewood, mostly waste from the cabin construction, was stacked handy to the stove.

Davis Bracken's name would likely have faded into obscurity were it not for an unexpected encounter with the well-known writer Horace Kephart, who had recently published his first edition of *Our Southern Highlanders*, a series of essays on the peculiar customs of the Smoky Mountain people.

Kephart, in the company of a federal revenue agent in pursuit of a moonshiner, was traveling down the old Indian Gap road into Tennessee when the two were overtaken by darkness. Kephart and the revenue agent eventually stumbled into a cabin in what is now the Chimney Tops Picnic Area. This cabin was the home of Davis Bracken and his wife. The Brackens took Kephart in, fed him supper, and gave him a place to sleep for the night. Kephart later incorporated the story of this encounter in an expanded edition of *Our Southern Highlanders* published in 1922, casting Bracken under the pseudonym Jasper Finn. Of all the impressions Bracken made on him, Kephart only recorded that "there are mighty few cowards in the mountains, and subsequent event proved he was not one of them." The "subsequent events" to which Kephart alluded involved Bracken's shooting and killing an intoxicated moonshiner named Newman who dared to step up onto the porch of Bracken's cabin while brandishing a gun.

From the Grassy Patch parking lot, the Alum Cave Trail proceeds forty-five yards to Walker Camp Prong, crossing on a wooden footbridge. A hundred and twenty yards farther, the trail clears Alum Cave Creek on a similar bridge and then begins coursing through great arbors of tall rhododendrons shaded by large American beech trees. The grade remains easy and never far from Alum Cave Creek. About a half-mile above the Grassy Patch, the trail enters a rough opening where the vegetation recedes and dim vestiges of an old manway can be seen to the left extending up the side of the mountain.

The manway, which dates to the early Cherokee, is the oldest trail to Alum Cave Bluff. It was once described as a mile-and-a-half scramble up the side of a steep ridge through a tunnel of rhododendron. Although it remained in use until the 1920s, it was probably never much of a trail.

When this direct route to Alum Cave Bluff was abandoned, a new trail was installed that adhered to the creek bottom. The newer course crossed Alum Cave Creek at this point and proceeded a short distance upstream before crossing back and turning up the east side of Styx Branch to the mouth of Arch Rock. The trail remained on the east side of Styx Branch until Labor Day 1951, when a thunderstorm near the summit of Mount Le Conte deposited four inches of rain in less than an hour, sending a wall of water surging out of Huggins Hell and down Styx Branch. According to Harvey Broome, who visited the area shortly after the flood, "half the trail from Grassy Patch to Arch Rock was gone, undercut, or obliterated by debris. The creek was littered with boulders, trees, branches, and twigs. There was no certainty as to its prior course. Its bed had been drastically changed shifting in some places as much as 100 feet."

The power of the flood was unbelievable. Broome noted that log jams were numerous. Some were as large as two medium size houses and composed of some of the largest trees in the area. Twigs were flung into the jams with such force that they created breastworks head-high and solidly meshed. In the aftermath of the flood, the Alum Cave Trail was redirected to remain on the west side of Alum Cave Creek and then upstream along its tributary, Styx Branch.

A little over a mile above the Grassy Patch, the trail crosses Styx Branch, proceeds 200 yards upstream, then crosses back. Two hundred yards farther, it crosses Styx Branch a third time. All three crossings are on footlogs. Twenty-five yards beyond the third footlog, the trail enters Arch Rock, a natural tunnel-like hole that extends through a solid, rib-like, rock outcropping that slants down from the adjacent slope to the stream. The hole, although twenty feet high at its lower end, is barely high enough at the top to permit a full-grown person to stand erect. The trail proceeds through the hole on a stone staircase accompanied by a wire-cable handrail.

The inside edges of Arch Rock are sharp and jagged, indicating that the hole is a result of the fracturing action of cold and ice rather than the wearing of water erosion. The slanting rib is defined geologically as having been formed of compressed sediments of oceanic mud and scientifically identified as Anakeesta formation. During the intense upheavals that formed the mountains, these sedimentary layers were thrust upward into a perpendicular plane. Water seeping into the exposed crevices of the upturned strata freezes in colder weather, thus fracturing the rock. At Arch Rock, the upended sediments are apparently weaker on the sides than on the exposed outer edges, allowing the erosion to occur through the center of the slant.

Once through Arch Rock, the Alum Cave Trail proceeds along a narrow rock ledge 120 yards to a fourth and final footlog over Styx Branch. Upstream are massive arbors of rhododendron interspersed with colossal red spruces straight as shipmasts and rugged old birch trees which, as Harvey Broome once noted, "softened the rigid ranks of the spruces." The place which inspired Broome's comment is known as Huggins Hell, a terrain of uncompromising ruggedness even by Smoky Mountain standards.

"Hell" is a Smoky Mountain colloquialism referring to any dense impenetrable thicket of rhododendron and laurel covering an extended area of mountain terrain. According to a bit of mountain lore preserved by Paul Fink, the name "Huggins Hell" is attributed to a certain gentleman named Huggins who "vowed he'd explore the wilderness if it took him to Hell. He was never heard from again, and popularly was supposed to have carried out the alternative."

A hundred and forty-five yards beyond the final Styx Branch crossing, the trail encounters a gully-like wash-out that is the result of another incident of excessive water.

In the early evening of June 28, 1993, a heavy thunderstorm plowed into the face of Mount Le Conte and released several inches of rainwater onto the upper reaches of Huggins Hell. The water gathered quickly along the higher slopes, forming a torrent that was sent roaring down the narrow defile. The weight of the moisture in the humus and the scouring action of the rainwater, which could not be absorbed, combined in a devastating way to harrow a raw gash in the mountainside. Huge trees were clipped with such force that they toppled upstream. The smaller vegetation and soil cover were stripped away, leaving freshly scoured bedrock.

This highland flood is estimated to have been twenty feet high. It struck quickly, meting out its destruction in less than five minutes. In the process a seam of highly acidic Anakeesta rock was left exposed. The distinct smell of sulfur is evidence that the caustic effluent is still leaching out.

Beyond the wash-out, the grade stiffens noticeably as the trail winds through stands of red spruce for about 600 yards to emerge onto a heath bald covered in low impenetrable thickets of mountain laurel and tussocks of sand myrtle. The small bare prominence in the middle of the heath is known as Inspiration Point.

Inspiration Point is the premier vantage point on the Alum Cave Trail, offering views into the depths of the upper Sugarlands fastness. Two rugged knife-edge ridges appear immediately to the west, across the deep defile below. The closer of the two, Little Duckhawk Peak, is distinguished by an impressive hole in its side as though it had been shot through with a cannonball. Its twin, Big Duckhawk Peak, can be seen only where it rises above its smaller sibling. The Duckhawk Peaks are of the same Anakeesta formation as Arch Rock. The fracturing action that formed the hole in Arch Rock is responsible for the cannonball hole in Little Duckhawk Peak.

On April 26, 1842, an itinerant botanist named Samuel Botsford Buckley and a companion known only as Dr. Hammer climbed out onto Little Duckhawk Peak while searching for plant specimens. Buckley later recorded that he found himself "on a narrow ledge of loose rocks with precipices several hundred feet deep on both side. It was a fearful place. With a palpitating heart I crept back, and hastened down the mountain."

The high peak south of Inspiration Point is Mount Mingus (5,802 feet). Immediately to the west of Mount Mingus the long high ridgeline of Sugarland Mountain (5,495 feet) extends for thirteen miles, separating the Little Pigeon River drainage from that of the Little River. The upper end of Sugarland Mountain is anchored to the main Smoky divide near Mount Collins (6,188 feet) about five miles beyond Mount Mingus. Its lower end reaches to Fighting Creek Gap at Little River Road. Buttressed to the near-vertical north slope of Sugarland Mountain are two distinct peaks known as the Chimney Tops (4,501 feet). From Inspiration Point they appear just over the lower end of Little Duckhawk Peak.

To the east, the Boulevard appears as the high meander extending from the summit of Mount Le Conte to the main Smoky divide. From the Boulevard, Anakeesta Ridge slants sharply down, forming the eastern perimeter of Huggins Hell.

From Inspiration Point, the trail turns north and out of the heath and into the cooler confines of a red spruce grove. Within 400 yards it reaches a set of stone steps that climbs a hundred yards to the base of Alum Cave Bluff, another remarkable geologic landmark.

Alum Cave Bluff is not a cave in the true sense of the word, but an enormous jutting ledge at the butt-end of a ridgeline. The height from floor level to the outer edge of the overhang is over a hundred feet, and the projection from the back of the bluff about sixty feet. The length of the entire formation is greater than a hundred yards.

According to Smoky Mountain legend, Alum Cave was discovered by Yonaguska, chief of the Middle Town Cherokee while, as a youth, tracking a bear. Another tradition holds that Ephraim Mingus, eldest son of Jacob Mingus of Oconaluftee, was the first white man to visit the cave when he was taken there by an Indian guide. Sometime around 1838, Ephraim Mingus engaged in a partnership with five others to form the Epsom Salts Manufacturing Company with the intent of mining the abundance of minerals found in the cave. These included alum, Epson salts, saltpeter, magnesia, and copperas.

The Epsom Salts Manufacturing Company operated in Alum Cave until at least 1842, and may have ceased then because of the great difficulty in transporting the minerals down the mountain. When James M. Safford, Tennessee state geologist, reported on a visit to the cave in 1855, he made no reference to the mining operation, thus implicating that it was no longer in operation, but he did comment that "there was a wagon load of each of the salts on the floor of the cave . . . the Epson salts being at one end, and the alum at the other." Another traveler, known only as R of Tennessee, who visited the cave four years later, made a similar observation. "At the lower edge of the cave are immense beds of almost pure alum. At the upper part . . . are larger beds of sulphate of magnesia, and Epson salts."

When the company began mining the cave, camps were set up, and water vats and log hoppers were built to process the salts. These fixtures were likely located below the trail near the stone steps. When Buckley visited Alum Cave in 1842, he commented on seeing a "small hut which had been used by the workmen while experimenting with the manufacture of epsom salts." Buckley's only observation was that the hut had a stone floor.

William Johnson, who visited Alum Cave in 1913, reported that "near the front edge there were a number of timbers and rocks piled up in a regular fashion and we were told that they were the remains of the try-works that had been operated by the Confederate Army." At the conclusion of the Civil War, mining in Alum Cave apparently ceased.

From Alum Cave Bluff, the trail climbs steeply on a rocky course to a ledge along the face of a cliff that forms the western flank of Peregrine Peak. The thinness of intervening vegetation permits superb views south to Mount Mingus, Sugarland Mountain, and down along the spines of the Duckhawk Peaks. Two hundred yards above Alum Cave, the trail circles right along the ledge. After an additional 200 yards, the climb peaks and the trail turns and starts down. Just at the turn, an access path exits left about ten yards out to a rocky projection known as the Pulpit.

From the Pulpit the entire south face of the summit of Mount Le Conte is visible. Cliff Top (6,555 feet) is identifiable as the distinct notch at the west end of the summit. The highest point on the skyline is High Top (6,593 feet). Myrtle Point (6,444 feet) is the slight peak near a notch just to the right of High Top. The three peaks were known collectively by the earliest settlers as Bull Head. Arnold Guyot, the Swiss geologist who charted the high peaks of the Smokies in 1859, referred to the mountain as "the Group of Bull Head, Tennessee," and identified the three main peaks as "Central Peak, or Mount Le Conte," "West Peak, or Mount Curtis," and "North Peak, or Mount Safford." Subsequent to Guyot's report, Central Peak was changed to High Top and the name Mount Le Conte applied to the whole massif. "North Peak or Mount Safford" was named by Guyot for James Safford, state geologist of Tennessee and later professor at Vanderbilt University, an early scientific explorer in the Smokies. Mount Safford was later renamed Myrtle Point, for the billowing tussocks of Huber's sand myrtle that grow there. West Peak or Mount Curtis was later renamed Cliff Top.

In Guyot's time the distinctive cone-shaped peak just west of Cliff Top was known as Balsam Point. This peak was later renamed West Point (6,344 feet).

From the Pulpit, the trail descends for a little more than a quarter of a mile to a saddle ridge connecting Peregrine Peak with the south face of Le Conte. From the low point along the ridge, the trail begins a steep rocky three-quarter-mile climb into the upper reaches of Huggins Hell. A long log notched into stair-steps mitigates the worst of the climb.

The eastern hemlocks and hardwoods maintain a fairly equal balance along this ridge, though red spruces begin to displace the hardwoods as elevation is gained. Spruces reach their lowest elevation at about 4,800 feet. Hemlocks extend well above that elevation, and the two are often found side by side. The needles of the spruce are short like those of the hemlock, but are sharply pointed and arise from all surfaces of the twig. Hemlocks are much larger than mature spruce at this elevation, so trees over fifteen inches in diameter are unlikely to be spruce.

At the head of the climb, the trail executes a sharp switchback left assisted by a wooden stairway, then starts across the south face of Le Conte. In a few places along the face where the trail is notched out of the solid rock, the view is straight down rather than out over the mountain gulf.

Up to this point, the trail is in transition from cove hardwoods to the balsam zone. The vegetation pattern changes as the trail progresses across the face of the mountain. The woods become more open, and the rhododendron subsides. The spruces lessen, and the Fraser firs begin appearing. Just short of a half-mile beyond the switchback, the trail passes through a wide open space that was cleared by an earth slide caused by the cloudburst on Labor Day 1951.

On the steeper slopes along the south face of Le Conte, the soil and tree roots are confined to a relatively shallow depth, usually no more than eighteen inches. During a heavy rainstorm, the water reaches the underlying bedrock quickly and, having no place to seep, pools up and runs down the rock. The flowing water loosens the soil-root mass and sends the vegetation sliding down the slope, leaving a scar on the face of the mountain.

In the sixty years since the slide, grass has covered much of the scar, and trees have gained purchase on the perimeter. Because of hostile climate conditions, short growing seasons, and the paucity of remaining soil, it may well be a hundred years or so before the scar is completely forested.

Rugel's Indian plantain, also formerly known as Rugel's ragwort and not known to exist anywhere except in the high Smokies, is found frequently along this stretch of the trail. It was named after its first collector, Ferdinand Rugel, who accompanied Buckley here in 1842. The ragwort's flowers are an inconspicuous creamy-tan growing on stiff, erect, purple stalks.

Conspicuous on the rock surfaces beginning in early April are the small-leaf rosettes of Michaux's saxifrage, whose loose cluster of small white leaves open in mid-summer. Michaux's saxifrage and other high-elevation plant species are nourished by groundwater which seeps through the cliff faces of Le Conte.

Here, Fraser firs begin appearing with greater frequency. Unlike red spruces, which produce needles on all surfaces of the twig, the firs grow their needles roughly in two wing-like ranks. Needles of the spruce are sharply pointed and leave pegs when they fall while those of the fir are notched at the top and fall without leaving pegs.

Beyond the slide scar, the trail pursues a winding course along a narrow shelf cut into the near-vertical cliff. Wire cables are affixed to the cliff wall in the more treacherous places for the benefit of nervous hikers and for safety during the coldest seasons when the seepages across the rock surfaces turn to sheets of ice. Tussocks of sand myrtle growing on the small crags flaring out from the sides of the cliff herald the entrance to a corridor of young densely growing fir trees. The trail climbs through the firs, crosses the ridgeline that connects Cliff Top with West Point, and then turns and follows an easy 200-yard course to terminate in an intersection with the Rainbow Falls Trail.

Until 1983, a gate post stood in a clearing near the end of the Alum Cave Trail. The post, a remainder of a temporary camp pitched in the clearing in 1924, was erected as part of a fence to deter pack horses from wandering off the cliff. At that time, the only horse trail to Le Conte was by Rainbow Falls. Colonel David

Chapman, chair of the Park Commission for Tennessee, suggested making an additional trail that would show off the mountains to their fullest advantage. Chapman asked Andy Huff, proprietor of the Mountain View Hotel in Gatlinburg, to retain Will Ramsay and Wiley Oakley to cut a trail from the top of Mount Le Conte to Alum Cave Bluff. Enlisting the aid of others, Ramsay and Oakley cut much of the upper end of the present-day Alum Cave Trail, completing their work during the summer of 1924. Later, crews from the Civilian Conservation Corps improved the trail by blasting out obstacles and building stone retaining walls. The trail generally retains the course marked by Huff and his men.

Two hundred yards beyond its intersection with the Alum Cave Trail, the Rainbow Falls Trail enters a shallow basin that harbors Le Conte Lodge, a hostel compound that marks the provisional center of Mount Le Conte.

RAINBOW FALLS TRAIL

Cherokee Orchard Road to the summit of Mount Le Conte—6.7 miles.

POINT OF DEPARTURE: In Gatlinburg, follow Airport Road 1.0 mile to the entrance to the park boundary, where the name changes to Cherokee Orchard Road. Follow Cherokee Orchard Road 2.5 miles to the large parking lot on the right. The Rainbow Falls Trail begins near the south end of the parking lot.

QUAD MAP: Mount Le Conte 165-NW

0.0—Cherokee Orchard Road.
0.1—Trillium Gap Trail exits left 8.8 miles to the summit of Mount Le Conte.
1.9—Le Conte Creek. Footlog.
2.7—Le Conte Creek. Footlog.
2.8—Rainbow Falls.
3.3—Le Conte Creek.
4.2—Overlook.
5.5—Access exits left to Rocky Spur.
5.5—Alternate access to Rocky Spur.
6.0—Bull Head Trail exits right 5.9 miles to the Old Sugarlands Trail.
6.6—Alum Cave Trail exits right 5.0 miles to Newfound Gap Road at the Grassy Patch.
6.6—Access trail exits right to Cliff Top.
6.7—Entrance to Le Conte Lodge.
6.7—Boulevard Trail. Trillium Gap Trail.

From its beginning in Cherokee Orchard to its terminus on Mount Le Conte, the Rainbow Falls Trail gains nearly four thousand feet of elevation over a distance of almost seven miles, making it one of the longer steady climbs in the Smokies. Completed in 1934 by the Park Service, the modern Rainbow Falls Trail begins at the upper corner of the first large parking area on Cherokee Orchard Road. As it leaves the road, the trail proceeds toward Le Conte Creek for 120 yards before intersecting the Trillium Gap Trail angling across the upper end of the Cherokee Orchard tract. Beyond the intersection and on the approach to Le Conte Creek, the Rainbow Falls Trail enters a wide bench flanking both sides of the stream. Once, when traveling this part of the trail, Harvey Broome recalled having "the feeling of moving upward through a wide shallow trough with the soft rush of the creek at the bottom." At some point in ancient time, nature had poured onto the trough a "tumbled floor of huge boulders and slivers of rock," some the size of an ordinary room. The trail leads over, around, and through this confusion of boulders, soon entering into a forest of giant trees—yellow poplars, eastern hemlocks, white basswoods, yellow buckeyes, Carolina silverbells, shagbark hickories, and a variety of oaks and maples.

The precursor to the Rainbow Falls Trail was a rudimentary streamside trace that adhered closely to Le Conte Creek until the stream dwindled out near the summit of the mountain. Le Conte Creek was once known by the local mountaineers as Mill Creek, the name changed by the Park Nomenclature Committee to reduce the number of Mill Creeks in the Smokies. The earlier trail stayed to the east side of Mill Creek until it reached Rainbow Falls, where it crossed to a hemlock tree leaning against the cliff a hundred feet west of the falls. Hikers climbed the tree to reach the top of Rainbow Falls. From there, the trail resumed its course along Mill Creek, crossing the stream several times until its headwaters disappeared beneath the thick humus of a boreal forest about a quarter-mile below the mountain's summit.

Early travelers on the original trace mention a barn two miles downstream from Rainbow Falls as a well-known point of departure. The barn stood in what was later a parking lot just to the right of the trailhead. The parking lot was abandoned when Cherokee Road was improved. The barn belonged to the Cherokee Orchard Company, which had purchased a thousand acres along Mill Creek about two miles above Gatlinburg. The soil, moisture, and climatic conditions of the north-facing slope at this elevation were favorable for growing apple trees. At one time the company had approximately three hundred acres planted in apples trees and ornamental nursery plants. The company added a road leading up to the orchard from Gatlinburg that later came to be called Cherokee Orchard Road, a name that has persisted to the present.

After a mile, the Rainbow Falls Trail circles away from the stream and climbs onto a drier exposure. Trailing arbutus, teaberry, galax, and rhododendron are the most noticeable flowering species, with Table Mountain pine the most prevalent forest cover. Visible to the east is the round dome of Bull Head (4,282 feet) and, above it, Balsam Point (5,818 feet). Across to the south is Cove Mountain.

Within the next half-mile, the trail executes a sharp switchback right to follow a narrow berm ranging high along the slope. The trail eases out of the dry-ridge exposure and, a half-mile above the switchback, crosses Le Conte Creek on a long slender footlog. The trail then proceeds into the gloom of a hemlock stand, gaining elevation with the assistance of a series of climbing switchbacks. After a second feeder stream, the trail drops briefly to cross Le Conte Creek, again on a footlog.

Visible upstream through the overarching branches of trees is a high fortress-like crag that Harvey Broome once described as "set back in a kind of ethereal diorama, cold and unreachable." Hemlocks diffuse intruding sunbeams into a pale yellow twilight, imbuing the stone gray walls of the crag with tinctures of color. The massive amphitheater is crowned by a protruding ledge over which descends Rainbow Falls.

 On an August evening in 1926, Broome and Richard Gilmore, manager of the Cherokee Orchard and Nursery Company, completed a night hike to Rainbow Falls. Broome later reported that

> the stream, swelled by recent rains, was galloping by in a rushing, surging roar, and it plunged over the cliff in a mad, gleeful frenzy. This walled cliff over which the stream poured was faintly visible at a distance of a hundred yards—through the irregular lattice work of the branching trees, lighted as it was by stray and vagrant beams of light. The water, impeded in its mad descent by the pressure of the air, was molded into tiny beads of spray, which reflecting the chance light took on a ghostly pallor like a huge, quivering, unearthly curtain of mystery. As the moisture-laden air was chilled and unfriendly, and as I drew up to the foot of the falls, it swept out in a drenching, horizontal current of dampness from its splattering base.

Usually at this elevation Le Conte Creek is a rather thin stream, and much of the water plunging over the ledge disperses into a mist before striking a flat solid surface eighty-three feet below. Sunlight reflecting off the descending mist casts a rainbow across the face of the falls, thus suggesting the name. When the air is sufficiently cold, the mist freezes as it descends, forming a tremendous, jagged, cone-shaped pinnacle of ice. White, motionless, and almost luminescent against the stark gray cliff, the cone commands the entire amphitheater. Broome, a frequent visitor to Rainbow Falls in wintertime, once described the remarkable color of the ice as "opaque with a faint trace of blue—so delicate it seems to come and go with the variations of light."

The ice cone itself is truncated at the top, hollow inside, and its wide base sprawled out on the flat rock rostrum at the foot of the falls. A trickle of water falls into the open end of the cone. Clinging to the ice are thousands of tiny, elongated, black dots that are continuously shifting in irregular patterns. These are snow fleas.

◆ Rainbow Falls rarely freezes from top to bottom. November 1925 was an exception. When informed of this rarity by Paul Adams, the young caretaker of the camp on the summit of Le Conte, a fledgling photographer from Knoxville named Jim Thompson traveled to the mountains to capture on film the completely frozen Rainbow Falls. Thompson's photograph was dispersed across the country as an illustration for dozens of magazine articles, soon becoming one of the most widely recognized images of the Great Smoky Mountains. This photograph, as well as many others taken by Thompson, played an instrumental role in the media campaign to establish a national park in the Smokies.

Seventy-five yards upstream, the Rainbow Falls Trail crosses back over Le Conte Creek on a footlog that is anchored to the rocks just below the base of the falls. A tumble of large boulders guards the lower end and flanks of the amphitheater, making any direct approach to the falls forbidding.

When it leaves Rainbow Falls, the trail resumes a rocky course, proceeding five hundred yards to a small stream that trickles over a fifteen-foot precipice of stratified rock and onto the trail before seeping off to find Le Conte Creek. In springtime Dutchman's-breeches, sweet white violets, witch-hobble, and white erect trilliums bring touches of brilliant whiteness to the somber grays, browns, and greens of the ancient undisturbed forest flanking the stream. Within the next hundred yards, the trail executes a sharp switchback. Two hundred yards beyond, a feeder stream is followed immediately by a double-switchback. Four hundred yards beyond the double-switchback, the trail crosses Le Conte Creek for the final time. At this elevation the trail enters the lower fringes of the boreal zone, where red spruce and yellow birch trees compete for space among the boulders. Here, trees have often been forced to germinate on bare rock, and sustain themselves by wrapping tentacle-like roots tightly around the boulders, seeking the soil collected in crevices in the rock.

The appearance of Table Mountain pine, mountain laurel, and galax signals that the trail has exited the boreal stands and moved into the drier conditions of the southwest corner of Rocky Spur, a substantial ridge that springs from the face of Le Conte about a thousand feet below the summit. Here, the grade eases perceptibly. After the trail circles the end of Rocky Spur, it proceeds along the northeast exposure to a vantage point overlooking Gatlinburg and Pigeon Forge. Cove Mountain rises directly behind the city of Gatlinburg. Immediately below are the rugged slopes of Scratch Britches.

Rocky Spur is composed of sedimentary rock running in parallel layers of massive ledges and cliffs. Except for a few exposures, the hard sandstone skeleton of the spur is hidden by stands of boreal species—red spruce, Fraser fir, mountain maple, and yellow birch. To negotiate this terrain, the trail proceeds about a half-mile along the north flank of the spur and then completes three wide switchbacks that circumnavigate the high bluffs and position the trail on the south flank. The switch-backs are separated by intervals of about a quarter-mile. A hundred and fifty yards beyond the third switchback, the trail completes a final, tight, circling switchback that places it on an upward trajectory just below the spine of Rocky Spur.

By the time the trail passes through this complex of switchbacks, it is well into the boreal zone. Birches and spruces are most prevalent, with thickets of fir forming up in corridors. About 250 yards above the circling switchback, an access trail exits sharply back to the left and up to the top of Rocky Spur. It then continues a hundred yards along the spine of the spur before looping back to the main trail.

The access to the top of Rocky Spur starts up through dense balsam growth before breaking out into a rock garden bearing masses of ground-hugging sand myrtle so dense that the pathway is almost completely submerged beneath the growth. Trees are scarce, affording a superb view deep into the Roaring Fork drainage. To the south, the enormous north face of Mount Le Conte looms in astonishing bold relief. West Point (6,344 feet) appears slightly to the right. Progressing eastward are Cliff Top (6,555 feet), High Top (6,593 feet), and Myrtle Point (6,444 feet). A second vantage point fifty yards further along Rocky Spur opens out over the distinctive heath bald known as Brushy Mountain (4,911 feet). Beyond Brushy Mountain and commanding the gulf of Greenbrier basin is Pinnacle Lead, extending northward from the main Smoky divide at Old Black. Seventy-five yards beyond the second vantage point, the Rocky Spur access returns to the Rainbow Falls Trail fifty-five yards above the point where it initially exited the main trail.

Here, the Rainbow Falls Trail begins curling off the flank of Rocky Spur on a southeasterly course angling steeply upward toward West Point. Within a half-mile it intersects the Bull Head Trail just beneath West Point. At the intersection the Bull Head Trail terminates. The Rainbow Falls Trail turns sharply left and angles up across the north face of Mount Le Conte.

For the remainder, the trail keeps to a narrow track of loosely shifting stones, ascending deeper into a forest of closely growing firs. A half-mile above its junction with the Bull Head Trail, the Rainbow Falls Trail intersects the upper terminus of the Alum Cave Trail. Within the next 130 yards, the trail meets an access path on the right leading to Cliff Top. On the left is the main entrance to the Le Conte Lodge compound.

The access to Cliff Top is a 300-yard deeply eroded rut that climbs steeply through a stand of boreal forest. Moss and wood sorrel obscure a spongy humus floor soft with the disintegration of ages of ancient fir forest. The familiar sweet aroma associated with Christmas trees pervades. Most of the larger fir trees are dead or dying, victims of the balsam wooly adelgid, a tiny aphid that burrows under the bark and feeds on the tender parts of the trees. The firs retain their dead needles for a year or so, though rusty red in color. Thereafter they are mere poles, gaunt vestiges of once-splendid trees. Fortunately, the balsam wooly adelgid cannot penetrate the bark of the younger firs, giving sufficient time for the production of seeds. Where dying trees leave openings in the forest cover, the fir seedlings thrive, resulting in the thick young stands that cluster on the slopes below the summit of Cliff Top.

Cliff Top is one of the premier vantage points in the Smokies. It is covered with stands of windswept balsams and scattered patches of rhododendron. The precipitous south side is draped in masses of billowing sand myrtle which, in mid-June, yield rich pink and white blossoms. In the intermediate distance, the long steep-sided Sugarland Mountain forms the opposing watershed for the Sugarland Valley drainage. Far below, near the lowest visible point in the drainage, are the distinct twin peaks of the Chimney Tops, appearing tiny and insignificant. Beyond Sugarland Mountain is the long meander of the main Smoky divide from Clingmans Dome (6,643 feet) to Thunderhead (5,527 feet). To the west in the evening, when the sky is clear, the sun can be seen setting beyond the far distant Cumberland Plateau.

At the top of the climb, the access trail to Cliff Top intersects a 500-yard path that traces the length of the cliff's edge. At its eastern end, the cliff trail intersects the Boulevard Trail in a grassy gap just below the Mount Le Conte Shelter.

Across the Rainbow Falls Trail from the lower end of the access to Cliff Top are steps descending into the Le Conte Lodge compound, a commercial operation offering meals and sleeping accommodations to visitors with prior registration.

The earliest recorded human improvement found on the summit of Mount Le Conte was a rudimentary lean-to near Basin Spring along the lower east corner of the current compound. In July 1925, while search for the spring, Paul Adams unintentionally discovered the lean-to which he found to be rotting and fairly dilapidated. It was similar to another lean-to which Adams had discovered and repaired on his first trip to Le Conte in 1918. Between the time of Adam's first visit and his return in 1925, at least two other camps were built on Le Conte. The first was an eight-by-six-foot pole cabin built in 1921 by Davis Bracken and his son Andy. It stood in a natural clearing in the vicinity of the upper terminus of the Alum Cave Trail. The clearing was later fenced in with smooth wire, and a gate was positioned where a trail crossed the field.

The second camp was a makeshift bark lean-to erected around 1922 just below the summit of Cliff Top. It has been suggested that the camp was built by Will Ramsey and Wiley Oakley under the direction of Andy Huff as a camp for men hired by Huff to clear out and improve the old trail that was the precursor to the current Rainbow Falls Trail. On his 1925 visit, Paul Adams occupied a tarpaper-covered shack maintained for rangers and visitors from the Champion Fibre Company, which owned the mountain. The tarpaper camp probably occupied the same site as the bark lean-to built by Ramsey and Oakley. In the summer of 1925, Adams was retained by the Great Smoky Mountains Conservation Association, an organization formed to seek national park status for the Smokies, to dismantle the tarpaper shack and build a lodge nearer Basin Spring. To assist this effort, Adams cut a path between the tarpaper camp and Basin Spring. Adams's path was later appropriated as the access to Cliff Top.

During the winter of 1925–26, Adams built the first lodge at the new camp, a fifteen-by-twenty-foot structure that stood just west of the present Le Conte Lodge. It was constructed of notched spruce and fir logs and fitted with a floor made of four-foot puncheons set on joists spaced two feet apart. The cracks were chinked with a mixture of clay and moss, and the roof was shingled with shakes riven from fir. The rear eight feet of the lodge were reserved for bunks made of poles notched into the sides of the walls. The building had one window and a door made of thin seven-foot puncheons opening to the inside. It was heated by a "drum heater" stove placed near the center of the room.

Paul Adams operated his camp on Mount Le Conte only until May 10, 1926, after which the management was taken over by Jack Huff and Will Ramsey. Huff began immediately building a larger lodge, a thirty-four-by-twenty-four-foot cabin that was popularly christened "The House that Jack Built." Huff's lodge was constructed entirely of balsam wood with trunks laid lengthwise. The chinks were filled with moss from which ferns and shamrock-like wood sorrel grew all the way from the ground to the eaves. The roof was of boards, waterproofed with tarpaper weighted down with gravel.

The floor of the lodge was hard dry clay. One end of the lodge was occupied by a fireplace made of rocks and bordered with board seats. A straight-back bench extended across the room in front of the fireplace. The door, three feet wide and four feet six inches high, stood in the wall opposite the fireplace.

Bunk beds, sixteen upper and sixteen lower, were arranged on the door end of the lodge. They were made of floor boarding covered with thick layers of balsam branches and finished with blankets placed over the branches. Guests slept fully clothed, four abreast, with no separate accommodations for men and women. The fire was kept going all night with the door and windows open regardless of weather.

Since the time of the Adams and Huff cabins, Le Conte Lodge has grown to a large compound occupying much of the basin below Cliff Top. It now includes a dining hall, recreation lodge, and several guest cabins.

From the steps leading into Le Conte Lodge, the Rainbow Falls Trail proceeds a final forty yards along the upper side of the compound to terminate in a three-way intersection with the Boulevard Trail and the Trillium Gap Trail. The Boulevard Trail leads in straight from the east end of Mount Le Conte. The Trillium Gap Trail leads in from the left along the eastern perimeter of the Le Conte compound. All three trails terminate at the intersection.

TRILLIUM GAP TRAIL

Cherokee Orchard to the summit of Mount Le Conte—8.9 miles.

POINT OF DEPARTURE: Follow directions to the Rainbow Falls Trail. The Trillium Gap Trail begins 120 yards up the Rainbow Falls Trail.

QUAD MAP: Mount Le Conte 165-NW

0.0—Old Sugarlands Trail.

0.1—Rainbow Falls Trail exits right 6.6 miles to the summit of Mount Le Conte.

0.7—Baskins Creek Trail exits left 50 yards to cross the Roaring Fork Motor Nature Trail, then 2.7 miles to the Roaring Fork Motor Nature Trail.

2.4—Access path exits left to the Roaring Fork Motor Nature Trail.

3.6—Grotto Falls.

5.3—Trillium Gap. Brushy Mountain Trail exits straight 4.5 miles to the Porters Creek Trail and left 0.4 mile to the summit of Brushy Mountain.

6.7—Switchback at Twin Falls.

8.9—Basin Spring. Access path exits right into the Le Conte Lodge compound.

8.9—Boulevard Trail. Rainbow Falls Trail.

Mount Le Conte is the crown jewel of the Great Smoky Mountains. It stands apart from the main Smoky divide, a looming eminence measuring one mile from its base to its summit. The north face of Le Conte forms a barrier to the oceans of moisture-laden air drifting in from the Gulf of Mexico, chilling them into the heavy rains that account for the abundant moisture on the northern slopes of Mount Le Conte.

In this cool moist environment, diversity shows no constraint. All the great trees of the Smokies are here—giant eastern hemlocks, Carolina silverbells, yellow buckeyes, red and silver maples, and American beeches. Wildflowers bloom. Dog-hobble and rhododendron congregate in thick lush masses. At the higher elevations are the boreal species—red spruces, Fraser firs, yellow birches, mountain maples, and mountain ashes.

Officially, the lower terminus of the Trillium Gap Trail resides on the Old Sugarlands Trail sixty-five yards down-trail from Cherokee Orchard Road. From the trailhead it proceeds only 130 yards to intersect the Rainbow Falls Trail. Since the Rainbow Falls Trail leaves from the parking area adjacent to Cherokee Orchard Road, hikers most frequently access the Trillium Gap Trail by way of the Rainbow Falls Trail, a distance of 120 yards, rather than hiking down the Old Sugarlands Trail, then back up the Trillium Gap Trail. Consequently, the 130-yard "rump" between the Old Sugarlands Trail and the Rainbow Falls Trail, a faint trace that winds through clusters of daffodils, is rarely used. It is maintained primarily to allow horse access from the Old Sugarlands Trail to the Trillium Gap Trail.

From its intersection with the Rainbow Falls Trail, the Trillium Gap Trail enters an easy excursion that angles upward through old clearings of Cherokee Orchard.

Cherokee Orchard was originally a commercial venture operated by Knoxville businessman Matt Whittle. The orchard included a thousand-acre tract of mountain land on the north side of Mount Le Conte on which Whittle cultivated forty-seven varieties of apples and several types of ornamental nursery plants. The business was permitted to continue operation on the mountain for several years after the founding of the park. After Whittle abandoned his apple orchard, the name Cherokee Orchard remained as a Smoky Mountain place-name.

The Trillium Gap Trail winds a little more than a half-mile to reach the perimeter of Cherokee Orchard and intersect the upper terminus of the Baskins Creek Trail which exits fifty yards to the Roaring Fork Motor Nature Trail. The trail then eases onto a narrow track that begins plying the lower slopes of Scratch Britches.

In the early history of human inhabitation of the lower slopes of Le Conte, Scratch Britches was considered remote even by Smoky Mountaineer standards. Noah "Bud" Ogle (whose cabin at Junglebrook is preserved by the Park Service) once possessed a parcel of land on Scratch Britches not far above the trail line. On the land was a small ramshackle cabin. In 1904, when Ogle's daughter, Rebecca Ann, age fifteen, married Wiley Oakley, age nineteen, the bride's father made the cabin available as a first home for the newlyweds. The Oakleys' closest neighbors were about a mile away. Wiley, who would later achieve fame as a Smoky Mountain storyteller, called Rebecca Ann his "Golden-Haired Bride of Scratch Britches Mountain," and the two lived on Scratch Britches for four years before problems with rattlesnakes under the cabin floor forced them to leave. Their adventures on Scratch Britches supplied fodder for many of Wiley's tall tales, a few of which he later incorporated into two semi-biographical collections of stories, *Roamin' with the Roamin' Man of the Smoky Mountains* and *Restin'*.

Travel across the lower reaches of Scratch Britches soon gives way to a course circumnavigating the base of Piney Mountain, the transition marked by the increasing steepness of the adjacent slopes. The trail maintains a moderate climb, but narrows to a single-file berm to negotiate the contours. Until completing its course around Piney Mountain, the trail remains in sight of the Roaring Fork Motor Nature Trail. When the trail crosses Rocky Spur Branch, it leaves Piney Mountain and enters a cool moist environment of more moderately sloped terrain.

All of the great cove-hardwood species are here. One of the more conspicuous, the Fraser magnolia, is easily identifiable by its large leaves shaped somewhat like giant spear points. The leaves exhibit two lobes at their bases called "auricles" for their fancied resemblance to ears. Another distinctive feature is the large number of shoots sprouting from the roots at the base of the tree. In early summer, Fraser magnolias sport large floppy white flowers which bloom high in the upper boughs and thus are not readily noticeable from the trail.

In places along this section of the trail, large glades of wildflowers blanket the slopes. Sweet white violet, spring beauty, trout lily, large-flowered bellwort, Solomon's-seal, purple wakerobin, black cohosh, squirrel-corn, yellow violet, Fraser's sedge, great chickweed, pipsissewa, blue cohosh, and rattlesnake plantain bloom in late April or early May. In early May when the Carolina silverbells shed their blooms, the trail and wildflower glades are carpeted with bright white bell-shaped blossoms.

A quarter-mile beyond the Rocky Spur Branch crossing, the trail intersects an access trail on the left leading up 250 yards from the Roaring Fork Motor Nature Trail. This access, often called the Grotto Falls Trail, affords a more immediate access to the falls and functions to shorten the Trillium Gap route to the summit of Le Conte by two-and-a-half miles. The so-called Grotto Falls Trail is available as an option only when the one-way Roaring Fork Motor Nature Trail is open to vehicle traffic, generally from the first of June until the end of November.

Here, the trail continues through cove-hardwood stands, eventually passing through another wildflower glade, crossing the headwaters of a tributary of Rocky Spur Branch and then entering the upper reaches of Spruce Flats, a rocky bench shaded by hemlocks.

 The earliest predecessor to the current Trillium Gap Trail was built in 1926 under the supervision of Paul Adams, a young man who had been retained a year earlier by the Smoky Mountain Conservation Association to build the first lodge on the summit of Mount Le Conte. Adams concluded that the most suitable route to Le Conte through Trillium Gap should begin from a rudimentary road leading up from Gatlinburg along Roaring Fork Creek to Sherman Clabo's cabin. The Clabo cabin stood just north of the modern Roaring Fork Motor Nature Trail, roughly a half-mile above the western end of the Grapeyard Ridge Trail. Adams received permission from Clabo to use a private sled track that ran above the cabin and through Spruce Flats. Adams cut a new trail from Spruce Flats to Trillium Gap and then on to the summit of Mount Le Conte. The current Trillium Gap Trail follows the old Adams track from Spruce Flats as far as Trillium Gap.

The Trillium Gap Trail soon converges on Roaring Fork in a narrow steep-sided gorge flanked by a noble forest of Carolina silverbells, black cherries, yellow poplars, silver maples, and eastern hemlocks. Rhododendron forms a dense understory extending from the stream's edge to the top of the slope. As the trail proceeds into the gorge, the track becomes considerably rockier.

Roaring Fork, one of the more steeply pitched stream courses in the Smokies, is graced by a continuous succession of falls, cascades, and plunge pools. The best-known of these, Grotto Falls, stands at the head of the gorge where Roaring Fork rushes through an opening in a cliff and over the brow of a rock overhang into an eighteen-foot free-fall that pools at the base of the falls. The name Grotto is suggested by a cavity beneath the overhang that is sufficiently deep to permit hikers to pass behind the falling water without getting wet. When the Trillium Gap Trail reaches the back of the grotto, it circles behind the waterfall and then turns downstream and begins edging out of the Roaring Fork gorge.

Roaring Fork is fed by underground tributaries which can be heard rumbling against the rocks as it seeks subterranean outlets to the parent stream. Here, the slopes are strewn with talus from the higher cliffs, masking the streams that irrigate this remarkable botanical enclave. During the last ice age, the bare projecting rocks on the exposed higher elevations of Mount Le Conte, riven by intense cold and frost action, broke free and tumbled, producing the boulder fields that flank the trail near Roaring Fork.

From Roaring Fork the trail angles up into stands of huge Carolina silverbells and yellow buckeyes, the only two flowering trees that are conspicuous at this elevation along the Trillium Gap Trail.

Carolina silverbells can be identified by their profuse clusters of white bell-shaped flowers that blanket the trail when the trees drop their petals, usually in mid-May. The bark of the silverbells is checkered and, as the trees mature, takes on a purplish hue. Yellow buckeyes, which also bloom in mid-May, have compound leaves with five leaflets arrayed in circular order and upright clusters of tubular yellow and pink flowers. The fruit of the buckeye tree, also conveniently called "buckeyes," are brown nut-like spheres with a pale spot suggesting a buck's eye. In late summer the spine-covered buckeye burrs fall to the ground where their husks will open slowly as the buckeye sends down roots. Each husk contains a pair of buckeyes. According to Smoky Mountain lore, one is edible and the other poisonous.

An increase in the rockiness of the terrain signals the approach to Surry Fork, a fast-moving stream which, like Roaring Fork, is fed by underground tributaries. According to research compiled by Alan Coggins in *Place Names of the Smokies,* Surry is a corruption of the name Sarah, in particular, a Sarah Bohanan who lived on the lower reaches of Surry Fork.

After crossing Surry Fork, the trail proceeds through a more open forest for almost a half-mile before leveling out at Trillium Gap, a low saddle-shaped swag in the long steeply pitched ridge that connects Brushy Mountain with the summit of Mount Le Conte.

Before the park was established in 1934, Horace Albright, director of the National Park Service, visited the Smokies on several occasions to help promote the idea of the park. On one visit he was taken by horseback up the old Adams trail to Grotto Falls and then to the saddle gap on the ridge between Le Conte and Brushy Mountain. The gap was then known as Grassy Gap. Albright was so impressed with the beautiful display of trilliums along the trail that he suggested the gap be called Trillium Gap. Either out of deference or agreement, Grassy Gap later became known as Trillium Gap.

As a name, Trillium Gap was an unfortunate choice as trilliums are conspicuously absent in the gap. Wildflowers Albright might have noticed as he approached the gap are spring beauty, Dutchman's-breeches, sweet white violet, black cohosh, trout lily, Rugel's Indian plantain, toothwort, and skunk goldenrod. Albright would likely have seen a large number of beech trees in the gap. Beech trees are identifiable by their smooth gray bark and long slender buds. In winter they are easily recognized by their brittle tan leaves that remain on the trees until new leaves appear in spring. Because they have the capacity to withstand the heavy windthrows that frequently visit the higher gaps in the Smokies, the beeches are often the only tree species that survive there. With the first frost, the spiny-husked fruit of the beech opens up to release a triangular-shaped nut.

Since beeches are the dominant tree in Trillium Gap, it was occasionally referred to by local mountaineers as Beech Gap. The beeches here are interspersed by a few maples and shade a small clearing of rich mountain grass and a carpet of white fringed phacelia.

At Trillium Gap, the trail meets its eastern counterpart, the Brushy Mountain Trail, entering from the opposite side. At the intersection, the Brushy Mountain Trail turns north and climbs a half-mile to the summit of Brushy Mountain. The Trillium Gap Trail turns right and follows the ridge 3.6 miles to the summit of Mount Le Conte.

From Trillium Gap, the old Adams trail stayed to the spine of the ridge and proceeded directly to High Top on the summit of Mount Le Conte. In blazing the trail, Adams had to work around a high bluff halfway between the gap and the summit. The course Adams chose followed the ridgeline to the base of the bluff beyond which horses were unable to continue. Early travelers on the Adams trail left their horses in a small bench at the foot of the bluff then proceeded by foot on a manway the final thousand feet directly to High Top, where it intersected a trace running between Le Conte Lodge and Myrtle Point. Accounts of Smoky Mountains Hiking Club excursions to Le Conte record that the Adams trail from the gap to the summit was "exhaustingly steep for almost a mile," following "along what seemed to have been an old bear trace." When crews from the Civilian Conservation Corps later rehabilitated this section of the old Adams trace, they altered it considerably, lengthening it by two miles.

The Trillium Gap Trail exits the gap along the western flank of the ridge, passing through large hemlocks and a field of boulders, and then begins a grueling mushy trudge compounded by the ruggedness of the terrain and water seepages draining the higher cliffs of Mount Le Conte.

Slightly less than a mile and a half above the gap, the trail completes a sharp left turn above a narrow steep-sided gorge that channels Roaring Fork. At the bottom of the gorge, Roaring Fork slithers in parallel streams 125 feet over a near-vertical rock-face in a cascade has long been known unofficially as Twin Falls. The ruggedness of the intervening terrain prohibits any easy access to the base of the falls.

About 300 yards above Twin Falls, Roaring Fork flows gently over a crescent-shaped edge and spreads to a thin sheen over a hemisphere of bald rock. In the late 1920s, photographer Jim Thompson captured on film two remarkable pictures of this small waterfall, naming it Dome Falls. Thompson's photographs of Dome Falls were widely distributed in a variety of national publications, instantly projecting them into the ranks of the most recognized images of the Great Smoky Mountains.

At the turn, the Trillium Gap Trail moderates considerably as it begins an east-ward trajectory across the face of the intervening bluff and through a corridor of thick-set fir trees. Where there are breaks in the forest cover, Brushy Mountain is visible below, identifiable by its contrasting pale-green heath covering a rounded summit. Farther along, the firs subside, replaced by ranks of colossal red spruce trees arrayed along the narrow spines of projecting finger ridges.

For the final ascent, the trail turns south for a steep one-mile pull over a stony single-file track through what was at one time a densely growing stand of boreal forest. The boreal stands are now only ghosts of their former selves, reduced to sun-bleached masses of gray-white boles. The spruce trees still stand, stately and tall, pagoda-shaped, with their characteristic pointed tops, but the older firs are all dead, victims of the balsam woolly adelgid, a tiny sap-sucking aphid that burrows into the bark of mature trees.

Fir seedlings grow fairly quickly to a height of a few inches and then slack to an extremely slow rate of growth. As long as the seedlings remain in the shade of larger trees, they continue growing at the slow pace, often as long as ten years. When an opening in the tree canopy allows sunlight to reach the forest floor, the seedlings are "released" and begin growing very rapidly to fill the vacancy. The elimination of the large fir trees by the balsam woolly adelgid has triggered an explosion of young fir growth competing for space on the slope flanking the trail.

Basin Spring, a weak outlet just to the left of the trail, heralds the approach into the Le Conte Lodge compound at the summit of Mount Le Conte. Water from

Basin Spring dribbles out onto the trail and trickles off with deliberation into the thick weedy undergrowth, then drips down the face of Le Conte to converge with hundreds of other rills that eventually form up the headwaters of Roaring Fork. A few feet down-trail of Basin Spring, an access path on the left marks the entrance to a large clearing that was once use for stabling horses traveling to the lodge. Above Basin Spring, a path on the right leads into the lower corner of the lodge compound. A hundred yards above the spring, the Trillium Gap Trail terminates in a three-way intersection with the Boulevard Trail and the Rainbow Falls Trail. The Boulevard Trail leads in from the left along the summit of Mount Le Conte. The Rainbow Falls Trail leads in from the right after passing along the upper side of the lodge compound. All three trails terminate at the intersection.

BULL HEAD TRAIL

Old Sugarlands Trail to the Rainbow Falls Trail—5.9 miles.
POINT OF DEPARTURE: Follow directions to the Rainbow Falls Trail. The Old Sugarlands Trail ends just below the parking area for the Rainbow Falls Trail. The Bull Head Trail begins 0.4 mile down the Old Sugarlands Trail.
QUAD MAP: Mount Le Conte 165-NW

0.0—Old Sugarlands Trail.
2.5—The Pulpit.
2.8—Creek.
3.0—Overlook.
3.4—Overlook.
5.9—Rainbow Falls Trail exits straight 0.7 mile to Le Conte Lodge.

Bull Head is a literal translation of the word "Uskwalena," the name given to a minor Cherokee chief who was famed within his own tribe for his grotesquely shapen head. When Swiss geologist Arnold Guyot visited the mountains in 1860, he learned that the name Bull Head was being used by mountaineers to identify the three peaks that are now known collectively as Mount Le Conte. In the interest of scientific preciseness, Guyot recognized the peaks aggregately as "the group of Bull Head." If there was ever any association between Uskwalena and the group of Bull Head, it likely originated with the fancied resemblance of the shape of the mountain to that of a bull's head. When viewed from the north at a distance, the three peaks spaced equidistant across the broad summit of Mount Le Conte could conceivably be imaged by Uskwalena's fellow tribesmen as in the likeness of the head of a bull.

Whatever its origin, the aggregate designation Bull Head fell out of use, yielding to the demands of scientific rigor for assigning individual names to specific peaks.

Subsequently, each of the peaks of Mount Le Conte went through an evolution of names, but by the end of the nineteenth century they were fixed as Cliff Top, High Top, and Myrtle Point. The name Bull Head survives, but only as a minor peak far down the western flank of Le Conte.

The Bull Head Trail is a steep course that climbs through some of the most rugged terrain in the Smokies. It begins along the Old Sugarlands Trail about a half-mile southwest of Cherokee Orchard Road and proceeds slowly uphill through an area that was once farmland. The old farm fields are now grown up in yellow poplar of uniform diameter interspersed with some red maple and yellow birch and a few small eastern hemlocks. The forest floor is quite free of undergrowth, indicating that the fields were likely pasture land rather than plowed ground.

An interesting plant found along this section of the trail is the buffalo-nut or oil nut, a shrub of medium height with bright green leaves and bearing a poisonous pear-shaped fruit a little more than an inch in diameter. The shrub is partially parasitic and thrives on other green plant roots. Its flowers, which bloom in April, are arrayed in flaccid spikes. When the botanist Samuel Botsford Buckley passed through here in 1858, he found the shrub growing in abundance "in the edge of some woods fenced into a wheat field." He further noted that the fruit is "so oily that it will burn like a candle if a wick be drawn through it."

After the first half-mile, the course becomes rocky, largely the result of crossing through a boulder field. The boulder field is the result of the ice age which last visited the Great Smoky Mountains perhaps 20,000 years ago. The Smokies were well south of the leading edge of the ice sheets and were never visited by glaciers, although the region did experience a more rigorous climate than now. The bare projecting rocks along the north face of Mount Le Conte, cracked by the intense cold and frost action, broke free and tumbled, producing boulder fields on the lower slopes. In the boulder field, trees begin exhibiting more variations in girth and are spaced farther apart.

Closed oak stands yielding to copses of pitch pine and Table Mountain pine herald the transition from west-facing slopes to the south-facing exposures of Bull Head. A sharp turn on a ridgeline completes the transition and directs the trail into an exceptionally rugged terrain of massive rock cliffs and overhangs.

Within 300 yards, a severe switchback left redirects the trail back across the cliff face. Along here, Gatlinburg is visible below with Cove Mountain immediately behind. Beyond is the eastern end of the Chilhowee Range, and to the right are Pigeon Forge and Sevierville with Douglas Lake in the distance. A switchback to the right sends the trail back across the cliff face a third time.

Another sharp turn to the left directs the trail away from the cliffs and onto a long south-facing "saddle" between Bull Head and Balsam Point. Here, the grade moderates appreciably as the trail enters a pine-heath stand.

South-facing slopes in the Smokies are often forested in pine-heath and pine-oak stands since these species can tolerate the extremes of climate that occur on these exposures. Here, winters are more severe and summers more intense. Southern exposures experience brief inundations during frequent showers, rapid drying in the direct sunlight, then periods of aridity until the next rain. The north-facing slopes, on the other hand, tend to support broad-leafed trees in associations commonly known as cove hardwoods. Here, the sun's angles are more acute and the air slightly cooler and more humid.

The heath growing in the saddle is too high to permit any viewing; however, a rock conveniently at the left of the trail offers an elevated place on which to stand and look over the growth and down onto the long gentle sweep of the Sugarlands. When Buckley passed this way in 1842, the Sugarlands were a patchwork of fields and forests interspersed with an occasional cabin or barn. The slope has now returned to forest. In the fall, dogwoods, sumacs, and sassafrases mass together with sourwoods, black gums, red and silver maples, and yellow poplars to imbue the landscape with an extravaganza of colors.

The trail enters a level stretch for 200 yards, then drops into a slight dip occupied by a four-foot-high stacked-rock platform known as the Pulpit. The platform was built by corpsmen of the Civilian Conservation Corps in the 1930s while upgrading the Bull Head Trail. From the vantage point atop the Pulpit, an observer may enjoy views of Scratch Britches Mountain, Rocky Spur, Mount Winnesoka, English Mountain, and Douglas Lake. Up to the right in the sight-line of the trail is Balsam Point (5,181 feet).

When it leaves the Pulpit, the trail enters a thicket of rhododendron so tall that it arches completely over like a bower. This is a fine example of the rhododendron "tunnels" that frequently shade Smoky Mountain trails. The tunnel is especially attractive when in bloom in late June. At the far end, the trail enters an extended enclave of mixed hemlock-hardwood stands irrigated by a couple of insignificant streams.

At this elevation, flowering plants are especially prevalent. Groundcover spring flowers include trilliums, squirrel corn, Dutchman's-breeches, white fringed phacelia, and rue anemone. Later-blooming wildflowers include black cohosh and early meadow rue. Conspicuous among the shrubs are wild hydrangea, having tan bark and flat clusters of off-white blooms, and witch-hobble with similar snow-white clusters and very dark bark. Only two flowering trees are found at this elevation along the Bull Head Trail. The Carolina silverbell is identifiable by its clusters of white bell-shaped flowers that adorn the trail when the tree drops its petals. Less noticeable is the yellow buckeye, which grows sparingly along the trail.

The Bull Head Trail does not cross the top of Balsam Point, but circles around its south end and into another heath slick where a solid phalanx of rhododendron and mountain laurel forms up on both sides of the trail. At a break in the heath, a

rock ledge projects out over the mountainside, affording a vantage point for surveying the main Smoky divide from Clingmans Dome (6,643 feet) to Thunderhead
(5,527 feet). Sugarland Mountain is the long high ridge in the intermediate distance
extending west from Mount Collins (6,188 feet) to Fighting Creek Gap. In the
sight-line beyond Fighting Greek Gap is the rounded peak of Blanket Mountain
(4,609 feet).

As the trail approaches the brow of Balsam Point, it completes a sharp switchback left then climbs 185 yards to an equally sharp switchback right to begin its
long final climb. The view at the first switchback is of the upper end of Sugarland
Mountain and Mount Mingus (5,802 feet). At this elevation, the cove hardwoods
have completely disappeared, and the forest is almost entirely red spruce with a
few yellow birches and American beeches interspersed. When executing the second
switchback, the trail charts a one-mile, rigidly straight trajectory up the south flank
of the ridge between Balsam Point and West Point. At the top of the climb, the trail
switches over to the north side of the ridge, where the views are northwest across
the Tennessee Valley. Rocky Spur is the prominent lead in the foreground. Beyond
Rocky Spur lies the low flattened ridge of English Mountain. Douglas Lake extends
down the valley beyond Sevierville. Pigeon Forge is below to the left, and farther
left is Gatlinburg. At night, these towns as well as far-off Knoxville, Dandridge, and
Newport appear as puddles of light in the valley.

On the north side of the ridge, the Bull Head Trail resumes a straight but fairly
level course, following a bed of loose shifting stones. Fraser firs and a few mountain
ash trees enter the mix with the red spruce. West Point (6,344 feet) looms straight
ahead. A quarter-mile after switching to the north side of the ridge and just below
West Point, the Bull Head Trail terminates when the Rainbow Falls Trail merges in
from the left. At the intersection, the Rainbow Falls Trail turns and proceeds 0.7 mile
to Le Conte Lodge on the summit of Mount Le Conte.

BASKINS CREEK TRAIL

Roaring Fork Motor Nature Trail to the Trillium Gap Trail—2.7 miles.
POINT OF DEPARTURE: Follow directions to the Rainbow Falls Trail, continuing
on Cherokee Orchard Road until its juncture with the one-way Roaring Fork
Motor Nature Trail. Three hundred and fifty yards above the road junction,
the Roaring Fork Motor Nature Trail crosses the Baskins Creek Trail, then
continues another mile to intersect the lower terminus of the trail. The
Roaring Fork Motor Nature Trail is closed in winter.
QUAD MAP: Mount Le Conte 165-NW

0.0—Roaring Fork Motor Nature Trail.
0.1—Bales Cemetery.

1.2—Manway exits right. Baskins Creek.

1.3—Access path exits right 0.2 mile to Baskins Creek Falls.

1.5—Access path exits right 300 yards to Baskins Creek Cemetery.

1.8—Falls Branch.

2.7—Roaring Fork Motor Nature Trail.

2.7—Trillium Gap Trail.

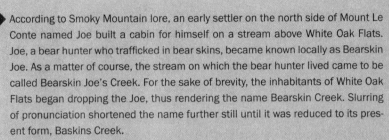

According to Smoky Mountain lore, an early settler on the north side of Mount Le Conte named Joe built a cabin for himself on a stream above White Oak Flats. Joe, a bear hunter who trafficked in bear skins, became known locally as Bearskin Joe. As a matter of course, the stream on which the bear hunter lived came to be called Bearskin Joe's Creek. For the sake of brevity, the inhabitants of White Oak Flats began dropping the Joe, thus rendering the name Bearskin Creek. Slurring of pronunciation shortened the name further still until it was reduced to its present form, Baskins Creek.

In Bearskin Joe's time, cabins and farms ranged along Baskins Creek from its headwaters on Piney Mountain to its mouth in White Oak Flats, now the town of Gatlinburg. Trails leading up Baskins Creek connected White Oak Flats with settlements in Cherokee Orchard, Spruce Flats, and Roaring Fork. The present Baskins Creek Trail traces the courses of the trails that once linked these mountain communities.

In addition to offering easy access to Baskins Creek Falls, the Baskins Creek Trail serves as a connector between the Grapeyard Ridge Trail and the Trillium Gap Trail. From its lower end, the Baskins Creek Trail begins at the parking area on Roaring Fork Motor Nature Trail sixty yards up the road from the western terminus of the Grapeyard Ridge Trail. The upper end of the Baskins Creek Trail is a slightly more confusing proposition. It actually resides on the Trillium Gap Trail fifty yards above the point where the Roaring Fork Motor Nature Trail crosses the Baskins Creek Trail. Because hikers access the trail from the road, the 50-yard rump is frequently ignored.

Access to the falls is about equidistant from either end of the trail. However, in winter months when the Roaring Fork road is closed to automobile traffic, the upper end of the trail is more easily accessed, reached by hiking 350 yards up the Roaring Fork road from the point where it leaves Cherokee Orchard Road.

From its lower end, the Baskins Creek Trail leaves the Roaring Fork road and follows an old settler's trace ninety yards to the Bales Cemetery. The cemetery is built up along its lower side with stone terracing, forming a level ground for the dozen or so fieldstones that mark the gravesites. In the interest of preserving the fragile terracing that supports the graveyard, the cemetery is closed to visitors. Remnants of the old fencing that once enclosed the cemetery can still be seen on the terraced ground inside the modern woven-wire fence line.

The trail circles below the cemetery, then drops to cross a dry bed of Rocky Spur Branch before beginning an easy angling ascent of the flank separating the Rocky Spur drainage from that of Baskins Creek. Upon clearing the ridgeline at a sharp turn to the left, the trail descends steeply, following a ravine for a quarter-mile, then easing out onto a downstream course along Baskins Creek.

Ten yards prior to crossing Baskins Creek, the trail intersects a manway on the right that leads down the stream and into a small cove below Baskins Creek Falls. The distance to the cove is about a half-mile. Where the trail crosses Baskins Creek, the stream is deep and usually difficult to rock hop. After crossing, the trail switches back and into a low interval between Baskins Creek and Falls Branch, where it follows an easy course 300 yards to intersect on the right an access path leading downstream along Falls Branch a quarter-mile to Baskins Creek Falls.

The access path is a level course along Falls Branch except for the final approach where it clears a slight rise and then enters an exceedingly steep descent to the base of a great sandstone bluff. The bluff is an imposing natural edifice that guards the upper end of a wide flat hollow. Near the center of the amphitheater, Falls Branch flows over the upper edge of a cliff and drops thirty-five feet to form Baskins Creek Falls.

Water from the falls does not pool at the base of the bluff, but gathers quickly into a stream and runs off into the grassy fields below. At the falls, a manway crosses the stream and wanders down through the field where it again crosses Falls Branch at its confluence with Baskins Creek. Technically, the waterfall is on Falls Branch; however, given its proximity to the parent stream, it is known as Baskins Creek Falls.

The manway continues downstream, passing occasional ruins of cabin sites before exiting the park above Gatlinburg. This route is easily discerned and suitably level but requires some wet stream crossings. Just below the confluence of Falls Branch and Baskins Creek, the manway leading downstream from the falls intersects the manway that leaves the main trail where it crosses Baskins Creek.

Three hundred and sixty yards above the point where the Baskins Creek Trail passes the access path to the falls, the trail intersects another access path leading right 300 yards to the Baskins Creek Cemetery. Perched on a small knoll above the stream, the tiny plot bears a little more than two dozen graves, all but one marked with thin weather-worn fieldstones.

When it leaves the access to the cemetery, the trail turns and enters a steep hollow, climbing 440 yards before crossing Falls Branch. The stream here is not deep, but not always easy to rock hop. The trail climbs for another half-mile to clear a minor ridge shaded by Table Mountain pines, dry-ridge hardwoods, and mountain laurel. On the descent, the north face of Mount Le Conte and Bull Head come into view.

As the trail descends, it enters a gentle terrain shaded by fine stands of northern red oak, red maple, striped maple, eastern hemlock, chestnut oak, and black gum.

The descent continues for almost a half-mile until reaching the Roaring Fork Motor Nature Trail. The Baskins Creek Trail crosses the road, proceeds another fifty yards, and terminates into the Trillium Gap Trail. Where it crosses the road, the Baskins Creek Trail is 350 yards above the junction where the Roaring Fork Motor Nature Trail turns off Cherokee Orchard Road.

TWIN CREEKS TRAIL

Cherokee Orchard Road at the park boundary to the Noah "Bud" Ogle
   Nature Trail—1.9 miles.
POINT OF DEPARTURE: In Gatlinburg, drive Airport Road 1.0 mile to the
   entrance to the park. The Twin Creeks Trail begins on the left of the road
   just inside the park boundary.
QUAD MAPS: Mount Le Conte 165-NW
Gatlinburg 157-NE

0.0—Cherokee Orchard Road.
0.4—Watercrease Branch. Footlog. Grassy Branch Horse Trail.
1.2—Road to Twin Creeks Resource Center.
1.4—Tributary of Le Conte Creek.
1.9—Noah "Bud" Ogle Nature Trail.

The Twin Creeks Trail, one of the shortest in the park, begins at the park boundary in Gatlinburg, runs through old farmlands and homesites, and then terminates at the Noah "Bud" Ogle Nature Trail. From start to finish, the trail is rarely more than a hundred yards or so from Cherokee Orchard Road. The trail received its name because, for much of its upper course, it remains in a narrow intervale that separates Le Conte Creek from its major tributary.

The trail leaves from the right side of Cherokee Orchard Road just inside the park boundary and follows what was likely an old farm road, passing through a stand of eastern hemlock and a tall chimney on the left that is buried in honeysuckle. Seven hundred yards above the road, the trail crosses Watercrease Branch on a short footlog with a handrail. Immediately beyond the footlog, the trail intersects the Grassy Branch Horse Trail crossing from Cherokee Orchard Road en route to the Sugarlands.

From this juncture, the trail winds through a rocky bottomland flanking the confluence of Le Conte Creek and Watercrease Branch. Stone walls, piles of rocks, and thin stands of struggling second growth betray the sites of former farms and cornfields.

After a little more than a mile, the trail reaches a paved road that leads to the Twin Creeks Resource Center, a facility maintained by the Park Service for the study of the rich and diverse plant and wildlife of these mountains. On the right is a newly constructed research facility.

After crossing the road, the trail resumes its winding through old farm fields, following a minor re-route that circumnavigates the new research facility. Four hundred and seventy yards above the road, the trail crosses a nameless tributary of Le Conte Creek in a fairly easy rock-hop. Above the stream crossing, scattered clusters of traditional boxwoods approximate the locations of former homesites. About a half-mile farther, the Twins Creeks Trail terminates into the Noah "Bud" Ogle Nature Trail. About 300 yards to the left, the nature trail reaches the Noah "Bud" Ogle place and Cherokee Orchard Road.

The Noah "Bud" Ogle place, known popularly as Junglebrook, is a homestead now preserved by the Park Service as an example of the log cabin structures that were once indigenous to the Smokies. On the site is a large "saddlebag" type cabin consisting of two halves built around a central chimney. The right half was built shortly after Ogle and his wife Cindy moved to Junglebrook in 1879. The left half was added as more space was needed for their expanding family. Both "halves" have front and back doors, and porches extend along the full length of the front and back of the cabin. Through a flume built of wood, water from a nearby spring was delivered to a rough wooden trough next to the house.

Above the cabin is a four-crib log barn with lofts and a high frame roof. The lower part of the barn is constructed of large poplar logs that are, like many pioneer structures in the Smokies, joined at the corners with dove-tailed notching.

In the 1920s when the Tennessee Park Commission was acquiring land for the newly proposed national park, the 660-acre Junglebrook tract was one parcel that went to a "jury of view" of four persons who valued the land about $140,000 less than its owner demanded. When this decision was appealed, a full jury reduced the legal value another $15,000. The owner received about $26 per acre for the land, hardly enough to cover the cost of the lawyers who represented him. Junglebook, like much of the land in the Smokies, essentially was stolen. It was the contention of many landowners in the Smokies that the Park Commission, through legal manipulation, had acquired their land for scandalous prices. As a result, there was considerable enmity between many of the local residents and the Park Commission.

◆ SUGARLANDS ◆

The upper end of the Sugarlands section is the heart of the Great Smokies, an exceptionally rugged chasm that separates the imposing south face of Mount Le Conte from the steep-sided flank of Sugarland Mountain. The lower end of the Sugarlands descends in a majestic sweep from the west flank of Le Conte to the bottomlands of the West Prong of the Little Pigeon River. The name Sugarlands originates from the abundance of sugar maple trees that grow on the lower slopes of the adjacent mountain sides. Today, the Sugarlands are recognized as the low-lying intervale that harbors the Sugarlands Visitor Center and the Park Headquarters building.

One of the oldest trans-mountain aboriginal trails over the Smokies crossed into Tennessee at Indian Gap and then down through the defile between Mount Le Conte and Sugarland Mountain. The aboriginal trace was first improved by the Cherokee crossing the main divide from their villages on the Oconaluftee and Tuckasegee rivers to the Great Indian War Path in Tennessee. It was upgraded by the Oconaluftee Turnpike Company in 1832 and then again by a force of Cherokee under the command of Col. William Holland Thomas during the Civil War. With the arrival of the National Park in 1934, the upper part of this historic trail was rehabilitated and is now incorporated into the Road Prong Trail and the lower half of the Chimney Tops Trail. The upper half of the Chimney Tops Trail terminates at one of the more spectacular vantage points in the Smokies.

In addition to these two historic courses, only four other trails are included in the Sugarlands section. The Gatlinburg Trail and Old Sugarlands Trail remain generally in the lowland bottoms. The Sugarland Mountain Trail traces the spine of its namesake while the Huskey Gap Trail crosses Sugarland Mountain to Little River in the Elkmont section.

The Mile 53 Backcountry Campsite (#21) is the only backcountry campsite included in the Sugarlands section. However, since it is near the end of the Huskey Gap Trail, it may reasonably be considered as being in the Elkmont section.

From the Sugarlands Visitor Center, the Sugarland Mountain Trail is reached by driving west on Little River Road to Fighting Creek Gap. All other trails in this section except the Road Prong Trail are directly accessible from Newfound Gap Road (US441). The Road Prong Trail begins 0.9 mile up the Chimney Tops Trail.

CHIMNEY TOPS TRAIL

Newfound Gap Road to the Chimney Tops—2.0 miles.

POINT OF DEPARTURE: From the Sugarlands Visitor Center, drive Newfound Gap Road (US441) 6.7 miles to a parking area along the right side of the road. The Chimney Tops Trail begins at the low rock wall along the parking lot.

QUAD MAPS: Mount Le Conte 165-NW
Clingmans Dome 165-SW

0.0—Parking area on Newfound Gap Road.
0.9—Road Prong Trail exits left 2.4 miles to the Appalachian Trail at Indian Gap.
2.0—The Chimncy Tops.

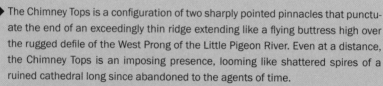

The Chimney Tops is a configuration of two sharply pointed pinnacles that punctuate the end of an exceedingly thin ridge extending like a flying buttress high over the rugged defile of the West Prong of the Little Pigeon River. Even at a distance, the Chimney Tops is an imposing presence, looming like shattered spires of a ruined cathedral long since abandoned to the agents of time.

The Cherokee moniker for the Chimney Tops is "Duniskwalguni," meaning "forked antlers," perhaps a reference to the Cherokee's understanding of the mountain as being two peaks emanating from a common base. The modern designation, Chimney Tops, or simply "the Chimneys," was bequeathed by the white pioneers who generally referred to a stack formation of rock that extends above the surrounding terrain as a "chimney." A hole down the center of the taller spire of the Chimney Tops reinforces and popularizes the name.

The trail to the "forked antlers" is actually pieced together from remnants of two older trails. The first mile is part of the old Thomas Road which passes north over the main Smoky divide at Indian Gap and descends along the Road Prong of the West Prong of the Little Pigeon into the Sugarlands. The last 200 yards are part of an old manway that followed the spine of a connecting spur between Sugarland Mountain and the peaks of the Chimney Tops. In 1963 sections of these older tracks were connected by a graded trail, thus forming the present Chimney Tops Trail.

During the early years of the twentieth century, the local mountaineers often crossed the Road Prong and Walker Prong via the well-known Le Conte Ford just above the point where the two streams converged to form the West Prong of the Little Pigeon. The ford provided access from the Thomas Road to Alum Cave and the old Bear Pen Hollow Trail leading to the summit of Mount Le Conte.

The Chimney Tops Trail begins from the parking area along Newfound Gap Road about a hundred yards above the old Le Conte Ford. The trail descends 120 yards to Walker Prong, crosses on a study bridge, then proceeds another seventy yards to cross Road Prong on a similar bridge. Immediately beyond the Road Prong crossing, the trail turns sharply left and follows the old Thomas trace upstream. The trail is a wide well-maintained track coursing through dense stands of yellow birch and eastern hemlock shading arbors of rhododendron.

About a quarter-mile above the second stream crossing, the trail again approaches Road Prong, crosses on a bridge, and climbs to a course higher above the stream. Beyond the bridge, the trail remains on an easy grade, following the contours of the stream gorge. The stream itself is rarely visible, buried beneath a riot of growth.

The trail continues with little variation for nearly a half-mile until it crosses Road Prong a final time, again on a wooden bridge. It then climbs a hundred yards to intersect the lower terminus of the Road Prong Trail in a thinly forested gradient known as Beech Flats. Here, the Chimney Tops Trail turns right, proceeds on an easy course out of Beech Flats, and, within 200 yards, enters a narrow V-shaped hollow that is angled upward at a steep tilt. In the hollow, the grade stiffens considerably, and the track becomes increasingly rocky. The hollow is remarkably free of understory, and the trees, mostly yellow buckeyes, are astonishingly large.

Seven hundred yards up into the hollow, the climb lessens when the trail turns abruptly left and shifts out of the buckeye association and into stands of great red spruces shading an understory of rhododendron. At a switchback ninety yards farther, the trail charts a quarter-mile trajectory across the nearly perpendicular north-facing slope of Sugarland Mountain. From here to the base of the Chimney Tops, the track remains wide, the grade easy, and the course impeded only by a couple of heavy seepages and minor scrambles around cliff outcroppings.

The Chimneys are suspended from the side of Sugarland Mountain by a thin stratum of upwardly thrust metamorphic slate, its edge covered by a latticework of roots supporting wind-agonized spruces that have managed to grapple the bare rock. The trail eases onto the spur and then negotiates a circumspect course seventy-five yards to the base of the taller of the two Chimney Tops peaks. The climb to the summit entails a 50-yard hand-over-hand scramble up the steeply pitched bald-rock pinnacle that marks the outer end of the projecting spur. Save where the surface has been worn bare by generations of hikers uprooting the tenuously anchored vegetation in an effort to gain purchase, the Chimneys are mantled with dense bracken and sand myrtle. Such are the climate and nature of this region of the Smokies that a rock cliff, whenever it is not strictly vertical, will hold moisture and vegetation.

The taller of the two spires is aptly distinguished by a near-vertical hole some three feet by five feet running down twenty-five feet to where it turns to the outside. In the manner of a chimney, a current of cool air continuously blows up through the hole from below. Near the hole, the top of the spire is wider than its thickness some feet farther down. The taller spire is linked to the shorter by a razor-thin spur, one of the few, true, knife-edge ridges in the Smokies. The surface along the spine of the connecting spur is exceedingly rugged and treacherous, making any attempt to access the lower spire a dangerous undertaking.

The Chimney Tops affords one of the most remarkable vantage points in the Smokies. The open exposure and the vertical drop on either side of the pinnacle engender an exhilaration of standing precariously close to a precipitous edge. Far below, the West Prong of the Little Pigeon winds its way out to the Sugarlands. Looming across the river gorge is the massive south face of Mount Le Conte (6,593 feet), and on its eastern flank, the high tortuous Boulevard suspended between Mount Le Conte and the main Smoky divide. Closer and to the east is Mount Mingus (5,802 feet), a heavily forested promontory that marks the end of Mingus Lead.

The grander views are perhaps those to the west, where the receding ranges of mountains are defined by subtle gradations in color rather than by any fixed landmarks or boundaries. Most immediate is Sugarland Mountain, extending from behind the Chimney Tops to some indeterminate point in the western distance. Beyond are the hazy outlines of the higher peaks that distinguish the western end of the Smoky divide. Separating Sugarland Mountain from the western sweep of Mount Le Conte is the immense forested valley of the Sugarlands of which the Chimney Tops affords a commanding view.

ROAD PRONG TRAIL

Chimney Tops Trail at Beech Flats to the Appalachian Trail at Indian Gap— 2.4 miles.

POINT OF DEPARTURE: Follow directions to the Chimney Tops Trail. The Road Prong Trail begins 0.9 mile up the Chimney Tops Trail.

QUAD MAPS: Mount Le Conte 165-NW
Clingmans Dome 165-SW

0.0—Beech Flats. Chimney Tops Trail exits right 1.1 miles to the Chimney Tops.
0.4—Trinkling Falls.
0.5—Standing Rock Ford. Footlog.
0.6—Indian Grave Gap.
0.8—Talking Falls.
2.4—Indian Gap. Appalachian Trail. Clingmans Dome Road.

The precursor to the Road Prong Trail is an ancient Cherokee trace that crossed the high divide of the Smokies at Indian Gap, descended into the Sugarlands and then to the Great Indian War Path leading out of Tennessee. The claim has been advanced that the Spanish explorer Hernando De Soto ventured into the Smokies, crossed the mountain at Indian Gap, and descended into Tennessee along the old

Cherokee track. The evidence supporting this claim is not considered conclusive; nonetheless Horace Kephart, after consulting sources in the Library of Congress, suggested that "it now seems likely that De Soto in 1540, went up the Lufty, through Indian Gap and out through Tennessee. This was before the founding of Jamestown, and long before the Pilgrims landed at Plymouth Rock." The kernel of truth in Kephart's speculation is that the Indian Gap Road was the oldest trail over the mountain and likely the only course available were De Soto to have attempted such a crossing.

There is evidence that the Cherokee had long abandoned this over-mountain trail by the time of the white settlers. Nevertheless, William Davenport, during his survey of the state-line divide in 1821, recognized the trail and identified it as a "beach 29th mile Indian path at the head of deep cr." Davenport later commented that, "if there is ever a wagon road through the Big Smoky mountains, it must go through this gap." Apparently acting on Davenport's observation, the North Carolina legislature during the 1831–32 session granted rights to the Oconaluftee Turnpike Company to upgrade the Indian trace to a usable road. Nevertheless, by the time Arnold Guyot passed through Indian Gap in 1860, he would note that the turnpike was the "one tolerable road, or rather mule path, . . . found to cross from the great valley of Tennessee into the interior basins of North Carolina." Guyot understood the place where the road crossed the mountain to be called "Road Gap."

This "mule path" was converted into an operable wagon road during the Civil War by a force of six hundred Cherokee under the direction of Confederate Colonel William Holland "Little Will" Thomas and used thereafter primarily for directing troops and munitions across the mountain. What sort of road it must have been even in its prime may be judged from the fact that a detachment of General Robert Vance's Confederates had to dismount their cannons from the carriages and drag them over the boulders to descend the mountain.

After the war, the road, known variously as the Indian Gap Road, the Thomas Road, and the Oconaluftee Turnpike, was used sparingly by local farmers and traders. The hardships they endured cannot be overestimated. Lurching and groaning down the steep rough road, their wagons would often reach some point beyond which progress was nearly impossible. The wagons would occasionally slide on water-slickened boulders, turning over and spilling their contents into the nearby stream, or worse, under the stress and strain of hauling over an uneven surface, collapse over a snapped axle.

By the time Horace Kephart had passed this way in the early twentieth century, wagon usage had ceased. The only commercial traffic was the occasional drover herding cattle or hogs over the mountain to the markets in Knoxville. The improvements made by Thomas's legion of Cherokee had been obliterated by the agents of time and its width reduced by the unceasing encroachments of undergrowth.

Just prior to the outbreak of the Civil War, a traveler into the Smokies known only as R of Tennessee ventured up the old Indian trace from the Tennessee side.

Later, commenting on his experience, he wrote, "I seemed to be riding through some vast graveyard—so solemn and gloomy did everything appear." Fifty years later Horace Kephart stopped briefly in Indian Gap and, contemplating his first visit into the Sugarlands, made an observation similar to that of R of Tennessee. "This was the beginning of the Sugarlands," Kephart later wrote, "a country full of ill fame, hidden deep in remote gorges, difficult to access, tenanted by a sparse population who preferred to be a law unto themselves. Beyond was a steep and rocky trail, going down, down along a brawling torrent into the gloom of narrow gulfs that were choked with laurel and spruce and balsam."

The Road Prong Trail begins halfway along the Chimney Tops Trail in a gently sloped, thinly forested gradient known as Beech Flats. While hiking through Beech Flats in 1950, Harvey Broome described the trail as a mere pathway through a thicket of American beech sprouts, but remembered it thirty years earlier being the width of a wagon road and running through a clearing which was blocked off above and below by pole gates to restrain the cattle that browsed there. In the ninety years since Broome's first visit, the clearing has now all but vanished in a copse of slender beech trees. The soil in Beech Flats must have been severely compacted by the grazing cattle since the trees would normally have been much larger after the passage of this much time.

The Road Prong Trail follows a single-file path out the upper end of Beech Flats and onto a wet, rocky, deeply rutted track flanked on either side by solid phalanxes of rhododendron that arch overhead, casting the trail in a funereal gloom. On the left and secluded in the rhododendron, the fast-moving Road Prong can be heard rushing headlong in a maelstrom. Three hundred yards above Beech Flats, the stream negotiates two attractive waterfalls. The first entails a small cliff over which the stream plunges into a shallow basin. Immediately upstream, rushing water is channeled down a long sliding cascade into a deep pool of remarkable clarity. A photograph of this cascade taken by noted Smoky Mountain photographer Jim Thompson appeared in several national publications promoting the establishment of a national park in the Smokies. The picture was often affixed with the caption of either "Trickling Falls" or "Trinkling Falls." Neither name was widely recognized, and consequently, neither was accepted into Smoky Mountain nomenclature.

Eight hundred yards above Beech Flats, the trail crosses Road Prong at Standing Rock Ford. The ford derives its name from a thin slab of rock about fifteen feet high and twenty feet wide affixed like an axe blade into the ground along the trail forty yards above the stream crossing. Until 2008, when the Park Service installed a slender footlog over the stream, Standing Rock Ford could be crossed only by wading Road Prong. From Standing Rock Ford, the trail climbs away from the stream and enters the edge of Indian Grave Flats, a former clearing now totally engulfed in rhododendron and gnarled beech trees.

The name Indian Grave Flats originates from the occasion of a skirmish near Cherokee, North Carolina, in which Union troops retreated over the Smoky divide through Indian Gap, taking with them several Cherokee forcibly conscripted as guides. The troops camped for the night not far above Standing Rock Ford. The next morning, an old Indian, either unwilling or unable to continue, was shot and left to die. Pursuing Confederates found the wounded Indian and cared for him until he died. They buried him in a shallow grave along the road. Animals later clawed up the remains, and the bleaching bones were seen afterwards by passersby. The site of the Union camp and the place where the Indian was buried is now known as Indian Grave Flats.

Indian Grave Flats has likely long been used as a wayside camp by early travelers along the road. Workers hauling Epsom salts manufactured at nearby Alum Cave Bluff as well as military detachments patrolling the mountains during the war took advantage of the respite that the flats offered from the ubiquitous steepness. There is evidence that Davis Bracken, the Sugarlands native who built the widely known possession cabin in Grassy Patch at the foot of the Alum Cave Trail, also built a cabin in Indian Grave Flats for the Champion Fibre Company. When Harvey Broome passed through here as a young man, he noted that the flats consisted of a two-acre clearing harboring two pole cabins.

The trail continues on its wet rocky course, passing through patches of ferns, dog-hobble, and prostrate bluets, soon coming into sight of another attractive cascade where Road Prong is funneled into a narrow aperture separating two massive boulders. The juxtaposition of the boulders forces the stream into an abrupt ninety-degree turn where it fans out and plunges into a pool so deep that its bottom is lost in the ambient gloom. The volume of water in the pool is augmented by an ancillary stream that crosses the trail and flows into Road Prong at the base of the falls. During the early part of the twentieth century, sporadic references were made to this waterfall by the names "Talking Falls" and "Two Rock Falls." Neither name was widely accepted in popular nomenclature, and both soon passed completely out of use.

When R of Tennessee passed through this way, he was told a story which illustrates something of the dangers and difficulties of early travel in the high Smokies. A young man from South Carolina by the name of Psatter endeavored to cross the mountain against the advice of the local mountaineers, who suspected a snowstorm was coming on. The storm came, and to protect himself from the elements, Psatter crawled under an overhanging rock near a waterfall. The temperature plummeted, and the young man froze to death. A week later he was found by hunters, sitting upright with both eyes pecked out by birds. The hunters dug a grave and buried him by the trail. This incident occurred a few years before the Civil War, prior to the trail being improved to accommodate the road.

From the falls, the trail climbs away from the stream, passing briefly through a rock-strewn terrain whose boulders are covered in thick mats of moss. Here, the trail begins edging into the lower fringes of the boreal zone, marked by sporadic occurrences of yellow birch, red spruce, and mountain maple. The trail soon returns to its streamside course where seepages and standing pools leave the path extremely wet. Early travelers along here occasionally mentioned seeing a rudimentary trail that crossed the stream and proceeded up a deep ravine leading to the top of Sugarland Mountain at Bear Pen Gap. This trace was used by lumbermen traveling between their homes in the upper Sugarlands to the logging camps on Rough Creek and Little River.

The Road Prong Trail soon enters a narrow draw where it becomes intimately engaged with the stream, crossing it a half-dozen times in the span of a hundred yards. In places the trail is indistinguishable from the stream. Obstructing blow-downs of massive eastern hemlocks and entangling thickets of witch-hobble obscure the original track, forcing the trail into a provisional course. Crimson bee-balm, pink turtlehead, and monkshood congregate in the sunlit openings left in the wake of the blow-downs. The stream itself separates into channels, making it more difficult to discern the hiking track. When storms rage and the water runs high, this section of the Road Prong Trail can offer some of the most exhilarating, yet frustrating, hiking in the Smokies.

The trail engages its final half-mile when it leaves the stream and enters the boreal zone where spruces and firs share space with birches, mountain maples, yellow buckeyes, and black cherries. This final upper stretch is a remnant of the old Thomas Road. The grade here is steep, the track an unstable bed of loosely shifting slate-like rocks irregularly impeded by encroaching weedy undergrowth. A thin copse of beeches heralds the approach into Indian Gap, where the Road Prong Trail terminates into the Appalachian Trail on the state-line divide. Above the trail intersection, an apron of closely cropped grass separates the wilderness from the paved parking lot that accompanies Clingmans Dome Road, which passes on the North Carolina side of the gap.

OLD SUGARLANDS TRAIL

Newfound Gap Road to Cherokee Orchard Road—3.9 miles.

POINT OF DEPARTURE: From the parking area adjacent to the Park Headquarters building, cross Newfound Gap Road (US441) to the stone bridge over the West Prong of the Little Pigeon River. The Old Sugarlands Trail begins at the far end of the bridge.

QUAD MAPS: Gatlinburg 157-NE
Mount Le Conte 165-NW

0.0—Newfound Gap Road at the bridge over Little Pigeon River near Park Headquarters.

0.1—Twomile Branch bridle path exits left. Rock quarry.

0.7—Grassy Branch bridle path exits left.

1.5—T-junction at old CCC camp.

1.7—Junction. Roadbed turns right to old Pi Beta Phi Settlement School site.

3.2—Twomile Lead bridle path exits left.

3.3—Twomile Branch bridle path exits left.

3.5—Bull Head Trail exits right 5.9 miles to the Rainbow Falls Trail.

3.8—Le Conte Creek. Bridge.

3.9—Trillium Gap Trail exits right 8.9 miles to the summit of Mount Le Conte.

3.9—Cherokee Orchard Road.

The Sugarlands is a magisterial sweep of wooded mountain terrain extending from the western flank of Mount Le Conte down to the West Prong of the Little Pigeon at Fighting Creek. It is bounded on the north by Balsam Point and Bull Head Mountain and on the south by Sugarland Mountain. Prior to the coming of the park, the lower reaches of the Sugarlands harbored a thriving farm community populated with frame houses, barns, crossroads stores, blacksmith shops, gristmills, churches, and schools. Stonewalls and split-rail fences cross-hatched the slopes, lining the roads and circumscribing the farm buildings, fields, and orchards. Roads entered on all sides, connecting the Sugarlands with communities over the adjacent mountains. An old wagon road along the east side of the West Prong was the main artery through the Sugarlands. The wagon track was later upgraded to a road and designated as state highway TN71. Later still, after the establishment of the park, it was appropriated as the Old Sugarlands Trail.

The Old Sugarlands Trail begins within sight of the Sugarlands Visitor Center. The trailhead is at the east end of the stone bridge where Newfound Gap Road crosses the West Prong of the Little Pigeon River near the front of the Park Headquarters building. Fifty yards down-trail a bridle path, Twomile Branch Spur, intersects the Old Sugarlands Trail from the left. Here, the main trail veers slightly to the right and follows upstream to a high bluff once used as a quarry supplying stone and gravel for building the first paved roads through the mountains. Beyond the quarry, the trail proceeds a short distance before turning away from the stream and climbing a narrow rocky course. Traces of the old wagon road can be seen below in the bottomland where Caleb Trentham once operated a large mill. Trentham constructed a dam across the Little Pigeon that impounded water sufficient to propel a turbine powering a grist mill and a saw mill. Nothing remains of the dam, although clusters of daffodils and Spanish sword and piles of stacked rock testify to the location of houses and outbuildings that accompanied the mills.

A little more than half-mile above the quarry, the Old Sugarlands Trail curls left into a hollow drained by a nameless stream. Here, it encounters a rather confusing intersection with the Grassy Branch bridle path. The bridle path continues on the graded track, proceeding to the Twomile Branch Spur on the ridge above. The Old Sugarlands Trail drops abruptly off to the right, leaving the graded course to follow a narrow rough track down to the stream. It crosses the stream, turns back out of the hollow, and then immediately mounts a wide remarkably level berm that once served as a roadbed for TN71. Crested dwarf irises and sweet white violets are plentiful in the transition interval.

The trail follows the roadbed on a straight course for just over a quarter-mile before reaching a bridge over Bull Head Branch.

 On the left, immediately prior to the bridge crossing, is the former site of a farm once known as the Ranson Sims place. The farm was later purchased by Crockett Maples, who was for many years the postmaster for the Sugarlands. Maples's postal route took him into Gatlinburg, where he picked up the mail at Ogle's store. His delivery route led up Le Conte Creek to Cherokee Orchard, then over Bull Head Mountain and into the Sugarlands. Maples would then proceed down through the Sugarlands, crossing the West Prong and then up Fighting Creek toward Elkmont. By the time he had returned home to the Sugarlands, Maples had traveled over thirty miles.

Just above the old Ranson Sims place stood the house store of John Whaley. Like many of the shopkeepers in the Sugarlands, Whaley operated his store out of his home, using one room in the house for displaying merchandise. Between the Sims place and Whaley's store, a wagon track exited the main road and proceeded down to a ford in the river. Beyond the ford, the wagon track proceeded up the side of Sugarland Mountain to Huskey Gap.

After crossing Bull Head Branch, the Old Sugarlands Trail continues on the straight level roadbed, but distances itself considerably from the river to follow the course of Bull Head Branch. A half-mile farther, the trail enters an old road junction where it turns immediately to the left. The right fork of the junction, now somewhat obscured, turns down toward the river to where it once crossed on an old wooden bridge. The right fork proceeded along the bottomland on the far side of the river a short distance, then turned up the side of Sugarland Mountain to intersect the road coming up from the Ranson Sims place. The part of the old right fork between the river and Newfound Gap Road has been incorporated into one of the park's quiet walkways. That part beyond Newfound Gap Road was adopted as the Huskey Gap Trail.

At the old bridge crossing of the West Prong, there once stood a one-room, framed, weatherboard building known as the Old Bridge School. The school was set by the side of the road with the front facing the road and the bridge. There was a rock fence on the up-stream side of the school, separating it and Richard Ownby's general house store. The Old Bridge School was one of four schools to have been in operation in the Sugarlands vicinity. The others were a school in Huskey Gap, the Bracken School at the upper end of the Sugarlands, and the Pi Beta Phi School near the Sugarlands Cemetery. The county built the Pi Beta Phi School from logs taken from the Bracken School. Students from the Bracken School and the Old Bridge School were transferred to the newer school, where they were taught by teachers supplied from the Pi Beta Phi Settlement School in Gatlinburg.

When the Old Sugarlands Trail completes the left turn away from the fork leading to the river, it proceeds a hundred yards to a T-junction. The trail turns right. Immediately after completing the turn, it intersects a faint path on the left leading into a clearing that was occupied from 1933 until 1942 by a large Civilian Conservation Corps camp. The space is scattered with several noticeable remains from the camp. Most interesting is a tall facade that appears to have been some kind of announcement board. Nearby is a low rock wall configured in a circle about twelve feet in diameter.

Two hundred yards beyond the T-junction, the Old Sugarlands Trail enters a crossroads formerly known as Bull Head Fork. Here, the Old Sugarlands Trail proceeds straight on the wider track. The fork to the right is part of a main artery through the Sugarlands that once provided access to the Sugarlands Cemetery and the Pi Beta Phi School.

From Bull Head Fork, the Old Sugarlands Trail charts a course leading over the lower end of Bull Head Mountain. It follows briefly along a tributary of Bull Head Branch and through the upper end of the CCC camp. An abandoned garbage dump, remnants of a few building foundations, and a nearby concrete weir are the most readily noticeable artifacts from the camp. The trail widens to a macadam road as it begins climbing over the mountain. To the left beds of irises and daffodils, a stone foundation, and an abandoned washtub mark the site of one of the last houses before the trail leaves the Sugarlands.

At it gains elevation, the road reaches the dry-ridge conditions of a pine-oak mix. A long hairpin switchback directs the road to a broad ridgeline where it intersects the upper end of the Twomile Lead Spur. A hundred yards farther, it intersects the upper end of the Twomile Branch Spur.

Three hundred yards beyond the Twomile Branch Spur intersection, the Old Sugarlands Trail passes the lower terminus of the Bullhead Trail on the right. The grade levels noticeably and eases into the cooler confines of rhododendron, oaks, and hemlocks. A stone wall on the right betrays a former farm site nestled in a rocky niche along Le Conte Creek. Le Conte Creek is then crossed on a footlog, and fifty yards farther, the trail intersects on the right the rump end of the Trillium Gap Trail. The rump, considered officially part of the Trillium Gap Trail, is a rarely used 130-yard connector between the Old Sugarlands Trail and the Rainbow Falls Trail. Sixty-five yards beyond the Trillium Gap Trail intersection, the Old Sugarlands Trail terminates into Cherokee Orchard Road. To the right is the lower terminus of the Rainbow Falls Trail.

HUSKEY GAP TRAIL

Newfound Gap Road to the Little River Trail—4.1 miles.
POINT OF DEPARTURE: From the Sugarlands Visitor Center, drive south 1.5 miles along Newfound Gap Road (US441). The Huskey Gap Trail begins on the right directly across from a small parking area.
QUAD MAP: Gatlinburg 157-NE

0.0—Newfound Gap Road.
2.0—Huskey Gap. Sugarland Mountain Trail exits left 8.8 miles to the Appalachian Trail and right 3.1 miles to Little River Road at Fighting Creek Gap.
2.4—Big Medicine Branch.
2.8—Phoebe Branch.
3.7—Sugar Orchard Branch.
4.0—Access path exits left 100 yards to the Mile 53 Backcountry Campsite (#21).
4.0—First Branch.
4.1—Second Branch.
4.1—Little River Trail.

A mile and a half above the Sugarlands Visitor Center and along the north side of Newfound Gap Road, a parking lot stands adjacent to the head of a quiet walkway leading down to a bottomland along the Little Pigeon River. The quiet walkway follows the lower part of an old trans-mountain road that linked the pioneer settlements in the Sugarlands with those on Little River. Immediately across the highway from the parking area is the northern terminus of the Huskey Gap Trail. The Huskey Gap Trail, however, does not adhere precisely to the old settlers' trace but follows a newer graded course that closely approximates the route of the old road.

From Newfound Gap Road, the Huskey Gap Trail climbs on a single-file track into old-field stands of slender yellow poplars, pignut hickories, and red maples interspersed with copses of eastern hemlocks. In springtime, crested dwarf iris, sweet white violet, hepatica, yellow trillium, rue anemone, little brown jug, squaw-root, and may-apple are attractive diversions along the trail. A quarter-mile above the highway, the trail clears a small feeder stream. Beyond the stream and down to the right is a short section of stone wall marking a former farm site. Below the wall is a noticeable trace of the old settlement road to Huskey Gap.

After continuing on a fairly stiff grade for three-quarters of a mile, the trail approaches a field of boulders where, during the summer months, pale jewel weeds grow in great profusion along Flint Rock Branch. Just a short distance downstream is a crossroad that once marked the intersection of the old Huskey Gap road with another settlement road that led up from the lower end of the Sugarlands.

The boulder fields are the result of rocks riven from the higher cliffs on Sugarland Mountain by the fracturing action of intense freezing during the most recent ice age. Soil among the boulders is often poor, and where the soil is poor, grapevines frequently thrive. Above the Flint Rock crossing, prolific grapevine growth has suffocated other vegetation, leaving openings in the forest cover that afford unlikely vantage points. Through these openings the whole lower sweep of the Sugarlands is visible as far down as Gatlinburg. Immediately beyond Gatlinburg is Cove Mountain with Mount Harrison (3,310 feet) as its most prominent peak. Far to the east, at the head of the Sugarlands drainage, are Balsam Point (5,181 feet) and Mount Le Conte (6,593 feet). Sighted in the distance between Cove Mountain and Mount Le Conte is the distinctive anvil-shaped English Mountain.

At this elevation Solomon's-seal, bloodroot, and large-flowered bellwort enter into the wildflower mix. Higher up, the trail negotiates the end of a ridge point where the grade moderates. Here, it enters into dry-ridge stands of sugar and red maple, pignut hickory, Fraser magnolia, and a variety of oaks with an understory of mountain laurel and low woody xerophylic growth interspersed with the occasional flame azalea.

Stands of black gum trees, conspicuous in the fall by their brilliant red leaves, herald the approach into Huskey Gap, a long shallow dip in the ridgeline of Sugarland Mountain. Down and to the right are faint traces of the old settlement road into the gap. Between the settlement road and the trail there once stood a log schoolhouse built in 1893 to serve children of the families living in the Sugarlands and on Little River. The Huskey Gap school was abandoned when the newer Bridge School was built in the Sugarlands near the bridge where the Huskey Gap settlement road crossed the Little Pigeon River. The Huskey Gap schoolhouse later burned. The charred timbers could still be seen well into the twentieth century.

When it enters Huskey Gap, the trail intersects the Sugarland Mountain Trail following along the ridgeline. The latter trail proceeds northwest 3.1 miles to Little River Road at Fighting Creek Gap and southeast 8.8 miles to the Appalachian Trail near Mount Collins.

From the gap, the Huskey Gap Trail descends on an easy grade following a single-file, hard-packed, dirt track through hedges of mountain laurel. It wends down the flank of Sugarland Mountain and into an open forest of widely spaced second-growth hardwoods. Except for a crossing of Big Medicine Branch 700 yards below the gap and a crossing of Phoebe Branch about a half-mile farther on, the trail descends with little variation in grade, forest cover, and general trail conditions until it passes through an old farm field and eases into an upstream course high above Little River.

The trail descends along Little River for about 150 yards to cross Sugar Orchard Branch. It then turns away from Little River and crosses a bottomland 180 yards to an access path that exits left a hundred yards to the Mile 53 Backcountry Campsite (#21), one of the newest campsites in the park. The Mile 53 Camp currently shares the number 21 with the Big Medicine Branch Backcountry Campsite on the Sugarland Mountain Trail, which is being discontinued as a campsite. The name Mile 53 refers to notations on topographic maps showing the camp to be fifty-three miles upstream of the confluence of Little River with the Tennessee.

The Mile 53 Camp is situated on a large gradient that was once a farm field tilled by Ben Parton. The slope still remains exceptionally open, bereft of understory and shaded by meager stands of thin sugar maples and yellow poplars. The camp exhibits no natural perimeters, giving an initial impression that it is a large camp; nevertheless, the ground is pitched a bit too steeply to afford many excellent tent sites. The camp's two food-storage cables are convenient, but the closest water is in Sugar Orchard Branch.

From the campsite, the Huskey Gap Trail continues through the old Ben Parton farm, crosses First Branch, then eases onto an old roadbed. The trail follows the road along Little River for 200 yards before crossing Second Branch and terminating into the Little River Trail. The Little River Trail proceeds downstream 2.9 miles to its trailhead at Elkmont and upstream 0.9 mile to the Goshen Prong Trail.

GATLINBURG TRAIL

River Road in Gatlinburg to the Sugarlands Visitor Center—1.9 miles.
POINT OF DEPARTURE: In Gatlinburg, drive River Road to the south end of town, where it terminates into the parkway (US441). The Gatlinburg Trail begins near the end of River Road.
QUAD MAP: Gatlinburg 157-NE

0.0—Gatlinburg. River Road near intersection with US441.
0.5—West Prong of the Little Pigeon River. Footbridge.
0.7—Chimney ruins.
0.9—Viaduct for the Gatlinburg Bypass.
1.4—Park Service maintenance compound.
1.7—Asphalt trail at Park Headquarters building.
1.9—Sugarlands Visitor Center.

When settlers of European descent first entered the cove that now harbors the town of Gatlinburg, Tennessee, they found a cleared bottomland occupied by a few Indian huts. The settlers, like the Indians before them, probably entered the cove along the Great Indian War Path, an ancient Cherokee trace that crossed the main Smoky divide at Indian Gap, linking the Cherokee valley towns with the overhill villages. Soon after their arrival, the settlers christened the cove White Oak Flats, a name that has failed to survive except in the single instance of White Oak Flats Baptist Church.

White Oak Flats Baptist, organized in 1835, was the first church in Gatlinburg. Worship services were held in a log house built by mountaineers along the banks of Baskins Creek on a site now occupied by the Arrowcraft Shop near the Pi Beta Phi Elementary School. In 1835, the church building was only partially complete. It had a hard-beaten smooth earth floor and a single window at one end behind the pulpit so the preacher could see to read his text. At the opposite end, a door of rough hand-hewn boards usually stood open to admit air and light. The congregants sat upon benches of split logs with auger holes bored at the four corners and inserted with pegs that served as legs.

Soon afterward, other churches came to White Oak Flats. One, the New Hampshire Baptist Gatlinites, was organized by Radford Gatlin, a merchant for whom the town was later named. Gatlin came with his wife to White Oak Flats about 1850. He was reported to be a shrewd businessman and operated a store at the fork in the main road where US321 now exits from US441 at the north end of town.

Radford Gatlin apparently alienated himself from much of the citizenry of White Oak Flats. He possessed an overbearing manner and preached a strongly secessionist doctrine in a community of strong Unionist sentiment. Much of the hard feelings against Gatlin, however, originated with his harsh treatment of a "slave woman" he brought from North Carolina. Gatlin's enemies testified that he was a hard cruel man who abused his slave woman. When she died, Gatlin declared that she was fit for no more than to be dragged out to a sinkhole and dumped in.

Tradition differs as to how the town came to be named after such an unpopular miscreant as Radford Gatlin. Gatlin had agreed to house the U.S. Post Office in his store, and supposedly the government named the post office "Gatlinburg," a designation that eventually was applied to the whole town. Another account suggests that Gatlin was asked to leave on the condition that the town be named for him. One night after an unusually fiery speech supporting the Confederate cause, Gatlin was visited by a band of masked men, given a severe beating, and ordered to leave White Oak Flats. He left and was never heard from again.

As Gatlinburg grew, it expanded along the banks of the West Prong of the Little Pigeon River. Settlers moving upstream began encroaching on the lower end of a large cove that later became known as the Sugarlands. As the Sugarlands developed into its own separate community, a serviceable wagon road was cut along the river between the two mountain hamlets. This first mountaineer road was later replaced by a modern paved track (TN71) which, in turn, was superseded by US441, the current highway crossing the main Smoky divide between Gatlinburg and Cherokee, North Carolina.

The Gatlinburg Trail begins at the south end of town, where the Gatlinburg city limits abuts the park boundary. The trail has two points of origin only a few yards apart. Both are along River Road near its intersection with US441. The lower access, a hundred yards long, and the upper, sixty yards long, appear to receive equal use. When they converge, the Gatlinburg Trail charts an easy course along the West Prong of the Little Pigeon River following a wide light-gravel track. A stone wall, an enduring remnant from the settlement era, forms up on the left. A short distance beyond the wall, the trail angles away from the river, makes a tangent encounter with US441, then turns away and crosses the West Prong on a wide wooden footbridge.

Before the advent of the park, mountaineers crossed the river here on a long narrow footlog suspended high over the stream. As a young girl living in the Sugarlands, Gladys Trentham once watched a man who was known to have an affinity for moonshine attempt to negotiate the footlog over the West Prong. Before reaching the far end of the footlog, the man slipped and fell to his death in the torrent below.

Two hundred and thirty-five yards beyond the footbridge, the trail passes a chimney ruin standing immediately on the left side. Twenty-five yards farther, it passes a second chimney. Unlike the dry-stacked and mud-chinked chimneys most commonly found in the Smokies, these are mortared with concrete, suggesting that they are of a more modern vintage. At the top of the rise above the chimney ruins, an unusual semicircular set of steps on the right leads to a level tract that bears the outlines of a former house. This, like the chimneys, was likely not a settler's home, but a summer retreat for rusticators from outside of the mountains.

From here, the trail descends the rise, returns to a streamside course, and then passes underneath a highway viaduct that is part of the Gatlinburg Bypass. After continuing along the river for the better part of a half-mile, the trail approaches the lower end of the Park Service maintenance compound. The compound is situated on a bottomland tract and consists of an assortment of utility buildings and open sheds sheltering various pieces of heavy equipment and construction material. The bottom was the site of the former Fighting Creek School.

There is an enduring Smoky Mountain legend that contends that the name Fighting Creek School originated from an incident of two mountaineers engaged in an altercation over the issue of where best to locate a proposed schoolhouse. The fight, if it even actually took place, was of such renown that it engendered the name not only for the school, but for nearby Fighting Creek and Fighting Creek Gap at the foot of Sugarland Mountain.

The Gatlinburg Trail follows the river for 530 yards as it circumnavigates the maintenance compound and merges onto a paved road that leads out of the compound and circles around a bend in the river to intersect US441. Six hundred and fifty-five yards up the paved road, the Gatlinburg Trail turns left onto an asphalt track that proceeds immediately along the front of the large stone building that is the Park Service headquarters.

Prior to the park, the grassy lawn in front of the Park Service headquarters building was occupied by a church building known as Evans Chapel, founded in 1832. A church stood in this field until 1933. The cemetery that accompanied the church is along the road behind the headquarters building.

The headquarters was built by the Civilian Conservation Corps during 1939–40 with the main lobby being modeled after the historic Blount Mansion in Knoxville. The stone on the outside of the building was quarried near the old settler's community of Ravensford near the Oconaluftee Visitor Center in North Carolina. The wood paneling on the inside was salvaged from local American chestnut trees that had been infected by a killing blight.

After the asphalt track passes the headquarters building, it turns slightly and intersects the Fighting Creek nature trail exiting on the right. The nature trail is a short loop that leads to a small log cabin standing in a farm field once owned by Noah McCarter. From here, the Gatlinburg Trail turns up and approaches the back of the Sugarlands Visitor Center. Built in 1960, the visitor center contains an auditorium, museum, gift shop, and visitor information desk in the main building. A smaller building with public restrooms is separated from the main building by an open breeze-way. The Gatlinburg Trail passes through the breeze-way and terminates at the parking lot in front of the Sugarlands Visitor Center.

SUGARLAND MOUNTAIN TRAIL

Little River Road at Fighting Gap to the Appalachian Trail at Mount Collins—11.9 miles.

POINT OF DEPARTURE: From the Sugarlands Visitor Center, drive Little River Road 3.7 miles to Fighting Creek Gap. The Sugarland Mountain Trail begins in the gap directly across the road from the Laurel Falls Trail.

QUAD MAPS: Gatlinburg 157-NE

Mount Le Conte 165-NW

Clingmans Dome 165-SW

0.0—Fighting Creek Gap. Little River Road. Laurel Falls Trail.

1.4—Mids Gap.

3.1—Huskey Gap. Huskey Gap Trail exits left 2.0 miles to Newfound Gap Road and right 2.1 miles to the Little River Trail.

4.0—Big Medicine Branch. Former Medicine Branch Bluff Backcountry Campsite.

7.2—Rough Creek Trail exits right 2.8 miles to the Little River Trail.

8.7—Manway to the Chimney Tops.

11.5—Spring at Moccasin Branch.

11.6—Mount Collins Shelter.

11.9—Appalachian Trail.

Sugarland Mountain is a high razor-thin ridge springing at right angles into Tennessee from the backbone of the Smoky divide and separating the valley of the West Prong of the Little Pigeon River from that of Little River. Extending over twelve miles from the state-line divide near Mount Collins to Fighting Creek Gap on Little River Road, Sugarland Mountain is an imposing immanence. Without a significant gap in its ridgeline, it forms an intimidating rampart difficult to scale from either side.

The lower terminus of the Sugarland Mountain Trail is anchored in Fighting Creek Gap directly across Little River Road from the trailhead for the popular Laurel Falls Trail. Smoky Mountain lore alludes to several origins of the name Fighting Creek Gap. One of the more current versions refers to a long-standing heated disagreement among local mountaineers concerning a suitable location for a schoolhouse to be built along the large stream that drains the southern slopes of Cove Mountain. The stream was subsequently named Fighting Creek. Fighting Creek Gap, by virtue of association, was so named because of its proximity to the headwaters of the stream.

There is nothing subtle about the beginning of the Sugarland Mountain Trail. When the trail leaves Little River Road, it turns abruptly left and begins switching sharply in and out of deep ravines as it climbs steeply out of Fighting Creek Gap. Because the lower end of Sugarland Mountain is splayed out in ramifying ridges, the trail must either maneuver around the ridges or climb over them to reach the spine of the divide. The first mile, though an arduous climb, is not without its attractions. In springtime the adjacent slopes are festooned with rue anemones, birdfoot violets, yellow trilliums, great chickweeds, common cinquefoils, smooth yellow violets, and may-apple. Higher up, halberd-leaved violets, Clinton's lilies, blue cohosh, Solomon's-seal, and wild geraniums are spotted occasionally. Where there are openings in the forest cover, Balsam Point (5,818 feet) and Mount Le Conte (6,593 feet) can be seen presiding in the intermediate distance while below is the long graceful sweep of the Fighting Creek watershed.

Over the course of the first three miles, the trail has several steep upward and downward pitches. The first significant descent occurs one mile above Fighting Creek Gap where the trail enters a long even drop into Mids Gap, a saddle-shaped notch in the ridgeline that once harbored a trans-mountain pass between Elkmont on Little River and the farm settlements on Fighting Creek.

From Mids Gap, the trail climbs steadily through a dry-ridge pine mix for approximately a mile and a half before leveling and easing into a long drop to Huskey Gap. Halfway between Mids Gap and Huskey Gap, the trail passes a minor vantage point that offers a fine view of the south front of Mount Le Conte and the long graceful sweep of its western flank extending down into the Sugarlands. In Huskey Gap, the Sugarland Mountain Trail intersects the trans-mountain Huskey Gap Trail linking the Sugarlands with the upper Little River Valley.

> During the early years of human settlement in the Smokies, only a few families lived in the Sugarlands and on the upper reaches of Little River. Settlers cut a rough road across Sugarland Mountain at Huskey Gap, thus connecting the two communities. Later a log schoolhouse, likely the first in the Sugarlands vicinity, was built along the road in Huskey Gap. Children from both sides of Sugarland Mountain attended the school. Sometime after 1900 the schoolhouse was destroyed by fire. Charred logs from the old school building could still be seen in Huskey Gap as late as 1916. During this early period, the trail was used extensively by inhabitants of the Sugarlands crossing through the Huskey Gap to work in the logging camps on Little River.

The Sugarland Mountain Trail eases out of Huskey Gap on a single-file track through a tight corridor of laurel, then into pine stands of such density that needles shed from the trees accumulate in layers two inches deep on the path. One mile above Huskey Gap, the trail circles into a gently sloped rock-strewn amphitheater shaded by tall widely spaced cove hardwoods, notably Carolina silverbells and black cherries. The understory is remarkably thin. During spring, displays of large-flowered trilliums, yellow trilliums, sweet white violets, smooth yellow violets, may-apples, birdfoot violets, large-flowered bellworts, and great chickweeds brighten the basin. Situated in the center of the amphitheater and straddling the trail is a galled spot that marks the site of the disused Medicine Branch Bluff Backcountry Campsite.

From Big Medicine Branch, the trail circles out onto a dry ridge-point and then switches back into another moist hollow. This pattern repeats through three iterations before the trail starts a long descent to an intersection with the Rough Creek Trail. From any of the exposed points along this interval, there are good glimpses through open woods and down west-facing slopes to Little River. Blanket Mountain (4,609 feet) is the prominent point in the intermediate distance just beyond the river, and Silers Bald (5,607 feet) is conspicuous as the high point on the main Smoky divide. Two miles above Big Medicine Branch, the trail circles into a gently sloped terrain shaded by tall, slender, widely spaced oak trees. The stroll through this woodland is a deceiving prelude to what Horace Kephart once described as "the profound and dismal depths" that flank the main ridgeline of Sugarland Mountain.

As the trail circles out of this woodland bowl, it enters the drier conditions of a southern exposure where the vegetation is largely xerophytic. Ground pine, galax, partridge-berry, mountain laurel, and Table Mountain pine are the most evident. A long steady descent heralds the approach to a nameless minor swag harboring the upper terminus of the Rough Creek Trail.

In the late nineteenth century three trans-mountain trails crossed Sugarland Mountain. One passed through Mids Gap, one through Huskey Gap, and another started from the Goshen Prong vicinity of Little River and followed a streamside course up Rough Creek to the crest of Sugarland Mountain. The latter trail then traced the spine of Sugarland Mountain a hundred yards or so to Bear Pen Gap where it turned left and descended down the mountainside to the old Indian Gap Road (now the Road Prong Trail) just above Standing Rock Ford. At that time there was no long trail along the crest of Sugarland Mountain. By the middle of the twentieth century, when the Sugarland Trail was cut along Sugarland Mountain, the old trail up Rough Creek was re-routed to intersect the new Sugarland Mountain Trail about four miles above Huskey Gap. This new re-routed section was named the Rough Creek Trail. The section that descended on the north side of Sugarland Mountain to the old Indian Gap Road was abandoned. It has since become clogged with blow-downs and impassable thickets of rhododendron and dog-hobble.

From the Rough Creek Trail junction, the Sugarland Mountain Trail climbs to the spine of Sugarland Mountain, a knife edge which, in places, is no more than six feet across. The trail remains on the spine for only a short distance before deviating around a high knob shaded by a copse of towering eastern hemlocks. The trail passes through the hemlocks and into a more open exposure bearing a northern hardwood mix of red maple, white basswood, yellow buckeye, and northern red oak. Sunlight here is sufficient for prostrate bluets, spring beauties, and sweet white violets to thrive and thick patches of mountain grass to spring up along the trail's edge.

Ever-steepening slopes on either side press the trail to the center of another knife-edge where, down to the unfathomable depths on the Tennessee side, ranks upon ranks of colossal hemlocks and red spruces cling to the near-vertical declivity. Far below, the West Prong of Little Pigeon traces the bottom of the deep defile which is bounded on the north by the immensity of Mount Le Conte and its great outlier, Balsam Point. On the North Carolina side, the mountain falls away to the vast basin of the East Prong of Little River, formed in the angle between the main Smoky divide and its powerful spur, Sugarland Mountain.

The distance along the knife-edge is not far, perhaps a quarter-mile. Its upper end was once marked by a large yellow birch bearing a blaze indicating the head of an old manway that descended to the Chimney Tops, an aptly named pinnacle at the end of a flying buttress that hangs in a balance high over the Sugarland Valley. The birch tree is now reduced to a broken snag, and the manway has degenerated to a difficult and dangerous bushwhack. Once the birch snag is passed, the grade stiffens noticeably, and the Sugarland Mountain Trail enters the boreal zone.

Beyond the knife-edge, the declivity of the Sugarland divide moderates, its flanks rolling off into dense forest on either side. Readily noticeable is a wide band of great yellow birches, a superb example of virgin forest left uncut by the lumber companies. The trail proceeds through the birches and into a long, steady, climbing course that angles across a slope of spring beauties. In late summer, Turk's-cap lilies, rosy twisted stalks, and wood-betonies can be seen along this section of the trail. The birches that shade the spring beauties soon begin sharing space with towering red spruces and the occasional thicket of Fraser firs. Here, the turfs of grass that softened much of the earlier trail begin giving way to a rockier course. The higher the trail climbs into the boreal zone, the more it degenerates into a rough, rutted track.

Red spruce, fire cherry, and a densely growing corridor of Fraser fir are reliable indicators that the trail is reaching higher elevations and approaching its terminus. In an opening at the left of the trail, the headwaters of Moccasin Branch form up from a weak spring accoutred with a white vinyl pipe. The Moccasin Branch Spring is the only water available along the upper end of the trail and the closest source for the nearby Mount Collins Shelter.

The Mount Collins Shelter, 250 yards up-trail from the spring, resides on a large level bench of spongy boreal turf heavily shaded by beautiful rich balsam woods. A well-worn path winds fifty yards through the balsams to a small clearing with a vintage, three-sided shelter. Large boles of fallen spruces below the shelter afford an attractive setting in the cool shade of the balsams.

Beyond the shelter, the Sugarland Mountain Trail winds on a level course 555 yards through balsam woods to terminate into the Appalachian Trail just below the summit of Mount Collins. During the wet seasons, this section of the trail often becomes saturated with water, leaving the track a sticky mire. Four hundred and eighty yards down the Appalachian Trail, a short outlet path on the right exits fifty-five yards to Clingmans Dome Road immediately across from the upper terminus of the Fork Ridge Trail.

✦ ELKMONT ✦

The Elkmont section incorporates the triangle formed by Sugarland Mountain, the main Smoky divide, and Miry Ridge and harbors the drainages of Little River and Jakes Creek. Most of the woodlands in the basin were clear-cut during the early years of the twentieth century by the Little River Lumber Company. When the lumber company departed, outsiders moved in, building summer cottages along Jakes Creek and forming social associations designated as the Appalachian Club and the Wonderland Club. Today, the former site of the lumber town is occupied by Elkmont Campground, and a selected contingent of the rusticators' cabins as well as the Appalachian Club house have been restored as historic sites.

Seven trails visit the Elkmont section, four of which follow old railroad berms. The Little River Trail is a main artery following up the river to Three Forks under the lee of Clingmans Dome. The Miry Ridge Trail and Goshen Prong Trail climb to the Appalachian Trail on the state-line divide. The Rough Creek Trail climbs to the spine of Sugarland Mountain and the Jakes Creek Trail to Blanket Mountain. The Meigs Mountain Trail exits Elkmont on a lateral course into Tremont. The Cucumber Gap Trail is a short utility course linking Little River and Jakes Creek.

The Elkmont section is abundantly supplied with backcountry campsites—two each on the Little River Trail and Meigs Mountain Trail and one each on the Goshen Prong, Jakes Creek, and Miry Ridge trails. An eighth camp, the Mile 53 Backcountry Campsite on the Huskey Gap Trail, is treated in the Sugarlands section, though it is less than a quarter-mile from the Little River Trail. The two camps on the Little River Trail and those on the Goshen Prong Trail and Jakes Creek Trail are the sites of old logging camps. The camp on the Miry Ridge Trail was once associated with a "gant" lot used by herders to hold cattle. The remaining three camps in the Elkmont section are former homesites.

To reach the trails in the Elkmont section, drive from the Sugarlands Visitor Center west along Little River Road 4.9 miles to the entrance road to Elkmont Campground. Continue on the entrance road 2.0 miles to the campground; then turn left and follow the secondary road 0.6 mile to a parking area that marks the head of the Little River Trail. The secondary road continues another 200 yards to a parking area at the head of the Jakes Creek Trail.

LITTLE RIVER TRAIL

Elkmont to the Three Forks Backcountry Campsite (#30)—6.2 miles.
POINT OF DEPARTURE: From the Sugarlands Visitor Center, drive Little River Road 4.9 miles to the entrance to Elkmont. Turn left and drive 2.0 miles to

the campground and a secondary road that exits on the left. Proceed on the secondary road 0.6 mile to a small parking area. The Little River Trail begins at the head of the parking area.

QUAD MAPS: Gatlinburg 157-NE

Silers Bald 157-SE

0.0—Barrier at end of road above Elkmont.

2.1—Huskey Branch. Bridge.

2.4—Cucumber Gap Trail exits right 2.4 miles to the Jakes Creek Trail.

2.7—Little River. Bridge.

2.8—Huskey Gap Trail exits left 2.1 miles to the Sugarland Mountain Trail.

3.3—Groundhog Branch. Bridge.

3.7—Lost Creek. Bridge.

3.7—Goshen Prong Trail exits right 7.6 miles to the Appalachian Trail.

4.3—Feeder stream. Bridge.

4.3—Rough Creek.

4.4—Rough Creek. Rough Creek Backcountry Campsite (#24).

4.5—Rough Creek Trail exits left 2.8 miles to the Sugarland Mountain Trail.

5.9—Meigs Post Prong.

6.2—Little River.

6.2—Spud Town Branch.

6.2—Three Forks Backcountry Campsite (#30).

The Little River Trail is one of the more popular in the park. From beginning to end, it follows an easy streamside course tracing a railroad grade that remained when the Little River Lumber Company ceased operation on this part of Little River in 1918. Even before the lumber company left, outsiders began acquiring rights to property along the railroad lines above Elkmont and building rustic cabins for summer retreats. The cabins along the Little River line became known as Millionaires' Row. At this time, automobiles could be driven over the rail grade as far up as the Goshen Prong junction and then along Goshen Prong on a spur line to the old Fish Camp. Later, the road was blocked about a mile above Millionaires' Row. When the last of the leases on the Elkmont cabins expired in 1992, the road was blocked even farther downstream at the junction where the road up Jakes Creek forks from the old Little River Road.

The Little River Trail begins at the junction on a paved track that remains from the time of the summer rusticators. Immediately to the left are the stone gates that led to Happy Landings, a summer house built by Col. W. B. Townsend, president of the Little River Lumber Company, for his third wife, Alice. Directly across the trail from Happy Landings is Alice Townsend's old carriage house. Happy Landings was destroyed by fire several years ago, but the carriage house survived and was later converted into a residence. It still shows unmistakable signs of its equestrian origin.

The cabins on Little River were owned by outsiders who held long-term leases from the Park Service. As the leases expired, the cabins were abandoned and allowed to become dilapidated. Less than a half-dozen buildings remain standing on each side of the trail. All are in hazardous condition and, by Park Service edict, are not to be entered.

On the right, about 200 yards above the trailhead, a wide access leads immediately into a grassy clearing and to a fine stone building that was once the Foust cabin. A quaint stone bridge leads from the edge of the clearing to another summer home that once belonged to Lindsay Young. On the mountain slope between the Faust and Young cabins there occurs annually one of the most remarkable natural phenomena in the entire western hemisphere. Every evening for two weeks beginning around the second week in June, fireflies come out on the slope around ten o'clock and begin blinking as fireflies do. Within a few minutes the blinking of the thousands of fireflies becomes synchronized. The pattern appears to be six seconds of total darkness followed by thousands of fireflies lighting up in six simultaneous blinks before returning to another six-second period of darkness. Sometimes the fireflies all blink simultaneously and sometimes the synchronization appears as a sequence of waves. The synchronized fireflies on Little River are thought to share this trait with only two or three other colonies of fireflies worldwide.

When the Little River Trail passes the last house going upstream, the pavement yields to a light-gravel track. The trail continues on the gravel track following the big stream for three-quarters of a mile before entering a turnaround that marks the previous end-point of the old Little River Road. When the Little River Trail was first opened in the 1970s, it began at the end of this turnaround.

Beyond the turnaround, the Little River Trail initially remains near the river. A half-mile upstream, bends in the river force occasional intervals of separation between the stream and trail. About a mile above the turnaround, the Little River Trail executes a tangent encounter with the river precisely where the trail passes over Huskey Branch on a wooden bridge. On the right, along the side of the bridge, Huskey Branch cascades in reckless abandon down a long, tortuous, steeply pitched crevice, finishing its fall below the bridge. From beneath the bridge, the stream dashes out violently into Little River, which is passing by swiftly immediately below the left side of the bridge. When mountain streams are swollen with rainfall and snowmelt, particularly in March and April, the raging surge down the Huskey Branch cascade is a mesmerizing display of water.

Four hundred and forty yards above the Huskey Branch bridge, the trail intersects the eastern terminus of the Cucumber Gap Trail, a lateral connector that leads over the adjacent watershed to the Jakes Creek Trail. Six hundred yards beyond the Cucumber Gap junction, the Little River Trail crosses the river on a wooden bridge and then proceeds an additional eighty yards to intersect the western terminus of the Huskey Gap Trail, a trans-mountain course that links Little River with the Sugarlands.

From the Huskey Gap junction, the Little River Trail remains fairly close to the river, first crossing a wooden bridge over Groundhog Branch after a half-mile and then, 600 yards farther, passing through a boggy tract immediately preceding a bridge over Lost Creek. Fifty yards beyond the bridge, the trail enters an unconventional Y-shaped intersection that marks the lower terminus of the Goshen Prong Trail. The unusual configuration of the intersection is the result of the trails following the smooth, outwardly curving trajectories of an old railroad junction. In the fork of the rail junction, the Little River Lumber Company maintained a commissary for the loggers and their families, who lived in portable "stringtowns" arranged along the sides of the rail lines.

At the Goshen Prong junction, the Little River Trail turns left onto a rougher rocky course. A half-mile up, it crosses a feeder stream on a bridge that rests on a stone retaining wall remaining from the logging period. Seventy yards above the bridge, the trail encounters a 25-yard stretch of exceedingly uneven ground where it is forced to negotiate a long angular crossing of a natural sluice of Rough Creek. Though the stream is fairly shallow, it is broken up by an accumulation of rocks, making the footing here rather treacherous. A hundred and forty-five yards upstream, the trail crosses the main channel of Rough Creek and enters immediately into the Rough Creek Backcountry Campsite (#24). The crossing to the campsite usually requires wading.

The main part of the Rough Creek Camp extends over a slender plot of rough terrain along the right side of the trail. The site is level, but the prevalence of rocks scattered across the camp restricts the number of good tent sites. Water and a food-storage cable are convenient at the lower end of the camp. On a slight knoll directly across the trail is a small secluded annex site that is suitable for a couple of tents. A second food-storage cable is found on the left a few yards up-trail from the annex. On the right side of the trail and about fifty yards above the main campsite a second annex is cloistered in a tight thicket of rhododendron. The second annex is quite level and clean, but suitable for only one tent.

One hundred and twenty-five yards above the upper annex, the trail intersects the lower terminus of the Rough Creek Trail, which leads 2.8 miles to the Sugarland Mountain Trail. Three hundred yards beyond this junction, the Little River Trail negotiates a feeder stream and then, 200 yards farther, a difficult double-crossing of another feeder. Here the trail enters a low hummocky terrain. The track remains rough and the grade easy, still tracing the old railroad bed.

During the time when the Little River Lumber Company was clear-cutting the upper reaches of the river basin, loggers lived in portable houses that were lined up in stringtowns within a few feet of the railroad tracks. Florence Cope Bush, whose family once lived upstream at Three Forks, later recorded her recollections of the stringtown houses in *Dorie: Woman of the Mountains*. The houses were "varied in size and in the number of windows and doors in each unit. . . . Both the inside and outside of the units were made from rough lumber. Tar paper was used as an insulation between the walls, linoleum covered the splintery floors inside. Most of the units were painted barn red."

Since all portable units had to be moved on railroad flatcars, Bush explains that "the structure couldn't be longer than twelve to fourteen feet and wider than eight feet. Each had a hole in the top and bottom, covered with tin that could be removed—leaving a place for a heavy chain and hook to be dropped . . . down from the ceiling through the floor to steel crossbars that made an "X" just under the hole in the floor." When the house had to be moved, the hook was fastened to the crossbars and a crane lifted the house and put it on a flatcar. The house itself was placed on a "house seat," a pallet-like structure made from poles. When the house was moved, the house seat was dismantled and moved to the next site.

Slightly less than a mile and a half above the Rough Creek junction, the trail crosses Meigs Post Prong, proceeds 500 yards to cross Little River, and then another 120 yards to Spud Town Branch. There are no bridges at either of these streams, and fording is rarely easy. The collapsed remnant of the old railroad bridge that once carried logging trains across Little River lies in the stream. Railroad bridges also once spanned Meigs Post Prong and Spud Town Branch, but now only a few timbers remain scattered about in the stream bed.

The Little River Trail terminates in the Three Forks Backcountry Campsite (#30) on the far side of Spud Town Branch.

The name Three Forks remains from the loggers' reference to the basin where Little River, Spud Town Branch, and Grouse Creek converge. According to an anecdote recorded by Vic Weals in *Last Train to Elkmont*, the name Spud Town Branch is the result of an incorrect understanding of the words Spud Tongue Branch. Spud Tongue refers to the business end of a tanbark spud used by loggers to peel bark from logs. The incorrect name was recorded by the U.S. Geological Survey and has remained ever since.

Prior to the backcountry camp, Three Forks was occupied by the Little River Lumber Company's Camp 19, sometimes known as the Higdon Camp. Refuse from the logging camp, particularly rusting remains from the garbage dumps, can still be found outside the perimeter of the backcountry campsite. The Three Forks

Camp is situated in a level clearing of about a half-acre enclosed by patches of dog-hobble and shaded by slender second-growth yellow poplars. The camp easily accommodates a dozen tent sites, and both water and food-storage cables are convenient. Remoteness and the difficulty of the stream crossings act as barriers to entry that help make the Three Forks Camp one of the nicer backcountry campsites in the park.

GOSHEN PRONG TRAIL

Little River Trail to the Appalachian Trail—7.6 miles.
POINT OF DEPARTURE: Hike 3.7 miles up the Little River Trail. The Goshen Prong Trail begins on the right.
QUAD MAP: Silers Bald 157-SE

0.0—Little River Trail at Fish Camp Fork.
0.1—Little River. Bridge.
1.2—Road turnaround.
1.3—Feeder stream.
1.4—War Branch.
2.1—Former Camp Rock Backcountry Campsite.
2.2—Battle Hollow.
3.0—Fish Camp Prong.
3.2—Fish Camp Prong.
3.2—Access path exits left to the Camp Rock Backcountry Campsite (#23).
3.3—Manway to the old Lower Buckeye Gap Backcountry Campsite.
4.4—End of railroad grade.
5.0—Cave.
7.6—Appalachian Trail.

While clear-cutting the slopes flanking Little River and its tributaries, the Little River Lumber Company extended rail lines up along the larger tributaries to gain access to the more remote timber at the higher elevations. Afterward, when the loggers finished on Little River, the company took up the rails and moved them to other sites, leaving a network of graded berms that would later be appropriated as hiking trails. The Goshen Prong Trail follows one such berm, tracing a grade along Fish Camp Prong before turning and ascending the rugged Goshen Prong drainage to the main Smoky divide.

At its lower terminus the Goshen Prong Trail is engaged with the Little River Trail in a remarkably smooth Y-shaped junction. The junction reflects the rounded configuration of the old rail bed where a single rail line separated into two uniformly diverging lines. In the wye of the rail junction there once stood a large wooden building that served as a commissary for the men and women working with the lumber company. The junction was known as Fish Camp Fork.

When it leaves Fish Camp Fork, the Goshen Prong Trail follows a wide level track for 200 yards before encountering a metal frame bridge spanning Little River. Beyond the bridge the trail continues on its level track, soon settling into an easy course along Fish Camp Prong.

Fish Camp Prong is a large stream with a variegated constitution. In places, it flows evenly over remarkably level ledges the width of the stream. At others, it rushes madly through narrow chutes, and yet at others it is gliding over dome-shaped shields. At times it can be seen composing itself in deep placid pools. Along both sides of the stream are bottomlands once completely cleared of timber. Where the forest has been slow to recover, horse nettle, smooth yellow and sweet white violets, pale and spotted jewel weeds, trilliums, bedstraw, crested dwarf iris, white fringed phacelia, may-apples, Indian cucumber roots, and toothworts are conspicuous.

One mile above the bridge, Coon Hollow empties into the far side of Fish Camp Prong in an attractive cascade. A hundred and thirty-five yards beyond the cascade, the trail widens into a turnaround. From this juncture the trail continues its level course on the old rail berm, albeit on a much narrower track. Two hundred and ten yards above the turnaround, another feeder stream intervenes. Where the trail crosses, there can be seen the stone understructures that once supported a railroad bridge. Understructures such as this are the more conspicuous remnants of the logging era, although bits of coal, miscellaneous pieces of industrial metal, and cinders remain scattered along the way.

Beyond the feeder stream the trail follows closely along Fish Camp Prong for 200 yards to a rocky bluff where War Branch spills across the path in search of the larger stream. War Branch, along with nearby Hostility Branch and Battle Hollow, suggest that the area may have been the setting for some incidence of collective combat. This apparently is not the case. A local mountaineer once informed Paul Fink that the colorful name refers to the terrain, rugged and heavily infested with laurel, being "so horse-tile ye had to battle yer way through."

Two miles above the bridge crossing over Little River and to the left of the trail a large overhanging rock presides over what was once the site of the Camp Rock Backcountry Campsite. The site here was abandoned late in the twentieth century and the camp reestablished a mile upstream.

Three-quarters of a mile above the old Camp Rock site, the trail degenerates into an exceedingly rocky course as it crosses Battle Hollow. After the better part of a mile, the trail completes a rather difficult crossing of Fish Camp Prong and then proceeds to cross a parcel of low level ground that is actually an almond-shaped island separating two divergent streams of Fish Camp Prong. At the head of the island, 335 yards farther, the trail executes another difficult crossing of Fish Camp Prong and immediately enters a large flat where Goshen Prong and Ash Camp Prong converge with Fish Camp Prong.

Prior to the lumbering era, the island and surrounding vicinity were occupied by a local fishing camp. When the lumber company arrived, a rail line was extended the length of the island and along the main stream with spur lines running up both tributaries. The fishing camp was replaced by a small settlement that included a general store, a church-schoolhouse building, and at least thirteen houses for the loggers. At the time of the loggers' settlement, Goshen Prong was occasionally referred to as Spradlin Prong in deference to Nathan Spradlin, who lived on the stream with his wife and family. Ash Camp Prong was then known as both Powder Prong and Middle Prong.

Sixty-five yards beyond the second crossing of Fish Camp Prong, the trail encounters an access path on the left leading about a hundred yards to the new Rock Camp Backcountry Campsite (#23). The camp is situated on the old logging settlement grounds, a large level plat commanded by a high bluff on the back side. The site is slightly terraced, effectively dividing it into two distinct camps, both of which are quite attractive and free of trees. A food-storage cable is suspended near the upper camp, and water is available below the lower site where the trail crosses Fish Camp Prong.

Eighty yards above the point where the access path enters the campsite, the Goshen Prong Trail turns and leaves Fish Camp Prong for a course up Goshen Prong. At the turn, a readily noticeable manway exits from the right side of the trail. Approximately a mile long, the manway crosses Fish Camp Prong and proceeds to a nexus of small clearings that once constituted the Lower Buckeye Gap Backcountry Campsite. The camp was abandoned early in the twenty-first century and is no longer considered an official campsite.

After the turn, the grade stiffens noticeably though the trail remains on the old railroad bed. It stays high and away from Goshen Prong for a mile before dropping to a tangent encounter with the stream. Here, Goshen Prong flows uniformly over a level rock ledge and then bolts down through a narrow rocky chute. The trail veers left, leaves the railroad grade, and begins a steep climb up the flank of Goshen Ridge and away from the stream.

At this elevation the trail is in a transition zone where red spruce and yellow birches gradually begin displacing the eastern hemlocks and cove hardwoods. A half-mile after leaving the railroad grade, the trail executes a sharp turn right to cross a large feeder stream cascading down a jagged face of up-turned rock strata. The grade stiffens another few degrees and proceeds 105 yards to a rocky cave immediately to the left of the trail. The cave, about fifty feet deep, has a fairly level floor and is high enough to stand upright. Seepage keeps the cave's floor perpetually damp.

By the time the trail reaches the cave, it is in the balsam zone. Red spruces, yellow birches, and American beeches are dominant with Fraser firs now entering the mix. As the trail gains elevation, the steepness increases, and the track degenerates into a bed of flat loosely shifting stones convoluted with gnarled roots of encroaching spruce and birch trees. In places, weak streams percolate out from the slopes and use the trail as a path of least resistance down the mountain. These conditions persist for the better part of the final two miles as the Goshen Prong Trail continues climbing, eventually reaching the state-line divide and terminating into the Appalachian Trail 2.2 miles west of Clingmans Dome.

ROUGH CREEK TRAIL

Little River Trail to the Sugarland Mountain Trail—2.8 miles.
POINT OF DEPARTURE: Hike 4.5 miles up the Little River Trail. The Rough Fork Trail begins on the left.
QUAD MAPS: Silers Bald 157-SE
Gatlinburg 157-NE

0.0—Little River Trail.
0.5—Rough Creek.
1.4—Rough Creek.
1.9—Rough Creek.
2.8—Sugarland Mountain Trail.

Early maps of the Smokies indicate a trail running along the full length of Rough Creek up to Bear Pen Gap on the ridgeline of Sugarland Mountain and then descending to the Road Prong Trail near Standing Rock Ford. From the scant written records of the trail, it appears to have been a rudimentary track used by mountaineers traveling from their homes in the upper end of the Sugarlands to the logging camps on Little River. When the Rough Creek Trail was graded by enlistees of the Civilian Conservation Corps and officially adopted by the Park Service in the 1930s, it was made to start from the end of the gravel road where the Goshen Prong Trail exits from the Little River Trail. The old Rough Creek track followed up the railroad bed that is now the Little River Trail and continued through the Rough Creek Backcountry Campsite (#24). Just beyond the campsite, the trail turned away from Little River and proceeded into the Rough Creek drainage. Instead of continuing northeast on to Bear Pen Gap as the old rudimentary track did, the park trail followed the stream for the first two miles, then turned back sharply to ascend Sugarland Mountain on a lower trajectory. This first official Rough Creek Trail was almost three-and-a-half miles long.

As late as 1973, when Dick Murlless and Constance Stallings completed the Sierra Club *Hiker's Guide to the Smokies*, the Rough Creek Trail still started at the Goshen Prong junction, and there was no official Little River Trail. A few years later, when the Little River Trail was authorized and opened to Three Forks, the Rough Creek Trail was shortened by a little over a half-mile and made to start at the junction just above the Rough Creek Campsite.

From where it now begins, the Rough Creek Trail exits from the Little River Trail and enters quickly onto an easy course through stands of American holly, yellow birch, and American beech. Though the tree species along the trail vary with changes in elevation and environmental conditions, all trees here are second-growth. During the second decade of the twentieth century, the Little River Lumber Company built a rail line up the hollow and, using heavy mechanized equipment, proceeded to strip the adjacent slopes completely bare of trees.

A transition into stands of yellow poplar and eastern hemlock heralds the approach to Rough Creek, which is crossed a half-mile above the trailhead. A hundred and fifty yards above the crossing, a large feeder stream cascades in an attractive near-vertical plunge into Rough Creek. The grade stiffens a bit and for a short interval adheres closely to the stream. It soon edges away and eventually eases onto an old roadbed that enters a flat open ground that once harbored a rail junction and logging camp. Galvanized buckets, sections of wire rope, barrel hoops, and miscellaneous pieces of machinery lie nearby. On the left is a pile of rusting cans marking what may have likely been the camp dump.

The logging camp on Rough Creek was operated by the Little River Lumber Company under contract with the Champion Fibre Company. Champion owned the timberland high on the upper reaches of Rough Creek where access was limited from the North Carolina side. It was more economical for Champion to bring the spruce timber down into Tennessee and retain the Little River Lumber Company to mill and freight it to Champion's pulp mill in Canton, North Carolina, than to haul the raw timber back over the Smoky divide to their own sawmills.

In *Our Southern Highlanders*, Horace Kephart recounts a fascinating story in which he accompanies a police detective named Mr. Quick and a Cherokee guide, Ketch, on a raid into the Sugarlands in pursuit of three fugitives of the surname Ruff. At one point the pursuit leads Kephart and his companions over Sugarland Mountain and down to the camp on Rough Creek, which Kephart calls Barradale's. The camp was then new, and Kephart describes it as having a "flume, portable mill and cook-house just finished, and shacks under construction."

Kephart was invited to join the camp for lunch and so took his place with the loggers at the long table. He became immediately aware that "the crew ate in a silence that fairly gave one the creeps. It seemed ominous of trouble all around." He had earlier been told that in some logging camps in the Smokies all unnecessary talking at meals was prohibited. When Kephart inquired why the men were treated like convicts, the camp boss responded, "If you had to run a hell-roarin' bunch like mine, you'd know why. Their idea of conversation is argument; their idea of argument is a rumpus. I can't afford that when there's two hundred dollars' worth of crockery lyin' handy."

At a feeder stream above the old logging camp, the trail leaves the roadbed and drops to cross Rough Creek a second time. Beyond, the forest cover remains fairly open with partridge-berry and dog-hobble conspicuous as ground cover. White basswood, Carolina silverbell, American beech, eastern hemlock, and red maple enter the forest mix. After an easy half-mile, the trail encounters a couple of feeder streams and then crosses Rough Creek for the third and final time to begin a three-quarter-mile assault of the flank of Sugarland Mountain. The final climb is much steeper than the streamside course, and seepages keep the track wet and rocky. In places the track is no more than a narrow berm. Halfway up, a cliff commands the right side of the trail. Here, the grade moderates a bit as the trail begins a long approach into a small featureless junction where it terminates into the Sugarland Mountain Trail. From here, the Sugarland Mountain Trail climbs east 4.7 miles to the Appalachian Trail at Mount Collins and descends west 4.1 miles to intersect the Huskey Gap Trail.

JAKES CREEK TRAIL

Elkmont to the Miry Ridge Trail and Panther Creek Trail at Jakes Gap—3.7 miles.

POINT OF DEPARTURE: Follow directions to the Little River Trail, and continue driving on the road another 200 yards to the parking area on Jakes Creek. The Jakes Creek Trail begins on the old road above the parking area.

QUAD MAPS: Gatlinburg 157-NE
Silers Bald 157-SE

0.0—Parking area on Jakes Creek Road above Elkmont.
0.4—Old parking area. Trail leaves Jakes Creek Road. Gate.
0.7—Cucumber Gap Trail exits left 2.4 miles to the Little River Trail.
0.8—Meigs Mountain Trail exits right 6.1 miles to the Meigs Creek Trail and Lumber Ridge Trail at Buckhorn Gap.
1.3—Manway exits right 225 yards to the Avent Cabin.
1.6—Roadbed ends. Waterdog Branch. Footlog.
1.7—Newt Prong.
2.3—Jakes Creek.
2.4—Switchback.
3.0—Lower Jakes Gap Backcountry Campsite (#27).
3.7—Miry Ridge Trail exits left 5.0 miles to the Appalachian Trail. Panther Creek Trail exits straight 2.3 miles to the Middle Prong Trail. Manway exits right 0.9 mile to Blanket Mountain.

When the Little River Lumber Company began logging the upper reaches of the Little River watershed, the company established a logging settlement at the confluence of Jakes Creek and Little River. The settlement included a commissary, company boarding house, hotel, theater, general store, infirmary, and houses for company employees. The logging town was adjacent to an older community of mountain farms with its own stores, churches, schools, and houses. The area including both the logging town and the mountain community soon became known as Elkmont.

In the wake of their clear-cutting the slopes of the Little River watershed, the lumber company began selling cottage lots to well-to-do outsiders envisioning rustic summer resorts in the Smokies. Over eighty cottages were built, mostly along Jakes Creek. The rusticators organized themselves as the Appalachian Club and built a large fine clubhouse, a swimming hole, and other recreational amenities. With the coming of the park, the right of ownership of Elkmont was taken over by the federal government. The mountaineers were granted the option to sell their property to the government or receive lifetime leases to remain on their farms. The cottage owners were given the option of a lifetime lease or a "time-of-years" lease. In 1989 Lem Ownby, the last mountaineer remaining in Elkmont, died, and by 1992 the last of the "time-of-years" leases expired and the land was left to return to wilderness.

An early account attributes the origin of the name Elkmont to an old man by the name of Nick Smith. Smith was a well-known hunter and farmer who had an intense dislike of Indians. It was said that he would kill an Indian with as much pride as he would kill a bear or deer. He wore a coonskin cap, buckskin leggings, and a red hunting shirt. His hair was long and unkempt and his beard shaggy. Sometime shortly after the Civil War, Smith was hunting in the vicinity of Elkmont and killed a large buck whose horns were long and sported several prongs on each horn. Smith took from the head of the elk, as he called it, one of the horns. With his hunting knife, he split the branch of a hickory tree and placed the horn on the split end. The tree continued to grow, taking the horn up with it until reaching a great height. Nick Smith named the place Elk Mountain, not for the elk, but to commemorate his heroic deed. Elk Mountain was later shortened to Elkmont, the name which survives today.

A later tradition contends that the name was inspired by the occasion of the Knoxville Elks organization visit here for a summer jamboree. The event prompted the Little River Lumber Company to attach the name Elkmont to their newly built logging settlement.

Until Lem Ownby died and the last of the cottage leases expired, the road along Jakes Creek was required to remain open. Accordingly, the Jakes Creek Trail began above the "last house" on Jakes Creek Road, where a secondary road angles up to the left. In 2010 a paved parking area was built near the entrance to the Elkmont Cemetery and the trailhead shifted almost a half-mile back down Jakes Creek Road.

The Jakes Creek Trail begins above Elkmont at the upper end of the parking area on the old Jakes Creek Road. From the parking area, the trail follows Jakes Creek Road as it passes along the fronts of the cottages that were once the summer homes of affluent rusticators.

Most of the cottages are in an advanced state of deterioration, some even to the point of collapsing. In the interest of public safety, passersby are prohibited by Park Service edict from visiting the premises or entering the buildings. Nevertheless, encountering these silent ghostly relics of a bygone era, all in various stages of succumbing to the inexorable agents of time and nature, is no less an edifying experience than that of contemplating the most purely natural phenomena in the Smokies. Arranged side-by-side on the narrow strip of rocky terrain that separates the creek from the road, the cottages are no more than a few feet from their neighbors and in a conspicuous variety of shapes and designs.

The cottages extend along Jakes Creek Road for the better part of a half-mile to where the road widens momentarily at the foot of the original trailhead for the Jakes Creek Trail. Here, the trail leaves Jakes Creek Road and follow a secondary road that climbs away and into a shallow hollow. The main road crosses Jakes Creek and continues for a third of a mile to terminate at what was once the Lem Ownby homeplace.

When it leaves the main road, the Jakes Creek Trail climbs on an easy grade for about a third of a mile before encountering the Cucumber Gap Trail leading in on the left from Little River. Here, the Jakes Creek Trail turns and begins descending, proceeding only ninety yards before intersecting the eastern terminus of the Meigs Mountain Trail leading in from the right.

Almost a half-mile beyond the Meigs Mountain Trail junction, a manway exits to the right and leads 225 yards across Jakes Creek to the Avent Cabin. The head of the manway is difficult to discern as it drops off below the edge of the trail. A long footlog over Jakes Creek entails not having to wade the stream.

> The Avent Cabin consists of a 24.5-by-17.5-foot one-room log structure with an 8.0-by-11.0-foot board-and-batten addition that served as a kitchen. The original log cabin, built in 1850, was the home of Sam and Minnie Cook. In 1918, the cabin was purchased by Frank and Mayna Avent, who added the kitchen annex, large glass picture windows, and a fireplace. Mayna, an artist, used the cabin as a studio from about 1919 until 1940. She died in 1959, and in 1993 the cabin became the possession of the National Park Service. It is now listed on the National Register of Historic Places.

Three-quarters of a mile beyond the Meigs Mountain Trail junction, the road-bed ends. The Jakes Creek Trail continues on a narrow track, proceeding only forty yards before crossing Waterdog Branch on a footlog. The trail clears a small rise and then, 130 yards farther, crosses Newt Prong. Crossing Newt Prong is generally easy but can be difficult when the stream is running high.

 In April 1922, a spark from a logging skidder ignited a slash pile, resulting in a wildfire that destroyed several acres of woodland, stacks of cut timber, and several pieces of logging equipment along Jakes Creek. From the ashes of the burned-over landscape sprang fire cherry trees that today are one of the primary species in this second-growth forest. Carpets of ferns and scattered clusters of rhododendron make up much of the understory.

The trail continues on an old railroad trace, climbing on a moderate grade through the fire-scald for slightly more than three-quarters of a mile before crossing Jakes Creek. Jakes Creek is a large fast-moving stream that deviates very little from a direct course down the mountain. Though the trail follows the stream from this point, it rarely gets close enough to be considered a streamside course.

One hundred and fifty yards above the stream crossing, the trail negotiates a switchback and then continues on up along the stream. In a couple of places, feeder streams seeking Jakes Creek run in the trail for a short distance. Slightly more than half a mile above the switchback, an access path exits left to the Lower Jakes Gap Backcountry Campsite (#27), a large camp spread out on three distinct plats arrayed along the slope between the trail and the stream.

Just where the access path enters the camp it encounters a large boulder, a fire ring, and a food-storage cable. To the right and beyond the boulder is a large level site that gives the appearance of a fine camping spot, notwithstanding that the ground is a bit rough and uneven. There are a couple of suitable tent sites, particularly on a small annex situated along the lower side of the site. This part of the camp is fairly close to the food-storage cable, but a bit removed from the water source.

To the left and below the boulder is a larger plat that affords more suitable tent sites than the upper camp. A food-storage cable is suspended along one side, and the stream is about forty yards in back of the camp. Conveniently situated in the middle of the camp is a low boulder of the right height to serve as a rough table and sitting bench.

About thirty yards below the middle camp, a third campsite occupies a small level bench immediately above Jakes Creek. The upper side of the camp is defined by a low flat-topped boulder that serves as a fine camp table and sitting bench. Water is immediate, although the closest food-storage cable is in the middle camp.

When it leaves the Lower Jakes Gap Camp, the trail follows the railroad grade an additional three-quarters of a mile and then curls up onto a ridgeline to terminate in Jakes Gap, an exceptionally wide flat swag separating Dripping Spring Mountain from Blanket Mountain. Rising into the gap from the opposite side is the

Panther Creek Trail leading up from the Middle Prong Trail in Tremont. On the left, the Miry Ridge Trail begins, circumnavigating the western end of Dripping Spring Mountain to proceed five miles to the Appalachian Trail near Buckeye Gap. On the right, an unmaintained access path leads nearly a mile to the summit of Blanket Mountain and the former site of the Blanket Mountain fire tower.

There is no consensus as to the origin of the names Jakes Gap and Jakes Creek. Andy Gregory, a well-known local surveyor, contends that the creek and gap were named for Jake Halman. Gregory gives no further justification for the origin of the name other than that Halman was a mountaineer. Other lesser-known sources suggest the creek was named for a Jake Houser, a Jake Cattern, or a Jake Parton. It is implied that they all lived on the stream.

The access path to Blanket Mountain exits out of Jakes Gap and proceeds through a corridor of stunted dry-ridge mix interspersed with mountain laurel and rhododendron before ending in a large grassy tract that marks the summit of the mountain. Beginning sometime in the late 1920s, the clearing was occupied by a sturdy thirty-five-foot wooden tower known as the State Lookout Station. The look-out was accompanied by a tiny wooden cabin. In 1949, the tower and cabin were dismantled and replaced with a metal frame fire tower and a modern warden's cabin. These structures were later dismantled and removed, leaving only the base supports of the tower and ruins of the cabin. Since the clearing is completely enclosed by high vegetation, there are no views from the summit. The summit does, however, afford a nice place for a lunch break.

In 1797 Benjamin Hawkins was commissioned by Secretary of War James McHenry to survey the boundary separating the Indian lands from those of the white settlers as stipulated by the 1791 Treaty of the Holston. Beginning at Fort Southwest Point (near present-day Kingston, Tennessee), the Hawkins party proceeded on a course south seventy-six degrees east into "the Great Iron Mountain," crossing over what was probably Bote Mountain and a stream that has been identified as the West Prong of Little River. Somewhere in the vicinity of Blanket Mountain the course was lost by the surveyors. The only account of this final part of the survey survives in the surveyor's field notes: "This line terminates at the 30th mile from Holston, in the midst of mountains which cannot be passed by horses and is extremely difficult for footmen."

By the time the Hawkins survey had been aborted, another treaty was in the works. Because white settlers had encroached on the Indian side of the boundary, the Cherokee were being asked to cede more territory to the federal government. Duly authorized and signed in 1798, the Treaty of Tellico offered clearer demarcations of the line separating the Indian territory from that of the settlers.

In 1802, Indian Commissioner Return Jonathan Meigs was authorized to re-draw the Tellico line to clear up some discrepancies. Meigs apparently followed the old Hawkins line to its terminus at Blanket Mountain. Leaving the pack horses behind because of rough terrain, the Meigs party climbed to the Smoky divide near Mount Collins and sighted back to a marker on the summit of Blanket Mountain to determine the point that an extended Hawkins line would intersect with the state line between Tennessee and North Carolina. The survey party marked the point of intersection with a spruce post. The marker later became known as Meigs Post. Tradition contends that the object Meigs sighted in fixing the survey line was a bright Indian blanket—thus the origin of the name Blanket Mountain. (The history of the Hawkins line, Meigs Post, and Blanket Mountain is treated in a fine article by Ron Petersen, "Two Early Boundary Lines with the Cherokee Nation," in the *Journal of Cherokee Studies* 6, no. 1 [1981]).

CUCUMBER GAP TRAIL

Jakes Creek Trail to the Little River Trail—2.4 miles.
POINT OF DEPARTURE: Hike 0.7 mile up the Jakes Creek Trail. The Cucumber Gap Trail begins on the left.
QUAD MAP: Gatlinburg 157-NE

0.0—Jakes Creek Trail.
0.3—Tulip Branch.
1.1—Cucumber Gap. Bent Arm manway.
2.0—Huskey Branch.
2.4—Little River Trail exits left 2.4 miles to Elkmont.

The Cucumber Gap Trail is a lateral connector that is frequently traveled as the middle part of an easy five-and-a-half-mile loop that begins in Elkmont on the Jakes Creek Trail and returns to Elkmont by the Little River Trail. From its Jakes Creek end, the Cucumber Gap Trail starts up into a moderate climb on a wide gravel track where the adjacent slopes are gentle gradients forested in tall slender white basswoods, yellow poplars, mountain maples, and eastern hemlocks heavily burdened with thick strands of wild grapevines reaching a hundred feet to the tree canopies. The prevalence of grapevines is often an indicator of poor or depleted soil on which other undergrowth species do not thrive.

Six hundred yards above the trailhead, the Cucumber Gap Trail crosses Tulip Branch, formerly known as Poplar Branch and so-named for the prevalence of large yellow poplars that grew in the vicinity before being felled by loggers. After crossing Tulip Branch, the trail levels out for the next quarter-mile. Spring beauties, cut-leaved toothworts, hepaticae, and pink turtleheads can be seen on the slopes.

Just after completing its first mile, the trail encounters the lower terminus of the Bent Arm manway as it enters the south side of Cucumber Gap, a wide level interlude in the ridgeline between Bent Arm and Burnt Mountain. The manway, which leads to the Miry Ridge Trail near the site of the original Dripping Spring Mountain Backcountry Campsite, has not been maintained since the middle of the twentieth century and thus is not recommended as a hiking trail.

 The name Cucumber Gap likely originates from the prevalence of cucumber trees, a hardy species that tends to occur as scattered species rather than in groves. The cucumber tree produces a long bumpy fruit that bears some resemblance to a cucumber.

Beyond Cucumber Gap the trail begins descending into rocky terrain and soon finds a course along a small stream leading into a somewhat boggy, rhododendron and dog-hobble infested bottom. Trout lilies, bloodroots, trilliums, and patches of crimson bee-balms are scattered beneath the canopies of tall second-growth cove-hardwood stands. A mile below the gap, the trail completes a crossing of Huskey Branch that may be slightly difficult when the stream is running high.

Beyond Huskey Branch, the trail eases onto a wide smooth track of negligible grade that proceeds almost a half-mile to terminate into the Little River Trail. This lower part of the Cucumber Gap Trail was likely a logging road that connected to the rail line following up Little River.

MEIGS MOUNTAIN TRAIL

Jakes Creek Trail to the Lumber Ridge Trail and Meigs Creek Trail at
  Buckhorn Gap—6.1 miles.
POINT OF DEPARTURE: Hike 0.8 miles up the Jakes Creek Trail. The Meigs
  Mountain Trail begins on the right.
QUAD MAPS: Gatlinburg 157-NE
Wear Cove 157-NW

0.0—Jakes Creek Trail.
0.1—Jakes Creek. Footlog.
0.2—Manway to the former Lem Ownby homeplace.
1.0—Shields Branch.
1.9—King Branch Backcountry Campsite (#20).
2.0—Kiver Branch.
2.1—Blanket Creek.

4.1—Curry Mountain Trail exits right 3.3 miles to Little River Road at Metcalf Bottoms.

4.4—Access path exits right to the Meigs Mountain Cemetery.

4.6—Upper Henderson Backcountry Campsite (#19).

5.2—Upper Buckhorn Gap.

6.1—Buckhorn Gap. Meigs Creek Trail exits right 3.5 miles to Little River Road at the Sinks. Lumber Ridge Trail exits straight 4.1 miles to the Great Smoky Mountains Institute at Tremont.

Meigs Mountain is a long ridge oriented on an east-west axis between Elkmont and Tremont with its back to the main Smoky divide and its north face shadowing the Little River gorge. The Meigs Mountain Trail follows the axis, adhering to the transition zone between the declivities of the north face and the more gentle gradient sloping to the river.

Meigs Mountain was visited in 1802 by its namesake, Return Jonathan Meigs, during his command of a survey party attempting an on-the-ground verification of the Hawkins Line as stipulated by the Treaty of the Holston of 1791. An earlier attempt to survey the line by a party under the direction of Benjamin Hawkins was not completed. The effort was abandoned, according to the surveyor's field notes, "in the midst of mountains which cannot be passed by horses and is extremely difficult for footmen." Meigs eventually completed the Hawkins Line, but only after bypassing the tangle of mountains that had confounded the Hawkins party, climbing to the main Smoky divide at Mount Collins, and sighting back to a colorful marker placed on Blanket Mountain, a high peak just south of Meigs Mountain. The marker used by Meigs was apparently a brightly colored Indian blanket—the source of the name Blanket Mountain.

The more intriguing story of Return Jonathan Meigs concerns the origin of his name. It seems that sometime in the early eighteenth century a young suitor named Jonathan Meigs became enamored with a Quaker girl who was reluctant to embark on the great adventure of matrimony. Young Jonathan's ardent proposals were always met with a "not now" response by the lass. Jonathan was persistent, and the familiar turndown did not deter him from asking. Once, after yet another attempt on bended knee, the "not now" was followed by a glimmer of encouragement. The Quaker girl was still not ready for marriage, but advised her suitor to "return, Jonathan Meigs, return."

Jonathan Meigs did return, and finally the young lass was ready. A wedding date was set. Solemn vows were exchanged. Jonathan Meigs and his bride became husband and wife. Soon afterwards a child was born. In honor of his mother's words of encouragement, the child was named Return Jonathan Meigs.

In 1801, Return Jonathan Meigs was appointed Indian commissioner by the U.S. secretary of war and was later authorized to survey the Cherokee boundary through the country officially identified as "the Great Iron or Smoky Mountain." The next year Meigs completed the survey, spending considerable time on the mountain that now bears his name. At the time, Meigs commented that "the backwoodsmen and the Indians could give us very little information, for neither had explored the great Iron Mountain anywhere near the part where the direction of our line would take us."

It would be nearly a century after Meigs's survey before the broad lower slope of Meigs Mountain would be settled by a few venturesome pioneers. Not until the twentieth century, when the lumber companies built a rail line up Little River and established logging camps at Elkmont and Tremont, did Meigs Mountain become easily accessible to the outside world.

From its Elkmont end, the Meigs Mountain Trail begins along the Jakes Creek Trail, descending 250 yards to a footlog suspended over Jakes Creek. Immediately beyond the footlog, a manway exits to the right, leading downstream about a hundred yards to a gravel road and grassy field that was once the home of Lem Ownby, the last permanent living resident in Elkmont. Upon his death in 1989, Lem Ownby's cabin was immediately razed by the Park Service. A small horse barn was later built near the old cabin site and the pasture fields fenced in. The gravel road continues another 675 yards back to the head of the Jakes Creek Trail.

After crossing Jakes Creek, the Meigs Mountain Trail climbs out of the drainage, clears a slight ridge, and then descends to a bottomland along Shields Branch. At the top of the climb, an odd U-shaped stone structure is noticeable to the left of the trail. It is one of the more unusual artifacts remaining from the pioneer era.

During the dry season, Shields Branch may hardly be noticed. During the wetter season, three spring-branch headwaters of the stream will intervene. None of the three is necessarily easy to cross. Beyond the stream, the trail remains fairly level, winding across the bottom through thickets of rhododendron.

A half-mile beyond Shields Branch the trail clears another ridge gap and then descends steeply 550 yards to cross a nameless stream and enter the King Branch Backcountry Campsite (#20). The camp is situated on a large slightly pitched gradient ranging along the upper side of the trail. A few trees are interspersed among the half-dozen or so level spots that suffice as suitable camping spots. Water is readily available at the edge of the camp, and a food-storage cable is convenient along the upper back corner.

At this juncture, the trail begins following an old roadbed with a stone wall bordering the upper side. The King Branch Camp occupies the old homesite that once marked the end of the road. The road maintains an easy grade across the bottom, first crossing Kiver Branch 250 yards below the camp and then Blanket Creek 150 yards farther along. Both crossings can be difficult. A large iron switching mechanism remaining from the logging era lies abandoned at the second crossing.

From here, the terrain becomes noticeably more rugged as the trail completes an easy half-mile climb to clear a minor ridge gap. For the next mile and a half, the trail plies the contours of the mountain and crosses as many as five streams. The first is Sugar Maple Branch. The next four are headwater prongs of Mannis Branch. During the drier seasons, all five may completely disappear.

After crossing the last stream, the trail rises to intersect the upper terminus of the Curry Mountain Trail, an old course that leads in from Metcalf Bottoms on Little River. Until the coming of the park, this junction was occupied by a school-house. From here, the Meigs Mountain Trail veers to the left and follows the course of the older road. Four hundred and twenty yards beyond the intersection, an access path exits right and leads fifty yards to the Meigs Mountain Cemetery, a small grassy plat that harbors a few worn fieldstones and two modern headstones.

Three hundred and ninety yards beyond the cemetery access, the trail enters a rough galled spot that was once occupied by a cabin, barn, and smokehouse. It was the home of the Andy Brackin family. The clearing is now appropriated by the Upper Henderson Backcountry Campsite (#19), a small badly sloped gradient that enjoys a ruggedly attractive mountain setting but affords a less than ideal camping site. The trail passes through the middle of the campsite, which lies under the lee of a ridge and heavily shaded by forest, thus rarely visited by direct sunlight. There are no more than three or four level spots, and these are terraced plots built up with dirt in-fill. When it rains, the terraced plots pool run-off from the slopes and become slightly muddy.

Water is readily accessible from a fine spring immediately below the smaller rougher site along the lower side of the trail. A food-storage cable is suspended across the middle of the campsite. All that remains from the former Brackin residence is the spring and a rusty washtub abandoned below the campsite.

From the Upper Henderson Camp, the trail descends on an easy course for slightly more than a half-mile to Upper Buckhorn Gap, crossing, in the interval, as many as five small streams, none of which may be running during the drier seasons. The first four are spring branches of Henderson Prong. The fifth is Bunch Prong.

Upper Buckhorn Gap once harbored an intersection. A secondary trail passed through the gap and continued on to an old mountain farm in Honey Cove. In 1971, the Youth Conservation Corps built a twelve-person shelter by a fine spring in the cove. The shelter has since been torn down and the trail abandoned to the agents of nature.

From Upper Buckhorn Gap the Meigs Mountain Trail turns and descends a mile to Buckhorn Gap to enter a four-way intersection. On the right, the Meigs Creek Trail exits to the Sinks on Little River Road. Straight on, the Lumber Ridge Trail exits to the Great Smoky Mountains Institute at Tremont. On the left, a well-defined manway exits to Spruce Flats Falls on the Middle Prong of Little River. All four trails terminate in Buckhorn Gap.

MIRY RIDGE TRAIL

Jakes Creek Trail and Panther Creek Trail at Jakes Gap to the Appalachian Trail—5.0 miles.

POINT OF DEPARTURE: Hike 3.7 miles to the end of the Jakes Creek Trail. The Miry Ridge Trail begins from the left side of Jakes Gap.

QUAD MAP: Silers Bald 157-SE

0.0—Jakes Gap. Jakes Creek Trail. Panther Creek Trail. Manway to the summit of Blanket Mountain.

1.2—Fire-scald.

1.9—Pierces Improvement. Access path exits left 200 yards to the Dripping Spring Mountain Backcountry Campsite (#26).

2.4—Bent Arm manway. Former Dripping Spring Mountain Campsite.

2.5—Lynn Camp Prong Trail exits right 3.7 miles to the Middle Prong Trail and Greenbrier Ridge Trail at Indian Flats.

4.7—Spring.

5.0—Appalachian Trail.

The Miry Ridge Trail is a remote course that crosses Dripping Spring Mountain and then traces the length of Miry Ridge. The trail's lower end resides in Jakes Gap, which can be approached by way of the Jakes Creek Trail out of Elkmont or from Tremont by a combination of the Middle Prong and Panther Creek trails.

Before the advent of the park, Dripping Spring Mountain was reached by a manway up a small ravine that adhered generally to the course of Newt Prong. When he was fifteen years old and on his first adventure into the Smoky Mountains backcountry, Harvey Broome hiked to Silers Bald along this manway up the face of Dripping Spring Mountain. He later described this provisional route as "slippery and inhumanly steep." Paul Fisk, who also traveled along this manway, remarked that "part of the trail is very steep, like that up the head of Bear Pen Hollow," and "water oozes everywhere through the blanket of moss covering the ledges."

The current Miry Ridge Trail circumvents the "slippery and inhumanily steep" course by leaving Jakes Gap and circling around the west end of Dripping Spring Mountain and out along Log Ridge, a short spur that extends from the southwest corner of the main mountain. Here, the slopes are forested in sugar maple, white basswood, black cherry, and Carolina silverbell trees interspersed with pockets of eastern hemlocks. A half-mile out of Jakes Gap, the trail makes a U-turn at the end of Log Ridge and returns to Dripping Spring Mountain, the vegetation changing to a drier mix of sourwood, chestnut oak, mountain laurel, galax, trailing arbutus, and wintergreen sharing the slopes with the occasional saplings of American chestnut. Before they were decimated by blight in the early years of the twentieth century, the American chestnut was a primary species on many of the Smoky Mountain slopes, in some places comprising as much as eighty percent of the forest cover. The abundant mast was a reliable source of food for bears and turkeys, and the tree's straight-grained, rot-resistant timber was an excellent wood for pioneer craftsmen.

In 1922, a spark from a logging skidder ignited a wildfire that swept up the Jakes Creek drainage and over the top of Dripping Spring Mountain. A remnant fire-scald lies along the trail just slightly over a mile above Jakes Gap. It appears as a steeply pitched parched gradient extending from the trail to the top of the ridge and bearing rough, low-growing, woody vegetation. A narrow gravel path runs up through the vegetation to the ridgeline.

From the fire-scald, much of the state-line divide between Thunderhead (5,527 feet) and Siler Bald (5,607 feet) is visible. That part which cannot be seen is obscured by Mellinger Death Ridge intervening in the intermediate distance across the Lynn Camp Prong drainage.

As the name implies, Mellinger Death Ridge is the scene of a particularly grim episode in Smoky Mountain history. There are several versions of the story, but it appears that sometime in 1903 a heavy bear trap was set on a dim little-used trail on the mountain now known as Mellinger Death Ridge. Contrary to all local custom, the bear trap was unmarked. Jasper Mellinger, a blacksmith, was crossing the mountain from Elkmont to the Everett Mine on Hazel Creek. Mellinger blundered into the bear trap and was caught, the heavy jaws of the contraption breaking his leg. He could not free himself.

According to Jim Shelton, a mountaineer who knew Jasper Mellinger, the man who set the trap was Old Art Huskey. When Huskey went to check on the bear trap, he took with him a boy who was a playmate of Shelton's. When Huskey and the boy found Mellinger, he had been in the trap for several days and was nearly dead. As Shelton tells the story, "when old Art sees he's just about dead anyhow, he got this boy a club and made him just made him knock that old man in the head and finish killing him. He covered him up with brush."

Two years later, a man named Burt Ownby was herding cattle near where Old Art Huskey and the boy had killed Jasper Mellinger. According to Jim Shelton, Burt Ownby was so near-sighted he could hardly see. While checking on his cattle, he stumbled over something, then got down on his knees to look at it and decided it was a cow's skull. Ownby hollered at his companions, saying "here's one's a died." When his companions stepped down to see, they explained to Burt that he had found the skull of a human, not that of a cow.

The law was called, and an investigation was completed. They found every bone of the man's body except one-half of a leg bone, and concluded that some animal had carried it off. The authorities identified the bones as those of Jasper Mellinger by the clothing and the contents of his pockets.

Jim Shelton concludes the story by saying, "this boy now, he tuk sick to die. . . . When he tuk sick to die people was goin' in to see him. Someone asked him if he's prepared to die. The boy said 'all I hate about dying is daddy made me finish killing that old man, hit him in the head with a stick, finish killing him.' He said, 'that worries me.'"

Horace Kephart was told the story of Jasper Mellinger when he and his bear-hunting companions stumbled upon a similarly unmarked bear trap on the North Carolina side of the Smokies. In Tennessee, Kephart was told, it was a penitentiary offence to set out an unmarked bear trap. There were no such restrictions in North Carolina.

When it leaves the fire-scald, the Miry Ridge Trail descends gradually through groves of hemlocks for three-quarters of a mile to enter what appears as an extended shallow gap with low weedy undergrowth and shaded by large widely spaced yellow buckeyes, black cherries, American beeches, and red maples. This semi-clearing, once known as Pierces Improvement, marks the transition point between Dripping Spring Mountain and Miry Ridge.

During the time when near-sighted Burt Ownby was a herder in the Smokies, Pierces Improvement was a "gant" lot for holding cattle before herding them down the mountain to Elkmont and then to the markets in Knoxville. Gant, a corruption of the word gaunt, refers to the fact that the cattle lose more weight the longer they are penned up waiting for the owners to herd them off the mountain. For many years after the gant lot on Pierces was abandoned, the remains of a herders' cabin and fenced area of pasture could be seen.

Harvey Broome spent his first night out under the stars in the Smoky Mountain backcountry at Pierces Improvement, sleeping "in a rude enclosure constructed around the 'claim cabin' of a lumber company." The site of the claim cabin is likely to have been at the head of Newt Prong near what is now the Dripping Spring Mountain Backcountry Campsite (#26). The campsite is reached by a 200-yard access path that exits from the left side of the trail.

The Dripping Spring Mountain Campsite is situated on a slender tract extended along the ridgeline above the Miry Ridge Trail. The east end of the camp is an open grassy plot with a fire-ring in the center. Immediately to the west is an additional tract heavily shaded by large hemlocks. Both the grassy plot and the shaded tract are excellent campsites with ample level ground for tents.

Beginning at the east side of the grassy plot, an access path leads down the steep back side of the ridge seventy-five yards to a thin spring that dribbles through a vinyl pipe and into a messy bog. The spring here is not reliable. When it is dry, water may be found at the site of the old Dripping Spring Mountain Backcountry Campsite a half-mile farther down the Miry Ridge Trail.

The camp's food-storage cable is suspended near where the access path from the Miry Ridge Trail enters the grassy plot. More convenient to the camp in the shaded tract is a metal foot-locker-style food-storage bin. The food locker is set on the ground at the far end of the campsite.

Upon leaving Pierces Improvement, the Miry Ridge Trail descends gently on a rather rough track while it negotiates the transition from Dripping Spring Mountain to Miry Ridge. The adjacent slopes are fairly open, bearing little understory and festooned in spring with prostrate bluets, spring beauties, and great chickweeds. A half-mile below Pierces Improvement, the trail encounters the upper terminus of the old Bent Arm manway leading out along the adjacent ridge to Cucumber Gap. On the right fifty yards down-trail is the former site of the Dripping Spring Mountain Backcountry Camp. Except under the driest conditions, water can be found about 200 yards down the slope below the old campsite.

One hundred and eighty yards beyond the old campsite, the Miry Ridge Trail intersects the upper terminus of the Lynn Camp Prong Trail. From this junction on, horse traffic is not permitted on the Miry Ridge Trail, and thus the track immediately ameliorates from a rough course to that of a smooth, soft, loamy surface. In springtime, witch hazel, white erect trilliums, and spring beauties are conspicuously abundant.

Miry Ridge itself is a near-vertical stratum of broken quartz, worn at its apex such that its upper edges retain water. When it rains, fallen leaves and decayed vegetation accumulated in the trough turns into a malodorous, black, sticky mire, thus suggesting the name Miry Ridge.

Three-quarters of a mile beyond the Lynn Camp Prong junction, the trail reaches a small knob that marks the high point of Ben Parton Lookout, a short flat promontory extending from the east flank of Miry Ridge. For several years, Ben Parton was retained by the Little River Lumber Company to maintain a possession cabin on the mountain as a means of maintaining clear title to the timberland. Parton had a lookout post on the promontory, affording him a vantage point for spotting trespassers attempting to establish squatters' rights in the Fish Camp Prong drainage.

A half-mile above the Ben Parton Lookout, the trail circles to the east side of Miry Ridge and onto a dry-ridge course confined to a narrow corridor of thickly growing mountain laurel. During late spring the corridor sports an abundance of painted trilliums. Mountain ash and American beech interspersed with the occasional red spruce are the more conspicuous tree species. There is nothing peculiar about spruce trees being found among beech stand, except that spruce on Miry Ridge mark the westernmost point where this tree can be found in the Smokies. Some have speculated that beech stands in the gaps along the Smoky divide have hindered the advancement of red spruce westward along the divide. Others have suggested that the arrested westward migration is attributable to specific environmental conditions created by the last ice age. In either case, the red spruce are rare in the Smokies west of Miry Ridge.

A half-mile prior to reaching its terminus, the trail eases off Miry Ridge and into a long transition onto the north flank of the main Smoky divide. In the transition, the trail passes through an unmixed stand of beech trees shading slopes of thickly growing white erect trilliums. After passing a spring, the trail continues for another quarter-mile before sliding inconspicuously up and onto the state-line divide and intersecting the Appalachian Trail 290 yards above Buckeye Gap.

◆ BOUNDARY ◆

The Boundary section includes those trails along the northern perimeter of the park between the Sugarlands and Whiteoak Sink and north of Little River Road. The Cove Mountain Trail, Little Greenbrier Trail, Roundtop Trail, and Chestnut Top Trail trace the boundary ridgelines while the three remaining trails in this section climb to the boundary ridgelines. All of the trails in this section are available to hikers only.

The Boundary section includes three of the most popular attractions in the park: Laurel Falls on the Laurel Falls Trail, Little Greenbrier School on the Metcalf Bottoms Trail, and the Walker Sisters Cabin on the Little Brier Gap Trail. The trails to these landmarks are connectors between Little River Road and the boundary trails. There are no backcountry campsites in the Boundary section.

All the trails in the Boundary section can be accessed directly from roads—the Cove Mountain Trail at the Park Headquarters building; the Little Greenbrier, Little Brier Gap, and Roundtop trails from Wear Cove Gap Road; the Metcalf Bottoms Trail from the Metcalf Bottoms Picnic Area; the Laurel Falls Trail from Little River Road; and the Chestnut Top Trail from the Townsend Wye. In wintertime, however, the half-mile gravel access road to the Little Brier Gap Trail is closed.

COVE MOUNTAIN TRAIL

Park Headquarters to Cove Mountain fire tower—8.5 miles.

POINT OF DEPARTURE: From the parking area adjacent to the Park Headquarters building at the Sugarlands, proceed to the parking area about 150 yards behind the building. The Cove Mountain Trail begins beside the stone bridge over Fighting Creek.

QUAD MAP: Gatlinburg 157-NE

0.0—Fighting Creek. Parking area behind the Park Headquarters building.
0.1—Cataract Falls.
0.5—Double Gourd Branch.
1.0—Dry Pond Branch.
3.0—Holy Butt.
8.4—Laurel Falls Trail exits left 4.0 miles to Little River Road at Fighting Gap.
8.5—Cove Mountain fire tower.

The Cove Mountain Trail begins directly behind the Park Headquarters building at the west end of the bridge over Fighting Creek. The trail follows Fighting Creek downstream on a wide, level, spongy course for 200 yards until reaching the base of Cataract Falls, where thin streamlets of Cataract Branch cascade forty feet down a deeply creviced cliff face, collect in a shallow pool at the base of the falls, and then ease off across the trail to join Fighting Creek.

When it leaves Cataract Falls, the trail narrows considerably, entering a slow steady climb that continues almost unabated for the next eight miles. Six hundred yards beyond the falls, Double Gourd Branch slithers down a narrow fissure in the rock face along the left side of the trail and splashes out into the trail. The trail continues climbing, working up and onto a dry ridge high above Fighting Creek. Along here, Robin's-plantain, crested dwarf irises, sweet white violets, and foamflowers are prevalent in early spring.

At the end of the first mile, the trail turns and proceeds through a gap to cross Dry Pond Branch. In an old clearing near the stream crossing, a few rotting timbers and crumbled remains of a chimney mark the site of a former cabin. Above and below the cabin site, outlines of old farm fields are still distinguishable. Once beyond the stream, the trail returns to its northerly course and proceeds along Dry Pond Branch for three-quarters of a mile to the park boundary. For most of the way, the trail is separated from Dry Pond Branch by a high hedgerow of leggy rhododendron. Rhododendron is perhaps the most ubiquitous plant species in the Smokies. It is found in every watershed in the park and grows at all elevations. Those along this stretch of the Cove Mountain Trail are particularly attractive in early summer when their large white blossoms festoon the trail's edge.

The trail reaches the park boundary at the property line of a private residence, turns immediately left, and picks up an old farm road following a westerly course along the boundary line. The boundary enjoys a southern exposure forested in laurel and pine. Unfortunately, the southern pine beetle has wreaked considerable damage to much of this forest, and consequently many of the pines here are dead or dying. At occasional intervals, the trail swings out momentarily on an eastern exposure, affording superb views of Mount Le Conte (6,593 feet), Balsam Point (5,818 feet), and the long westerly sweep of the Sugarlands. To the right of the Le Conte massif, Mount Mingus (5,802 feet) appears as the high point near the head of Sugarland Mountain, the long slender ridge descending in the intermediate distance. On a clear day when sunlight is penetrating directly into the deep recesses of the mountains, the distinctive peaks of the Chimney Tops can be seen projecting from the side of Sugarland Mountain. Farther to the right and in the far distance, the main Smoky divide marks the high southern rim of the Little River basin.

The trail continues climbing, generally following the contours and switching alternately between exposed dry-ridge pine conditions and the more sheltered oak-hardwood habitats. In places, the trail is cushioned with thick layers of deciduous leaves and, in others, by deep accumulations of pine needles. Everywhere the track remains wide, smooth, free of obstruction, and edged with turfs of grass. A short spur trail leading out of the park marks the beginning of a climb around the end of a bulge in the ridgeline that was said to be known originally as Holly Butt, presumably named after the holly tree. A butt, as distinguished from a butte, is a topographical feature evidenced by an abruptly broken-off mountain ridge, as in the butt end of a log. There is still extant an old story of a mountain woman named Aunt Lydia who lived on a nearby stream named Holly Branch. Being a God-fearing woman, Aunt Lydia shortened the name of the stream to Holy Branch. The name of the mountain was later changed to Holy Butt to correspond with that of the stream.

When it leaves Holy Butt, the trail approaches the park boundary momentarily before turning away to begin a one-mile climb to Mount Harrison (3,310 feet). Over this interval, the trail completes three tangent approaches to the boundary where Gatlinburg can be glimpsed down along the northern slope. As it approaches Mount Harrison, the trail drifts southward along a spur before crossing over and turning back toward the boundary. From here until its terminus at the highest point on Cove Mountain, the trail remains close along the boundary, tracing the high ridgeline between Mount Harrison and Cove Mountain. Notwithstanding the ridge one mile west of Mount Harrison known as Phils View, there are no good vantage points along this section of the boundary. Hikers from the early years of the Smoky Mountains Hiking Club recorded that "one of the finest panoramic views of the Smokies is from a point on the trail a mile west of Mount Harrison." Elsewhere the hikers wrote that "more peaks can be seen from this point than any other place in the mountains," specifying that one could view the entire Smoky range from Mount Guyot to Gregory Bald. In wintertime, when leaf coverage is reduced, one can certainly discern the outline of the Smoky divide, but in the eighty years that have transpired since the Hiking Club first visited Cove Mountain, things have changed on Phils View.

From Phils View the trail descends into a slight swag where the course along the ridgeline follows parallel to an old jeep road. The slopes on the north side of the boundary are part of the Cove Mountain Wildlife Management Area, which in the fall is open for deer, bear, and boar hunting. Where there are openings in the forest cover, Wears Cove can be seen out beyond the base of Cove Mountain.

The highest point in this section of the Smokies is a featureless peak formed by the conjunction of Cove Mountain and Chinquapin Ridge. As it approaches the summit, the Cove Mountain Trail merges into a well-maintained jeep road and then proceeds 200 yards before intersecting the Laurel Falls Trail leading up on the left along Chinquapin Ridge. The Cove Mountain Trail continues another 180 yards to terminate at the base of a steel-frame fire tower that is now used for monitoring air quality. The Cove Mountain tower is situated on the corner of a one-acre clearing that is bare except for a thin covering of grass. Steps leading up the tower are blocked above the second landing by a metal compartment housing the air-monitoring equipment.

Unfortunately, the second landing is not above the tops of the surrounding trees. If it were otherwise, the Cove Mountain tower would afford the same grand panoramic views that early Smoky Mountain hikers once enjoyed from Phils View.

LAUREL FALLS TRAIL

Little River Road at Fighting Creek Gap to the Cove Mountain Trail—4.0 miles.

POINT OF DEPARTURE: From the Sugarlands Visitor Center, drive Little River Road 3.7 miles to Fighting Creek Gap. The Laurel Falls Trail begins in the gap across the road from the Sugarland Mountain Trail.

QUAD MAP: Gatlinburg 157-NE

0.0—Fighting Creek Gap. Little River Road. Sugarland Mountain Trail.
0.8—Bench.
1.3—Laurel Falls.
1.4—Switchback.
3.1—Little Greenbrier Trail exits left 4.3 miles to Wear Cove Gap Road.
4.0—Cove Mountain Trail exits right 8.4 miles to the Park Headquarters building in the Sugarlands and left 0.1 mile to the Cove Mountain fire tower.

The Laurel Falls Trail is one of the most popular in the park. It offers a gentle ascent on a paved track of just slightly more than a mile to Laurel Falls, a sixty-foot cascade that is among the more attractive displays of water in the Smokies.

The trail begins in Fighting Creek Gap, the lowest point in the long Sugarland Mountain ridgeline that separates the Little Pigeon River watershed from that of the Little River. The gap is a large mis-proportioned saddle-shaped swag that also harbors the lower terminus of the Sugarland Mountain Trail as well as accommodating the trans-mountain crossing of Little River Road. While compiling research for *Place Names in the Smokies,* Allan Coggins uncovered no less than five traditions concerning the origin of the name Fighting Creek. One of the more enduring involves two mountaineers by the names of Owensby and Cole who had a big quarrel and nearly had a "fit." No actual fighting took place, but the stream near where the two men faced off has since been known as Fighting Creek. Some have suggested that the confrontation was the result of continuous bickering over the location of a schoolhouse.

As it starts out of Fighting Creek Gap, the Laurel Falls Trail turns immediately onto a paved track following a sinuous course three-quarters of a mile into a deep draw that drains Laurel Branch. The forest cover consists of a dry-woods mix of sourwoods, oaks, and maples interspersed with stands of pine, most of which are suffering from infestations of pine-bark beetles. When the trail approaches the Laurel Branch draw, it turns right and proceeds into the steep-sided defile on a level berm cut into the mountain rock by Civilian Conservation Corp crews in 1935. From this point, Blanket Mountain (4,609 feet) is clearly visible back across the Little River watershed, conspicuous as the high knob anchoring the end of Dripping Spring Mountain.

The cut berm remains high over Laurel Branch, which can be heard rushing violently as it sluices through a narrow chasm known as Devils Chute. A half-mile into the defile, the trail reaches the stream at Laurel Falls, where the water drops thirty feet to a rock ledge and then spills fifteen feet farther down a bare, uneven, rocky gradient onto a wide shelf-like basin. The stream collects momentarily in a shallow pool before moving off and plunging over a fifteen-foot precipice to resume its course as Laurel Branch.

The display of water at Laurel Falls is especially attractive when the stream is running high. The basin is not large enough to pool the excess water, and thus the flow spews forcefully off the lower cliff. The lower falls can best be seen by circling through the amphitheater and proceeding downstream along the lower side.

The paved track ends at Laurel Falls. The trail, however, continues beyond the falls, passing directly through the pool at the base of the upper falls. Water in the pool is not deep, but an unsightly concrete walkway built across the basin assures a dry crossing. On the far side of the pool, a gently sloped rock apron affords a superb place to sit and enjoy the soothing sounds of falling water.

The trail continues on a steeper course that is rocky and perpetually wet from seepages seeking the main stream. Three hundred yards beyond the falls, it executes a sharp switchback right and enters a short run through a tunnel of rhododendron. A half-mile above the falls and on a softer, more even track, the trail emerges into a disjunct enclave of virgin cove-hardwood forest fortuitously spared the fire and logger's axe that devastated much of the forest elsewhere in the Smokies. A sparse undisturbed understory nourished by ages of decaying old-growth forest is shaded by Fraser magnolias, white basswoods, yellow buckeyes, yellow poplars, and eastern hemlocks of enormous proportions.

The trail soon leaves the deep-woods solitude of this ancient forest and rolls up onto Chinquapin Ridge, where conditions are more conducive to dry woods species of red and white oaks, stripped maples, and sourwoods. Chinquapin Ridge is supposedly named for the chinquapin oak tree. The chinquapin oak, however, is not native to the Smokies, but it is closely related to the American chestnut, which once grew abundantly on these slopes. It is likely that the naming of the ridge originated from a mistaken identity of the chestnut as a chinquapin, which it resembles in appearance.

Just where the trail emerges onto Chinquapin Ridge, it intersects the upper terminus of the Little Greenbrier Trail leading in from Wear Cove Gap Road. Over the short interval that the Laurel Falls Trail remains on the Chinquapin ridgeline, it affords a few obstructed views into Wear Cove.

When it rolls off the ridgeline, the trail begins negotiating a long transition from the flank of Chinquapin Ridge to that of Cove Mountain. The climb remains moderate and in dry woods conditions. The appearance of a stand of slender widely spaced hardwoods shading a low, remarkably uniform understory of woody heath heralds the approach to the summit of the Cove Mountain ridgeline. On the approach, the sparseness of the forest cover affords an exceptional view across the Sugarlands to the west face of Mount Le Conte. The Laurel Falls Trail terminates in an intersection with the Cove Mountain Trail 180 yards below a grassy opening where the latter trail terminates at the foot of the Cove Mountain fire tower. The fire tower is not usable as a vantage point as its steps are blocked at the second landing by a metal compartment housing air-monitoring equipment.

METCALF BOTTOMS TRAIL

Wear Cove Gap Road at Metcalf Bottoms to the Little Greenbrier Schoolhouse—0.7 mile.

POINT OF DEPARTURE: From the Sugarlands Visitor Center, drive Little River Road 9.5 miles to the Metcalf Bottoms Picnic Area, or, from the Townsend Wye, drive Little River Road 9.3 miles. The Metcalf Bottoms Trail begins back of the picnic area at the far end of the bridge over Little River.

QUAD MAP: Wear Cove 157-NW

0.0—Metcalf Bottoms. Wear Cove Gap Road.
0.5—Little Brier Branch. Footlog.
0.6—Little Brier Branch. Footlog. Little Greenbrier Schoolhouse.
0.7—Gravel road outlet to Wear Cove Gap Road. Little Brier Gap Trail.

The Metcalf Bottoms Trail, less than a mile in length, is one of the easier hikes in the park. The trailhead is near the Metcalf Bottoms Picnic Area, where Wear Cove Gap Road crosses on a bridge over Little River. The trail starts out from the road on a level course following Little River upstream 200 yards before turning away and mounting a rough jeep track that climbs a low ridge.

Clumps of Spanish sword indicate a former homesite now occupied by a water tank that serves the Metcalf Bottoms Picnic Area. Just beyond the water tank, the trail clears a minor ridge where it leaves the roadbed for a single-file track descending sharply to Little Brier Branch.

The trail along Little Brier Branch is level, winding through a bottomland that was once completely cleared and occupied by mountain farms. The trail crosses the stream on a footlog and then, 125 yards farther on, negotiates a step-log over a feeder stream. Twenty-five yards beyond the step-log, the trail crosses Little Brier Branch a second time on a footlog and immediately enters a maintained clearing that harbors the Little Greenbrier Schoolhouse.

◆ The schoolhouse is a large one-room log cabin constructed of massive poplar timbers and bearing a split-shingle roof. Moveable straight-backed wooden benches for the schoolchildren are arranged on a floor of puncheons, split logs finished on one side. A door stands at the front of the building and a blackboard occupies the wall on the opposite end. Windows on both sides of the schoolhouse allow light into the room.

Land for the school was donated by William Abbott and the poplar timbers by Ephriam Ogle. The school was opened on January 1, 1882, with Richard Perryman as the first teacher.

The building was considered by the community to be too valuable an asset to be used solely as a school; thus it was also commissioned as a church until a proper church house was built nearby in 1924. The church is no longer here. It was sold and moved out of Little Greenbrier in 1936. The church cemetery, however, still remains, occupying the slope immediately in front of the schoolhouse.

The Metcalf Bottoms Trail passes in front of the schoolhouse and exits the schoolyard to terminate in a gravel parking lot that is adjacent to a one-lane gravel track leading in a half-mile from Wear Cove Gap Road. Above the cemetery, the gravel track forks, the lower fork circling down into the parking area. The upper fork, blocked by a gate and inaccessible to automobiles, proceeds into Five Sisters Cove, where it terminates at the Walker Sisters Cabin. The gate also marks the trailhead for the Little Brier Gap Trail. The gravel track affords an alternate access to the Little Greenbrier Schoolhouse, but it is closed to automobile traffic during the winter months.

LITTLE BRIER GAP TRAIL

Little Greenbrier Schoolhouse to the Little Greenbrier Trail at Little Brier Gap—1.4 miles.

POINT OF DEPARTURE: Follow directions to the Metcalf Bottoms Trail, and hike to the end of the trail. The Little Brier Gap Trail begins on the road above the Little Greenbrier Schoolhouse. Except during the winter season, the Little Brier Gap Trail can also be reached by automobile along a gravel track leading off Wear Cove Gap Road 0.4 mile above the Metcalf Bottoms Picnic Area.

QUAD MAP: Wear Cove 157-NW

0.0—Road above Little Greenbrier Schoolhouse.
0.5—Little Brier Branch. Footlog.
1.1—Road to Walker Sisters Cabin.
1.4—Little Brier Gap. Little Greenbrier Trail exits left 1.9 miles to Wear Cove Gap Road and right 2.4 miles to the Laurel Falls Trail.

For most of the year, the lower terminus of the Little Brier Gap Trail can be accessed by a half-mile one-lane gravel track that exits Wear Cove Gap Road 0.4 mile above Metcalf Bottoms and leads to the Little Greenbrier Schoolhouse. During the winter months, the gravel track is closed, and the only easy access to the lower terminus of the Little Brier Trail is along the Metcalf Bottoms Trail.

The Little Brier Gap Trail begins at the gate blocking the road above the parking area adjacent to the schoolhouse. The road was once a mountaineer's trace that connected Metcalf Bottoms with the upper reaches of Little Greenbrier. The trail follows the road, remaining on the slope above the bottomland flanking Little Brier Branch. A half-mile along the road, the trail drops down along the stream and crosses on a long footlog. The road itself fords the creek on a concrete causeway.

The trail remains in the bottomland, proceeding upstream on a leisurely course another half-mile before reaching a point where the road forks. The more prominent right fork circles back and down along Straight Cove Branch to the Walker Sisters Cabin. The Little Brier Gap Trail proceeds on the less noticeable left fork.

 A quarter-mile up the right fork, the road terminates at the Walker Sisters Cabin in Five Sisters Cove, named for the Walker sisters Margaret, Polly, Martha, Louisa, and Hettie, who steadfastly maintained their home in this cove until the last of them died in 1964. The road first passes a springhouse and then approaches the front of the cabin, one of the very few original mid-nineteenth-century log structures remaining in the park. The cabin is a three-room, two-story house with a front porch along the length of a kitchen annex. The main room at the front of the cabin served at the sleeping quarters as well as the primary living space.

Brice McFalls is thought to have made the first improvements on the land in Five Sisters Cove in the 1840s, building a cabin about 400 yards from where the Walker Sisters Cabin now stands. Wiley King, a grandfather of the sisters, later started building what is now the main part of the Walker Sisters Cabin. His sons completed it the year after King's death in 1859.

According to research by Robert R. Madden and T. Russell Jones published in Mountain Home, John N. Walker married Wiley King's daughter, Margaret Jane, in 1866 and moved with his family into the King cabin sometime in the 1870s. The expanding Walker family soon outgrew the house. To provide more room, John Walker dismantled the old McFalls cabin and reconstructed it as a kitchen addition to his cabin. Walker added the porch at the same time.

Over the years, John and Margaret Jane Walker added several outbuildings around the house, including a barn, pig-pen, smokehouse, apple house, springhouse, blacksmith shop, and a combination corncrib and gear shed. One building conspicuously missing was the outhouse. The Walker family used the woods, the women appropriating those below the house, the men those above. Of the outbuildings, only the springhouse and corncrib/gear-shed remain.

The Walkers also constructed a tar kiln, ash hopper, charcoal-making pit, and drying racks. They maintained a grist mill on a nearby stream and cleared land for a garden and corn patch which they protected with split-rail and stone fences. They kept a poultry yard and on nearby slopes planted orchards of apple, plum, cherry, peach, and chestnut trees.

When John and Margaret Jane died, five of their daughters remained on the farm, continuing the Smoky Mountain tradition of self-reliance with an unfailing adherence to the value of hard work instilled in them by their father and mother. Though after 1934 the Walker sisters were living within the newly established Great Smoky Mountains National Park, they maintained their privacy and relative obscurity until an article published in the *Saturday Evening Post* in 1946 brought national attention to the sisters' quaint anachronistic mountain life.

At the road fork, the Little Brier Trail continues straight, following along Little Brier Branch. A quarter-mile above the fork, the road ends, but the trail continues as a single-file track climbing to the back of the cove. After 290 yards on the single-file track, the trail rises into Little Brier Gap and terminates into the Little Greenbrier Trail running along the park boundary between Wear Cove Gap Road and the Laurel Falls Trail on Chinquapin Ridge. On the opposite side of the gap, a jeep track leads out of the Park to Robeson Road in Wear Cove.

LITTLE GREENBRIER TRAIL

Wear Cove Gap Road to the Laurel Falls Trail—4.3 miles.

POINT OF DEPARTURE: Follow directions to the Metcalf Bottoms Trail. After crossing the bridge over Little River, drive along Wear Cove Gap Road 1.2 miles to the park boundary at Wear Cove Gap. The Little Greenbrier Trail begins on the right just below the gap.

QUAD MAP: Wear Cove 157-NW

0.0—Wear Cove Gap Road.

1.9—Little Brier Gap. Little Brier Gap Trail exits right 1.4 miles to the Little Greenbrier Schoolhouse.

4.3—Laurel Falls Trail exits right 3.1 miles to Little River Road at Fighting Gap and left 0.9 mile to the Cove Mountain Trail.

The Little Greenbrier Trail, an infrequently used course that follows the park boundary immediately south of Wear Cove, affords some of the best vantage points anywhere along the northern perimeter of the park. When it leaves Wear Cove Gap Road, the trail starts climbing on a west-facing dry-ridge shaded by a pine-oak mix.

As it gains elevation, the cone-shaped Roundtop Mountain (3,071 feet) comes into clear view on the right. A quarter-mile above the road, the trail circles around a ridge point to an east face where Cove Mountain (4,077 feet) forms up as the prominent peak to the east.

Two hundred yards after circling the point, the trail reaches a ridgeline that marks the boundary between the park and Wear Cove. At various intervals, openings in the forest cover offer views down into the bottom of the cove.

During the geological upheavals that formed the Great Smoky Mountains, the Carolina Shale Belt formation crunched into the North American plate in a mountain-building event called the Acadian orogeny. During the collision, igneous rocks skidded over the North American limestone plate, folding and buckling up into high mountains. The orogeny took place over millions of years, the overthrust moving prodigiously slowly. Here, the overthrust was left at such a low angle that the eroding agents of nature wore through the hanging wall, exposing the underlying limestone substrata that now form the floor of Wear Cove. Because limestone readily percolates water and is resistant to erosion, the soil in Wear Cove retains its fertility.

After a quarter-mile run along the ridgeline, the trail rolls off to complete a transition onto Little Mountain, a slender ridge that extends obliquely across the boundary and down along Five Sisters Cove to the vicinity of the Little Greenbrier Schoolhouse. From the vantage of Little Mountain, Cove Mountain stands in bold relief to the east. The trail returns to the boundary line briefly and then drops easily into Little Brier Gap, where it intersects the upper terminus of the Little Brier Gap Trail leading up from the Little Greenbrier Schoolhouse and the Walker Sisters Cabin in Five Sisters Cove. On the opposite side of the gap, a jeep track descends out of the park to Robeson Road in Wear Cove.

At Little Brier Gap, the Little Greenbrier Trail becomes a steep relentless climb. It initially proceeds southward but soon edges into an easterly course as it plies the flank of Cove Mountain. Here, Roundtop Mountain again comes into view as well as the west end of Wear Cove with Bates Mountain in the immediate distance and Chilhowee Mountain beyond.

Boulder fields intervene. The grade remains steep, but the track does not become rough or uneven. Almost two miles above Little Brier Gap, the trail reaches a false gap on the crest of Rocky Ridge, a short spur that extends from the flank of Chinquapin Ridge. From here, Cold Spring Knob (5,220 feet) appears as the high peak on the main Smoky divide directly across the Little River gorge. Silers Bald (5,607 feet) is the next high peak to the left on the divide with Brier Knob (5,215 feet) and Thunderhead (5,527 feet) on the right. Gregory Bald (4,949 feet) is visible near the west end of the divide.

Along the crest of Rocky Ridge, the grade moderates nicely, and the trail proceeds through a corridor of mountain laurel while making a smooth quarter-mile transition from Rocky Ridge to Chinquapin Ridge. The Little Greenbrier Trail terminates into the Laurel Falls Trail on the wide flat spine of Chinquapin Ridge. One mile to the left along the Laurel Falls Trail is the summit of Cove Mountain. Almost two miles down-trail is Laurel Falls, one of the most popular natural landmarks in the Smokies.

ROUNDTOP TRAIL

Wear Cove Gap Road to Little River at the Townsend Wye—7.5 miles.
POINT OF DEPARTURE: Follow directions to the Metcalf Bottoms Trail. After
   crossing the bridge over Little River, drive Wear Cove Gap Road 1.2 miles to
   the park boundary at Wear Cove Gap. The Roundtop Trail begins on the left
   200 yards back down the road from the park boundary.
QUAD MAP: Wear Cove 157-NW

0.0—Wear Cove Gap Road.
2.5—Joint Ridge.
7.5—Little River. Townsend Wye.

A long-forgotten book, *Haywood's History of Tennessee*, deals with tales of the struggles of the pioneer settlers in their desperate encounters with the Indians who resisted encroachment on their hunting grounds in Tennessee. At one point the narrative states that the war-like Cherokee made pilgrimages over the Smoky Mountains along a trail that led through Wear Cove. The Cherokee's great campground en route was a place they called Tuckaleechee, meaning "drowned muskrat." The Tuckaleechee camp was located at a bend in Little River just above the present site of Townsend.

Early settlers attested to other old blackened campsites along the Cherokee's warpath, as well as numerous arrowheads, cemeteries, and a trail that led south from Wear Cove through the gap in the high mountain that surrounds the valley. This south gap, the low point just east of Roundtop, was first known as Indian Camp Gap. It is currently known as Wear Cove Gap.

Legends contend that the first white men into Wear Cove were two pioneers named Piercefield and Crowson. When the Indians found the two hewing out homes in the wilderness, they killed Piercefield, but Crowson escaped his pursuers, finding refuge in a settlement on the Little Pigeon River. The Indians erected a pole at the gap marking the north entrance to Wear Cove and affixed the hands and scalp of Piercefield on the pole as a mute, but eloquent, warning to other would-be settlers. Later, settlers entering from the north side of Wear Cove would pursue the Indians through Indian Camp Gap, eventually catching them in their camp at a place that would later become known as Metcalf Bottoms.

On the old Cherokee trail through Indian Camp Gap, about a quarter-mile on the Wear Cove side, there is a famous mineral spring in a small depression in a small knob projecting from Roundtop Mountain about a mile below the summit. The spring's long-time owner, Alfred Line, operated a hotel there known as the Summer Resort of Line Spring. The water in Line Spring is chalybeate with many beneficial minerals, particularly iron. It was claimed that this water never failed to benefit the sick and invalid with the exception of those suffering with tuberculosis. Apparently the iron carbonation in the water was injurious to consumptives.

With the white settlement of Metcalf Bottoms, the ancient trace through Indian Camp Gap was widened to a wagon road, and then later, with the advent of the park, paved and named Wear Cove Gap Road. The Roundtop Trail begins in an inconspicuous cut in the wilderness along the road about 200 yards south of the park boundary at Wear Cove Gap. The trail is an infrequently used moderately steep course along the northern perimeter of the park between Wear Cove Gap Road and Little River at the Townsend Wye. The Roundtop Trail is particularly interesting in the winter, when the absence of foliage permits views of many of the major peaks in the western end of the Smokies. Because the trail ends in a crossing of Little River, it can, at times, be difficult if not impossible to complete.

When it leaves Wear Cove Gap Road, the Roundtop Trail enters a winding climb. A half-mile above the road, it circles south to clear a minor ridge point where Roundtop (3,071 feet) appears prominently as the cone-shaped peak immediately to the west. To the east, Cove Mountain (4,077 feet) is the high peak presiding over Little Greenbrier Cove and Metcalf Bottoms. After clearing the ridge point, the trail turns back north and encounters the park boundary for the first time, permitting fleeting views into Wear Cove.

After visiting the boundary briefly, the trail turns south again for a winding two-mile circumnavigation of Joint Ridge, a spur that extends south from the flank of Roundtop. Here, the trail is initially on an east-facing slope, where pink lady's-slipper, spiderwort, Solomon's-seal, pink turtlehead, pipsissewa, sweet white violet, coreopsis, and blue-eyed grass are among the more conspicuous wildflower species. As the trail approaches the end of Joint Ridge, Meigs Mountain appears as the long ridge in the intermediate distance. Beyond Meigs Mountain is the main Smoky divide with Silers Bald (5,607 feet), Cold Spring Knob (5,220 feet), Brier Knob (5,215 feet), and Thunderhead (5,527 feet) being readily noticeable. Blanket Mountain (4,609 feet) is the peak appearing at the east end of Meigs Mountain and just below Cold Spring Knob. Farther out toward the end of Joint Ridge, Clingmans Dome (6,643 feet), Mount Collins (6,188 feet), and Mount Le Conte (6,593 feet) can be seen back toward the east. Once the trail clears the end of Joint Ridge, much of the western end of the Smoky divide between Thunderhead and Gregory Bald (4,949 feet) comes into view.

Upon reaching the west flank of Joint Ridge, the Roundtop Trail descends into the wide bottom of a hollow that harbors three or four wet-weather streams. Weeds abound, and dead hemlock boles are the primary forest cover. At the bottom, the trail turns and begins an easy half-mile climb out of the hollow and onto a dry southwestern exposure. Here it begins an easy descent where there are occasional views into Tuckaleechee Cove and beyond to the Chilhowee Mountains.

Shortly beyond the Tuckaleechee view, the trail enters a downward climb that ranks among the two or three steepest short climbs in the Smokies. The trail descends for 200 yards on a narrow track that slants badly from left to right and is cushioned with layers of friction-free pine needles that make it difficult to procure traction. The first fifty yards of the descent are exceedingly steep. The descent ends in a sharp switchback that directs the trail into a hollow drained by Cane Creek.

A quarter-mile beyond the Cane Creek drainage, the trail encounters the boundary for only the second time. Again, it visits only briefly, then returns to another southern exposure where, for the next half-mile, the track is very narrow and perched precariously on the slope. Weeds are abundant.

Conditions moderate noticeably when the trail turns and begins a two-mile drop to Little River. Initially the descent is almost imperceptible, winding gently along the contours of a meandering ridgeline. After a mile, the windings gradually become increasingly tighter and the grade increasingly steeper. For the final half-mile, it treads on a ledge cut into the cliff high above the Little River gorge before dropping sharply to reach the stream.

As the Roundtop Trail approaches Little River, the track forks. The fork to the right proceeds seventy-five yards to a large pool formed by the confluence of Little River and the West Prong. Here, the river is widest and generally easier to cross. That to the left is the original course of the Roundtop Trail which terminated at a swinging bridge over Little River. Damage from floodwaters frequently compromised the safety of the bridge, and thus it was dismantled and removed. The eye-bolts that once anchored the bridge's cables to the ground can be seen beside the trail.

Across Little River, the Roundtop Trail terminates at the Townsend Wye, the distinct junction that interconnects Townsend Road, Little River Road, and Laurel Creek Road. When Little River is high, the Townsend Wye cannot be reached from the end of the Roundtop Trail.

CHESTNUT TOP TRAIL

Townsend Wye to the Schoolhouse Gap Trail—4.3 miles.

POINT OF DEPARTURE: From the Sugarlands Visitor Center drive Little River Road to its intersection with Townsend Road at the Townsend Wye, or enter the park from Townsend and drive one mile to the wye. The Chestnut Top Trail begins across the parking area long Townsend Road 100 yards below the wye.

QUAD MAP: Wear Cove 157-NW

0.0—Townsend Wye.

0.7—Switchback at top of climb.

2.8—Bryant Gap.

4.3—Schoolhouse Gap Trail exits left 2.0 miles to Laurel Creek Road and right 0.2 mile to the Scott Mountain Trail at Schoolhouse Gap.

The Chestnut Top Trail begins at an opening in a split-rail fence about a hundred yards downstream of the Townsend Wye, a distinctive junction that marks the intersection of Townsend Road, Little River Road, and Laurel Creek Road. The wye was originally formed when the Little River Lumber Company built a rail line to conform to the Y-shaped confluence of Little River and the West Prong. A connecting section of track was built between the arms of the Y-shaped line, allowing trains to turn around without the need for a turntable. The wye was configured so that the option was available to direct rail traffic into the mountains up along either stream, both going and returning.

When the trail leaves Townsend Road, it angles steeply away from the wye on a narrow berm cut into the bluff that forms the truncated eastern end of Chestnut Lead. The bluff is the remainder of eons of the Little River wearing through the hard core rock of the lead. Below, the road and river run in close parallel courses out of the mountains and into Tuckaleechee Cove. Crested dwarf iris, bloodroot, rue anemone, hepatica, toothwort, spring beauty, Jack-in-the-pulpit, fire pink, and trillium are a few of the dozens of wildflower species that bloom along this initial half-mile of the Chestnut Top Trail. Few trails in the Smokies matches the Chestnut Top Trail for variety and abundance of wildflowers over such a short interval.

A half-mile above the road, the open fields of Tuckaleechee Cove and the buildings of Townsend come into view. Within the next quarter-mile, the trail leaves the cooler confines of the Little River gorge, circling through a long switchback to reach the crest of Chestnut Top Lead where dry-ridge hardwoods and pine stands are prevalent. For the remainder of its course, the trail alternates at irregular intervals between concentrations of the hardwoods and the pines. The grade is rarely steep, and the trail remains uniformly smooth and often well cushioned by leaves and pine needles. Occasionally visible to the south is the meander of the main Smoky divide and to the north, the open spaces of Tuckaleechee Cove.

One tree that is conspicuously absent from Chestnut Top Lead is the one for which it is named—the American chestnut. At one time, the American chestnut was the most dominant tree species on many of the mid-elevation slopes in the Smokies.

Sometime during the early twentieth century, a fungus transported into New York City on ornamental nursery plants developed into a blight that eventually spread into the Smokies, killing all the mature chestnut trees. The chestnut was valued by the settlers for its smooth grain and rot-resisting wood and by the foraging bears and turkeys for its dependable masts. Since its wood is slow to rot, large gray boles of fallen chestnut trees can be seen along many of the trails in the mountains. The blight, however, does not necessarily kill the trees' roots. Young chestnuts spring up from the old root systems, appearing as low-growing sprouts identifiable by their coarsely serrated oblong leaves.

Almost three miles beyond the Townsend Wye, the trail reaches the top of its climb, then descends for a half-mile to Bryant Gap. After a slight climb to circum-navigate the cone-shaped Chestnut Top Mountain, the trail eases into a gentle half-mile descent to terminate into the Schoolhouse Gap Trail. The Schoolhouse Gap Trail leads left two miles to Laurel Creek Road near the lower terminus of the Bote Mountain Trail.

◆ TREMONT ◆

The Tremont section includes the large basin south of the main Smoky divide bounded on the west by Bote Mountain and on the east by the configuration of Miry Ridge and Blanket Mountain. Defeat Ridge and Meigs Mountain preside over the interior of the basin, which is drained principally by the West Prong and Middle Prong of Little River and Lynn Camp Prong.

The provisional center of Tremont is Walker Fields, currently the site of the Great Smoky Mountains Institute at Tremont. Walker Fields was first settled in 1859 by "Black Bill" Walker, the patriarch of an extended family that infiltrated the coves and hollows of this isolated niche of the Smokies and persisted as a remarkable anachronism of their eighteenth-century forebears. Tremont was opened to the outside world by the Little River Lumber Company entering in 1920 to harvest timber for the mills downstream in Townsend, Tennessee.

Railroad berms left by the lumber company form a small network of trails that probe into the upper reaches of the Tremont section. Following these berms, the Middle Prong Trail is the primary artery from which the Panther Creek Trail climbs to Blanket Mountain, the Lynn Camp Prong Trail to Miry Ridge, and the Greenbrier Ridge Trail to the Appalachian Trail on the state-line divide. South of Meigs Mountain, three trails following old setters' traces climb to the Meigs Mountain Trail leading in from Elkmont—the Curry Mountain Trail beginning in Metcalf Bottoms, the Meigs Creek Trail beginning at the Sinks, and the Lumber Ridge Trail beginning at the Great Smoky Mountains Institute at Tremont. Also beginning at the institute is the West Prong Trail, climbing west to the Bote Mountain Trail.

The Tremont section harbors only two backcountry campsites, one each on the West Prong Trail and the Lynn Camp Prong Trail. Both are on the sites of old logging camps. There are no campgrounds in the Tremont section, but large campgrounds are available in Cades Cove seven miles up Laurel Creek Road and in Elkmont about twice the distance east on Little River Road.

To reach the Tremont section, enter the park from Townsend and drive one mile to the Townsend Wye, the distinctive intersection of Townsend Road, Little River Road, and Laurel Creek Road. Turn right onto Laurel Creek Road, and proceed 0.2 mile to Tremont Road, which exits on the left. Walker Fields and the Great Smoky Mountains Institute at Tremont are 2.3 miles up Tremont Road. Beyond this point the road continues as a gravel track to its terminus at the head of the Middle Prong Trail. All but two trails in this section can be reached directly or indirectly from Tremont Road. The trailhead for the Meigs Mountain Trail is at the Sinks, 7.3 miles up Little River Road from the Townsend Wye. The Curry Mountain Trail begins on Little River Road at Metcalf Bottoms, 9.3 miles from the Townsend Wye.

CURRY MOUNTAIN TRAIL

Metcalf Bottoms to the Meigs Mountain Trail—3.3 miles.

POINT OF DEPARTURE: From the Sugarlands Visitor Center, drive west on Little River Road 9.5 miles to the Metcalf Bottoms Picnic Area or from the Townsend Wye, drive east 9.3 miles. The Curry Mountain Trail begins across the Little River Road from the east end of the picnic area.

QUAD MAP: Wear Cove 157-NW

0.0—Metcalf Bottoms. Little River Road.

1.9—Curry Gap.

3.3—Meigs Mountain Trail exits left 4.1 miles to the Jakes Creek Trail near Elkmont and right 2.0 miles to the Meigs Creek Trail and Lumber Ridge Trail in Buckhorn Gap.

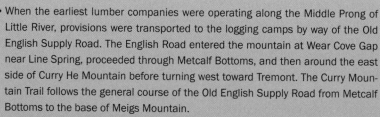

When the earliest lumber companies were operating along the Middle Prong of Little River, provisions were transported to the logging camps by way of the Old English Supply Road. The English Road entered the mountain at Wear Cove Gap near Line Spring, proceeded through Metcalf Bottoms, and then around the east side of Curry He Mountain before turning west toward Tremont. The Curry Mountain Trail follows the general course of the Old English Supply Road from Metcalf Bottoms to the base of Meigs Mountain.

The trail's name is suggested by its proximity to Curry He Mountain and Curry She Mountain. The origin of the mountains' names, however, is the result of the white settlers' misunderstanding and corruption of a Cherokee word. According to Paul Fink's version of this incident, "a certain plant much favored by the Cherokee as a spring salad and call by them gura grew here in abundance. A Cherokee pointed out the place to his white companion, saying 'Guri-hi,' adding the locative syllable 'hi' to mean 'Guri is there.' The white man, ignorant of the plant, thought what was meant was simply the name of the knob, and before long garbled that into Curry He. Some local wag, or perhaps and early feminist, thought the fair sex should not be slighted, and consequently christened a nearby peak Curry She."

The Curry Mountain Trail begins along Little River Road across from the Metcalf Bottoms Picnic Area. The trail climbs out of the bottoms and away from the highway following a dug road that angles up along the northeast face of Curry He Mountain on an easy grade through old-field stands of tall slender yellow poplars. A small stream, Breakfast Branch, is crossed a half-mile above Metcalf Bottoms, where the poplars begin yielding to a mix of eastern hemlocks and oak stands. Farther up, the hemlocks occur in stands of such density that ground plants are almost completely shaded out.

About two miles above Metcalf Bottoms, the trail turns left into a draw drained by Curry Prong, then climbs 250 yards to Curry Gap, a shallow pass that separates Curry He Mountain from its close sibling, Curry She Mountain. Except during the wetter season, Curry Prong is usually dry at this elevation.

At Curry Gap, the trail leaves the hemlock-hardwood mix for a steep quarter-mile climb that tops out in a level run through dry-ridge pine stands on Long Arm Ridge. At a short digression where the trail negotiates a minor bunion on Long Arm Ridge, Cove Mountain (4,077 feet) comes into view with Roundtop (3,071 feet) and Tuckaleechee Cove beyond and farther to the west.

A switchback right directs the trail to the south flank of Long Arm Ridge with Meigs Mountain forming up straight ahead and Blanket Mountain (4,609 feet) appearing as the high peak to the left. Shortly, the Curry Mountain Trail eases off Long Arm Ridge and onto a fairly level course along the southeast flank of Curry She Mountain.

Irregularly spaced chestnut fence posts conspicuous along the left side of the roadbed betray old settlement fields that once occupied the gentle slopes of Curry She Mountain. Trailing arbutus, teaberry, and galax line the roadbed, which is lightly shaded by a low growth of sourwood, oak, and pine trees. The appearance of tall arbors of mountain laurel a mile beyond the switchback heralds the approach into a long smooth curve that terminates in an intersection with the Meigs Mountain Trail. The intersection was once occupied by a schoolhouse. From the intersection, the Meigs Mountain Trail leads east 4.1 miles to the Jakes Creek Trail above Elkmont and west 2.0 miles to an intersection with the Meigs Creek and Lumber Ridge trails at Buckhorn Gap. The Meigs Mountain Cemetery is 420 yards west along the Meigs Mountain Trail.

MEIGS CREEK TRAIL

The Sinks on Little River Road to the Meigs Mountain Trail and Lumber Ridge Trail at Buckhorn Gap—3.5 miles.

POINT OF DEPARTURE: From the Sugarlands Visitor Center, drive west on Little River Road 11.5 miles to the Sinks, or, from the Townsend Wye, drive east 7.3 miles. The Meigs Mountain Trail begins at the back of the stone platform overlooking the Sinks.

QUAD MAP: Wear Cove 157-NW

0.0—Little River Road. The Sinks.
1.4—First crossing of Meigs Creek.
1.7—Fourth crossing of Meigs Creek.
1.8—Access to cascade.
2.4—Eleventh crossing of Meigs Creek.

2.5—Curry Prong.

2.7—Henderson Prong.

2.8—Meigs Creek.

2.8—Bunches Prong.

3.5—Buckhorn Gap. Meigs Mountain Trail exits left 6.1 miles to the Jakes Creek Trail. Lumber Ridge Trail exits right 4.1 miles to the Great Smoky Mountains Institute at Tremont.

The Meigs Creek Trail begins at the Sinks, a kink in Little River where the stream drops with great violence off a bedrock ledge and into a cauldron of swirling turbulence. The Sinks were formed eons ago when the constant flow of Little River wore through a narrow neck of a horseshoe bend in the river, forcing a straightened course through the mountain. The abandoned meander remains, beginning along the lower corner of the Meigs Creek Trail parking area, where it loops away and then returns to the river a short distance below the Sinks, thus forming a large circular amphitheater.

The current appearance of the Sinks is the result of dynamite used by the Little River Lumber Company to clear out a log jamb in the stream. As a consequence, the Sinks themselves are now one of the most violent displays of water anywhere in the Smokies. Undertow generated by the force of water plunging into the pools is credited for the Sinks' well-earned reputation as one of the most dangerous places in the park, being responsible for a high number of deaths by drowning.

In 2011, the Park Service completed construction of an attractive, yet unobtrusive, stone overlook immediately by the Sinks that permits visitors to enjoy proximity to the display of plunging water without the risk of slipping on wet rocks and tumbling into the turbulence. The Meigs Creek Trail begins at the overlook, crossing a stone plaza, then climbing a low rocky rim before dropping into the old meander that was once the Little River stream bed. In the meander, the trail is frequently damp, almost marshy, from rainwater that still seeks the old river bed. The trail wanders a short distance along the meander before reaching the back of the amphitheater, where it completes a U-turn to the right and angles up what was once the bank of Little River.

Between 1892 and 1896, Henry Stinnett operated a pounding mill in the meander. It was powered by water directed through a flume from a large spring at the back of the amphitheater. In 1880 Stinnett had built a mill on the next tributary upstream on Little River, a stream that later became known as Pounding Mill Branch.

When the Meigs Creek Trail leaves the old river bed meander, it turns sharply left and climbs to a course high above the Little River gorge. A half-mile above the meander, the trail turns away from the river and descends 400 yards to the first crossing of Meigs Creek.

The Meigs Creek Trail entails fifteen stream crossings. All are fairly easy rock-hops. However, in the event of rising water from rain storms, a few of the crossings may not be routine. With one exception, the first eleven crossings are of Meigs Creek. The exception is the seventh crossing, which clears a large feeder stream. The upper four crossings clear Curry Prong, Henderson Prong, Meigs Creek, and Bunch Prong, in that order. The shortest interval between stream crossings is thirty-eight yards. The longest is 430 yards. In only five instances is the distance between crossings more than 200 yards. When the trail approaches Meigs Creek for the first time, it crosses immediately and turns upstream on an easy course that begins this irregular cadence of stream crossings.

Two hundred and twenty yards beyond the fourth crossing, an access path exits right to a narrow, steeply pitched, natural channel through which Meigs Creek rushes furiously before plunging over a ten-foot cascade. Thirty yards beyond the fifth crossing, the adjacent slopes yield to a wide, flat, creek bottom that is heavily infested with rhododendron. The trail winds through the bottom until the eighth crossing, marked by a large beech tree on the left. Beyond this point, the adjacent slopes converge, pressing the trail closer to the stream.

After the eleventh crossing, the trail enters another bottomland where American holly trees began appearing with noticeable frequency among stands of eastern hemlocks. As it circles through the bottomland, the trail completes the sequence of Curry Prong, Henderson Prong, Meigs Creek, and Bunch Prong. Beyond the last crossing, the trail angles away from the bottom, climbing a final half-mile to a four-way intersection at Buckhorn Gap. Entering from the left, the Meigs Mountain Trail leads in 6.1 miles from the Jakes Creek Trail near Elkmont. On the right, the Lumber Ridge Trail leads in 4.1 miles from the Great Smoky Mountains Institute at Tremont. Between the two, a well-defined manway enters the gap leading in from Spruce Flats Falls on the Middle Prong of Little River. All four trails terminate in Buckhorn Gap.

LUMBER RIDGE TRAIL

Great Smoky Mountains Institute at Tremont to the Meigs Creek Trail and Meigs Mountain Trail at Buckhorn Gap—4.1 miles.

POINT OF DEPARTURE: From the Sugarlands Visitor Center, drive Little River Road to the Townsend Wye, then proceed straight on Laurel Creek Road 0.2 mile to Tremont Road. Turn left onto Tremont Road, and proceed 2.3 miles

to the Great Smoky Mountains Institute. The Lumber Ridge Trail begins on the north end of Caylor Lodge above the parking area for the institute.
QUAD MAP: Wear Cove 157-NW

0.0—Walker Fields. Great Smoky Mountains Institute.
0.3—Switchback.
0.5—False gap. Manway exits right.
0.7—Manway exits right.
2.3—Gap in ridgeline.
4.1—Buckhorn Gap. Meigs Creek Trail exits left 3.5 miles to Little River Road at the Sinks. Meigs Mountain Trail exits straight 6.1 miles to the Jakes Creek Trail. Manway exits right 3.0 miles to Spruce Flats Falls.

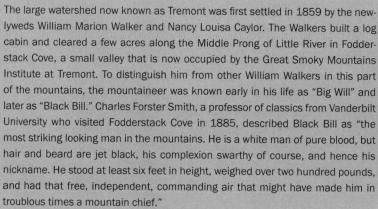

The large watershed now known as Tremont was first settled in 1859 by the new-lyweds William Marion Walker and Nancy Louisa Caylor. The Walkers built a log cabin and cleared a few acres along the Middle Prong of Little River in Fodder-stack Cove, a small valley that is now occupied by the Great Smoky Mountains Institute at Tremont. To distinguish him from other William Walkers in this part of the mountains, the mountaineer was known early in his life as "Big Will" and later as "Black Bill." Charles Forster Smith, a professor of classics from Vanderbilt University who visited Fodderstack Cove in 1885, described Black Bill as "the most striking looking man in the mountains. He is a white man of pure blood, but hair and beard are jet black, his complexion swarthy of course, and hence his nickname. He stood at least six feet in height, weighed over two hundred pounds, and had that free, independent, commanding air that might have made him in troublous times a mountain chief."

Black Bill and Nancy Caylor had twelve children. Walker later acquired two com-mon-law wives, fathering several other children by Mary Ann Moore and Mary (Moll) Stinnett. It has been estimated that Black Bill Walker fathered over twenty-six children between his wives and various other women in the mountains. To his lasting credit, Walker cared generously for all of his children and their mothers, maintaining homes for them in his settlement of "four cabins and a little corn mill."

Another outsider, Frank Carpenter, after visiting Fodderstack Cove in 1889, recorded, "The path to Walker's is only a mountain trail, zigzagging from side to side of the stream, and sometimes requiring careful attention to tell when it crosses on some fallen tree-trunk and threads its way among the thicket. We reached Walker's at eleven o'clock—a rude log-cabin at the highest point of the cove, situated on a high bank above the reach of floods. It is surrounded by a tiny farm of a few acres, with the forest within two hundred feet of the house." The visi-tor stayed for the night at Bill and Nancy Walker's cabin, eating a supper of bacon, cornpone, and honey, and, after watching the stars through the wide cracks in the roof, fell asleep.

At its best, the path to the Walker's cabin was an unimproved sled track and remained so until Black Bill's death in 1919. Shortly thereafter, the Little River Lumber Company acquired the timber rights to the Tremont watershed, including Fodderstack Cove, and graded a rail line up the Middle Prong and on to the upper reaches of the drainage. Col. W. B. Townsend, president of the lumber company, appropriated Black Bill's former settlement as the site for Camp Margaret Townsend to be operated by the Knoxville Girl Scout Council. Even then, the cove could only be reached by logging train or by hiking five miles along the railroad tracks. Today, the cove is known as Walker Fields and is occupied by the Great Smoky Mountains Institute at Tremont and can be reached by a paved road following the old railroad grade.

For several years Walker Fields could be approached from Elkmont by way of the Meigs Mountain Trail, a ten-mile course that extended along the length of Meigs Mountain from Elkmont. Sometime in the 1970s, the last four miles of the Meigs Mountain Trail were ceded and incorporated into the newly named Lumber Ridge Trail. Today, the Lumber Ridge Trail begins above what is now the parking area for the Great Smoky Mountains Institute at the north end of a dormitory, Caylor Hall. Fittingly, the dormitory is named in recognition of the first settler in the cove, Black Bill's legally wedded wife, Nancy Louisa Caylor.

The Lumber Ridge Trail leaves Walker Fields on a well-worn track that circles up and into a steep climb above the Middle Prong. Six hundred yards above Walker Fields, the trail executes a wide switchback around a rocky knob, then levels out on a short ridgeline. Three hundred and thirty-five yards beyond the switchback, the trail enters a false gap marking the transition onto the flank of Mill Ridge. Noticeable on the right side of the gap is a manway that leads back down the mountain to Walker Fields.

At this juncture, the trail turns north and begins climbing along the flank of Mill Ridge in the direction of the larger Lumber Ridge. Along here, the forest cover consists largely of dry-ridge species of pine and oak. Occasionally, the trail diverges into a cloistered hollow that harbors cove-hardwood stands shading a slope festooned with a variety of wildflowers, crested dwarf iris and spring beauty being the most conspicuous.

The transition from Mill Ridge to Lumber Ridge is seamless, recognizable only by the appearance of an odd "saddle" in the ridgeline, indicating that the trail has reached a low point along Lumber Ridge. The trail descends from the saddle for about a half-mile before leveling out for a nice easy one-mile approach into Buckhorn Gap. In Buckhorn Gap the Lumber Ridge Trail enters a three-way intersection with the Meigs Creek Trail leading up from the Sinks and the Meigs Mountain Trail leading in from Elkmont. All three trails terminate in Buckhorn Gap.

Along the right side of Buckhorn Gap a well-worn manway exits, leading down to an abandoned railroad grade that follows Spruce Flats Branch to its confluence with the Middle Prong of Little River. As it approaches the river, Spruce Flats Branch flows through a deep narrow gorge guarded on one side by a sheer slope and on the other by intersecting rows of fortress-like cliffs, gathering momentum for a plunge over four separate precipices known collectively as Spruce Flats Falls. The upper falls, a forty-foot cascade, is hidden in the dark recesses of the gorge, almost inaccessible. Seventy-five feet below, at a crook in the stream, the second falls descends in a picturesque display of water dropping from a rhododendron-cloistered notch in the cliff twenty feet onto a flat rock basin. The outer rim of the basin, only twenty feet from the base of the second fall, forms the edge of the third falls, a straight plunge of nearly thirty feet onto a jumble of boulders. A hundred feet downstream, the stream cascades sixty feet into a deep rock-rimmed pool, gathers momentarily, then rushes off to join the river a few feet below.

Another well-worn manway leads from the base of Spruce Flats Falls a mile downstream along the Middle Prong to the upper end of Walker Fields. The manway is a cliff-side course that affords some exceptional vantage points for surveying the rugged Middle Prong gorge. The Lumber Ridge Trail combined with the two manways makes a nice eight-mile loop out and back to Walker Fields.

WEST PRONG TRAIL

Tremont Road near the Great Smoky Mountains Institute to the Bote
  Mountain Trail—2.7 miles.
POINT OF DEPARTURE: Follow directions to the Lumber Ridge Trail. The West
  Prong Trail begins across the road from the entrance to the Great Smoky
  Mountains Institute.
QUAD MAPS: Wear Cove 157-NW
Thunderhead Mountain 157-SW

0.0—Tremont Road. Parking area. Dorsey Branch Trail exits right.
0.1—Access path exits right 100 yards to the Walker Valley Cemetery.
0.3—Access path exits right 300 yards to the Walker Valley Cemetery.
1.1—Upper end of Dorsey Branch Trail enters on right.
2.1—West Prong Backcountry Campsite (#18).
2.1—West Prong. Footlog.
2.7—Bote Mountain Trail exits right 1.2 miles to Laurel Creek Road and left
  5.7 miles to Spence Field.

As Tremont Road approaches the entrance to the Great Smoky Mountains Institute at Tremont, it meets a road exiting twenty-five yards to a gravel parking lot on the right. On the upper edge of the gravel lot is a windowless utility building. The West Prong Trail begins along the side of the utility building.

Just when the West Prong Trail leaves the gravel lot, it bears left at an intersection with two manways. That on the right is the old Dorsey Branch Trail. The second proceeds straight sixty-five yards to a knoll that harbors the Walker Valley Cemetery. Forty yards beyond the intersection, the West Prong Trail intersects a third manway exiting on the right and leading eighty yards to the cemetery. A well-maintained split-rail fence with a fine wooden gate encloses the cemetery with its mix of worn fieldstones and modern tombstones arranged in neat rows along the knoll.

From the cemetery access, the West Prong Trail climbs a circumnavigating course along the foot of Fodderstack Mountain. Five hundred and forty-five yards into the climb, it intersects another access leading 490 yards back down a draw to the front entrance of the cemetery. The trail continues climbing the flank of Fodderstack, winding through a dry-woods mix of pines, chestnut oaks, and sourwoods. A mile above the trailhead, the upper end of the old Dorsey Branch Trail intersects from the right. Until sometime in the late 1990s, this trail was marked and identified by a weather-beaten sign affixed to a short post about a foot off the ground.

The Dorsey Branch Trail, used for instructional purposes by the Great Smoky Mountains Institute at Tremont, is a well-marked, one-and-a-half-mile course that winds around the lower fringes of Fodderstack Mountain. In an earlier era, this area was known as the Spicewoods, and the trail linked the settlement homes here with those in the bottomlands along the Middle Prong of Little River. Today, it functions as a suitable off-the-beaten-path alternative to climbing around Fodderstack.

From its lower terminus at the gravel parking lot, the Dorsey Branch Trail climbs to the foot of the knoll that harbors the Walker Valley Cemetery. Here, the trail is high and almost directly over Tremont Road and the Middle Prong. Beyond the knoll, the trail proceeds about 200 yards, then turns to the left and begins working up the Dorsey Branch drainage. At one point, a path leaves the trail to the left and descends to the stream. At this junction, the trail leaves the draw and begins a sinuous journey through a gentle mountain terrain that was once cleared farmland.

Halfway along, the trail passes the first of two former cabin sites. The first is on a small knoll occupied by the collapsed remains of a stacked-rock chimney. The second, a quarter-mile up-trail, is marked by a crumbled chimney whose stone are much more widely scattered. Above the chimney sites, the Dorsey Branch Trail negotiates a low flat ridge, clears a couple of low knolls, then rises to terminate into the West Prong Trail.

Just beyond its upper intersection with the Dorsey Branch Trail manway, the West Prong Trail begins a winding one-mile descent to the West Prong of Little

River. As it approaches the stream, the trail enters the West Prong Backcountry Campsite (#18).

The West Prong Camp is a large site divided into two unequal halves by the stream. It is then further divided into quadrants by the bisecting trail. The quadrant immediately to the right is the largest, a level barren parcel of ground shaded by a few large sycamore trees. The site is a bit rough and readily exposed to the trail on two sides. A small, messy, feeder stream meanders along the back of the camp, separating it from the food-storage cable.

On the left, a path leads upstream through a rhododendron thicket fifty yards to the second quadrant where a small camp is sequestered in the laurel between the West Prong and the feeder stream. The camp is quite attractive with tent sites on a flat along the main stream and on a slight rise near the feeder. A food-storage cable is suspended along the feeder side of the camp.

The trail crosses the West Prong on a footlog. To the left is the smallest of the four campsites. It is sufficiently distant from the trail to be secluded, but occupies somewhat rough and uneven ground. The closest food-storage cable is back across the West Prong.

On the right after crossing the footlog, a path leads a hundred yards downstream to the nicest of the four sites of the West Prong Camp. The site is small, but attractive, more heavily shaded than its siblings and suitably secluded nicely along the stream. The camp enjoys its own food-storage cable.

For many years the West Prong Trail crossed the stream on a low footlog several yards downstream of the camp in the first quadrant. After crossing, it intersected the access path just above the camp in the fourth quadrant. The trail then followed upstream on what is now the access to the camp in the fourth quadrant.

The West Prong Trail now crosses the stream on a large footlog in the middle of the camp. It turns downstream for fifty yards, then switches sharply left and begins climbing the flank of Bote Mountain. The climb is uniform and fairly easy, rising from the lushness of the streamside environment to the dry exposure of a south face. About three-quarters of a mile above the West Prong Camp, the trail terminates into the Bote Mountain Trail, a ridgeline course that climbs from Laurel Creek Road to Spence Field.

In 1972, the Park Service opened the Finley Cane Trail to link with the West Prong and others to form a long connector between Tremont and Cades Cove. The eastern end of the Finley Cane Trail is found on the Bote Mountain Trail 560 yards above the upper terminus of the West Prong Trail.

MIDDLE PRONG TRAIL

Tremont Road to the Greenbrier Ridge Trail and Lynn Camp Prong Trail in Indian Flats—4.1 miles.

POINT OF DEPARTURE: Follow directions to the West Prong Trail, but remain on Tremont Road another 3.1 miles until it ends at a parking area adjacent to a bridge over Lynn Camp Prong. The Middle Prong Trail begins on the bridge.
QUAD MAP: Thunderhead Mountain 157-SW

0.0—Tremont Road. Bridge.
0.4—Cascade.
0.5—Bench at upper end of cascade.
1.9—Benchmark.
2.3—Panther Creek Trail exits left 2.3 miles to the Jakes Creek Trail and Miry Ridge Trail.
3.5—Indian Flats Prong. Bridge.
4.1—Greenbrier Ridge Trail exits right 4.2 miles to the Appalachian Trail. Lynn Camp Prong Trail exits left 3.7 miles to the Miry Ridge Trail.

Where Thunderhead Prong and Lynn Camp Prong converge to form the Middle Prong of Little River, the Little River Lumber Company established a lumber town initially known as Tarpaper Camp. The name was changed to Tremont following a suggestion by Flo Drew and Stuart NcNeil, secretary and office manager, respectively, for Col. W. B. Townsend, president of the lumber company. During the logging era, a railroad line along Middle Prong crossed Lynn Camp Prong on a trestle just above the point where the two tributaries converge. Below the trestle, in what is now the parking area at the trailhead for the Middle Prong Trail, the lumber company maintained a large machine shop, a schoolhouse that also saw duty as a church and theater, and houses for company employees. Directly across the road from the parking area was a sand house where locomotives were fueled with coal and sand. A water tank stood on the same side a few yards back down the road. On the left at the foot of the trestle was a powerhouse for generating electricity. The foundation of the powerhouse is still visible.

Immediately across the trestle the rail line forked, the right fork following Thunderhead Prong and the left proceeding up Lynn Camp Prong. A general store with a post office stood in the wye formed by the rail junction. Across Lynn Camp Prong from the wye was the Tremont Hotel, a two-story frame building with twenty-two rooms and managed by Mrs. Earnest Headrick. The hotel, reached by a swinging footbridge, served company employees. Later it was promoted as a resort for outsiders.

The Middle Prong Trail begins on a metal bridge that rests on the stone abutment that once supported the railroad trestle. A few yards beyond the bridge, the trail makes a smooth turn to the left, tracing the unmistakable course of the old railroad wye. The right fork out of the wye is an unmaintained course that continues up Thunderhead Prong to Defeat Ridge.

From its beginning until its end at Indian Flats, the Middle Prong Trail remains on the old railroad berm. At the lower elevations, the trail is an exceptionally wide, light-gravel track with an easy grade and adheres closely to Lynn Camp Prong. Five hundred and eighty-five yards above the wye, the trail starts into a wide climbing turn that conforms to a double-bend in the stream. At the bend, the big stream cascades down a steeply pitched scarp eighty feet through a three-foot sluice worn into the rock. At the bottom of the sluice, the water plunges fifty feet, hitting a solid ledge with such force that the stream is deflected into a spray. At the edge of the trail, a split-log bench is conveniently placed for sitting and enjoying the display of falling water.

A hundred yards up-trail, a second split-log bench marks a short path to a crag jutting out over the upper end of the cascade. The sound and violence of the rushing turbulence combined with proximity to water falling from a great height are mesmerizing. The cliffs which bound the far side of the cascade are identified on an early map as Rattlesnake Bluffs.

During the 1890s, before the Little River Lumber Company descended on the Smokies with their heavily mechanized, clear-cutting operation, the slopes along Lynn Camp Prong were selectively logged by the J. L. English Lumber Company. English felled trees along the creek bottom, hauling them into the stream with teams of oxen and horses. With water unleashed from temporary splash dams, the logs were floated downstream to rail lines where they could then be transported to a sawmill in Rockwood, Tennessee.

The splash dams were log structures, often well over two hundred feet wide and twenty feet high. Most were built with wide spillways, although some were simply blasted with dynamite to release the impounded water. The dams were placed at strategic places along the streams and tributaries with the release of water synchronized to maximize the volume of flow.

Four hundred and fifty yards above the cascade at Rattlesnake Bluffs, the trail passes the mouth of Marks Creek, where a few remnant timbers of a splash dam lie in the bed of Lynn Camp Prong. Though not discernable from the trail, the scar of a skid road remains along the north side of Marks Creek.

Lynn Camp Prong at this elevation is a succession of placid pools linked by channels of fast-moving water. Along the banks are sycamores, white basswoods, yellow poplars, and yellow birches shading toothworts, Jack-in-the-pulpits, pale jewel weeds, rue anemones, and foamflowers. Because of the prevalence of basswoods, also known as American linden trees, there is some suggestion that the name Lynn is derived from "linden." Others contend that the number of pools on the stream invoked among the Scots settlers the archaic "linn," a word of Gaelic origin meaning "a pool at the base of a waterfall."

About three-quarters of a mile above the mouth of Marks Creek, the Middle Prong Trail crosses Woodchuck Branch and eases into a level stretch that once was occupied by a stringtown, a row of box-like portable buildings, usually about twelve feet square, set a along a rail line to provide housing for the loggers and their families. On Lynn Camp Prong, the stringtown consisted of two rows of houses, one each along either side of the rail line.

Near the lower end of the former Lynn Camp stringtown, an access path exits right fifty yards to the shell of a stripped-down antique Cadillac. The car, owned by a supervisor for the Civilian Conservation Corps, was pushed off the road and abandoned when it ceased to run.

The middle of the former stringtown is now marked by a brass U.S. Geological Survey benchmark (2,515 feet) affixed to a granite stone along the side of the trail. Seven hundred yards beyond the benchmark, the Middle Prong Trail intersects the lower terminus of the Panther Creek Trail angling off to the left. The Panther Creek Trail immediately crosses Lynn Camp Prong and begins climbing to Jakes Gap.

A half-mile above the Panther Creek junction, the Middle Prong Trail approaches Doghobble Branch. On the approach, the trail passes on the right the site of the former Lynn Camp School, which served children living in the nearby stringtowns and lumber camps.

Four hundred yards above the Doghobble Branch crossing, the trail leaves Lynn Camp Prong and eases into a course along Indian Flats Prong. The transition is not readily apparent. It marks, however, the entrance to a former CCC camp. Built in 1933, the camp operated for eight years. A brick chimney on the left, a scattering of concrete foundations, and a grassy clearing athwart the trail are the most conspicuous remnants of the camp. A lone steel rail lying in the clearing is a reminder that the place was once the domain of the loggers before becoming a home to the corpsmen.

A mile above the Panther Creek junction, the trail begins climbing, executes a pair of switchbacks, and then crosses Indian Flats Prong on a bridge, all within a quarter-mile. From the bridge, the trail circles up seventy-five yards to a junction above the stream. At the right of the junction stands a stone abutment that once supported a long railroad trestle that spanned Indian Flats Prong.

Beyond the abutment, the course becomes steeper and markedly more rugged, however a succession of switchbacks mitigates the severity of the climb. At the second switchback, an access path exits right 170 yards to the base of the uppermost of four successive cascades known as Indian Flats Falls.

The upper falls drops twenty feet into a small pool bounded on one side by an island of small round stones. A few yards downstream, Indian Flats Prong clears a bluff, striking a ledge part-way down that projects the flow across the rim of a circular pool. At the base of the third and smallest of the falls, the water collects momentarily before descending the fourth and final bluff and resuming its course. Pitfall and obstruction make an approach to the lower three falls a difficult proposition.

From the access to Indian Flat Falls, the trail climbs a final quarter-mile to a wide looping switchback and then terminates in a three-way intersection with the Greenbrier Ridge Trail and the Lynn Camp Prong Trail. The Greenbrier Ridge Trail exits the switchback on a narrow track that traverses a flat bottom flanking Indian Flats Prong before climbing to the Appalachian Trail. The Lynn Camp Prong Trail follows through the switchback on the railroad trace, then wends up into the mountains to terminate into the Miry Ridge Trail.

PANTHER CREEK TRAIL

Middle Prong Trail to the Jakes Creek Trail and the Miry Ridge Trail at Jakes Gap—2.3 miles.

POINT OF DEPARTURE: Hike 2.3 miles up the Middle Prong Trail. The Panther Creek Trail begins at the stream crossing on the left.

QUAD MAPS: Thunderhead Mountain 157-SW
Silers Bald 157-SE

0.0—Middle Prong Trail. Lynn Camp Prong.
0.1—Switchback.
0.3—Panther Creek.
0.8—Panther Creek.
1.0—Panther Creek.
1.3—Panther Creek.
2.3—Jakes Gap. Miry Ridge Trail exits right 5.0 miles to the Appalachian Trail. Jakes Creek Trail exits straight 3.7 miles to Elkmont. Manway exits left 0.9 mile to the summit of Blanket Mountain.

The Panther Creek Trail is a lateral connector providing access from the Middle Prong Trail to Jakes Gap, where it terminates in a crossroads intersection with the Jakes Creek Trail and the Miry Ridge Trail. When the Panther Creek Trail leaves the Middle Prong Trail, it ventures only forty yards before negotiating a difficult crossing of Lynn Camp Prong. When the stream is running high, the crossing here may be considered dangerous.

Sixty yards beyond the stream crossing, the trail completes a switchback onto an old railroad grade that is now little more than a rocky, washed-out gully along Panther Creek. The condition of the trail is attributable to its steepness, water erosion, and the action of horse traffic churning up the soil while digging in for the climb.

Three hundred and sixty yards above the switchback, the trail crosses Panther Creek for the first time. A half-mile farther, the trail approaches the stream at a shallow angle. The stream here is not deep, but the angle of approach makes for a long crossing. Immediately, the trail clears a second channel of Panther Creek to complete what is essentially a double-crossing. Seventy yards beyond the double-crossing, the trail executes a sharp switchback right. For much of its lower course Panther Creek is a shallow stream dispersed widely over a boulder-filled terrain; however, dog-hobble and rhododendron clog the stream bed, keeping it well sequestered from the trail.

From the last switchback, the trail ascends the flank of Timber Ridge to another railroad grade where it turns right and continues up the Panther Creek drainage on a course well above the stream. Within a half-mile, the Panther Creek Trail drops to cross the stream again. This is the first of eight stream crossings that occur within the next mile. Over this interval, the track is wet and muddy, subject to dozens of rills crossing the trail in search of the larger stream.

The onset of dry-ridge hardwood conditions signals the approach to Jakes Gap, a wide saddle in the ridgeline between Blanket Mountain and Dripping Spring Mountain. In the gap, the Panther Creek Trail terminates in a four-way intersection with the Jakes Creek Trail rising into the gap from the opposite side and the Miry Ridge Trail leading out to the west end of Dripping Spring Mountain. Exiting on the left, a well-marked manway leads about a mile to Blanket Mountain following an old jeep track servicing a fire tower that once stood on the summit of the mountain.

GREENBRIER RIDGE TRAIL

Junction of the Middle Prong Trail and Lynn Camp Prong Trail in Indian Flats to the Appalachian Trail at Sams Gap—4.2 miles.

POINT OF DEPARTURE: Hike 4.1 miles to the end of the Middle Prong Trail. The Greenbrier Ridge Trail begins on the right.

QUAD MAP: Thunderhead Mountain 157-SW

0.0—Indian Flats. Middle Prong Trail. Lynn Camp Prong Trail.
0.4—Indian Flats Prong.
0.6—John Frank Walker Branch.
1.4—Double Trestle Branch.
1.8—Switchback.
2.6—Switchback.
4.2—Sams Gap. Appalachian Trail.

The Greenbrier Ridge Trail, a well-maintained lightly traveled course that probes the upper reaches of the Middle Prong watershed, is one of the best in the Smokies for observing the succession pattern of tree species regenerating on slopes that were cut-over and badly burned by logging operations. Fire cherries are among the first to claim ground on the burned slopes while yellow poplars prevail in the flat drier places and eastern hemlocks seek the cooler shaded hollows. Higher up, red and silver maples and sweet birches are common, sharing space with occasional stands of yellow buckeyes and Carolina silverbells. Higher still, white and chestnut oaks are the prevalent species.

The Greenbrier Ridge Trail shares a trailhead with the Lynn Camp Prong Trail in an old railroad switchback that marks the upper terminus of the Middle Prong Trail. The Lynn Camp Prong Trail follows through the switchback and then remains on the railroad bed climbing the flank of Miry Ridge. The Greenbrier Ridge Trail exits the side of the switchback and proceeds on a smooth narrow track across a bottom that flanks Indian Flats Prong.

Two hundred yards beyond the switchback, the Greenbrier Ridge Trail begins a half-mile climb through a tangle of dog-hobble and rhododendron before executing a difficult crossing of Indian Flats Prong. A thick wire cable lays the full width of the stream where the trail crosses. It was likely once suspended from a skidder used by the loggers to transport timber off the mountain and down to the rail lines.

Three hundred and twenty yards above the Indian Flats Prong crossing, the trail clears John Frank Walker Branch in an easy rock-hop, and then, after almost another mile, reaches the headwaters of Double Trestle Branch. The intervals between the crossings are somewhat rough, particularly near the streams.

The next notable landmark is a sharp switchback that places the trail on the spine of Davis Ridge, named for the Knoxville socialite Anne Davis, who, with her husband Willis Davis, was instrumental in galvanizing the movement to establish a national park in the Smokies. Prior to the park, local mountaineers knew the mountain as Greenbrier Ridge, a name that survives in the trail.

The Greenbrier Ridge Trail remains on the crest of Davis Ridge for only a few yards before rolling off and following the contours of the west flank. In wintertime when foliage is thin, Thunderhead (5,527 feet) can be seen as the high point on the main Smoky divide at the head of Defeat Ridge, the powerful spur descending into Tennessee. A second switchback almost a mile farther directs the trail back toward the ridgeline on a slight descent. Before reaching the ridgeline, the trail cuts across an abrasion where the slope has been scoured of all vegetation except for the larger trees. In places, the ground has been excoriated down to bedrock. The abraded swath extends a considerable distance up and down the slope, no wider than a few feet, a jarring testimony to Smoky Mountain storms which can mete out heavy rainfall concentrated in a single draw, sending a torrent down the mountain and wreaking havoc on the landscape.

When the trail reaches the ridgeline, large hemlocks prevail, shading thickets of leggy rhododendron. The course here is remarkably level and the ground soft and spongy. In all, conditions are more suggestive of a low-elevation cove-hardwood environment than of a high dry-ridge exposure.

When the trail eases out of the hemlocks, it leaves the ridgeline for a final moderate climb that circumnavigates Mount Davis, a peak on the main Smoky divide that was named for Willis P. Davis in recognition of his role as president of the Smoky Mountain Conservation Association. The original petition to honor both Anne and Willis Davis recommended that the name Davis be affixed to nearby Cold Spring Knob. The U.S. Geological Survey rejected the proposal but responded by agreeing to recognize the two separately in Davis Ridge and Mount Davis.

A weak spring and clusters of wild golden-glows and Curtis' asters herald the approach into Sams Gap, where the Greenbrier Trail terminates into the Appalachian Trail. Sams Gap was named for Sam Cook, a Smoky Mountaineer who settled in the lower reaches of Middle Prong. Along the Appalachian Trail, 555 yards west of Sams Gap, is the Derrick Knob Shelter.

LYNN CAMP PRONG TRAIL

Junction of the Middle Prong Trail and Greenbrier Ridge Trail in Indian Flats to the Miry Ridge Trail—3.7 miles.

POINT OF DEPARTURE: Hike 4.1 miles to the end of the Middle Prong Trail. The Lynn Camp Prong Trail begins on the left.

QUAD MAPS: Thunderhead Mountain 157-SW
Silers Bald 157-SE

0.0—Indian Flats. Middle Prong Trail. Greenbrier Trail.
1.5—Marks Cove Backcountry Campsite (#28).
1.6—Buckeye Cove.
3.7—Miry Ridge Trail exits right 2.5 miles to the Appalachian Trail and left 2.5 miles to the Jakes Creek Trail and Panther Creek Trail at Jakes Gap.

The Lynn Camp Prong Trail begins in a switchback where the Middle Prong Trail terminates in a junction with the Greenbrier Ridge Trail. The Greenbrier Ridge Trail exits the switchback and proceeds across a creek bottom. The Lynn Camp Prong Trail follows through the switchback, then along the old railroad grade up the flank of Miry Ridge.

The first mile is easy, coursing through one of the last areas in the Smokies to be logged. Fraser magnolias, Carolina silverbells, yellow poplars, American beeches, black cherries, and sourwoods are recovering nicely. In April and early May, carpets of white fringed phacelia and large colonies of creeping phlox blanket the flanking slopes.

A mile and a half above the trailhead, the Lynn Camp Prong Trail makes a ninety-degree turn right and leaves the rail grade. The rail grade continues straight for seventy-five yards to enter the Marks Cove Backcountry Campsite (#28).

The Marks Cove Camp is divided into two unequal halves separated by Lynn Camp Prong. The nearer site is on an old railroad siding, level and grassy but forlorn and unattractive, more akin to a construction site than a wilderness retreat. A food-storage cable is suspended below the lower side of the camp over a swath of cleared underbrush.

Across Lynn Camp Prong lies the second campsite, small and similar to the first, but without the worst of the roughness. The food-storage cable is suspended over a hummock along the side of the camp. Beyond the hummock and down the slope is a heavily shaded, dog-hobble-infested, bare, gritty ground that affords an additional campsite. The lower site has the advantage of being secluded and without the coarseness of the rail grade, but it tends to be somewhat gloomy and damp. Water is convenient, but the cable is not. The access path to the camp proceeds through the middle of the two sites and then continues as an unmaintained manway along Dripping Spring Branch to reach the Miry Ridge Trail at the end of Log Ridge.

When the Lynn Camp Prong Trail turns and leaves the railroad grade, it climbs on a narrow, steep, rocky, muddy gully into Buckeye Cove. These conditions are maintained by horses churning the ground to gain traction for the climb. Except for a crossing at Buckeye Cove Branch, trail conditions improve very little from this point until the end on Miry Ridge.

Above Buckeye Cove, the fire cherries were the first to regenerate on the burnt-over slopes left by the Little River Lumber Company. Though still prevalent, the fire cherries are being slowly displaced by a mix of cove hardwoods taking advantage of favorable succession conditions. Higher up, where seepages running off Miry Ridge keep the slopes irrigated, there is a greater diversity of tree species, particularly groves of eastern hemlocks and black cherries. The cherry trees on Lynn Camp Prong are convenient to some of the more rugged Smoky Mountain terrain where bears often den. Late in summer, when the fruit ripen, bears may occasionally be seen filching cherries.

Beyond the cherry grove, the trail curls up and onto the spine of Miry Ridge to terminate into the Miry Ridge Trail an equidistant 2.5 miles from the Appalachian Trail along the state-line divide and Jakes Gap near Blanket Mountain.

◆ WHITEOAK SINK ◆

Over the millennia following the geological upheavals that formed the Great Smoky Mountains, wind and water eroded through the thinner low-hanging overthrusts, leaving a nexus of limestone coves in the northwest quadrant of the Smokies—Tuckaleechee Cove and Dry Valley along the boundary just outside the park, and Cades Cove, Whiteoak Sink, and Big Spring Cove just inside. These limestone coves are among the most fertile and arable land in the mountains and hence attracted some of the earliest settlers into the Smokies. In the 1830s, a party of Cherokee under the direction of Reverend Isaac Anderson built a road from Dry Valley through Whiteoak Sink and up along the spine of Bote Mountain to Spence Field, providing access to the fine grazing ranges on the main Smoky divide. Soon thereafter, other roads were built, mostly sled tracks connecting the farms in Whiteoak Sink and Big Spring Cove with the Anderson Road. These old farm roads are the predecessors of the small network of trails that are included in the Whiteoak Sink section.

Only seven trails visit the Whiteoak Sink section. The Schoolhouse Gap Trail and Bote Mountain Trail generally follow the course of the Anderson Road, the former along the eastern rim of Whiteoak Sink and the latter up Bote Mountain. The Scott Mountain Trail circles the northern and western rim of the sink before exiting to Cades Cove. The Finley Cane, Lead Cove, Crib Gap, and Turkeypen Ridge trails all exit Big Spring Cove, the first two climbing to Bote Mountain, the Crib Gap Trail exiting for Cades Cove, and the Turkeypen Ridge reaching Dosey Gap at the entrance to Whiteoak Sink. Except for the Bote Mountain Trail, all trails in this section are fairly short and easy to hike. All except the Scott Mountain Trail can be accessed directly from Laurel Creek Road.

The Turkeypen Ridge Backcountry Campsite (#6) on the Scott Mountain Trail is the only backcountry campsite in the Whiteoak Sink section. However it is only 180 yards from the west end of the trail and thus more easily reached from the Cades Cove section.

BOTE MOUNTAIN TRAIL

Laurel Creek Road to the Appalachian Trail at Spence Field—6.9 miles.

POINT OF DEPARTURE: From the Townsend Wye, drive 3.4 miles west on Laurel Creek Road. The Bote Mountain Trail begins on the left side of the road. Parking is available at the Schoolhouse Gap Trail 250 yards farther up Laurel Creek Road.

QUAD MAPS: Wear Cove 157-NW
Thunderhead Mountain 157-SW

0.0—Laurel Creek Road.

1.2—West Prong Trail exits left 2.7 miles to Tremont Road at the Great Smoky Mountains Institute.

1.5—Finley Cane Trail exits right 2.8 miles to the Lead Cove Trail and Turkeypen Ridge Trail at Laurel Creek Road.

3.5—Hickory Tree Gap.

4.0—Sandy Gap. Lead Cove Trail exits right 1.8 miles to the Finley Cane Trail and Turkeypen Ridge Trail at Laurel Creek Road.

5.2—Anthony Creek Trail exits right 3.6 miles to the Cades Cove Picnic Area.

5.5—Road turnaround.

6.9—Spence Field. Appalachian Trail.

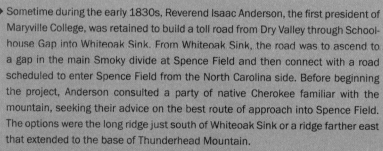

Sometime during the early 1830s, Reverend Isaac Anderson, the first president of Maryville College, was retained to build a toll road from Dry Valley through Schoolhouse Gap into Whiteoak Sink. From Whiteoak Sink, the road was to ascend to a gap in the main Smoky divide at Spence Field and then connect with a road scheduled to enter Spence Field from the North Carolina side. Before beginning the project, Anderson consulted a party of native Cherokee familiar with the mountain, seeking their advice on the best route of approach into Spence Field. The options were the long ridge just south of Whiteoak Sink or a ridge farther east that extended to the base of Thunderhead Mountain.

To gauge the consensus of opinion, Anderson took a poll among the Cherokee. The Indians voted for the ridge south of Whiteoak Sink. Since the Cherokee language has no sound for the letter "v," the closest being the sound for "b," the Indians voiced their consensus with a "bote." Since that time, the ridge has been known as Bote Mountain. The ridge farther east, the one not chosen, was subsequently christened Defeat Ridge.

A variation on this story collected by W. H. Camp during a scientific expedition into the Smokies contends that the vote was taken among the local settlers. The vote ended in a tie. One of the settlers, a native of northern Europe who had not voted, was solicited to break the tie. He responded, "I bote vor dis vun."

Anderson and his party of Cherokee completed the road almost to Spence Field. The North Carolina counterpart, which was projected to begin in Walhallow, South Carolina, and follow through Rabun Gap, cross the Little Tennessee River and on up Chambers Creek, then through DeLosier Gap and Haw Gap, and on into Spence Field, was never started. The Anderson Road, as it later came to be known, was then appropriated by herders driving cattle to the grazing ranges on the high Smoky divide.

In July 1887, a group of students from the University of Tennessee ventured up Bote Mountain to Spence Field following the Anderson Road. One of the party later wrote, "For a mile and a half the trail lies in the bed of the creek. The laurel growing down close to the bank forbids one to tread upon the solid earth. The scenery along this creek is grand. Here and there large trees, blown down by the storms, would be found lying across the ravine, great rocks rising up on either sides, the thick foliage shutting out the sun's rays. The clear water now rushing in cataracts over the larger stones, now gliding quietly among the lesser ones, and the sweet perfume of the laurel and rhododendron floating upon the breeze. What a delightful place to be in."

Frank Carpenter, a traveler on Bote Mountain in 1890, noted that "many years ago a road was surveyed and partly graded towards the top of Thunderhead, but was given up. The storms have done their best to efface it; but there still remains a terrace, making a fairly easy path for several miles." When Carpenter and his companions reached the end of the road, they "then followed a stony trail through rhododendron bushes, which rose far above our heads." By the time the Smoky Mountains Hiking Club was venturing up Bote Mountain in 1928, the Anderson Road had deteriorated to "an old washed-out and badly deformed wagon road."

With the advent of the park, young men with the Civilian Conservation Corps rehabilitated the Anderson Road sufficiently for automobiles to enter Spence Field. Even as late as the 1960s, automobiles were permitted on certain occasions to travel Bote Mountain as far as the end of the original Anderson Road.

From Laurel Creek Road, the Bote Mountain Trail enters a cool hemlock-darkened hollow following the course that was improved by the CCC. The trail is wide and smooth, and initially there is little grade. About a mile above the road, the course deteriorates noticeably as it climbs a quarter-mile through a hard-packed red-clay gully to intersect the upper terminus of the West Prong Trail entering on the left. Here, the grade levels and the trail surface changes to a consistency of sand. Five hundred and sixty yards beyond the West Prong intersection, the Bote Mountain Trail intersects on the right the upper terminus of the Finley Cane Trail.

Immediately above the Finley Cane junction, the Bote Mountain Trail becomes steeper and degenerates to a state redolent of the "old washed-out and badly deformed wagon road" encountered by the hiking club in 1928.

Almost two miles above the Finley Cane junction, the trail eases through Hickory Tree Gap and onto a level ridgeline that was burned by fire from a lightning strike in 1987. Table Mountain pine was the first tree species to claim space on the burned-over slopes with blackberry thickets and other rough browse forming the understory. At several places along the fire-scald, Thunderhead and Defeat Ridge come into clear view.

The trail remains level for the better part of a half-mile, then climbs another half-mile to Sandy Gap and an intersection with the upper terminus of the Lead Cove Trail. Here, the trail ratchets up a few more notches in steepness and continues grinding up the rough track for a mile and a quarter to an intersection with the upper terminus of the Anthony Creek Trail. The deterioration of this part of the Bote Mountain Trail is largely the result of horses having to dig in to gain purchase for the climb. The digging action loosens the soil which then washes away with rain-water, leaving only rough loose stones for the trail bed.

Hidden in the rhododendron immediately across from the Anthony Creek Trail is the west end of an old CCC trail connecting Bote Mountain with Defeat Ridge. The old trail terminates on Defeat Ridge just below a landmark known as the Chimney Rock. The trail is now largely obscured by heavy undergrowth and blow-downs.

Five hundred and eighty yards above its intersection with the Anthony Creek Trail, the Bote Mountain Trail enters a turnaround that marks the point reached by the Cherokee before they stopped work on the old Anderson Road. Beyond the turn-around, the grade remains stiff but the track narrows to a deep rough rut, continuing as thus for a mile before yellow birches begin yielding to Allegheny serviceberry trees along the indefinite lower fringe of Spence Field.

Harvey Broome once noted that "there was a time when Spence Field was as close-cropped as a lawn and when its fringe of trees was well-defined. Then there were galled spots where the grazing animals had eaten too closely and the rains had gullied through the turf, leaving bare patches of minimal soil." Years later, when Broome returned to Spence Field, he noted that "the sod is long, tough, and matted. Small saplings and laurel clumps are edging in." Patches of mountain grass now indicate places where the field once extended, but the encroachment of the woody growth Broome noted has completely obscured the well-defined fringe of his early visit to the bald.

The Bote Mountain Trail soon passes a spring which was once inside the perim-eter of Spence Field. Two hundred yards above the spring, the trail terminates into the Appalachian Trail. A hundred and ten yards to the right along the Appalachian Trail, the Eagle Creek Trail leads 290 yards to the Spence Field Shelter. To the left, the Appalachian Trail winds a mile through the grassy sward to the foot of Thunderhead Mountain.

SCHOOLHOUSE GAP TRAIL

Laurel Creek Road to the Scott Mountain Trail at Schoolhouse Gap—2.2
  miles.
  POINT OF DEPARTURE: Follow directions to the Bote Mountain Trail. The
  Schoolhouse Gap Trail begins at the parking lot on the right 250 yards farther up Laurel Creek Road.

QUAD MAPS: Wear Cove 157-NW
Kinzel Springs 148-NE

0.0—Laurel Creek Road.
1.1—Dosey Gap. Turkeypen Ridge Trail exits left 3.6 miles to the Finley Cane
Trail and Lead Cove Trail on Laurel Creek Road.
1.1—Access path exits left into Whiteoak Sink.
2.0—Chestnut Top Trail exits right 4.3 miles to the Townsend Wye.
2.2—Schoolhouse Gap. Scott Mountain Trail exits left 3.6 miles to the
Crooked Arm Ridge Trail and Indian Grave Gap Trail.

Sometime in the mid-1830s, the president of Maryville College, Reverend Isaac Anderson, was retained to supervise the construction of a road from Dry Valley to the main Smoky divide at Spence Field, where it was intended to connect with a similar road being built up the North Carolina side of the mountain. The road, known provisionally as the Anderson Turnpike or the McCampbell-Anderson Turnpike, passed from Dry Valley through Schoolhouse Gap and into Whiteoak Sink. It then exited the sink near Dosey Gap and followed down the middle of Spence Branch to Laurel Creek, where it crossed and ascended an unnamed stream to the crest of Bote Mountain and eventually into Spence Field. The road leading up from North Carolina was never completed.

Carlos Campbell once recorded having heard from Smoky Mountaineers that Spence Branch was formerly known as "Near Branch" and the unnamed stream on the south side draining Bote Mountain as "Far Branch." Near Branch and Far Branch empty into Laurel Creek within a short distance of one another. The Schoolhouse Gap Trail begins from a small parking area along Laurel Creek Road just above the confluences of the three streams. The trail quickly picks up the course of the old Anderson Road following up Near Branch (Spence Branch). When it was being used by mountaineers, the Anderson Road actually ran in the middle of the stream. Wagons being dragged up and down Near Branch wore tracks in the hard rock shield of the stream bed that are still visible today.

The Schoolhouse Gap Trail follows a wide track that courses easily through a few old settlement clearings until reaching Dosey Gap a mile above Laurel Creek Road. Here, it intersects the east terminus of the Turkeypen Ridge Trail ranging in from Big Spring Cove. Sixty-five yards beyond the Turkeypen junction, an access path exits left leading into Whiteoak Sink, a limestone basin of several acres completely enclosed by mountains and once inhabited by pioneering families.

The access to Whiteoak Sink wends through a hummocky perimeter of pines and hemlocks for nearly 700 yards before splitting into two divergent courses. The right fork goes up and over a "rim" and into the sink. On clearing the rim, it skids a hundred feet down an exceedingly steep, badly galled track to the edge of Rainbow

Hole, a deep cave sheltered by a high rocky bluff. Directly over this forbidding hole, a nameless stream drops over the cliff and into the maw, seeking a subterranean passage out of the sink. With the proper angle of sunlight, spray from the waterfall forms a rainbow over the great fissure, thus prompting the name Rainbow Hole.

The left fork engages an easier and more sinuous half-mile course around the perimeter before easing onto the floor of the sink and reuniting with its right fork counterpart about 100 yards west of Rainbow Hole. Because of severe erosion on the "skid" down to Rainbow Hole, it is strongly recommended that Whiteoak Sink be entered and Rainbow Hole approached by the left fork.

Almost three hundred billion years ago, the Carolina Shale Belt formation crunched into North America in a mountain-building event called the Acadian orogeny. During the collision, igneous rock skidded over the North American limestone plates, folding and buckling up into high mountains much in the way a floor rug bunches up when scooted by a clumsy foot. The orogeny took place over millions of years, the overthrust moving almost imperceptibly, perhaps less than the speed of a growing fingernail. In some places the mountain-forming action left "windows," openings in the overthrust where the underlying limestone strata remained exposed. Whiteoak Sink is an example of such a limestone window.

The overthrust action of the Acadian orogeny can be seen at Rainbow Hole. Noticeable about midway up the cliff above the hole are two strata of rock. The lower stratum appears horizontal while the upper rests directly upon the lower at an upthrust angle. The horizontal stratum is part of the original limestone plate that was crunched by the colliding Carolina Shale Belt, which is seen here as the angling upper stratum.

Where the left fork rejoins the right, the access trail starts out across the wide open floor of Whiteoak Sink. The sink is home to a great variety of wildflowers, but most striking are the beds of creeping phlox that occasionally cover the entire floor of the basin.

Rainwater draining from nearby Turkeypen Ridge collects in rocky channels that empty their contents onto the floor of Whiteoak Sink, where loose sieve-like layers of rocks allow the stream to percolate out of sight. On rare occasions when the run-off is of such volume that the water cannot be quickly absorbed, the excess drains into Blow Hole, a small cave at the base of a high bluff 200 yards across the sink. Blow Hole's colorful name is suggested by a steady current of cool air that is often blowing outward from the cave's mouth. Visitors are strongly encouraged by the Park Service to refrain from approaching Blow Hole in an effort to protect bats living there from becoming infected with a contagious and deadly white nose fungus.

Bob Spence, whose father began grazing cattle on Spence Field in 1830, died during a snowstorm at his home in Whiteoak Sink. The snow was so deep that it was not possible to move his body to a cemetery in Tuckaleechee Cove.

The younger Spence was then buried on one of the ledges above the Blow Hole cave.

A manway noticeable to the right of the bluff behind Blow Hole follows the course of the old Anderson Road into the sink from Schoolhouse Gap. The manway also passes another large sinkhole known as Scott Mountain Cave.

From Dosey Gap, the Schoolhouse Gap Trail continues on an easy grade circling the rim of the Whiteoak Sink basin. A mile above Dosey Gap, it intersects the western terminus of the Chestnut Top Trail leading in from the Townsend Wye. About 370 yards above the Chestnut Top junction, the Schoolhouse Gap Trail reaches the park boundary at Schoolhouse Gap, where it terminates into the eastern end of the Scott Mountain Trail. On the left side of the gap is the manway leading past Scott Mountain Cave and into Whiteoak Sink.

 According to information gleaned by Pete Prince from interviews with Inez Burns and Randolph Shields, between 1872 and 1886 Schoolhouse Gap was the site of a small building in which the Reverend Charles H. Gibson held church services on Sunday and taught school during the remainder of the week. All that remains as a testament of the school is the name Schoolhouse Gap.

SCOTT MOUNTAIN TRAIL

Schoolhouse Gap to the Crooked Arm Ridge Trail and Indian Grave Gap Trail—3.6 miles.

POINT OF DEPARTURE: Hike to Schoolhouse Gap at the end of the Schoolhouse Gap Trail. The Scott Mountain Trail begins in Schoolhouse Gap.

QUAD MAPS: Kinzel Springs 148-NE

Cades Cove 148-SE

0.0—Schoolhouse Gap. Manway to Whiteoak Sink.

3.5—Turkeypen Ridge Backcountry Campsite (#6).

3.6—Crooked Arm Ridge Trail exits left 2.2 miles to the Rich Mountain Loop Trail. Indian Grave Gap Trail exits right 3.7 miles to Rich Mountain Road.

Scott Mountain is a low-elevation range along the northern perimeter of the Great Smoky Mountains that separates the limestone coves of Whiteoak Sink from those of Dry Valley. During the geological upheavals that formed the Great Smoky Mountains, continental plates of igneous rock skidded over the North American limestone strata, folding and buckling up into high mountains. The overthrusts that were once on either side of Scott Mountain were left as such a low angle that the eroding agents of nature wore through the hanging wall of igneous rock, exposing the underlying limestone that now forms the floors of Whiteoak Sink and Dry Valley.

Following along the Scott Mountain ridgeline is the Scott Mountain Trail, extending from Schoolhouse Gap on the eastern perimeter of Whiteoak Sink to the junction of Scott Mountain with Rich Mountain above Cades Cove. Schoolhouse Gap was long recognized by Smoky Mountaineers as a suitable pass between Dry Valley and Whiteoak Sink. In the 1830s, the gap was occupied by the so-called Anderson Road, a rudimentary wagon track that proceeded from Dry Valley through the gap and then up along the spine of Bote Mountain to the crest of the main Smoky divide at Spence Field. In Spence Field, the Anderson Road was to have connected with a similar road being built up from the North Carolina side. The North Carolina road was never completed. Today, Schoolhouse Gap straddles the park boundary and harbors the upper terminus of the Schoolhouse Gap Trail and the eastern terminus of the Scott Mountain Trail.

The Scott Mountain Trail begins at the end of the Schoolhouse Gap Trail immediately across the road from a modern house that sits just outside the park boundary. As it leaves Schoolhouse Gap, the trail enters a slow climb around the outer rim of Whiteoak Sink. Just below the point where the trail leaves the gap, a manway exits on a lower course, circling down along Scott Mountain Cave and into Whiteoak Sink.

About a half-mile above the gap, the trail returns to the crest of Scott Mountain for a short ridge run that affords views of the tidy farms and green fields that dot Dry Valley and Tuckaleechee Cove. South, across Whiteoak Sink, Thunderhead (5,527 feet) appears as the high peak on the state-line divide.

When the trail rolls off the ridgeline, it begins following the curvature of Scott Mountain around the circumference of Whiteoak Sink. The flanking terrain becomes rugged and the trail a narrow weed-infested berm adhering precariously to an ever-steepening slope. Large northern red oak, white basswood, yellow poplar, Carolina silverbell, and pignut hickory are the more prevalent tree species. In places, vines hang thickly on the trees and in others trilliums blanket acres of mountain slope. Other wildflower species, noticeably squirrel corn, Dutchman's-breeches, sweet white violet, and blue-eyed grass are interspersed among the trilliums.

A mile and a half above Schoolhouse Gap, the Scott Mountain Trail leaves the rim of Whiteoak Sink and climbs onto a southern exposure where the main Smoky divide from Silers Bald (5,607 feet) to Gregory Bald (4,949 feet) comes into view with Thunderhead appearing immediately to the south. The grade moderates noticeably while the forest cover changes to white and chestnut oaks shading a dry-ridge mix of galax, mountain laurel, flame azalea, and rhododendron. High grass grows abundantly in the trail. Twice the trail leaves the exposure for a diversion into shaded hollows where ferns dot the slopes and the poplars and silverbells re-appear along with Fraser magnolias.

After remaining on the exposure for about a mile, the trail turns and edges out to cross Turkeypen Ridge before resuming on the southern exposure. After another mile, the trail circles out to cross a minor finger ridge. On the return it reaches the Turkeypen Ridge Backcountry Campsite (#6).

The Turkeypen Ridge Camp is situated astride the saddle of a ridgeline in the shape of a hyperbolic paraboloid. The main part of the camp occupies the low point in the ridgeline with a small annex on the rise above the saddle. Both sites are small and, as the terrain is gently rolling, afford very few level spots. The camp is, nonetheless, quite attractive, especially the upper site with its grassy turf and fine wintertime view of Thunderhead. A food-storage cable is suspended in the upper camp, and water is available from a weak spring branch a hundred yards down the ridge opposite the entrance to the camp. The slope to the stream is very steep and unmarked. The better alternative may be to hike back down the Scott Mountain Trail 300 yards to the point where the stream crosses the trail.

A hundred and eighty yards beyond the Turkeypen Ridge Camp, the Scott Mountain Trail terminates in a three-way intersection with the upper terminus of the Crooked Arm Ridge Trail and the eastern terminus of the Indian Grave Gap Trail. The Crooked Arm Ridge Trail descends 2.2 miles to the Rich Mount Loop Trail near Cades Cove Loop Road. The Indian Grave Gap Trail crosses Rich Mountain 3.7 miles to Rich Mountain Road.

FINLEY CANE TRAIL

Laurel Creek Road at Big Spring Cove to the Bote Mountain Trail—2.8 miles.
POINT OF DEPARTURE: From the Townsend Wye, drive 5.7 miles west on Laurel Creek Road to Big Spring Cove. The Finley Cane Trail begins on the left side of the road at a trailhead it shares with the Lead Cove Trail.
QUAD MAP: Thunderhead Mountain 157-SW

0.0—Laurel Creek Road. Lead Cove Trail. Turkeypen Ridge Trail.
0.1—Sugar Cove Prong.
0.2—Access path exits left under Laurel Creek Road 245 yards to the Turkeypen Ridge Trail and Crib Gap Trail.
0.2—Big Spring sinkhole.
0.8—Laurel Cove Creek.
0.8—Hickory Tree Branch.
1.8—Finley Cove Creek.
2.8—Bote Mountain Trail exits right 5.4 miles to the Appalachian Trail at Spence Field and left 1.5 miles to Laurel Creek Road.

Immediately east of Cades Cove is Big Spring Cove, a limestone sink which at one time harbored several settlement farms connected by a network of wagon roads. One of these roads provided access out of Big Spring Cove to the old Anderson Road along the crest of Bote Mountain. With the advent of the park, this old wagon trace was abandoned and remained largely unused until the early 1970s, when it was upgraded to Park Service specifications and christened the Finley Cane Trail. While the Finley Cane Trail is an enjoyable hike in and of itself, its chief value lies in its role as a connector between the Turkeypen Ridge–Lead Cove–Crib Gap nexus of trails to the west and the Bote Mountain–West Prong–Schoolhouse Gap configuration to the east.

The Finley Cane Trail begins along the upper side of Laurel Creek Road at an intersection it shares with the lower terminus of the Lead Cove Trail and immediately across the road from the western terminus of the Turkeypen Ridge Trail. As it eases off the road, the Finley Cane Trail turns immediately left and proceeds on a rocky course downstream between Laurel Creek Road and Sugar Cove Prong. After 140 yards, it crosses the stream and charts an easy course across Big Spring Cove. About 220 yards beyond the stream crossing, an access path cuts sharply left, leading back across Sugar Cove Prong, through a tunnel under the road, and on to an intersection with the Turkeypen Ridge Trail and the eastern terminus of the Crib Gap Trail. The access path is a wet muddy course used primarily by horse traffic.

Fifty-six feet beyond the horse access, the Finley Cane Trail reaches two large sinkholes, one behind the other. The larger of the two is the Big Spring whence the cove gets its name. Around the perimeter are several pairs of wooden posts, remnants of rail fences for restraining cattle attracted to water standing in the hole.

Beyond the sinkhole, the trail passes through stands of pines and Fraser magnolias, crosses a small feeder stream, then begins climbing the north flank of Bote Mountain. Where the grade stiffens slightly, the trail enters a corridor of rhododendron, continuing for 300 yards before dropping slightly to cross, first, Laurel Cove Creek, and then, seventy yards farther along, Hickory Tree Branch. Here the trail eases into a mature cove-hardwood forest of large stately oaks, hickories, eastern hemlocks, and yellow poplars shading a thin understory of low browse. These trees are not the giants of the virgin stands, but they do nevertheless comprise a remarkable forest, especially the yellow poplars that extend seventy or eighty feet to the lowest limbs.

About a mile beyond the Hickory Tree crossing, the trail passes over a slight rise and drops to Finley Cove Creek. At this elevation, Finley Cove Creek is usually dry. Where the trail crosses, a small thicket of cane flanks the stream bed. In the Smokies, cane generally prefers a wet streamside environment. This patch is an exception but likely supplies the origin of the trail's name. From here, the trail climbs easily through dry-woods conditions to terminate into the Bote Mountain Trail.

LEAD COVE TRAIL

Laurel Creek Road at Big Spring Cove to the Bote Mountain Trail at Sandy
Gap—1.8 miles.

POINT OF DEPARTURE: Follow directions to the Finley Cane Trail. The Lead
Cove Trail shares a trailhead with the Finley Cane Trail.

QUAD MAP: Thunderhead Mountain 157-SW

0.0—Laurel Creek Road. Finley Cane Trail. Turkeypen Ridge Trail.
0.4—Sugar Cove Prong.
1.4—Laurel Cove Creek.
1.8—Sandy Gap. Bote Mountain Trail exits right 2.9 miles to the Appalachian
Trail and left 4.0 miles to Laurel Creek Road.

The Lead Cove Trail was once part of a network of old wagon roads that fanned out
from Big Spring Cove, a limestone sink that ranges along the upper end of Laurel
Creek. At one time the trail was known locally as the Sandy Gap Trail as it terminated on Bote Mountain at Sandy Gap. The trail was abandoned until 1970, at
which time it was rehabilitated and christened the Lead Cove Trail. The newer name
is an allusion to anecdotal evidence that lead ore was hauled down the trail in wagons
during the Civil War. This may well have been the case, but the source of the ore has
not since been determined.

The trail begins at the edge of Laurel Creek Road in an intersection it shares
with the western terminus of the Finley Cane Trail. Immediately across the road is
the western terminus of the Turkeypen Ridge Trail. The Lead Cove Trail starts up
quickly on a rough track along Laurel Creek Road. After 150 yards, it turns sharply
left onto a wider track that proceeds through old farm fields in the bottomland
flanking Sugar Cove Prong. The land's fertility was apparently severely depleted by
over-farming as now in places the old fields show evidence of struggling to return to
wilderness.

Six hundred and seventy yards above Laurel Creek Road, the trail negotiates
two branches of Sugar Cove Prong twenty yards apart, after which the grade become
markedly steeper. Two hundred yards above the stream crossings, the trail reaches
the fallen remains of a cabin once occupied by the Gibson Tipton family, likely
arriving with the influx of several Tiptons in 1821. Here, the grade stiffens another
few degrees and the track pressed into the more restricted confines of a narrowing
stream gorge. The hollow is moist and heavily shaded, a suitable environment for
squaw-roots, white wood asters, bloodroots, goldenrods, and a variety of trilliums.

About a half-mile above the cabin ruins, the trail turns sharply left and leaves the
hollow for a final 700-yard climb up the flank of Bote Mountain. The trail continues
over this interval with little variation while offering a few obstructed views across

Big Spring Cove to the park boundary at Scott Mountain. The trail soon rolls up into Sandy Gap and terminates into the Bote Mountain Trail three miles below the Appalachian Trail at Spence Field.

TURKEYPEN RIDGE TRAIL

Laurel Creek Road at Big Spring Cove to the Schoolhouse Gap Trail at Dosey Gap—3.6 miles.

POINT OF DEPARTURE: Follow directions to the Finley Cane Trail. The Turkeypen Ridge Trail begins across Laurel Creek Road from the trailhead for the Finley Cane Trail.

QUAD MAPS: Thunderhead Mountain 157-SW
Wear Cove 157-NW

0.0—Laurel Creek Road. Finley Cane Trail. Lead Cove Trail.
0.2—Crib Gap Trail exits left 1.6 miles to the Anthony Creek Trail. Access path exits right, leading through a tunnel under Laurel Creek Road 245 yards to the Finley Cane Trail.
0.3—Laurel Creek.
1.4—Pinkroot Branch.
3.6—Dosey Gap. Schoolhouse Gap Trail exits right 1.1 miles to Laurel Creek Road and left 1.1 miles to the Scott Mountain Trail at Schoolhouse Gap.

The Turkeypen Ridge Trail is part of a former network of wagon roads that linked Big Spring Cove with the mountain communities beyond the surrounding ridges. The trail's western terminus is anchored along Laurel Creek Road just opposite an intersection marking the lower terminus of both the Finley Cane Trail and Lead Cove Trail, themselves part of the old wagon network. When it leaves Laurel Creek Road, the Turkeypen Ridge Trail drops into the flat bottomland of Big Spring Cove and proceeds 325 yards to intersect the eastern terminus of the Crib Gap Trail, another spoke in the old wagon-road configuration. The Crib Gap Trail exits back left to clear the rim of Big Spring Cove and enter the Cades Cove basin along the Anthony Creek Trail. At the junction with the Crib Gap Trail, an access path exits the Turkeypen Ridge Trail on the right and proceeds 245 yards to a tunnel under Laurel Creek Road and on to the Finley Creek Trail. The access is a wet muddy course used primarily by horse traffic.

A hundred and seventy-five yards beyond the Crib Gap junction, the Turkeypen Ridge Trail negotiates an easy crossing of Laurel Creek and then, fifty-five yards farther, crosses a nameless tributary. The trail then enters an easy climb that angles up the side of the ridge adjacent to a wide-bottomed hollow that is an appendage of Big Spring Cove. On the left, stacked piles of rocks and pieces of an abandoned stove are the most visible testaments to the pioneering era. The hollow is drained by a nameless tributary flanked by old farm fields that are slowly being reclaimed by the wilderness.

A half-mile above the Laurel Creek crossing, the trail leaves Big Spring Cove through a small gap leading onto the flank of Turkeypen Ridge. A quarter-mile beyond the gap, it crosses a small feeder stream and then a quarter-mile farther along enters a slight draw where Pinkroot Branch spills over a rugged outcropping of stratified rock and splashes out onto the trail. Pinkroot is the Smoky Mountain vernacular for a slender, trumpet-shaped wildflower that is red on the outside and yellow on the inside or throat of the trumpet. The flower, rare in the Smokies, is more commonly known as Indian-pink.

From here, the trail stays along the eastern flank of Turkeypen Ridge, venturing occasionally out onto the drier exposures where pines, laurel, and galax are prevalent before retreating back into cooler, more moist, conditions of the hollows where trillium, crested dwarf iris, Carolina vetch, and flame azalea are common in spring. The trail follows the crest of Turkeypen Ridge for a short interval before entering a final half-mile descent to Dosey Gap. During the descent, the trail passes first through a pine stand that has been severely damaged by pine-bark beetles. It completes a run through dry-ridge oaks and pines to terminate at Dosey Gap in an intersection with the Schoolhouse Gap Trail. The gap is named for Anderson Dosey, a Civil War veteran who farmed in nearby Whiteoak Sink. An access path into the sink lies along the Schoolhouse Gap Trail sixty-five yards above the trail intersection. The Schoolhouse Gap Trail continues beyond the access 1.1 miles to the Scott Mountain Trail at Schoolhouse Gap.

CRIB GAP TRAIL

Turkeypen Ridge Trail to the Anthony Creek Trail—1.6 miles.
POINT OF DEPARTURE: Follow directions to the Turkeypen Ridge Trail. The Crib Gap Trail begins 325 yards down the Turkeypen Ridge Trail.
QUAD MAPS: Thunderhead Mountain 157-SW
Cades Cove 148-SE

0.0—Turkeypen Ridge Trail.
0.1—Feeder stream.
0.7—Laurel Creek Road.
1.1—Crib Gap.
1.4—Feeder stream.
1.6—Anthony Creek Trail exits right 380 yards to the Cades Cove Picnic Area.

The Crib Gap Trail is a lateral connector that links Big Spring Cove with the eastern end of Cades Cove. It is not one of the more pleasant hikes in the Smokies as it is never far from automobile traffic and is frequently occupied by horses traveling between the Anthony Creek Trail and Turkeypen Ridge Trail.

The Crib Gap Trail begins 325 yards down the Turkeypen Ridge Trail at a crossroads junction with the Turkeypen Ridge Trail and a 245-yard connector that passes under Laurel Creek Road to intersect the Finley Cane Trail. When it leaves the junction, the Crib Gap Trail winds 190 yards through a creek bottom before crossing a small feeder stream and turning to follow the course of another stream. Soon, the trail leaves the second stream, its course becoming steeper, rockier, and a bit difficult to negotiate.

The trail climbs steadily through thinly forested second-growth farm fields occupied by occasional stone piles remaining from the efforts of settlers to clear the fields for tilling or for pasture land. About three-quarters of a mile above the trailhead, the Crib Gap Trail crosses over Laurel Creek Road. The crossing is at an angle, making it a little difficult to pick up the trail immediately on the opposite side.

From Laurel Creek Road, the trail starts up a low rise. At the apex of the rise and to the left about fifty yards up the slope, the ruins of a stone building are visible. All that remains intact is a single deftly constructed corner of dry-stacked rock. Judging from the building's footprint, the back was embedded into the hillside and the front rested on a low terrace. There is little that remains to suggest what purpose the building served. The terrain is too badly sloped for it to have been a farm out-building, and the distance from water would suggest that it was not a homeplace.

The trail descends the rise to a course low along Laurel Creek Road for about forty yards, then turns and proceeds into the back of a steep-sided hollow. A sharp switchback reverses the trail out of the hollow and onto a stiff climb along a narrow berm 300 yards to Crib Gap.

Crib Gap is the primary landmark on the watershed separating Cades Cove from the Tremont drainage. Rain falling on the west side of Crib Gap flows into Anthony Creek, then Abrams Creek, and then to the Little Tennessee River. Rain falling on the east side runs off first into Laurel Creek, then Little River before eventually finding its way into the Tennessee River.

The trail clears Crib Gap just above a cut in the mountain where Laurel Creek Road passes through the gap. As the trail descends, it leaves the dry-ridge pine stands and eases into a grove of hemlocks. A tributary of Anthony Creek is crossed before the trail clears another small rise and drops to a wide light-gravel track. A half-mile along the gravel track, the Crib Gap Trail terminates into the Anthony Creek Trail 380 yards above the Cades Cove Picnic Area.

✦ CADES COVE ✦

"Cades Cove is the dream of the Smoky Mountains." Thus the Reverend Isaac P. Martin, a Methodist circuit-riding preacher, summed up the account of his first visit to Cades Cove in 1890. Martin approached Cades Cove from the north on an old trace over Rich Mountain.

> My first glimpse of the Cove was through openings in the forest, but presently I came to a cliff from which I could see almost the entire cove which nestles there among the crest of the great mountains. I had never seen anything quite so beautiful. Thunderhead Mountain, standing 5530 feet, rose to the southeast, rising nearly 3000 feet above the level of Cade's Cove.
> On the shoulder of Thunderhead nestled Spense Field, forever attesting man's desire to dwell on the lofty heights. A little further away to the southwest was Gregory's Bald with its park-like trees and its meadows in the sunlight.

In the 120 years since Isaac Martin first visited Cades Cove, nothing has diminished the primacy of the cove's wilderness. Here, a community was born, grew, prospered, and died, yet the wilderness remains as the cove's most enduring and ever-present quality. The superlatives called forth by Isaac Martin on the occasion of his first visit are no less valid today than they were in 1890.

Cades Cove is a remarkably flat limestone basin four miles long and a mile wide, completely surrounded by high mountains. Thunderhead and the main Smoky divide define the cove's southern boundary and Rich Mountain the northern. The cove's east end is enclosed by Bote Mountain and its west by the enmeshment of Hatcher Mountain and Hannah Mountain.

The cove is drained by Abrams Creek, the largest stream in the Smokies whose course lies entirely within the park. Around the cove's perimeter, Cades Cove Loop Road traces a touring course that passes several restored artifacts of nineteenth-century Appalachian architecture. Of particular interest are the John Oliver Cabin, the oldest log building in the cove, and Cable Mill, a remainder from the cove's industrial past. The loop road passes log cabins, barns, farm fields, churches, and cemeteries that were an integral part of the thriving settlement that once inhabited this fertile bottomland.

All trails in the Cades Cove section lie outside the perimeter of Cades Cove Loop Road. Along the north side of the cove is a network of trails that visit Rich Mountain, the long ridge that separates Cades Cove from Dry Valley. These include the Rich Mountain Loop, Crooked Arm Ridge, Indian Grave Gap, and Rich Mountain trails. The first three of these form a loop suitable for a one-day hike.

Beyond the west end of the loop road is the largest concentration of trails, mostly low-elevation courses that explore the lower reaches of Abrams Creek and the northwest corner of the park. The Abrams Falls Trail is by far the most popular of the westernmost trails and features Abrams Falls, one of the most notable landmarks in the Smokies.

The Hannah Mountain, Gregory Ridge, and Gregory Bald trails proceed generally on southerly courses, the latter two climbing to the main Smoky divide. The Hannah Mountain and Gregory Ridge trails connect with the Gregory Bald Trail, which reaches the famed bald that is today as attractive as it was when Isaac Martin extolled it beauties.

From the east end of Cades Cove, the Anthony Creek Trail provides a primary access to Spence Field and on to Thunderhead while the Russell Field Trail climbs to the Appalachian Trail at Russell Field.

The Cades Coves section harbors thirteen backcountry campsites spaced over eleven of the eighteen trails in this section. As the result of a windstorm in 2001, the two camps on the Beard Cane Trail were severely damaged and currently are closed to camping. The Cades Cove section is also served by two campgrounds. Cades Cove Campground and Picnic Area anchor the east end of the loop road, and Abrams Creek Campground is found along the stream on the western boundary of the park.

The easiest access to the Cades Cove section is from the east, driving in from the Sugarlands Visitor Center on Little River Road or entering the park on Townsend Road. Little River Road and Townsend Road intersect Laurel Creek Road at the Townsend Wye. Cades Cove Loop Road begins seven miles west of the Townsend Wye at the end of Laurel Creek Road.

The entrance to Abrams Creek Campground offers an alternate access to the boundary trails in the northwest corner of the Cades Cove section. To reach the campground, drive from Walland, Tennessee, on the Foothills Parkway eighteen miles to US129. Turn left onto US129, proceed a hundred yards, and turn left on Happy Valley Road. Follow Happy Valley Road six miles to Happy Valley Loop Road, turn right, and proceed another mile to the Abrams Creek Ranger Station. The campground is another half-mile beyond the ranger station.

ANTHONY CREEK TRAIL

Cades Cove Picnic Area to the Bote Mountain Trail—3.6 miles.

POINT OF DEPARTURE: From the Townsend Wye, drive 7.0 miles to the end of Laurel Creek Road and turn left into the Cades Cove Picnic Area. The Anthony Creek Trail begins at the far end of the picnic area.

QUAD MAPS: Cades Cove 148-SE

Thunderhead Mountain 157-SW

0.0—Cades Cove Picnic Area.

0.2—Crib Gap Trail exits left 1.6 miles to the Turkeypen Ridge Trail.

0.3—Horse camp.

0.6—Anthony Creek. Bridge.

1.0—Anthony Creek. Footlog.

1.1—Anthony Creek. Bridge.

1.6—Left Prong of Anthony Creek. Footlog. Russell Field Trail exits right 3.5 miles to the Appalachian Trail at Russell Field.

2.0—Anthony Creek. Footlog.

2.9—Anthony Creek Backcountry Campsite (#9).

3.0—Switchback.

3.6—Bote Mountain Trail exits right 1.7 miles to Spence Field and left 5.2 miles to Laurel Creek Road.

The Anthony Creek Trail an archetypical Smoky Mountain path. Hard by a rushing stream, its course is steep and rocky, rising through a deep cove-hardwood forest that is home to a variety of wildlife. It is among the more popular trails in the Smokies as it affords one of the shortest routes to Spence Field and Thunderhead Mountain, two of the premier attractions in the western end of the park.

The Anthony Creek Trail begins at the upper end of the Cades Cove Picnic Area on a wide gravel jeep track that courses through a bottom flanking the stream for which the trail is named. The name apparently originated with John (Jackie) Anthony Jr., who settled on the stream a mile or so above the picnic area. Little is known of John Anthony Jr. except that when he arrived in Cades Cove he had either been indicted or convicted of some crime in North Carolina and was running from the law.

Three hundred and eighty yards above the picnic area, the trail intersects the Crib Gap Trail leading up from Big Spring Cove. A hundred and fifty yards farther, the trail proceeds through the middle of a horse camp and on into a bottomland shaded by stands of eastern hemlock. Five hundred and sixty yards beyond the horse camp, the trail crosses Anthony Creek on a wooden bridge, then crosses back after another 560 yards, this time on a footlog. Three hundred and fifty-five yards farther, it crosses again for the third time. The third crossing is on a wooden bridge.

After the third crossing, the grade steepens noticeably, and the track becomes a bit rockier as it eases out of the bottom and into more mountainous terrain. After a half-mile, the trail enters a galled gradient that harbors the confluence of Anthony Creek and the Left Prong of Anthony Creek. A footlog over the Left Prong leads ninety yards to the middle of the galled area and an intersection with the lower terminus of the Russell Field Trail. A few yards above the intersection, the Anthony Creek Trail returns to the shade of the cove hardwoods and onto a narrower course along the main stream.

When it leaves the intersection, the Anthony Creek Trail proceeds 700 yards to a footlog that marks the fifth and final stream crossing. From here, the grade begins alternating between moderate steepness and intervals of level ground as it charts a course higher up the slope and away from the stream. A little more than a mile above the final footlog, the trail crosses two feeder streams twenty yards apart. Three hundred and sixty yards farther, a short access path on the right exits to the Anthony Creek Backcountry Campsite (#9).

The Anthony Creek Camp is arranged on three distinct plats spaced along a sloped bench above the stream. The lower site is the largest and deftly enclosed by large fallen boles arranged around the perimeter of the camp. The middle camp is the second in size. It is less shaded, somewhat rougher, and with parameters a bit too poorly defined for the camp to retain any distinctive character. The upper site, though small, is concentrated around a fire ring nicely sheltered on one side by a large boulder and quaintly shaded by a few tall leggy rhododendrons. A food-storage cable is suspended in the upper camp and another between the middle and lower. Water is accessible below the bench in nearby Anthony Creek.

A hundred and forty yards above the campsite, the trail executes a switchback and leaves the stream drainage for a strenuous half-mile climb up the flank of Bote Mountain. From a few places along the way, contrasting pale greens of the farm fields in Cades Cove can be seen beyond the darker shades of the woodland ridges of the Anthony Creek watershed. When the Anthony Creek Trail reaches the main ridgeline of Bote Mountain, it terminates into the Bote Mountain Trail 1.7 miles below Spence Field.

RUSSELL FIELD TRAIL

Anthony Creek Trail to the Appalachian Trail at Russell Field—3.5 miles.
POINT OF DEPARTURE: Hike 1.6 miles up the Anthony Creek Trail. The Russell Field Trail begins on the right.
QUAD MAPS: Cades Cove 148-SE
Thunderhead Mountain 157-SW

0.0—Anthony Creek Trail.
0.2—Feeder stream.
0.7—Left Prong of Anthony Creek. Footlog.
0.8—Feeder stream.
0.9—Leadbetter Ridge Backcountry Campsite (#10).
1.8—Switchback.
3.4—Access path to spring.
3.5—Russell Field Shelter. Appalachian Trail.

Like many trails in the Smokies, the Russell Field Trail is pieced together from sections of rehabilitated manways connected by graded trail. An old dead-end settler's manway leading up the Left Prong of Anthony Creek was extended by the Park Service with a graded track that climbs to the spine of Leadbetter Ridge. Here, the graded extension was spliced into another manway that followed the ridgeline up and into Russell Field.

The Russell Field Trail begins along the Anthony Creek Trail a little more than a mile and a half above the Cades Cove Picnic Area in an open gradient that harbors the confluence of Anthony Creek and the Left Prong. The trail climbs immediately into a cove-hardwood association of northern red oak, yellow buckeye, sugar maple, yellow poplar, Fraser magnolia, and eastern hemlock, then proceeds along the Left Prong 435 yards to cross a nameless feeder stream. Above the stream crossing, rhododendron thickets enter the understory while hemlocks become the prevalent tree species.

A half-mile above the feeder stream, the trail crosses the Left Prong on a footlog. Two hundred and fifteen yards farther, it executes a difficult rock-hop across a large tributary of the Left Prong, then eighty yards farther, rises up alongside the Leadbetter Ridge Backcountry Campsite (#10).

The Leadbetter Camp is divided into an upper and a lower site, neither of which is particularly level and both beset with surface roots. The upper site is the nicer, with a couple of suitable plats that are discretely secluded from the trail and the lower camp by a thick hedge of rhododendron. The lower site is larger, a bit rougher, and pitched more steeply, but is tucked in nicely among a copse of large hemlocks. A food-storage cable is suspended in the lower camp, and water is readily available at the stream crossing.

When it leaves the campsite, the trail becomes a bit steeper as it pushes into one of the few remaining old growth stands in the Cades Coves section of the Smokies. Most noticeable are the large hemlocks and northern red oaks. Four hundred and sixty yards above the campsite, the trail executes a switchback away from the stream and begins ascending the steep flank of Leadbetter Ridge. Here, the forest cover begins to grade from the hardwood mix to an exposed dry-ridge association of maples, oaks, Table Mountain pine, and mountain laurel shading a ground cover of galax. The climb continues for over a half-mile until reaching the spine of Leadbetter Ridge, where the trail turns sharply left and levels out for an easy course over a soft track along the ridgeline. Occasional breaks in the dry-ridge cover afford views north into Cades Cove and across to Rich Mountain (3,686 feet), and south to Thunderhead (5,527 feet) on the state-line divide. After a half-mile along the ridgeline, the trail returns to climbing, continuing for another mile before entering the lower northwest corner of Russell Field.

Prior to the coming of the park, Russell Field was a rolling expanse of several hundred acres situated on a wide spur that extends obliquely from the main Smoky divide at McCampbell Knob to Pole Knob, a high point which punctuates the end of the spur. The field was partially cleared by John Russell, a Cades Cove resident for whom the bald was named. For many years, herders and their families lived on Russell Field, building cabins and barns, tending gardens, and herding cattle that fed on the rich mountain grass that grew there. With the cessation of grazing on the Smoky Mountain balds, Allegheny serviceberries, yellow birches, American beeches, rhododendron, and mountain laurel have encroached on the perimeter, reducing Russell Field to a fraction of its original size.

The trail curls up onto the crest of the field where it is still a partially cleared grassy turf, then turns down for a long drop into a dell harboring the messy headwaters of Russell Field Branch. The trail approaches the stream but does not cross, circling around and above the stream's headwater to an access path that leads fifty yards down to a spring. A steep 210-yard climb above the spring, leads to the Russell Field Shelter where the trail terminates immediately into the Appalachian Trail. The spring at the head of Russell Field Branch is the closest source of water to the shelter.

RICH MOUNTAIN LOOP TRAIL

Cades Cove Loop Road to the Indian Grave Gap Trail—3.3 miles.

POINT OF DEPARTURE: From the Townsend Wye, drive 7.0 miles to the end of Laurel Creek Road and the entrance to Cades Cove Loop Road. The Rich Mountain Loop Trail begins on the right just past the entrance to Cades Cove Loop Road.

QUAD MAPS: Cades Cove 148-SE
Kinzel Springs 148-NE

0.0—Cades Cove Loop Road.
0.4—Crooked Arm Branch.
0.5—Crooked Arm Ridge Trail exits right 2.2 miles to the Indian Grave Gap Trail and Scott Mountain Trail.
1.0—Harrison Branch.
1.4—Access path exits left to the John Oliver Cabin.
1.7—Marthas Branch.
3.0—Switchback. Overlook.
3.3—Indian Grave Gap Trail exits left 1.1 miles to Rich Mountain Road and right 2.6 miles to the Crooked Arm Ridge Trail and Scott Mountain Trail.

The Rich Mountain Loop Trail is not a loop in the true sense of the word; nevertheless it is considered the primary leg of an eight-mile circuit that incorporates the Crooked Arm Ridge Trail and part of the Indian Grave Gap Trail to complete a return journey from Cades Cove to the top of Rich Mountain and back.

The Rich Mountain Loop Trail begins on the right a few feet beyond the entrance to the eleven-mile Cades Cove Loop Road. Initially the trail proceeds on a course parallel to the road but quickly begins gaining some separation. About 300 yards beyond the trailhead, the course veers to the right onto an old farm road through woodlands just outside the perimeter of a cleared farm field.

Within a half-mile of leaving Cades Cove Loop Road, the trail reaches a wide crossing of Crooked Arm Branch and, thirty yards farther, intersects the lower terminus of the Crooked Arm Ridge Trail leading up to the east end of Rich Mountain. The grade remains easy as the trail circles through low sparse woodlands that share more affinity with the flat expanse of the cove than the rugged terrain of Rich Mountain. Thirty yards beyond the Crooked Arm Ridge junction, the trail crosses a feeder stream, and then 500 yards farther, crosses another feeder. After another 440 yards, Harrison Branch is crossed. Although the slopes between these streams receive ample sunlight and moisture, they are remarkably free of undergrowth and wildflowers. This may be explained in part by the presence of Japanese grass, an invasive ground-cover that was introduced to the cove in the 1960s and tends to crowd out native wildflowers. Five hundred and ninety yards beyond the Harrison Branch crossing, the Rich Mountain Loop Trail emerges from the woods and makes a tangent pass of a clearing that harbors the John Oliver Cabin.

 According to long-standing tradition, John Oliver, his wife, Lucretia, and daughter, Polly, were the first permanent white settlers in Cades Cove, arriving in 1818, one year prior to the Calhoun Treaty which ceded these mountains away from the Cherokee. The Olivers most likely came to Cades Cove in the early fall, entering from nearby Tuckaleechee Cove on an old Indian trace through Rich Gap. They spent their first night in an abandoned Indian hut, then moved to the upper end of the cove and built a crude cabin under the lee of Rich Mountain. A pile of stones resting twenty yards north of the present cabin is thought to be the chimney of this first dwelling. The Olivers lived here through the winter, surviving on dried pumpkins set out by a benevolent Cherokee.

The next summer, Oliver dug a sixty-four-foot well and walled it up with smooth glen stones gathered from the fields. Sometime in the early 1820s he replaced the crude first shelter with the cabin that now stands in the clearing. Oliver later added a log barn with two pens and a thrashing floor. The Olivers grazed their cattle in summer on the rich grass along Abrams Creek, then drove them into the canebrakes at the lower end of the cove to forage and find protection during the winter.

Exiting along the lower side of the cabin yard is an access path used by visitors walking in from the nearby Cades Cove Loop Road.

When it passes the cabin, the Rich Mountain Loop Trail turns right and begins climbing the face of Rich Mountain along Marthas Branch, a stream named for John and Lucretia Oliver's second child. About 500 yards upstream, the trail reaches a chimney ruin on the right that serviced a cabin likely built sometime prior to the Civil War. Within 150 yards of the chimney ruin, the trail negotiates the first of four crossings of Marthas Branch. Each of the crossings is easy, and all occur within an interval of about a half-mile. Here, the grade becomes markedly steeper, the course rocky, and, in several places, wet from seepages. When it leaves Martha Branch, the trail turns west and follows a narrow berm for nearly three-quarters of a mile until reaching a switchback on the spine of Cave Ridge. The ridge is named for its proximity to Gregory Cave, which lies in Cades Cove at the foot of the ridge.

The switchback on Cave Ridge affords the only good vantage point on the Rich Mountain Loop Trail. Below is the long expanse of Cades Cove appearing as a contrasting patchwork of fields. Three thousand feet above the floor of the cove, the western end of the main Smoky divide is visible from Gregory Bald (4,949 feet) to Thunderhead (5,527 feet), to Silers Bald (5,607 feet), and on to the ragged western shoulder of Mount Buckley (6,575 feet), and then to Clingmans Dome (6,643 feet).

During the geological upheavals that formed the Great Smoky Mountains, older layers of rock were thrust up and over the newer. Here, the overthrust was left at such an angle that the hanging wall was worn through by rain and wind, exposing the underlying formation, a limestone substrate that forms the floor of Cades Cove. Because limestone readily percolates rainwater and is resistant to erosion, the soil in Cades Cove retains its fertility, yielding a very rich flora.

While standing on Rich Mountain and looking down into Cades Cove, Supreme Court Justice William Douglas once asked a local mountaineer, "Why is this Rich Mountain? Was there a settler by that name?"

"Because hit's rich," he answered.

The mountaineer explained his response by pointing out that the mountain and the cove contained lots of limestone. "They burn it to get lime. And sometimes they put a bit of lime in every hill of corn for fertilizer."

Cades Cove is part of a territory once ruled by Old Abram of Chilhowee, a famous warrior chief who led the Cherokee against the Watauga settlement. Tradition holds that the cove was named for Old Abram's wife, Kate. A later and perhaps more reliable tradition claims that Cades Cove is named for Chief Kade, a lessor-known successor to Old Abram.

From the switchback, the trail turns and climbs steeply along the spine of Cave Ridge through stands of oak, pine, and mountain laurel 650 yards to terminate into the Indian Grave Gap Trail in an inconspicuous junction near the western end of Rich Mountain.

CROOKED ARM RIDGE TRAIL

Rich Mountain Loop Trail to the Indian Grave Gap Trail and Scott Mountain Trail—2.2 miles.

POINT OF DEPARTURE: Hike 0.5 mile up the Rich Mountain Loop Trail. The Crooked Arm Ridge Trail begins on the right.

QUAD MAPS: Cades Cove 148-SE

Kinzel Springs 148-NE

0.0—Rich Mountain Loop Trail.

0.2—Crooked Arm Falls.

0.4—Crooked Arm Branch.

1.2—Switchback. Overlook.

1.9—Switchback. Overlook.

2.0—Trail split.

2.2—Indian Grave Gap Trail exits left 3.7 miles to Rich Mountain Road. Scott Mountain Trail exits right 3.6 miles to the Schoolhouse Gap Trail.

The Crooked Arm Ridge Trail is part of a frequently used loop that begins along Cades Cove Loop Road and follows in succession the Rich Mountain Loop Trail, the Crooked Arm Ridge Trail, and the Indian Grave Gap Trail before returning to Cades Cove Loop Road by the Rich Mountain Loop Trail.

The Crooked Arm Ridge Trail begins a half-mile up the Rich Mountain Loop Trail and climbs quickly to a streamside course along Crooked Arm Branch. About 400 yards upstream, Crooked Arm Falls slides with little perturbation twenty-five feet down a bare face of rock. A thin layer of humus accumulated on the immediate sides of the waterfall is an indicator that the stream rarely flows profusely.

The trail continues up the hollow, passing 250 yards through stands of eastern hemlock before crossing Crooked Arm Branch and entering into a steep climb up the flank of Crooked Arm Ridge. Switchbacks mitigate the steepness, nevertheless the climb remains strenuous. When the trail reaches the ridgeline, the grade moderates momentarily, and the hemlocks give way to a mix of hardwoods, noticeably oaks, maples, and hickories.

The switchbacks afford opportunities for scenic viewing into Cades Cove. At one of the better views, a mile above the waterfall, the eastern end of the cove can be seen as far as Cades Cove Campground. From another switchback three-quarters of a mile up-trail, the mid-section of the cove is clearly visible where Sparks Lane crosses through old farm fields.

Three hundred and twenty-five yards above the last overlook, the trail splits. The right fork climbs to a low knoll while that to the left maintains a lower course. The two forks reconnect eighty yards beyond at the foot of the knoll. The Sierra Club *Hiker's Guide to the Smokies* notes that there was once a backcountry campsite on Crooked Arm Ridge. The probable location was on the knoll. The site appears suitable for a small camp, but lack of proximity to water likely led to its demise.

After the trail rejoins itself, it continues another eighty yards to terminate in a three-way intersection with the eastern end of the Indian Grave Gap Trail and the western end of the Scott Mountain Trail. Both trails exit out along the park boundary. The Indian Grave Gap Trail follows the crest of Rich Mountain 3.7 miles to Rich Mountain Road. The Scott Mountain Trail proceeds east 3.6 miles to Schoolhouse Gap. A hundred and eighty yards down along the Scott Mountain Trail is the Turkeypen Ridge Backcountry Campsite (#8).

INDIAN GRAVE GAP TRAIL

Rich Mountain Road to the Crooked Arm Ridge Trail and Scott Mountain
Trail—3.7 miles.

POINT OF DEPARTURE: Follow directions to the Rich Mountain Loop Trail,
and then drive along Cades Cove Loop Road to the Cades Cove Missionary
Baptist Church. At the church, turn right and proceed 2.2 miles up Rich
Mountain Road, a one-way gravel track that exits into Dry Valley through
Rich Gap. The Indian Grave Gap Trail begins on the right side of the road.

QUAD MAPS: Cades Cove 148-SE
Kinzel Springs 148-NE

0.0—Rich Mountain Road.

0.6—Indian Grave Gap.

1.1—Rich Mountain Loop Trail exits right 3.3 miles to Cades Cove Loop
Road.

1.9—Rich Mountain Trail exits left 2.3 miles to Rich Mountain Road at Rich
Mountain Gap on the park boundary.

2.1—Access path exits left to the summit of Cerulean Knob.

2.3—Alternate access to Cerulean Knob.

2.5—Overlook.

3.7—Crooked Arm Ridge Trail exits right 2.2 miles to the Rich Mountain
Loop Trail. Scott Mountain Trail exits left 3.6 miles to the Schoolhouse Gap
Trail.

The Indian Grave Gap Trail begins 2.2 miles up Rich Mountain Road, a one-way gravel track that leaves Cades Cove Loop Road at the Cades Cove Missionary Baptist Church and exits the park at Rich Mountain Gap. The trailhead can be difficult to notice as it angles back from the road.

The trail starts out as an old jeep track, wide but a bit rough and rutted. It begins climbing immediately and soon emerges from the forest cover and into a fire-scald where burned-over pine and oak stands afford some long views down the length of Cades Cove. After a little more than a half-mile, the trail rises into Indian Grave Gap, where the jeep track appears to end. Slightly to the left, the trace of an old roadbed can be seen leading out of the gap and down the mountain. The roadbed marks the course of the original Rich Mountain Road, which was cut by the earliest white settlers in Cades Cove. The settlers' trace followed the course of an earlier Indian trail.

 Though the Cherokee apparently did not make it a practice to bury their dead in Cades Cove, there is evidence of stone burial mounds along the ridge immediately west of Indian Grave Gap. A traveler to Cades Cove in the late nineteenth century recorded seeing an Indian grave at the top of the mountain along the old Rich Mountain Road. He described it as "a huge pile of stones marking the resting place of perhaps one of the first owners of this fair vale." The stone mounds may have been a well-known landmark in the early history of the cove and likely the origin for the name Indian Grave Gap.

A half-mile beyond Indian Grave Gap, the trail reaches the upper terminus of the Rich Mountain Loop Trail leading up on the right from Cades Cove Loop Road. From here, the Indian Grave Gap Trail makes a short climb to a ridgeline, where it remains for much of the way until intersecting the upper terminus of the Rich Mountain Trail leading up on the left from the park boundary at Rich Mountain Gap. Visible from the intersection is the Rich Mountain Backcountry Campsite (#5), 110 yards down the Rich Mountain Trail. The interval between the junction with the Rich Mountain Loop Trail and that of the Rich Mountain Trail is about three-quarters of a mile.

When the Indian Grave Gap Trail intersects the Rich Mountain Trail, the grade moderates noticeably. For the next 400 yards, the trail remains just below the ridgeline as it approaches Cerulean Knob (3,686 feet), the highest point on Rich Mountain. The trail passes below the summit; however, an access path exits on the left leading about a hundred yards to the top of the knob which was once occupied by the Rich Mountain fire tower. A space of level ground on the left side of the access path marks the former site of a warden's cabin. All that remains is a stone cistern about eighteen inches deep and thirty-six inches in diameter and built flush with the ground. The cistern was likely the only water supply for the cabin.

The summit of Cerulean Knob is flat and sports a thin turf of short grass. On one side are concrete stanchions that once supported the frame metal fire tower. There are no views from the knob, but it is an excellent place to stop for a lunch break. An over-grown path exits the east side of the knob and returns to the Indian Grave Gap Trail.

Beyond Cerulean Knob, the trail edges momentarily onto the Rich Mountain ridgeline, where openings in the forest cover permit superb views down into Dry Valley and up the length of Tuckaleechee Cove. In the intermediate distance is the Chilhowee range. On a clear day Fort Loudoun Lake and the city of Knoxville can be seen in the distance with the Cumberland Mountains being discernible where the blue of the sky meets the blue of the horizon.

From here, the trail remains on a fairly level course following a well-maintained track along the park boundary out to the eastern end of Rich Mountain. Where the trail coincides with the ridgeline there are occasional views into Dry Valley and Tuckaleechee Cove and a few obscured glimpses into Cades Cove. About a mile below Cerulean Knob, a manway intervenes, leading out along the boundary; otherwise the course remains uniform and uneventful until passing through a clearing beneath a power line and then dropping quickly to terminate in a three-way intersection with the upper end of the Crooked Arm Ridge Trail and the west end of the Scott Mountain Trail.

The Scott Mountain Trail exits on the left and leads 180 yards to the Turkeypen Ridge Backcountry Campsite (#6) and then continues almost four miles to Schoolhouse Gap. The Crooked Arm Ridge Trail exits on the right to the Rich Mountain Loop Trail.

RICH MOUNTAIN TRAIL

Rich Mountain Road at Rich Mountain Gap to the Indian Grave Gap
   Trail—2.3 miles.
POINT OF DEPARTURE: Follow directions to the Indian Grave Gap Trail, but
   continue on Rich Mountain Road to the park boundary at Rich Mountain
   Gap. The Rich Mountain Trail begins on the right about a hundred yards
   back down the road.
QUAD MAPS: Cades Cove 148-SE
Kinzel Springs 148-NE

0.0—Rich Mountain Gap. Rich Mountain Road.
0.2—Switchback.
0.3—Sinkhole.
1.2—Overlook.
1.9—Headwaters of Hesse Creek.
2.3—Rich Mountain Backcountry Campsite (#5).
2.3—Indian Grave Gap Trail exits right 1.9 miles to Rich Mountain Road and
   left 0.2 mile to Cerulean Knob.

The lower terminus of the Rich Mountain Trail lies along Rich Mountain Road about a hundred yards inside the park boundary at Rich Mountain Gap. There are two options for reaching the trailhead. From within the park, follow Cades Cove Loop Road three miles to Rich Mountain Road, a one-way gravel track that exits to the right near the Missionary Baptist Church. However, Rich Mountain Road is closed in winter, and Cades Cove Loop Road is closed Wednesday and Saturday mornings from May through September. From outside the park, Rich Mountain Gap can be approached from US321 in Kinzel Springs. Turn right off US321 onto Old Tuckaleechee Road, and follow it to the Tuckaleechee Cove Methodist Church at Old Cades Cove Road. Turn right on Old Cades Cove Road, and follow it into the park at Rich Mountain Gap.

The Rich Mountain Trail is a steep course which climbs from Rich Mountain Gap to the crest of Rich Mountain near Cerulean Knob. When it leaves the gap, the trail winds a short distance through old fields before picking up the trace of a road-bed that ascends the adjacent ridge. The roadbed is part of an earlier Rich Mountain Road that was built in the 1820s by the first white settlers into Cades Cove. The road allegedly followed an earlier Indian trace. Other parts of the older road can be seen rising into Indian Grave Gap on the Indian Grave Gap Trail.

A quarter-mile above Rich Mountain Gap, the trail reaches the ridgeline, where it turns left at a switchback and leaves the roadbed. Sixty-five yards beyond the switchback, the trail passes a deep sinkhole, a geological formation similar to the much larger Bull Cave just off the Ace Gap Trail near Rich Mountain Gap.

A half-mile above the switchback, openings in the forest cover permit glimpses out over the western end of the park, particularly the ridges of Beard Cane and Hatcher Mountains. Within the next half-mile the trail climbs to the park boundary and an overlook that affords a superb view into Dry Valley and down along the length of Tuckaleechee Cove. Hikers from the Smoky Mountains Hiking Club in 1930 claimed to be able to see from this point across Cove Mountain to Mount Le Conte. To do so, the line of sight would have had to adhere just to the north side of Cerulean Knob, the prominent peak on Rich Mountain.

After continuing to climb for another three-quarters of a mile, the trail enters a short hollow and proceeds alongside the headwaters of Hesse Creek. Hesse Creek at this elevation is a slow-moving course resembling more the proverbial babbling brook than a vigorously dashing mountain stream. The stream is submerged in a swampy confusion of rhododendron, yet sports a ten-foot waterfall that can be attractive when there is sufficient rainfall. The trail adheres closely to the stream as it proceeds up the draw. It then crosses over the stream and adjacent slope, then circles into another draw that harbors the Rich Mountain Backcountry Campsite (#5). The distance from the crossing at Hesse Creek to the campsite is 540 yards.

The Rich Mountain Camp was once occupied by a shelter built by the Youth Conservation Corps in 1972. The shelter was dismantled a few years ago and replaced by the backcountry camp. The camp is situated in a shallow draw between the two peaks of Double Mountain. The adjacent slopes are open and gently sloped, making the camp an attractive site. The draw is slightly pitched and rather bowl-shaped; thus there is not an abundance of nice level plats for tents. A food-storage cable is suspended across the draw below the camp. Water is plentiful from Hesse Creek and can be reached either by walking down the draw or back down the trail to the stream crossing.

One hundred yards above the campsite, the Rich Mountain Trail reaches a ridge-line at the top of the draw to terminate into the Indian Grave Gap Trail. A left turn onto the Indian Grave Gap Trail leads 425 yards to an access path that climbs to the old Rich Mountain fire tower site on the summit of Cerulean Knob. The Indian Grave Gap Trail continues on to the Crooked Arm Ridge Trail which descends to the Rich Mountain Loop Trail which, in turn, climbs around and back to the Indian Grave Gap Trail, thus making a nice loop. A right turn on the Indian Grave Gap Trail leads two miles to Rich Mountain Road, which can be hiked back to the trailhead at Rich Mountain Gap.

ACE GAP TRAIL

Rich Mountain Road to the Beard Cane Trail at Blair Gap—5.5 miles.

POINT OF DEPARTURE: Follow directions to the Indian Grave Gap Trail, but continue on Rich Mountain Road to the park boundary at Rich Mountain Gap. The Ace Gap Trail begins on the left side of the gap.

QUAD MAP: Kinzel Springs 148-NE

0.0—Rich Mountain Gap. Rich Mountain Road. Access path exits left 200 yards to Bull Cave.

2.3—Kelly Gap.

4.6—Ace Gap.

5.5—Blair Gap. Beard Cane Trail exits left 4.2 miles to the Cooper Road Trail. Manway exits straight to Cane Creek in Miller Cove.

Long before the incursion of white settlers into the western end of the Great Smoky Mountains, the Cherokee had established a trail through Rich Mountain Gap that afforded sure passage between Tuckaleechee and Cades Cove. The first settlers into Cades Cove came by way of Rich Mountain Gap, following the old

Indian trace that descended into the cove near the site of the present Missionary Baptist Church. Records indicate that the cove settlers returned regularly to Tuckaleechee, usually to trade at George Snider's store for items they could not make themselves. Within a few years, the cove farmers were driving cattle over this same Indian trace through Rich Mountain Gap to be sold at the markets in Maryville.

According to Smoky Mountain legend, a bull once got separated from the herd during a cattle drive over the mountain, straying just as he reached the crossing at Rich Mountain Gap. The bull wandered a few hundred yards off the gap on the Cades Cove side of the mountain, fell into a deep sinkhole, and soon perished. The sinkhole at Rich Mountain Gap has since been known as Bull Cave.

An access path to Bull Cave exits on the west side of Rich Mountain Gap following a narrow etching in the turf that leads 200 yards down the mountain to the sinkhole. Halfway along, a smaller sinkhole lies to the left. The last few yards of the descent to Bull Cave are exceedingly steep. Down and to the left of the path, a gaping hole of enormous proportions appears, ominous, even somewhat frightening. The terrain on all sides is nearly vertical, converging to a single vortex as though compelled by some unseen force of the sinkhole itself. A small stream seeps from a crevice in the mountain wall and, having no outlet except the sinkhole, drops into the maw of Bull Cave. Direct sunlight rarely reaches the bottom of the gulf, leaving the sinkhole in a perpetual funereal gloom.

Explorers have determined that Bull Cave is well over 7,000 feet long and reaches a depth of 741 feet, making it the second-deepest known cave in the eastern United States. The terrain immediately around the cave is exceedingly treacherous, sloping very steeply to a fifty-foot drop into the sink. Entrance into Bull Cave is strictly forbidden without direct permission from the Park Service.

The Ace Gap Trail begins in Rich Mountain Gap immediately adjacent to the access path to Bull Cave. Rich Mountain Gap is the lowest point along the range and straddles the park's northern boundary. When it leaves the gap, the trail moves away from the boundary and begins following the contours of Rich Mountain on such course as to remain at the same general elevation. The trail circles around the rim of the depression that harbors Bull Cave on a path that is exceedingly rocky and rough for the first hundred yards or so, but soon evens out into a hard-packed dirt track. With few exceptions, the trail surface remains uniformly hard and even, occasionally softened by pine needles or the detritus of deciduous leaves. The grade remains easy, the trail gaining and losing little elevation and continuously alternating between a dry-ridge pine association and cove-hardwood stands.

The Ace Gap Trail was built primarily as a utility connector between Rich Mountain Road and the northwest corner of the park, and thus it is fairly scarce of outstanding landmarks and scenic views. However, in wintertime, the trail affords some fine views down onto nearby Cades Cove Mountain and across the cove to the higher peaks along the main Smoky divide. Most opportunities for views will occur within the two miles between the point of leaving Rich Mountain Gap and where the trail returns to the park boundary at Kelly Gap.

Kelly Gap is a narrow swag once occupied by the Kelly Gap Backcountry Campsite. The gap is a remarkably level plat extending to the left of the trail and configured into something of a maze by boles of several large, fallen, hemlock trees. The fallen trees parceled the camp nicely into a patchwork of individual tent sites, although the camp is situated in a low place that is prone to collecting run-off from rain storms. The source of water for the campsite was from a weak stream at the very back of the gap.

In two places within the next mile, the Ace Gap Trail has been re-routed from where it once strayed beyond the boundary and out of the park.

The single instance that resulted in the length of the trail being shortened was occasioned by a boundary dispute initiated by a former governor of Tennessee, Don Sunquist, who had purchased property adjacent to the trail and contiguous with the Park boundary. Boundary disputes have long been a staple of Smoky Mountain history. The first land claims in nearby Cades Cove were strictly illegal as the Indian treaties in force at that time clearly indicated that all land in the cove was outside of the U.S. territories and belonged to the Cherokee. By the middle of the nineteenth century, Cades Cove had become thoroughly settled, resulting in a veritable patchwork of overlapping property claims. Most often, boundary disputes were engendered by the failure of settlers to register their claims with the government or by the consequences of imprecise surveys accompanying those deeds that were registered.

A little more than a mile beyond Kelly Gap, the trail drops into Ace Gap, a shallow dip distinguished by an old railroad cut angled acutely across the trail. A rail line leading up Davis Branch from just west of Kinzel Springs crossed over the mountain at Ace Gap and descended into the Hesse Creek basin at the foot of Hurricane Mountain. Sometime in the first decade of the twentieth century the Little River Lumber Company had developed plans for logging Hesse Creek and its tributaries, Beard Cane Creek and Cane Creek, but landowners in Miller Cove and the lower reaches of Hesse Creek opposed to the lumbering operations refused either to sell the land or to negotiate a right-of-way for a rail line, thus denying the lumber company easy access to the timber. Rather than contest the issue, the Little River Lumber Company opted to incur the expense of transporting the logs up and over Hurricane Mountain through Ace Gap. The company maintained a small shelter at the gap in which loggers would gather to play cards, thus suggesting the name Ace Gap.

On the left a few yards above the gap, a rough clearing marks the site of the former Ace Gap Backcountry Campsite. The Ace Gap site was always one of the poorest camps in the park, situated on an extremely unattractive, badly galled, steeply pitched gradient. The only convenient source of water was from a weak unreliable stream down the slope in back of the campsite. This camp, like that at Kelly Gap, was abandoned around the turn of the twentieth-first century.

When it leaves Ace Gap, the trail completes a gentle climb along the crest of Hurricane Mountain before beginning a half-mile descent to its terminus at Blair Gap. Here, it enters a three-way intersection with the Beard Cane Trail rising in sharply on the left and a manway entering from the opposite side of the gap. The Beard Cane Trail leads 4.2 miles south to a crossroads junction with the Cooper Road Trail and Hatcher Mountain Trail. The manway follows the crest of Hurricane Mountain to intersect an extension of the Cane Creek Trail that lies outside the park boundary.

GREGORY RIDGE TRAIL

Forge Creek Road to the Gregory Bald Trail at Rich Gap—5.0 miles.

POINT OF DEPARTURE: Drive 5.4 miles on the one-way Cades Cove Loop Road to the entrance to the Cable Mill parking area. Continue straight 2.2 miles on the gravel Forge Creek Road to the turnaround at the end. The Gregory Ridge Trail begins at the end of the turnaround.

QUAD MAP: Cades Cove 148-SE

0.0—Forge Creek Road turnaround.
0.3—Forge Creek. Footlog.
1.4—Big Poplar stump.
1.8—Forge Creek. Footlog.
1.9—Forge Creek. Footlog.
2.0—Forge Creek Backcountry Campsite (#12).
2.9—Whale Rock.
5.0—Rich Gap. Gregory Bald Trail exits right 0.7 mile to Gregory Bald and left 2.1 miles to the Appalachian Trail.

The most popular route for hikers visiting Gregory Bald is the Gregory Ridge Trail. Technically, this trail does not reach Gregory Bald, but terminates into the Gregory Bald Trail about three-quarters of a mile below the bald. For all practical purposes, however, the Gregory Ridge Trail is the most convenient option for accessing Gregory Bald.

Access to the Gregory Ridge Trail is from a turnaround at the end of Forge Creek Road that exits from Cades Cove Loop Road near the Cades Cove Visitor Center.

Forge Creek Road was first established sometime in the early 1830s when Daniel D. Foute, the proprietor of the Montvale Springs resort hotel, was granted a charter to build a four-foot-wide horse trail from his hotel, through the Chilhowees to Cades Cove and then along the old Indian trail up Ekaneetlee Branch to the stateline divide. A few years later Foute had sections of the horse trail improved and widened to accommodate wagon traffic. Part of the improved section followed the course of the current Forge Creek Road and passed through an area then known as Chestnut Flats.

An early settler in Chestnut Flats was George W. Powell, a moonshine distiller who grew splendid orchards on the hilly terrain around the flats. Moonshining soon brought Powell into conflict with the law, and his notoriety for lawlessness spread as swiftly as his reputation for making brandy. An article in a local newspaper, *The Maryville Index*, illustrates Powell's decline into lawlessness:

> Deputy Elias Cooper on a recent raid in Chestnut Flats, Blount County, a few days since, accompanied by eight men, visited the isolated rum mill of George Powell where they seized 11 tubs of beer and mash, 4 tubs of pomice, 130 gallons of brandy singlings, 5 bushels of meal, 2 bushels of rye, 2 bushels of malt. The revenue squad also arrested Powell, the engineer of the mash mill, who subsequently escaped while the men and women of the household were abusing and threatening the officers. The captured property was destroyed. The officers, who immediately started for the city on foot, while passing an unfrequented place in the mountains, the squad was fired upon by parties in ambush—and a lively fusillade ensued. About 40 shots were fired by their assailants, the revenue squad returned the fire, but with what effect they were unable to ascertain. The attacking party remained in ambush. None of the revenue officers were wounded, though a bullet found its way through the clothing of Bennet Ledbetter with the revenue raiders.

Records uncovered by historian Durwood Dunn suggest that Powell's illicit business was but a single clue to the social circumstances of Chestnut Flats. Dunn explains that "in time Chestnut Flat became the scene of innumerable drunken brawls. Not infrequently men were murdered in the course of these inebriated disputes over cards, cock-fighting, shooting matches, or prostitutes. Sober cove residents shuddered to think that their own sons, husbands, or brothers might be attracted to these forbidden pleasures. But in such an atmosphere of lawlessness, criminals from other parts of Tennessee and North Carolina were the ones primarily drawn into the flats."

Chestnut Flats attracted outlaws of all descriptions who drank, gambled, whored, and shot each other. In time, these inhabitants of the Chestnut Flats became intermarried. But family relations and sharing the common profession of illicit distilling did not prevent the inhabitants from killing each other. An article from *The Maryville Times* states,

On September 26, John Harvey Burchfield was killed at his home in the mountains near George Powell's. Theodore Rose and Will Burchfield, son of Sam, of the Flats, went to Harvey B's home and raised a quarrel over some old grudge when Rose pulled a revolver and shot once. Harvey then took Rose's pistol away from him, but Will B. who was standing near gave Rose his revolver with which he finished the job. Dr.s Blankenship and Martin of this place reached there the next evening and found Burchfield shot in three places, once through the upper part of the lung, a little below the heart, and in his right arm, with a 38 caliber revolver. He died the next morning at 1 o'clock. A wife and three small children are left in destitute circumstances without any means of support. Both Rose and Will Burchfield had been drinking and were quarrelsome when they arrived at the home of Harvey Burchfield.

But, as Dunn points out, the mountaineer men were not the only social renegades: "Among the flats women, sexual promiscuity became rampant. Prostitution flourished as the flats became the red-light district for a much larger region. Unmarried women had numerous children, often each by a different father. One woman reportedly had three men killed over her. Occasionally liaisons lasted several years, but marriages were infrequent."

Forge Creek Road terminates near the upper end of Chestnut Flats in a turnaround at what was later the Willie Myer place. Willie and his wife operated a lodge here which catered to hikers stopping over on their way to Gregory Bald. During a visit to Cades Cove in 1937, Eleanor Roosevelt enjoyed lunch at the Myers' lodge before hiking to see the famed Big Poplar on Forge Creek.

The Gregory Ridge Trail begins along the upper edge of a turnaround that marks the end of Forge Creek Road. The trail rises quickly on a wide track amply cushioned with the needles of white pines and eastern hemlocks. Below, Forge Creek courses through a bottomland that still shows evidence of having once been farmed. After a quarter-mile, the trail drops to the bottomland and then passes through an abandoned farm field to cross a footlog over the stream just above the mouth of Bower Creek. According to the Sierra Club *Hiker's Guide to the Smokies,* inhabitants of Cades Cove considered the mouth of Bower Creek to mark the point of origin of Forge Creek. Above this point Forge Creek was then known as Marion Creek, named for Marion Burchfield, who lived in a cove farther up the mountain.

Noticeable on the right about 200 yards above the stream crossing is a scar indicating the course of a road that once led up Bower Creek into Tiptons Sugar Cove and then along the spine of Gregory Ridge. Before the advent of the park, the old road up Gregory Ridge was frequently used by hikers going to Gregory Bald and was then known as the Fork Ridge Trail. The upper part of the Fork Ridge Trail was later incorporated into the current Gregory Ridge Trail.

A half-mile above the stream crossing, the trail leaves the last of the old farm fields and enters a hollow whose bottom is congested with great masses of rhododendron from which large trees rise up as though protruding through blankets of ground-level fog. Virgin stands of yellow poplar, hemlock, white oak, white basswood, Fraser magnolia, Carolina silverbell, and northern red oak compose a stateliness that Harvey Broome compared to "the hushed containment of a cathedral but also a feeling of openness and expansiveness which no cathedral ever had. There was both closure and space under those enormous leafy domes supported by columns of living trees."

As the trail climbs, it moves into a slightly cooler environment of a grove of exceptionally large hemlocks.

Along here are the basal remains of the Big Poplar visited by Eleanor Roosevelt in 1937. Because of its size, the Big Poplar was a destination point for hiking parties until late into the twentieth century. In 1948 Harvey Broome noticed that the duff around the Big Poplar had been pulverized by visitors who stood around it for photographs. The duff had washed away, leaving only compacted mineral soil on its upper side. Broome wondered then how long the great tree could survive such treatment. The Big Poplar did not live much longer afterward.

Many of the earliest white settlers entering Cades Cove from the east did so by way of an ancient Cherokee trace crossing over the main Smoky divide through Ekaneetlee Gap and then descending along Ekaneetlee Branch to Forge Creek and out through Chestnut Flats to the cove. The settlers later developed their own roads into North Carolina, leaving the old Ekaneetlee trace to become a little-used manway. Until its demise, the Big Poplar stood as a well-recognized totem marking the point where the ancient Cherokee trace left Forge Creek and proceeded up to Ekaneetlee Gap. The manway has long since been abandoned and is not recommended.

The Gregory Ridge Trail crosses Forge Creek a second time a mile and a half above the first crossing, and then, 180 yards farther, crosses a third time. All of the crossings are on footlogs. Sixty-eight yards above the third crossing, the trail enters the Forge Creek Backcountry Campsite (#12). The camp is situated on two distinct plats about forty yards apart and shaded by large old-growth trees. The site farthest from the trail is small, suitable for only one or two tents. The nearer site is larger and suitably level, but is somewhat diminished in attractiveness by its wide exposure to the trail. The camp is served by a convenient food-storage cable, and the water source is nearby Forge Creek.

After circumnavigating the campsite, the Gregory Ridge Trail enters a narrow draw drained by Forge Creek. Here, the grade stiffens considerably as the trail begins inching away from the stream. Six hundred yards above the campsite, a sharp right turn directs the trail out of the cove-hardwood cover and into a strenuous grind up and across a dry, burned-over, sawbrier-infested exposure of sporadic oaks and pines. Compounding the steepness are progressively rocky conditions and the absence of forest cover to ameliorate the effects of heat and direct sunlight. The exposed climb breaks off after slightly more than a half-mile at a large sandstone outcropping that is referred to provisionally as either Whale Rock or Elephant Rock, depending on whether the observer fancies it to resemble a whale or an elephant.

At Whale Rock, the trail turns south and falls in with the old course of the Fork Ridge Trail that once ascended directly up the spine of Gregory Ridge from the mouth of Bower Creek. The course up Gregory Ridge remains steep, climbing through a dry-ridge mix of sourwoods, pines, and oaks until reaching a cooler environment of cove hardwoods. Visible on the left at various intervals is the high ridgeline of the main Smoky divide between Doe Knob and Mollies Ridge. Higher up the trail, Spence Field and Thunderhead (5,527 feet) can be seen farther down the divide. At other intervals a few obstructed views into Cades Cove appear on the right.

The appearance of tufts of thick grass and stands of slender American beech and yellow birch trees signals the approach to Rich Gap, where the Gregory Ridge Trail terminates into the Gregory Bald Trail. Immediately across the gap an axuillary trail leads 560 yards to Moore Spring. The Gregory Bald Trail leads right three-quarters of a mile to the summit of Gregory Bald and 2.1 miles east to the Appalachian Trail at Doe Knob.

GREGORY BALD TRAIL

Parson Branch Road at Sams Gap to the Appalachian Trail at Doe Knob—7.3 miles.

POINT OF DEPARTURE: Follow directions to the Gregory Ridge Trail. Just before reaching the end of Forge Creek Road, turn right on the one-way gravel Parson Branch Road and drive 3.2 miles to Sams Gap. The Gregory Ridge Trail begins on the left side of Sams Gap. Parson Branch Road is closed during the winter. A difficult alternate to Sams Gap is by way of the Hannah Mountain Trail.

QUAD MAPS: Cades Cove 148-SE
Calderwood 148-SW

0.0—Sams Gap. Parson Branch Road. Hannah Mountain Trail exits right 9.5 miles to the Abrams Falls Trail and Hatcher Mountain Trail.
3.3—Panther Gap.
3.9—Water source for the campsite.

4.1—Sheep Pen Gap. Sheep Pen Gap Backcountry Campsite (#13). Wolf Ridge Trail exits 0.7 mile to Parson Bald.

4.5—Gregory Bald.

5.0—Access path exits right 250 yards to Moore Spring.

5.2—Rich Gap. Gregory Ridge Trail exits left 5.0 miles to Forge Creek Road. Access path exits right 560 yards to Moore Spring.

5.3—Long Hungry Ridge Trail exits right 4.5 miles to the Twentymile Creek Trail.

6.2—Forge Knob.

7.3—Buck Gap.

7.3—Appalachian Trail at Doe Knob.

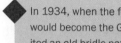

In 1934, when the federal government officially assumed control of the land that would become the Great Smoky Mountains National Park, the Park Service inherited an old bridle path built by Daniel D. Foute for the convenience of his guests at the Montvale Springs Hotel. The bridle path climbed Hannah Mountain to Sams Gap and then on up to the main Smoky divide at Sheep Pen Gap. From here it turned east and followed the divide a short distance to Gregory Bald. Later, the part of Foute's bridle path between Sheep Pen Gap and Gregory Bald was incorporated into the newly designated Appalachian Trail, which was initially designed to follow the entire length of the main Smoky divide and exit the mountains at Deal Gap on US129. The remainder of the bridle path became known as the Hannah Mountain Trail.

Over time, several changes were wrought. By 1945, the Appalachian Trail had been redirected at Doe Knob to exit the Smokies near Fontana Dam. Subsequently, the Hannah Mountain Trail was shortened, made to stop where Parson Branch Road passes through Sams Gap, and from the residuum of this process, a new trail was designated. The remainder of the old Hannah Mountain Trail between Sams Gap and Sheep Pen Gap was pieced together with that of the old Appalachian Trail between Sheep Pen Gap and Doe Knob and christened the Gregory Bald Trail. A three-quarter mile section of the western runt end of the old Appalachian Trail was incorporated in the Wolf Ridge Trail and the remainder was abandoned.

The Gregory Bald Trail begins in Sams Gap. Sams Gap not only marks the lower terminus of the Gregory Bald Trail, but also harbors the upper terminus of the Hannah Mountain Trail and the one-way Parson Branch Road leading out of Cades Cove and down to US129 near Calderwood. The Gregory Bald Trail can be reached by automobile along Parson Branch Road. During the winter season the road is closed. Then, the Gregory Bald Trail can be reached either by hiking the Hannah Mountain Trail or Parson Branch Road up from the end of Forge Creek Road.

The Gregory Bald Trail eases out of Sams Gap on a fairly level track cushioned with layers of pine needles. Shortly, the trail begins to climb, moving quickly into a second-growth cove-hardwood mix while plying the contours of the adjacent slopes. When the trail edges out onto drier exposures, pines are prominent, but generally it stays in the cooler recesses of the hollows and shaded ridges.

Three miles above Sams Gap, the trail enters Panther Gap, a gentle saddle-shaped swag fringed with a collar of grass. Here, the trail turns south and begins a one-mile climb into Sheep Pen Gap. Occasional tufts of mountain grass shaded by remarkably slender American beeches and red maples outline roughly the perimeter of the grazing range that once extended a considerable distance from the top of the mountain. The forest becomes more open and park-like with numerous small grassy areas containing considerable dry browse. About 300 yards prior to reaching Sheep Pen Gap, the trail passes two headwater springs of Panther Creek lying less than ten yards apart. Both are miry mud-holes churned up by horses led down to drink from the water; nevertheless, these are the only sources of water between here and Moore Spring on the east side of Gregory Bald.

Sheep Pen Gap is a large, level, grassy swag shaded by widely spaced yellow birches and harboring the Sheep Pen Backcountry Campsite (#13), one of the most attractive campsites in the park. Situated fortuitously between Parson Bald and Gregory Bald, Sheep Pen Gap shares something of the open expanse of a bald, yet retains the protection and intimacy of a gap. The result is a park-like setting whose perimeters shade imperceptibly into the ambient wilderness. The camp is large and level, and affords the option of camping in open sunlight or in the cover of shade. A food-storage cable is suspended along the Wolf Ridge Trail at the upper end of the camp. Water, unfortunately, is available only from the rather messy spring 300 yards back down the trail.

Along the east side of the gap, the Gregory Bald Trail meets the upper terminus of the Wolf Ridge Trail leading in from nearby Parson Bald. At the intersection, the Gregory Bald Trail turns sharply left and climbs a rough rocky track along the main Smoky divide. Three-quarters of a mile above the gap, it breaks out of the forest cover and onto the vast rounded sward of Gregory Bald.

The earliest written reference to Gregory Bald is from field notes recorded by William Davenport while surveying the boundary between Tennessee and North Carolina in 1821. At one point in his notes, Davenport mentions "a red oak 54th mile at Equenutty path to Cades Cove." The "Equenutty path" refers to an ancient Cherokee trace that crossed the Smoky Mountains at Ekaneetlee Gap about four miles east of Gregory Bald. Working west along the boundary, Davenport reached "the top of the bald spot in sight of Tellessee Old Town." The town he refers to was a Cherokee village on the Little Tennessee River that would have been visible from a high opening west of Ekaneetlee Gap. Davenport then soon reaches a "red oak . . . in the edge of the second bald spot," as if to say that the two bald spots are in close proximity. It is clear from the circumstances of his survey that the two bald spots Davenport identified are Gregory Bald and Parson Bald. Oddly, he does not mention a bald spot in reference to Thunderhead, Spence Field, or Russell Field, evidence perhaps that only Gregory and Parson were natural balds. Afterward and for the duration of the nineteenth century, maps of the Great Smoky Mountains identified the peak at Gregory's as "Bald Spot."

Though several inhabitants of Cades Cove herded cattle on Gregory Bald, Russell Gregory, for whom the bald was named, was the first to build a cabin there. It was a cylindrical stone structure with large windows that he called "portholes." In the evenings, Gregory would poke his rifle, "old Long Tom," out through one of the portholes and shoot deer drawn to the salt licks set out for cattle. Although there is long-standing speculation that Gregory is a natural bald, some inhabitants of Cades Cove are certain that Russell Gregory cleared part of the area.

A traveler to Gregory Bald in 1900, known only as B.G., recorded seeing stone pens, ostensibly for confining sheep that frequently grazed in the sward. According to Cades Cove native Randolph Shields, sheep "kept close to or on the crest while cattle often drifted into hollows. Even exploding bolts of lightning usually failed to drive them from the heights." Another early twentieth-century visitor to the Smokies, William Hinklin, mentions watching a ram fight on Gregory. "Hundreds of sheep were gathered around in a large circle, watching a big league butting bout. Two old rams were in the center doing all they could to butt out each other's brains. Their heads were bloody but unbowed and they stuck doggedly at it. From a distance of 75 feet they would charge in unison, their horns crashing with terrific impact, turn about, dash back for some distance and charge again."

Mrs. John Oliver of Cades Cove once mentioned that she "had it from the older folks long dead" that Gregory Bald was "originally a blueberry meadow" and had "always been bald." To some extent, B.G. confirms Mrs. Oliver's sources, describing Gregory Bald as "a rim of stunted oaks border[ing] the bare summit which is perhaps 30 acres in extent, covered with fine grass and dotted with scattering huckleberry bushes," but mentions nothing of the azaleas for which Gregory is well known. Randolph Shields once commented to Harvey Broome that, during the time he was a boy, Gregory had none of the azaleas for which it has become noted. Thirty-four years after B.G.'s visit and grazing on the bald had ceased, Broome could write that Gregory Bald "looked well kept" and that "the gorgeous azalea clumps of diverse hues, running from pure white through all the pinks, yellow, salmon, and flames, to deep saturated reds, were ranged in such delightfully unstudied stands around the edges that it seems as though it had been done by design." Broome estimated the bald to be fifty grassy acres with a few scattered plants springing up in the sward, but the great masses were found on the dividing line between forest and fell.

Today, Gregory Bald is considerably smaller than the estimates by either B.G. or Harvey Broome. The azaleas are no longer "delightfully unstudied stands around the edges," but are clustered in great labyrinths along the crest of the sward. Those on Gregory are flame azaleas, first noted by botanist William Bartram and of which he wrote: "the epithet fiery I annex to this most celebrated species of azalea, as being expressions of the appearance of its flower." The Gregory azaleas blossom the third week in June and are arguably the most remarkable floral display anywhere in the Smokies.

Gregory Bald still looks "well kept," like a carefully tended park. The views into North Carolina are not as extensive as those enjoyed by William Davenport, but those toward Tennessee afford splendid vistas down into the lower end of Cades Cove. On a clear day, the main Smoky divide can be seen meandering to the east as far as Spence Field and Thunderhead.

A grove of dead standing oaks, bleak and completely free of bark, occupies the lower east end of the sward. The sight is striking and aptly described in an observation by Edwin Way Till. "For a great tree death comes as a gradual transformation. Its vitality ebbs slowly. Even when life has abandoned it entirely it remains a majestic thing. On some hilltop a dead tree may dominate the landscape for miles around. Alone among living things it retains its character and dignity after death. Plants wither; animals disintegrate. But a dead tree may be as arresting, as filled with personality, in death as it is in life."

Among the dead trees, the Gregory Ridge Trail collects itself and exits the bald for a three-quarter-mile descent into Rich Gap. This end of Gregory, B.G. noted, was not bald, but covered in a great profusion of ferns. Today the ferns are much diminished, and the slopes show signs of having once been cleared for grazing. Three hundred yards below the bald, a slightly overgrown manway exits on the right, circling out to Moore Spring before looping back to join the Gregory Ridge Trail at Rich Gap. The Gregory Ridge Trail continues descending on the state-line divide 350 yards to reach Rich Gap and a crossroads intersection with the upper terminus of the Gregory Ridge Trail and the lower end of the manway circling in from Moore Spring.

From Rich Gap the manway to Moore Spring is 560 yards. Moore Spring includes a dell on the lower east flank of Gregory Bald that harbors a small clearing and a bold spring issuing from beneath a large flat rock. Moore Spring is the most reliable source of water on Gregory and was likely the site of several early camps.

The spring's namesake is the Reverend Frank Moore, minister of New Providence Presbyterian Church in Maryville, Tennessee, who in 1895 retained Julius Gregg and Carson Birchfield of Cades Cove to build a cabin here. Moore paid Gregg and

Birchfield twenty-five dollars for the work. Five years later when B.G. stopped by Moore Spring, he observed that the cabin consisted of two contiguous structures. "Built on to the main cabin is a little log annex, most of the floor space being taken up with a bunk at the end, and a hearth built against the chimney, but no fireplace or outlet for the smoke except through the various cracks in the walls and roof." He also "found a dozen people comfortably domiciled in the main cabin, three husbands and their wives, two children and several young brothers and sisters." Mostly likely the men were herders living here with their families while tending cattle on the bald. Later, in 1910, Charles Forster Smith, a professor of classics at Vanderbilt University, stopped by Moore Spring on an excursion through the Smokies. He left no record of his experience there other than the brief remark that the cabin was "the dirtiest human hovel I have ever looked into."

The Gregory Bald Trail continues through the intersection and proceeds 135 yards to the east end of Rich Gap to intersect the upper terminus of the Long Hungry Ridge Trail leading in from North Carolina.

Early in the twentieth century, the east side of Rich Gap was known as Gant Lot. The name was derived from a fenced enclosure that stood near the junction with the Long Hungry Ridge Trail and was used by herders in late summer and early fall for holding cattle for their owners to retrieve in November and drive them to market. If an owner was late in coming to claim his stock, the cattle would lose weight and become lean or "gaunt" from being penned up in the lot—thus the name Gant Lot. During the time Gant Lot was operative, Rich Gap was cleared of trees, allowing unobstructed views into Cades Cove.

When it leaves Rich Gap, the Gregory Bald Trail climbs briefly and then settles into a steep half-mile descent before beginning a short easy climb to Forge Knob. From Forge Knob the trail drops steeply again, negotiates a couple of minor bumps, then enters Brier Lick Gap. Bedstraw, fire pink, sundrops, flame azalea, spiderwort, black-eyed Susan, and galax are among the wide diversity of flowering species conspicuous along this interval. Beyond Brier Lick Gap the trail edges off into Tennessee and climbs around Brier Lick Knob before returning to the state line at Buck Gap. When it exits Buck Gap, the trail crosses a gentle terrain along the north side of Doe Knob, where it terminates into the Appalachian Trail approaching along the main divide. At the junction, the Appalachian Trail turns south around Doe Knob and leaves the main divide, descending along Twentymile Ridge to Fontana Dam.

ABRAMS FALLS TRAIL

Abrams Falls parking area to the Hannah Mountain Trail and Hatcher
  Mountain Trail—4.2 miles.
POINT OF DEPARTURE: Drive 5.0 miles on the one-way Cades Cove Loop Road,
  and turn onto the gravel road exiting to the right. The gravel road terminates
  in a parking area. Just beyond the end of the parking area, the Abrams Falls
  Trail begins on a wooden bridge over Abrams Creek.
QUAD MAPS: Cades Cove 148-SE
Calderwood 148-SW

0.0—Abrams Creek. Bridge.
0.1—Access path exits right 0.5 mile to the Elijah Oliver Cabin.
0.7—Footlog.
1.1—Arbutus Ridge.
1.8—Stony Branch. Footlog.
2.4—Wilson Branch. Footlog.
2.5—Access path exits left 85 yards to Abrams Falls.
3.5—Footlog.
3.7—Footlog.
4.2—Hannah Mountain Trail exits left 1.9 miles to the Rabbit Creek Trail
  at Scott Gap and 9.5 miles to Parson Branch Road at Sams Gap. Hatcher
  Mountain Trail exits right 0.2 mile to the Little Bottoms Trail.

The Abrams Falls Trail, readily accessible from Cades Cove Loop Road, is one of
the most popular in the Smokies. It affords a pleasant stroll along a wide mountain stream that leads to a powerful twenty-five-foot waterfall situated in a place of
exceptional rugged beauty. The trail begins in the extreme west end of Cades Cove at
the juncture where Abrams Creek leaves the cove and enters the mountain fastness.
It was near here that John Oliver, a descendent of the first settlers in Cades Cove,
operated a lodge that became a recognized landmark in this end of the Smokies.
Travelers going to Abrams Falls or nearby Gregory Bald often stayed at the Oliver
Lodge before venturing into the higher-elevation backcountry of the mountains.
Accommodation for a week's stay at the Oliver Lodge was fourteen dollars.

Abrams Creek is the largest stream completely within the boundaries of the
park. Eighteen smaller streams descend the slopes of the Cades Cove basin and empty
into Abrams Creek as it meanders on a westerly course though the cove's open fields.
The stream exits the lower end of the cove through an aperture in the mountains
and then winds through a narrow forest-clad gorge to its confluence with Chilhowee
Lake near the southeast corner of the park.

"Abrams" is a truncation of "Abraham," the name of the erstwhile chief of the Cherokee noted for his leadership in the last Indian attack on the Watauga settlement. Chief Abram presided over Chilhowee Village on the Little Tennessee near the mouth the stream that now bears his name.

The Abrams Falls Trail begins on a long wooden bridge spanning Abrams Creek. Immediately at the far end of the bridge, the trail intersects a well-maintained access path to the right that leads a half-mile to the Elijah Oliver Cabin. At the end of the bridge, the Abrams Falls Trail turns left and proceeds downstream along Abrams Creek. Here, the trail is wide and smooth with little perceptible grade. The stream flows slightly below the grade of the trail and separated from it by a barrier of luxuriant rhododendron whose leggy boughs frequently extend completely over the path.

Abrams Creek is remarkably free of boulders. Its bed is a hard shield of waterworn rock whose ledges, scallops, and furrows shape the stream's abundance of falls, pools, and channels. The stream does not dash madly about, rushing down the mountain in a spectacular torrent of moving water, but ripples along in a peaceful uniform flow.

When the trail completes the first mile, it leaves the stream and climbs Arbutus Ridge. The name is suggested by the rare beauty of the white-petal trailing arbutus flower which is common in this part of the mountains in the early spring. Arbutus Ridge is oriented perpendicularly to Abrams Creek, thus forcing the stream to alter its course to circumnavigate the end of the ridge. When the trail reaches the ridgeline, Abrams Creek can be seen veering away to execute a mile-long loop around the butt end of Arbutus Ridge. Down-trail the stream is seen completing the loop and returning to its westerly course. Native mountaineers often referred to this section of Abrams Creek as the Horseshoe, owing to the configuration of the creek's bend. The distance across Arbutus Ridge at the neck of the Horseshoe is about a hundred yards.

From the crest of Arbutus Ridge, the trail descends sharply to resume its streamside course along Abrams Creek. White pines presiding over patches of galax and thickets of mountain laurel provide the principal forest cover. The most attractive flowering species noticeable on this part of the trail is perhaps the fringed polygala, also known as gay wings and flowering wintergreen. This flower, three to four inches tall, sports striking orchard-pink petals that blossom usually in April or early May. The fringed polygala is rare to the Smokies but is most likely to be found in pine stands.

Slightly less than a mile beyond Arbutus Ridge, the trail crosses Stony Branch on a footlog and then climbs up and away from the stream to clear Little Shoe Ridge where the stream enters another horseshoe-like bend. Seven hundred yards beyond the Stony Branch crossing, the trail drops sharply to a footlog over Wilson Branch, where it turns and proceeds eighty yards to Abrams Creek. Here, an access path exits left, crossing back over Wilson Branch on a footlog and proceeding a short distance to the base of Abrams Falls.

Abrams Falls is a wide bluff over which the stream plunges twenty-five feet into one of the deepest pools in the Smokies. Level benches of solid rock near the base of the falls provide splendid places for enjoying proximity to the mesmerizing violence of falling water. On the far side of the pool, the bluff is framed by overhanging rhododendron and mountain laurel that scale the steep outer banks of the stream. Occasionally otters can be seen cavorting on the edges of the pool, scrambling up the rock faces and sliding down again on the moss-slickened scarps. The rush of water, the falls, the deep pool, and the undeniable ruggedness of the immediate terrain make this a place of surpassing Smoky Mountain beauty.

The Abrams Falls Trail continues downstream for nearly two miles before terminating in a three-way intersection with the Hannah Mountain Trail and Hatcher Mountain Trail. This last section follows the course of Abrams Creek, generally proceeding on a narrow berm affixed to the steep slope high above the stream gorge. Twice the trail descends, first to clear Kreider Branch and then Oak Flats Branch, both on footlogs. After a long gradual final descent to Abrams Creek, the trail reaches its intersection with the lower terminus of the Hannah Mountain Trail and the southern terminus of the Hatcher Mountain Trail. At this junction, the Hannah Mountain Trail immediately fords Abrams Creek, climbs to an intersection with the Rabbit Creek Trail, and then continues to Parson Branch Road at Sams Gap. Abrams Creek at this point is wide and deep. Even when the water is running low, fording the stream is not necessarily easy. When it is running high, the stream is difficult if not dangerous to cross. The Hatcher Mountain Trail continues downstream 350 yards to intersect the eastern terminus of the Little Bottoms Trail before turning to ascend Hatcher Mountain and on to a crossroads intersection with the Cooper Road Trail and Beard Cane Trail.

RABBIT CREEK TRAIL

Abrams Falls Trail parking area to Abrams Creek Ranger Station—7.8 miles.

POINT OF DEPARTURE: Follow directions to the Abrams Falls Trail. The Rabbit Creek Trail begins on Mill Creek 50 yards to the left of the bridge at the head of the Abrams Falls Trail.

QUAD MAP: Cades Cove 148-SE

0.0—Mill Creek.
2.3—Andy McCully Ridge.
4.1—Rabbit Creek Backcountry Campsite (#15). Rabbit Creek.
5.1—Scott Gap. Scott Gap Backcountry Campsite (#16). Hannah Mountain

Trail exits left 7.6 miles to Parson Branch Road and right 1.9 miles to the Abrams Falls Trail and Hatcher Mountain Trail.

6.1—Pine Mountain.

7.6—Abrams Creek. Footlog.

7.8—Abrams Creek Ranger Station.

Within ten years after being settled by its first white inhabitants, Cades Cove was disturbed by the noise and violence of heavy industry. Sometime in the 1840s Daniel D. Foute, an entrepreneur and owner of a well-known resort at nearby Montvale Springs, established a new business enterprise, the Cades Cove Bloomery Forge, along Forge Creek just above the present site of the John Cable Mill. Low-grade iron ore was readily available in the nearby mountains, prompting the building of iron forges on the Tennessee side of the Smokies, though Foute's would be the only one in Cades Cove.

This primitive method of making iron utilized a bloomery where the ore, heated to an incandescent mass in a charcoal fire, had the impurities hammered out under repeated blows of a ponderous hammer on a forge. Charcoal to fire the furnaces was made in huge pits on nearby "coaling grounds" where pine trees were felled, stacked, covered with earth, and fired.

"Black Bill" Walker, a notable bear hunter from the Tremont area, once described the forge: "I never heerd sech a racity-rack! Ye'd think the heavens was fallin' down! Them fellers aworkin' thar in the sweat an' gaum reminded me more of the gate to the bad place! And at night, ye c'd see the red light of hit acrost the mount'ins fer miles an' hear thet hammer thumpin' tell hit seemed to jar the earth into a quake."

Since Foute needed cheap transportation to make his business profitable, operation of the forge was the incentive for many of the roads constructed in the lower end of Cades Cove. One such road, later known as the Rabbit Creek Road, was cut into the mountains to provide access to the charcoal needed to fire the forge. The road fell into disrepair when Foute's forge was closed down in 1848, but was later gradually improved and extended until it became serviceable as an outlet to neighboring communities in Happy Valley and along the lower reaches of Abrams Creek. The Rabbit Creek Road was never used extensively for commercial traffic and perhaps was best remembered by the cove inhabitants as the major escape route for renegade soldiers leading stolen cattle and horses out of the cove during the Civil War.

The modern Rabbit Creek Trail follows the course of the old road from the west end of Cades Cove to the lower end of Abrams Creek. It begins near the confluence of Mill Creek and Abrams Creek at a trailhead it shares with the Abrams Falls Trail. The latter proceeds over a sturdy bridge that spans Abrams Creek while the Rabbit Creek Trail plunges immediately into Mill Creek just opposite the mouth of Victory

Branch. Mill Creek is not a difficult crossing even with the water high and running, but rarely is the water level low enough to allow rock hopping. Once across Mill Creek, the trail proceeds up the middle of Victory Branch. A few yards up the stream bed, the trail veers from Victory Branch and climbs a rough track toward the Coon Butt end of Andy McCully Ridge.

Along the lower elevations, the hiking is quite pleasant with the trail coursing through a deep hollow forested in eastern hemlocks and bearing a thick understory of rhododendron. Occasionally the trail returns to the stream bed. Sometimes the trail is in the stream itself, sometimes just at the stream's edge. Eventually, it edges away from the cooler recesses and, after crossing More Licker Branch, climbs into the drier environment of a pine-hardwood mix.

When the trail reaches Coon Butt, the grade levels for a hundred yards or so. In the time of Foute's forge, a trail exited Rabbit Creek Road along this level stretch and proceeded south to nearby Coalen Ground Ridge, where charcoal was produced as fuel for firing the forges. The ridge was stripped of its pine, the wood ricked and covered with earth, and then fired. The charcoal was then hauled down the "coaling" road to the forge in Cades Cove. The old track to Coalen Ground Ridge forks as it reaches the ridge, the right prong proceeding to Parson Branch Road and that to the left dropping down to another road built by Foute and now known as Forge Creek Road. This network of roads is all likely part of the Foute enterprise, given the proximity of the Coalen Ground to the old Cades Cove forge.

Andy McCully Ridge is named for a man who at one time farmed the land along the crest of the ridge. The trail here is sometime smooth and even and sometimes rough and rutted, but always retaining its character as a road and everywhere coursing through a dry-ridge pine-hardwood mix. After it crosses the ridge, the trail begins a long winding descent to Rabbit Creek. Whenever the trail switches back into the cooler hollows, particularly as it gets nearer Rabbit Creek, it enters a lush cove-hardwood environment of large trees shading a wide variety of wildflowers.

The appearance of the Rabbit Creek Backcountry Campsite (#15) heralds the trail's approach to Rabbit Creek. Prior to the advent of the park, the camp marked the intersection of the trail with a manway leading upstream along Rabbit Creek to Parson Branch Road. The larger part of the Rabbit Creek Camp is situated to the left of the trail on a spacious, fairly level gradient above the stream. The camp is spread out under a canopy of tall slender pines, red maples, and hemlocks. Across the trail and down by the stream is a small annex with a capacity for only one or two tents. This lower site enjoys the ambience of the nearby stream, but is cramped and a bit worn and damp.

The trail crosses Rabbit Creek just above its confluence with Hannah Branch. When the water level is low, the stream can often be negotiated by hopping among the boulders just up-stream of the crossing. Where the trail fords, the stream bed is smooth and level. Even after a heavy rain, Rabbit Creek is an easy stream to wade.

Just beyond the stream crossing is the beginning of one of the finer stretches of hiking trail anywhere in the Smokies. Adjacent steep-sided ridges converge from either side, forming a deep gorge of such narrow proportions that the trail is forced into the stream that drains the hollow. Trees with straight trunks, towering like gigantic columns with scarcely a noticeable taper, extend seventy or eighty feet to the nearest limb. What little sunlight reaches the bottom of the gorge is filtered by the high overarching canopy, imparting the silence and grandeur of a natural cathedral.

The trail climbs through the gorge one mile until it enters Scott Gap and intersects the Hannah Mountain Trail. George Scott maintained a home and farm to the left of the trail just below the gap. At the junction of the two trails, an access path exits 175 yards down the mountain to the Scott Gap Backcountry Campsite (#16), a gentle gradient situated under a thin cover of pines, sweet gums, red maples, and yellow poplars. The camp is spacious, but given the slope and roughness of the terrain, there are few suitable tent sites. Water is available from a very weak stream below the campsite.

When George Scott farmed this slope, a manway continued from the area of the camp down the drainage, following Pardon Creek to Abrams Creek, where it connected with a road leading to Happy Valley. Until recently the campsite itself was occupied by the Scott Gap Shelter, a shallow open structure built in the fashion of a log cabin. Concrete foundation posts from the dismantled shelter can still be seen near the upper end of the campsite.

The forest cover changes abruptly from the cove hardwoods to a dry-ridge pine mix when the trail leaves Scott Gap and begins a mile-long climb to the crest of Pine Mountain. A sharp right-hand turn marks the end of the climb and the beginning of a long winding descent to a bottomland along Abrams Creek. The forest on the descent is largely a hardwood cover blended with stands of white pines. The bottomland is little more than a narrow intervale separating Abrams Creek from Pine Mountain, but apparently wide enough to support a farm. Evidence of old homesites is scattered along the bottom, but for much of the year all but a single chimney ruin is obscured by the overgrowth of weeds and low woody browse.

The Rabbit Creek Trail finishes it course with a crossing of Abrams Creek on a long sturdy footlog, followed by an easy 200-yard excursion to a light-gravel track leading out to Abrams Creek Road. The trail ends at the road. Directly across the road is the Abrams Creek Ranger Station. A half-mile down the road is Abrams Creek Campground.

WET BOTTOM TRAIL

Cooper Road Trail to the parking area adjacent to the Abrams Falls Trail and Rabbit Creek Trail—1.0 mile.

POINT OF DEPARTURE: Follow directions to the Abrams Falls Trail. The Wet
Bottom Trail begins on the right between the parking area and the wooden
bridge at the head of the Abrams Falls Trail. The alternate option is to drive
4.3 miles on Cades Cove Loop Road to the Cooper Road Trail, then hike
310 yards up the Cooper Road Trail. The Wet Bottom Trail begins on the
left.

QUAD MAP: Cades Cove 148-SE

0.0—Cooper Road Trail.

0.2—Follows access path to the Elijah Oliver Place. Feeder stream. Footlog.

0.4—Exits access path to the Elijah Oliver Place.

0.5—Floodplain enclosure.

0.8—Abrams Creek.

1.0—Access path from parking area to the Abrams Falls Trail and Rabbit
Creek Trail.

The Wet Bottom Trail is maintained primarily as a horse access connecting the Cooper
Road Trail and Rabbit Creek Trail; nevertheless it ranks among the most interesting of the short trails in the Smokies. The lower end of the Wet Bottom Trail is
located about halfway along the path leading from the parking area to the bridge
over Abrams Creek that marks the trailhead to Abrams Falls. The upper end of the
Wet Bottom Trail is along the Cooper Road Trail 310 yards up above Cades Cove
Loop Road. Because of its proximity to the parking area, the lower end is the more
convenient trailhead. However, because of a wide crossing of Abrams Creek near the
lower end, the trail's course is easier to describe by beginning at the upper end.

When leaving the Cooper Road Trail, the Wet Bottom Trail drops onto a thinly
forested, gently pitched gradient alongside a small nameless stream. On the far side
of the stream is a large cleared farm field characteristic of much of the bottomland in
Cades Cove.

Three hundred and seventy yards down-trail, the Wet Bottom Trail reaches a
wide light-gravel track that serves as an access path between Cades Cove Loop Road
and the Elijah Oliver Place. At this juncture, the Wet Bottom Trail turns right onto
the light-gravel track, crosses the stream on a short footlog, then proceeds in the
direction of the Elijah Oliver Place. Seventy-five yards beyond the stream, the trail
passes in front of a large barn built by John Oliver sometime around 1900. The barn
is now used by the Park Service to store pieces of lumber scavenged from various
cabins and barns around Cades Cove.

Three hundred and sixty-five yards down the light-gravel track, the Wet Bottom
Trail exits to the left and follows a faint single-file track into the woods. The light-
gravel track continues for another 290 yards to a cleared slope occupied by the Elijah
Oliver Cabin.

The Elijah Oliver Cabin was built prior to the Civil War and consists of a stand-alone one-room structure connected by a narrow "dog-trot" to a smaller unit that was used as a kitchen. The walls of both rooms were made of widely spaced spit logs chinked with mud. Roughly planed boards nailed horizontally on the inside covered the mud chinking. Porches were built on both units. Sometime later, one side of the cabin's front porch was framed in with boards, creating a small annex that was used as a bedroom, particularly for strangers seeking lodging for the night. Mountaineer families deemed it inhospitable to refuse lodging to travelers passing through the mountains.

Three rough-hewn log outbuildings plus a springhouse accompany the cabin. Water is supplied to the springhouse by a series of long wooden half-pipes running from a small spring to a heavy wooden trough built into the wall of the springhouse. Another half-pipe catches the overflow from the trough and drains it away. The half-pipes are made of poles shaved down on one side with the inner pulp cored out.

The Elijah Oliver Place can also be reached by another path leading in on the lower south corner of the clearing. This path is a half-mile course that begins along the Abrams Falls Trail just at the point where it crosses Abrams Creek on a wooden bridge.

When the Wet Bottom Trail exits the light-gravel track, it winds through an old field once tilled and planted in tobacco and corn by Elijah Oliver. A hundred and eighty-five yards across the field, the trail encounters a wire fence set parallel to a wet-weather stream. The fence was put up in 1984 as part of the Abrams Creek Floodplain Enclosure and is intended to keep wild hogs out of the floodplain to protect a variety of flora and fauna, many of which are rare within the park.

After following the fence and wet-weather stream for 220 yards, the trail, the fence, and the stream part ways, with the trail continuing across the floodplain toward Abrams Creek. Abrams Creek runs through the floodplain in a cut-bank stream bed. The stream is remarkably free of boulders and flows with little sound or perturbation. The water level is rarely below knee-deep and often much higher. Near the banks of the stream, evidence of beaver activity is visible on trees gnawed in tell-tale fashion just above ground level. A greater concentration of beaver activity can be found off-trail a hundred yards upstream.

Along Abrams Creek, the trail crosses a low swale through which the course can be difficult to discern. The course remains parallel to Abrams Creek until the stream makes a readily discernable bend across the path. Here, the trail crosses Abrams Creek and then proceeds 280 yards downstream through delightfully attractive woodlands to terminate on the access path from the parking area to the Abrams Falls Trail. Abrams Creek here is wide, deep, and anything but easy to cross. To avoid a wet crossing, an alternate route is available along a faint manway that leads downstream to the gravel access path connecting the Abrams Falls Trail to the Elijah Oliver Place. Tuning left on the Oliver access, the stream can be crossed on the bridge at the head of the Abrams Falls Trail.

Conversely, hikers wishing to begin from the parking area at the lower end of the Wet Bottoms Trail, but not wanting to wade the stream, can begin along the Elijah Oliver access. Going upstream on the Oliver access, the manway exits on the right in search of the Wet Bottom Trail just where Abrams Creek turns away. Another suitable alternative is to remain on the Oliver access until reaching the cabin, then turning onto the light-gravel track to pick up the Wet Bottom Trail just beyond the barn.

HANNAH MOUNTAIN TRAIL

Junction of the Abrams Falls Trail and Hatcher Mountain Trail to Parson
   Branch Road at Sams Gap—9.5 miles.
   POINT OF DEPARTURE: Hike to the end of the Abrams Falls Trail. The Hannah
   Mountain Trail begins on the left at the edge of Abrams Creek.
   QUAD MAP: Calderwood 148-SW

0.0—Abrams Falls Trail. Hatcher Mountain Trail. Abrams Creek.
1.9—Scott Gap. Access path exits 175 yards to the Scott Gap Backcountry
   Campsite (#16). Rabbit Creek Trail exits left 5.1 miles to the Abrams Falls
   Trail parking area and right 2.7 miles to the Abrams Creek Ranger Station.
5.1—Flint Gap. Flint Gap Backcountry Campsite (#14).
7.6—Big Poplar.
9.5—Sams Gap. Parson Branch Road. Gregory Bald Trail exits 4.5 miles to
   Gregory Bald.

The Hannah Mountain Trail affords one of the very best hiking surfaces of any trail in the Great Smoky Mountains. The grade is always easy and the track smooth, free of obstruction, and cushioned underfoot with thick carpets of pine needles.

The trail was originally cut in 1840 by a crew of Cherokee hired by Daniel D. Foute to provide ready access from his resort hotel at Montvale Springs to Gregory Bald. In addition to the usual guests at the hotel, men and women of literary distinction, notably Mary Noailles Murfree and Sidney Lanier, traveled Foute's trail to the main Smoky divide for adventure, recreation, and perhaps inspiration for their literary strivings. Murfree, who wrote under the pseudonym Charles Egbert Craddock, achieved fame in the 1880s for several novels set in Cades Cove, particularly *In the Tennessee Mountains* (1884) and *The Prophet of the Great Smoky Mountains*

(1885). Sidney Lanier's grandfather, Sterling Lanier, was manager of the Mont-vale Springs hotel in the 1850s, and the grandson often availed himself of the opportunities to accompany traveling parties along the Foute trail to Gregory Bald and points farther along the spine of the Smokies. Lanier published several short vignettes and a longer tale, *Tiger-Lilies* (1867), in which Smoky Mountain inhabitants were presented in a devastating caricature.

The most difficult part of the Hannah Mountain Trail is the first hundred yards, where it fords Abrams Creek and begins climbing away from the stream. Abrams Creek is wide and deep at this juncture and, after rain, crossing can be extremely difficult. Beyond the stream the trail skirts the edge of a creek bottom forested in huge eastern hemlocks with a thick understory of rhododendron. The trail soon eases away from the stream drainage, and the hemlocks yield to a pine-hardwood mix.

Two miles above Abrams Creek, the trail enters Scott Gap and intersects the Rabbit Creek Trail, another old Foute road that once connected Cades Cove with Happy Valley. At the junction, an access path on the right exits 175 yards down to the Scott Gap Backcountry Campsite (#16).

The Scott Gap Camp is situated on a gentle gradient under a thin cover of white pines, sweet gums, red maples, and yellow poplars. The camp is not particularly small, but given the slope and roughness of the terrain, there are but few suitable tent sites. The source of water is a weak stream just below the campsite.

The campsite was previously occupied by the Scott Gap Shelter, a shallow, three-sided structure built in the fashion of a log cabin and capable of accommodating eight campers. Unlike the newer shelters along the Appalachian Trail, the Scott Gap Shelter had no protective fencing on the open side and was without a built-in fireplace. Remains of the shelter's foundations are readily noticed along the upper end of the camp. The long gentle slope of mountain below the camp was once farmed by George Scott, the mountaineer for whom the gap is named. Scott's homeplace is now occupied by the campsite.

When leaving Scott Gap, the trail continues on its gentle grade through stands of white pine, pignut hickory, red maple, and a variety of oaks until nearing the crest of Polecat Ridge and entering an area of dry-ridge pines. It soon drops away from the ridgeline and enters the cooler recesses of the Polecat Branch drainage, where seepages drain into the trail. A sharp left-hand turn marks the end of the descent and the beginning of a one-mile climb into Flint Gap and the Flint Gap Backcountry Campsite (#14).

Flint Gap is a saddle-shaped configuration with the campsite straddling the trail. A food-storage cable is suspended on the right of the trail opposite a fire ring that marks the center of the camp. The better tent sites, found a few yards up-trail on a slight rise to the right, are nicely cushioned with pine needles. The terrain in Flint Gap is a bit rolling, affording a scarcity of level spots. Though the setting can be considered attractive, the trail consumes much of middle area of the camp. Water can be found in a weak stream about a hundred yards down the south side of the gap. During the drier seasons it may be necessary to descend a hundred yards farther to find the stream. A larger stream crosses 400 yards up-trail and may be a more reliable source for water.

Beyond Flint Gap, the trail follows the contours along the northwest slope of Hannah Mountain, affording some nice views down into the heavily forested Hannah Branch drainage. After working its way up and around to an eastern exposure, the trail reaches the crest of Hannah Mountain and continues on or near the ridgeline to its terminus at Sams Gap. Just prior to reaching the ridgeline, the trail passes through a lush hardwood forest shaded by the adjacent Mount Lanier, named for the famed poet who once traveled this route on his visits to the high Smokies.

From the time of the earliest settlers in Cades Cove, herders drove livestock to the highland meadows along the western end of the Smokies to graze on the rich mountain grass growing there. Above Cades Cove there were four major ranges—Spence Field, the Dan Lawson range, Gregory Bald, and the Hannah Mountain range. The Hannah Mountain range was the westernmost of the four, lying astride the wide rolling spine of Hannah Mountain between Sams Gap and Mount Lanier. Although the mountain has since been reclaimed by stands of pine forest, remnant patches of the grass once grazed by highland cattle can be seen in several places along the trail.

The Morton Butler Lumber Company logged several sections of Hannah Mountain during the 1930s; nevertheless there were some trees that escaped the lumberman's axe. One fine example is a massive yellow poplar at the trail's edge two-and-a-half miles above Flint Gap. Seeing this tree can only suggest to the modern hiker what the Smoky Mountain forests must have looked like when Murfree and Lanier were riding their horses along Foute's trail to visit Gregory Bald.

According to Smoky Mountain lore, one of the Cherokee hired by Foute to build the trail died while on Hannah Mountain. His body is reputed to have been buried on the ridge just to the left of the trail a quarter-mile prior to reaching its terminus at Sams Gap.

Two miles beyond the big poplar, the Hannah Mountain Trail enters Sams Gap at a gravel parking along the edge of Parson Branch Road. Across the road, the Gregory Bald Trail exits Sams Gap and climbs 4.5 miles to Gregory Bald. Parson

Branch Road, a one-way gravel track suitable for automobile traffic, leads up from Forge Creek Road in Cades Cove and descends to US129 near Calderwood Dam.

HATCHER MOUNTAIN TRAIL

Junction of the Abrams Falls Trail and Hannah Mountain Trail to the Cooper
  Road Trail and Beard Cane Trail—2.8 miles
POINT OF DEPARTURE: Hike to the end of the Abrams Falls Trail. The Hatcher
  Mountain Trail begins on the right.
QUAD MAPS: Calderwood 148-SW
Blockhouse 148-NW

0.0—Abrams Falls Trail. Hannah Mountain Trail.
0.2—Little Bottoms Trail exits left 2.3 miles to the Cooper Road Trail.
2.8—Cooper Road Trail exits left 4.9 miles to Abrams Creek Campground
  and right 5.6 miles to Cades Cove Loop Road. Beard Cane Trail exits straight
  4.2 miles to the Ace Gap Trail at Blair Gap.

The Hatcher Mountain Trail is a short connector used primarily as an access route between a network of trails along Abrams Creek and those extending into the extreme northwest corner of the park. At its lower terminus the Hatcher Mountain Trail connects with the western terminus of the Abrams Falls Trail and the lower terminus of the Hannah Mountain Trail at the point where the latter crosses Abrams Creek. Three hundred and fifty yards above this junction, the Hatcher Mountain Trail meets the eastern terminus of the Little Bottoms Trail leading in along Abrams Creek. At its upper end the Hatcher Mountain Trail enters a crossroads intersection with the Cooper Road Trail and the southern terminus of the Beard Cane Trail. The Cooper Road Trail connects Cades Cove Loop Road with Abrams Creek Campground while the Beard Cane Trail proceeds to the park boundary at Blair Gap to intersect the western terminus of the Ace Gap Trail.

Beginning at its lower terminus along Abrams Creek, the Hatcher Mountain Trail turns immediately away from the stream, winds to its intersection with the Little Bottoms Trail, and then settles into a steady climb on a rough track up the south end of Hatcher Mountain. Looking back down the trail from this elevation, the beauty and the ruggedness of the Abrams Creek gorge can be readily appreciated.

Within the first mile, the trail clears the end of the mountain and moves into the moist cooler environment of the Oak Flats drainage. The trail here is level, remarkably even, and smooth underfoot. Eastern hemlocks and white pine are the dominant tree species on the top of the ridge while the cove-hardwood species are prevalent on the steeper slopes below the trail.

Emerging from the shade of the Oak Flats drainage, the trail remains just below the crest of Hatcher Mountain until it terminates at the crossroads intersection. This last stretch traverses the mountain from the south to north through an open dry-ridge mix of Virginia and pitch pine, pignut hickory, chestnut oak, and silver maple. Much of the path here is a coarse track of sandy sedimentary consistency studded with small pebbles of quartz. The trail is in some places a bit rutted, but rarely rough or uneven.

COOPER ROAD TRAIL

Abrams Creek Campground to Cades Cove Loop Road—10.5 miles.

POINT OF DEPARTURE: From Maryville, drive US321 to the Foothills Parkway, turn left, and continue until the parkway terminates into US129. Turn left on US129, proceed a hundred yards, and turn left on Happy Valley Road. From Fontana, drive NC28 to US129 and continue to Happy Valley Road. Drive Happy Valley Road 6.0 miles to Happy Valley Loop Road, turn right, and proceed 1.0 mile to the parking area just beyond the Abrams Creek Ranger Station. Hike along the gravel road 0.4 mile to Abrams Creek Campground. The Cooper Road Trail begins at the upper end of the campground.

QUAD MAPS: Calderwood 148-SW
Blockhouse 148-NW
Kinzel Springs 148-NE
Cades Cove 148-SE

0.0—Abrams Creek Campground.

0.6—Kingfisher Creek.

0.9—Cooper Road Backcountry Campsite (#1). Little Bottoms Trail exits right 2.3 miles to the Hatcher Mountain Trail.

2.5—Gold Mine Gap. Gold Mine Trail exits left 0.8 mile to the park boundary.

3.1—Cane Gap. Cane Creek Trail exits left 2.1 miles to the park boundary.

4.9—Beard Cane Trail exits left 4.2 miles to the Ace Gap Trail at Blair Gap. Hatcher Mountain Trail exits right 2.6 miles to the Little Bottoms Trail and 2.8 miles to the Abrams Falls Trail and Hannah Mountain Trail.

6.3—Wilson Branch.

7.3—Stony Branch.

9.2—Arbutus Branch.

10.3—Wet Bottom Trail exits right 1.0 mile to the Abrams Falls Trail and Rabbit Creek Trail.

10.5—Cades Cove Loop Road.

Sometime in the late 1820s, land speculator and entrepreneur Daniel D. Foute moved into Blount County, Tennessee and began accumulating vast tracts of mountain property, much of it in the western end of the Great Smokies. His first major venture was the acquisition of 6,300 acres that included a mineral spring where in 1832 he established the resort hotel Montvale Springs. Foute later procured extensive tracts of mountain land between the Chilhowees and Cades Cove, and soon after built a bloomery forge near the confluence of Mill and Forge creeks in the lower end of the cove. In the interest of serving guests at his hotel, Foute received a charter from the state of Tennessee to construct a four-foot-wide horse trail from his property at Montvale through the Chilhowee range to Cades Cove, then along an old Indian trace up Ekaneetlee Branch to the main divide at Ekaneetlee Gap. The horse trail apparently was never completed, lacking the last few miles into Ekaneetlee Gap.

Around 1840, Foute received permission to widen the section of horse trail from Chilhowee to Cades Cove to accommodate wagon traffic. Foute hired Joe Cooper to supervise the construction. When finished, Cooper's road provided the primary access from Cades Cove to Maryville and to the outside world. Sometime after the park was established, the road was closed and the wagon track became known as the Cooper Road Trail.

The Cooper Road Trail begins at the upper end of Abrams Creek Campground and follows a wide, smooth, light-gravel track through an attractive corridor of tall white pines. The farther the Cooper Road Trail proceeds into the mountains, the more it begins to exhibit the characteristics of a wagon road, becoming rutted in places and worn to bare rock on the steeper grades. Soon, the trail clears a low rise over a sweeping bend in Abrams Creek where eastern hemlocks, red maples, Fraser magnolias, and American hollies come into the mix with the pines. A half-mile above the campground, a feeder stream seeking Kingfisher Creek may entail a wet crossing, but even when rock-hopping is not feasible, the crossing is never difficult.

Below the trail and to the right, at the confluence of Kingfisher Creek and Abrams Creek, is the site of the former Carson's Iron Works, a forge that operated until the mid-1840s. It was later known as the Abrams Creek Forge and may have been acquired by Daniel Foute. In any case, the Cooper Road was instrumental to the Carson operation, providing access to the ore mines and coaling grounds as well as to the markets beyond the mountains.

Slightly less than a mile above Abrams Creek Campground, the Cooper Road Trail intersects the Little Bottoms Trail on the right, and then, a few feet beyond, enters the Cooper Road Backcountry Campsite (#1). The Cooper Road Camp is one of the nicer in the park. It is level, spacious, and conveniently cushioned by layers of pine and hemlock needles. Large hemlocks and tall thickets of rhododendron shade the camp, and water is convenient from Kingfisher Creek along the back side of the camp. A food-storage cable is suspended near the trail intersection.

When it leaves the campsite, the trail enters stands of hemlocks sharing space with yellow poplars. The trail retains it character as a rough wagon road, wide and rutted, passing through occasional muddy puddles. A mile and a half beyond the campsite, it reaches Gold Mine Gap, where it intersects the eastern terminus of the Gold Mine Trail, a very rough road that leads out of the park and is used primarily by horse traffic. The Gold Mine Trail was once part of the network of Foute roads, leading out over the adjacent ridge into the Flats and then across Chilhowee Mountain. The trail today is less than a mile long and terminates at the park boundary.

A half-mile beyond Gold Mine Gap, the Cooper Road Trail descends to Cane Gap, an open dell harboring the southern terminus of the Cane Creek Trail. At this juncture the Cooper Road Trail turns sharply right and begins a steady climb to the crest of Hatcher Mountain. The road course here is dry and sandy, heavily eroded, and often encumbered with roots and rocks. Cattle drives were responsible for much of the early erosion of Cooper Road as this was a primary route for cattle grazing on Gregory Bald and Yellow Sulfur to be herded out of the cove. Yellow Sulfur was a small grazing range that extended along the top of Hatcher Mountain at the head of Beard Cane.

When the Cooper Road Trail reaches the crest of Hatcher Mountain, it enters a badly galled crossroad that marks the intersection of Cooper Road with the Hatcher Mountain Trail exiting right along Hatcher Mountain to Abrams Creek and the Beard Cane Trail leading left to Blair Gap. The intersection still bears scars of its history as a cattle trail.

When it leaves the intersection, the Cooper Road Trail descends steadily on a rough rocky course for about a half-mile before crossing a tributary of Beard Cane Creek. The steepness moderates, and the roughness subsides as the trail proceeds for nearly another mile to the coolness of a shaded hollow where it immediately crosses a tributary of Wilson Branch. A hundred and sixty yards farther, the trail completes a messy crossing of Wilson Branch and then turns and proceeds up the hollow following the course of a small feeder stream.

At the head of the draw, the trail crosses the feeder and enters into a steep climb to the crest of Stony Ridge. On this side of the ridge the deciduous species are more prevalent, and the track is often nicely cushioned in layers of leaves. Upon clearing Stony Ridge, the trail descends about a quarter-mile to an easy crossing of Stony Branch and then turns and starts into a half-mile climb to the crest of Arbutus Ridge. As it eases onto the ridge, the trail turns sharply back to the left to follow the ridgeline briefly before dropping off for a steep descent into the Arbutus Branch drainage. Here, the course winds considerably, following closely the contours of the slope on a track that is wide, smooth, free of obstruction, and shaded by pines. One mile farther, the descent ends at a tributary of Arbutus Branch.

After crossing the stream, the grade remains fairly level for 500 yards before crossing Arbutus Branch on a concrete causeway. The trail then proceeds downstream for a short distance before turning away for a one-mile approach into Cades Cove. The course remains wide, smooth, and amply cushioned with pine needles. Three hundred and ten yards before terminating into Cades Cove Loop Road, the Cooper Road Trail intersects the upper terminus of the Wet Bottom Trail leading in from the parking area adjacent to the trailhead to Abrams Falls. The Cooper Road Trail ends where Cades Cove Loop Road makes a ninety-degree turn and descends to the nearby parking area for the Elijah Oliver Place.

LITTLE BOTTOMS TRAIL

Cooper Road Trail to the Hatcher Mountain Trail—2.3 miles.

POINT OF DEPARTURE: Hike the Cooper Road Trail 0.9 mile to the Cooper Road Backcountry Campsite (#1). The Little Bottoms Trail begins on the right.

QUAD MAP: Calderwood 148-SW

0.0—Cooper Road Trail. Cooper Road Backcountry Campsite (#1).
0.1—Kingfisher Creek.
0.7—Buck Shank Branch.
1.2—Mill Branch.
1.6—Little Bottoms Backcountry Campsite (#17).
2.3—Hatcher Mountain Trail exits left 2.6 miles to the intersection of the Cooper Road Trail and Beard Cane Trail and right 0.2 mile to the intersection of the Abrams Falls Trail and Hannah Mountain Trail.

The Little Bottoms Trail affords one of the most exhilarating hiking experiences anywhere in the Smokies. For much of its course the trail is turning and twisting, cutting sharply around latticeworks of roots and jagged rock outcroppings as it negotiates a narrow berm that often seems barely fixed to the steep mountain slope. At times the trail is high above the beautiful Abrams Creek gorge, and at others it is within only a few feet of the stream itself.

The Little Bottoms Trail begins at the Cooper Road Backcountry Campsite (#1) along the Cooper Road Trail one mile above Abrams Creek Campground. The first hundred yards of the Little Bottoms Trail are a deceiving prelude to what soon follows. After a short easy stroll through old-field stands of white pine and eastern hemlock, the trail crosses Kingfisher Creek and a few steps beyond enters an exceedingly steep 300-yard climb to the crest of a narrow ridge. Once at the top, the trail levels momentarily, then enters an equally steep drop to begin one of the wildest stretches of trail in the Smokies.

The Little Bottoms Trail is not a graded course, but a relic from a time when mountaineers engraved a track in the slope above the stream simply by their comings and goings. Because its track is so steep and narrow, this trail was known to old-timers as "the goat trail." In places it is little more than an etching in the ground not much wider than a hiker's boot. When not climbing around a tree or protruding roots, "the goat trail" is often edging along some treacherous jut of rock.

At the bottom of the descent, the trail offers a brief respite when it crosses Buck Shank Branch and settles into a level stretch close along the edge of Abrams Creek. The trail continues by the stream for perhaps 200 yards before resuming as "the goat trail."

A mile and a quarter into its course, the trail drops again to the stream, crossing Mill Branch and entering a bottomland of ten to twelve acres that straddles Abrams Creek. Even by Smoky Mountain standards, this would have been considered a small settlement, thus suggesting the name Little Bottoms. The bottom was once tilled as a Smoky Mountain farm and still harbors ruins of an old farm building. A segment of rock fencing and several cairns of gathered stones are tangible reminders of the bottom's agrarian heritage.

The former settlement farm is now occupied by the Little Bottoms Backcountry Campsite (#17), the largest and one of the nicer backcountry campsites in the park. It is situated on a slight gradient of approximately four acres overlooking Abrams Creek. A half-dozen distinct camping sites are parceled across the old farmyard, and the camp is serviced by three widely spaced food-storage cables. Much of the area is nicely carpeted with needles from the scattering of second-growth old-field pines shading the camp.

Three hundred yards beyond the Little Bottoms Camp, the trail crosses a small nameless stream and then enters the most challenging segment of its course. Here, the trail climbs high above the Abrams Creek gorge and then inches along an exceedingly rugged declivity that drops steeply to the stream. The berm is narrow and requires constant stepping up, down, and around to circumnavigate trees and negotiate intruding rocks and roots. At one juncture, the trail edges out onto a rough ledge hacked into the cliff face where the track is little more than a bed of loosely shifting shale. These difficulties subside only when the trail begins a final descent to its terminus at an intersection with the Hatcher Mountain Trail. Three hundred and fifty yards below the trail junction, the Hatcher Mountain Trail intersects the western end of the Abrams Falls Trail and the lower terminus of the Hannah Mountain Trail.

GOLD MINE TRAIL

Cooper Road Trail at Gold Mine Gap to the park boundary—0.8 mile.
POINT OF DEPARTURE: Hike 2.5 miles up the Cooper Road Trail. The Gold Mine Trail begins on the left.
QUAD MAP: Blockhouse 148-NW

0.0—Gold Mine Gap. Cooper Road Trail.
0.8—Park boundary.

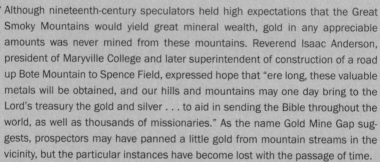

Although nineteenth-century speculators held high expectations that the Great Smoky Mountains would yield great mineral wealth, gold in any appreciable amounts was never mined from these mountains. Reverend Isaac Anderson, president of Maryville College and later superintendent of construction of a road up Bote Mountain to Spence Field, expressed hope that "ere long, these valuable metals will be obtained, and our hills and mountains may one day bring to the Lord's treasury the gold and silver . . . to aid in sending the Bible throughout the world, as well as thousands of missionaries." As the name Gold Mine Gap suggests, prospectors may have panned a little gold from mountain streams in the vicinity, but the particular instances have become lost with the passage of time.

Whatever the origin of its name, Gold Mine Road was built by Daniel D. Foute as an access to the Cooper Road into Cades Cove. The original Gold Mine Road ascended the valley slopes of the Chilhowees, crossed the Flats, and joined the Cooper Road at Gold Mine Gap. Today the Gold Mine Trail is a short rump that traces the old Foute road from Gold Mine Gap to the park boundary, a distance of less than a mile. A quarter-mile beyond the park boundary, the old Foute track meets a paved road at the Top of the World Estates. From that point the old road has been obliterated.

Early accounts of hikers entering the Smokies via the Flats mention the Monkey House. The name Monkey House is associated with Dr. Felix T. Oswald, a scholar who ventured to the Smokies from Ohio in the summer of 1885 to spend time at the Montvale Springs hotel. He persuaded the proprietor of the hotel to build him a cabin in the Flats of Chilhowee Mountain. The cabin was exceptionally well built, having two rooms separated by a "dog trot" and sporting two elaborate chimneys. Dr. Oswald spent the summers of 1886 and 1887 at the cabin while writing *Household Remedies* and was known locally as the "monkey man" because his only companion was a pet monkey. In 1922 Oswald was killed in a streetcar accident in Cincinnati. For many years after his death, the cabin was referred to as the Monkey House and used as a hunting lodge. It stood on the right side of Gold Mine Road less than a quarter-mile beyond the park boundary.

The Gold Mine Trail begins where the Cooper Road Trail enters Gold Mine Gap. Except for one level stretch through a rhododendron tunnel, the entire Gold Mine trail is a steady climb up a rough rutted wagon track. In June, the rhododendrons bloom profusely, making the stroll through the tunnel a pleasant experience. In rainy weather, run-offs collect in the hard-packed ruts, making for a slippery hiking surface.

CANE CREEK TRAIL

Cooper Road Trail at Cane Gap to the park boundary at Hurricane
   Mountain—2.1 miles.
POINT OF DEPARTURE: Hike 3.1 miles up the Cooper Road Trail. The Cane
   Creek Trail begins on the left.
QUAD MAP: Blockhouse 148-NW

0.0—Cane Gap. Cooper Road Trail.
0.6—Cane Creek Backcountry Campsite (#2).
1.3—Access path exits left 30 yards to the Buchanan Cemetery.
2.1—Park boundary.

The Cane Creek Trail runs a straight course along the trough of a narrow watershed drained by Cane Creek. It begins as a wagon road in Cane Gap, an open dell once known as the Buchanan Place and now marked by the intersection of the Cane Creek Trail and Cooper Road Trail.

During the second decade of the twentieth century the Little River Lumber Company moved into Cane Creek and began clear-cutting the entire watershed. When the lumber company departed, a few families in addition to the Buchanans scattered out along Cane Creek, building homes and tilling farmland. The terrain here is exceptionally moist, and the adjacent ridges keep the watershed shaded for much of the time, resulting in conditions that are excellent for wildflowers but rather poor for farming.

When it leaves Cane Gap, the trail descends to the stream and remains along the bottom of the watershed until terminating at the park boundary, two miles farther. In some places the trail is even and soft underfoot; at others it is steeper and a bit rough, but always beneath a cover of slender second-growth hardwoods. The trail alternates between level ground and undulating terrain, and over its course executes several crossings of Cane Creek and its tributaries.

Slightly over a half-mile beyond Cane Gap, the trail enters a small parcel of creek bottom nestled in a wide arc of Cane Creek where the Cane Creek Backcountry Campsite (#2) resides along the side of the bottom away from the stream. The camp is quite level with several excellent tents sites and is shaded by a sparse scattering of oaks, maples, and pines. The stream is blocked from the camp by a thick partition of rhododendron, but water is readily accessible at both ends of the bottom.

Less than a quarter-mile beyond the campsite, the Buchanan Cemetery occupies a low knoll thirty yards above the left side of the trail. Adjacent to the cemetery is the former site of the Cane Creek School. The cemetery and the school are testimonies to the fact that this insignificant hollow in the Great Smoky Mountains was once sufficiently settled to sustain a community.

Beyond the cemetery, the trail diminishes to a narrow trace that threads its way through tangled thickets of understory. It continues for slightly less than a mile before reaching the park boundary at an undistinguished spot in the woods. The trail continues as a passable route into Miller Cove, but hiking is discouraged by inhospitable no-trespassing signs posted at trail's end. Within a quarter-mile, the passage beyond the park boundary intersects, near the confluence of Cane Creek and Hesse Creek, the western terminus of a manway following along Hurricane Mountain to Blair Gap where it meets the Ace Gap Trail and Beard Cane Trail.

BEARD CANE TRAIL

Cooper Road Trail to the Ace Gap Trail at Blair Gap—4.2 miles.
POINT OF DEPARTURE: Hike 4.9 miles up the Cooper Road Trail. The Beard Cane Trail begins on the left.
QUAD MAPS: Blockhouse 148-NW
Kinzel Springs 148-NE

0.0—Cooper Road Trail. Hatcher Mountain Trail.
1.0—Beard Cane Backcountry Campsite (#11).
3.6—Hesse Creek Backcountry Campsite (#3).
3.7—Hesse Creek.
4.2—Blair Gap. Ace Gap Trail exits right 5.5 miles to Rich Mountain Road. Manway exits left to Cane Creek in Miller Cove.

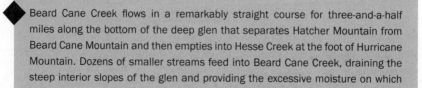

Beard Cane Creek flows in a remarkably straight course for three-and-a-half miles along the bottom of the deep glen that separates Hatcher Mountain from Beard Cane Mountain and then empties into Hesse Creek at the foot of Hurricane Mountain. Dozens of smaller streams feed into Beard Cane Creek, draining the steep interior slopes of the glen and providing the excessive moisture on which great forests thrive. Before the watershed was logged by the Little River Lumber Company, the Beard Cane drainage was thick with great hardwoods standing tall and straight to reach what little sunlight filtered into the narrow ravine. Today, nearly ninety years since the area was clear-cut by the lumbermen, the trees have returned, tall and slender, with scarcely a taper and reaching sixty, seventy, perhaps eighty feet to the first limb. The high canopy shades out the sunlight, casting a perpetual gloom over the silent open forest.

When the Little River Lumber Company first began logging the Hesse Creek basin, a railroad line was run along Beard Cane Creek to facilitate the retrieval of cut timber. The rail line adhered closely to the stream, running a straight course with remarkably little change in elevation. The modern Beard Cane Trail appropriates the bed of the abandoned rail line.

Access to either terminus of the Beard Cane Trail is difficult. The trail may be approached from Rich Mountain Gap, Cades Cove Loop Road, or Abrams Creek Campground. In either case, the distance is at least five miles.

The southern terminus of the Beard Cane Trail lies in a nameless gap in Hatcher Mountain that harbors a crossroads intersection with the Hatcher Mountain Trail and Cooper Road Trail. From this junction, the Beard Cane Trail works its way north through a narrow pass between Hatcher Mountain and Wedge Ridge then descends steadily a half-mile on a hard-packed track to cross Beard Cane Creek at the bottom of the glen. As it descends, the trail leaves the open dry-ridge pine stands for the gloom of deep woods.

At the stream crossing, the trail picks up the railroad trace, following it until crossing Hesse Creek three miles farther. Along the way, multiple stream crossings intervene. In some places the track is rocky and uneven; in others the loam is a sticky morass, but nowhere on its course along the stream does the trail betray even the slightest grade.

After a mile, the trail approaches Beard Cane Backcountry Campsite (#11), a small level tract fitted between the trail and the stream. The camp is an attractive setting tucked in among a thicket of rhododendron and shaded by slender trees. Like every place else in the Beard Cane watershed, the camp area is damp and, during a heavy rain, apt to become wet and boggy.

For the next two-and-a-half miles, there are no appreciable changes in either the trail conditions or the surrounding forest environment. The exception occurs in springtime when this wet protected environment literally explodes with wildflowers. One species, rare to the Smokies but indigenous along Beard Cane Creek, is the beautiful fringed polygala. Only three to four inches tall and flowering in May, the fringed polygala bears a reddish-pink, winged bloom. It is also known as gay wings and flowering wintergreen.

Before reaching its crossing of Hesse Creek, the trail turns away from Beard Cane Creek and enters a wide flat occupied by the Hesse Creek Backcountry Campsite (#3). The camp is situated on a level bench above Hesse Creek and shaded with slender hemlocks. The site is spacious, offering several suitable tents sites and the opportunity to spread out among the trees.

At this juncture, the old lumber company rail line turned up Hesse Creek and proceeded to another flat near the confluence of Shell and Hesse creeks. Here the lumber company maintained a camp to house loggers, naming it Eldorado. Some have speculated that the name was suggested by the richness of the timber resources in the Hesse Creek drainage, but more than likely it was named for Calvin Post's earlier, but unsuccessful, mining venture of the same name at the head of Hesse Creek near Rich Mountain Gap. The stream that flows by Eldorado was named for John Hess, a Swiss immigrant who operated a mill near the mouth of Hesse Creek in Miller Cove.

Immediately beyond the Hesse Creek Camp, the trail crosses Hesse Creek and begins a steep 400-foot climb up the face of Hurricane Mountain to terminate in Blair Gap. The origin of the name Hurricane Mountain is uncertain. Inhabitants of the area occasionally refer to the mountain and the Hesse watershed collectively as "the Hurricane" with reference to some unspecified hurricane or large storm that blew down a great many trees. Ironically, in the spring of 2011 a major windstorm descended on Hurricane Mountain with such force that it left a swath of fallen trees the length of the Beard Cane Creek, destroying the campsites and making the trail virtually impossible to travel. The occurrence of the latter-day storm is eerily reminiscent of whatever event that may have been the occasion for the origin of the name.

At Blair Gap, the Beard Cane Trail reaches the park boundary and enters a three-way intersection with the Ace Gap Trail leading in from Rich Mountain Road and an unmaintained manway along Hurricane Mountain that connects with an extension of the Cane Creek Trail lying outside of the park.

♦ APPALACHIAN TRAIL ♦

In the October 1921 issue of the *Journal of the American Institute of Architecture,* forester and conservationist Benton MacKaye published "An Appalachian Trail: A Project in Regional Planning," in which he proposed the building of "a 'long trail' over the full length of the Appalachian skyline, from the highest peak in the north to the highest peak in the south." MacKaye based his proposal on the premise that people need escape from the "high powered tension of the economic scramble" that characterized American life in the early twentieth century. His vision precipitated in the creation of the Appalachian Trail (AT), an ingenious trail system that continues for more than two thousand miles from Springer Mountain in Georgia to Mount Katahdin in Maine.

The realization of the AT through the Great Smoky Mountains is much the result of the foresight and effort of the Smoky Mountains Hiking Club. Founded in 1924, early members of the club were instrumental in blazing a course along the main Smoky divide and fostering the trail's inclusion in the AT system. The original course charted by the club followed the state-line divide between North Carolina and Tennessee, entering the southwest corner of the Smokies at Deals Gap and exiting the northeast corner at Davenport Gap. With the advent of Fontana Lake in 1945, the course of the AT was changed, routing it off the divide into North Carolina at Doe Knob and along the spine of Twentymile Ridge to Fontana Dam where it now exits the park.

Within the Great Smoky Mountains National Park, the AT completes 71.6 miles and traverses more than a dozen peaks whose elevations are greater than six thousand feet. Along the main Smoky divide, it rarely dips below five thousand feet. Thunderhead, Clingmans Dome, Charlies Bunion, and Mount Cammerer are a few of the more notable peaks along the trail that afford surpassing vantage points for surveying the rugged Southern Appalachian highlands where the forest cover ranges from the boreal world of spruce-fir stands, to splendid beech gaps, to ragged semi-balds, to dry-ridge deciduous stands. Abundance of rain and cool atmospheric conditions are conducive to a proliferation of wildflower species, some rare, and others that blanket entire mountain slopes.

The descriptive narrative of the AT assumes a beginning from the Fontana Dam end of the trail and proceeds east to Davenport Gap. The choice is arbitrary, but corresponds to the direction more frequently used by through-hikers.

Camping on the AT inside the park is permitted only in the twelve shelters spaced at half-day hiking intervals along the main divide or in the Birch Spring Gap Backcountry Campsite (#113) on Twentymile Ridge. The trail passes immediately by the shelters at Mollies Ridge, Russell Field, Derrick Knob, Silers Bald, and Double

Spring Gap. Those at Icewater Spring, Tricorner Knob, Cosby Knob, and Davenport Gap are reached by short access paths and may not necessarily be visible from the AT itself. The shelter in Spence Field is 290 yards down the Eagle Creek Trail; that on Mount Collins is 540 yards down the Sugarland Mountain Trail; and that near Pecks Corner is 655 yards down the Hughes Ridge Trail. All shelters have been upgraded with wooden benches and bar-width tables covered by extended roof-lines.

Backpackers staying in any of the shelters or backcountry campsites must make reservations with the Backcountry Reservation Office. Reservations can be made online at https://smokiespermits.nps.gov/, by calling the Backcountry Office at (423) 436-1297 or 436-1231 between 8 a.m. and 5 p.m., or in person at the Sugarlands Visitor Center two miles south of Gatlinburg on US441 (Newfound Gap Road). Reservations may be made up to one month prior to the first day of the trip.

The fee for camping in the shelters is $4.00 per night for each camper up to a maximum of $20.00 per person. Campers may not stay consecutive nights at any shelter or at the Birch Spring Gap Backcountry Campsite (#113).

APPALACHIAN TRAIL

Fontana Dam Road at the Lakeshore Trail to TN32/NC284 at Davenport Gap—71.6 miles.

POINT OF DEPARTURE: Cross Fontana Dam and drive 0.7 mile to the end of Fontana Dam Road. The Appalachian Trail begins on the left at the end of the road.

0.0—End of Fontana Dam Road. Western terminus of the Lakeshore Trail.

3.4—Access path exits right 150 yards to the Shuckstack fire tower.

3.7—Sassafras Gap. Lost Cove Trail exits right 2.7 miles to the Lakeshore Trail. Twentymile Trail exits left 5.0 miles to the Twentymile Ranger Station.

4.3—Red Ridge Gap.

4.6—Access path exits left to Birch Spring Gap Backcountry Campsite (#113).

6.8—Gregory Bald Trail exits left 2.8 miles to Gregory Bald.

6.9—Doe Knob.

7.4—Mud Gap.

8.3—Ekaneetlee Gap.

10.0—Lawson Gant Lot. Mollies Ridge Shelter.

11.8—Little Abrams Gap.

12.2—Big Abrams Gap.

13.2—Russell Field Shelter. Russell Field Trail exits left 3.5 miles to the Anthony Creek Trail.

14.7—Mount Squires (Little Bald).

16.1—Spence Field. Eagle Creek Trail exits right 290 yards to the Spence Field Shelter.

16.1—Bote Mountain Trail exits left 6.9 miles to Laurel Creek Road.

16.5—Jenkins Ridge Trail exits right 8.9 miles to the Hazel Creek Trail.

17.2—Rocky Top.

17.9—Thunderhead.

18.6—Beechnut Gap.

18.7—Brier Knob.

20.5—Starkey Gap.

21.3—Sugartree Gap.

22.3—Derrick Knob Shelter.

22.4—Big Chestnut Bald.

22.7—Sams Gap. Greenbrier Ridge Trail exits lefts 4.2 miles to the Middle Prong Trail and Lynn Camp Prong Trail.

22.8—Mount Davis.

23.6—Hemlock Knob.

24.6—Cold Spring Knob.

25.0—Miry Ridge Trail exits left 5.0 miles to the Jakes Creek Trail and Panther Creek Trail.

25.2—Buckeye Gap.

27.9—Silers Bald Shelter.

28.1—Silers Bald.

28.3—Welch Ridge Trail exits right 6.7 miles to High Rocks.

28.7—The Narrows.

29.6—Double Spring Gap. Double Spring Gap Shelter.

30.2—Goshen Prong Trail exits left 7.6 miles to the Little River Trail.

31.6—Mount Buckley.

32.1—Clingmans Dome Bypass Trail exits right 0.5 mile to the Forney Ridge Trail.

32.4—Access path exits right 75 yards to the Clingmans Dome Observation Tower.

34.4—Collins Gap.

35.4—Mount Collins.

35.9—Sugarland Mountain Trail exits left 540 yards to the Mount Collins Shelter.

36.1—Access path exits right 55 yards to Clingmans Dome Road and the Fork Ridge Trail.

38.6—Indian Gap. Road Prong Trail exits left 2.4 miles to the Chimney Tops Trail at Beech Flats.

40.3—Newfound Gap. Newfound Gap Road (US441).

42.0—Sweat Heifer Creek Trail exits right 3.7 miles to the Kephart Prong Shelter.

43.1—Boulevard Trail exits left 5.4 miles to the summit of Mount Le Conte.

43.3—Access path exits right to the Icewater Spring Shelter.

43.4—Icewater Spring.

44.3—Access path exits left to Charlies Bunion.

44.4—Access path returns on left from Charlies Bunion.

44.7—Fire-scald.

44.8—Dry Sluice Gap Trail exits right 4.2 miles to the Cabin Flats Trail.

45.8—Porters Gap.

47.0—False Gap.

48.4—Laurel Top.

49.5—Bradley View.

50.8—Pecks Corner. Hughes Ridge Trail exits right 655 yards to the Pecks Corner Shelter.

51.7—Eagle Rocks.

52.5—Copper Gap.

53.6—Mount Sequoyah.

54.9—Mount Chapman.

56.0—Access path exits right to the Tricorner Knob Shelter.

56.1—Balsam Mountain Trail exits right 10.1 miles to Balsam Mountain Road at Pin Oak Gap.

57.9—Guyot Spring.

58.0—Access path to the summit of Mount Guyot.

58.8—Deer Creek Gap.

59.8—Snake Den Ridge Trail exits left 5.3 miles to Cosby Campground.

62.1—Camel Gap Trail exits right 4.7 miles to the Big Creek Trail at Walnut Bottom.

63.7—Access path exits right to the Cosby Knob Shelter.

64.4—Low Gap. Low Gap Trail exits right 2.5 miles to the Big Creek Trail at Walnut Bottom and left 2.9 miles to Cosby Campground.

66.5—Mount Cammerer Trail exits left 0.6 mile to the Mount Cammerer Lookout Tower.

68.8—Lower Mount Cammerer Trail exits left 7.5 miles to Cosby Campground.

69.7—Chestnut Branch Trail exits right 2.1 miles to Big Creek Road.

70.8—Access path exits left to the Davenport Gap Shelter.

71.6—Davenport Gap. TN32/NC284.

Technically, the Appalachian Trail (AT) enters the Great Smoky Mountains National Park at Fontana Dam, following a paved track known as Fontana Dam Road. The trail remains on the road as it circles around the lower end of Fontana Lake three-quarters of a mile to a parking area adjacent to the western end of the Lakeshore Trail.

Conventionally, the AT begins where the pavement of Fontana Dam Road yields to a jeep track that marks the beginning of the Lakeshore Trail. At the point of transition, the AT makes an inconspicuous exit from the human improvements of the road, pavement, dam, and lake and ventures immediately into the Smoky Mountain fastness on a narrow hard-packed dirt track. The trail gains elevation rapidly, winding through a mix of yellow poplar, sassafras, and redbud, soon giving way to a dry-ridge association of oaks and maples. The climb continues unabated until the trail turns abruptly left below a slight rock-strewn draw. Originally the AT did not turn at this point, but followed up the draw directly to a minor peak known as Little Shuckstack, then turned and traced the connecting ridgeline to the summit of its bigger sibling, Shuckstack.

When the trail turns at the foot of the draw, the grade moderates, then continues for 500 yards before edging out onto a slate outcropping completely abraded of vegetation. From the outcropping, Cheoah Lake can be seen below, as well as Canepatch Ridge, the prominent spur extending down to the lake. Sheep Knob is the distinctive peak immediately to the west.

When it leaves the outcropping, the trail descends for a little more than a hundred yards through high weedy growth before starting into an extremely steep 600-yard climb to the ridgeline west of Shuckstack. At the ridgeline, the trail cuts sharply back to the east, tracing the spine of the ridge for only a few yards before reaching an odd intersection where the AT rolls off to the north side of the ridge to follow an old roadbed. The track which continues east on the ridgeline climbs on a rough winding course 150 yards to the summit of Shuckstack (4,020 feet), a sharp pinnacle that punctuates the south end of Twentymile Ridge. The name "Shuckstack" is suggested by the peak's resemblance to a standing sheaf of cornstalks when viewed from a distance.

 On the summit of Shuckstack, which slopes off steeply on three sides, stands a sixty-foot steel fire tower built in 1934 by the Works Progress Administration. From a vantage point atop the tower, the Little Tennessee River appears below, anchored at its upper end by Fontana Lake, where rugged green-clad mountains rise almost vertically from the water's edge. The north shore of the lake defines the south boundary of the park. Across Fontana Lake are the Yellow Creek Mountains with High Top (3,786 feet) the highest point on the range, visible just above the Fontana Marina embayment, which is to the left of Fontana Dam. The Cheoah Mountains are visible beyond the Yellow Creek Mountains with Cheoah Bald (4,062 feet) and Wauchecha Bald (4,390 feet) being the noticeable peaks to the left and right, respectively, of High Top. Southwest of the tower and below is Sheep Knob (3,860 feet), a small point on the short ridge extending down to the river. Directly over the ridge and across the river are the Unicoi Mountains.

Due east is High Rocks (5,190 feet), a prominent pinnacle that once harbored a fire tower similar to that on Shuckstack. The fire tower on High Rocks was dismantled and removed in the 1980s.

To the north is the looming ridgeline of the main Smoky divide. Gregory Bald (4,949 feet) is the dominant peak to the west, with Thunderhead (5,527 feet), Silers Bald (5,607 feet), and Clingmans Dome (6,643 feet) appearing progressively east along the divide.

A small warden's cabin built of chestnut logs once stood near the foot of the fire tower. The cabin was removed in the late 1980s, but the stone chimney still remains, along with the foundation and a concrete water cistern.

When it exits the odd intersection, the AT begins following a road once used for vehicle access to the fire tower. The trail descends along the road on a fairly steep grade for 600 yards, then enters Sassafras Gap where the Lost Cove Trail rises up into the gap from the east side and the Twentymile Trail enters on the west. Both trails terminate in Sassafras Gap. At the gap, the road turns down the mountain on the Twentymile Trail. The AT continues north on a narrower track along the spine of Twentymile Ridge.

After the AT climbs out of Sassafras Gap, it levels out for a short interval, then drops into Red Ridge Gap. Within the next 500 yards, it climbs out of Red Ridge Gap and drops into Birch Spring Gap, where an access path on the left leads down a draw 150 yards to the Birch Spring Gap Backcountry Campsite (#113).

For many years the Birch Spring Gap site was occupied by a low dungeon-like shelter that sat with its back flush against the mountain slope and facing a spring. The shelter was torn down early in the twenty-first century, leaving only its stone back wall embedded in the slope. The current backcountry camp consists of seven separate tent sites spaced out down the draw. Five sites are across the spring from the old shelter site and considerably downstream. The remaining two are at the end of the access path that continues behind of the old shelter site.

Because of the steepness of the terrain, the tent sites consist of terraced plots built up with logs and back-filled with dirt. Though nice and level, the back-fill tends to muddiness when it rains. The camp affords two food-storage cables, though they are not convenient to some of the tent sites. Water is available at the spring immediately in front of the former shelter site. In the drier seasons, Birch Spring may become quite feeble, but rarely does it disappear completely.

From Birch Spring Gap, the AT climbs for the better part of a half-mile and then enters an easier, modulating course that circumnavigates Greer Knob. It soon edges up along the west flank of Doe Knob to intersect the east terminus of the Gregory Bald Trail running along the spine of the main Smoky divide.

Since its day as a grazing range, Doe Knob has recovered to a sparsely forested slope with a thin understory, a setting having more affinity with a park than a mountain fastness. The AT circles around the knob on an easy course and then descends to Mud Gap.

 During the early years of the twentieth century, Greer Knob and Doe Knob were summer grazing ranges for cattle driven up from Cades Cove. The lower knob is named for Andy Greer, a resident of Cades Cove who was known to have herded cattle here. Prior to 1947, the AT through the Smokies remained on the state-line divide for its entirety and did not turn down into North Carolina at Doe Knob. It continued to Gregory Bald and Parson Bald before exiting the Smokies at Deals Gap. The re-route at Doe Knob was implemented to direct the trail to a more suitable course over the newly built Fontana Dam. For the hiker beginning at the Fontana Dam end, the AT turns east at Doe Knob onto the main Smoky divide and continues following the divide until exiting the park at Davenport Gap.

Just a few paces after starting down to Mud Gap, a large birch tree can be seen on the left of the trail standing up off the ground, supported only by its roots. As a seed, the birch tree germinated on a fallen log, sending its roots into the rotting host. In the early stages of colonization, the tree would appear to be perched on the log itself. Later, as the tree grew, its roots girdled the log as if embracing it, until finally reaching to the ground. When the nurse log eventually fully decayed, the birch was left with its roots like curved stilts, propping the trunk well off the ground and nothing but a cavity where the fallen log once lay.

The trail descends a half-mile to Mud Gap, then rises gently to clear Powell Knob prior to completing a gradual three-quarter-mile drop into Ekaneetlee Gap (3,868 feet), the lowest point of elevation along the spine of the Smoky divide.

 Ekaneetlee, a corruption of the Cherokee word Egwanulti meaning "by the river," identifies one of the oldest human landmarks in the Smokies. An ancient Cherokee trace crossed over the mountain through Ekanteelee Gap connecting the overhill towns in North Carolina with the Great Indian War Path in Tennessee. The Indian trace followed Ekaneetlee Creek upstream from Eagle Creek and then descended into Cades Cove along Ekaneetlee Branch. Early settlers from South Carolina entered Cades Cove through Ekaneetlee Gap and would later journey back to the gap, leading cattle to graze on the grassy highland balds. Superseded by better trails and roads, the old Indian trace fell into disuse and eventually degenerated to an impassible track.

Because of its strategic location and proximity to water, Ekaneetlee Gap has long been regarded as a camping place for wayfarers on the Smoky divide. For a brief period in the 1920s, the gap even sported a small cabin built near the creek on the Tennessee side by the Oliver family of Cades Cove.

From Ekaneetlee Gap, the AT rolls off the ridgeline into North Carolina for a short excursion through rhododendron thickets, then loops back onto the ridgeline and into a park-like setting similar to that on Doe Knob. About a mile above the gap, the trail enters a half-mile section that was re-routed in 2002 to circumvent a steep, badly eroded gully that led to a high point known at various times as Bear Pen Knob, the Lawson Range, and Lawson Gant Lot. Here, the ridgeline opens out into a flat expanse of several acres. During the tenure of the herders, the range was covered in a carpet of grass six to ten inches deep. The name, Gant Lot, suggests that the range once harbored a cattle pen used for holding browsing stock before they were herded down the mountain and to the markets.

Though slowly returning to woodland, the Lawson Range still bears vestiges of its grazing heritage. The most conspicuous feature on the range now is the Mollies Ridge Shelter, a three-sided stone structure facing east into a spacious yard of closely cropped turf and with its back to a rolling gradient of weedy undergrowth. A roof overhang projecting from the side wall of the shelter protects a table and benches. Water is available from a spring 150 yards down the Tennessee side. Though accoutered with a pipe, the spring is not entirely reliable and occasionally goes completely dry.

Mollies Ridge, a short spur extending down into Tennessee from the highest point on the Lawson Range, is punctuated at its lower end by a knob known as Mollies Butt.

 According to legend, Mollies Butt is haunted by the ghost of a young Cherokee maiden who froze to death while searching nearby for a lost hunter. Harvey Broome recorded this story as told to him by Uncle Eph Pruett of Sassafras Cove:

> Now, I allus heerd her genuwine name war Molly—she wuz a Cherokee Injun gal—but people what couldn' read er cipher none got to callin' her Mollie. She wuz sweet on White Eagle Button—a halfbreed. The'r tribe come to Cades Cove hyar from t'other side o' the mountain fer to hunt. Button went a-huntin' toward yander knob, and didn' come back. Leastways he didn' turn up till yars later. Mollie hankered atter him. That's whut some says, but I never heerd o' no Injun gal a-follerin' atter a man. Mabe she war teched; some says that. Leastways she follered atter him, and thet night thar come a big freeze, and jist frizzed the sperrit outen her body. I say hit died out. I can't see no differ in freezin' a body's sperrit out and in jist dyin' it out. But I'm tellin' hit to you'ins the way hit was tol' to me. And her sperrit ar' still knockin' about up on that thar mountain. The white folks when they first settled hyar called hit "Old Butt" for White Eagle. But ez they kep' comin' back fr'm huntin' with tales o' sump'm flittin' through the trees, what they said wuz Mollie's sperrit—they got to callin' hit Mollies Butt.

I never seed no sperrit; hit'd pleasure me to call hit Old Butt. But there's them thet has seed hit. They say her sperrit's brighter'n moonlight in January, 'n' jest as bright ez moonlight in August, 'cause nobody never claimed to hav seed it in August. Some says hit's darker'n fog. Some says hit's warmer'n freezin'. Others says hit's colder'n hell. Some says they hev walked right through it. I says hit ar' jest one o' them passels o' cold air whut any hunter knows aboutn. Some claims her shadder gets offen the Butt and over to the Sugar Cove, 'cause they's felten cold spots thar. Some says these hyar roads follers her tracks through the woods, 'cause she allus went the easy way. I dunno. But they's the way Mollies Butt got named, and I'm tellin' hit to you'uns jest the way I heerd it fr'm ol' Aunt Cindy Tomey, when I wusn't big enough to make spittin' balls.

Like most legends, the story of Mollie has many variations, but most contend that she froze to death. One account, however, suggests that she was eaten by a bear called Spider Foot. The descendants of Spider Foot were thought to be exceptionally vigorous, and most never ventured far from Mollies Butt. If there is any truth to the bear story, it rests with the understanding that bears inhabited the Mollies Butt vicinity because of its proximity to some of the Smokies' prime chestnut forests, a favorite source of food for those foragers.

From Lawson Range, the AT climbs steeply for about 400 yards before easing through the Devils Tater Patch (4,775 feet). At the end of the Devils Tater Patch, the AT executes a sharp switchback left, leaves the ridgeline, and plunges into heavy concentrations of rhododendron. Although descending, the grade is not particularly steep. Two additional switchbacks at intervals of 600 and 500 yards mitigate the descent into Little Abrams Gap where the trail returns to the ridgeline. A little less than a mile farther, the trail drops into the slightly larger Big Abrams Gap. The names were assigned to the gaps as a tribute to the Cherokee Chief who lived in Chilhowee village at the mouth of Abrams Creek. Previously, these gaps were known to the local mountaineers as Little Mill Creek Gap and Big Mill Creek Gap in recognition of their proximity to the headwaters of the big stream that drains into the lower end of Cades Cove.

From Big Abrams Gap, the trail edges off onto the North Carolina side of the ridge and proceeds on a gradual climb through beech stands for slightly over a mile before entering Russell Field, another of the former grazing ranges on the main divide.

Two of the earliest owners of Russell Field were William Murry of Chilhowee and Joseph Estabrook, president of East Tennessee College (later the University of Tennessee). In 1833, Murry and Estabrook were among a group of eleven investors in the so-called Anderson Road which was proposed to cross the mountain from Tennessee to North Carolina through nearby Spence Field.

Russell Field was named for early settler John Russell who began grazing sheep on the balds along the Smoky divide a quarter-century prior to the Civil War. Early travelers to Russell Field commented on seeing a herder's cabin on the bald which may have been the log cabin which John Russell built sometime in the mid-1830s. During its heyday as a grazing range, Russell Field was described as "a beautiful rolling grassy expanse of several hundred acres nestling in the depression where two ridges join." Sometime late in the nineteenth century the Cooper family lived here year-round, raising cattle, maintaining a large garden, and harvesting hay which they put up in barns. In 1930, hikers with the newly formed Smoky Mountains Hiking Club found remnants of the Cooper place—two ramshackle cabins and a dilapidated barn in the field.

As a young man, Harvey Broome noticed that the upper end of Russell Field was dotted with stumps. Broome surmised that the field had at one time been enlarged for grazing, leading him to ponder the possibility that the grassy balds of the Smoky Mountains were the result of human activity rather than naturally occurring phenomena.

Since the time of Broome's visit, the wilderness has reclaimed much of Russell Field, reducing the cleared space to a few acres astride the state-line divide. The Russell Field Shelter now occupies the clearing, facing east along the divide. The shelter is a three-sided stone structure with an extended roof that covers an enclosure of tables and benches. The Russell Field Trail, leading up from Cades Cove, passes in front of the shelter to intersect the AT along the North Carolina side of the divide. Water is available from a messy rill 210 yards down the Russell Field Trail.

As it leaves Russell Field, the AT remains on the broad crest of the Smoky divide, winding an easy course through old highland clearings shaded by scattered oaks, American beeches, and Allegheny serviceberries. Though the slopes immediately east of Russell Field were not cleared for farming, the forest cover was kept thin by the persistent rooting of domestic hogs that were turned free to roam the mountains.

A mile and a half beyond Russell Field, the trail rises into a small clearing once known to the Smoky Mountaineers as Little Bald. In 1953 Little Bald was renamed Mount Squires in honor of Mark Squires, a senator from North Carolina who played an instrumental role in bringing the Great Smoky Mountain Park movement to fruition.

Beyond Mount Squires, the trail continues with little deviation in grade and little variation in forest cover for another mile to reach the western end of Spence Field, an enormous grassy sward extending along the divide almost two miles to the foot of Thunderhead Mountain.

James Spence, for whom the field is named, was the first white settler to maintain a cabin here, arriving sometime around 1830. Spence occupied his cabin on the mountain during the warmer months, but returned to his home in Whiteoak Sink for the winter. (Just outside of Whiteoak Sink is a small stream that was for many years known as Spence Deadening Branch. The name was later shortened to Spence Branch.)

When James Spence first arrived on Spence Field, there may well have been a small clearing maintained by the Cherokee as a hunting ground, although as late as 1869 most of the mountain around the field was covered in beech stands. By 1870 settlers began clearing the gently rolling slopes of the mountain, first girdling the buckeye trees so that cattle brought to graze in the fields would not be poisoned from eating the buckeyes. Spence Field continued to be expanded by clearing for several years afterward. Passersby noted stumps on the perimeter of the field as late as 1906. When grazing ceased in 1936, Spence Field was a grassy expanse almost two mile long and extended a considerable distance down both the Tennessee and North Carolina sides of the mountain. Its turf was as close-clipped as a lawn and the perimeter well-defined by a fringe of trees.

Eben Alexander, a visitor to Spence Field in the 1880s, mentioned that the original cabin built by James Spence was gone but a newer one bearing Spence's name had been erected. Early maps of the Smokies locate the Spence cabin (sometimes called the Spencer cabin) on the Tennessee side of the clearing. A student from the University of Tennessee visiting in the summer of 1887 estimated the Spence cabin to be twenty-five feet by twenty feet with one door, no windows, and floored with puncheons. He gave no indication of the cabin having a chimney or fireplace except to say that he and his companions all slept in the cabin with their feet to the fire. This is likely the same building visited by W. L. Hinklin in 1903 when he witnessed a cabin being crowded with wild hogs rushing in for safety when hearing the screams of a nearby eagle.

The first cabin built on the North Carolina side of Spence Field may have been as late as 1905. A few years later this cabin was destroyed when lightening "shivered its timbers." This cabin was replaced by another which was described as being about twenty feet long and fifteen feet wide, built of logs and having two rooms, a loft, and a big stone fireplace. The loft was reached by a ladder nailed to the side of the cabin. The shelter, used primarily by herders and hunting parties, was infested with fleas and wood mice. By 1926 the foundation was sagging, and the whole floor titled badly.

This last cabin in Spence Field was built by Tom Sparks, a Cades Cove native who often stayed on the mountain throughout the summer, herding cattle for his neighbors in the cove. The cabin stood below the ridgeline just west of the fine spring that forms a headwater for Eagle Creek. (This is the same spring that now serves the Spence Field Shelter.) On July 16, 1926, Tom Sparks was staying at the cabin with his son Asa Sparks, son-in-law Fonze Cable, two grandsons Braney and Robert (Buster) Cable, and a young man named Earl Cameron who worked as an occasional hired hand for the Sparks family. That evening Tom Sparks was fixing dinner for his grandsons and young Cameron. Cameron had been acting a bit surly during the day, perhaps as the result of being accused of taking Spark's wallet. Cameron had also broken the house rule concerning guns. Any armed person coming into the two-room cabin was supposed to toss his weapon on a nearby bed and leave it there until he departed. At dinnertime, Cameron entered the cabin, went immediately into the cabin bedroom, and stretched out on the iron bed with the weapons, refusing to join the others at dinner.

Tom Sparks was by nature a generous and gracious man who had the peculiar habit of remaining standing at dinner until everyone else had been seated and served. While Earl Cameron was sulking in the bedroom, Sparks was standing and waiting. Cameron eventually came out of the bedroom brandishing one of the grandsons' pistols. Pointing the pistol at Sparks, Cameron backed out through the cabin door. Sparks, unarmed, followed, but did not go outside of the cabin. The younger grandson, Buster, standing only a few feet away, watched as Cameron fired twice. Both bullets entered Tom Sparks's stomach, and he died instantly.

Earl Cameron dropped the pistol and ran off across Spence Field. He was later apprehended near his home in Sunshine, Tennessee, near Tuckaleechee Cove. Because the cabin stood on the North Carolina side of Spence Field, the murder trial was held in Bryson City. Buster Cable, the most immediate witness to the killing, was not allowed to testify during the trial. He was eleven years of age at the time and thus considered too young to be a legally reliable witness.

The cabin in which Tom Sparks died was the last to stand in Spence Field. Just east of the site of the last Spence cabin is the modern Spence Field Shelter, located 290 yards down the Eagle Creek Trail.

The AT intersects the Eagle Creek Trail at the west end of Spence Field just below the ridgeline on the Tennessee side. A hundred and ten yards farther, the AT meets the upper terminus of the Bote Mountain Trail leading up from Laurel Creek Road. From here, the AT edges out into the open spaces of Spence Field and begins a gently winding course that works up and over the succession of hills that were once roamed by hundreds of cattle, sheep, horses, and hogs. The University of Tennessee student who visited Spence Field in 1887 recorded seeing a herd "composed of 500 head of cattle, forty hogs, and thirty young mules and horses." He commented that "Occasionally, a bear, pressed for hunger, kills and makes a meal of a calf. However, this is rare."

During its tenure as a grazing range, Spence Field appeared from a distance to be shaped like an enormous saddle, with the light fresh green of the grass reminding one of a saddle-cloth extending a considerable distance down the slope to the dark green of the forest. In the seventy-five years since grazing has ceased on Spence Field, encroaching rhododendron and Allegheny serviceberry trees have effaced the neatly defined perimeter. Of the hundreds of acres that once comprised the two-mile-long bald, only about thirty retain any appearance of a clearing.

Five hundred and fifty yards beyond the Bote Mountain Trail intersection, the AT meets the upper terminus of the Jenkins Ridge Trail leading in on the right from Hazel Creek. A hundred yards or so down into North Carolina from the trail junction is a fine spring. Near it there once stood a six-person backcountry shelter. Several years ago the shelter was dismantled and the camp abandoned. Subsequently the spring has become submerged beneath the thickets of rhododendron that have spread up and into Spence Field, making the old shelter site difficult to locate.

The east end of Spence Field is defined without precision as the point where the gentle gradient of the sward yields to the steeper terrain of Thunderhead Mountain. Older convention claims that Thunderhead is the name bestowed collectively to the group of naturally bald peaks immediately east of Spence Field with Rocky Top being the distinctive "naked" peak and Laurel Top being the highest. The name Thunderhead is suggested by an arrangement of dome-shaped rocks on the top of the mountain which, seen from the cove below, have the appearance of thunder-head clouds. Later convention contends that Thunderhead Mountain is comprised of three peaks—Rocky Top being the western-most, Thunderhead the middle and highest, and Laurel Top a less conspicuous point on the east flank.

The trail first traverses Rocky Top, unmistakable with its welter of bleached-out rocks accompanied by a few gnarled storm-agonized trees. Herders like Tom Sparks often used the bowl-shaped pits on the surface of the rocks as receptacles for salting cattle. As the salt was leached out by rains or scattered by the cattle, the area around Rocky Top became bare, or, as the settlers would say, "naked ground."

The view from Rocky Top is unsurpassed. To the west is the grassy expanse of Spence Field, and beyond is the meander of the state line as far as Gregory Bald (4,949 feet). Extending into North Carolina is Twentymile Ridge, punctuated on its end by Shuckstack (4,020 feet) with its metal frame fire tower. Visible below Shuckstack are Fontana Dam and the blue waters of Fontana Lake. Immediately to the south are waves of mountains of great peaks and ridges, forest clad, solid, ranging in bold relief yet with subtle gradations in color.

Below on the Tennessee side are the patchwork fields of Cades Cove, and beyond are the Chilhowee Mountains and the Tennessee Valley. At night, the lights of Mary-ville are bright in the foreground, with the beacon atop Blount Memorial Hospital particularly noticeable. The lights of Knoxville can be seen to the right, forty miles away.

From Rocky Top the trail climbs three-quarters of a mile to the highest point on Thunderhead, which is covered with a thick heavy growth of rhododendron that blooms late in June with red and pink blossoms. There are no views from the top of Thunderhead except that into North Carolina afforded by a perch of stacked rock upon which one can stand and peer over the rhododendron hedge.

The AT crosses the top of Thunderhead (5,527 feet) through a narrow pass in the rhododendron, eases into Tennessee to circumnavigate Laurel Top, and then descends on one of the steepest courses in the Smokies. The track is rocky and without switchbacks. The descent continues unabated for three-quarters of a mile until reaching Beechnut Gap, a spacious swag that slopes gently into Tennessee. Seventy-five yards down the slope, water seeps from beneath the detritus of beech leaves to collect in pools that form the headwaters of Thunderhead Prong.

For the next mile and a half, the trail remains in beech and serviceberry stands while negotiating a succession of minor, closely spaced gaps and knobs. The knobs are low and, with the exception of a couple of exceedingly steep places, the climbing is not difficult. The gaps are attractive and tend to be wide and sloping into Tennessee. When Horace Kephart sojourned in this part of the Smokies, the North Carolina side of the divide between Laurel Top and Brier Knob was a burned-over slope known as the Firescald. The Firescald overlooks the gristly drainage separating Killpecker and Saddleback Ridges with their welter of abrupt spurs, jagged crags, and gloomy depths choked with impenetrable tangles of rhododendron and mountain laurel.

A short, but wickedly steep, climb out of Mineral Gap marks the onset of a level course that remains just below the ridgeline on the North Carolina side for a 500-yard approach to Brier Knob (5,215 feet). As it clears Brier Knob, the trail enters on a steep, rocky, half-mile descent that ranks among the most strenuous climbs in the Smokies. Nineteenth-century visitors to Brier Knob remarked that it was open on the top with superb views and subsequently surmised that the knob was a natural bald. By 1921, when John Oliver travel the Firescald and over Brier Knob, he would comment on having come "in contact with great briar patches, many of which were higher than our horses' backs."

At the base of Brier Knob, the trail reaches Starkey Gap, a distinctive V-shaped notch in the ridgeline. The grade moderates considerably as the trail climbs out of Starkey Gap to clear a nameless knob that marks the junction of the Sevier–Blount County line with the state-line divide. The trail then descends into Sugartree Gap, a long, gently sloped, saddle-shaped swag shaded by yellow birch, American beech, yellow buckeye, and a variety of oak trees interspersed among the sugar maples that suggest the gap's name.

Leaving Sugartree Gap, the trail returns to its modulating course, advancing more in the upward climb than the downward. A mile beyond Sugartree Gap, the ridgeline widens into the flat expanse of the western end of Big Chestnut Bald as the trail approaches Derrick Knob Shelter.

Derrick Knob Shelter is a three-sided stone structure recently modernized with an overhanging roof covering an attachment of benches and tables. The shelter stands a little to the Tennessee side and faces into the long, nearly level, western flank of Big Chestnut Bald. Two food-storage cables are suspended along the front yard of the cabin. The water source is a spring on the Tennessee side at the end of a path that angles from the front of the shelter for fifty yards and then turns sharply and doubles back for another fifty yards.

Big Chestnut Bald was formerly known as Derrick Knob, named for Asa Derrick, the high sheriff of Sevier County. Assisted by his two oldest sons, Derrick built a cabin on the bald just prior to the Civil War. As Union and Confederate troops crossed over the Smokies, the Derrick cabin and nearby spring became a well-known stopping place. There is evidence that the cabin survived several years after the war. A land transaction of September 3, 1873, for a tract located in the upper end of the Tremont area of Sevier County mentions "a state line leading to the Derrick Cabin in North Carolina."

The Derrick cabin was torn down in 1879 by Thomas Joshua Calhoun, a Smoky Mountaineer who owned considerable acreage on the upper reaches of Hazel Creek. In 1882, Calhoun's neighbor from Bone Valley, Crate Hall, started construction on a new cabin near the site of the old Derrick shelter. At that time, Derrick Knob was a cleared spot estimated to be around fifty to seventy acres and covered with a thick turf of grass eight to ten inches high. The Crate Hall cabin quickly became a significant fixture on the Smoky divide, its prominence indicated by the bald itself becoming widely known as Halls Cabin.

Horace Kephart, who visited Halls Cabin shortly after arriving in the Smokies in 1904, described it as a "hut built years ago for temporary lodgment of cattle-men herding on the grassy 'balds' of the Smokies. A sagging clapboard roof covered its two rooms and the open space between them we called our 'entry.' The State line between North Carolina and Tennessee ran through this unenclosed hallway. The Carolina room had a puncheon floor and a clapboard table, also better bunks than its mates." The cabin reportedly was blown down by high winds within a few years of Kephart's visit.

Around the time of Kephart's first visit to Halls Cabin a group of outdoorsmen associated informally as the Appalachian Hunting and Fishing Club built a sturdier cabin near the spring. The cabin's location is marked on a 1906 North Carolina geological survey map of Hazel Creek, which identifies it as the "A. H. & F. Club House." However, the club house inherited the name of its predecessor and was thereafter known as Halls Cabin. Joseph Bowles, a bear hunter who camped at the club cabin in 1914, referred to the club house specifically as Halls Cabin and noted that it was "so constructed that one-half rests on North Carolina soil, while the other half is in Tennessee. The chimney—a two-sided affair—rests right on the line, throwing the kitchen end of the cabin in Tennessee and the sleeping quarters in North Carolina." The sleeping bunks were arranged along the walls. In the same year, a traveler named Don Beeson stopped at Halls Cabin. Beeson maintained a diary in which he refers to the shelter as Halls Cabin and comments that it "was strongly built of logs on end, with a split-shingle roof that seems waterproof. The window openings are closed with batten doors fastened on the inside. The chimney rises in the center of the one room, three sides of which are taken up with bunks supplied with loose hay and straw mattresses of the early Victorian period and not cleaned since." In a newspaper article written in 1921, John Oliver mentioned that the last Halls Cabin had burned to the ground several years earlier. All that remained was the large double-chimney.

From the Derrick Knob Shelter, the AT climbs 250 yards to clear the summit of Big Chestnut Bald then drops sharply for about 300 yards to Sams Gap, where it intersects the Greenbrier Ridge Trail leading up from the Indian Flats vicinity of Tremont. From this juncture, the trail veers into North Carolina to circumnavigate Mount Davis and then settles into a long easy course that adheres to the center of the wide crest of the divide. Here, the forest cover is almost exclusively beech and birch interspersed with an occasional hemlock.

Prior to 1941, Mount Davis was known as Greenbrier Knob. The name was changed to recognize Anne and Willis P. Davis, an influential couple from Knoxville who initiated the successful movement to establish the Great Smoky Mountains National Park. After seeing national parks in the western United States, the Davises returned to Tennessee with the question: "Why can't we have a national park in the Smokies?" Anne and Willis Davis made their initial inquiries in 1923, and twenty years later President Franklin Delano Roosevelt was in Newfound Gap formally dedicating the Smokies as America's newest national park.

The original petition to recognize the Davises for their effort to bring a national park to the Smokies recommended that their names be affixed to nearby Cold Spring Knob. The U.S. Geological Survey rejected this request but responded by agreeing to recognize Willis Davis for his role as president of the Smoky Mountain Conservation Association by changing Greenbrier Knob to Davis Knob and a similar tribute to Anne Davis by changing Greenbrier Ridge to Davis Ridge.

One mile beyond Sams Gap, the trail completes an easy crossing over Hemlock Knob then begins a difficult mile-long grind to the top of Cold Spring Knob. Immediately upon reaching the summit, the trail starts down the far side, proceeding on an even steeper course that drops a half-mile to Buckeye Gap. Three hundred yards prior to reaching Buckeye Gap, the Miry Ridge Trail merges in from Tennessee, having ascended from the vicinity of Blanket Mountain.

At Buckeye Gap, Harvey Broome once wrote, "the earth dipped quickly from the east and rose as quickly to the west, and dropped off sharply to the north and south—all in beautiful, rounded, merging curves, like those of a saddle. It was a perfect hyperbolic paraboloid." Today, Buckeye Gap harbors a small clearing surrounded by buckeyes, beeches, birches, and maples. In 1921 the gap was occupied by a logging camp built by the Ritter Lumber Company to service their operation on the upper Proctor Creek drainage. The camp's dining hall, which had a fireplace at each end, could accommodate thirty-five people. The bunkhouse adjoined the dining hall. Water for the camp was accessible 200 yards down into North Carolina from a spring that forms the headwaters of Proctor Creek. For many years, debris from the camp could be seen scattered throughout the gap.

Beyond Buckeye Gap, the trail adheres firmly to the state-line divide on a fairly easy course that proceeds through old grazing ranges. During the grazing era, the ground was a tough firm turf. Today it is a spongy sod shaded by beech, birch, and Allegheny serviceberry trees interspersed with stands of pin cherries, Carolina silverbells, and the occasional red spruce. Although red spruces are prevalent elsewhere on the high Smoky divide, they are fairly scarce this far west and are believed not to be found west of Cold Spring Knob. The silverbells and serviceberries both bloom in early June and, after pollination, drop their blossoms in a dazzling display of brilliant whiteness.

Two-and-a-half miles beyond Buckeye Gap, the trail eases into a grassy dell that harbors the Silers Bald Shelter. The shelter is of stone and has been recently upgraded with an extended roof and accoutered with tables and benches in the same fashion as other shelters along the divide. A food-storage cable is suspended nearby, and the water source is a fine spring tucked in a small depression twenty-five yards down the Tennessee side.

Accounts written by early visitors to Silers Bald refer to old shacks and lean-tos seen down in the dell near the spring. The earliest of these were likely built by herders tending cattle for Jesse Richardson Siler, a Franklin, North Carolina, resident who owned several hundred acres on the bald. In 1904, the estate of Jesse Siler sold 1,683 acres of the bald to W. Scott Adams for four dollars an acre. Adams subsequently established the Siler Meadow Mining and Lumber Company with the intent of extracting copper ore from seams running through the bald. A few mines shafts were sunk, but the operation proved to be uneconomical and was soon abandoned. Paul Fink, an avid Smoky Mountain explorer, mentions that, well into the twentieth century, "the almost obliterated old copper workings" on Silers could still be seen. Today, only remnants of a few old mine shafts can be found down on the North Carolina slopes.

When operations ceased, the miners' shacks were appropriated for provisional camps by the occasional traveler or hunting party on the bald. Hodge Mathes mentions discovering a herdsman's shelter of rude poles standing a considerable distance from the spring. As late as 1928, hikers with the Smoky Mountains Hiking Club would report finding a tar-paper lean-to standing almost squarely across the state-line divide about thirty yards from the spring. Eight years earlier John Oliver had passed by and camped at the lean-to.

In 1863 When Arnold Guyot published the results of his scientific measurements of the high peaks on the Smoky divide, he identified the high point on Silers Bald as Big Stone Mountain, claiming he could uncover no name for the bald currently in use by the local mountaineers. The name Silers Meadow came into use sometime in the mid-nineteenth century and remained current until it was changed to Silers Bald by the U.S. Geological Survey in 1932.

The highest point on Silers Bald is a straw-colored grassy peak 420 yards up-trail from the shelter. Visible from the summit immediately to the east is the ragged western shoulder of Mount Buckley and Clingmans Dome. On the left, a path leads seventy-five yards to a vantage point overlooking a vast triangular basin formed by Miry Ridge, Sugarland Mountain, and the state-line divide.

On one bitter, cold, winter evening Horace Kephart looked down from this north-facing vantage point on Silers Bald, gazing into the basin below. He later recalled that the view from Silers revealed "a weird and forbidding land. Vast labyrinths of rhododendron covered those profound and dismal depths, impenetrable, sunless in winter, dead but for the murky evergreen of shrubs and spruces. The place was unearthly in its dreariness and desolation."

Three hundred and ten yards down from the summit of Silers, the AT meets the upper terminus of the Welch Ridge Trail, a ridgeline course that extends 6.7 miles to High Rocks. Beyond the junction with the Welch Ridge Trail, steepening slopes on either side press the AT to the center of a straitened corridor of upturned strata known as the Narrows. Troughs and pits in the strata and rollings in the underlying sod render the track wickedly uneven. Gnarled stunted trees cleave to the ends and sides of the steeply slanted rock. In wintertime, winds howling up from the depths below issue a deep-toned guttural roar as they sweep over the thin ridgeline. Here, the rich palettes of hardwoods that are dominant in the western Smokies begin yielding to the serried dark-green ranks of the balsams which do battle along the peaks of the eastern Smokies.

Beyond the Narrows, the ridgeline widens considerably as the trail climbs on a leisurely course for a half-mile to a small grassy semi-bald at Jenkins Knob. After another half-mile through rich woods of beech and Allegheny serviceberry, the trail eases into a grassy opening occupied by the Double Spring Gap Shelter.

The name Double Spring Gap is suggested by two free-flowing springs about seventy-five yards apart, one each in Tennessee and North Carolina, and both within ten feet elevation of the ridgeline. Water from the spring on the North Carolina side issues from a pipe and into a rock basin before scrambling down a rocky face in search of Forney Creek. On the Tennessee side, the water seeps imperceptibly out of a messy mould and gathers in a slow-moving rill that forms the headwater of Fish Camp Prong.

The shelter at Double Spring Gap resides in an attractive setting situated slightly on the Tennessee side facing into North Carolina. On the slope that forms the east end of the gap, a remarkably uniform stand of thin beech trees is shaded in the background by a rank of tall red spruces. In June, the slope west of the shelter is brightened with a carpet of spring beauties. In front of the shelter is a spacious grassy lawn. A food-storage cable is suspended behind the shelter near the path leading to the spring in Tennessee.

When the AT leaves Double Spring Gap, it enters a relentless climb that affords little relief until reaching the summit of Clingmans Dome almost three miles away. Initially, the climb is not particularly demanding. The vegetation alternates between spruce-birch stands, closely growing fir thickets, grassy semi-balds, and copses of beeches and serviceberries. Slightly more than half a mile out of the gap, the AT intersects the Goshen Prong Trail leading up from Little River.

About a mile above the Goshen Prong junction, the grade steepens noticeably. A half-mile farther, near the foot of Mount Buckley, the AT exacts yet another level of stringency, proceeding along the edges of sharply upturned strata of rock, soon emerging from beneath the shading vegetation and onto a ragged semi-bald.

John Oliver once described this east flank of Mount Buckley as being "as sharp as a razor-back hog, saw-tooth like." While being led along this saw-toothed ridge, Oliver's horse, Billy, lost his footing on a slick shield of rock, tumbled over and down, becoming lodged in the space between two sharp strata with every foot straight up. Billy was extracted from his predicament only through strenuous pulling by two men and a great exertion by the horse himself. Once regaining his composure, Billy would have enjoyed superb views deep into ranks of North Carolina mountains. Looking across the bald, he would have been able to peer down into the great gulf between Forney Ridge and Welch Ridge as far down as Fontana Lake. Billy's views into Tennessee, however, would have been limited to the narrowest places where the trail is pressed to the spine of Mount Buckley.

In 1859, Samuel Botsford Buckley, an itinerant botanist from New York, engaged Senator Thomas Lanier Clingman of North Carolina to accompany him on an excursion to measure the elevation of the highest peak in the Smokies. With the assistance of Robert Collins, a guide from Oconaluftee, and Dr. Samuel Love of Asheville, Buckley and Clingman traveled up to a high point then known as Smoky Dome. At Smoky Dome, Buckley and Clingman took readings on a barometer. These measurements would later be compared with similar readings from a stationary barometer in Waynesville, North Carolina, being monitored by John Le Conte, a geologist from the University of South Carolina. When the two explorers returned from the mountains, John Le Conte calculated from the readings of the barometers the elevation of Smoky Dome to be 6,755 feet above sea level. Buckley immediately published a report of the findings and named the peak Mount Buckley. Clingman quickly responded with a protest that he was in fact the one who instigated the expedition, conducted the measurements, and thus his name should be honored with the highest peak. A bitter controversy followed. It was not settled until Arnold Guyot, the highly regarded Swiss geologist from Princeton, ventured to Smoky Dome the next year and discovered its elevation to be only 6,660 feet. Reflecting perhaps on Clingman's political position making the senator's case more persuasive to the local North Carolinians than that of the outsider Buckley, Guyot designated the highest peak as Clingmans

Dome and the peak on its western shoulder as Mount Buckley. In addition, Guyot identified two peaks north of Clingmans as Mount Love and Mount Collins. All four of these names later became formally authorized in Smoky Mountain nomenclature by the U.S. Geological Survey.

When clearing the summit of Mount Buckley, the AT eases into a slight swag where it intersects the Clingmans Dome Bypass Trail leading up from the Forney Ridge Parking area. The AT then continues 460 yards to Clingmans Dome, penetrating deeper into the boreal zone.

The AT does not actually cross the summit of Clingmans Dome but passes a little below on the Tennessee side. A 75-yard access path leads from the trail to the foot of a concrete ramp that circles 375 feet to the top of the 45-foot Clingmans Dome Observation Tower on the summit of the dome. From the tower, the most prominent mountain in view is Mount Le Conte immediately to the north. East of Le Conte is the high meander of the Smoky divide stretching to Mount Guyot, at 6,621 feet, the second-highest point in the Smokies. On the west, the Smoky divide is seen stretching to Thunderhead and beyond, buttressed on both sides by powerful ridges. To the south is Fontana Lake and beyond, waves upon waves of mountains rolling deep into North Carolina. On the very clearest days, Mount Mitchell, the highest point in eastern North America, is visible east of the dome.

The current concrete observation deck was not the first tower to occupy the summit of Clingmans Dome. A crudely constructed wooden survey tower was built in the late 1920s and used sporadically by the occasional hiking party until its center pole was shattered by a strike of lightening. In 1935, the Civilian Conservation Corps constructed a sturdy forty-foot wooden tower with a viewing deck for visitors to the newly established Great Smoky Mountains National Park. The CCC tower was later dismantled to make room for the modern concrete tower.

Before an opening was cleared in the forest for the towers, it was said that the large balsams on Clingmans Dome were so thickly grown that the rays of the sun never reached the ground. The kernel of truth in this hyperbole is somewhat confirmed by Paul Fink's observation in 1927 that "the top of the Dome bore as heavy a stand of spruce and balsam as we had ever seen. There was not a single spot from which to see out."

As a young man in 1915, Harvey Broome visited Clingmans Dome and captured something of the enchantment of an undisturbed, primeval, Smoky Mountain boreal forest: "At the summit of Clingmans we entered a dim, thickset stand of evergreens. . . . The memory of that dark and closely growing timber has remained with me all of my life." Broome later became a champion for wilderness areas. He was one of the founders of the Wilderness Society and worked tirelessly to stop the Clingmans Dome Road from being extended along the crest of the western Smoky divide. Broom certainly would have agreed with former Secretary of the Interior Stewart Udall, who called the concrete tower on Clingmans "a mistake."

The Cherokee called the peak Ku-wa-hi, meaning "Place of Mulberries." It was home of the Great White Bear, chief of all bears in the Smokies, and considered one of four conclaves where the bears danced before retreating into hibernation. Early settlers referred to the peak as Smoky Dome; however, a traveler known only as R of Tennessee, who visited the Smokies during the time of the Buckley-Clingman controversy, mentions having heard the highest peak in the Smokies called "Quonacatoosa." The writer offers no explanation for the name or of its origin.

At 6,643 feet above sea level, Clingmans Dome is the highest point in the Smokies and the third-highest in eastern North America. It was considered to be the second-highest point in the east until 1993 when a U.S. Geological Survey measurement based on satellite GPS technology revised the elevation of Mount Craig in North Carolina upward to 6,647 feet. The revised elevation, considered to be accurate to within four inches, is four feet higher than that of Clingmans Dome. The elevation of Clingmans Dome is based upon a conventional optical survey done in 1920, and until the dome can be measured by GPS, Mount Craig will continue to claim the distinction of being as the second-highest point in eastern North America.

Where the AT passes below the summit, its elevation is 6,625 feet, making this the highest point reached during its entire 2,175-mile journey from Georgia to Maine. As it rolls off Clingmans Dome, the trail follows a narrow, winding, rocky course into an open saddle that separates the summit of the dome from its long eastern shoulder, Mount Love. After clearing Mount Love, the trail enters a mile-long descent into Collins Gap, winding through a remarkable forest of massive red spruces straight as ship masts and interspersed with rugged old birches. Collins Gap and nearby Mount Collins were named for Robert Collins, the Smoky Mountain guide from Oconaluftee who, at the behest of Colonel Robert Love, cut a six-mile path to Clingmans Dome to assist the scientist Arnold Guyot in his explorations of the high peaks on the Smoky divide. Prior to that time, North Carolinians referred to the gap as Deep Gap.

After a moderately steep one-mile climb out of Collins Gap, the trail reaches the top of Mount Collins (6,188 feet), a flat-topped mountain that once harbored a significant Indian boundary marker.

As the result of the Treaty of the Holston in 1791, Colonel Benjamin Hawkins was commissioned to survey the line that was to separate the Indian lands from those of the white settlers. Beginning at Fort Southwest Point, near present-day Kingston, Tennessee, Hawkins and his surveyors charted a line south 76 degrees east, thus determining that the Indian boundary crossed the high Smoky divide at Mount Collins. Immediately disputes ensued, necessitating a remedy in the form of the 1798 Treaty of Tellico. The newer treaty required that the Hawkins Line be re-surveyed.

In 1802, Indian Commissioner Return J. Meigs commanded a party instructed to survey the Hawkins Line and fix the point where the Indian boundary crossed the divide. According to Meigs's journal, at the point where the boundary inter- sected the state-line divide, the survey party "Erected a Post of Spruce Pine 15 Inches in diameter, Six feet high, Painted at top, drawing a line from top to Bottom to designate our Course & marked on the north side U.S. 1802 R.J. Meigs A.W. D. T. Freeman U.S.S. & on the South side O.N. U. & E. Cherokee Chiefs. Erected a mound of stone around the post of about 2 Tons of Stone, which with difficulty we collected. having no Tools for digging."

Meigs Post was rarely, if ever, visited for most of the nineteenth century. How- ever, because of its significance as a fixed point on the state line, the marker was frequently cited as a reference point for land transactions. According to a well- known and persistent rumor, a Smoky Mountaineer named Ben Parton, who was retained to maintain possession cabins for the Little River Lumber Company, was instructed by the company's president, Colonel W. B. Townsend, to move Meigs Post, rocks and all, west along the divide to the head of Miry Ridge, putatively to increase the company's land holdings. The actual location of Meigs Post then became the subject of several highly contested lawsuits, some of which gener- ated other conflicting surveys. Ben Parton never admitted to having moved Meigs Post; nevertheless, whenever the subject was broached in his presence, the mountaineer would come up fighting. Later the Little River Lumber Company qui- etly had the post returned to Mount Collins, a tacit admission that the company had knowledge of the post's removal.

Almost sixty years after Return J. Meigs erected the post, Arnold Guyot measured the peak on which it stood and identified it as Mount Collins. At the time of Guyot's visit, the peak was considerably easier to access from the North Carolina side owing to the comparatively gentler slope. The peak was difficult to ascend from Tennessee and very rarely approached from that side. Consequently the mountain was always better known by North Carolinians than by Tennesseans. Oddly, however, the peak came to be known among Tennesseans as both Meigs Post and Mount Collins, but never had a name of its own among North Carolinians. They simply referred to it as "the main high top where the Fork Ridge tops out on Smoky."

In 1928, at the request of North Carolinians, the U.S. Geological Survey named this "un-named" peak Mount Kephart, and in so doing set off a bitter controversy between Tennesseans and North Carolinians. Tennesseans contended that the peak's name should remain Mount Collins, citing the authority of Arnold Guyot and pointing out that this name was recognized in court cases. North Carolinians countered by pointing out that Guyot's place-names were difficult to reconcile with specific peaks and that in all but a very few instances, the Guyot names were never commonly accepted. The core of the dispute, it appears, centered on a suspicion by North Carolinians that Tennesseans were plotting to have Kephart's name removed from the peak so that they could have it replaced with that of Colonel David Chapman, a businessman from Knoxville who had played a major role in the movement to establish the Great Smoky Mountains National Park. North Carolinians, who considered Kephart one of their own and were justifiably proud of Kephart's *Our Southern Highlanders* as well as his contribution to the park movement, were not reticent in their response to the Tennesseans. The U.S. Geological Survey resolved the dispute in 1932 by reassigning the name Mount Kephart to the high peak on the Smoky divide that anchors the east end of the Boulevard and returning the name Mount Collins to the peak marked by Meigs Post.

When leaving Mount Collins, the AT descends on a gentle grade through a superb forest of great red spruces interspersed with occasional thickets of Fraser fir and gnarled old birch trees. The forest floor is damp, if not wet, and covered in yellowish-green spongy humus. Slightly less than a half-mile down, the terrain becomes level, and on the right the Sugarland Mountain Trail leads in from Tennessee to terminate into the AT.

Five hundred and forty yards down the Sugarland Mountain Trail an access path exits right fifty yards to the Mount Collins Shelter, which resides on a large level bench of spongy boreal turf shaded by balsam woods. The shelter is a vintage three-sided structure upgraded in the same manner as the others along the AT. A food-storage cable is suspended immediately behind the shelter. The closest source of water, however, is from a spring at the head of Moccasin Branch, 250 yards farther down the Sugarland Mountain Trail. The spring is just off the trail to the right and marked by a white vinyl pipe.

From its intersection with the Sugarland Mountain Trail, the AT winds through balsam flats for 480 yards before meeting an access path on the right leading fifty-five yards to Clingmans Dome Road and the upper terminus of the Fork Ridge Trail.

From here, the AT enters a long descent that is interrupted with short intermittent climbs. Up or down, the grade remains moderate. Though still in the boreal zone, the balsam stands become thinner, less robust, and increasingly interspersed with patches of thornless blackberries and turfs of thick mountain grass. Almost three miles below its junction with the Sugarland Mountain Trail, the AT breaks out into Indian Gap (5,272 feet), a close-cropped grassy clearing that shares space with Clingmans Dome Road and a parking lot.

Historically, Indian Gap is among the most significant landmarks in the Smokies by virtue of its having once harbored an ancient Indian trace that crossed over the mountain from North Carolina and joined the Great Indian War Path leading out of Tennessee. There is evidence that the Cherokee had long abandoned this over-mountain trail by the time of the white settlers; nevertheless, William Davenport, during his survey of the state-line divide in 1821, recognized the trail and identified it as a "beach 29th mile Indian path at the head of deep cr." Davenport later commented that, "if there is ever a wagon road through the Big Smoky mountains, it must go through this gap." Apparently acting on Davenport's observation, the North Carolina legislature during the 1831–32 session granted rights to the Oconaluftee Turnpike Company to upgrade the Indian trace to a usable road. Corresponding improvements on the Tennessee side were never forthcoming, although provisional upgrades were made during the Civil War by Cherokee in the Thomas Legion of the Confederate Army, enabling soldiers to cross into Tennessee as well as gain access to mineral deposits at Alum Cave.

Three years after Davenport's survey, Pleasant M. Wear of Sevier County received a grant of fifty acres of Smoky Mountain land that included Indian Gap. At about the time of Wear's purchase, a cabin was built in the gap along the trail about a hundred feet down the Tennessee side. For the next hundred years there was a cabin of some sort in the gap. William Johnson, traveling through Indian Gap in 1914, remarked on seeing three cabins built by a hunting party around the turn of the century. Two remained in fine condition, and one had lost a roof.

Since the time of Wear's purchase, Indian Gap has served as a center for cattle-ranging activities and a camping place for surveyors, timber rangers, and traveling parties in search of recreation and adventure. A party from Minnesota camping here for several weeks in 1896 described the gap as being a "fine grass plot, about an acre in extent, which lies on the mountain range like a blanket on a horse's back."

In 1924, shortly after the Champion Fibre Company had acquired a large tract of timber land that included Indian Gap, the company's president, Ruben Robertson, built in the gap Timber Top Lodge as a private retreat for himself and guests. The lodge stood by the old Oconaluftee Turnpike trace on the North Carolina side. It was rustic in appearance but well apportioned for convenience. In 1931 the lodge was leased from Robertson by Jack Huff and operated as a hostel under the name Balsam Lodge. Huff's lodge was open to the public and could accommodate eighteen guests. The lodge remained in use until May 9, 1958, when it was destroyed by fire. A group of students from the Asheville Boy's School was staying at the lodge when one of the boys accidently knocked over an oil lamp, sending the lodge up in flames.

Today much of historic Indian Gap has been obliterated by Clingmans Dome Road and a large parking lot. The AT swings low along the Tennessee side through the only grassy remnant in the gap. Here, it intersects the upper terminus of the

Road Prong Trail, itself a vestige of the old Thomas Road into Tennessee. All traces of the Oconaluftee Turnpike rising into the gap from North Carolina have been obscured by pavement.

The AT exits the north end of Indian Gap, remaining on the Tennessee side as it climbs steeply through a transition of birch and spruce yielding to beech stands. About 500 yards above the gap, the trail reaches the spine of Mingus Lead, where an opening in the forest cover affords a superb view of Mount Le Conte. Most noticeable are the Duckhawk Peaks clad in their pale green heath and projecting sharply from the face of the mountain. Alum Cave can be distinguished as the gray niche just above the Duckhawk Peaks.

Within a few yards, the trail is blocked by a fenced enclosure that straddles a short section of Mingus Lead. The enclosure keeps out wild boars intent on rooting among the stands of beech and fir. In late spring, thick carpets of spring beauties are the most visually striking plant life within the fenced area. The trail clears the fence on a metal stile, proceeds 180 yards across the enclosure, then exits on another stile.

From here the trail enters a steep descent while completing a transition from Mingus Lead to the west flank of the main Smoky divide, alternating between airy copses of beech trees and the gloom of spruce stands. A little more than a half-mile down, the grade moderates as the trail emerges from a spruce cover. Near here, on the right, a faint path angles up to a stone wall that supports Clingmans Dome Road. The path leads to a tunnel that passes beneath the road. Until it was boarded up several years ago, the tunnel provided access to a trail leading back along the east side of the road and connected with an old trail that once followed the course of the Oconaluftee Turnpike.

After passing the access path, the trail follows a moderate grade on a narrow berm bordered by witch-hobble, mountain maple, and the occasional spruce. Over this interval, Clingmans Dome Road remains nearby on a parallel course. The trail and road soon converge where the trail executes a short climb and pops up into Newfound Gap.

Newfound Gap (5,046 feet) came by its name when it was discovered by surveyors, perhaps as early as the 1850s, to be a lower-elevation pass over the high Smokies than the well-known Indian Gap. When planning the first modern highway over the mountain, the ancient route through Indian Gap was abandoned in favor of the pass at Newfound Gap. What was once an insignificant beech gap on the crest of the divide was widened to accommodate the highway and a large parking lot. As it crosses the road, the AT passes from the Tennessee to the North Carolina side of Newfound Gap, skirting the parking lot, which is wholly in North Carolina. A stone retaining wall along the far side of the parking lot affords a fine vantage point for surveying the upper reaches of the vast Oconaluftee River drainage.

On the left, where the trail leaves the pavement and returns to the wilderness, a high curved stone dais marks the occasion of the official opening of the Great Smoky Mountains National Park on September 2, 1940. The dais was built specifically for the event in which President Franklin Delano Roosevelt traveled to Newfound Gap and dedicated the new national park to "the free American people."

When leaving Newfound Gap, the AT returns quickly to the balsams, climbing first for about a half-mile on the North Carolina side before switching into Tennessee. On both sides the slopes are steep, particularly in Tennessee. The cliffs are rarely bare, covered with a solid mantle of stunted trees rooted in every crevice. The trail is steep and shares the raw ruggedness of the terrain. Up and to the left the bold contour of Mount Le Conte commands an intervening gulf that may well be over a half-mile in depth.

Where the trail returns to the ridgeline, the mountain is remarkably flat and broad. The course is level and winds among large spruce and birch trees shading a grassy turf. Two miles above Newfound Gap, the AT intersects the upper terminus of the Sweat Heifer Creek Trail. A small bench twenty-five yards down the Sweat Heifer Creek Trail offers a fine place to sit and gaze out over the great ranges of mountains that extend deep into North Carolina.

The AT continues on its easy excursion for another mile, first passing Mount Ambler, then approaching the foot of Mount Kephart, where it intersects the eastern terminus of the Boulevard Trail leading 5.4 miles to the summit of Mount Le Conte.

 Mount Ambler was named for Chase P. Ambler in recognition of his effort in fomenting the first organized impetus to establish a national park in the Great Smoky Mountains. Ambler, a physician, moved from Ohio to Asheville in 1899 and a year later was successful in garnering support from the Asheville Board of Trade in organizing the Appalachian National Park Association. In its bylaws, the association stated that "its objective shall be establishment of a national park somewhere in the Southern Appalachian mountains." Ambler died in 1932 and thus did not live to see the full fruition of his vision for a national park in the Great Smoky Mountains.

At its intersection with the Boulevard, the AT turns sharply right into North Carolina and wends on a pleasant course 530 yards through a thin balsam grove to reach a grassy bench that harbors the Icewater Spring Shelter. The shelter is nicely situated with its back to Mount Kephart and overlooking the deep declivity that separates the main Smoky divide from Richland Mountain. In front of the shelter is a small plat of grassy turf fringed by high weeds. A food-storage cable and a composting toilet are found a short distance beyond the south end of the shelter. Water is available thirty yards down-trail at Icewater Spring. The spring is in the middle of the trail.

The AT passes behind the shelter. Beyond Icewater Spring, it becomes steeper, rockier, and saturated with water from rogue rills escaping from the spring. The descent continues for a half-mile until the trail switches to the Tennessee side to circumnavigate a sharply pointed knob that was at one time considered part of the Charlies Bunion configuration.

The confusion regarding the nomenclature relating to Charlies Bunion is reflected in a trail guide published by the Appalachian Trail Conference in 1950. In describing the course of the AT east of Newfound Gap, the guide indicates "at 2.85 m. swing to Tenn. side and pass around left side of precipitous west (lower) peak of Charlies Bunion at 4 m. . . . Beyond, cross to N.C. side, touch state line at 4.05 m. and pass around the highest peak of Charlies Bunion. The lower or west peak is sometimes called Fodder Stack; the eastern or higher peak being called Charlies Bunion." In 1960, at the request of the Carolina Mountain Club, the U.S. Geological Survey considered naming the lower or west peak Masa Knob in honor of George Masa, the Japanese photographer who worked tirelessly with Horace Kephart in promoting the effort to establish a national park in the Smokies. In a letter of request to the survey, the club recommended "that the name Masa's Pinnacle be given one of the peaks of what used to be known as 'The Fodderstacks'— one of which has been renamed humorously 'Charlies Bunion' and the other one can be called Masa's Pinnacle." The next year, the survey officially designated the lower peak immediately west of Charlies Bunion as Masa Knob.

Just beyond Masa Knob the trail inches back to the divide for a short excursion along a catwalk ridgeline. After dropping briefly back into North Carolina, it switches again to the Tennessee side and rolls out to Charlies Bunion, a bald rock protrusion buttressed on its Tennessee side by a razor-thin spur projecting out from the side of the mountain. The sheer ruggedness and precarious steepness of Charlies Bunion make it one of the premier vantage points in the Smokies.

In 1925, wind-aided fire sparked by a logging operation swept up the North Carolina slope, scorching the area around Charlies Bunion. Prior to the fire the Bunion was densely matted with a spongy humus, shaded with stands of fir, and bearing few visible traces of the rock beneath. Two years after the fire, a thunderstorm plowed into the mountain, releasing a torrent of water onto Charlies Bunion. The burnt, water-soaked earth could not maintain its grip and slid off into the ravine below, carrying with it every vestige of vegetation and leaving a bare rocky protrusion. The tree trunks swept away in the flood are still visible, piled like kindling in the narrow naked defiles below. On Labor Day 1951, a second cloudburst visited Charlies Bunion, washing away the thin vegetation that had managed to gain a tenuous hold on the scoured rock. Today, Charlies Bunion is still largely devoid of plant life, dotted with a few wind-agonized trees and clumps of sand myrtle and remaining, as Harvey Broome once remarked, "a barren monument to man's carelessness with fire and nature's excess with water."

The AT actually passes behind Charlies Bunion on a lesser-used path. What appears to be the main trail is an access path that loops out and around the Bunion to a small knob that anchors a flying buttress of bare rock suspended out over the cliff's edge. The spine of the buttress is extremely narrow, its sides falling away precipitously into the depths below. In is an altogether unparalleled window into the ruggedness that underlies the eastern end of the Smoky divide.

Charlies Bunion overlooks the vast Greenbrier basin, which is defined on the west by the steep-sided Mount Kephart, on the south by the meander of the Smoky divide, and on the east by the powerful Pinnacle Lead. Pinnacle Lead is anchored to the Smoky divide at the base of Old Black and punctuated on its extended end by Greenbrier Pinnacle. Just beyond Greenbrier Pinnacle the cliffs of the Catstairs appear as white vertical scars on the green slope.

Towering over Mount Kephart is Myrtle Point, a superb vantage point that marks the east end of Mount Le Conte. Visible just north of Myrtle Point is a large slide scar on the slope of the Boulevard. North of Mount Kephart is Brushy Mountain, distinguished by its pale green heath bald. In the intermediate distance and down to the left is the aptly named Horseshoe Mountain and, on the right, Porters Mountain appears as the long ridge extending into Greenbrier Cove.

Immediately to the east are the Sawteeth, a section of the main Smoky divide that derives its name from the unending succession of jagged little peaks that line the narrow ridgeline at fairly regular intervals. The peaks range in various heights from a few feet to nearly a hundred. The ridgeline scarcely averages over ten feet in width and, in places, not even a foot. Early travelers who managed to reach the Sawteeth remarked that it was practically impossible to climb over the "teeth," making it necessary to go below them along steep cliffs. Loose slate and crumbling rocks made climbing the ridge perilous. In many places, the mountain drops off almost perpendicularly for hundreds of feet on both sides. Horace Kephart described the Sawteeth as "the most rugged and difficult part of the Smokies (and of the United States east of Canada)." With the building of the AT, the ridgelines were graded to hold a trail, so the jagged "blades" of the Sawteeth could be conveniently circumnavigated.

In the fall of 1929, Horace Kephart and George Masa were camped on Bradley Fork, a short distance above Cabin Flats at a place known as the Washout Camp. During their stay, Masa and a local guide named Charlie Connor decided to venture to the main Smoky divide and explore the Sawteeth. Kephart remained in camp. Masa and Connor's explorations took them over the distinctive protrusion that was burned over by the fire in 1925. When the men returned to the Washout

Camp, the guide gave an account of their adventures to Kephart, apparently mentioning their climb over the knob at the head of the fire-scald. Connor commented that "when we went over the little knoll my feet were hurtin'" and made a reference to a bunion on his foot. Kephart, who was a member of the North Carolina Nomenclature Committee, responded with "Good; we'll put it down on a government map." From thence the burned-over knob on the Smoky divide has been known as Charlies Bunion. Originally, it seems, Kephart christened the landmark as "Charlie Connors Bunion," but the name was later shortened during the official deliberations on Smoky Mountain nomenclature.

At the point where the access path splits off to approach Charlies Bunion, the AT proceeds around the back side of the Bunion. The main trail is rejoined by the circling access path 150 yards down-trail. From here, the AT descends 300 yards through a belt of beech trees to enter a clearing where the mountain has been slow in recovering from the fire of 1925. Down the slope, a thin copse of beech trees is slowly reclaiming the shallow defile where the fire swept up the mountain. Above the trail, only low weedy growth has managed to gain purchase while a few fir and spruce encroach gingerly on the perimeter.

Midway across the fire-scald, a path of loose rock leads up about a hundred yards to one of the "teeth" on the ridgeline. These teeth are exposed ends of sharply upturned strata of rock of only a few feet thickness. The scouring effect of the fire and flood has left a "window" exposing the geological formations that underlie the divide from Mount Kephart to Laurel Top. Because the fire-scald is devoid of heavy vegetation, this point on the Sawteeth affords splendid views south into the Oconaluftee drainage and into the sea of mountains extending into North Carolina as well as north across the Greenbrier basin and out into the Tennessee Valley.

When it exits the far side of the fire-scald, the trail descends for about 150 yards before easing back onto the ridgeline at Dry Sluice Gap.

Immediately on the left a barely recognizable opening marks the upper end of an exceedingly treacherous manway leading down the near-vertical slope for several hundred feet before leveling out into the upper end of Porters Flat. This manway, once part of an old Indian trace linking the Cherokee villages in Oconaluftee and those in Porters Flat, is one of the earliest trails traversing the high Smoky divide. The Dry Sluice Gap manway may likely have been more heavily used by the Cherokee than the trail over Indian Gap as it appears on several of the earliest maps of the Smokies in absence of the one through Indian Gap.

Three hundred yards beyond the fire-scald, the AT intersects the upper terminus of the Dry Sluice Gap Trail following up along Richland Mountain. The Dry Sluice Gap Trail, which descends into the Bradley Fork drainage, likely follows the North Carolina part of the old Indian manway between Oconaluftee and Porters Flat.

Dry Sluice refers to a spring that sinks beneath the surface, its water flowing in a subterranean channel for some distance. Given the topography around Dry Sluice Gap, it is likely the spring to which the name refers is on the Tennessee side of the mountain.

A mile beyond its intersection with the Dry Sluice Gap Trail, the AT drops into an unimpressive swag known as Porters Gap.

The gap was named for James P. H. Porter, a prominent settler in Sevier County who owned land on the mountain and possibly lived in nearby Porters Flat. Porter is said to have used a trail that passed through the gap when traveling to the settlements on the Oconaluftee or to visit his friend William Holland Thomas who had a trading post on Soco Creek. After the defeat of Thomas's legion during the Battle of Gatlinburg in 1863, some of his troops made their way back into North Carolina through Porters Gap. As the soldiers were leading their horses along a precipitous ledge, two of the horses slipped, fell over a cliff, and died as a result of the fall. Their saddles were hung up in a tree in the gap and left to rot. H. C. Wilburn has recorded that the remains of the saddles had been seen by people still living well into the twentieth century.

According to another story preserved by Wilburn, Porters Gap was once known by North Carolinians as Rhinehart Gap. The gap apparently lay along the boundary of a tract of mountain land being surveyed by a man named Ledbetter. One of Ledbetter's assistants on the survey was named Rhinehart. When the survey party reached the gap, Ledbetter became seriously ill. Others in the party proceeded to get the sick man down the mountain to their camp at Cabin Flats on Bradley Fork. After arriving at camp, Ledbetter became worse and could proceed no farther. Rhinehart, who was a giant of a man, lifted the sick man to his shoulders and set him astride his neck. He then proceeded down a rough narrow manway toward the settlements at Bradleytown near what is now Smokemont Campground. After about three miles, Ledbetter cried for water and requested to rest. He was eased to the ground and placed in as comfortable position as possible, reclining against the sloping roots of a large poplar tree. He was given water from Rhinehart's hat, and then immediately expired. It has been surmised that he died from "camp colic."

Sometime after Ledbetter's death, Rhinehart returned to the gap and finished the survey—hence the name Rhinehart Gap. For many years afterward, the tree where the surveyor died was known to the settlers along Bradley Fork as the Ledbetter Poplar.

A variation on this story preserved by John Preston Arthur contends that it was W. W. Rhinehart who died and that it was Eli Arrington who carried the sick man down the mountain to Bradley Fork. Arthur places the incident in 1863 and records that the man died of milk-sickness.

Although Porters Gap is well within the section that Kephart described as "the most rugged and difficult part of the Smokies," it was apparently a significant landmark for the early settlers. Hodge Mathes, traveling through here in 1914, mentioned seeing a flat sandstone slab leaning against a tree and bearing the rude inscription "Porters Gap" with a number of names and initials. Dan Beeson, who accompanied Mathes on this trip, elsewhere described the slab as "an old broken tombstone" marking the point where a poor trail crossed the main divide.

The AT exits Porters Gap for a short climb and then begins a long easy descent into False Gap, a slight dip in the ridgeline a little more than a mile east of Porters. From the left side of the gap a faint path winds 250 yards steeply down through beech stands to the remains of the False Gap Shelter. The ruin is a three-sided structure similar in design to the other shelters in the park. The shelter's stone shell is completely intact, but the roof and all the wooden bunk structure are gone. Forty yards in back of the shelter is a bold spring augmented by a black vinyl pipe.

From False Gap, the trail continues on what Harvey Broome described as a "promiscuous ramble of the state line," being successively steep and level, or delightful and difficult. At first it remains just below the ridgeline on the Tennessee side as it climbs out of the gap. Within a half-mile it executes a hairpin turn to the right, levels out, and returns to the ridgeline. As the trail completes the hairpin, the distinct cone-shaped summit of Laurel Top (5,907 feet) comes into view.

After an easy interlude of a half-mile, much of it along a narrow ridge, the trail deviates again to the Tennessee side to circumnavigate Laurel Top. The grade here is stiff and climbs on a narrow track of loose slaty rock through the heavy gloom of a boreal forest. When it reaches the top of the climb, the trail executes another sharp turn right similar to that below Laurel Top. Again the grade levels and returns to the ridgeline. At the turn, Mount Chapman (6,417 feet) and Mount Guyot (6,621 feet) come into full view.

Beyond Laurel Top, the crest of the ridgeline is as narrow as a plank and wall-steep on either side. Before the ridgelines were leveled to make the trail, Harvey Broome noticed that they were even narrower, "being made up of horizontal strata of slaty rock, truncated at each end and resting crosswise like cordwood, and almost as unstable." The near-vertical slope supports only light vegetation that is not sufficiently high to block views into Tennessee and North Carolina.

About a mile beyond Laurel Top, the trail reaches a low fifteen-foot block of rock, smooth on its sides, flat on top, and aligned like a low thick wall between the trail and the mountain slope. The view from the top of the rock is down the Bradley Fork drainage, thus suggesting the name Bradley View. Bradley View is among the finest natural venues in the Smokies for sitting comfortably and enjoying a panorama of mountains. Immediately to the right is Richland Mountain, and on the left is Hughes Ridge. Visible back down the divide are the outlines of the Sawteeth and the summit of Mount Kephart. Farther along and beyond Richland Mountain is the rounded eminence of Clingmans Dome.

Beyond Bradley View, a short steep descent prefaces a mile of easy grade leading to Pecks Corner and an intersection with the upper terminus of the Hughes Ridge Trail. Over this interval the main divide becomes slightly rounded and forested in birch trees. The AT does not cross over the top of Pecks Corner but eases along a cliff on the North Carolina side to a rough galled pitch where it intersects the Hughes Ridge Trail. Six hundred and fifty-five yards down the Hughes Ridge Trail is the Pecks Corner Shelter.

Pecks Corner is an old survey meet for a mountain tract once owned by Judge Peck of Dandridge, Tennessee. The configuration of Hughes Ridge and the main Smoky divide is such that early surveyors and travelers approaching Pecks Corner along the state line often deviated onto Hughes Ridge thinking they were on the main divide, realizing their error only after having descended well into North Carolina.

The five miles east of Pecks Corner has been and remains still the most remote section of the Smoky divide. Neither from Tennessee nor North Carolina does anything resembling a trail or manway climb to meet the AT between Pecks Corner and Tricorner Knob. Horace Kephart, a backwoodsman familiar with the people and places of the Smokies, once confessed that he knew "but few men who have ever followed this part of the divide." He described it as "an uninhabited wilderness so rough that you could not make seven miles a day in it to save your life, even if you knew the course, and there is no trail at all." Dan Beeson, a traveler along the divide in 1914, was more explicit than Kephart in his description of this part of the divide: "There are places where you have to climb up or down the ends of boulders ten or twelve feet high or walk a fallen tree across a hole whose depth you can only guess at on account of the thickness of the undergrowth which hides the face of the earth completely."

Beyond Pecks Corner the ever steepening slopes on either side press the trail to the spine of the divide, and for a mile the trail stays on the ridgeline, climbing on a stiff grade until leveling out at Eagle Rocks, an exposed edge of escarpment that flares out over a hideously steep drop into the Greenbrier basin. Three hundred and sixty yards farther up-trail is another outcropping similar to Eagle Rocks. Far below, a network of rugged defiles is defined by ridges of varying size, shape, and gradations of color.

When leaving Eagle Rocks, the AT enters a moderately steep half-mile drop to a low wet spot that was known by early Smoky Mountaineers as Copper Gap. The origin of the name Copper Gap has apparently vanished with the passage of time.

At Copper Gap, the trail enters a difficult climb that veers into Tennessee and into the rich gloom of unmolested balsam stands. Here, one may sense the ineffable remoteness of the wilderness and the touch of solitude and solace more than any other place in the Smokies. One mile above Copper Gap, the climb eases markedly as it returns to the state line to clear the summit of Mount Sequoyah (5,945 feet). By this point, the spine of the divide has become more rounded, reflecting a change in the underlying geology from that of the Anakeesta formation, which is prone to fracturing into crags and outcroppings, to that of Thunderhead Sandstone, which tends to erode more evenly into smooth contours.

 Prior to being named Mount Sequoyah, this peak had the provisional name Three Brothers, which Arnold Guyot had assigned to the mountain during his scientific explorations in 1859. The reason behind Guyot's choice of names is unclear. The shape of the mountain does not warrant the name, and there appears to be nothing about Guyot's trip that involved brothers. Like several of the names Guyot assigned to Smoky Mountain peaks, Three Brothers was not generally accepted outside of the scientific community. The name Sequoyah was affixed to the peak in 1932 by the U.S. Geological Survey in recognition of George Gist, inventor of the Cherokee syllabary.

Upon leaving Mount Sequoyah, the trail remains on the state line, dropping into a moderately steep half-mile descent to a wet nameless swag that, at the first sign of warm weather, is carpeted in the bright whiteness of spring beauties. The trail then deviates into North Carolina, following a moderate grade to the circus-tent-shaped peak, Mount Chapman.

 Mount Chapman was once known as Mount Lumadaha. The name Lumadaha, purported to be a Cherokee word, was actually concocted by hiking companions Lucien Green, Marshall Wilson, Dave Huffine, and Harvey Broome by stringing together the first two letters of their first names. Lumadaha first entered common usage in the 1928 edition of the *Handbook of the Smoky Mountains Hiking Club* and soon afterward began appearing in an assortment of respectable journals featuring articles on the Great Smoky Mountains. Suspicions aroused by the fact that one of the syllables does not occur in the Cherokee language eventually led to the word's demise as a legitimate Smoky Mountain place-name. Long before Lumadaha surfaced, though, Arnold Guyot recorded that Samuel Botsford Buckley had already named the peak Mount Alexander, probably in honor of Stephen Alexander, a professor of botany at Princeton University. Although Alexander was not a fictitious person, the name did not survive as long as Lumadaha.

In 1932 the U.S. Geological Survey officially named the peak Mount Chapman in recognition of Colonel David C. Chapman, a Knoxville businessman who was the main driving force in bringing to fruition the efforts to establish a national park in the Great Smoky Mountains.

By the time the AT reaches Mount Chapman, the topography has become markedly less rugged and access to the divide much easier. During their excursion in 1914, hiking companions Dan Beeson and Hodge Mathes encountered cattle on the peak. The two followed a faint cattle trail down the mountain in search of water. A short distance below the ridgeline they found a clear cold spring with cattle trails leading off in several directions. In following one of these back to the ridgeline, they stumbled across a small shelter about six feet square. Farther up the trail they spotted behind a big spruce tree a soap box with two one-gallon jugs inside. Mount Chapman was then remote enough, yet accessible enough, to sustain a moonshine operation.

The AT passes below the summit of Mount Chapman on a steep rocky climb before returning briefly to the main divide and beginning a mile-long descent to a nameless gap that harbors an access path to the Tricorner Knob Shelter. Over this mile, the trail leaves and returns to the ridgeline at irregular intervals, always descending on a rocky grade. Just beyond the point where it bottoms out, the trail meets the access path to the shelter angling to the right. The distance to the shelter is a hundred yards.

Like most of the shelters on the AT, the one at Tricorner Knob has been upgraded with an extended roofline, skylights, and benches. The shelter is situated at the head of a menacingly deep ravine that is fringed all around with tall spruce trees. A bold pipe-assisted spring issues forth immediately in front of the shelter and runs off into the ravine. The shelter is confined on its lower side and front by the ravine and spring and on its upper side by the adjacent slope, depriving it of the sense of spaciousness. Paucity of space requires the service of a composting toilet that stands about fifty yards beyond the spring on a site that was once occupied by a second shelter.

A hundred and thirty yards beyond its intersection with the access path, the AT meets the upper terminus of the Balsam Mountain Trail circling in below the summit of Tricorner Knob. The name Tricorner Knob is suggested by the convergence of the corners of Haywood and Swain counties in North Carolina and Sevier County in Tennessee on the summit of the nearby peak. Tricorner Knob also marks the point where the Balsam Mountain range joins the main Smoky divide.

The AT eases into Tennessee for a quarter-mile circumnavigation of Tricorner Knob, returns to the state line momentarily, and then veers back into Tennessee as it circles wide around Mount Guyot.

Mount Guyot, the second-highest peak in the Smokies, was given its name by Samuel Botsford Buckley in recognition of the famed Swiss geologist Arnold Guyot, who spent much of his professional career studying the Appalachian mountain system. Guyot published the results of his early work in 1861 after spending much of 1859 in the Smokies measuring the high peaks along the state-line divide. In 1863 Guyot collated the notes from his Smokies expedition in an eighteen-page manuscript. However, the manuscript was never published. It was filed in the archives of the U.S. Geodetic Survey and remained there until it was discovered in 1929 by Myron Avery, chairman of the Appalachian Trail Conference. Avery subsequently published Guyot's manuscript as "Notes on the Geography of the Mountain District of Western North Carolina" in the *North Carolina Historical Review*.

Immediately after his sojourn in the Smokies, Guyot engaged his nephew, Ernest Sandoz, to construct a hand-drawn map of the high Smoky divide using his notes and measurements. The Guyot map was soon thereafter used as the source for maps printed for Union forces during the Civil War.

Although Guyot measured the peak that bears his name as well as its closest neighbor, Old Black, he did not recognize that either peak stood on the state line, believing them to be "wholly in the state of Tennessee." Furthermore, he did not measure any peaks on the state line east of Old Black but did measure those on Balsam Mountain, leading to speculation that Guyot erroneously understood the boundary between Tennessee and North Carolina to follow the crests of Mount Sterling Ridge and Balsam Mountain. Sandoz was cognizant of the fact that the state line did not follow Balsam Mountain; nevertheless, on the map he corroborates Guyot's error by placing Mount Guyot and Old Black as outliers standing wholly in Tennessee. In a letter to Myron Avery, George Masa confirms that Guyot's error may have originated from guidance he received from the local mountaineers, many of whom believed that the boundary between the two states did in fact follow Mount Sterling Ridge and Balsam Mountain. Masa contends that Guyot approached the state line along an old Indian trace known as the Raven Fork Trail, which split off the old Indian Gap Trail near Ravensford and led up Raven Fork, then Straight Fork, and then to the crest of Balsam Mountain near Big Cataloochee. It is surmised that, once Guyot reached the ridgeline of Balsam Mountain, he understood himself to be on the boundary between Tennessee and North Carolina.

Mount Guyot has a flat half-mile-long summit that is aligned squarely along the divide. The trail swings deep into Tennessee to avoid the summit, passing the headwaters of two springs, the second of which is known as Guyot Spring. A few yards beyond Guyot Spring, a rough manway leads up about 500 yards to the top of the mountain.

While traveling over the summit of Mount Guyot in 1914, Dan Beeson remarked that "the mountain is so densely wooded, covered with small balsams four feet apart, that you can't see over the surrounding region except in a very unsatisfactory way at one place on the west side. . . . Half the trees are dead and the ground covered with thick green moist moss that squirts when you step on it. You could get lonesome here on a bright day in June with all your friends and a brass band."

As Beeson noted, there are no views from Mount Guyot. The climb to the summit reaches a tiny clearing that was once occupied by a crude pole tower that government engineers built in the 1920s while surveying the mountains. Around the clearing the tops of the spruce and fir are so closely overlapping that only a dim light filters down from above, giving the place a gloomy funereal cast. The undergrowth is sparse, with scattered clumps of wood sorrel over the thick green moss that Beeson noted.

When it sweeps around the east end of Mount Guyot, the AT returns to the state line and drops into a shallow gap separating Guyot from Old Black (6,370 feet).

Early visitors to this part of the Smokies remarked on seeing a bear pen or trap that stood in the open bench below the Tennessee side of the gap. According to historian Paul Fink, bear traps in the Smokies were of two kinds. One was a log deadfall weighted with rocks and heavy logs and propped up on one end with a stout pole. Bait, usually of meat or honeycomb, was attached to the pole. When the bait was taken, the contraption fell on the bear, crushing it to death. The other was a pen of lighter but stronger timbers roofed over with poles. The pen was propped up high on one side so the bear could walk under to the bait. Taking the bait tripped a trigger that dropped the whole pen down on the bear, holding it captive until the hunter returned.

The name Old Black is suggested by the concentration of darkness found in the heart of the densely growing fir stands that thrive there. At its summit, the corners of Cocke and Sevier counties in Tennessee and Haywood County in North Carolina converge in a configuration mirroring that at Tricorner Knob. The trail does not cross the summit of Old Black but deviates into Tennessee to circumnavigate the peak before returning to the state line at an attractive glade known as Deer Creek Gap. The clearing at Deer Creek Gap is not a natural bald but the result of a logging fire that swept up from Big Creek and burned sections of the divide.

When Paul Fink traversed this part of the Smokies in the summer of 1919, he noted that the whole basin of Big Creek had been cut over and everything of any size had been taken for the pulp mills. "Then, as usual, fire had gotten out in the slash and completed the devastation, burning everything, even the organic matter on the forest floor, leaving the bare soil to erode and wash away under the heavy rainfall. A few straggling bushes of firecherry, laurel and blackberry were making a feeble effort to cover over the scars."

The two acres in Deer Gap are now covered with grass and patches of blueberry and thornless blackberry bushes. In the middle of the clearing is a flat slab of concrete that was used at one time as a pad for landing helicopters.

To the west, Mount Guyot is clearly visible with Balsam Mountain and its prominent peak, Luftee Knob (6,234 feet), extending out to the south. Angling across on the far side of the Big Creek drainage is Mount Sterling Ridge. On a clear day the Mount Sterling fire tower (5,842 feet) can be seen on the east end of the ridge.

From Deer Creek Gap, the AT enters a moderate descent that continues with little variation until reaching Camel Gap in a little more than three miles. Much of this part of the divide was consumed by the fire that visited Deer Creek Gap. Mountain ash and fire cherry were among the first tree species to germinate on the fire-scald, followed by birches and Allegheny serviceberries. Where the vegetation has been slower in recovering, openings afford points for surveying the basin formed by Balsam Mountain, Mount Sterling Ridge, and the Smoky divide.

One mile below Deer Creek Gap, the trail deviates into North Carolina to circle around Inadu Knob and intersect the Snake Den Ridge Trail leading up from Cosby Campground. Inadu, a Cherokee word for snake, is one of the few place-names of Indian origin to have survived in the Smokies. The impetus for the name is somewhat underscored by the proximity of the so-named Snake Den Mountain.

From its intersection with the Snake Den Ridge Trail, the AT continues descending, first circling around Camel Hump and then entering laurel-infested Camel Gap to intersect the Camel Gap Trail leading in from the upper reaches of the Big Creek drainage. The origin of the name Camel is likely a function of corrupt pronunciation. There is some suggestion that the name refers to a Camel family from Cosby, but the more plausible explanation is that the name is a slurring of the word Campbell.

At Camel Gap, the AT begins climbing, first clearing Ross Knob, and then descending through a wide parabolic swing into North Carolina, thereby avoiding a climb over Cosby Knob. At the vertex of the detour, an access path exits on the right fifty yards to a wide draw that harbors the Cosby Knob Shelter. The shelter commands a fine position overlooking a defile drained by Rocky Branch. The stream's headwater is a bold spring found immediately along the far side of the shelter. The camp is served by two food-storage cables suspended down below the front of the shelter and by a composting toilet just off the access path.

Beyond the access path, the AT continues its steep rocky descent for three-quarters of a mile before entering Low Gap, a V-shaped notch in the divide harboring a grassy opening surrounded by slender birch and beech trees. Passing through the gap is the Low Gap Trail connecting Walnut Bottom on Big Creek in North Carolina with Cosby Campground in Tennessee. This trail follows a remnant of the Raven Fork Trail, an Indian trace that split off the ancient Indian Gap Trail near Ravensford and crossed over the Smoky divide through Low Gap. The Low Gap Trail is the only trail in the park that traverses the state boundary without changing names.

The AT climbs steeply out of Low Gap for a mile to a small grassy opening near Sunup Knob and, after another mile, reaches an intersection with the Mount Cammerer Trail exiting to the left.

MOUNT CAMMERER TRAIL

Appalachian Trail to the Mount Cammerer Lookout Tower—0.6 mile.

The Mount Cammerer Trail is a rugged short course that follows the spine of the Smoky divide for a half-mile before ending abruptly at a rocky promontory crowned by a stone observation tower. The trail begins as a moderately easy excursion that wanders most of the way through laurel thickets. It then descends on a winding course to a small notch in the ridgeline known as Sharptop Gap. For the remaining 225 yards to the tower, the trail clambers up and over the fractured ends of upturned strata of rock where encroaching thickets of laurel and rhododendron press the trail into the jagged troughs. The troughs act as receptacles, retaining water and accumulating leaves and other detritus which decompose into a rotting mixture of sticky black mire.

The capacity of the rock strata on Mount Cammerer for retaining water was noted by William Davenport while following the Strother survey line into the Smokies. Davenport recorded in his journal that he proceeded "to the top of the Smoky mountain at a spring on the extreme height of the mountain." The "top of the Smoky mountain" in this instance is Mount Cammerer, and what Davenport described as a spring was only a furrow in the solid rock that always contains water replenished by rain and dew.

At the end of the trail and perched precariously atop a prominent outcropping of Mount Cammerer (4,928 feet) is a squat, two-story, octagonal lookout tower that resembles a fourteenth-century Norman turret without the castle. The lookout tower was built according to the "organic style" or the so-called "Yosemite model," a design adapted for rocky outcroppings in the national parks in the western states.

Construction on the tower was started in 1937 by young men of the Civilian Conservation Corps under the direction of Marshall Fox, the project's master stonemason. The white granite used in the construction was quarried a short distance below the tower and hauled up by hand. When completed in September 1939, the tower had an enclosed observation deck built over a storage cellar. The deck had windows on all sides and was encircled by a wooden catwalk. The tower was originally christened White Rock Lookout.

The tower was abandoned in 1966 and soon fell into disrepair. The catwalk rotted away, the roof partially collapsed, and some of the steps leading into the observation deck were displaced. Under the direction of the Friends of the Great Smoky Mountains National Park and the Appalachian Trailways Association, the Mount Cammerer Lookout Tower was restored in 1996 to look exactly as it had in 1939 when dedicated as the White Rock Lookout.

Old-timers from Tennessee may remember when Mount Cammerer was called White Rock, and those from North Carolina may know it still as Sharp Top. The name Sharp Top, which appears on some early Smoky Mountain maps, likely originates from the slanting knife-like appearance of the point of the promontory when seen from the North Carolina side. The cliff on the north side of Sharp Top is covered with a chalky lichen which from a distance resembles a large white rock. Inasmuch as the white cliff is readily noticeable from the valleys below to the north, the name White Rock became popular in Tennessee vernacular. In 1942 the name of the mountain was officially fixed as Mount Cammerer in memory of Arno B. Cammerer, who was director of the National Park Service from 1933 until 1940. It was Cammerer who persuaded John D. Rockefeller Jr. to match the state and local funding to establish the park, resulting in a $5 million contribution. Cammerer's effort may well have been the watershed event that transformed the dream of a park into a reality.

The Mount Cammerer Lookout Tower does not sit on the summit of Mount Cammerer. The summit is near the junction where the Mount Cammerer Trail exits the AT while the tower punctuates the east end of Cammerer Ridge. Nonetheless, the 360-degree view from the tower is among the very finest in the Smokies. Mount Sterling Ridge is the most dominant mountain in view, extending across the entire southern vista. On a clear day, the sixty-foot Mount Sterling fire tower can be seen atop the knob that marks the east end of the ridge. West, along the meander of the Smoky divide, Mount Guyot is the highest peak with Balsam Mountain, punctuated by Luftee Knob and Big Cataloochee, extending southward. The broad peak to the east is Snowbird Mountain. Beyond it, and discernible by its bright grassy expanse, is Max Patch. To the north, the Smoky Mountains fall away to the complex array of foothills and ridges of the Tennessee Valley. Conspicuous in the valley below are Douglas Lake and a short section of I-40 just south of Newport, Tennessee.

APPALACHIAN TRAIL

When the AT leaves the intersection with the Mount Cammerer Trail, it turns down into North Carolina and onto one of the most difficult long grades in the Smokies. Going up, it is an interminable grind. Going down, it is a relentless jarring ordeal. While surveying this part of the state line in 1799, John Strother recorded in his field book that "the country is absolutely desert, impenetrable and impossible to get over." After several days, Strother managed to reach Mount Cammerer, which he later identified on a map as a "high pinnacle on the Smokey mn." At this point Strother gave up and abandoned the survey.

A half-mile below its intersection with the Mount Cammerer Trail, the AT turns sharply right at a bare rock rampart that, if climbed, affords superb views of the Big Creek and Pigeon river valleys. From here, the trail works back toward the east end of Cammerer Ridge and into a potter's field of boulders that have broken free from the higher ridges and come to rest on the slopes below. A wide double-switchback completes the course through the boulders, and soon the trail edges back toward ridgeline. On the approach, the trail passes a faint access path on the right that leads twenty yards to a fine spring. A short distance below the spring, the trail reaches the ridgeline and intersects the upper terminus of the Lower Mount Cammerer Trail leading in 7.5 miles from Cosby Campground.

The grade moderates as the AT continues along the spine of the divide for another mile until reaching the upper terminus of the Chestnut Branch Trail leading up 2.1 miles from Big Creek Road. At this point, the grade again becomes steeper. One mile farther, an access path on the left leads a hundred yards to a former house site now occupied by the Davenport Gap Shelter. The shelter is situated on a level bench facing downward into a wide hollow. It was one of the first to be upgraded with an overhanging roof but remains the only shelter not accompanied by a food-storage cable. Water is convenient from a spring just at the side of the shelter, although the spring tends to be somewhat unreliable in the drier seasons. The grade moderates again as the AT completes its final mile within the park, dropping into Davenport Gap and terminating into TN32/NC284 a narrow, winding, gravel track that connects Cataloochee with Cosby.

When John Strother surveyed the state line in 1799, he recorded in his journal of having seen a trail he identified as the "Cataloochee Turnpike," an ancient Indian trace that served as a connecting route between the Rutherford War Trace in North Carolina and the Great Indian War Path in Tennessee. In Strother's time the Cataloochee trace was not a turnpike in the true sense of the word. Historian H. C. Wilburn suspects that the road most likely had fallen into disuse as the Cherokee abandoned their settlements along the Pigeon River beginning with the Indian wars of the 1760s. By the early 1800s, settlers were on Jonathan Creek in North Carolina and in the Cosby area of Tennessee; hence there was likely frequent traveling on the Cataloochee Turnpike between the two settlements by the time of William Davenport's survey in 1821.

Davenport recorded in his field journal of having marked the beginning point of his survey with a stone in the gap at the place where the "Cattaluche track" crossed the state line at what is now Davenport Gap. The General Assembly of the State of Tennessee acknowledged the marker as "a stone set up on the north side of Cataloochee Turnpike Road, and marked on the west side, Ten. 1821, and on the east side N.C. 1821." The stone was later moved when the Cataloochee track was widened to accommodate TN32/NC284.

◆ BIG CREEK ◆

The Big Creek section is defined as the large basin bounded along its north side by the main Smoky divide, south by Mount Sterling Ridge, and west by Balsam Mountain with its east end open, allowing Big Creek to escape to the Pigeon River.

White settlers, following the abandoned trace of the Cataloochee Indian Track, began drifting into the area and inhabiting the lower bottoms of Big Creek by the mid-eighteenth century. However, with access blocked on the lower end by the Pigeon River and surrounded on all sides by steep mountains, travel into Big Creek remained difficult until well into the twentieth century. Edward Guerrant, a circuit-riding minister traveling in the eastern Smokies during the closing years of the nineteenth century, recorded the following account of his first visit to Big Creek. "Over rocks and stumps and trees, where there was not even a path, we made our way down to the mouth of the gorge in the mountain. . . . The way we went was up a rushing, roaring stream, which came down five hundred feet in a half-mile, like a dozen cataracts of Lodore. It was magnificent, but it was not a road; but it was worth a trip to one who never saw nature in her wildest mood, and most magnificent dress."

Big Creek remained sparsely settled until 1890 when the Scottish Land and Timber Company moved in and established a selective-cutting operation along the stream near its confluence with the Pigeon River. By the beginning of the twentieth century Scottish Land and Timber had departed, and a succession of more-mechanized lumber concerns descended on the watershed, laying rail lines, building mill towns and camps, and clear-cutting the slopes nearly to the rim of the basin.

During the heyday of the loggers, houses sprang up near the mills and camps accompanied by the occasional church building and a schoolhouse. When the lumber companies departed, the loggers left and the mills closed down, leaving only a few mountaineer families to carry on tilling the hardscrabble farms in the bigger bottoms of Big Creek.

With the advent of the park in 1934, the main rail grade up Big Creek was rehabilitated and appropriated as the Big Creek Trail which currently forms the backbone of an array of trails branching out and up the ridges that enclose the basin. The Chestnut Branch Trail, Low Gap Trail, and Camel Gap Trail each climb north to the Appalachian Trail on the main divide. The Baxter Creek Trail and Swallow Fork Trail climb south to the spine of Mount Sterling Ridge. The Gunter Fork Trail exits the western end of the basin and climbs to the crest of Balsam Mountain. Two additional trails, the Mount Sterling Trail and the Mount Sterling Ridge Trail, range along the high ridge that forms the south rim of the Big Creek basin.

Backcountry camping in the Big Creek section is limited to three camps, the Lower Walnut Bottom Backcountry Campsite (#37), the Upper Walnut Bottom Backcountry Campsite (#36), and the Mount Sterling Backcountry Campsite (#38). The two camps in Walnut Bottom are old logging venues. The Lower Walnut Bottom Camp is one of the more attractive backcountry camps in the park while its upper sibling is generally reserved as a horse camp. The Mount Sterling Camp, at the intersection of the Baxter Creek Trail and Mount Sterling Trail on the summit of Mount Sterling, registers the highest elevation of any backcountry campsite in the Smokies.

Along the perimeter of the Big Creek basin are the Davenport Gap Shelter, the Cosby Shelter, and the Laurel Gap Shelter. The Davenport Shelter resides along the Appalachian Trail 1.9 miles below the upper end of the Chestnut Branch Trail, the Cosby Shelter is 0.7 mile west of Low Gap on the Appalachian Trail, and the Laurel Gap Shelter is on the Balsam Mountain Trail 280 yards south of the upper terminus of the Gunter Fork Trail.

To reach the Big Creek section, take the Waterville Exit (451) off I-40 and cross the bridge over the Pigeon River. Turn left and proceed one mile to the Carolina Power and Light plant and Big Creek Road. Though the power plant is situated at the confluence of Big Creek and the Pigeon River, water for driving the turbines comes from neither stream. On the south side of Scottish Mountain, Cataloochee Creek is diverted into a tunnel, fourteen feet in diameter and bored through six miles of solid rock, and channeled into the power plant. The tailrace boils out into the Pigeon River.

At the power plant, Big Creek Road turns and proceeds another 1.3 miles to the park boundary and an intersection with NC284, a gravel road that follows the old Cataloochee Indian Track. The intersection was for many years known as Mount Sterling Post Office. NC284 leads south to Mount Sterling Gap and the Mount Sterling Trail and then descends into Cataloochee. Going north, NC284 leads to the state-line divide at Davenport Gap, where it crosses the Appalachian Trail. At the state line the road become TN32 and continues to Cosby, Tennessee.

Big Creek Road continues through the intersection 0.2 mile to the Big Creek Ranger Station. About a mile beyond the ranger station, the road terminates in a parking area near Big Creek Campground and Picnic Area just below the trailhead for the Big Creek Trail.

BIG CREEK TRAIL

Big Creek Road to the Camel Gap Trail at Walnut Bottom—5.8 miles.

POINT OF DEPARTURE: From Knoxville, drive on I-40 east 60 miles to the Waterville exit or from Asheville follow I-40 west 50 miles. At the Waterville exit, cross the Pigeon River and proceed upstream to the Carolina Power and Light Company plant, turn, and proceed 2.0 miles to an intersection with NC284. Pass through the intersection onto Big Creek Road. Continue past the Big Creek Ranger Station 0.7 mile to the parking area above the Big Creek Picnic Area. The Big Creek Trail begins on the right where the road turns down to the parking area.

QUAD MAPS: Waterville 173-SE

Cove Creek Gap 174-NE

Luftee Knob 174-NW

0.0—Big Creek Road.

1.0—Access path exits right 200 feet to the Rock House.

1.4—Midnight Hole.

2.0—Mouse Creek Falls.

2.3—Big Creek. Bridge.

2.8—Brakeshoe Spring.

4.5—Flint Rock Cove Creek. Concrete causeway.

5.1—Walnut Bottom. Swallow Fork Trail exits left 4.0 miles to the Mount Sterling Ridge Trail at Pretty Hollow Gap.

5.2—Big Creek. Bridge.

5.3—Lower Walnut Bottom Backcountry Campsite (#37).

5.3—Low Gap Trail exits right 2.5 miles to the Appalachian Trail at Low Gap.

5.7—Upper Walnut Bottom Backcountry Campsite (#36).

5.8—Camel Gap Trail exits straight 4.7 miles to the Appalachian Trail at Camel Gap.

The main Smoky divide is separated from Mount Sterling Ridge by a deep elongated basin breached at its eastern end by a narrow aperture where Big Creek escapes to the Pigeon River. The floor of the basin, three thousand feet below the adjacent ridges, is defined by the wide stream distinguished for its abundant pools, exceedingly large boulders, and water of remarkable clarity.

During the early years of the twentieth century when commercial logging concerns in the Big Creek watershed were advancing to highly mechanized operations capable of clear-cutting on the higher slopes, rail lines were extended into remote reaches of the basin to expedite hauling timber out of the mountains. With the advent of the park, the main rail line, which adhered closely to the stream, was adopted by Civilian Conservation Corps workers as a jeep road and then later appropriated by the Park Service as the Big Creek Trail. Over its entire length, the trail is wide, smooth, and follows an easy grade.

The entrance into the Big Creek basin is along Big Creek Road, which leaves NC284 and proceeds upstream. About three-quarters of a mile beyond the Big Creek Ranger Station, the road turns downhill into a large parking area. The Big Creek Trail begins along the road where it turns to approach the parking area.

The trail is separated from the stream by a wide bottomland that was once occupied by sawmill operations of the Champion Lumber Company. The trail stays to the north edge of the bottomland, maintaining an easy climb along the adjacent slope. Within a half-mile, the bottomland yields to converging ridges, marshalling the trail into closer proximity with the stream.

After another half-mile, the trail enters a long straight stretch that roughly mirrors the course of the stream. On the slopes to the right, under sheer cliffs and overhanging ledges, dozens of huge rocks, split and upheaved, lie tumbled and scattered in great confusion, thrown at all angles upon the slopes. At an indeterminate point where the trail and stream appear to be in closest proximity, a beech tree cantilevered slightly out over the right side of the trail marks the head of a faint two-hundred-foot scramble up the talus to the Rock House, a juxtaposition of boulders under an overhang that forms a large roomy alcove. The Rock House has two vertical walls joined at a precise right angle and its interior sheltered by a remarkably level twenty-five foot "ceiling." The walls and ceiling joints are noticeably trim, making the ceiling overhang appear to have been fitted to the dimensions of the walls. Early settlers on Big Creek reportedly inhabited the Rock House temporarily while building more permanent accommodations along the stream.

A half-mile above the Rock House, the trail reaches Midnight Hole, one of the larger pools on Big Creek and arguably one of the most attractive in all of the Smokies. Here, Big Creek flows through a pinched opening between two boulders, then fans out into a translucent sheet of water that falls ten feet to a pool. The pool is fifteen feet deep at the base of the falls and extends eighty feet downstream to a depth of only a foot. Water in the stream is of such clarity that the pebbles on the bottom of the deepest parts of Midnight Hole are visible. Except where escaping at the downstream end, there appears to be little movement on the surface of the pool, the force of the falls being efficiently absorbed by the volume of impounded water.

A little more than a half-mile upstream of Midnight Hole, Mouse Creek Falls makes a spectacular near-vertical plunge into Big Creek, cascading fifty feet down the face of a rocky cliff. During the logging era, an access road passed between Mouse Creek Falls and Big Creek. The falls drops onto the track of the old road before cascading a final ten feet into Big Creek. A hitching post along the trail marks an access path that climbs over a low berm and down to the edge of Big Creek opposite Mouse Creek Falls.

Four hundred and fifty yards upstream of the falls, a sturdy bridge spans Big Creek where it collects in another of its deep crystal-clear pools. The exceptional translucence of the water in Big Creek has been noted by early visitors to the Smokies.

While commenting on fishing in Big Creek, outdoorsman Jim Gasque, author of *Hunting and Fishing in the Great Smoky Mountains,* remarks, "Many trout could be seen, but because of the extreme clarity of the water it was almost impossible . . . to make a cast and remain undiscovered." Gasque concludes with the comment that some fishermen pass on Big Creek because its clear water make the pools too difficult to fish.

From this juncture the trail remains in close proximity to the stream, affording opportunities to explore the large boulders and pools that characterize Big Creek. Across the stream are pockets of bottomland that were cleared by the lumbermen but proved to be too rocky for farming. The terrain on the left is a succession of rocky cliffs separated from the trail by infestations of rhododendron and dog-hobble. At one point a half-mile above the bridge and where the cliffs encroach closely upon the trail, small rills from Brakeshoe Spring exit crevices in the moss-covered rocks and drip out onto the trail bed. Sometime in the early twentieth century, a railroad engineer with the lumber company placed a locomotive brakeshoe on the rock below the spring. Acting as a basin, the curvature of the brakeshoe collected the drip from the spring, affording passersby a convenient source of drinking water. The brakeshoe remained in place for half a century until it was filched sometime in the mid-1970s.

The trail continues its easy course along the stream, first crossing Flint Rock Cove Creek on a concrete causeway and then proceeding another half-mile to enter Walnut Bottom, an enclosed cove once occupied by a logging camp. The approach to Walnut Bottom is marked by the lower terminus of the Swallow Fork Trail exiting left four miles to Mount Sterling Ridge at Pretty Hollow Gap. A hundred and thirty-five yards beyond the Swallow Fork junction, the Big Creek Trail crosses the stream on a wide wooden bridge and enters the expansive Lower Walnut Bottom Backcountry Campsite (#37).

The Lower Walnut Bottom Camp is divided by the trail into two unequal parts. The smaller of the two occupies a fine level tract along the right side of the trail, bounded firmly on the back side by a wooded slope, and shaded by a few large buckeyes. The camp offers several excellent tent sites with ready access to a food-storage cable and the stream.

The larger part of the campsite is situated on a strip of bottomland fitted deftly in a slight bend in Big Creek. Entrance to the campsite is through a small annex separated from the main site by a berm of hummocky ground. The annex affords an excellent camping site, though it is a bit exposed to the main trail. Beyond the hummocks is a wide parcel of smooth level ground bordered by clusters of rhododendron and shaded by a mix of eastern hemlocks and hardwoods. During the early years of the twentieth century, the bottom was occupied by facilities serving the Champion Lumber Company. The bare, smooth, unencumbered ground of the camp is the residue of the logging operation. Because of its size, its smooth level ground, and its proximity to Big Creek, the streamside part of the Lower Walnut Bottom Camp ranks among the finer campsites in the park.

Immediately above the campsite, the Big Creek Trail intersects the southern terminus of the Low Gap Trail, which climbs 2.5 miles to the Appalachian Trail at Low Gap and then descends 2.9 miles to Cosby Campground in Tennessee.

Seven hundred yards above the Low Gap intersection, the Big Creek Trail reaches the Upper Walnut Bottom Backcountry Campsite (#36), a horse camp situated on a level strip of ground flush against the trail's edge. The site is open and fairly roomy but enjoys little of the attractiveness of its larger sibling at the lower end of Walnut Bottom.

Ninety yards above the Upper Walnut Bottom Camp, the Big Creek Trail terminates into the lower terminus of the Camel Gap Trail. There is no noticeable junction. Rather than intersecting, the two trails connect end-to-end. Their point of connection is not discernable except for the presence of a Park Service trail sign. The Camel Gap Trail continues along the same railroad grade traced by the Big Creek Trail, leading just over a half-mile to an intersection with the lower terminus of the Gunter Fork Trail before exiting Walnut Bottom for a course into the upper reaches of Big Creek.

CHESTNUT BRANCH TRAIL

Big Creek Road to the Appalachian Trail—2.1 miles.

POINT OF DEPARTURE: Follow directions to the Big Creek Trail. The Chestnut Branch Trail begins 50 yards above the Big Creek Ranger Station.

QUAD MAPS: Waterville 173-SE
Hartford 173-SW

0.0—Big Creek Road.
1.1—Switchback.
2.1—Appalachian Trail exits right 1.9 miles to Davenport Gap and left 3.2 miles to the Mount Cammerer Trail.

The precursor to the Chestnut Branch Trail is a logging road cut along the stream by the Scottish Land and Timber Company operating in the Big Creek drainage around 1890. After the lumber company departed, settlers moved into the area, building houses and tilling farms along the abandoned lumber road.

One of the more prominent settlers on Chestnut Branch, a tributary of Big Creek, was A. W. Hopkins, who operated an overshot grist mill at the mouth of the stream near the Chestnut Branch Trail. There is some indication that Hopkins may have also maintained a sawmill on the same site. In either case, the ground flanking the lower stretch of the Chestnut Branch Trail was so severely compacted by heavy use that in the interim the forest has recovered only to a thin mix of struggling pines and hemlocks.

Another settler family on Chestnut Branch was Zilphie Sutton's. When Joseph Hall, a professor of linguistics at Columbia University, interviewed Zilphie Sutton in 1937, she explained that White Rock (Mount Cammerer) was once known as Old Mother, a name also used locally for Chestnut Branch. In Zilphie Sutton's day the principal route to White Rock was up the old Scottish Land and Timber logging road—thus the common name Old Mother for both the mountain peak and the stream.

The Chestnut Branch Trail begins along Big Creek Road a few yards up from the Big Creek Ranger Station. The trail starts steeply but quickly moderates to an easier grade when it enters a stand of old-field hemlocks and pines. The trail continues with little variation in grade, eventually working its way into stands of yellow poplar, American beech, and a variety of oaks while passing the occasional rock wall and chestnut fence post that mark places of former human inhabitation.

A half-mile above Big Cove Road, the forest cover gives way to a clearing once occupied by a mission school and church started by Presbyterians in 1920. Adjacent to the school property was the Garfield Jenkins place. Jenkins maintained a grist mill that stood on the opposite side of Chestnut Branch not far above the site of the mission school. Broken crockery, discarded washtubs, a rusty bed frame, an extension of stove pipe, and miscellaneous sheets of metal scattered up and down the trail are a few of the more noticeable artifacts remaining from the settlement era.

Above the clearing, the drainage narrows noticeably where the trail crosses a feeder stream and enters a closed oak association. The trail soon reaches another clearing before switching away from Chestnut Branch and onto a steeper grade. At this juncture, the trail leaves the old Scottish Land and Timber trace to follow a newer roadbed that ascends the adjacent ridge. In Zilphie Sutton's day the old timber road extended 500 yards farther up Chestnut Branch and served another half-dozen families living along the creek bottoms. The road which the Chestnut Branch Trail now follows served a single farm situated on a tributary of Chestnut Branch.

When it turns to leave the old timber trace, the trail proceeds 180 yards to a switchback, then 200 yards to a second switchback. It then clears a ridge and levels out on a moderately easy grade. Four stream crossings intervene before the trail enters a thin copse of second-growth poplars now occupying what was once a mountain settlement. The old-field poplars mark the onset of a steep half-mile approach to a minor swag on the main Smoky divide where the Chestnut Branch Trail terminates into the Appalachian Trail. Slightly less than two miles down the divide, the Appalachian Trail reaches the park boundary at Davenport Gap. Three miles up the main divide, the Appalachian Trail intersects the Mount Cammerer Trail, leading a half-mile out to the summit of Old Mother and the Mount Cammerer Lookout Tower.

BAXTER CREEK TRAIL

Big Creek Picnic Area to Mount Sterling—6.1 miles.

POINT OF DEPARTURE: Follow directions to the Big Creek Trail. The Baxter Creek Trail begins below the Big Creek Picnic Area on the metal bridge over Big Creek.

QUAD MAPS: Waterville 173-SE
Cove Creek Gap 174-NE

0.0—Big Creek Road. Big Creek Picnic Area.
0.4—Access path exits right 560 yards to standing chimney ruins.
1.3—Baxter Creek.
4.3—Switchback. Big Branch manway exits left.
5.9—Access path exits right 260 yards to spring.
6.1—Mount Sterling. Fire tower. Mount Sterling Backcountry Campsite (#38). Mount Sterling Trail.

From its beginning on Big Creek to its terminus at the summit of Mount Sterling, the Baxter Creek Trail climbs four thousand feet, ascending from old-field stands of second-growth poplar and maple and then through various iterations of cove hardwood, northern hardwood, and a hemlock-spruce associations before finishing in the boreal gloom of a spruce-fir forest. All of the great trees of the Smokies are here in a panoply of riot and diversity unmatched by all but the most fecund forests in North America.

The Baxter Creek Trail begins on a slender steel bridge that spans Big Creek just below the Big Creek Picnic Area. At the far end of the bridge, the trail turns right and proceeds on an easy course around the base of a truncated ridge whose bare massive cliffs form a rampart commanding a wide fertile intervale flanking Big Creek. Ferns, toothwort, foamflower, and hepatica thrive in the seepages from the cliffs. Rangy rhododendron and thickets of dog-hobble cloister the trail. The trail soon moves out of the rhododendron bottom and into stands of yellow poplar whose slender boles extend straight as ramrods seventy or eighty feet over an understory of thin eastern hemlocks.

 The bottomland flanking Big Creek was logged by the earliest timber companies to enter the watershed and soon thereafter was inhabited by farming settlers and workers from the nearby lumber mills. Various artifacts of former human inhabitation remain scattered throughout the area. A particularly impressive example can be seen 560 yards along the trail, where a well-worn access path exits to the right and proceeds a little over a quarter-mile to a massive stone chimney that was once part of a lodge. The chimney stands sixty feet high and is constructed of glen stones stacked without mortar.

Along the upper edge of the bottom, the grade stiffens. The track becomes narrow and appreciably rougher as it enters a wide draw channeling Baxter Creek. Great cliffs preside over a rugged boulder-strewn terrain shaded by large poplars, hickories, and red maples. Three-quarters of a mile upstream, the trail crosses Baxter Creek and enters a lateral course tracing the contours of the lower fringe ridges of Mount Sterling. When the trail crosses a ridge point, it is often cloistered in tall leggy rhododendron whose over-reaching branches form a tunnel over the path. In the more moist recesses, hemlocks, Fraser magnolias, striped maples, black gums, yellow buckeyes, sourwoods, Carolina silverbells, and sassafras grade into the mix. Large boles of dead American chestnuts remain as stark reminders of the long-vanished tree that was once the most dominant tree species on these slopes. Higher up, American beech and black cherry join in noticeable numbers. Along this stretch there are no outstanding vantage points, only a brief glimpse of Mount Cammerer when the trail rises to clear a small ridge overlooking the Big Creek drainage.

After negotiating a final ridge point, the trail reaches the solace and solitude of a hemlock forest where the tall, stately, widely spaced evergreens share space with gnarled old maples and beeches. The slopes here are steep and heavily encumbered with boulders. The large old trees have thrived on this rugged terrain through an adaptation Doris Gove aptly describes as an ingenious complex of "aerial roots, twisted trunks, and counterbalanced branches." Higher up the mountain, the deciduous species fade from the mix, and the red spruce appear, heralding the approach to the boreal zone. The trail through the transition is long and arduous, the track often little more than a slight berm etched onto the steeply sloped mountainside.

After little more than four miles, the trail climbs into a slight swag along the crest of Mount Sterling Ridge. Here, a sharp switchback to the right marks what was once the intersection of the Baxter Creek Trail and the now disused Big Branch Trail.

 Prior to the coming of the park, a mountaineer's trace followed the spine of Mount Sterling Ridge from the summit of Mount Sterling to a point on Big Creek near the lower terminus of the Baxter Creek Trail. The lower part of the old trace was a streamside course along Big Branch, whence the trail got its name. Except for the remnant now incorporated into the Baxter Creek Trail, the Big Branch trace was abandoned by the Park Service and survives now only as an excessively overgrown manway.

At the switchback, the trail enters a steep course that generally follows the spine of Mount Sterling Ridge. The hemlocks transition out, replaced by the increasing occurrence of large red spruce trees. Where conditions are relatively drier, rhododendron and weeds appear as the understory. In the cooler, more moist recesses, there is little understory aside from ferns and the occasional Fraser fir. After two additional switchbacks, the trail narrows noticeably and proceeds into a rhododendron corridor shaded by a birch-spruce association.

Near the end of the rhododendron corridor, a double-switchback ushers the trail off the ridge and into a more rugged terrain where it is forced into a winding course among large boulders. There is relatively little understory, only thick mats of spongy moss blanketing the rocks. The trail is soft underfoot, cushioned by ages of needles shed by thick-set stands of spruce and fir. A sweet, resinous smell permeates. The trees grow so closely together that no direct sunlight reaches the forest floor, perpetuating an eternal twilight in which a palpable quietness pervades. This is the boreal forest primeval.

The trail continues its steep ascent, soon moving onto a drier exposure and proceeding through a tight corridor of closely spaced firs interspersed with large birch and spruce trees. Four hundred yards from trail's end, a well-worn path exits right 260 yards down the mountain to a small spring secluded in a bed of jewel weeds. The spring is accoutered with a pipe and affords the only convenient source of water on Mount Sterling.

The summit of Mount Sterling is a gently sloped gradient of close-cropped turf encircled by stands of fir and spruce. The Baxter Creek Trail terminates on the summit near the base of the Mount Sterling fire tower, where it completes an end-to-end connection with the upper terminus of the Mount Sterling Trail. The trail intersection coincides with the highest point on the mountain and immediately adjacent to the Mount Sterling Backcountry Campsite (#38). For details on the fire tower and campsite, refer to the Mount Sterling Trail.

SWALLOW FORK TRAIL

Big Creek Trail at lower Walnut Bottom to the Mount Sterling Ridge Trail at Pretty Hollow Gap—4.0 miles.

POINT OF DEPARTURE: Hike the Big Creek Trail 5.1 miles to Walnut Bottom. The Swallow Fork Trail begins on the left just below the bridge crossing Big Creek at the entrance to the Lower Walnut Bottom Backcountry Campsite (#37).

QUAD MAP: Luftee Knob 174-NW

0.0—Walnut Bottom. Big Creek Trail.

1.0—Swallow Fork. Footlog.

1.2—McGinty Creek.

2.6—Switchback.

3.1—Switchback.

4.0—Pretty Hollow Gap. Mount Sterling Ridge Trail exits left 1.4 miles to the Mount Sterling Trail and right 3.9 miles to the Balsam Mountain Trail. Pretty Hollow Gap Trail exits straight 5.6 miles to Cataloochee Road at Beech Grove School.

Near the lower end of Walnut Bottom, the Big Creek Trail crosses a sturdy wooden bridge and immediately enters the Lower Walnut Bottom Backcountry Campsite (#37). A hundred and thirty-five yards downstream of the bridge, the Swallow Fork Trail exits the Big Creek Trail and proceeds on a long leisurely course across the eastern edge of Walnut Bottom, a remarkably flat interval that harbors the confluence of Swallow Fork and Big Creek.

Prior to the arrival of the lumber companies, the bottomland around the confluence of the two streams was cleared and occupied by settlement farms. On commenting about Walnut Bottom, Zilphie Sutton of Chestnut Branch once said "it was thick of houses, thick of people up thar then." Little evidence of these farms and homeplaces remains today. What the logging operations did not obliterate the passage of time has obscured. Scattered piles of fieldstones, the occasional apple tree, and a couple of trail-side springs are the most noticeable relics of Walnut Bottom's settlement heritage.

Within the first quarter-mile, the Swallow Fork Trail approaches Big Creek from a high vantage point, affording a fine view across the stream and into the Walnut Bottom interval. Here, the trail steers left, crosses a feeder stream, and proceeds into the Swallow Fork drainage. Thin stands of red maple, yellow poplar, red oak, and American beech are slowly reclaiming the old fields that were once heavily eroded by farming and logging.

After a half-mile, the trail crosses a second feeder stream while maintaining its easy grade through second-growth fields, then ascends to a streamside course along Swallow Fork. At one mile, the trail completes its only crossing of Swallow Fork, clearing the stream on a footlog. Noticeable on the right just above the stream crossing is a small level clearing that was once occupied by a backcountry campsite. Opposite the old campsite, Swallow Fork cascades in an attractive step-wise fashion down through a succession of shallow pools, the water spilling limpidly over the outer rim of each pool and filling into the one below. This graduation of pools is a harbinger that the grade is quickly to become stiffer.

Four hundred and fifty yards above the footlog crossing, the trail enters a slight switchback crossing McGinty Creek and then turns up into a narrow draw. The water of McGinty Creek flows down the mountain through a trough of fractured upturned rock strata, pooling momentarily in the trail before dashing off to join Swallow Creek below. At this juncture, the trail is climbing in a southeasterly direction but still following the course of Swallow Fork. It continues with very little deviation in either direction or grade but gains over six hundred feet in a little over a mile. After eventually crossing a headwater tributary of Swallow Fork, the trail completes a sharp switchback and then, eight hundred yards farther, executes a second switchback that repositions it on a steeply angled course up and across the north flank of Mount Sterling Ridge. Rock bluffs and outcroppings define the terrain. The trail surface becomes markedly uneven. Minor vantage points offer fine glimpses of a few prominent landmarks along the Smoky divide—Low Gap (4,424 feet), Cosby Knob (5,180 feet), Old Black (6,370 feet), and Mount Guyot (6,621 feet).

A half-mile above the second switchback the grade eases, the track becomes less rugged, and the trail enters a fine copse of beech trees. The Swallow Fork Trail remains in the beeches as it angles up and into Pretty Hollow Gap, a small grassy opening on the crest of Mount Sterling Ridge. Here, the Swallow Fork Trail terminates in a crossroads intersection with the Mount Sterling Ridge Trail and the upper terminus of the Pretty Hollow Gap Trail. The Mount Sterling Ridge Trail follows the ridgeline while the Pretty Hollow Gap Trail rises into the gap from the opposite side.

LOW GAP TRAIL (NORTH CAROLINA)

Big Creek Trail at Walnut Bottom to the Appalachian Trail at Low Gap—2.5 miles.

POINT OF DEPARTURE: Hike the Big Creek Trail 5.3 miles to the Lower Walnut Bottom Backcountry Campsite (#37). The Low Gap Trail begins on the right at the upper end of the campsite.

QUAD MAP: Luftee Knob 174-NW

0.0—Walnut Bottom. Big Creek Trail.

0.1—Chestnut Cove Creek.

0.4—Feeder stream. Cemetery.

1.1—Feeder stream. Spring.

2.0—Low Gap Branch.

2.5—Low Gap. Appalachian Trail. The Low Gap Trail (Tennessee) continues 2.9 miles to Cosby Campground.

When settlers of European descent first began moving into the Oconaluftee River Valley, they found an abandoned Indian trace that proceeded up Raven Fork and then along Straight Fork to the flank of Balsam Mountain. The Indian trace then crossed over Balsam Mountain and descended along Gunter Fork to Walnut Bottom on Big Creek. After crossing to the north side of Walnut Bottom, it climbed to the main Smoky divide, passing through Low Gap and descending into Tennessee. That part of the Indian trace between Walnut Bottom and Low Gap was claimed by the settlers as a mountaineers' access between the settlements on Big Creek and those in Cosby, Tennessee. With the advent of the park, the settlers' trace was upgraded to Park Service specifications and officially designated as the Low Gap Trail.

Under the current Park Service configuration, the Low Gap Trail climbs 2.5 miles from Walnut Bottom to Low Gap and then descends 2.9 miles to Cosby Campground. It is the only trail in the park that traverses the state-line divide between North Carolina and Tennessee without changing names. For the sake of consistency in grouping trails according to geographical sections, the North Carolina part of the Low Gap Trail is treated in the Big Creek section while that in Tennessee is found in the Cosby section.

The Low Gap Trail begins along the Big Creek Trail immediately above the Lower Walnut Bottom Backcountry Campsite (#37) and climbs steeply 220 yards to a rocky crossing of Chestnut Cove Creek. At this juncture, the trail eases into a nice level course running parallel to Big Creek but separated from the stream by a bottomland.

Four hundred and sixty yards beyond the Chestnut Cove Creek crossing, the trail crosses a feeder stream while passing below a small knoll on the left which harbors an old cemetery occupied by nine gravesites. About a hundred yards beyond the cemetery knoll, the trail turns away from Big Creek and into a steep climbing course parallel to Low Gap Branch. Evidence of field clearings and old homesites is unmistakable. Most conspicuous is a fine spring sheltered by a dry-laid rock wall and covered by a large flat stone. The spring is on a feeder stream immediately to the left of the trail. It is likely that a log springhouse once stood over the spring, providing cool storage for milk, butter, eggs, and other perishables.

On the right immediately beyond the spring, the skeletal remains of a chimney preside over the remnants of a cast iron stove. In the vicinity are fragmented sections of rock walls and stone piles which, together with the spring and chimney, were once part of the Dan Gunter homeplace.

Higher up, the trail become rockier and begins winding through a boulder field under the cover of large yellow poplars. A mile above the Gunter place, the trail crosses Low Gap Branch and then proceeds about a 150 yards to a switchback that directs the course onto a spur ridge for a final approach into Low Gap. From the spur, Cosby Knob (5,180 feet) appears to the left as the high point on the Smoky divide. Back and below is a fine view of the Low Gap Branch drainage. In late spring the slopes on the approach are distinguished by the dazzling white blossoms of the Carolina silverbell trees that thrive there.

When the trail reaches Low Gap, a deep V-shaped notch in the state-line divide, it crosses the Appalachian Trail before beginning a 2.9-mile descent to Cosby Campground in Tennessee. Proceeding west out of the gap, the Appalachian Trail leads three-quarters of a mile to the Cosby Knob Shelter. To the east it continues two miles to the Mount Cammerer Trail, which then leads a half-mile to the Mount Cammerer Lookout Tower.

CAMEL GAP TRAIL

Big Creek Trail at Walnut Bottom to the Appalachian Trail at Camel Gap—
    4.7 miles.
POINT OF DEPARTURE: Hike 5.8 miles to the end of the Big Creek Trail. The
    Camel Gap Trail begins where the Big Creek Trail ends.
QUAD MAP: Luftee Knob 174-NW

0.0—Walnut Bottom. Big Creek Trail.
0.6—Gunter Fork Trail exits left 4.1 miles to the Balsam Mountain Trail.
1.2—Rocky Branch.
3.4—Switchback.
4.7—Camel Gap. Appalachian Trail.

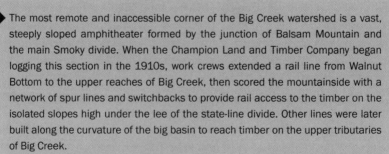

The most remote and inaccessible corner of the Big Creek watershed is a vast, steeply sloped amphitheater formed by the junction of Balsam Mountain and the main Smoky divide. When the Champion Land and Timber Company began logging this section in the 1910s, work crews extended a rail line from Walnut Bottom to the upper reaches of Big Creek, then scored the mountainside with a network of spur lines and switchbacks to provide rail access to the timber on the isolated slopes high under the lee of the state-line divide. Other lines were later built along the curvature of the big basin to reach timber on the upper tributaries of Big Creek.

When Champion discontinued operation in the Smoky Mountains, the railroad grades remained as the most convenient routes through the rugged trackless Big Creek terrain. Most of the graded lines on the upper reaches of Big Creek have been allowed to return to wilderness, but a few were incorporated into what is now the Camel Gap Trail. Because of its remoteness, the Camel Gap Trail is one of the lesser used trails and leads into some of the less-frequently visited backcountry in all of the Smokies.

The lower terminus of the Camel Gap Trail coincides with the upper terminus of the Big Creek Trail at a point that is not even distinguished by a junction but marked only by a Park Service trail sign. Following an old railroad grade, the Big Creek Trail proceeds to the upper end of Walnut Bottom and then comes to an abrupt stop at an arbitrary point ninety yards above the Upper Walnut Bottom Backcountry Campsite (#36). The Camel Gap Trail simply picks up at that point and continues following the rail grade upstream.

When it leaves Walnut Bottom, the Camel Gap Trail proceeds on an easy level course through bottomland flanking Big Creek. Much of the land here was heavily abused by the logging operations, and forest growth has been a bit tentative in reclaiming the wilderness. After little more than a half-mile, the Camel Gap Trail intersects the lower terminus of the Gunter Fork Trail. The Gunter Fork Trail exits left, immediately crosses Big Creek, then climbs to the crest of Balsam Mountain.

At this juncture, the Camel Gap Trail eases out of the bottomland and into a low hummocky terrain strewn with boulders. Large eastern hemlocks and a variety of oaks appear in great profusion. Dense thickets of rhododendron and dog-hobble form the understory. Through here, the trail continues tracing the grade of the old rail line though it occasionally drifts away from the stream. Big Creek at this elevation is a remarkably attractive stream characterized by large boulders and deep pools, rapidly flowing cataracts, and charming falls cloistered in luxuriant arbors of rhododendron.

Little elevation is gained until the trail reaches Rocky Branch one mile above the trailhead. It crosses a nameless tributary 500 yards farther along and then settles into a long, modulating course that remains high above Big Creek. A cove-hardwood mix of oaks, white basswood, American beech, red and sugar maple, and hemlock shades the slopes while the stream, mostly hidden from sight, courses through a wide flat that is heavily infested with rhododendron. Almost a half-dozen feeder streams intervene at various intervals as they make their way to Big Creek.

A conspicuous stand of beech trees heralds the approach to a switchback that directs the trail up and away from the Big Creek drainage. Near this point, Big Creek is joined by Yellow Creek, a large tributary that drains the south face of Inadu Knob. Yellow Creek is worth pointing out only as a reminder that the Camel Gap Trail was once known as the Yellow Creek Trail. The name change was implemented to accommodate the fact that the official trail now terminates at Camel Gap on the state-line divide.

On completing the switchback, the trail passes through a corridor of rhododendron and then reaches a fairly level clearing that was likely the site of some heavy industrial use by the logging operations. Sawbriers abound in a thin copse of beech trees interspersed with the occasional basswood, yellow birch, and Fraser magnolia. Beyond the clearing, the trail passes back through the upper end of the same beech stand encountered below the switchback. The grade stiffens, and the forest begins showing the first signs of transition to a northern hardwood mix. Over the next 300 yards, the trail proceeds on an easterly course across a south-facing exposure, then veers north and enters the moist, cool, shaded environs of a high-elevation ravine. While yet on the southern exposure, openings in the forest cover permit views back toward Balsam Mountain and its prominent peak, Luftee Knob (6,234 feet). Once the trail completes its transition from the southern exposure and gains some elevation, Cosby Knob (5,180 feet) comes into view, looming high on the state-line divide. The vast sweep of the Big Creek basin appears below. Across the gulf is the long Mount Sterling Ridge punctuated prominently on its west end by Big Cataloochee Mountain (6,155 feet) and on its east by Mount Sterling (5,842 feet).

For the most part, the trail surface remains smooth underfoot and unimpeded by rocks. As it reaches higher elevations, however, the surface becomes rockier and the grade increases noticeably. Here, the northern hardwoods begin yielding to the boreal species. Thickset stands of Fraser fir herald the trail's approach into Camel Gap, where it terminates into the Appalachian Trail.

 Some sources suggest that Camel Gap was named for a Camel family from Cosby, Tennessee, while others contend that Camel is a corruption of the name Campbell. In either case, the particular individual or family for whom the gap was named is apparently unknown.

GUNTER FORK TRAIL

Camel Gap Trail to the Balsam Mountain Trail—4.1 miles.

POINT OF DEPARTURE: Hike 5.8 miles to the end of the Big Creek Trail and then 0.6 mile up the Camel Gap Trail. The Gunter Fork Trail begins on the left.

QUAD MAP: Luftee Knob 174-NW

0.0—Camel Gap Trail.
0.1—Big Creek.
0.3—Gunter Fork.
0.9—Gunter Fork.

1.4—Gunter Fork. Pool.
1.7—Gunter Fork. Double-crossing.
1.8—Gunter Fork Cascades.
1.9—Gunter Fork.
2.2—Switchback.
4.1—Balsam Mountain Trail.

> Gunter Fork is a small stream so named because it flows from its headwaters on Balsam Mountain into Big Creek at a point adjacent to a fifty-acre tract once farmed by George W. Gunter and his wife, Polly. George and Polly may well have been the last private landowners living on the upper reaches of Big Creek. A deed of trust executed on April 1, 1911, documents that most of the mountain land in the Big Creek watershed was conveyed to the newly formed Champion Land and Timber Company. One exception noted in the conveyance document is the fifty acres belonging to the Gunters.
>
> When Champion was operating on Big Creek, the company built a lumber camp in Walnut Bottom, a wide intervale below the confluence of Gunter Fork and Big Creek. Logging crews from the Walnut Bottom camp gained access to timber on the higher elevations over rail lines built up along the various tributaries of Big Creek. With the advent of the park, sections of the abandoned rail grade along Gunter Fork were adopted for hiking trails.

The lower terminus of the Gunter Fork Trail is situated along the Camel Gap Trail about a half-mile above the upper end of Walnut Bottom. When it leaves the Camel Gap Trail, the Gunter Fork Trail proceeds a hundred yards, then crosses Big Creek. Rarely is Big Creek sufficiently shallow at this point to be crossed by rock hopping. Most often the opposite bank can be reached by wading, although, after heavy rainstorms the stream becomes a raging torrent that can be dangerously difficult if not impossible to cross.

Beyond Big Creek, the Gunter Fork Trail strikes an easy course through a bottomland that is slowly reclaiming some semblance of its primeval grandeur. Thickets of rhododendron and dog-hobble are shaded by a mix of yellow birches, red maples, and yellow poplars. The trail quickly picks up the old rail grade and eases into a streamside course along Gunter Fork.

After a quarter-mile, the trail crosses Gunter Fork and 200 yards farther crosses a small feeder stream, at which point the grade stiffens perceptibly. The trail continues its streamside course for another half-mile before approaching Gunter Fork a second time. The trail does not cross immediately but angles away from the stream and onto an even steeper grade. Over this interval, the trail works its way along the flank of the Gunter Fork drainage, not straying far from the stream itself. When the trail eventually completes the second crossing, it continues another half-mile before approaching Gunter Fork again. Shortly after the third crossing, the trail completes a sharp turn that brings it back to the stream just above an attractive pool.

The pool is fifteen yards below the right side of the trail. Immediately above the pool, flanking boulders press Gunter Fork to a thin stream cascading thirty feet down a near-vertical slide and into a triangular-shaped basin that fans out from the base of the falls. Water collecting in the pool seeps out over the thin outer rim of the basin and runs off quickly down the mountain.

Beyond the pool, the trail narrows to a smooth berm and proceeds on a leisurely streamside course for about 600 yards before approaching what appear to be two channels of Gunter Fork separated by a thirty-foot wedge of boulder-strewn ground. The trail crosses both channels, turns upstream, and proceeds sixty yards to the base of Gunter Fork Cascade, a steeply pitched shield of bare rock that extends 150 feet upward from the edge of the trail. Though flanked on both sides by forest and heavy undergrowth, the exposed rock is free of vegetation except for patches of moss. A well-defined line is etched diagonally across the face of the rock, demarcating a smooth surface below the line from a knobby granular surface above. Thin sheets of water glide noiselessly down the face, forming a cascade that is remarkable both for its length and unconventional beauty. On a clear day, the water's limpid movements scintillate in the sunlight. When conditions are sufficiently cold, the surface bears a glaze of ice beneath which thin rivulets of water flit about on hurried courses down the incline.

The falling water collects momentarily in a small pool at the foot of the falls before dashing off to join Gunter Fork. The trail passes through the pool and proceeds another seventy-five yards to execute a switchback and cross Gunter Fork for the final time. When completing the switchback, the trail angles away from the stream and up along a narrow berm affixed to the steeply sloped mountainside.

The climb continues, following the contours of the northern face of Balsam Mountain. A half-mile above the switchback, a ridge point affords glimpses of the high Smoky divide ranging along the left. On the right Sevenmile Beech Ridge extends across and down to Big Creek. A half-mile farther, natural openings in the forest cover afford better views of Sevenmile Beech Ridge. Big Cataloochee Mountain (6,155 feet) is the high point anchoring the upper end of Sevenmile Beech Ridge, and Mount Sterling Ridge is the high range in the background. On the far left, the horizon is defined by the main Smoky divide. The more impressive views, however, may be down the vast draw of the Big Creek watershed, which opens out for an unobstructed view deep into the mountains of the Cherokee National Forest.

At this juncture, the forest cover begins a transition from a northern hardwood association of mostly hemlock, maple, and black cherry to that of yellow birch and red spruce. The trail remains moderately steep, but still tracing the contours as it edges onto a southerly course climbing to the crest of Balsam Mountain. As elevation is gained, the birches become the lesser species interspersed among the more dominant red spruce and Fraser fir. The terrain becomes noticeably rocky, and there is little undergrowth except for thick beds of feathery sphagnum moss that cover the rocks. In places the trail is so heavily shaded by the boreal species that little direct sunlight reaches the forest floor.

A half-mile from its upper terminus, the Gunter Fork Trail steers to a southeasterly course that runs roughly parallel to the Balsam Mountain ridgeline. Over this interval the trail remains in the boreal zone, rising to the crest of the mountain and terminating on the ridgeline in an intersection with the Balsam Mountain Trail.

MOUNT STERLING TRAIL

NC284 at Mount Sterling Gap to Mount Sterling—2.7 miles.

POINT OF DEPARTURE: From Knoxville, drive on I-40 east 60 miles to the Waterville exit or from Asheville follow I-40 west 50 miles. At the Waterville exit, cross the Pigeon River and proceed upstream to the Carolina Power and Light Company plant, turn, and proceed 2.0 miles to an intersection with NC284. Turn left onto NC284 and drive 6.7 miles to Mount Sterling Gap. The Mount Sterling Trail begins on the west side of the gap.

QUAD MAPS: Cove Creek Gap 174-NE
Luftee Knob 174-NW

0.0—Mount Sterling Gap. NC284.
0.5—Long Bunk Trail exits left 3.6 miles to the Little Cataloochee Trail.
2.3—Mount Sterling Ridge Trail exits left 5.3 miles to the Balsam Mountain Trail.
2.6—Mount Sterling Backcountry Campsite (#38).
2.7—Mount Sterling. Fire tower. Baxter Creek Trail descends 6.1 miles to Big Creek.

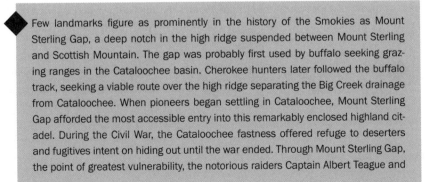

Few landmarks figure as prominently in the history of the Smokies as Mount Sterling Gap, a deep notch in the high ridge suspended between Mount Sterling and Scottish Mountain. The gap was probably first used by buffalo seeking grazing ranges in the Cataloochee basin. Cherokee hunters later followed the buffalo track, seeking a viable route over the high ridge separating the Big Creek drainage from Cataloochee. When pioneers began settling in Cataloochee, Mount Sterling Gap afforded the most accessible entry into this remarkably enclosed highland citadel. During the Civil War, the Cataloochee fastness offered refuge to deserters and fugitives intent on hiding out until the war ended. Through Mount Sterling Gap, the point of greatest vulnerability, the notorious raiders Captain Albert Teague and

Colonel George Kirk led detachments of bushwhackers into Cataloochee, seeking out deserters and enemy sympathizers while looting homes and farms.

Today Mount Sterling Gap harbors the north terminus of the Asbury Trail and the lower terminus of the Mount Sterling Trail as well as accommodating the passage of NC284, a gravel road linking Big Creek with Cataloochee. The Asbury Trail is a rehabilitated section of an old Indian trace known provisionally as the Cataloochee Indian Trail. It extends from Cove Creek Gap at the southeast corner of Cataloochee to Mount Sterling Gap at the cove's northeast corner. The trail is maintained for use by troops of the Boy Scouts of America.

The Mount Sterling Trail begins in Mount Sterling Gap along the west side of NC284 just opposite the northern terminus of the Asbury Trail. The Mount Sterling Trail starts up from the gap in a steep climb following a jeep track into a closed oak forest. Tall weeds abound. Wild golden-glows, purple asters, Joe-Pye-weeds, starry campions, and pale jewel weeds all bloom on the roadside in late summer.

After a half-mile, the grade moderates briefly when it reaches a flat grassy patch where the Long Bunk Trail leads in from Little Cataloochee. The trail returns immediately to its steep grade as it moves out of the closed oak association and into a spruce-hemlock mix where ferns, rhododendron, and witch-hobble constitute the primary understory. A quarter-mile beyond the Long Bunk junction, the trail completes a sharp turn to the right onto a drier exposure. Here, small hardwoods preside over an understory of tall leggy laurel. Galax, with their white spiky flowers in summer and copper-red leaves in winter, are conspicuous as well as the smooth red berries of yellow mandarins.

The trail continues for a half-mile along the drier slope before switching back left and entering a rough boulder-strewn terrain of big spruces and witch-hobble. The grade remains steep while the track becomes increasingly congested with obstructing roots and rocks. As elevation is gained, occasional openings in the forest cover afford fine views south across the Cataloochee basin. A densely growing corridor of Fraser fir heralds the trail's approach to the crest of Mount Sterling Ridge, where it enters a small grassy opening and intersects the eastern terminus of the Mount Sterling Ridge Trail.

When settlers first arrived in the eastern end of the Smokies, they found along the spine of Mount Sterling Ridge grassy fields which the Cherokee had given the colorful name "The Devil's Bedchamber." The settlers, being pragmatic, referred to these grassy ranges with the more prosaic monikers of Near Old Indian Field and Far Old Indian Field. These fields extended along the greater portion of Mount Sterling Ridge west from Mount Sterling to Balsam Mountain. Herders from Little Cataloochee would often drive grazing stock up from the range on Long Bunk to feed on the thick rich summer grass in the old Indian fields.

At its junction with the Mount Sterling Ridge Trail, the Mount Sterling Trail turns sharply right and follows the ridgeline through a remnant of the old Indian fields. Tall weeds and blackberry thickets congest the open areas while stands of fir encroach on the perimeters. A hitching post to the right of the trail marks the entrance to the lower section of the Mount Sterling Backcountry Campsite (#38).

The Mount Sterling Backcountry Camp flanks both sides of the trail. On the right is the lower camp, a gently sloping gradient heavily shaded by fir trees. While not a large tract, it does afford opportunities for campers to spread out. A little farther up the trail are two additional camping spots. The first is a small opening tucked discretely among the fir trees a few yards down the slope to the left. The second is a level plot at the summit of Mount Sterling that is carpeted in a sturdy turf of short grass. Each of the sites has its advantages, but all are equally attractive and pleasant places to camp. Camps on both sides of the trail are serviced by food-storage cables. That on the south side of the trail is near the middle of the camp while that on the north is a bit out of sight, below the camp in the down-trail direction. Water, unfortunately, is not readily available. The closest source is 410 yards down the Baxter Creek Trail where an access path leads 260 yards down to a fine spring.

Adjacent to the upper campsite is the Mount Sterling fire tower, a sixty-foot steel lookout built in 1935 by the Civilian Conservation Corps. The tower was accompanied by a warden's cabin, which stood nearby in the grassy clearing now occupied by the uppermost part of the backcountry camp. The cabin was accompanied by a cistern and privy.

On a clear day the tower affords magnificent 360-degree views. In the foreground is the entire Cataloochee basin delineated by the enclosing circle of high mountain ranges that form the basin's rim. Beyond the peaks of the Cataloochee Divide are the Plott Balsams and, at night, the lights of Waynesville, North Carolina. To the north is the high ridgeline of the main Smoky divide with the sharp peak of Mount Cammerer (4,928 feet) visible to the northwest and, farther west, Mount Guyot (6,621 feet), the fourth-highest peak east of the Mississippi. To the east, beyond the Pigeon River, is the grassy bald of Max Patch Mountain in the Pisgah National Forest. At night, if one looks to the northeast, Newport, Tennessee, appears as a puddle of light in the far-off valley. In wintertime, when the absence of foliage permits, the Little Cataloochee Baptist Church can be seen far down in the Cataloochee basin, appearing as a tiny solitary speck of white lost in a vastness of brown wilderness. The Mount Sterling Trail terminates at the foot of the tower in an intersection with the upper terminus of the Baxter Creek Trail leading up from Big Creek.

MOUNT STERLING RIDGE TRAIL

Mount Sterling Trail to the Balsam Mountain Trail—5.3 miles.

POINT OF DEPARTURE: Hike 2.3 miles up the Mount Sterling Trail. The Mount Sterling Ridge Trail begins on the left.

QUAD MAP: Luftee Knob 174-NW

0.0—Mount Sterling Trail.

1.4—Pretty Hollow Gap. Swallow Fork Trail exits right 4.0 miles to the Big Creek Trail at Walnut Bottom. Pretty Hollow Gap Trail exits left 5.6 miles to Cataloochee Road at Beech Grove School.

4.9—Lost Bottom Creek.

5.3—Balsam Mountain Trail.

Mount Sterling Ridge is a long high divide that separates the Cataloochee basin from the Big Creek drainage and forms a powerful buttress extending from the eastern flank of Balsam Mountain. Up until the latter part of the nineteenth century, it was mistakenly understood by many of the pioneer settlers in this part of the mountains that the state-line divide between North Carolina and Tennessee followed the spine of Mount Sterling Ridge and then along Balsam Mountain to the main Smoky divide at Tricorner Knob. When the famed Swiss geologist Arnold Guyot visited the mountains during the summer of 1859 to chart the high peaks of the Smokies, he apparently was informed by local guides that the state line traced Mount Sterling Ridge rather than along the high ridge immediately to the north. Years later, when Guyot cobbled his measurements and findings into a map, the high peaks currently known as Old Black and Mount Guyot were placed entirely within the state of Tennessee and Mount Cammerer was omitted, errors consistent with his mistaken assumption that the crest of Mount Sterling Ridge formed the state-line divide.

The eastern end of Mount Sterling Ridge is distinguished by a prominent balsam-clad peak that was known to the ancient Cherokee as "The Devil's Bedchamber." The Devil's Bedchamber was later named Mount Sterling, but was often referred to by the local mountaineers as Old Field Balsam. The Cherokee believed that the grassy balds spaced along the top of Mount Sterling Ridge were the devil's footprints leading from his bedchamber. The devil's footprints became known as the Near Old Indian Field and the Far Old Indian Field, or colloquially, as the Nigh Field and the Fur Field.

The origin of the name Mount Sterling has been obscured by the passage of time. One strain of Smoky Mountain lore contends that the peak was named for an unknown woodcutter from Kentucky by the name of Sterling. The particulars surrounding the incident that suggested the name have not survived. A tradition handed down by a mountain physician known as "Dr. Mac" claims that the peak got its name from a streak of lead that ran through a nearby creek. According to the story, a mountaineer took an axe and chopped out a large piece of the lead from which he fashioned homemade bullets. The bullets were soft and faded gray, leading some to think that they may have been silver—thus the name Sterling. But even these traditions are further clouded by notations on some of the earliest maps of the Great Smokies identifying the ridge as Mount Starling.

Although the Cherokee never established permanent settlements in either Cataloochee or Big Creek, hunting forays into the area left temporary camps in strategic sites, including the fields along Mount Sterling Ridge. When white settlers moved into the Smokies, the herders began ranging their cattle on the fields where the Indians once hunted, following the old Indian traces and wearing them into more permanent fixtures on the Smoky Mountain landscape. Since then, the cattle traces have been adopted as hiking trails furnished with trailheads and given proper names. The long Indian trail following Mount Sterling Ridge was subsequently separated into three distinct trails. As a result, the official Mount Sterling Ridge Trail begins at a crook in the Mount Sterling Trail a half-mile below the Devil's Bedchamber.

Beginning from its intersection with the Mount Sterling Trail, the Mount Sterling Ridge Trail descends westerly on a moderate grade through fine stands of red spruce and Fraser fir interspersed with yellow birch and American beech. Thick turfs of rich mountain grass constitute much of the sparse understory. The track is rocky in places and runs full of water during rainy periods. After almost a mile and a half, the trail proceeds through a copse of birch trees that heralds the approach into Pretty Hollow Gap, a long shallow saddle-shaped swag occupied by an open grassy clearing surrounded by stands of wind-stunted beeches. Here, the Mount Sterling Ridge Trail enters a crossroads intersection with the Swallow Fork Trail rising into the gap on the right and Pretty Hollow Gap Trail rising in on the left. Both trails terminate in Pretty Hollow Gap.

After passing through Pretty Hollow Gap, the Mount Sterling Ridge Trail climbs a quarter-mile out of the beeches and into a half-mile course where the ridgeline becomes fairly broad and flat. The beeches give way to a boreal mix of spruce and birch shading a very thin understory. Deeper into the spruce-birch forest, the crest of the mountain widens, flattening out into shallow basin where the trees are spaced increasingly farther apart. Low places in the basin are often saturated in water.

The appearance of another beech stand marks the beginning of a short rocky climb. By the time the trail reaches the end of the climb, it has rolled off the ridgeline onto the south flank of Big Butt, a short protruding stub of Big Cataloochee Mountain, and back into stands of red spruce and Fraser fir. The trail remains at this elevation on a remarkably level course for the next three miles until terminating into the Balsam Mountain Trail. Over this interval, several feeder streams and seepages intervene and the forest cover alternates among various permutations.

Initially, spruce and fir dominate with rhododendron appearing and disappearing as the density of the forest cover and environmental conditions dictate. When the trail works itself around to the more exposed contours, the beech and birch are more prevalent. In the shaded environments where conditions are wetter and cooler, stands of remarkably tall spruce and birch preside over an understory thick with ferns and hobblebush. In other places, thick copses of tall leggy rhododendrons crowd beneath the taller trees and, in yet others, where the forest cover is open, rich mountain grass and blackberry thickets cover the slopes.

A half-mile prior to reaching its western terminus, the trail veers into a slight hollow and crosses the headwaters of Lost Bottom Creek. In the stream bed and just below the point of crossing, several logs appear arranged in an orderly side-by-side fashion. This configuration is one of the few remnants along the trail of the extensive logging operations that were conducted on the lower southern slopes of Big Cataloochee Mountain.

 According to native legend, the broad summit of Big Cataloochee Mountain (6,155 feet) once bore some of the fiercest greenbrier growth in all the Smoky Mountains. So dense and impenetrable were these thickets that the briers are purported to still drip the blood of early pioneers. Fortunately, the Mount Sterling Ridge Trail stays well to the south of the summit of Big Cataloochee Mountain.

Beyond Lost Bottom Creek, the trail proceeds through stands of unusually tall spruce and birch before terminating in a small featureless junction with the Balsam Mountain Trail. One mile north of the junction, the upper terminus of the Gunter Fork Trail intersects the Balsam Mountain Trail. Three hundred yards south, a wide bench harbors the Laurel Gap Shelter.

◆ CATALOOCHEE ◆

Cataloochee, one of the least accessible quarters of the Smokies, is a complex watershed encompassed on all sides by high ridges that form imposing barriers of access from any direction. From the time of the earliest settlers, the easiest points of entry were through two high-elevation passes—Cove Creek Gap on the southeast corner of Cataloochee and Mount Sterling Gap on the northeast corner. But even then, travel into Cataloochee was a difficult undertaking. In his personal journal for November 30, 1810, Bishop Francis Asbury, a circuit-riding Methodist minister, entered, "Friday, our troubles began at the foaming, roaring stream, which hid the rocks. At Cataloochee I walked over a log. But O, the mountains height after height, and five miles over! After crossing other streams, and losing ourselves in the woods, we came in, about nine o'clock at night, to Vater Shuck's. What an awful day!"

Mount Sterling Ridge, Balsam Mountain, and the Cataloochee Divide form respectively the northern, western, and southern boundaries of the Cataloochee basin while a conjunction of White Oak Mountain and Scottish Mountain encloses the eastern end. A disarray of ramifying ridges segregates the basin into a complex of coves, the largest of which is Big Cataloochee, a remarkably flat expanse flanking Cataloochee Creek and Rough Fork. Before the arrival of the park in 1934, Big Cataloochee was farmland supporting an isolated agrarian community of nearly a thousand people. Of the approximately two hundred buildings once scattered across this picturesque landscape, only a fraction remain—the Palmer, Caldwell, and Woody houses, the Will Messer Barn, Beech Grove School, and Palmer Chapel. All of these are maintained by the Park Service and, except for the Woody house, can be reached by automobile. Outside of Cades Cove, Cataloochee contains the largest concentration of Appalachian architecture within the park.

Four other buildings—the Hannah Cabin, the Cook Cabin, the Little Cataloochee Missionary Baptist Church, and the stone walls of the Messer apple-house—stand in Little Cataloochee, a sub-cove high under the lee of Mount Sterling and separated from its larger sibling by Noland Mountain. Though geographically distinct, the two communities were joined by blood and marriage. Apple-growing formed the economic base of the tiny hamlet of Ola, the provisional center of the farming settlements clustered in Little Cataloochee.

Many of the Park Service trails in the Cataloochee section are appropriated from the old settlers' roads that led out of the basin. The McKee Branch Trail and Hemphill Bald Trail climb to the Cataloochee Divide, the Rough Fork Trail and Palmer Creek Trail to Balsam Mountain, and the Pretty Hollow Gap Trail to Mount Sterling Ridge. The Caldwell Fork Trail and its shorter companion, the Boogerman Trail, remain confined to the Caldwell Fork drainage.

The rim of the Cataloochee basin was at one time traced by a continuum of the Cataloochee Divide Trail, Hemphill Bald Trail, Polls Gap Trail, Mount Sterling Ridge Trail, and Asbury Trail. The Mount Sterling Ridge Trail is treated in the Big Creek section. The Polls Gap Trail, following Balsam Mountain between Polls Gap and Spruce Mountain, is disused and no longer an official trail. The Asbury Trail, following White Oak Mountain and Scottish Mountain between Cove Creek Gap and Mount Sterling Gap, is an unmaintained course providing access to a backcountry camp available for Boy Scout troops.

Little Cataloochee boasts only two trails—the Little Cataloochee Trail crossing Noland Mountain to Big Cataloochee and the Long Bunk Trail climbing toward Mount Sterling.

Backcountry camping in the Cataloochee section is limited to three campsites—the Caldwell Fork Backcountry Campsite (#41), Big Hemlock Backcountry Campsite (#40), and Pretty Hollow Backcountry Campsite (#39). All are in Big Cataloochee, and only the Big Hemlock Camp is closed to horses.

To reach Cataloochee from I-40, take Exit 20 onto US276 toward Maggie Valley and immediately beyond the south exit ramp, turn off US276 onto Cove Creek Road. From east or south of the park, follow US276 to I-40, turning left onto Cove Creek Road just as US276 approaches the south entrance ramp onto I-40. One mile down Cove Creek Road, a secondary road exits left to Suttontown. Cove Creek Road proceeds straight. The pavement soon ends but the road continues, climbing steeply on a narrow gravel track five miles to the park boundary at Cove Creek Gap.

At Cove Creek Gap, the Cataloochee Divide Trail begins on the left and the Asbury Trail on the right. Cove Creek Road continues through the gap, descending two miles to Sal Patch Gap to intersect the paved Cataloochee Road.

At Sal Patch Gap, the gravel track continues as NC284, intersecting Old Cataloochee Road at 2.3 miles, the Little Cataloochee Trail at 6.5 miles, Mount Sterling Gap at 8.9 miles, and Big Creek Road at 15.6 miles. The road from Sal Patch Gap to Big Creek Road is an exhausting drive but nevertheless offers an alternative entrance into Cataloochee from the Exit 451 (Waterville) off I-40.

From Sal Patch Gap, the paved Cataloochee Road descends three miles to cross Cataloochee Creek and intersect the southwest end of Old Cataloochee Road, a gravel track that leads to the Palmer house and then on to NC284. A mile beyond the Cataloochee Creek crossing, Cataloochee Road reaches Cataloochee Campground. From the campground, the road continues straight to the end of the cove, providing direct access to the Caldwell Fork Trail, Pretty Hollow Gap Trail, Big Fork Ridge Trail, and Rough Fork Trail as well as Palmer Chapel, Beech Grove School, and the Caldwell house.

CATALOOCHEE DIVIDE TRAIL

Cove Creek Road at Cove Creek Gap to the Hemphill Bald Trail at Double Gap—6.4 miles.

POINT OF DEPARTURE: From Knoxville drive I-40 east 80 miles, or from Asheville drive west 30 miles to the Maggie Valley exit onto US276. Turn immediately north off US276 onto Cove Creek Road and proceed 5.8 miles to the park boundary at Cove Creek Gap. The Cataloochee Divide Trail begins on the left side of Cove Creek Gap.

QUAD MAPS: Cove Creek Gap 174-NE

Dellwood 174-SE

0.0—Cove Creek Gap. Cove Creek Road. Asbury Trail.

1.3—Vantage point.

2.1—Panther Spring Gap.

4.3—Access path exits left 460 yards to the Appalachian Highland Science Learning Center.

4.6—McKee Branch Trail exits right 2.3 miles to the Caldwell Fork Trail. Access path exits left to the Ferguson Cabin.

6.0—The Swag.

6.4—Double Gap. Hemphill Bald Trail exits straight 5.5 miles to Heintooga Ridge Road and right 2.9 miles to the Caldwell Fork Trail.

Long before white settlers began drifting into the Cataloochee basin, the Cherokee called the place Ga-da-lu-tsi which, according to noted ethnologist James Mooney, roughly translates to "standing in a row." Ga-da-lu-tsi refers either to the high rim of mountains that encircle the basin or to the row upon row of stark pointed Fraser firs and red spruces that line the crests of the encompassing ridges. The settlers, stuttering over the Cherokee syllables, corrupted Ga-da-lu-tsi variously to Cataluche, Cattalooch, Cattylooche, Cataloucha, and Catalouche before finally fixing upon Cataloochee.

The Cataloochee basin is completely enclosed by mountains and bifurcated by a high ridge that separates Big Cataloochee from its sibling, Little Cataloochee. During the earliest period of settlement, two gaps along the eastern edge of the rim afforded the most suitable points of entry into the Cataloochee interior. At Mount Sterling Gap, a deep notch in the ridgeline proved to be the easiest point of access from Tennessee into Little Cataloochee while, to the south, Cove Creek Gap provided a point of entry into Big Cataloochee from Jonathan Creek. Long before the Cherokee, aboriginal Indian tribes entered through Mount Sterling and Cove Creek gaps on an ancient trace that was later known as the Cataloochee Track. This aboriginal trace was appropriated by the Cherokee as a route to their hunting grounds in Cataloochee as well as a byway between their villages on the Big Pigeon and towns in Jonathan Creek and Maggie Valley. Later, long hunters would follow game through the passes at Cove Creek Gap and Mount Sterling Gap, thus leading the way for herders and pioneer settlers who would soon discover the rich grazing ranges and fertile farmland in Cataloochee.

Cove Creek Gap marks the eastern end of the Cataloochee Divide, a high, slightly curved ridgeline that forms the long southern perimeter of the Cataloochee basin. This gap also marks the eastern terminus of the Cataloochee Divide Trail, which runs concurrent with the park boundary along the crest of the divide.

Sometime during the 1970s, the Park Service entertained a proposal for the so-called Circle the Smokies Road, a scenic highway that would have incorporated the Cataloochee Divide Trail as part of its route. Fortunately the road was never built. The trail, however, remains, easing out of Cove Creek Gap on a unexacting climb along the broad spine of the Cataloochee Divide and under a forest cover of fairly open second-growth hardwood stands of northern red, southern red, white, black, and chestnut oak; mountain and red maple; yellow birch; and pignut hickory. Open fields spaced irregularly along the south flank of the divide afford glimpses down into the Jonathan Creek drainage.

A readily noticeable break in the forest cover about a mile beyond Cove Creek Gap affords the only good vantage point along the trail for looking down into the Cataloochee basin from the divide. The open fields along the floor of the basin are not visible from this point, though one can, nonetheless, gain an appreciation for the isolation and wilderness geography of the enclosing mountains. In the intermediate distance, Noland Mountain slants across the basin, marking the boundary between Big and Little Cataloochee. Mount Sterling Ridge, anchored by Big Cataloochee Mountain (6,155 feet) on the west, forms the distant northern edge of the basin. Scottish Mountain (4,287 feet) appears as the prominent peak to the east. From here, the trail continues along the spine of the divide for almost a mile before reaching Panther Spring Gap, a rather insignificant dip in the ridgeline.

Because of its relative isolation and natural fortress-like protection, Cataloochee was visited by Cherokee hunters but never permanently inhabited by the Indians. In the early nineteenth century, a few white hunters ventured into the area, but settlers did not follow until about mid-century. According to Smoky Mountain lore, sometime before the basin was settled, a young girl from nearby Jonathan Creek was dragged screaming into the unknown Cataloochee wilderness by a panther. The place where the panther carried the girl across the divide and into the Cataloochee interior came to be known as Panther Spring Gap.

From Panther Spring Gap, the trail continues following the boundary while traversing several minor knobs. The trail remains on the ridgeline except when it diverts from the boundary to skirt the north side of two of the higher knobs, thus avoiding the climbs. Along much of the way, the trail is accompanied by a split-rail fence that separates the trail from a nearby wagon road. On the Cataloochee side of the trail, the slopes are shaded by a lush riot of rough northern hardwood species while on the Jonathan Creek side irregularly spaced clearings provide fine vantage points opening out onto the layers upon layers of mountains that extend deep into North Carolina. Two miles beyond Panther Spring Gap, an access path exits left from the trail and leads 460 yards to the Appalachian Highland Science Learning Center at Purchase Knob.

In 2001, Purchase Knob (5,086 feet) became the home of one of five initial learning centers created by Congress to support research in the national parks and disseminate the research findings to the American public. The building and 535 acres of land for the Appalachian Highland Science Learning Center were donated in 2000 by Kathryn McNeil and Voit Gilmore, who had maintained Purchase Knob as a summer home since 1964. Purchase Knob, which represents the largest donation of land to the Great Smoky Mountains National Park since its inception in 1934, is contiguous with the rest of the park along its boundary on the Cataloochee Divide.

When it leaves the access path exiting to the Learning Center, the trail continues following the boundary 450 yards to an intersection with the upper terminus of the McKee Branch Trail leading up from Cataloochee. On the left side of the intersection an access path exits to the Ferguson Cabin. A few yards out of the intersection, the access path forks. The left, or lower, fork is for hikers only. The right fork is for horses and hikers and continues above the cabin to connect with the road to the Appalachian Highland Science Learning Center. The distance from the McKee Branch intersection to the cabin is slightly less than a mile.

The one-room Ferguson Cabin was assembled from parts of an older "dog-trot" cabin originally built on Purchase Knob around 1874. Unlike most pioneer cabins in the Smokies which are propped up off the ground with rocks placed under the corners, the Ferguson Cabin sits on a stone foundation. It has one door, two windows, and a modest front porch. It resides at the highest elevation of any pioneer cabin in the Smokies.

When leaving the McKee Branch intersection, the Cataloochee Divide Trail again deviates off the ridgeline to skirt another high knob before rejoining the boundary along another split-rail fence originally built by the Civilian Conservation Corps in the 1930s. Along here, the track is frequently churned up by horse traffic, leaving wide pockets of mud unpleasant to hike through and difficult to circumnavigate. In places, boardwalks have been installed to provide an elevated hiking surface.

South, beyond the boundary fence, the landscape is a mix of ragged semi-balds, patches of woodland, and close-cropped expanses of green meadow grazed by browsing stock. The Swag, a private resort just outside the park boundary, sports neatly trimmed lawns. On the park side of the boundary, the slope is forested in a riot of yellow birch, red maple, white basswood, black locust, yellow buckeye, red maple, black cherry, eastern hemlock, and a variety of oaks, all of which obstruct any view into Cataloochee.

Beyond the Swag, the Cataloochee Divide Trail clears another minor knob and then descends into Double Gap to terminate in an intersection with the Hemphill Bald Trail approaching straight on along the divide. The distance from the Swag to Double Gap is slightly less than a half-mile. At the intersection, the Hemphill Bald Trail turns and descends 2.9 miles into Cataloochee.

CALDWELL FORK TRAIL

Cataloochee Road to the Rough Fork Trail—6.3 miles.

POINT OF DEPARTURE: Follow directions to the Cataloochee Divide Trail. At Cove Creek Gap, continue on Cataloochee Road 4.9 miles to Cataloochee Campground. The Caldwell Fork Trail begins on the left side of Cataloochee Road 200 yards beyond the entrance to the campground.

QUAD MAPS: Cove Creek Gap 174-NE

Dellwood 174-SE

Bunches Bald 174-SW

0.0—Cataloochee Road. Palmer Creek. Footlog.

0.8—Caldwell Fork. Footlog. Boogerman Trail exits left and loops 4.1 miles to return to the Caldwell Fork Trail.

2.8—Boogerman Trail enters from the left.

3.2—Big Fork Ridge Trail exits right 3.2 miles to Cataloochee Road.

3.2—McKee Branch Trail exits left 2.3 miles to the Cataloochee Divide Trail.

3.3—Access path exits left 40 yards to the Shelton-Caldwell gravesite.

3.6—Clontz Branch.

4.4—Stone wall.

4.5—Double Gap Branch.

4.6—Hemphill Bald Trail exits left 2.9 miles to the Cataloochee Divide Trail at Double Gap.

4.7—Caldwell Fork. Footlog.

4.8—Caldwell Fork Backcountry Campsite (#41).

5.1—Access path exits right 125 yards to big poplars.

6.3—Rough Fork Trail exits left 3.5 miles to Heintooga Ridge Road and the Hemphill Bald Trail and right 2.9 miles to Cataloochee Road.

During the latter days of the Civil War, Colonel George Kirk, a notorious raider who had deserted the Confederacy, rode into Cataloochee with a posse of Union renegades, looting farms and bushwhacking suspected Confederate sympathizers. Kirk and his men entered the Caldwell Fork wilderness looking for Levi Shelton and Ellsworth "Elzie" Caldwell, native Cataloochians accused of supporting the Confederacy. The raiders followed the ruffled surge of Caldwell Fork from the main basin of Cataloochee to where the stream winds through steep-sided ravines flanked by entanglements of dog-hobble and cavernous arbors of twisted, gnarled rhododendron.

In Kirk's day the upper reaches of Caldwell Fork were mostly wilderness. The first cabin he and his men encountered upstream was probably that of Jesse McGee, located near the junction of the current Caldwell Fork and McKee Branch trails. At the time, the McGee cabin was being occupied by Billy Caldwell, father of Elzie Caldwell and father-in-law of Levi Shelton. Failing to find Shelton and Caldwell, Kirk's marauders proceeded farther up the mountain to the Caldwell place and whipped the women, hoping to force them into revealing the whereabouts of the men. The women would not tell, so the soldiers waited until night when the women went to see the men. Kirk's men followed. They captured Shelton and Caldwell in their hiding place and led them to be executed at Rabbit Log Gap beside an old trail leading from Cataloochee across the divide to Caldwell Fork. (The Big Fork Ridge Trail now follows generally the course of this old trace). The bodies of the two men were thrown into the Sinkhole between Rough Fork and Caldwell Fork and covered with chestnut bark. Later, the bodies were retrieved and buried in a single grave on a hillside overlooking the Caldwell Fork Trail.

The Caldwell Fork Trail begins along the main road just west of Cataloochee Campground on a long footlog spanning Palmer Creek. Beyond the creek crossing, the trail winds through a bottomland forested in thin stands of second-growth pine. Initially the trail remains wide and level, following the remnants of an old farm road, but soon enters a streamside course along Caldwell Fork where surface conditions degenerate considerably. Except for the last mile, the Caldwell Fork Trail maintains an easy grade throughout, but the track itself is often rocky, uneven, and, in many places, wet and muddy.

Just less than a mile above the Palmer Creek crossing, the trail clears Caldwell Fork on a footlog. Then, within the next hundred feet, it intersects on the left the lower terminus of the Boogerman Trail leading up Palmer Branch. From here until it intersects the upper terminus of the Boogerman Trail two miles upstream, the Caldwell Fork Trail crosses the stream fifteen times, each time on a footlog. The footlogs afford some of the few openings in the high undergrowth from which enjoy the beauty of the splendid uncut forest. At times the trail is high above the stream; at others it is almost in the stream itself, but everywhere the trail and stream are cloistered in dense arbors of rhododendron.

Two miles above its intersection with the lower terminus of the Boogerman Trail, the Caldwell Fork Trail meets the upper terminus of the Boogerman Trail near the confluence of Snake Branch and Caldwell Fork. At the mouth of Snake Branch, J. L. Carson Messer once operated a stately, two-story, overshot gristmill. Water powering the mill's big wheel was channeled down a long millrace fed by the current of Snake Branch. Messer farmed the bottomland on the lower reaches of Snake Branch, and remnants of his home and farm buildings are visible along both sides of the Boogerman Trail just above the junction.

Over the next half-mile, the trail moves away from the stream to enter a flat that was once the most heavily settled area of the Caldwell Fork drainage. Here, trail conditions moderate considerably, becoming generally drier and less uneven. At the end of the half-mile, the trail crosses McKee Branch and immediately enters a galled spot where it intersects the upper terminus of the Big Fork Ridge Trail. Jesse McGee, one of the earliest settlers in Cataloochee, built a grist mill in 1861 on Caldwell Fork just opposite the mouth of McKee Branch. Down the Big Fork Ridge Trail and across Caldwell Fork once stood the one-room Caldwell Fork School built in 1927. A footlog conveyed the pupils across the stream and to the nearby McGee Trail that connected with a scattering of settlements on the slopes of the Cataloochee Divide. At the time students were attending the Caldwell Fork School, the nearby stream was known as McGee Branch and the trail as McGee Trail. In 1932 the U.S. Geographic Board inexplicably changed the landmarks to McKee Branch and McKee Branch Trail.

Seventy yards above the Big Fork Ridge Trail intersection, the Caldwell Fork Trail meets the lower terminus of the McKee Branch Trail leading down from the Cataloochee Divide Trail. Ninety yards beyond this junction, an inconspicuous path climbs left forty yards to an old roadbed flanked by a tiny enclosure bearing the graves of the murdered Levi Shelton and Elzie Caldwell.

 There are conflicting versions of the story of the two men buried here and the circumstances of their deaths. Although they were killed by Kirk's raiders, some contend that the two men were not Confederate soldiers but deserters hiding out to keep from being forced to join the war, as so many others did in this section of the mountains. In any event, they were caught and shot by Union troops and later buried here regardless of their military status. The graves are marked by two thick, irregularly shaped fieldstones bearing no inscriptions and separated from the wilderness by sagging strands of wire hanging on three chestnut posts along the longer edge of the gravesite. According to Smoky Mountain lore, the two were buried in a single grave. The second stone, tradition contends, marks the grave of an unknown woman.

The path to the Shelton-Caldwell gravesite continue for seventy yards, looping back to the Caldwell Fork Trail near the Deadening Fields, so called because of settler John Caldwell's practice of "deadening" virgin trees by paring off wide strips of bark from around the trunks and waiting for the trees to die. Afterward, Caldwell would burn the trees and clear the land for farming. The Deadening Fields bear few marks of Caldwell's old farm field except that the clearings are all now shaded by a struggling copse of scrawny, malnourished, second-growth pines.

The trail reaches the Deadening Fields and then climbs a bit to enter another large tract of rhododendron shaded by eastern hemlocks, white pines, and red maples. Here, the trail crosses several seepages and is pressed into a course closer to Caldwell Fork. It crosses Double Gap Branch and then enters an opening in the forest cover that harbors the lower terminus of the Hemphill Bald Trail leading down from the Cataloochee Divide Trail.

Two hundred and thirty-five yards beyond its junction with the Hemphill Bald Trail, the Caldwell Fork Trail descends to a footlog crossing Caldwell Fork, and then eighty yards farther enters a compound of several scattered camping spots known collectively as the Caldwell Fork Backcountry Campsite (#41). The sites nearer the trail are open and grassy. Those up the stream are secluded, hidden from view by thickets of rhododendron. The area around the camp was evidently graded for building sites as several level plats are clustered in tiers along the slope. The Caldwell Fork site affords excellent camping places, though it is often occupied by horses.

One-quarter-mile above the Caldwell Fork Camp, a path exits to the right leading 125 yards to three yellow poplar trees of staggering proportions, each within a few yards of the others. The largest of these rivals in size the giant poplar in Albright Grove, reputed to be the champion of the Smokies. The big poplars mark the fringe of a rich enclave of virgin forest concentrated along the upper end of Big Fork Ridge.

When it leaves the big poplars, the trail begins climbing Rough Fork Ridge and, as it does, penetrates deeper into the massive fecundity of this primeval woodland. Enormous boles of hemlocks and yellow poplars interspersed with large red maples, white basswoods, pignut hickories, and white oaks stand like irregularly spaced pillars of a great cathedral. The understory of striped maples and witch-hazel diminishes as the trail moves higher up the ridge and deeper into the old growth forest. A noticeable increase in steepness of the grade marks the onset of the last mile of the trail. At a featureless junction near the crest of the ridge, the Caldwell Fork Trail intersects the Rough Fork Trail leading up from Cataloochee Road. Originally the Rough Fork Trail was a settler's road extended by the Civilian Conservation Corps in 1935 to connect Cataloochee with Balsam Mountain at Polls Gap. The CCC trail was later officially designated by the Park Service as the Rough Fork Trail.

BOOGERMAN TRAIL

From the Caldwell Fork Trail and looping back to the Caldwell Fork Trail—
4.1 miles.

POINT OF DEPARTURE: Hike 0.8 mile up the Caldwell Fork Trail. The
Boogerman Trail begins on the left.

QUAD MAPS: Cove Creek Gap 174-NE
Dellwood 174-SE

0.0—Caldwell Fork Trail.
1.4—Access path exits right 40 yards to the Palmer Cemetery.
1.6—Palmer Branch.
2.5—Sag Branch.
3.4—Old gate post.
3.6—Snake Branch.
3.7—Snake Branch. Stone wall.
3.8—Access path exits right 180 yards to the Messer Cemetery.
4.0—Snake Branch.
4.1—Caldwell Fork Trail.

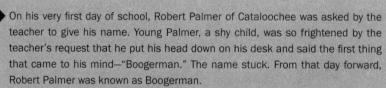

On his very first day of school, Robert Palmer of Cataloochee was asked by the teacher to give his name. Young Palmer, a shy child, was so frightened by the teacher's request that he put his head down on his desk and said the first thing that came to his mind—"Boogerman." The name stuck. From that day forward, Robert Palmer was known as Boogerman.

As a young man, Boogerman Palmer sought to escape the crowded Cataloochee valley by building a home in an isolated cove above Caldwell Fork, high under the lee of the Cataloochee Divide. Using only hand tools, he dug a serviceable road between the old Caldwell Fork road and his new home. Palmer's road was later re-routed and improved by the Youth Conservation Corps, and then afterward christened the Boogerman Trail.

The Boogerman Trail is a loop. It begins along the Caldwell Fork Trail and then completes a four-mile half-circle that terminates two miles up the Caldwell Fork Trail. When it leaves the Caldwell Fork junction, the Boogerman Trail climbs quickly out of the lush rhododendron and dog-hobble–encumbered hollow of Caldwell Fork and onto the drier northern flank of Den Ridge. When Boogerman Palmer owned the mountain along the Den Branch drainage, he did not permit lumber companies to cut timber on his property, and as a result many fine large trees flank both sides of the trail.

The trail proceeds in a steady climb along a narrow berm affixed to the steep-sided Den Ridge for about two miles before leveling off to enter a grove of tall white pines and yellow poplars. Shortly, the trail approaches an open space that once harbored Boogerman Palmer's home and farm. Palmer had constructed two log houses, a barn, and an assortment of farm buildings on this gently sloping gradient. No signs of the buildings remain today. There is, however, to the right of the trail a cleated iron wheel, perhaps a relic from some kind of implement used in mountain farming. Whatever the origin of the wheel, it is unlikely to have belonged to Palmer.

Soon after the trail passes through Palmer's farmstead, it turns and begins descending across a series of irregularly spaced stream seepages where huge boles of American chestnut lay scattered along the trail. Before a blight began killing the chestnut trees in the early years of the twentieth century, these trees comprised as much as sixty percent of the forest cover in some parts of the Smokies, providing an excellent smooth-grained, rot-resistant building material for the settlers as well as a reliable source of mast for bears and turkeys.

About a mile and a half above the trailhead, an access path exits to the right, leading forty yards to the Palmer Cemetery. Two hundred yards beyond the access path, the Boogerman Trail crosses Palmer Branch and then enters a succession of abandoned farm fields where spindly hemlocks and pines eke out a meager existence on depleted soil. A stone wall to the right of the trail is a salient reminder that this ground was once a pioneer farm.

Sag Branch, a mile beyond Palmer Branch, is the last stream crossing before the trail tops out and starts the downward journey back to Caldwell Fork. An old gate post, part of a collapsed fence line, stands on the left side of the trail about 500 yards below the downward turning point. A hundred and fifty yards farther down and on the right, a long stone wall extends perpendicularly to the trail. Two hundred yards beyond the stone wall, Snake Branch is crossed and then crossed again 200 yards farther on. Forty-five yards beyond the second crossing of Snake Branch, another stone wall forms up immediately on the right with the trail running between the steam and the wall for 200 yards. At the end of the 200 yards, an access path exits right to another perpendicular stone wall. The access proceeds around and along the upper side of the stone wall 180 yards to the Carson Messer Cemetery atop the adjacent ridge. The cemetery consists of a ten-foot-square level plat containing four stone markers and enclosed by a low barbed-wire fence. The stones bear no inscriptions but are known to mark the graves of two children of the Messer family.

A hundred yards below the cemetery access, a corner of stone marks the entrance to the site of what may have been a commercial building. The site is further defined by the outline ruins of a foundation. In the middle is a heavy piece of industrial equipment in the form of a narrow rail cradled by a slightly wider piece of metal of equal length. Standing upright on the rail is what appears to be a rack of metal rollers. The contraption may have been part of some farm equipment or perhaps associated with a large overshot mill that stood nearby at the mouth of Snake Branch. Whatever its origin, the equipment only adds to the testimony that the lower reaches of Snake Branch were a significant crossroads in the Caldwell Fork community.

Seventy-five yards below the building site, Snake Branch is crossed a final time. On the right, an access path exits left to the ruins and skeletal chimney of the old Carson Messer place. From this juncture, the Boogerman Trail crosses an unnamed feeder stream and then, 150 yards farther, exits a grove of white pines to terminate into the Caldwell Fork Trail.

BIG FORK RIDGE TRAIL

Cataloochee Road to the Caldwell Fork Trail—3.2 miles.

POINT OF DEPARTURE: Follow directions to the Caldwell Fork Trail. Continue on Cataloochee Road another 2.4 miles to a pull-over on the left side of the road. The Big Fork Ridge Trail begins on a footlog crossing Rough Fork.

QUAD MAP: Dellwood 174-SE

0.0—Cataloochee Road. Rough Fork.
1.2—Switchback.
1.8—Gap on Big Fork Ridge.
3.1—Caldwell Fork. Footlog.
3.2—Caldwell Fork Trail exits left 3.2 miles to Cataloochee Road and right 3.1 miles to the Rough Fork Trail.

Big Fork Ridge Trail is so named because it traverses a long low ridge that separates the Caldwell Fork drainage from that of Rough Fork. The trail begins at the southwest end of Cataloochee Road, first crossing Rough Fork on a long footlog and then entering a wide creek bottom that once harbored the Harrison Caldwell farm. Much of the bottom still has the appearance of abandoned farm fields, although white pines and yellow poplars are beginning to invade. Near the upper end of the bottom are the remains of a large wooden enclosure that was built by the Park Service as a temporary pen for holding elk when the animals were re-introduced into the Smokies in 2001.

Just beyond the old elk pen, the trail begins climbing the adjacent ridge on a nice even track that is overgrown with weeds. Here, the forest cover is largely red maple, eastern hemlock, and white pine. These conditions soon give way to a dry heath of mountain laurel and rhododendron, and the trail begins curling to the right into a short narrow cove. On entering the deeper recesses of the cove, the forest cover changes again to that of cove hardwoods shading a thin understory.

After crossing a couple of seepages, the trail switches sharply back to the southeast and climbs out of the cove, soon topping out in a slight swag on the crest of Big Fork Ridge.

From this juncture, the trail descends steadily into the Caldwell Fork drainage, working itself around the end of Rabbit Ridge. In places the course is smooth and even with only a few obstructions while in others it is deeply rutted and rough, churned up by the abuse of horse traffic. The forest cover, mostly dry-ridge hardwoods, occasionally yields to openings that offer glimpses into the Caldwell Fork basin and beyond to the Cataloochee Divide. The trail soon descends to a creek bottom shaded by spindly pines and tall leggy laurel. The bottom once harbored the Caldwell Fork School, one of only three schools in the entire Cataloochee basin.

 The Caldwell Fork School was established in 1927 for teaching grades one through seven. The schoolhouse consisted of one room whose only door faced the Goose Patch to the north across the Big Fork Ridge Trail. Three large windows on each side of the school let in the ambient light, and a fireplace on the end provided warmth. An outhouse stood behind the school, and a footlog over nearby Caldwell Fork provided the pupils access to the school from the settlements on the lower slopes of the Cataloochee Divide.

A short distance beyond the old school site, the Big Fork Ridge Trail crosses Caldwell Fork on a footlog and then climbs sharply up a rough rutted track 150 yards to terminate into the Caldwell Fork Trail. The lower terminus of the McKee Branch Trail is found seventy yards south along the Caldwell Fork Trail.

MCKEE BRANCH TRAIL

Caldwell Fork Trail to the Cataloochee Divide Trail—2.3 miles.
POINT OF DEPARTURE: Hike 3.2 miles up the Caldwell Fork Trail. The McKee Branch Trail begins on the left.
QUAD MAP: Dellwood 174-SE

0.0—Caldwell Fork Trail.

0.1—Access path exits left 260 yards to the Sutton-McGee Cemetery.

0.3—McKee Branch.

0.6—McKee Branch.

1.6—Double-switchback.

2.3—Cataloochee Divide Trail exits left 4.6 miles to Cove Creek Road and right 1.8 miles to the Hemphill Bald Trail at Double Gap.

The McKee Branch Trail begins at a wide intersection that was once a primary crossroads in the Caldwell Fork community, connecting the interior of Cataloochee with the world beyond the Cataloochee Divide. In the early years of settlement on Caldwell Fork, the McKee Branch Trail provided the most ready access from Cataloochee to Waynesville, the county seat. Today the trail is a rough steep track used primarily by horsemen to gain access to the trails on the Cataloochee Divide.

The McKee Branch Trail starts out as an easy stroll through stands of second-growth yellow poplar trees and then quickly enters an open field where the original Jessie McGee house was located. The field is slow in being reclaimed by the forest, but is nonetheless heavily overgrown with weeds and thick patches of crimson bee-balms. Noticeable among the weeds is a faint path exiting left down to McKee Branch. The path crosses the stream and proceeds 260 yards to the Sutton-McGee Cemetery, a well-kept square plot containing several fieldstones, none of which bear readable inscriptions.

 A modern headstone marks the only identifiable grave in the cemetery, that of Jessie McGee, one of the earliest settlers in Cataloochee and a veteran of the Confederate Army. On the stream near where he is buried, McGee once operated a grist mill which had been built sometime prior to the Civil War. Jessie McGee was not the only settler to operate a mill on McKee Branch. Around 1895, Solomon Sutton built a mill on the stream and operated it until 1916, when he moved out of Cataloochee.

Beyond the path to the cemetery, the trail passes through a mix of black walnut, red cedar, and black locust, species valued by pioneers for domestic use. Other evidence of farming and homesites is scattered throughout the fields flanking both sides of the trail, but the weedy undergrowth is so deep that much of it is difficult to see. There are, however, a chimney ruin and a few pieces of household refuse clearly visible just to the right of the trail.

Beyond the old fields, the trail climbs a bit, crosses McKee Branch, and then enters another flat area that was once tilled as farmland. At one time, this upper farmland was accessible not only by the McKee Branch route, but could be approached by a second trail leading up from Caldwell Fork and by two additional trails descending from the Cataloochee Divide. These trails have all but vanished.

At the upper end of the flat, the trail crosses the stream again and then becomes a steep rough track that, due to damage caused by horse traffic, is difficult to climb. In places the track is worn to the extent that water and decayed deciduous detritus collecting in the ruts leave a residue of sticky mire for a hiking surface. The trail remains a single-file track rarely diminishing in steepness and alternating between a hardwood-hemlock association and dry-ridge laurel and rhododendron stands as ambient conditions dictate. With little deviation in overall ruggedness, the trail continues until topping out and terminating into the Cataloochee Divide Trail.

ROUGH FORK TRAIL

Western end of Cataloochee Road to the Hemphill Bald Trail and Heintooga Ridge Road at Polls Gap—6.4 miles.

POINT OF DEPARTURE: Follow directions to the Caldwell Fork Trail. Continue on Cataloochee Road another 2.5 miles to the gate blocking the road. The Rough Fork Trail begins at the gate.

QUAD MAPS: Dellwood 174-SE
Bunches Bald 174-SW

0.0—Cataloochee Road.
0.5—Rough Fork. Footlog.
0.7—Rough Fork. Footlog.
0.8—Rough Fork. Footlog.
1.0—Woody Place.
1.4—Hurricane Creek. Footlog. Big Hemlock Backcountry Campsite (#40).
2.9—Caldwell Fork Trail exits left 1.2 miles to the big poplars and 6.3 miles to Cataloochee Road.
3.9—Railroad bed.
6.4—Polls Gap. Heintooga Ridge Road. Hemphill Bald Trail exits left 5.5 miles to the Cataloochee Divide Trail at Double Gap and 8.4 miles to the Caldwell Fork Trail.

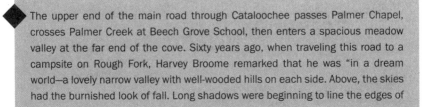

The upper end of the main road through Cataloochee passes Palmer Chapel, crosses Palmer Creek at Beech Grove School, then enters a spacious meadow valley at the far end of the cove. Sixty years ago, when traveling this road to a campsite on Rough Fork, Harvey Broome remarked that he was "in a dream world—a lovely narrow valley with well-wooded hills on each side. Above, the skies had the burnished look of fall. Long shadows were beginning to line the edges of the fields. The road went through meadow after meadow, fenced with rails, neatly cut, with the hay stacked and a little forelock twisting out around the pole to keep out the rain. Stock grazed in a few of the meadows. Here was a land in which the beauty of the wilds merged gently with appropriate, lovely, and beautiful husbandry of man. It was a place of perfection and a place to return to." In the time since Harvey Broome walked this road, much of the "beautiful husbandry of man" has succumbed to the "beauty of the wilds." Nevertheless, Cataloochee remains a dream world, still "a place of perfection."

Harvey Broome's road stops momentarily at the end of the last meadow, blocked by a gate marking the end of Cataloochee Road and the beginning of the Rough Fork Trail. Beyond the gate, the trail follows the old roadbed as it disappears into the gloom of the wilderness.

Initially the roadbed is wide and the surface even, affording an easy stroll over an imperceptible grade. It generally follows the course of nearby Rough Fork and is shaded by copses of virgin eastern hemlock interspersed with American beech, chestnut oak, ash, and yellow poplar. Wood sorrel and partridgeberry carpet the forest floor beneath the towering hemlocks. A little more than a half-mile beyond the gate, the trail crosses Rough Fork, a stream that was known as Ugly Fork until well into the twentieth century. After an interval of 345 yards, it crosses Rough Fork a second time, negotiates a wide bend, and crosses a third time eighty yards on. Each crossing is on a footlog. Four hundred yards above the third crossing, the trail enters an opening in the forest cover that harbors a white frame house known as the Woody Place.

Jonathan Woody first cleared this spot and built a one-room log cabin here in 1851. His son, Steve Woody, enlarged the house periodically, changing it from a log structure to a frame house. Between 1901 and 1910, he added bedrooms, a kitchen, and extended porches along the front and back. When the Woody Place was an operating farm, the forest was cleared high up the adjacent slopes and for a considerable distance along the stream. The farm included a barn, a tool shed, a wood shed, a chicken house, and a springhouse. Of the outbuildings, only the springhouse remains, standing a few yards to the right of the house.

Above the Woody house, the trail enters a low-lying patch of ground that becomes rather muddy during the wet seasons. Here, a forest of black locust, hemlock, and yellow poplar presides over a thin understory of witch-hazel and rhododendron. Almost a half-mile above the Woody Place, the trail crosses a footlog over Hurricane

Creek and then twenty yards farther meets an access path on the right leading into the Big Hemlock Backcountry Campsite (#40). The camp is fitted deftly in the angle formed by the confluence of Hurricane Creek and Rough Fork and situated on a low-lying tract of flat ground concealed by a labyrinth of rhododendron and shaded by huge hemlock trees. The access path winds through the labyrinth to several small camping sites of bare earth cloistered among the rhododendron. Any sunlight that reaches the camp is filtered through the high forest canopy, casting a perpetual gloom all around.

On leaving the Big Hemlock Camp, the trail engages in a steady climb onto the drier slope of Little Ridge where the hemlocks become interspersed with a wide variety of cove hardwoods. American beech, Fraser magnolia, red maple, white basswood, white oak, and northern red oak are the most prevalent. Throughout the climb, the trail traces the contours of Little Ridge, striving for a point along the crest of Big Fork Ridge.

A mile-and-a-half above the campsite, the trail intersects the upper terminus of the Caldwell Fork Trail about a mile above the Caldwell Fork Backcountry Campsite (#41) and the well-known big poplars. Beyond this junction, the Rough Fork Trail continues to climb, working itself up onto the spine of the ridge before leveling off to follow an old railroad trace into Polls Gap.

For the final two-and-a-half miles, the trail proceeds along an easy grade over a remarkably smooth berm. Prostrate bluets, crimson bee-balms, white snakeroots, and blackberries are common at this elevation. Where openings in the forest cover permit, there are some fine views of the Cataloochee Divide and the wide intervening Caldwell Fork watershed. Eventually red spruces appear, signaling that the trail is edging into the lower fringes of the balsam zone.

The Rough Fork Trail soon terminates in Polls Gap, a wide grassy swag that also harbors the western terminus of the Hemphill Bald Trail and the lower terminus of the disused Polls Gap Trail. The center of the gap is occupied by a paved parking area bounded on its lower side by Heintooga Ridge Road, connecting the Blue Ridge Parkway with Heintooga Campground and Balsam Mountain Road.

 For several years passersby through Polls Gap frequently remarked on seeing bleached bones of a milk cow scattered about the clearing. The cow belonged to an old woman named Polly Moody. It seems that Polly's menfolk drove her "springing" cow along with the others to graze the mountain ranges. As a result of the drive, the cow had difficulty at the time of her calving and, without attention, sickened and died. Polls Gap was named for Polly's cow. This account of the origin of the name, however, is not conclusive. Some early maps of the Smokies identify the place as Pauls Gap. Smoky Mountain old-timers have been known to claim that Polls Gap is a corruption of Pauls Gap, once named for an uncertain Paul.

HEMPHILL BALD TRAIL

Heintooga Ridge Road at Polls Gap to the Caldwell Fork Trail—8.4 miles.

POINT OF DEPARTURE: From the Oconaluftee Visitor Center, drive 0.7 mile south on Newfound Gap Road (US441), and turn east onto the Blue Ridge Parkway. Drive the parkway 11.0 miles to Wolf Laurel Gap, and turn left onto Heintooga Ridge Road, following it to the paved parking area in Polls Gap. The Hemphill Bald Trail begins from the east end of the gap.

QUAD MAPS: Bunches Bald 174-SW

Dellwood 174-SE

0.0—Polls Gap. Heintooga Ridge Road. Rough Fork Trail.

0.7—Sugartree Lick Gap.

1.4—Garrett Gap.

2.0—Buck Knob.

2.5—Maggot Spring Gap.

3.0—Sheepback Knob.

3.3—Little Bald Knob.

4.1—Pine Tree Gap.

4.8—Hemphill Bald.

5.5—Double Gap. Cataloochee Divide Trail exits straight 6.4 miles to Cove Creek Road at Cove Creek Gap.

6.0—Switchback.

6.5—Double Gap Branch headwater.

7.5—Double Gap Branch.

7.6—Double Gap Branch.

7.7—Double Gap Branch.

8.3—Double Gap Branch.

8.4—Caldwell Fork Trail exits right 4.6 miles to Cataloochee Road and left 1.7 miles to the Rough Fork Trail.

The southern end of Balsam Mountain is marked by Polls Gap, a gentle saddle-shaped aperture that harbors a three-way intersection of the Hemphill Bald Trail, the Rough Fork Trail, and the officially closed Polls Gap Trail as well as Heintooga Ridge Road, which rises into the west side of the gap for a quick tangential pass before continuing to the Heintooga Picnic Area. At the center of the gap, separating the road from the trailheads, is a small parking area.

The Hemphill Bald Trail starts out from the east end of Polls Gap, following a wide, level, smooth trace that was once a railroad grade for the Suncrest Lumber Company. Yellow birch is the most prevalent tree species regenerating on the slopes previously clear-cut by Suncrest with sugar maples becoming noticeable about a half-mile out from Polls Gap in an area known as Sugartree Licks.

The first noticeable change in grade is a mile and half beyond Polls Gap when the trail reaches the Cataloochee Divide and drops into Garretts Gap. From the gap, the trail enters an easy 500-yard climb around the north side of Buck Knob, where yellow buckeyes and mountain maples enter the forest mix. Upon circumnavigating Buck Knob, the trail returns to the crest of the divide and begins a gentle three-quarter-mile descent to Maggot Spring Gap.

The origin of the name Maggot Spring is not clear. Early maps of the Smokies identify the gap as Maggie Spring, suggesting that the current name is a corruption of Maggie. The proximity of Maggie Valley immediately to the south reinforces this contention. Other Smoky Mountain lore records that early hunters, seeing small, white, worm-like, juvenile insects in the bottom of the stream, mistakenly identified them as maggots and thus called it Maggot Spring. Regardless of the origin of the name, the spring is not in the gap.

From Maggot Spring Gap, the Hemphill Bald Trail resumes its easy cadence of climbing and descending along the spine of the Cataloochee Divide which, from this point, also corresponds with the park boundary. Over a two-mile interval, the trail visits Sheepback Knob, Little Bald Knob, Pine Tree Gap, and Hemphill Bald, the latter named for Thomas Hemphill, who settled just east of the bald in 1792. Rhododendron thickets enclose much of the trail, but where the slopes are more open, wild geranium, prostrate bluet, blue bead lily, false Solomon's-seal, wood-betony, and Jack-in-the pulpit may be seen.

Hemphill Bald affords a fine example of what much of the Cataloochee basin looked like before the advent of the park and the cleared slopes were allowed to return to wilderness. The "north half" of Hemphill Bald, which resides within the confines of the park and is forested in second-growth stands, contrasts sharply with the short-cropped grassy exposure of the outside "south half." Visible farther to the south is Ghost Town in the Sky, a western theme park on the top of Buck Mountain overlooking Maggie Valley. Beyond Maggie Valley are the Plott Balsam Mountains.

When it leaves the summit of Hemphill Bald, the trail enters a steep three-quarter-mile descent into Double Gap, progressing from a red spruce, yellow birch, northern red oak mix to that of second-growth stands of white basswood, mountain maple, eastern hemlock, and sugar maple. For most of the way the trail remains within the Cataloochee woods, offering no clear vantage points. At Double Gap, the Hemphill Bald Trail meets the western terminus of the Cataloochee Divide Trail approaching directly along the spine of the divide. Here, the Hemphill Bald Trail turns left and proceeds into the Cataloochee basin on a steep angling course across the north flank of the divide. The trail becomes progressively rougher, soon reaching a boulder-strewn terrain thick with vines and low woody infestations. A little more than a half-mile below Double Gap, the trail executes a sharp switchback across the boulder field. Seepages are frequent. In places where the slope is especially steep, openings in the forest cover permit views of Mount Sterling Ridge and glimpses of the main Smoky divide ranging beyond the Cataloochee basin.

Seven hundred yards below the switchback, the trail crosses the headwaters of Double Gap Branch. The trail continues descending steeply for a little more than a half-mile to a second switchback that directs it over a low ridge and into the Double Gap Branch drainage. On the ridge, black locust, greenbrier, and mountain laurel are prevalent. As the trail approaches the stream, hemlock and rhododendron become predominant.

Over the course of the next mile, the Hemphill Bald Trail crosses a couple of feeder streams and then crosses Double Gap Branch four times. Just prior to the third crossing, a large northern red oak can be seen to the right of the trail. This particular tree was once identified by the TVA Forestry Division as having superior timber-producing qualities and as a source for developing seed stock.

A little more than a half-mile below the third crossing, the trail clears Double Gap Branch for the final time before proceeding 250 yards to terminate into the Caldwell Fork Trail in a small opening in the forest cover. Near the intersection are a few piles of rocks which may be remnants of outbuildings from the Jim Sutton homeplace.

PRETTY HOLLOW GAP TRAIL

Cataloochee Road at Beech Grove School to the Mount Sterling Ridge Trail and the Swallow Fork Trail at Pretty Hollow Gap—5.6 miles.

POINT OF DEPARTURE: Follow directions to the Caldwell Fork Trail. Continue on Cataloochee Road to the parking area for the Beech Grove Schoolhouse. The Pretty Hollow Gap Trail begins on the jeep road along Palmer Creek.

QUAD MAPS: Cove Creek Gap 174-NE
Luftee Knob 174-NW

0.0—Cataloochee Road.
0.2—Horse camp.
0.3—Gate.
0.8—Little Cataloochee Trail exits right 5.4 miles to NC284.
1.5—Palmer Creek Trail exits left 3.3 miles to Balsam Mountain Road.
1.8—Pretty Hollow Backcountry Campsite (#39).
3.1—Pretty Hollow Creek. Footlog.
3.5—Pretty Hollow Creek. Footlog.
3.8—Pretty Hollow Creek. Footlog.
4.1—Onion Bed Branch.
5.6—Pretty Hollow Gap. Mount Sterling Ridge Trail exits left 3.9 miles to the Balsam Mountain Trail and right 1.4 miles to the Mount Sterling Trail. Swallow Fork Trail exits straight 4.0 miles to the Big Creek Trail.

The Pretty Hollow Gap Trail begins along Cataloochee Road where the road crosses Palmer Creek. As families moved into Cataloochee, a church, school, and post office were built around this junction, making it the provisional community center for the cove. In 1910 the Postal Service named the nearby post office "Nellie" in recognition of Nellie Palmer, Turkey George Palmer's daughter, who had won first prize in a baby contest.

Directly across Palmer Creek from the trailhead is Beech Grove School. Sometime around the turn of the twentieth century, the inhabitants of Big Cataloochee decided that an earlier schoolhouse that occupied this spot was too small. Steve Woody and George Caldwell, two prominent citizens of Cataloochee, were sent to the county seat at Waynesville, North Carolina, to seek funding from the county commission to pay carpenters and buy paint for a new school. The commissioners refused the request, claiming that they had no money and furthermore that Cataloochee did not pay enough taxes to warrant a new schoolhouse.

On the way home, one man said to the other, "I'll tell you what we'll do, we'll burn it down."

That night, the two went to the school and took out the tables, little sweaters, the books, and some dinner baskets. They covered all these with the blackboard in case it rained. They set fire to the school and agreed never to tell until only one was left alive. Soon, Cataloochee got money for a new schoolhouse.

Mountain children living up along Palmer Creek would walk to the Beech Grove School on a wide wagon road that extended into the higher reaches of Pretty Hollow. This road is now incorporated into the Pretty Hollow Gap Trail.

The Pretty Hollow Gap Trail begins on a wide jeep track following a streamside course along Palmer Creek. After the first quarter-mile, the trail passes an access road to a large horse camp on the right. At the upper end of the horse camp, the trail reaches a gate blocking vehicle traffic. At this point the grade stiffens. A half-mile beyond the gate, the Pretty Hollow Gap Trail meets the Little Cataloochee Trail exiting on the right. Here, the Pretty Hollow Gap Trail levels out again as it begins skirting a weedy clearing known as the John Mull Meadow.

Few particulars are known of John Mull, but he is thought to have been an early settler who once operated a mill on Palmer Creek. Originally the John Mull Meadow extended several hundred yards along the stream up to a bottomland known as Indian Flats near the confluence of Palmer Creek and Pretty Hollow Creek. Where it enters Indian Flats, the trail intersects the lower terminus of the Palmer Creek Trail just above the mouth of Pretty Hollow Creek. The Palmer Creek Trail immediately crosses its namesake on a long footlog.

At Indian Flats, the Pretty Hollow Gap Trail leaves Palmer Creek and narrows to a rough course following along Pretty Hollow Creek. Pretty Hollow Creek is an especially attractive fast-moving stream that drains a remarkably narrow hollow. The terrain here is so constricting that it affords little opportunity for the trail to diverge from the stream. Arbors of rhododendron cloister the stream for much of the way, affording little exposure to the trail.

Five hundred yards above the Palmer Creek junction, the trail enters the Pretty Hollow Backcountry Campsite (#39), a large attractive camp extending up a gentle gradient shaded by a grove of pine trees. The open spaciousness of the slope affords several separate camping sites. The camp is serviced by two food-storage cables, and water is available from Pretty Hollow Creek below and across the trail and from a small feeder stream running through the back of the camp.

Before the advent of the park, a house once belonging to Turkey George Palmer occupied the area below the camp. It was a six-room two-story building with two porches made of poplar and bore two chimneys of handmade brick. Turkey George lived here until a very old age, becoming one of the most colorful and noted citizens of Cataloochee.

When asked how he acquired his strange nickname, Turkey George gave the following account to Professor Joseph Hall of Columbia University, who later recorded it in *Smoky Mountains Folks and Their Lore*.

I had a patch of land in corn. The wild turkeys was about to eat it up, so I built a pen to try to catch 'em. The pen was ten foot each way, and I covered the top. Then I cut a ditch and run it into the pen and covered the ditch over with bark. I scattered corn in the ditch so as to draw the turkeys into the pen. Next mornin' they was nine big gobblers inside, an' one outside. I stopped up the hole an' got me a stick to kill 'em with. When I got in the pen, they riz up an' mighty nigh killed me instead; so I got out and fetched a hoe. When they stuck their heads betwixt the slats I knocked them with it. After that I built about three pens in the mountains an' caught two or three turkeys. That's why they call me "Turkey George," I reckon.

When it leaves the Pretty Hollow Camp, the trail passes an outpost of wooden stalls for hitching horses and then proceeds into one of the finest cove-hardwood stands anywhere in the Smokies. Huge sugar maples, yellow buckeyes, yellow poplars, and a variety of oaks cast a deep gloom over the narrow steep-sided hollow. The trail remains confined to a course close to the stream, but the stream itself remains out of sight, hidden beneath the masses of rhododendron and great boles of fallen trees. From this point, the trail begins a long steady climb that rarely abates until reaching Mount Sterling Ridge.

A little more than a mile above the campsite, the trail crosses Pretty Hollow Creek and then crosses twice again at intervals of 600 yards, each time on a footlog. It then veers sharply to the left and enters the Onion Bed Branch drainage. It is here that the cove earns the moniker "Pretty Hollow." The nearby fast-moving stream rushes about beneath the thickset rhododendron, hemlocks tower from the stream's edge, and wildflowers grow luxuriantly. Crimson bee-balm, ox eye daisy, wild golden-glows, great lobelia, foamflower, blue cohosh, and Clingmans hedge nettle all flourish here in their season. The trail remains a bit above the stream, affording a vantage point from which to enjoy the immense fecundity of this Smoky Mountain forest.

The trail soon crosses Onion Bed Branch and then loops back to Pretty Hollow Creek and continues its climb up the hollow. The grade increases incrementally as the trail enters a transition from the cove-hardwood mix to primarily hemlocks and pines. The hiking surface deteriorates to a thin, eroded berm etched into the steeply pitched slope. The stream runs far below while Indian Ridge rises straight up from the stream's edge to command the far side of Pretty Hollow.

The trail continues climbing with little variation in grade and surface condition as it edges out of the hemlock-pine stands and into the balsam zone. Mature yellow birch and mountain maple are prevalent among the red spruce and Fraser fir. Weeds encroaching closely on the path herald the long approach into Pretty Hollow Gap, a shallow saddle-shaped clearing straddling Mount Sterling Ridge. Here, the Pretty Hollow Gap Trail terminates into a crossroads intersection with the Mount Sterling Ridge Trail and the Swallow Fork Trail. The Mount Sterling Ridge Trail continues through the gap. The Swallow Fork Trail, leading in from the Big Creek Trail at Walnut Bottom, rises up into Pretty Hollow Gap from the opposite side to terminate in the intersection.

PALMER CREEK TRAIL

Pretty Hollow Gap Trail at Indian Flats to Balsam Mountain Road—3.3 miles.
POINT OF DEPARTURE: Hike 1.5 miles up the Pretty Hollow Gap Trail. The Palmer Creek Trail begins at a footlog crossing the stream on the left.
QUAD MAP: Luftee Knob 174-NW

0.0—Indian Flats. Pretty Hollow Gap Trail. Pretty Hollow Creek. Footlog.
1.1—Lost Bottom Creek. Footlog.
1.6—Beech Creek. Footlog.
3.2—Railroad bed. Access path exits right 25 yards to instrument tower.
3.3—Balsam Mountain Road.

The Palmer Creek Trail begins in Indian Flats, a bottomland flanking the confluence of Pretty Hollow and Palmer creeks that was once occupied by a Cherokee camp. The name Indian Flats, bequeathed by the earliest settlers in Cataloochee, still remains current in Smoky Mountain nomenclature.

In 1875, a young Cataloochean named Turkey George Palmer ventured up Pretty Hollow Creek to Indian Flats, where he found an ancient fireplace and several pieces of pottery scattered in an overgrown clearing. At the time of Turkey George's arrival, the stream running through the camp had been known as Indian Creek because of the considerable evidence of Indian occupancy along the creek bottom. Turkey George settled in the old Cherokee camp in Indian Flats and built a large house just upstream near the present Pretty Hollow Backcountry Campsite (#39). The house was a six-room, two-story frame building with two porches made of poplar and two chimneys of handmade brick. Turkey George lived here until a very old age, becoming one of the most colorful and noted citizens of Cataloochee.

Indian Flats now harbors the junction of the Pretty Hollow Gap Trail and the lower terminus of the Palmer Creek Trail. Beginning at this junction, the Palmer Creek Trail immediately mounts a footlog spanning Pretty Hollow Creek, crosses, and then traverses the upper end of Indian Flats to enter a narrow hollow sporting the finest northern hardwood forest in the Cataloochee basin. The hollow, drained by Palmer Creek, separates Shanty Mountain from the wide southern end of Butt Mountain. Though the trail follows the course of Palmer Creek, it maintains a polite distance, keeping high above the stream on a well-maintained berm affixed to the steep southern flank of Butt Mountain. For the first mile the grade is moderate, but gradually increases in steepness as the trail negotiates the lower contours of the mountain.

One mile above Indian Flats, conditions deteriorate, the course becoming considerably rugged. Here, it traverses a wide rock shield that serves as the bed for Palmer Creek and nearby Lost Bottom Creek. The trail then turns and enters a narrow hollow that channels Lost Bottom Creek. It crosses the stream on a footlog and climbs away.

A hundred yards above Lost Bottom Creek, the grade moderates, and the trail returns to tracing a course high above Palmer Creek. After a quarter-mile, it approaches the confluence of Beech Creek and Falling Rock Creek, the two streams converging to form Palmer Creek. The trail proceeds into the Beech Creek hollow, following the stream a hundred yards before crossing on a footlog. It then climbs out of the Beech Creek drainage and takes a course high up and along Falling Rock Creek.

Falling Rock Creek receives its name from a freak accident that occurred near the stream in 1922. According to Mark Hannah, a former resident and ranger in Cataloochee, the Reverend Wilson Camel and a companion from Cosby, Tennessee, came over to Turkey George Palmer's place to spend a few days in the mountains. The two decided to go up Palmer Creek to the mouth of Lost Bottom

Creek and fashion a campsite in the wilderness. They chose a suitable spot by a huge rock cliff.

It was spring, and the weather was still cool, so the two men gathered firewood enough to last through the night and built a great bonfire against the cliff. Apparently the fire heated the cliff face to a degree that the effect of expansion caused a slab of rock eight to ten feet high and ten inches thick to split off and drop down on its lower edge. The slab then toppled over and crushed the Reverend Camel, who was sleeping on the ground in front of the cliff.

The lone companion worked all night to pry the rock off the preacher. But all was in vain. When daybreak came, he waded down the creek (there was no trail at this date) to Turkey George's house and told what had happened. Some of the bigger boys and the teacher from the nearby Beech Grove School were quickly assembled to assist in carrying out the body.

The job of lifting the large rock was not easy. A stout maple sapling about sixteen feet long was cut and used with a bait rock, as it was called. The slab was pried from every angle with several poles. Wedges were placed under it to hold the weight, perhaps two tons. Eventually the men pulled the body out from under the rock and tied it to a stretcher made of two poles. Taking turns, four men at each turn, they carried the Reverend Camel's body down Palmer Creek until they arrived at Turkey George's house. Turkey George's wife, Martha, gave them a sheet to wrap the body before it was placed in a wagon for the trip over Mount Sterling Ridge to Cosby.

The basic facts of Reverend Camel's unfortunate altercation with the falling rock are captured by Elizabeth Powers in *Cataloochee: Lost Settlement of the Smokies*. Like many other stories of Smoky Mountain vintage, this one has resurfaced as a sub-plot in a work of historical fiction. In Wayne Caldwell's recent novel *Cataloochee*, Ed Camel is accompanied by Bud Harrogate on the fateful camping trip up Lost Bottom Creek. In Caldwell's fascinating retelling, the two men camp for the night beneath "a huge rock overhung from the mountain like a canopy awning thirty feet above a fancy storefront. The rock face was black with the remains of fires, many started long before white people came. Forgotten names carved in the rocks told of men who spoke English, and runic shapes burned in the rocks spoke of prehistory. 'The Cherokee, or whoever was here before them, took shelter here,' Camel said. 'So will we.'"

After crossing Beech Creek, the trail climbs to a higher elevation on the south slope of Trail Ridge, where a northern hardwood mix of red and sugar maples, American beeches, and yellow birches gives way to a dry-ridge association of chestnut and white oaks, pignut hickories, mountain laurel, and rhododendron with galax and trailing arbutus in the understory. Openings in the forest cover afford several views of Shanty Mountain to the south. The name for the mountain was suggested by a shack built and used by a black slave name Old Smart who once herded cattle for Mitchell Davidson, an early Cataloochee landowner from Jonathan Creek.

A 100-yard tunnel of over-reaching rhododendron heralds the approach to trail's end. On exiting the tunnel, the trail eases alongside an old railroad spur that extends a few hundred yards out along the spine of Trail Ridge. The Palmer Creek Trail quickly merges onto the old railway bed, where it immediately meets a path leading back down the railroad grade twenty-five yards to an instrument tower. Sixty yards beyond its junction with the access path, the Palmer Creek Trail terminates into Balsam Mountain Road, a one-way gravel track that begins at the end of Heintooga Ridge Road and continues through Round Bottom and into Big Cove.

LITTLE CATALOOCHEE TRAIL

Pretty Hollow Gap Trail to NC284—5.4 miles.

POINT OF DEPARTURE: Hike 0.8 mile up the Pretty Hollow Gap Trail. The Little Cataloochee Trail begins on the right.

QUAD MAP: Cove Creek Gap 174-NE

0.0—Pretty Hollow Gap Trail.
0.3—Little Davidson Branch.
1.0—Access path exits left 665 yards to the Burris Cemetery.
1.1—Davidson Creek.
1.5—Remains of log out-building.
1.6—Stone wall.
1.9—Davidson Gap.
2.7—Cook Cabin. Messer Apple-house.
3.4—Little Cataloochee Missionary Baptist Church.
3.9—Ola. Little Cataloochee Creek. Bridge.
4.2—Access path exits left 75 yards to the Hannah Cabin.
4.3—Long Bunk Trail exits left 3.6 miles to the Mount Sterling Trail.
5.4—NC284.

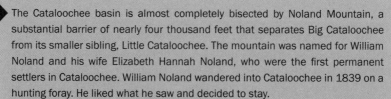

The Cataloochee basin is almost completely bisected by Noland Mountain, a substantial barrier of nearly four thousand feet that separates Big Cataloochee from its smaller sibling, Little Cataloochee. The mountain was named for William Noland and his wife Elizabeth Hannah Noland, who were the first permanent settlers in Cataloochee. William Noland wandered into Cataloochee in 1839 on a hunting foray. He liked what he saw and decided to stay.

When Cataloochee was being settled, the only suitable passway into Little Cataloochee over Noland Mountain was through a high swag now known as Davidson

Gap. Pioneer settlers carved a five-mile road up and through Davidson Gap that provided reliable access between the two coves. But even then, the travel through Davidson Gap was long and difficult. Raymond Caldwell, an inhabitant of Cataloochee who often traveled this road, once commented that "it was quite a chore to go through Davidson Gap. . . . It would take more than a day to go over to Little Cataloochee and back." The road Raymond Caldwell took over Davidson Gap was later engineered to park specification and officially sanctioned as the Little Cataloochee Trail.

The lower terminus of the Little Cataloochee Trail begins at a rather inconspicuous junction along the Pretty Hollow Gap Trail about a mile above the modern Cataloochee Road. The trail starts quickly into a climb over mountain farmland being reclaimed by old-field, second-growth forest. Within 525 yards, it crosses Little Davidson Branch and narrows to a single-file track. Three hundred yards farther, the trail enters a streamside course along Davidson Branch, following it into a deep glen of red and sugar maples, yellow poplars, American beeches, yellow birches, and Carolina silverbells shading a dense understory of rhododendron. Frequently the trail is either in Davidson Branch or negotiating seepages seeking the main stream. Along here and about a mile above the trailhead, an access path exits on the left and leads 665 yards to a cemetery of a single grave, that of a child of the surname Burris.

A hundred yards above the cemetery access, the trail enters a sharp turn to cross Davidson Creek, and then begins moving out of the glen. On the left, a conspicuous path leads a few feet to the ruins of an old log out-building. The few timbers that remain are chestnut. Their configuration suggests that the building was a twenty-by-twenty-square-foot structure embedded into the adjacent hillside. One corner of the cabin remains partially intact, affording a fine example of how the pioneers notched the logs to provide interlocking stability and then chinked the spaces between with mud to block out the elements.

Behind the log building, a stone retaining wall forms a terrace of level ground that may have been a building foundation. No building now stands here, but evidence strongly suggests that this was once a homesite. A few scattered bricks together with bits of glass and household refuse are strewn throughout the area. At the edge of the terrace stand two posts appearing conspicuously as part of a gate to a farmhouse yard.

When it leaves the homesite, the trail enters immediately into a steep climb that does not end until reaching Davidson Gap. Noticeable on the left is a stone wall that runs roughly parallel to the trail for no less than forty yards. The trail circles around the end of the wall and then begins following along the upper side. Until 2009, the Little Cataloochee Trail did not switch back at the head of the wall but proceeded directly to Davidson Gap. Because of erosion damage from horse traffic, the trail has been extended to include another switchback, thus lessening the grade for the final pull into the gap.

Davidson Gap was named for Mitchell Davidson, a resident of Jonathan Creek who was the earliest cattleman to graze livestock in Cataloochee. Out of the right side of the gap a faint path leads about a quarter-mile to Bald Top and then drops into Bald Gap, where it merges into an old manway that connected the post office at Nellie in Big Cataloochee with the road leading to the post office at Ola in Little Cataloochee. The manway was once used to convey mail between the two coves. Just above Bald Gap is Canadian Top which, at 4,060 feet, is the highest point on Noland Mountain. Canadian Top was named for Bill and Nancy Ewart, who settled here from Canada and were known locally as Bill and Nancy Canadian.

On leaving Davidson Gap, the trail descends steeply along a newly constructed surface that replaces another section heavily damaged by horse traffic. Shortly, a stone wall forms up on the right. The trail runs parallel to the wall, circles around the end, then doubles back along the wall's lower side. The wall extends a considerable distance to a corner where it turns and runs for another twenty yards or so. The trail does not approach the corner but turns down the mountain and away from the wall.

The stone wall marks the upper boundary of a large parcel of land once farmed by W. G. B. "Will" Messer, a businessman and the wealthiest resident of Little Cataloochee. Here, Messer built a log cabin that was reputed to have one of the finest stone chimneys in the area. He added a barn, an apple-house, and a spring-house. The apple-house was later removed and reconstructed at the Mountain Farm Museum back of the Oconaluftee Visitor Center on Newfound Gap Road. The barn was moved to a new site near the Cataloochee Ranger Station on the main road into Cataloochee where it is now known as the Messer Barn.

Within a half-mile, the trail completes its descent and approaches the Daniel J. Cook Cabin.

This cabin was built in the late 1850s by Dan Cook, perhaps the earliest settler in Little Cataloochee. The cabin stood on this site until 1975 when vandals destroyed the structure and the Park Service stored the remaining pieces in an effort to preserve the building. It was carefully restored in the fall of 1999 using traditional construction methods and only materials that would have been available to the settlers.

The Cook Cabin is a one-room log house that was originally built with floors of poplar puncheon, half-logs almost ten inches thick. When it was restored, a floor of sawmill lumber was installed as the original puncheons had been used in an earlier restoration of the Hannah cabin.

In one corner a stairway leads up to a full loft. At one end, the only window in the house flanks a stone fireplace. Doors on the three other walls open out onto a porch that surrounds the house on three sides. The house is covered with split shingles. The rear porch roof is a continuation of the main roof while that over the front porch is attached to the cabin wall a few feet below the eaves of the main roof. The Cook Cabin is one of the oldest and finest examples of a log structure anywhere in the Great Smoky Mountains National Park.

Directly across the road from the cabin are the ruins of an apple-house built by Will Messer in 1915. The building was once a two-story stone and lumber structure with walls almost two-and-a-half feet thick. The upper story walls were paneled in chestnut siding with a ten-inch space between the internal and external walls filled with sawdust for insulation. The apple-house was built into the side of a hill. Just behind the building is a trace of the old trail that passes through Bald Gap on Noland Mountain and once connected Little Cataloochee with the post office at Nellie in Big Cataloochee.

From the Cook Cabin, the trail widens to a road and begins an easy grade. It passes through stands of rhododendron and into open fields being reclaimed by second-growth forests. Old chestnut fence posts line the fields on both sides. Pieces of household effects, old washtubs and buckets, and stone retaining walls at road's edge all testify to the human activity that once abounded on this part of the mountain.

Less than a half-mile beyond the cabin, the trail reaches the Little Cataloochee Missionary Baptist Church standing prominently on a knoll of bare ground.

The church is a frame building bearing a belfry and set on an attractive foundation of river rocks painted white. The front door faces southwest and down the hill toward a fenced cemetery with the gravestones facing east. Pews inside the church are plain wooden right-angles whose hard board-straight backs are conducive for inhibiting naps during long sermons.

Worship services in the old Smoky Mountain churches were reverent, but often informal. Chronicler Horace Kephart noted that "during these services there is a good deal of running in and out by the men and boys, most of whom gradually congregate on the outside to whittle, gossip, drive bargains, and debate among themselves some point of dogma that is too good to keep still about." Usually the preacher was a circuit rider who expounded scripture and denounced sinners at the top of his voice for the better part of a Sunday afternoon, as long as "the spirit lasts."

When it leaves the church, the trail descends about a half-mile to Ola, a bottom-land that was once the community center of Little Cataloochee. On the left in the flat of the bottomland the trail approaches a spring lined with a rock wall. Presiding over the wall is a sturdy log post that was once likely part of an enclosure that sheltered the spring.

Will Messer purchased this bottomland and moved his family here from his farm near Davidson Gap around 1905. In 1910 he built the largest house in Little Cataloochee just across the road from the spring. The house was a stately structure containing eleven rooms serviced with running hot and cold water and illuminated by an acetylene lighting system. Beyond the house, Messer built several barns and mills, a blacksmith shop, and general store. Messer's store also served as the local post office, which the postal service designated as "Ola," named for Viola Messer, a daughter of Will and Rachel Cook Messer. As an extension, Ola became the accepted name for the small community that sprung up in Little Cataloochee. Nothing remains of Messer's farm at Ola except for a scattering of household items, an occasional row of fence posts, and a few noticeable non-native shrubs and flowers planted by the settlers.

At the lower end of Ola, the trail crosses Little Cataloochee Creek on a bridge and begins climbing out of the bottomland. A quarter-mile beyond the stream crossing, a road exits on the left seventy-five yards to the John Jackson Hannah Cabin.

In 1851, John Jackson Hannah, brother-in-law of William Noland, left his father's home, crossed Noland Mountain, and entered Little Cataloochee with his new wife, Martha Ann. Hannah forded Little Cataloochee Creek, ventured another 600 yards up the mountain, and built a small board cabin on a gently sloped gradient. Sometime before 1864, this first hovel was replaced by a larger one-room log cabin that still stands on its original site. The cabin is a simple structure of hand-hewn squared-off logs with chamfered notching at the corners. It has puncheon floors of wide boards of irregular width and a chimney of handmade bricks. A corner stairway leads to a low one-room loft. The roof is covered with split shingles and slopes to cover a low porch along the front of the cabin.

The yard was once enclosed by a rail fence. Inside the fence on the south corner Hannah kept bee gums. Beyond the upper back corner was a vegetable garden, and above the upper front corner Hannah maintained an orchard. The orchard contained an apple tree said to be thirty inches in diameter and widely claimed to be the largest in the world. On all sides of Hannah's cabin, except that facing the road, the slopes were cleared and tilled for crops.

After passing the access to the Hannah Cabin, the trail reaches a gravel road that circles around the mountain 260 yards to intersect with the Long Bunk Trail exiting left to the Mount Sterling Trail. The Little Cataloochee Trail continues along the gravel track for another mile before rising to terminate at an intersection with a larger gravel road, NC284.

In the waning days of the Civil War, a notorious Confederate bushwhacker named Captain Albert Teague entered Big Creek, intent on finding every man of draftable age he suspected of being a Union sympathizer. Teague finally captured three men—George and Henry Grooms and a simpleton named Mitchell Caldwell. He tied the men up and marched them on foot seven miles or so to Mount Sterling Gap, then along the "Cattalucha track" to Indian Grave Branch near the intersection of the Little Cataloochee Trail and NC284. Here, Teague stopped and ordered the three men executed by shooting. Teague's infamous deed has been recounted in so many versions that it has taken on the proportions of a folktale. Several variants are preserved in Elizabeth Powers's *Cataloochee: Lost Settlement in the Smokies*.

One version contends that Henry Grooms, a noted Smoky Mountain fiddler, was forced by his captors to play a last tune on his fiddle, which, incongruently, he had clutched as he stumbled along. He chose, fittingly, the famous "Bonaparte's Retreat," playing it much to the minor key, as musicians are wont to say. The song is uncommonly mournful, so that dogs often howl whenever it is being played. But evidently the music did not touch the hearts of Teague's war-hardened raiders. When the sweet plaintive strains of "Bonaparte's retreat were scarcely hushed in the deep-wooded silence of Cataloochee, the sharp report of firearms hushed the lives of Henry Grooms and his two companions."

Before dying, George Grooms was said to have cursed his captors, and Henry Grooms asked to pray. But the simpleton, Mitchell Caldwell, continued to stand and grin at his captors as they were about to shoot him. This so unnerved the executioners that they placed his hat over his face.

All three bodies were left lying in the road. Hours later, Eliza Grooms, Henry's wife, and a Sutton boy came with an ox hitched to a sled and carried the bodies back across the mountain. All three men were buried in the same grave in a single pine coffin.

The Grooms-Mitchell killing continues to be one of the most fascinating stories to come out of the Great Smoky Mountains. Charles Frazier, in his award-winning novel *Cold Mountain*, incorporates this story into the climactic episode of the deserter John Inman's attempt to escape as a fugitive from the war.

LONG BUNK TRAIL

Little Cataloochee at Ola to the Mount Sterling Trail—3.6 miles.

POINT OF DEPARTURE: Hike 4.3 miles up the Little Cataloochee Trail. The Long Bunk Trail begins on the left.

QUAD MAP: Cove Creek Gap 174-NE

0.0—Ola. Little Cataloochee Trail.
0.2—Hannah Cemetery.
2.3—Dude Branch. Pig Pen Flats.
3.6—Mount Sterling Trail exits right 0.5 mile to NC284 at Mount Sterling
Gap and left 2.2 miles to the Mount Sterling Backcountry Campsite (#38)
and Mount Sterling fire tower.

During the early years of the nineteenth century, hunters from Tennessee in search of food to feed their families ventured into Cataloochee, pursuing quarry of bear, deer, turkey, raccoon, and other wildlife seeking refuge in this isolated cove in the eastern Smokies. The hunters left their homes, entered into the wilderness, and pitched camps in the center of their hunting grounds. Once a fortnight they divided the kill and sent the meat home.

The hunters entered Cataloochee following an old Indian trace through Davenport Gap to Mount Sterling Gap, then turned and followed the ridge along what is now the Mount Sterling Trail. A quarter-mile up the ridge, the hunters turned south and descended into a hollow known then as the Bearwallow. At the Bearwallow, the hunters' trail turned southwest and proceeded a half-mile to the Hollow Log Camp. The camp was located on a flat ridge about 300 yards above Dude Creek on the north side of Long Bunk Mountain.

Leaving their children at home, wives of the hunters would saddle oxen and ride to the Hollow Log Camp to pick up the hunters' kill. After spending the night at the camp, the women would fill large leather bags with choice cuts of meat and leave early for the return trip home.

According to Mack Hannah, whose stories are recorded in *Cataloochee: Lost Settlement of the Smokies*, the women stored the meat at the home of Tobe Phillips, a famous bear hunter who lived on Tobes Creek in the northeast corner of the Smokies. As it was needed, the other families would come to the Phillips place to get their share of the meat.

A few years after the first hunters came to Hollow Log Camp, the herders arrived, driving their browsing stock to the rich grazing ranges along the flats of Long Bunk Mountain. Two of the best-known herders in the region were Richard Clark and Neddy McFalls, renegades who ranged cattle for the prominent landowner Mitchell Davidson. When a man named Zack White shot a deputy sheriff by the name of Rayburn, Clark and McFalls hid the outlaw near a big rock in a little flat a half-mile above the Lafayette Palmer house in Big Cataloochee, where for years the two herders carried him food.

Richard Clark is remembered for giving the name to Long Bunk, so-called for its fancied resemblance to a bunk. Neddy McFalls is distinguished in Smoky Mountain lore for his superstitions and his intense dislike of Indians. McFalls hunted with a rifle made by a man named Gillaspie who lived at the head of the French Broad River. Once, McFalls missed an easy shot at a buck and nothing could dissuade him from leaving Cataloochee and traveling miles to a female witch doctor who could remove the "spell" on his gun.

Neddy McFalls's grudge against all Indians was the consequence of his father's death at the hands of a Cherokee. In an act of revenge, McFalls persuaded his friend Sam McGaha to take aim with his Gillaspie rife at an unsuspecting Indian sitting on a log, telling him that the trigger was locked. Poor McGaha merely touched the trigger on McFalls's gun, only to see the Indian fall off the log dead. McFalls had "sprung" the trigger and tricked McGaha into wreaking his own revenge, perhaps salvaging his own conscience since he himself had not actually pulled the trigger.

Following the hunters and herders, the settlers arrived. They built homes on Long Bunk Mountain along a trace that was once known as the Pig Pen Trail and is now called the Long Bunk Trail.

The Long Bunk Trail begins from the Little Cataloochee Trail a mile below NC284 and just above the former settlement of Ola. From here, the trail climbs steadily on a gravel road through stands of oaks 350 yards to the Hannah Cemetery, a well-kept plot of nearly fifty graves. Buried here are John Jackson Hannah and his wife Martha Ann, two of the cove's earliest settlers. Sometime in the 1850s the Hannahs built the first log cabin in Little Cataloochee. Their second cabin, built in 1864, still stands off the Little Cataloochee Trail just below the Long Bunk trailhead.

As it leaves the cemetery, the trail diminishes to a single-file track, climbs briefly, then drops into the Flats of the Bunk, a level tract that once harbored several homes and farms. The Flats are slowly, but inexorably, being reclaimed by the wilderness, but there are still some remnants of the tract's pioneer past. On the left are a few fence posts and remains of an old cabin. On the right and across a small stream are a few pieces of an abandoned log outbuilding, perhaps a smokehouse or corncrib with the characteristic dovetailed notches in the timbers.

When the trail exits the Flats of the Bunk, it climbs around the north side of Long Bunk Mountain, generally tracing the contours of the slope. It gains sufficient elevation to afford some excellent views of nearby Scottish Mountain. The trail continues working its way around Long Bunk and eventually enters the Dude Creek drainage. Here, conditions become much more moist, the trees taller and of greater girth, and wildflowers flourish. As the trail begins rolling off the Bunk and down to a rendezvous with Dude Creek, it crosses several seepages, many encumbered by heavy weeds encroaching on the sides. When the trail crosses Dude Creek it enters a small bottomland once known as Pig Pen Flats. The name evidently is derived from the practice of settlers roaming their hogs on the flats. As late as the 1970s, the remains of a large pig pen could still be seen along the trail. Much of the land around this part of Dude Creek is flat and provided good farmland for the settlers. One of the inhabitants of Pig Pen Flats was Dude Hannah, a colorful mountaineer who lived for many years on the creek that bears his name. One of Dude's neighbors was his brother Ras, who was a notorious moonshiner on Long Bunk. Ras and his wife, Alice, once operated a still in Waycaster Laurel farther up Dude Creek.

In the pantheon of Smoky Mountain villains, there is perhaps none more notorious than that associated with the name "Dude." In 1883, a married woman named Nancy Conard Kerley took up with Dude Hannah, moving into his ramshackle cabin, which had not seen a woman's touch in twenty years. Nance, as she was called, grew up on nearby Conard Creek, and for most of her life had known Dude Hannah as a man whose penchant for moonshine made him irresponsible and violent. After leaving her husband and son, and moving in with Hannah, the woman came to be known by the locals as Nance Dude.

In October 1884, Nance Dude gave birth to a baby girl and named her Elizabeth Ann. Dude Hannah was in a Waynesville jail when his daughter was born and probably did not care what she was named or even whether she was born at all. The three lived in poverty for several years until one night, in a drunken rage, Hannah burned down the family cabin and disappeared. Homeless, Nance and the child were reduced to living off the charity of others.

In 1910, Elizabeth Ann became pregnant and bore a girl named Roberta Ann. Three years later and for reasons that were likely fostered by the harshness of their poverty, Nance Dude announced she was taking Roberta Ann over the mountain to an institutional foster home. It was later discovered that the grandmother had fastened the three-year-old up in a mountain cave and left her to die of exposure, hunger, and fright.

Nance Dude was convicted of murder and sentenced to prison. Fifteen years later, when she was eighty years old, Nance Dude was released from prison. She moved back to the mountains where she remained, becoming a figment of fright to those who lived near her. Nance Dude died in 1952 at the age of 104. In 1991, the various strains of the Nance Dude story were collated into a historical fiction work by Maurice Stanley and published as *The Legend of Nance Dude*.

On leaving Pig Pen Flats, the trail remains a narrow track climbing through attractive stands of large oak trees. It continues until clearing the adjacent ridge and then descends to cross the first of two streams that form Corell Branch. A knoll of lush grass and the second stream crossing immediately precede a final climb that terminates into the Mount Sterling Trail a half-mile above the point where NC284 crosses the mountain through Mount Sterling Gap.

◆ RAVEN FORK ◆

The Raven Fork section is defined as the basin bounded on the east by Balsam Mountain, on the west by Hughes Ridge, and divided into contiguous watersheds by Hyatt Ridge. Raven Fork drains the western side of the Hyatt Ridge divide, and its primary tributary, Straight Fork, drains the eastern. The main Smoky divide forms a high headwall along the upper end of the Raven Fork basin while its lower end grades into the bottomlands of the Qualla Boundary of the Cherokee Nation.

By the time white settlers had begun encroaching on Raven Fork in the early nineteenth century, the Cherokee had absorbed elements of European culture in an attempt to adjust to the influx of white settlers. For the most part, the Cherokee lived on farms and dressed like the white settlers. They maintained schools and established a republican form of government complete with a constitution and legislature. In 1820, gold was discovered on Cherokee territory, prompting the state of Georgia to expropriate their land by renouncing all treaties and revoking the Cherokee's personal legal rights. In 1833, with the Treaty of New Echota, the Cherokee ceded to the federal government all of their territory east of the Mississippi. Some of the Cherokee petitioned Congress for aid in averting the land grab, but to no avail. In the winter of 1838, sixteen thousand Cherokee were forcibly ousted from their ancestral homeland and made to walk on the infamous "Trail of Tears" to what later became known as the Oklahoma Territory. Several thousand perished to starvation and cold.

About a thousand Cherokee refused to leave, becoming renegades and hiding in the high recesses of the mountains where federal soldiers were unable to hunt them down. Many starved or froze to death, but those who survived became the nucleus of the Eastern Band of the Cherokee. To this remnant and their adopted chief, Col. William Holland Thomas, North Carolina courts later deeded the Qualla Boundary which includes much of the lower Raven Fork basin.

The Raven Fork section is the most isolated wilderness in the Smokies. Two roads encroach on the extreme southeastern corner of the basin. Balsam Mountain Road traces the lower east rim before circling down to meet Straight Fork Road approaching from the Qualla Boundary.

Of the seven trails in the Raven Fork section, the Balsam Mountain Trail and Hughes Ridge Trail remain on the perimeter while those reaching into the interior are confined to the lower part of the basin.

The Raven Fork section harbors three backcountry campsites and two shelters. The Laurel Gap Shelter and the Spruce Mountain Backcountry Campsite (#42) are ranged along the spine of Balsam Mountain, and the Pecks Corner Shelter is along the upper end of Hughes Ridge. In the interior of the basin, the McGee Spring Backcountry Campsite (#44) occupies a dell along Hyatt Ridge, and the Enloe

Creek Backcountry Campsite (#47) is situated on a bench overlooking Raven Fork. The vast upper interior of the Raven Fork watershed is without trails or campsites.

The Raven Fork section can be reached by automobile by way of either Balsam Mountain Road or Straight Fork Road. To reach Balsam Mountain Road, follow the Blue Ridge Parkway to Wolf Gap, 2.5 miles west of where the parkway intersects US19 at Soco Gap. At Wolf Gap, turn onto Heintooga Ridge Road, continuing until it terminates in a turnaround at the Heintooga Picnic Area. The gravel one-way Balsam Mountain Road begins at the turnaround and continues west 8.4 miles to meet Straight Fork Road in Round Bottom. Balsam Mountain Road is closed during the winter season.

To reach Straight Fork Road, drive US441 from the Oconaluftee Visitor Center south immediately beyond the entrance to the Blue Ridge Parkway and turn left onto Big Cove Road at the city limits of Cherokee, North Carolina. Follow Big Cove Road through the Qualla Boundary 9.0 miles to Straight Fork Road. Turn right and follow Straight Fork Road into the park. The Straight Fork terminates into Balsam Mountain Road near the trailhead for the Beech Gap Trail.

FLAT CREEK TRAIL

Turnaround at the end of Heintooga Ridge Road looping back to Heintooga Ridge Road—2.6 miles.

POINT OF DEPARTURE: From the Oconaluftee Visitor Center, drive south 0.7 mile on Newfound Gap Road (US441), and turn east onto the Blue Ridge Parkway. Drive the parkway 11.0 miles to Wolf Laurel Gap, and turn left onto Heintooga Ridge Road, following it to its end at Heintooga Campground and Picnic Area. The Flat Creek Trail begins on the left side of the turnaround at the end of the road.

QUAD MAP: Bunches Bald 174-SW

0.0—Turnaround at the end of Heintooga Ridge Road. Heintooga Campground and Picnic Area. Balsam Mountain Road.

0.1—Heintooga Overlook.

0.9—Flat Creek. Footlog.

0.9—Flat Creek.

1.0—Flat Creek.

1.2—Flat Creek. Footlog.

1.3—Flat Creek. Footlog.

1.8—Access path exits right to Flat Creek Falls.

2.3—Bunches Creek. Footlog.

2.5—Bunches Creek. Footlog.

2.6—Heintooga Ridge Road.

The Flat Creek Trail begins along the turnaround that marks the upper end of Heintooga Ridge Road and the beginning of Balsam Mountain Road, a one-way gravel track that leads into Big Cove. Adjacent to the turnaround are Heintooga Campground and Picnic Area. The Flat Creek Trail exits from the side of the turnaround on a roadbed circling around the end of the picnic area and into a grove of red spruce trees. A hundred and eighty yards beyond the turnaround the trail reaches Heintooga Overlook, which affords superb views across the Raven Fork drainage to Mount Guyot (6,621 feet) and the high Smoky divide.

Sixty yards beyond Heintooga Overlook, the trail leaves the roadbed and drops off right onto a narrow, hard-packed dirt track that descends gently through a woodland of red spruce, American beech, yellow birch, striped and red maple shading banks of ferns and turfs of thick grass.

The trail soon circles through a fine stand of red spruce and then drops into a bottomland to cross Flat Creek on a footlog. Eighty yards farther, it crosses back over the stream and then, after another twenty yards, crosses again. Over this interval, seepages in the trail make the track a bit wet and rocky. The flanking bottomland is thinly forested and bears a sparse understory. Four hundred and thirty yards below the third stream crossing, the trail again crosses Flat Creek on a footlog and then, ninety yards farther, crosses Flat Creek for the fifth and final time, again on a footlog. The trail continues its gentle descent for an additional half-mile before approaching on the right an access path exiting to Flat Creek Falls.

The access path angles 245 yards down toward the stream before reaching a junction where it forks. The left fork leads eighty yards to the bottom of the falls. The climb down is exceedingly steep and necessitates negotiating a rock shield which is treacherous when dry and perilous when wet. Dense undergrowth defends the stream, making a direct approach to the falls difficult. The lower part of the falls is a steeply pitched, V-shaped channel that is less than two feet wide and cut deep into a rock shield. From above, the steam emerges from beneath a shroud of rhododendron, dashes down the narrow chute, and disappears quickly into the hidden depths below. The ruggedness, the steepness, and the rushing fall of the water, all compacted in a small isolated niche, engenders a wonderfully pleasant wilderness experience.

The right fork leads about forty yards to the top of Flat Creek Falls. The only good vantage point here is a rock platform on the far side of the stream which can be difficult to reach. The platform is along the top of a steeply angled, smooth rock shield about fifteen feet wide at the top and tapering over a distance of twenty-five feet to the narrow channel below. Flat Creek descends from a ledge into a small pool and then onto the shield, where it glides evenly and with little sound or turbulence, a deceiving prelude to the violently rushing torrent that follows below.

At the point where the Flat Creek Trail passes the access path to the falls, it begins a short climb over a low ridge that separates the Flat Creek drainage from that of Bunches Creek. Thickets of Allegheny serviceberry, hawthorn, and black cherry mixed with birch and beech fashion a corridor that directs the trail over the ridge and down to Bunches Creek. A half-mile beyond the access to Flat Creek Falls, the trail crosses Bunches Creek on a footlog and then proceeds across the bottom for 260 yards to cross another footlog over a tributary of Bunches Creek. At this juncture, the trail starts into a final steep climb of 240 yards to terminate at Heintooga Ridge Road.

The lower trailhead is marked by a small pull-over along the side of Heintooga Ridge Road, permitting hikers to park here and follow the trail upstream to the Heintooga Overlook. The pull-over is just down the road from Polls Gap and the trailheads for the Rough Fork Trail and the Hemphill Bald Trail.

SPRUCE MOUNTAIN TRAIL

Balsam Mountain Road to the Spruce Mountain Backcountry Campsite (#42)—1.2 miles.

POINT OF DEPARTURE: Follow directions to the Flat Creek Trail. From the turn-around at the end of Heintooga Ridge Road, drive 5.9 miles on the one-way Balsam Mountain Road. The Spruce Mountain Trail begins on the right. (Balsam Mountain Road is closed in winter.)

QUAD MAP: Bunches Bald 174-SW

0.0—Balsam Mountain Road.
1.0—Intersection with the abandoned Polls Gap Trail.
1.2—Spruce Mountain Backcountry Campsite (#42).

The Spruce Mountain Trail is among the most isolated and inaccessible trails in the park. The only convenient access is 5.9 miles along the one-way Balsam Mountain Road, a gravel track which is closed during the winter season. At one time, the trail's upper end could be approached by the old Polls Gap Trail; however, this trail was officially closed several years ago and is now impassible.

The Spruce Mountain Trail follows a jeep road servicing a fire tower that once stood on the summit of the mountain. The trail starts up quickly from Balsam Mountain Road on a steep grade which is wide, even, and fairly free of rocks. Four hundred yard above Balsam Mountain Road, a small stream intervenes, pooling in a small rock basin at the edge of the trail. This stream is the nearest source of water when Bear Branch, the stream at the Spruce Mountain Backcountry Campsite (#42), is dry.

As it gains elevation, passing through northern hardwood stands, the jeep track yields to a grassy turf, pleasantly soft underfoot. A litte more little more than a half-mile above Balsam Mountain Road, the trail executes a sharp switchback right, and the hardwood stands begin yielding to the lower fringes of the balsam zone. Soon the grassy turf gives way to a surface of loosely shifting stones as the trail enters a fine grove of large red spruce trees.

The Spruce Mountain Trail reaches the crest of Balsam Mountain, where it once intersected the upper terminus of the Polls Gap Trail. At this juncture, the Spruce Mountain Trail turned left and traced the spine of Balsam Mountain a half-mile to a fire tower on the summit of Spruce Mountain. When the fire tower was abandoned, the trail was shortened by a half-mile to terminate in its junction with the Polls Gap Trail. Later, when the Polls Gap Trail was closed, the Spruce Mountain Trail was lengthened 230 yards to reach an access path that exits 115 yards to the Spruce Mountain Backcountry Campsite (#42).

The trail approaches the campsite after crossing and dropping down below the Balsam Mountain ridgeline. The camp is an open grassy patch situated along the lower edge of a spruce grove. The ground around the camp is level and affords several attractive tent sites. A food-storage cable is extended across the middle of the camp, and water is available from Bear Branch running off into the thickets from the back of the camp. Unfortunately, Bear Branch is not reliable during the drier seasons. The stream has been known to be dry even during the wetter seasons.

The Spruce Mountain Camp is one of the highest backcountry campsites in the Smokies and one of very few in the balsam zone. The spruce grove, the grassy turf, and the remoteness all combine to make this one of the more attractive campsites in the park.

BALSAM MOUNTAIN TRAIL

Balsam Mountain Road at Pin Oak Gap to the Appalachian Trail at Tricorner Knob—10.1 miles.

POINT OF DEPARTURE: Follow directions to the Flat Creek Trail. From the turn-around at the end of Heintooga Ridge Road, drive along Balsam Mountain Road 8.4 miles to Pin Oak Gap. The Balsam Mountain Trail begins on the right. (Balsam Mountain Road is closed in winter.)
QUAD MAPS: Luftee Knob 174-NW
Mount Guyot 165-NE

0.0—Pin Oak Gap. Balsam Mountain Road.
2.1—Ledge Bald.
2.3—Beech Gap. Beech Gap Trail exits left 2.5 miles to Round Bottom on Straight Fork Road.
3.6—Balsam High Top.
4.1—Laurel Gap. Laurel Gap Shelter.
4.3—Mount Sterling Ridge Trail exits right 5.3 miles to the Mount Sterling Trail.

5.2—Gunter Fork Trail exits right 4.1 miles to the Camel Gap Trail in Walnut Bottom.

7.2—Luftee Knob.

9.4—Mount Yonaguska.

10.1—Tricorner Knob. Appalachian Trail. Access trail to Tricorner Knob Shelter is 130 yards left along the Appalachian Trail.

Balsam Mountain is a long meandering ridge that extends south from the main Smoky divide at Tricorner Knob to the western end of the Cataloochee Divide. It was a nexus of settlement activity for the Cherokee as well as the earliest white settlers who ventured into the Smokies. What may have initially attracted settlers to this area was a rich grassland known as the Ledge, which ranges along the mountain between Balsam Corner and Spruce Mountain. Settlers on both sides of Balsam Mountain, Cataloochee on the east and Straight Fork on the west, herded cattle on the Ledge.

A prominent landmark on the Ledge is Pin Oak Gap, a deep cut in the Balsam Mountain ridgeline that was once known as Spanish Gap. The gap afforded the easiest access for herders driving cattle to the grassy balds on the Ledge from the Round Bottom area of Straight Fork. What was once a cattle track in Pin Oak Gap was adopted as a pioneer wagon road that, in turn, was incorporated into Balsam Mountain Road descending through the gap to Round Bottom.

Over its entire course, the Balsam Mountain Trail is a gradual climb tracing the ridgeline of Balsam Mountain from Pin Oak Gap to the main Smoky divide, where it terminates into the Appalachian Trail. When it leaves Pin Oak Gap, the trail follows a former settlement road, passing through remnants of the old grazing ranges which are now being overtaken by encroachments of American beech and yellow birch stands interspersed with various northern hardwood species. The climb remains gradual for the first mile and a half, at which point the grade stiffens noticeably to ascend a half-mile to Ledge Bald. Though Ledge Bald was once an open range, it is no longer a grassy sward, having succumbed to infestations of white snakeroot and incursions of second-growth forest cover.

Five hundred yards beyond Ledge Bald, the trail drops into a spacious tract of level grassy turf shaded by a few widely spaced trees. In the days of the Smoky Mountain herder, this park-like setting was known as the Big Swag. But for all of its domestic appearance, the Big Swag still remained a remote wilderness outpost. A party traveling on Balsam Mountain during the early part of the twentieth century recorded seeing cattle in the Big Swag. The cattle, attracted by noise made by the hikers, ran into the gap in anticipation of a delivery of salt blocks. The hikers noticed on the backs of a few cattle scars that were the result of attacking bears.

Today the Big Swag is known as Beech Gap. Here, the Beech Gap Trail exits on the left and descends to Round Bottom on Straight Fork Road. Noticeable along both sides of the gap are remnants of railroad lines used by the Suncrest Lumber Company when logging the upper slopes of Balsam Mountains during the early 1930s. Suncrest operated a logging camp in Beech Gap and positioned shanties alongside the rail lines for housing the loggers and their families.

When it eases out of Beech Gap, the Balsam Mountain Trail engages a moderate one-and-a-half-mile climb to Balsam High Top. Here, the trail passes through a tentative fringe of the balsam zone. Elevation is high enough to entice a few scattered red spruce and Fraser fir trees, but not sufficient to produce prolific growth. Nevertheless, an isolated pocket of rich spruce-fir growth heralds the approach to the flat summit of Balsam High Top.

The trail proceeds across Balsam High Top and down the opposite side, being in several places little more than a roughly eroded rut. The erosion is caused by the churning action of horses' hooves and the subsequent washing away by rainwater. At this elevation, particularly in the spruce-fir stands, Smoky Mountain surface soil is too fragile to withstand and recover quickly from abuse by horse traffic.

About 600 yards beyond Balsam High Top, the trail reaches Laurel Gap, an attractive half-acre of closely cropped grassy turf that harbors the Laurel Gap Shelter, one of only three backcountry shelters in the park that are not near the Appalachian Trail. The shelter was built in 1969 by the Youth Conservation Corps on the site of a former Civilian Conservation Corps sub-camp. It is a three-sided stone structure situated in the middle of a level bench facing east with its back to the trail. The shelter was upgraded and remodeled in 2011.

A food-storage cable is found a short distance to the right of the shelter, and water is available at the end of a 200-yard access path leading from the front of the shelter to the far edge of the gap and steeply down to an upper tributary of Lost Bottom Creek. Two hundred feet beyond, on a larger tributary, logs partially buried in the ground can be seen stacked in a side-by-side configuration. They were placed here in this manner by the logging crews to facilitate the movement of timber to a railroad line a mile below.

Upon leaving Laurel Gap, the trail climbs 300 yards to intersect the western terminus of the Mount Sterling Ridge Trail. At this junction the Balsam Mountain Trail turns sharply left to circumnavigate Balsam Corner and enter onto an easy grade that continues until the trail terminates on the main Smoky divide at Tricorner Knob. Balsam Corner marks the conjunction of Mount Sterling Ridge and the main ridge of Balsam Mountain. The name originates from its role as a boundary marker and was first mentioned in an 1898 deed which describes the marker as "a balsam on a rock at the junction of Mt. Sterling Ridge."

Slightly less than one mile above the Mount Sterling Ridge Trail junction, the Balsam Mountain Trail intersects the western terminus of the Gunter Fork Trail exiting to Walnut Bottom on Big Creek. A few yards beyond this junction, the trail returns to the ridgeline, following it for a quarter-mile before rolling off on the east flank where the striking white blossoms of witch-hobble and white erect trilliums are conspicuous among stands of American beeches and gnarled old yellow birch trees. Openings in the forest cover afford fine views down the Gunter Fork drainage and into the Big Creek basin where rows of ramifying ridges projecting down from the main Smoky divide enmesh with those of Mount Sterling Ridge.

After a half-mile on the eastern flank, the trail crosses over the Balsam Mountain ridgeline and into spruce-fir stands along the western flank. On the ridgeline and above the trail to the right is the high peak Luftee Knob, which was first measured by the famed Swiss geologist Arnold Guyot in 1859.

 In his "Notes on the Geography of the Mountain District of Western North Carolina," Guyot described Luftee Knob as "a remarkable conical peak." Guyot understood Luftee Knob to be "the beginning of the Smoky Mountain chain proper, which by general elevation both at its peaks and its crests, by its perfect continuity, its great roughness and difficulty of approach, may be called the master chain of the Appalachian system." Guyot's error in believing that Luftee Knob resides on the main Smoky Mountain divide was probably a reflection of a misunderstanding current among the local mountaineers that the state line followed Balsam Mountain. Although a survey had been run along the main divide by William Davenport in 1821, George Masa once noted that many old-timers living in this part of the mountains believed the state line between Tennessee and North Carolina followed the spine of Mount Sterling Ridge, then along Balsam Mountain, over Luftee Knob, and on to Tricorner Knob on the main Smoky divide.

An examination of Guyot's route into the Smokies may shed some light on the source of his error. On his first attempt to measure the high peaks, Guyot actually followed the true course of the main divide, beginning from a stone marker placed on the "Cataloochee turnpike" by William Davenport to indicate the boundary between Tennessee and North Carolina. Advancing through the wilderness from this point apparently proved to be insurmountable, so he retreated and tried again a year later. On his subsequent approach, it appears Guyot entered through the Oconaluftee River Valley, eventually reaching "Luftee Knob, head of Straight Fork of Oconaluftee River," a peak he refers to elsewhere as "The Pillar, head of Straight Fork of Oconaluftee River." Guyot concluded that the Pillar was "the beginning of the Smoky Mountain chain proper," thus reinforcing the local conviction that the state-line divide followed the spine of Balsam Mountain.

When Guyot reached the true state-line at Tricorner Knob, he could not have failed to notice two high peaks looming immediately to the east. These were the yet unnamed Mount Guyot and Old Black. After venturing out and measuring both peaks, the geologist returned to Tricorner Knob and then proceeded west along the divide without realizing both peaks were on the state line. In his notes Guyot incorrectly identifies both as being "wholly within the state of Tennessee."

The Balsam Mountain Trail passes below the summit of Luftee Knob. A faint access trail leads two hundred feet to the top. However, there is no vantage point, the density of intervening spruce and fir being characteristic of the impassable obstruction and pitfall that continually hindered Guyot in his quest to measure the high peaks of the eastern Smokies.

A half-mile beyond Luftee Knob, the trail circles immediately beneath the summit of a minor peak, Thermo Knob. The name is derived from Thermometer Knob, the name Guyot bequeathed to the peak after breaking a thermometer there. A mile farther, the trail passes beneath Mount Yonaguska, a peak Guyot identified as Raven Knob, likely to correspond with Raven Fork, the large stream whose tributaries drain the slopes below Mount Yonaguska. The peak's name was changed to Mount Yonaguska by the North Carolina Nomenclature Committee as a tribute to the famous Cherokee chief "Drowning Bear" who was successful in holding his people to the mountains, exhorting them to resist the debilitating influences of the white settlers, and to maintain the traditional Cherokee religion. In the interval between Luftee Knob and Mount Yonaguska, the trail enters an enclave of fir and spruce whose silence, stillness, and diffused light invoke imaginings of the enchanted forests of folklore.

Beyond Mount Yonaguska, the trail swings down to the right and into an attractive gap that once marked the upper terminus of the Hyatt Ridge Trail. According to the Sierra Club *Hiker's Guide to the Smokies,* the Hyatt Ridge Trail was still "newly opened" as late as 1973. A few years afterward, the upper five miles of the trail were abandoned, thus fixing the trail's terminus at the McGee Spring Backcountry Campsite (#44). The gap below Mount Yonaguska also marked the upper terminus of a trail yet older than the Hyatt Ridge course. This trail followed the spine of nearby Dashoge Ridge leading up six miles from the Three Forks headwaters of Raven Fork. Both of these old trails have vanished beneath the onslaughts of nature.

Beyond the gap, the Balsam Mountain Trail edges back toward the ridgeline and then proceeds a final half-mile to terminate into the Appalachian Trail on the stateline divide just west of Tricorner Knob. Access to the nearby Tricorner Knob Shelter is 130 yards west along the Appalachian Trail.

HYATT RIDGE TRAIL

Straight Fork Road at Round Bottom to the McGee Spring Backcountry Campsite (#44)—4.4 miles.

POINT OF DEPARTURE: From the Oconaluftee Visitor Center drive south to Big Cove Road near the park boundary at Cherokee, North Carolina. Turn left onto Big Cove Road and drive 9.0 miles to its intersection with Straight Fork Road. Turn right on Straight Fork Road, and drive 3.0 miles. The Hyatt Ridge Trail begins on the left side of the road.

QUAD MAPS: Bunches Bald 174-SW
Luftee Knob 174-NW

0.0—Straight Fork Road.
1.1—Hyatt Creek.
1.8—Low Gap. Enloe Creek Trail exits left 3.6 miles to the Hughes Ridge
Trail.
3.5—Beech Gap Trail exits right 2.8 miles to Straight Fork Road.
4.4—McGee Spring Backcountry Campsite (#44).

When the North Carolina Nomenclature Committee began identifying place-names found on the Carolina side of the Smokies, the committee uncovered frequent recurrences of identical names being used in multiple sections of the Smokies. The committee located, for example, several instances of Mill Creek, Big Creek, Laurel Branch, and Low Gap. One such Low Gap was found on Hyatt Ridge, a minor range that separates Raven Fork from its primary tributary, Straight Fork. Low Gap marked the intersection of two trails, one ascending from Raven Fork up the west flank of Hyatt Ridge, the other ascending from Straight Fork. The former track is now incorporated into the Enloe Creek Trail while the latter has become part of the Hyatt Ridge Trail, although the name Low Gap has been abandoned.

The Hyatt Ridge Trail begins along Straight Fork Road just upstream from the confluence of Hyatt Creek and Straight Fork. It climbs quickly out of the bottomland flanking Straight Fork and onto a rough jeep track that follows the course of the stream. Initially the grade is moderate, winding through stands of second-growth yellow poplar and sugar maple. During the growing season, encroachments by a virulent strain of stinging nettle reduce the track to a narrow file. Slightly less than a mile above the road, the trail crosses Hyatt Creek, where the grade becomes markedly steeper and oaks and eastern hemlocks enter the mix of tree species.

After crossing the stream, the trail continues for almost another mile before reaching the spine of Hyatt Ridge at the place once known as Low Gap. Here, the Hyatt Ridge Trail intersects the western terminus of the Enloe Creek Trail, then turns right, and climbs out of the gap. After about a half-mile, the grade eases to a pleasant stroll along the ridgeline before proceeding into a long drop to another gap. The hiking, nevertheless, remains easy. The woods are fairly open with boles of fallen American chestnut trees scattered across the forest floor. Spruce trees begin to appear.

After a moderate half-mile climb, the trail enters a level bench that marks the southern reach of Hyatt Bald. Here, it encounters the upper terminus of the west half of the Beech Gap Trail leading up from Straight Fork Road. From this juncture, the Hyatt Ridge Trail circles around the east flank of the bald and into a gentle gradient overrun with weeds and shaded by thin stands of chestnut oak, yellow birch, American beech, and red maple. The trail winds through the gradient for a hundred yards or so before dropping into a shallow basin that harbors the McGee Spring Backcountry Campsite (#44). The trail ends at the campsite.

The McGee Spring Camp is an open spacious site with spare slopes of wild-flowers along one side and stands of yellow buckeye and red spruce around the edges. In spite of its size, the camp has very few level spots that are free of dampness or standing water. The lower end of the camp is saturated in a network of seepages. The middle, while a bit drier, is rough and uneven. Along the upper periphery is a small detachment that is not ideal, but offers the best alternative. Clear water is available in abundance from McGee Spring, a small fissure in a rock outcropping a few yards below the campsite.

The Hyatt Ridge Trail did not always stop at the McGee Spring Camp. Instead of turning down into the campsite, the trail stayed on the ridge and continued for another two miles to Roses Gap, where it turned left and climbed onto Dashoge Ridge. Following Dashoge, the old trail crossed Mount Harrison and then terminated on Mount Yonaguska along the Balsam Mountain Trail about a half-mile below the state-line divide at Tricorner Knob. The point from which the old Hyatt Ridge Trail continued from the McGee Spring Camp also marked the upper end of the Breakneck Ridge Trail, which proceeded west from the bald and descended to Three Forks, the head of Raven Fork. Neither of these old courses can be hiked. Both have long since been submerged in undergrowth and blow-downs.

BEECH GAP TRAIL–WEST

Straight Fork Road at Round Bottom to the Hyatt Ridge Trail—2.8 miles.

POINT OF DEPARTURE: Follow directions to the Hyatt Ridge Trail and drive another 1.3 miles along Straight Fork Road to the bridge over Straight Fork. The Beech Gap Trail–West begins at the bridge on the left side of the road.

QUAD MAPS: Bunches Bald 174-SW

Luftee Knob 174-NW

0.0—Round Bottom. Straight Fork Road.

1.3—Grass Branch.

2.2—False gap.

2.8—Hyatt Ridge Trail exits right 0.9 mile to the McGee Spring Backcountry Campsite (#44) and left 3.5 miles to Straight Fork Road.

BEECH GAP TRAIL–EAST

Straight Fork Road at Round Bottom to the Balsam Mountain Trail at Beech Gap—2.5 miles.

POINT OF DEPARTURE: Follow directions to the Beech Gap Trail–West and continue another 285 yards on Straight Fork Road to the intersection with Balsam Mountain Road. The Beech Gap Trail–East begins on the left side of the road.

QUAD MAPS: Bunches Bald 174-SW
Luftee Knob 174-NW

0.0—Round Bottom. Straight Fork Road.
0.3—Thumper Branch.
0.4—Switchback.
2.0—Table Rock Branch.
2.5—Beech Gap. Balsam Mountain Trail exits left 7.8 miles to the
  Appalachian Trail and right 2.3 miles to Balsam Mountain Road at Pin
  Oak Gap.

The Beech Gap Trail is a lateral connector linking the Hyatt Ridge Trail with the Balsam Mountain Trail. Hyatt Ridge is separated from Balsam Mountain by the Straight Fork drainage, which harbors a wide intervale known as Round Bottom. Vehicle access into Round Bottom is along Straight Fork Road, that, in effect, bisects the Beech Gap Trail—one "half" ascending to the crest of Hyatt Ridge, the other to Balsam Mountain. Since both "halves" of the Beech Gap Trail are most likely to be accessed from Straight Fork Road, the trail is being treated here as though it were two separate trails provisionally identified as Beech Gap Trail–West and Beech Gap Trail–East.

The **Beech Gap Trail–West** begins along Straight Fork Road about seventy-five yards below the bridge over Straight Fork on a moderately level course that proceeds up the Straight Fork gorge. The slopes flanking the stream were denuded of trees by the Parson Pulp and Lumber Company through the 1920s. Over the eighty years since Parson departed from the Smokies, yellow poplars have proven to be the most prolific tree species regenerating along Straight Fork. In springtime, trilliums, rue anemones, prostrate bluets, white fringed phacelias, and Dutchman's-breeches are conspicuous on the lower slopes.

Soon the trail turns away from the stream, becoming markedly steeper, and degenerating to an uneven rocky course, particularly where feeder streams and seepages leach away the soil. After winding among the contours for a little more than a mile, the trail proceeds to the back of a hollow and crosses Grass Branch, where the stream trickles off a rock ledge and out onto the trail. At this juncture, the trail diminishes to a single-file track angling steeply up and across the flank of Hyatt Ridge. In wintertime or at openings in the forest cover, the long curvature of Balsam Mountain is visible across the Straight Fork drainage.

The trail proceeds with little variation in grade for slightly over a mile before leveling out momentarily and entering into what initially appears to be a gap. This occurrence, known in Smoky Mountain parlance as a "false gap," is noticeable when approaching the point of a finger ridge, particularly one that is level and fairly free of forest cover. As the trail rises to cross the ridge point, it often appears to the hiker to be a characteristic gap in the ridgeline which harbors an intersection marking the trail's end. On a steep climb such as the Beech Gap Trail, false gaps often give rise to false hopes. As a seasoned Smoky Mountaineer once expressed it, "You'll thank you're thar, but ye ain't."

At the false gap, the trail turns sharply left and climbs through open forests littered with fallen boles of American chestnut trees. More remarkable, however, are the extensive patches of trilliums that blanket the slopes on both sides of the trail for several hundred yards. Here, the trail remains a narrow file, but the track ameliorates to a softer cushion underfoot. The appearance of red spruce trees heralds the approach into a true gap where the Beech Gap Trail terminates in an intersection with the Hyatt Ridge Trail.

The **Beech Gap Trail–East** begins along Straight Fork Road 285 yards above the bridge over Straight Fork and just at the point where the road encounters a head-on intersection with the one-way Balsam Mountain Road. For the first seventy-five yards, the trail follows a level roadbed. It then turns sharply right, leaves the roadbed, and enters a stiff climb that does not ease until the trail terminates on Balsam Mountain. Early on, the trail follows a slightly rocky course as it winds through second-growth hardwood stands high above Straight Fork. It proceeds with little variation for nearly 700 yards before crossing Thumper Branch and then, 125 yards farther, executes a sharp switchback. Here, the track degenerates noticeably, worsened by large loosely shifting stones that turn underfoot.

From this juncture, the trail edges momentarily out onto a drier exposure before turning back into a hollow shaded with stands of large oaks and clusters of rhododendron and laurel. A mile above the switchback, it passes through an open weedy slope of seepages that marks the headwaters of Table Rock Branch. At this elevation, the trail is skirting what was once the perimeter of Ledge Bald. Stands of slender American beeches and sugar maples have taken over the bald but have not choked out the thick rich grassy turf that provided fodder for the cattle that once grazed on Balsam Mountain.

The appearance of red spruce heralds the approach into Beech Gap, where the trail terminates into the Balsam Mountain Trail. Beech Gap is a wide flat grassy swag that has more the appearance of a well-kept park than of a mountain ridge. There is very little undergrowth, and the few trees there are of a venerable vintage rather than the tall ramrod-straight Turks of the second-growth generation.

ENLOE CREEK TRAIL

Hyatt Ridge Trail to the Hughes Ridge Trail—3.6 miles.
POINT OF DEPARTURE: Hike 1.8 miles up the Hyatt Ridge Trail to the intersection in the gap. The Enloe Creek Trail begins from the west side of the gap.
QUAD MAPS: Bunches Bald 174-SW
Smokemont 165-SE

0.0—Hyatt Ridge Trail.
1.0—Raven Fork. Bridge. Enloe Creek Backcountry Campsite (#47).
2.0—Enloe Creek. Footlog.
3.4—False gap.
3.6—Hughes Ridge Trail exits right 4.6 miles to the Appalachian Trail at Pecks Corner and left 0.4 mile to the Chasteen Creek Trail.

Between Hughes Ridge and its eastern counterpart, Balsam Mountain, the vast Raven Fork basin harbors the most isolated and inaccessible wilderness area within the Great Smoky Mountains. All streams in the basin eventually drain to Raven Fork. Very few trails approach the Raven Fork wilderness, and only one, the Enloe Creek Trail, presumes to encroach on the interior, but even then, merely as a lateral connector traversing the basin's lower reaches.

Access to the Enloe Creek Trail is difficult. Its eastern terminus is anchored in a remote beech gap on Hyatt Ridge where it joins the Hyatt Ridge Trail. Its western terminus is fixed in an equally remote gap on Hughes Ridge, where it intersects the Hughes Ridge Trail.

Beginning at its eastern end, the Enloe Creek Trail drops quickly out of the beech gap and into a steep angling descent along the west flank of Hyatt Ridge, following a narrow hard-packed track through stands of second-growth cove hardwoods. After nearly a mile, the trail enters the Raven Fork gorge with the stream itself coming into view far below to the right. In quick succession, three tight switchbacks conduct the trail steeply down the flank of the mountain to the edge of Raven Fork, and then immediately to a metal frame bridge spanning the stream.

Raven Fork is without question the most rugged stream in the Smokies. As suggested by the enormous boulders and rocky cliffs at streamside, that stretch of Raven Fork downstream from the bridge is known as "the Gorges." Within the Gorges, access to Raven Fork is difficult, in many places entailing near vertical scrambles down high boulders whose surfaces have been worn smooth by the agents of nature. Here, the channels run deep and the current swift.

 There is some lack of agreement as well as some doubt as to the source of the name "Raven" as applied to the stream. According to H. C. Wilburn, the most common explanation currently given is associated with a high, jutting, rock cliff with many fissures and cracks found on the southern end of a spur of Hyatt Ridge. Former inhabitants of the area contend that, until the 1930s, ravens roosted on ledges in this rock. The place consequently became known as Raven Rocks. By the force of frequent reference to Raven Rocks, a corresponding Raven Fork was applied to the nearby stream.

Wilburn, however, is convinced that Raven Rocks is a recent manifestation and that the true source of the name is of older vintage. According to a tradition handed down to Wilburn by an old Smoky Mountaineer named Taylor Gass, there was a sub-chief of the Cherokee known as "the Raven" who is said to have lived on Raven Fork near the mouth of Mingo Creek, a place later known as the Hill Place. Sometime shortly after the Revolutionary War when white settlers began encroaching on Indian territory in and around the northwest corner of the Great Smoky Mountains, the Raven led a raiding party into the settlements, returning with several white scalps. In accordance with Cherokee custom, a great celebration and scalp-dance was held by the Raven and his warriors in which women and children participated. The scalp-dance took place on a tribal ceremony ground which was beside a deep place in the river. Enraged whites from the settlements tracked down the Raven and his war party to the ceremony ground and surprised them at the height of their celebrating. In the fight that followed, the Raven and some of his followers were killed. Others, in an effort to escape, took to the deep water and drowned. Wilburn believes the events took place in the 1780s.

Gass also told Wilburn that, when he was a boy, somewhere between twelve and fifteen years of age, an old Indian name Charlie Long showed him three white scalps—one of a man, slightly graying, one of a woman with long light hair, and the third of a child, fine and almost white. The scalps, said old Charlie, had been kept in his family for a long time. Furthermore, Charlie Long confided he was a descendent of the Raven.

The tradition passed down by Gass is corroborated to some extent by old place-names in the Smokies. The site where the Raven and his warriors were holding their scalp-dance is very likely the bottomland immediately below what more recently became known as the Hill Place. The Hill Place was formerly occupied by one of the Mingus families but was purchased in the 1840s by Col. William Thomas in his effort to secure the Cherokee a homeland in the Smokies. Old land grants indicate that the Hill Place was known as "Raven's old place" as early as 1812. The stream below the "Raven's old place" was cited as Raven's Creek as early as 1795.

At the far end of the bridge, the Enloe Creek Backcountry Campsite (#47) is fitted deftly on a small bench perched against a cliff high over Raven Fork. The fact that the name Enloe is assigned to a campsite on the edge of Raven Fork is a peculiar inconsistency in Smoky Mountain nomenclature. Enloe Creek does, however, empty into Raven Fork about a quarter-mile downstream of the campsite.

Notwithstanding the intrusion of the bridge, the Enloe Creek Camp setting is among the most attractive in the Smokies—a small plat of level ground partially turfed with grass, enclosed tightly on three sides by near-vertical cliffs, and exposed to a precipitous drop over the stream gorge on the open side. The more suitable part of the camp is along the upper side. Run-off during heavy rain tends to collect on the bare ground at the lower side of the camp.

Food-storage cables in the Enloe Creek camp are suspended from metal beams cantilevered from the end of the bridge framework. Campers who feel that the cable at full hoist is insufficient to evade the reach of marauding bears may opt for a nearby alternative maypole-type storage device. The "maypole" consists of series of hooks arranged around the perimeter of a metal disk affixed to the top of the pole. A second, shorter pole with a "fork" end is used to hoist packs onto the hooks. The pole storage is effective against bears, but is likewise out of reach of shorter campers.

The Enloe Creek Trail passes through the middle of the campsite and exits along the back corner near the maypole. It then angles steeply up the adjacent slope on a course roughly parallel to Raven Fork. Within a quarter-mile, the trail enters a long graduated veer to the right, edging away from the Raven Fork gorge and into the Enloe Creek drainage. At the point of transition, neither Raven Fork nor Enloe Creek is visible from the trail. Enloe Creek finally comes into view about a half-mile above the campsite, but even then only at a respectable distance. During the cooler seasons when intervening vegetation is not too dense, several small waterfalls and shoals can be seen gracing the slow-moving stream.

From the time of the earliest recreational visitors to the Smokies, Enloe Creek was noted as an excellent stream for deep-woods backcountry camping. Horace Kephart and George Masa occasionally camped on Enloe Creek, and Kelly Bennett, the pharmacist from Bryson City who was instrumental in promoting the new national park, was known to camp with his family high up on the stream. J. S. Coleman Jr., a newspaper editor for the *Asheville Times* who camped here during the summer of 1929, alluded to the fine campsites on Enloe Creek as being due to Enloe Creek, unlike most streams in the Smokies, not dashing down the mountain in a hurry to reach the larger stream below: "Within a mile or two of the main lead, Enloe flows gently along an almost level bed, leaving a fairly wide plain along its banks for a distance of nearly three miles."

Two miles above the campsite, the trail approaches Enloe Creek and crosses on a long slender footlog suspended low over the stream. It immediately climbs through an exceptionally wet, exceptionally rocky terrain that is almost hazardous to traverse. A hundred yards up, the trail eases onto a more suitable track and soon enters an old-growth cove-hardwood forest of remarkable fecundity. Wildflowers, weeds, and low woody growth encroach on the trail which is flanked by venerable red spruces, yellow buckeyes, yellow birches, and Carolina silverbells. The riot of growth in this enclosure is unmatched by all but a few enclaves of the Smokies.

A mile above the stream crossing, the trail completes a wide double-switchback that directs the trail away from the Enloe Creek drainage and onto the east flank of Hughes Ridge. The grade remains steep and the course narrow, but conditions become somewhat less rocky. Five hundred yards above the switchback, the trail passes through a false gap and into an open forest of second-growth hardwoods. Along here the slopes are blanketed with ranks of large-flower trilliums interspersed with wild geraniums and violets. Soon the Enloe Creek Trail terminates into the Hughes Ridge Trail in an attractive swag on the spine of Hughes Ridge.

HUGHES RIDGE TRAIL

Chasteen Creek Trail to the Appalachian Trail at Pecks Corner—5.0 miles.

POINT OF DEPARTURE: Hike to the end of the Chasteen Creek Trail, or hike to the end of the Enloe Creek Trail. The Hughes Ridge Trail begins at the end of the Chasteen Creek Trail and 0.4 miles down the ridge from the end of the Enloe Creek Trail.

QUAD MAPS: Smokemont 165-SE
Mount Guyot 165-NE

0.0—Chasteen Creek Trail.
0.4—Enloe Creek Trail exits right 3.6 miles to the Hyatt Ridge Trail.
2.9—Bradley Fork Trail exits left 7.3 miles to Smokemont Campground.
4.3—Utility shed.
4.7—Access path exits right 50 yards to the Pecks Corner Shelter.
5.0—Pecks Corner. Appalachian Trail.

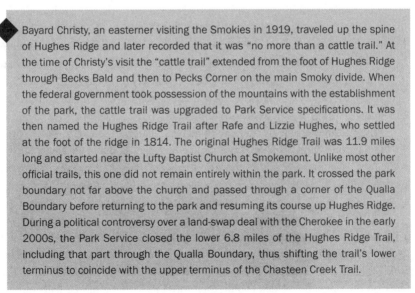

Bayard Christy, an easterner visiting the Smokies in 1919, traveled up the spine of Hughes Ridge and later recorded that it was "no more than a cattle trail." At the time of Christy's visit the "cattle trail" extended from the foot of Hughes Ridge through Becks Bald and then to Pecks Corner on the main Smoky divide. When the federal government took possession of the mountains with the establishment of the park, the cattle trail was upgraded to Park Service specifications. It was then named the Hughes Ridge Trail after Rafe and Lizzie Hughes, who settled at the foot of the ridge in 1814. The original Hughes Ridge Trail was 11.9 miles long and started near the Lufty Baptist Church at Smokemont. Unlike most other official trails, this one did not remain entirely within the park. It crossed the park boundary not far above the church and passed through a corner of the Qualla Boundary before returning to the park and resuming its course up Hughes Ridge. During a political controversy over a land-swap deal with the Cherokee in the early 2000s, the Park Service closed the lower 6.8 miles of the Hughes Ridge Trail, including that part through the Qualla Boundary, thus shifting the trail's lower terminus to coincide with the upper terminus of the Chasteen Creek Trail.

The Hughes Ridge Trail is difficult to access. The Chasteen Creek Trail and Enloe Creek Trail reach the Hughes Ridge Trail along its lower end, the Bradley Fork Trail along its midpoint, and the Appalachian Trail at the upper end, but all require long difficult hikes.

The lower end of the Hughes Ridge Trail is anchored in a featureless opening on the ridgeline where the Chasteen Creek Trail rolls up onto the ridge. When Bayard Christy ventured through here in 1919, the principal forest cover was American chestnut with a mix of chestnut oaks, sugar maples, black cherries, and some yellow poplars. The chestnuts later perished from a blight inadvertently imported into the United States on nursery plants. Flanking the trail are huge boles of fallen chestnuts that testify to the abundance of this tree on Hughes Ridge.

From here, the Hughes Ridge Trail starts on a moderate climb following a single-file track along the ridgeline. In places the track is a rough rut scoured by the run-off of heavy rainfall. In others it is even and soft underfoot. In early spring, flame azaleas are the most conspicuous flowering species, although wood-betony, spiderwort, bowman's root, fire pink, prostrate bluets, whorled loosestrife, painted trillium, and trailing arbutus grace the understory.

After nearly a half-mile, the trail intersects on the right the upper terminus of the Enloe Creek Trail leading up from Raven Fork. At this point, the Hughes Ridge Trail rolls off the ridgeline and begins an irregular cadence of moderate climbs and descents while negotiating a succession of minor knobs and swags. Over this interval the trail is soft underfoot, passing alternately through gaps darkened with eastern hemlocks, fields of wildflowers, and stands of second-growth cove hardwoods. About one-and-a-half miles above the Enloe Creek Trail junction, the Hughes Ridge Trail drops into a noticeable gap once known by Smoky Mountaineers as the Strawberry Patch. When an exploring party sponsored by the *Asheville Times* ventured here in 1929, they recorded having stopped in the Strawberry Patch to rest at a spring and enjoy the spectacular ferns growing on the slopes nearby. Photographs from the trip show ferns growing as high as a man's shoulder.

By the time the trail reaches the Strawberry Patch, it is in the lower fringe of the balsam zone. The occasional red spruce has already made an appearance and, as the trail continues ascending, the cove hardwoods begin giving way to American beeches, yellow birches, Fraser magnolias, and mountain maples. Higher-elevation flowering species like blue bead lilies and Canada mayflowers also begin to appear.

A mile above the Strawberry Patch, the trail enters a wide flat grassy gap where it intersects the upper terminus of the Bradley Fork Trail rising in from the left. During the early years of the Great Smoky Mountains National Park, the Bradley Fork Trail was a serviceable jeep road over which vehicles could reach Hughes Ridge. Once on the ridge, the vehicles could then travel to within almost a half-mile of the main Smoky divide. Vehicles no longer travel Hughes Ridge, but that part of the trail above the Bradley Fork intersection still bears signs of its former heritage as a jeep track. The track is often rough and rutted, full of loose stones, and congested with weeds. The course is generally a climb, in a couple of places fairly steeply. At irregular intervals the climbing is relieved by short occasional descents. On the last descent, the trail passes a small utility shack on the right that was once used as a horse patrol cabin, but now serves as a backcountry ranger and maintenance crew outpost. From here, the trail continues, descending another 700 yards to a small spruce gap that harbors the Pecks Corner Shelter.

The Pecks Corner Shelter is fifty yards along an access path to the right of the trail. It is situated at the north end of a deep V-shaped draw that extends precipitously down the mountain. The only water available is 150 yards down the draw at a bold pipe-assisted spring. The shelter has been recently remodeled with an extended roof that overhangs a small portico providing coverage for a table and a few benches. A pit toilet is readily accessible along the Hughes Ridge Trail just opposite the access path to the shelter.

This gap has likely been the site of a camp from the time of the earliest human visitors to this part of the Smokies. Bayard Christy recalled having been shown on the ridgeline nearby a low artificial mound that the Cherokee called Buffalo Grave. Whatever legend was attached to Buffalo Grave, Christy did not know. Whatever outpost the Cherokee may have had here was superseded by a surveyor's camp. Bayard Christy and Paul Fink both record seeing the remains of the surveyor's camp in 1919. By the time Harvey Broome visited in 1928, a cabin had replaced the surveyor's camp. Twenty-six years later Broome stayed at a shelter here, which he recalled as being "an open-front log shelter which blended unobtrusively into the surrounding woods."

In January 1955, a lone hiker named Charles Lindsley was traveling east along the Appalachian Trail, planning to spend the night in the same open-front shelter that Broome had visited a year earlier. On reaching Dry Sluice Gap at 2:30 in the afternoon, Lindsley found the Sawteeth covered in ice and buried in knee-deep snow that was deeper still in the drifts and wind-rows. The snow was frozen over with a thin crust that would not quite support his weight.

Lindsley found progress slow and exhausting. The footing was difficult and the going hard. It took him over three hours to reach Laurel Top, arriving as the last glow of day was fading. It was nearly three miles to the shelter on Hughes Ridge, and Lindsley seriously considered remaining on Laurel Top for the night. However, the prospect of a night in the shelter was more attractive than one in the snow on an open ridge, so he struggled on and reached Pecks Corner shortly after eight o'clock.

Lindsley turned down Hughes Ridge and in a few minutes entered the gap that harbored the shelter. Without a thought he turned off the trail and walked down the access path to the shelter only to discover it not to be where he expected. Lindsley was familiar with the camp yet found himself floundering around in the snow and brush. In the dark he could not discern the shelter, so he re-traced his steps to the trail and took off again in the direction it should have been. Still he found nothing. Returning to the trail once again, he carefully walked in the remembered direction. He reached the right spot. The trees and the slope of the ravine looked familiar, but no shelter. After looking around a bit, he found a few charred logs and the low stone foundation buried in the snow.

While absorbing this stunning disappointment, Lindsley vaguely noticed a pile of clothing near his feet. Poking at it idly with his walking stick, he found it to be hard. On closer inspection and using a flashlight, he discovered a hand and then the face of a man. Clearly the man was dead. There was no immediate evidence of foul play, but black smudges on the dead man's face and hand suggested that he had something to do with the fire that had burned down the shelter. The dead man was clad in light cotton pants and shirt and wore a light jacket. No shoes were on his feet, and he had no camping equipment, food, or utensils.

Since he was twelve miles from the nearest ranger station, Lindsley checked his initial impulse to run for help and settled into his sleeping bag in the snow and fixed supper. Throughout the night he turned over in his mind the many possibilities and finally concluded that his unfortunate companion had been dead about a week, caught in a bitter cold that had suddenly followed a spell of unseasonably warm weather. Lindsley figured the man had stopped at the shelter on the evening before the cold snap. After building a fire too close under the overhanging roof, he had escaped the shelter when it caught fire. Lindsley conjectured that the man must have lain down to sleep among the warm ruins of the shelter and had frozen in his sleep. The reason the man would be at Pecks Corner this time of year he could only guess.

The next morning Lindsley descended the Hughes Ridge Trail to a jeep track that is now the Bradley Fork Trail. After making a report to the park authorities, he accompanied three rangers on a return to the shelter by jeep. One of the rangers immediately recognized the victim as an Indian from the Cherokee reservation adjacent to the park. The ranger suspected that the man had been on a regular "milk run" from Tennessee to the reservation on the North Carolina side. Four two-quart jars of moonshine in the snow nearby confirmed the ranger's hunch. The fact that three jars were nearly half-empty explained why the man had been unable to handle his predicament. Knowledge of his mission had probably kept his family from reporting him missing or hunting for him. The rangers agreed with Lindsley's conclusion about the time and circumstances of the accident. The official verdict of the coroner was "death by exposure."

The open-faced stone structure that is now the Pecks Corner Shelter was built to replace the log shelter that was burned down by the unfortunate Indian.

When the Hughes Ridge Trail leaves the Pecks Corner Shelter, it climbs a rocky course 655 yards to terminate into the Appalachian Trail at a steeply pitched galled spot immediately below Pecks Corner, an old survey point on the state-line divide.

✦ OCONALUFTEE ✦

Oconaluftee is allegedly a corruption of the Cherokee word Egwanulti, which means "by the river" and refers to a network of small villages built along the stream by the Indians. The Cherokee name for the river itself seems to have been Nununyi, corresponding to the name of an Indian village that once stood near the present site of the Oconaluftee Visitor Center. Land grants issued by the state of North Carolina in the 1790s refer to the Oconaluftee as "Nuna," a name which probably resulted from the settlers' attempts to pronounce Nununyi.

The Oconaluftee River follows the seam of the Oconaluftee Fault, a fracture in the bedrock of the Great Smoky Mountains that makes the watershed particularly susceptible to erosion. Consequently, the bottoms flanking the stream in the Oconaluftee drainage are generally wider and more suitable for agriculture than those of most other watersheds in the mountains. The upper rim of the Oconaluftee basin is a vast curved headwall of the main Smoky divide between Newfound Gap and Pecks Corner. The basin is bounded on the east by Hughes Ridge and the west by Thomas Divide.

The Oconaluftee River basin was likely the site of the earliest white settlements in the Smokies. Not only did the settlers find abandoned Cherokee villages and fields ready for expropriation, but they discovered entry into the higher elevations expedited by ancient Indian trails leading across the mountain. One trail followed up the Raven Fork tributary to Straight Fork and then climbed up and over Balsam Mountain to Big Creek. Smoky Mountain legend contends that the Shawnee used this old trace as a warpath when advancing on the Cherokee in the Oconaluftee and Tuckasegee valleys. A second Cherokee trace proceeded upstream along the Oconaluftee, then followed the spine of Richland Mountain to cross the main Smoky divide and enter Tennessee at Dry Sluice Gap. A third remained along the Oconaluftee, eventually crossing the main divide at Indian Gap and exiting through Tennessee on the Great Indian War Path.

In 1831, the North Carolina General Assembly authorized the Oconaluftee Turnpike Company to build a wagon road up the Oconaluftee River and over the mountain at Indian Gap, following generally the course of the old Indian trail. The turnpike was completed in 1839 and for several years was operated as a toll road. During the Civil War, the road was upgraded by a force of six hundred Cherokee under the direction of Confederate Colonel William Holland Thomas and used by the warring armies dispatching troops and munitions across the mountains. What sort of road it may have been during its prime may be judged from the fact that a detachment of General Robert Vance's Confederates had to dismount their cannons from the carriages and drag them over the boulders. During the 1930s, sections of the road were incorporated into the course of the federal highway that now crosses the main divide at Newfound Gap.

The Oconaluftee section is divided along a north-south axis by US441, which provides access to the Oconaluftee Visitor Center and Smokemont Campground. On the west side of the highway, Mingus Creek, Newton Bald, and Kanati Fork trails climb from the river bottom to the spine of Thomas Divide. Most of the remaining trails in this section fan out in a nexus east of the river. All trails in this section are easily reached from US441.

The Oconaluftee section harbors four backcountry campsites and one shelter. The Newton Bald Backcountry Campsite (#52) is west of the river. The Lower Chasteen (#50), Upper Chasteen (#48), and Cabin Flats (#49) camps are east of Bradley Fork. The Kephart Prong Shelter resides in the middle of the Oconaluftee basin at the intersection of the Kephart Prong, Grassy Branch, and Sweat Heifer Creek trails.

OCONALUFTEE RIVER TRAIL

Oconaluftee Visitor Center to the park boundary at Cherokee, North Carolina—1.6 miles.

POINT OF DEPARTURE: From the Oconaluftee Visitor Center, walk around back to the Mountain Farm Museum. The Oconaluftee River Trail begins near the entrance to the museum.

QUAD MAPS: Smokemont 165-SE
Whittier 166-NE

0.0—Oconaluftee Visitor Center. Mountain Farm Museum.
0.2—Light-gravel track.
0.7—Blue Ridge Parkway viaduct.
1.1—Wooden bridge.
1.5—Big Cove Road.
1.6—Park boundary. Cherokee, North Carolina.

Archaeologists sifting through the loam of the Oconaluftee River basin have discovered evidence suggesting that the bottomland along the river was once inhabited by primitive tribes of Woodlands Indians as early as eight thousand years ago. More recently, the Cherokee built towns along the stream and referred to one of them as Egwanulti, meaning "by the river." Around 1790, white settlers began arriving in this part of the Smokies, displacing the Cherokee and corrupting Egwanulti to Oconaluftee, or Luftee, as it was familiarly known. Over time, variant spellings of this word began to appear on deeds, maps, and other records. The most common was Ocana Lufty, a name that was also given to the post office at the mouth of Couches Creek.

The Cherokee name for the river itself seems to have been Nununyi, corresponding with the name of a village that once stood near the present site of the Oconaluftee Visitor Center. Land grants issued by the state of North Carolina in the 1790s refer to the river as "Nuna," a name that probably resulted from the settlers' efforts to pronounce Nununyi. However, in an entry to Felix Walker in 1796, there is a reference "that this creek is called by John McDowell and others, Oconolufty."

In 1805 a settler, Abe Enloe ventured into this vicinity of the Smokies and settled on the banks of the Oconaluftee. According to an enduring strain of Smoky Mountain lore, Enloe brought with him an orphaned servant girl of about eighteen years of age named Nancy Hanks. Enloe had a daughter about the same age who was also named Nancy. Against the wishes of her family, the daughter Nancy eloped to Kentucky with a man named Thompson. Soon after the elopement, the servant girl Nancy became pregnant.

Stories vary on whether Nancy Hanks had her baby in the Enloe house or whether she was removed before the baby was born. In either case, the daughter, Nancy Enloe Thompson, reconciled with her parents, came back to her home on the Oconaluftee for a visit. On her return to Kentucky, she took Nancy Hanks, either pregnant or with infant son, to live with her. Soon after her removal to Kentucky, Nancy Hanks married Thomas Lincoln, the man who was later presumed to be the father of Abraham Lincoln.

The story of Abraham Lincoln's paternity was broached in an article published in the *Charlotte Observer* in 1893 by a writer who identified himself as a "Student of History" and who claimed that Abe Enloe was the real father of Abraham Lincoln. Whether true or not, the story quickly gained traction in several subsequent publications, most notably James H. Cathey's *Truth Is Stranger than Fiction: True Genesis of a Wonderful Man* and persists today as part and parcel of Smoky Mountain lore.

Thomas Robinson Dawley Jr., a government official visiting the Oconaluftee in 1907, was shown an old partially demolished log house that was then being used as a barn. Dawley was informed that in this house, Nancy Hanks, mother of Abraham Lincoln, served as a house girl. The original Enloe house was a two-storied cabin built of hewn logs and was the biggest and best in the county for miles around. It stood in an extensive piece of bottomland that now harbors the Oconaluftee Visitor Center and Mountain Farm Museum.

Bayard Christy, a traveler into the Oconaluftee River Valley when the Cherokee and white settlers were both living on the river bottoms, remarked on the differences in the living accommodations of the two races. The Indians' cabins, Christy noted, "were snuggled away behind thickets—hidden, like birds' nests—or perhaps pirated away on mountainsides. The white man builds by the wayside, and builds pretentiously; a white man's house in the woods always has that in appearance which jars; there is something raw about it. The Indian has here a wild animal trait; instead of pretentiousness, is the opposite quality; the tendency is for the Indian's home to merge into the surroundings, to belong where it stands, to attract attention only as a rock or the bark of a tree attracts—an integral part of a harmonious whole."

The Oconaluftee River Trail begins behind the Oconaluftee Visitor Center on a wide concrete sidewalk leading to the Mountain Farm Museum. At the entrance to the museum, the trail turns right onto a grassy track along the outside of a split-rail fence separating the museum compound from Abraham Enloe's old farm fields.

 The Mountain Farm Museum contains an impressive collection of original Smoky Mountain architecture and artifacts. It includes a cabin, barn, corncrib, outhouse, apple-barn, and other outbuildings and is intended to replicate the variety of buildings that would be found on a small Smoky Mountain family farm, the basic economic unit of the mountain frontier. The cabin, built at the end of the nineteenth century by John and Creasy Davis, stood on Thomas Divide above Indian Creek until it was moved to the museum in 1952. The apple-barn was used in a business operated by Will Messer, the wealthiest inhabitant in Little Cataloochee. These are two of only a few examples of representative pioneer architecture on the North Carolina side of the Smokies that survived burning by the Park Service.

Noticeable along the rail fence enclosing the museum compound are black walnut trees, a domesticated species planted by the settlers. At the lower end of the compound, the trail reaches the river, turns, and proceeds downstream on a light-gravel track.

At this elevation, the Oconaluftee River is a wide stream overhung with thick-limbed sycamores. The water appears clear emerald-green with many-colored stones of granite and transparent quartz forming a bottom pavement. Only the trail and a thin tree-line separate the river from Abraham Enloe's open fields.

A half-mile along the river, the trail passes under a viaduct of the Blue Ridge Parkway. By the time it reaches this point, it has left the pastoral setting of the farm and river to enter the noisy commotion of traffic on the parkway overpass, Big Cove Road across the river, and Newfound Gap Road nearby on the right. Along here the river bank appears fatigued and forlorn, worn down by continual visits by tourists.

Beyond the viaduct, the trail edges away from the stream and closer to Newfound Gap Road. After winding through woods for a half-mile, it then crosses a wooden bridge over a small stream. Almost a half-mile beyond the bridge, the trail crosses Big Cove Road and then continues for another hundred yards to terminate abruptly at a sidewalk that leads into the tourist town of Cherokee, North Carolina. Ironically, the Cherokee town possesses fully that quality which Bayard Christy noted of the white man's house in the woods. It "has that in appearance which jars."

MINGUS CREEK TRAIL

Mingus Mill on Newfound Gap Road to the Newton Bald Trail—5.8 miles.

POINT OF DEPARTURE: From the Oconaluftee Visitor Center drive north on Newfound Gap Road (US441) 0.5 mile to Mingus Mill. The Mingus Creek Trail begins at the end of the parking area adjacent to the mill.

QUAD MAP: Smokemont 165-SE

0.0—Mingus Mill parking area.
0.2—Mingus Creek. Bridge.
0.4—Mingus Creek. Bridge.
0.9—Mingus Creek. Bridge.
1.2—Feeder stream. Footlog.
1.2—Access road to the Mingus Creek Cemetery.
1.3—Madcap Branch.
2.2—Switchback.
2.9—Deeplow Gap Trail exits left 6.1 miles to the Indian Creek Trail.
5.8—Newton Bald. Newton Bald Trail exits left 0.6 mile to the Newton Bald Backcountry Campsite (#52) and right 4.8 miles to Newfound Gap Road.

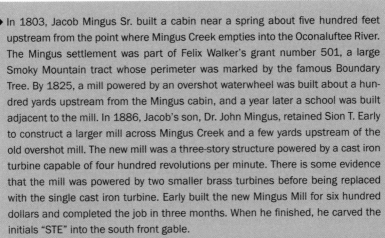

In 1803, Jacob Mingus Sr. built a cabin near a spring about five hundred feet upstream from the point where Mingus Creek empties into the Oconaluftee River. The Mingus settlement was part of Felix Walker's grant number 501, a large Smoky Mountain tract whose perimeter was marked by the famous Boundary Tree. By 1825, a mill powered by an overshot waterwheel was built about a hundred yards upstream from the Mingus cabin, and a year later a school was built adjacent to the mill. In 1886, Jacob's son, Dr. John Mingus, retained Sion T. Early to construct a larger mill across Mingus Creek and a few yards upstream of the old overshot mill. The new mill was a three-story structure powered by a cast iron turbine capable of four hundred revolutions per minute. There is some evidence that the mill was powered by two smaller brass turbines before being replaced with the single cast iron turbine. Early built the new Mingus Mill for six hundred dollars and completed the job in three months. When he finished, he carved the initials "STE" into the south front gable.

Mingus Mill with Sion Early's initials stands directly across Mingus Creek from the trailhead for the Mingus Creek Trail. The mill was rebuilt in 1937 and again in 1968. It is fully operational and open to the public from mid-March until mid-November.

The Mingus Creek Trail begins at the gate along the upper end of the parking area adjacent to the mill. About fifty yards to the right of the gate is an old slave cemetery occupied by a few unmarked fieldstones. The trail leaves the gate on a wide easy track along the stream near where a 150-yard sluice of oak boards diverts water from Mingus Creek to a wooden millrace that conducts the flow into the mill's penstock. At the upstream end a wooden gate regulates the flow into the millrace.

Seventy yards beyond the watergate, the trail crosses Mingus Creek on a wooden bridge. Three hundred and fifty yard farther, it crosses a second time on a bridge and then immediately enters a large open space once occupied by a Civilian Conservation Corps camp. Foundation remains of the officers' quarters, the corpsmen's barracks and mess hall, as well as various workshops, educational, and recreational buildings can still be recognized on the landscape. Part of the old camp is now used as a firing range by Park Service personnel. The firing range is to the right of the trail ninety yards above the second bridge. When the firing range is in use, the trail may be closed to public use.

Beyond the second bridge, the trail proceeds through cove-hardwood stands on an easy course along a wide jeep track a half-mile before crossing a third bridge over Mingus Creek. Two hundred and fifty yards above the bridge, the jeep track abruptly gives way to a narrower course that is a bit steeper and more uneven. Immediately to the right of the transition point, a noticeable path leads down to a low concrete weir across the stream. The weir was once part of an aqueduct supplying a water plant that stood nearby. Embedded in the concrete is a section of cast iron pipe that transported the water to the plant.

From this juncture, the trail winds through former farmsteads, crosses a feeder stream on a footlog, and then, 130 yards farther, enters an intersection. On the right, the wider track continues upstream along Mingus Creek, proceeding another three-quarters of mile to a path that leads eighty yards to the Mingus Creek Cemetery. At the intersection, the Mingus Creek Trail bears left, diminishes to a narrow track, and begins following Madcap Branch. The grade becomes markedly steeper as the course begins negotiating several crossings of Madcap Branch. The first, 180 yards above the trail junction, is a bit difficult. The remaining crossings are much easier and are spaced at irregular intervals over the next three-quarters of a mile.

One mile above the junction, the Mingus Creek Trail executes a sharp switch-back, the first of several that leverage the trail up the mountain and into a minor gap on a nameless ridge where it intersects the eastern terminus of the Deeplow Gap Trail. A lateral connector, the Deeplow Gap Trail enters the opposite side of the gap, leading in from the Indian Creek Trail by way of Deeplow Gap on Thomas Divide.

At its intersection with the Deeplow Gap Trail, the Mingus Creek Trail turns right and follows the ridgeline to Newton Bald. Initially the grade is easy, but it soon enters into a steep steady climb that remains below the ridgeline where a dry-ridge mix of pine and oak interspersed with a couple of mountain laurel tunnels makes up the main forest cover. About a mile and three-quarters above the Deeplow Gap Trail junction, the first of six switchbacks over an interval of 570 yards begins elevating the trail to the ridgeline for a long run through a rhododendron tunnel. Near the upper end of the tunnel, a live American chestnut tree stands just off to the right of the trail. The tree is about forty feet high, eight inches in diameter, and is identifiable by its coarsely serrated oblong leaves and the spine-covered husks that hold the chestnuts. This chestnut is one of only a few mature trees of this species still living in the Smokies. Until their demise from a parasitic fungus early in the twentieth century, the chestnuts were one of the dominant tree species in the Smokies, occasionally comprising most of the forest cover on the drier hardwood slopes like those flanking the Mingus Creek Trail.

About a half-mile above the rhododendron tunnel, the trail enters the southern perimeter of Newton Bald and terminates into the Newton Bald Trail. The Newton Bald Trail enters the bald from the east after climbing almost five miles from Newfound Gap Road at Smokemont, then continues west another half-mile to the Newton Bald Backcountry Campsite (#52).

NEWTON BALD TRAIL

Newfound Gap Road at Smokemont to the Thomas Divide Trail—5.5 miles.

POINT OF DEPARTURE: From the Oconaluftee Visitor Center drive north on Newfound Gap Road (US441) 3.2 miles to Smokemont Campground. The Newton Bald Trail begins on the left side of the road across from the entrance to the campground.

QUAD MAP: Smokemont 165-SE

0.0—Newfound Gap Road.
0.3—Bridle path.
0.4—Bridle path.
0.7—Bridle path.
2.8—Saddle gap.
4.8—Mingus Creek Trail exits left 5.8 miles to Mingus Mill on Newfound Gap Road.
5.4—Newton Bald Backcountry Campsite (#52).
5.5—Thomas Divide Trail.

The Newton Bald Trail is a steep rugged climb that gains nearly three thousand feet over a distance of slightly less than five miles; however, the trail makes restitution by affording one of the finest displays of spring wildflowers anywhere in the park. In order roughly by elevation, the Newton Bald Trail is home to large-flowered bellwort, trailing arbutus, Indian cucumber root, hepatica, galax, foamflower, blue and black cohosh, may-apple, wood anemone, yellow mandarin, Jack-in-the-pulpit, spiderwort, coreopsis, southern harebell, Dutchman's-pipe, Vasey's trillium, fire pink, rattlesnake plantain, Canada mayflower, jewel weed, crimson bee-balm, wild bergamot, white snakeroot, umbrella-leaf, pink lady's-slipper, goldenrod, black-eyed Susan, and flame azalea. Dog-hobble is prevalent at the lower elevations, and mountain laurel and rhododendron are frequent at several intervals along the trail. Several species of ferns are common and, as a special treat, stinging nettle and poison ivy share space in the ground cover.

The Newton Bald Trail begins immediately across Newfound Gap Road from the entrance to Smokemont Campground, leading out on a wide gravel track that follows a course parallel to the road for 265 yards before turning away and beginning the climb. Six hundred and ten yards above the trailhead, the Mingus Creek bridle path merges in on the left. A hundred and forty yards farther, the bridle path intersects the trail a second time and then completes a third intersection after another 420 yards.

Although the trail is not a streamside course, it does, nonetheless, cross several rills and seepages which are the home to many of the flowering species that prefer wetter conditions. In the intervals between the seeps, rhododendron and laurel tunnels are common. A particularly large seep and a false gap generally mark the halfway point to Newton Bald.

Four miles up, the trail reaches the perimeter of Newton Bald. Though it was once cleared for grazing livestock, Newton Bald is now completely reclaimed by second-growth forest; nevertheless, there remain tell-tale reminders of the bald's heritage as a grazing range. When it reaches the southern perimeter of the former bald, the climb abates and the trail intersects the upper terminus of the Mingus Creek Trail, leading in 5.8 miles from Newfound Gap Road at Mingus Mill. From this juncture, the Newton Bald Trail descends on a gentle course a half-mile to enter the Newton Bald Backcountry Campsite (#52).

The main part of the Newton Bald Camp is situated on the lower part of a narrow neck that bridges the western edge of the bald with the ridgeline of Thomas Divide. Fifty yards west of the main camp is a parcel of higher ground occupied by an annex site. Both sites are small. The camp in the swag is partially turfed in grass, but much of the space is occupied by a large fire ring and the trail passing down the middle. The remaining space is fairly level and suitable for four or five tents. A reliable spring can be found at the end of a very steep access path exiting the south side of the camp. A food-storage cable is suspended along the trail just where it drops off the bald and into the campsite.

The camp on the higher ground is a bare plat shaded by a few large trees. It enjoys the seclusion of being away from the trail, but is a bit far from the spring and the cable. It is not as large as the lower site, but still capable of billeting four or five tents.

The bald was named for Ebenezer Newton and his wife, Eleanor, who settled in a log cabin on a nearby stream that was for many years known as Newton Mill Creek. Newton and his wife lived in three different North Carolina counties without ever leaving their cabin on Newton Mill Creek. When the Newtons moved to the Smokies in the early 1820s, the bald was in Haywood County. When Macon County was formed in 1828, the boundary of the new county included "to the head of the waters of Newton's Mill Creek; thence down the said creek to Tuckaseega River." In 1851, Jackson County was carved out of Macon County, incorporating the Newtons' homeplace within the boundaries of this county. For the next half-century the major landmarks in this part of the Smokies were Newton Mill Creek and Newton Bald. Ebenezer Newton had died by the time the bald which bears his name was taken as part of Swain County.

Newton's homeplace was sold to Urill Cooper in 1873, and soon after, the stream came to be known as Cooper Mill Creek. For many years, the names Newton and Cooper were used interchangeably on land deeds.

The Newton Bald Trail proceeds through the lower campsite and then rolls off the ridgeline onto a level course that circumnavigates the higher camp. One hundred and sixty yards beyond the camp, the Newton Bald Trail terminates into the Thomas Divide Trail.

SMOKEMONT LOOP TRAIL

Smokemont Campground to the Bradley Fork Trail—3.9 miles.

POINT OF DEPARTURE: From the Oconaluftee Visitor Center drive north on Newfound Gap Road (US441) 3.2 miles to Smokemont Campground. The Smokemont Loop Trail begins on an old concrete bridge over the stream along the lower end of the campground.

QUAD MAP: Smokemont 165-SE

0.0—Smokemont Campground. Concrete bridge.
0.2—Exit roadbed.
0.3—Access path exits left to the Bradley Cemetery.
2.2—Switchback.
3.7—Feeder stream. Footlog.
3.8—Bradley Fork. Footlog.
3.9—Bradley Fork Trail exits right 1.7 miles to Smokemont Campground.

When white settlers first began encroaching on the Oconaluftee River Valley in the late nineteenth century, they found along the river bottom old fields abandoned by the Cherokee. The settlers appropriated these fields, building farms and homes and eventually developing small mountain communities along the river. One such settlement at the confluence of Bradley Fork and the Oconaluftee became known locally as Bradleytown.

During the early years of the twentieth century, the Champion Fibre Company purchased much of Bradleytown, dismantling the farms and building a large lumber mill and logging camp. Champion named the place Smokemont. When the lumber company departed, the Civilian Conservation Corps followed, building a camp where the old lumber mill once stood. With the departure of the CCC in the mid-twentieth century, the Park Service appropriated old Bradleytown as a tourist camp, subsequently naming it Smokemont Campground.

The Smokemont Loop Trail is technically not a loop. The name is suggested because it retains the quality of a loop when combined with the Bradley Fork Trail, which begins at the upper end of the campground and connects with the Smokemont Loop Trail almost two miles up-trail. The complete circuit from Smokemont Campground, up the Smokemont Loop Trail, and return to the campground by way of the Bradley Fork Trail is about six miles.

The Smokemont Loop Trail begins at the lower end of the campground on an old concrete bridge over Bradley Fork that once serviced a county road following up the Oconaluftee before the newer Newfound Gap Road was built by the federal government. Beyond the bridge, the trail follows the old county road through weedy clusters of great lobelias, wild golden-glows, Joe-pye-weeds, and black-eyed Susans for 340 yards before leaving the roadbed and turning up to the right on a conventional graded path. The trail climbs only a few yards before intersecting an access path that exits left down the slope to the Bradley Cemetery. The cemetery harbors about fifty graves, most of which are marked by weathered fieldstones.

The climb continues through a pine heath and into a dry-ridge mix of pignut hickories, yellow poplars, and scarlet and chestnut oaks. A noticeably level plot of grass shaded by a grove of eastern hemlock heralds a quarter-mile approach to a ridgeline where the trail executes a switchback right to begin a steep descent to Bradley Fork. From the ridgeline, Thomas Divide can be seen ranging along the far side of the Oconaluftee River Valley.

A mile below the switchback, the trail eases into a bottomland that was once cleared for farmland. At a footlog over a feeder stream, the Smokemont Loop Trail turns upstream along Bradley Fork and proceeds 120 yards to cross on a long springy footlog. Twenty-five yards above the footlog, the Smokemont Loop Trail terminates into the Bradley Fork Trail.

BRADLEY FORK TRAIL

Smokemont Campground to the Hughes Ridge Trail—7.3 miles.

POINT OF DEPARTURE: From the Oconaluftee Visitor Center drive north on Newfound Gap Road (US441) 3.2 miles to Smokemont Campground. The Bradley Fork Trail begins at the far upper end of the campground.

QUAD MAP: Smokemont 165-SE

0.0—Upper end of Smokemont Campground.

0.1—Horse trail exits right to the Tow String Horse Trail and the Lufty Baptist Church.

1.1—Bradley Fork. Bridge.

1.2—Chasteen Creek Trail exits right 4.0 miles to the Hughes Ridge Trail.

1.7—Smokemont Loop Trail exits left 3.9 miles to Smokemont Campground.

3.1—Bradley Fork. Bridge.

3.1—Bradley Fork. Bridge.

3.5—Bradley Fork. Bridge.

4.0—Road turnaround. Cabin Flats Trail exits left 0.9 mile to the Cabin Flats Backcountry Campsite (#49).

4.9—Taywa Creek. Two crossings. Bridges.

5.8—Feeder stream. Bridge.

7.3—Hughes Ridge Trail exits left 1.8 miles to the Pecks Corner Shelter and right 2.9 miles to the Chasteen Creek Trail.

The Bradley Fork Trail begins at the upper end of an extensive tract of bottomland now occupied by Smokemont Campground. For much of the nineteenth century this bottom was a mountain farm community known provisionally as Bradleytown, named for one of its earliest inhabitants, Isaac Bradley. By the beginning of the twentieth century, the Three M Lumber Company had moved into the lower end of Bradleytown, building a sawmill and introducing a railroad operated by a small steam engine. The engine pulled cars on wooden tracks on a ten-foot right-of-way running along the Oconaluftee River as far as Beech Flats. With the arrival of Three M, a post office was established in Bradleytown. The post office was given the address "Smokemont, NC," thus relegating the name "Bradley Town" to the anecdotes of history. By 1917 the Champion Fibre Company had purchased much of old Bradleytown and built on it a large mill town which adopted the name Smokemont.

Hikers from the Smoky Mountains Hiking Club visiting Smokemont in 1927 described it as a "company town, with a well-equipped commissary, a Post Office, and a Club house at which hotel accommodations can be obtained." In addition to the large mill operation, the hikers were fascinated by "the almost barren hill-sides, the maze of narrow gauge tracks, and bridges, little huts of the workers scattered along side, and the long string of cars loaded with great logs, being held back by the powerful donkey engine." Later hikers recall seeing deserted lumber shacks scattered at intervals along the stream on scarred mountainsides above the old mill town.

The twenty-first-century hiker along the Bradley Fork Trail is likely to be following the course of an old logging road or along the trace of a narrow gauge track left by the lumber companies. In 1935 young men from the Civilian Conservation Corps who were stationed in a camp near the lower terminus of the Bradley Fork Trail rehabilitated the abandoned trace along Bradley Fork to a superb jeep track. The first four miles of the trail follow a wide, level, well-graded, gritty bed of thin gravel and miry loam that affords an easy streamside excursion through the bottomland flanking the boulder-studded Bradley Fork. Over this interval the more common wildflowers are hepatica, crested dwarf iris, yellow mandarin, false Salomon's-seal, sweet white violet, buttercup, yellow trillium, large-flowered bellwort, crimson bee-balm, foamflower, partridge-berry, Fraser's sedge, wild geranium, and doll's eyes.

When it leaves Smokemont Campground, the Bradley Fork Trail enters a slight climb of 250 yards to intersect a horse trail on the right that circles back to the Tow String Horse Trail and the Lufty Baptist Church at the lower end of the campground. The name for the horse trail was originally Toe String, a reference to a string worn by a child to comfort an itching toe. Toe String was a fixture in Smoky Mountain placenames and used consistently in maps and land deeds until it was changed, likely as an inadvertent error, to Tow String by the Park Nomenclature Committee.

Another variant on the name Tow String derives from the process of converting flax into a fiber that can be spun into linen. Part of the process entails extracting the coarse fibers, the tow strings, from inside the stem of the flax plants by soaking them in water. It is from this process that the terms "tow sack" and "tow rope" are derived. The name may well have originated in Smoky Mountain nomenclature from references to the stream where the tow strings were soaked, Tow String Creek.

Immediately beyond the horse track, the Bradley Fork Trail begins ranging through tracts of bottomland that were once cultivated in farm fields. Today the former fields and the "almost barren hill-sides" are being reclaimed by vigorous growths of cove-hardwood stands. Nevertheless, remnants of the former human inhabitation are clearly visible, particularly where concentrations of activity around cabins, barns, and mills compacted the earth, leaving tell-tale clearings where vegetation is struggling to regain its place on the mountain.

A mile above Smokemont Campground, the trail crosses a wooden bridge over Chasteen Creek a hundred yards prior to reaching an intersection with the lower terminus of the Chasteen Creek Trail. During the nineteenth century this junction was part of the Chastain Reagan place which functioned as the provisional community center for upper Bradley Fork. The trail continues beyond the old Reagan place through second-growth farm fields for another half-mile before encountering on the left a path that drops down to a long springy footlog over Bradley Fork. The footlog marks the upper terminus of the Smokemont Loop Trail that begins on the lower west side of the campground and follows a course roughly parallel to the Bradley Fork Trail.

Beyond the Smokemont Loop junction, the Bradley Fork Trail continues on the jeep track for almost a mile and a half before crossing a sequential pair of wooden bridges that span Bradley Fork where the stream momentarily divides itself into two courses. The first bridge arches over to the "island" that divides Bradley Fork, and the second, thirty-five yards beyond, completes the crossing to the far bank. Beyond the crossings, the trail proceeds up the west side of Bradley Fork for 650 yards to another bridge that stands opposite the mouth of the violently cascading Taywa Creek. Ninety yards farther, a faint access path exiting on the right climbs steeply a hundred yards to a tiny cemetery harboring one grave, its simple marker bearing the inscription "daughter of Tom and Clarinda Huskey."

Thomas Jefferson Huskey was born July 11, 1822, in White Oak Flats (now Gatlinburg). He voted for Abraham Lincoln in 1860 and served in the Union Army. He and Clarinda were married in Sevier County, Tennessee, and soon afterward received a land grant of a hundred acres at twelve-and-a-half cents an acre at the mouth of Taywa Creek. At the time of his death on October 29, 1928, Tom Huskey was at 106 the oldest living man in Swain County, North Carolina.

A half-mile above the last bridge crossing, the trail enters a wide turnaround where it meets the lower terminus of the Cabin Flats Trail. Here, the Bradley Fork Trail hooks back sharply to the right and onto a moderately steep grassy track that curls up and around the end of Long Ridge. Within a quarter-mile, the trail veers into the hollow separating Long Ridge from the adjacent Mine Ridge where it charts a rocky course high above Taywa Creek. Until the mid-twentieth century, Taywa Creek was known as Upper Big Creek. The current name, a Cherokee word for "flying squirrel," was suggested by Asheville photographer George Masa and later officially adopted by the Park Nomenclature Committee.

A mile above the turnaround, the Bradley Fork Trail eases in alongside Taywa Creek, a fast-moving stream whose waters shift rapidly and with great ease down an extended succession of slides and gently sloped cascades. The space along the stream is occupied by tall hardwoods that filter what light seeps into the hollow. The trail soon crosses Taywa Creek twice, both times on wooden bridges seventy-five yards apart. At this point, the grade moderates noticeably as the trail skirts a small bottom that once harbored a cabin, a mill, and a few accessory buildings. Local mountaineers once knew the bottom as the Jim Chambers place and, before that, as the Rufus Floyd Licks.

As it eases out of the bottomland, the trail moves again to a higher course above the stream. The steepness returns, continuing for nearly a mile before reaching the confluence of two large streams that merge to form Taywa Creek. A bridge over the left-most stream marks the entrance into a tiny cove that was likely once occupied by a logger's shack. The shell of a large rusting washtub hangs conspicuously on a nearby tree as a tangible reminder of the cove's former domestication.

From this juncture, the stream is abandoned, and the course becomes a steep, narrow, exceedingly rough, rock-impeded grind up the flank of Hughes Ridge. A uniform cover of dry-ridge second-growth hardwood mix shades the trail for the next mile. Occasional patches of grass and a moderation in steepness herald the approach to a semi-bald on the crest of the ridge where the Bradley Fork Trail terminates into the Hughes Ridge Trail.

 Formerly, the bald extended farther down the mountain on all sides and the tree cover was much thinner, forming a grassy expanse that was appropriated by mountaineers for ranging browsing stock in the summer months. But even then, the bald was remote. Hikers on a well-promoted 1929 excursion to the Smokies sponsored by the *Asheville Times* recorded finding cattle on this part of Hughes Ridge, some of which bore claw marks from attacks by bears.

CHASTEEN CREEK TRAIL

Bradley Fork Trail to the Hughes Ridge Trail—4.0 miles.

POINT OF DEPARTURE: Hike 1.2 miles up the Bradley Fork Trail. The Chasteen Creek Trail begins on the right.

QUAD MAP: Smokemont 165-SE

0.0—Bradley Fork Trail.
0.1—Lower Chasteen Backcountry Campsite (#50).
0.2—Chasteen Creek. Bridge.
0.6—Access path exits left 25 yards to a hitching rack, then 180 yards to Chasteen Creek Falls.
2.2—Stream crossing.
2.4—Upper Chasteen Backcountry Campsite (#48).
2.8—Jeep track ends.
4.0—Hughes Ridge Trail exits left 5.0 miles to the Appalachian Trail at Pecks Corner.

According to a bit of Smoky Mountain lore recorded by H. C. Wilburn, the earliest human activity on Chasteen Creek included that of a Cherokee hunter referred to as Old Charlie who maintained a hunting camp near the mouth of the stream. The stream itself was then known as Charlie Branch. Old Charlie owned a black slave named Cudge who frequently accompanied the Indian on hunting trips to the camp. According to Cudge, on arrival at the camp Old Charlie would venture on up the stream some distance and later return with a supply of lead ore from which he would mold a supply of bullets for the hunt. Cudge also understood the Indian to say that in the vicinity there was also a vein of rock from which arrowheads, already formed, could be obtained. Acknowledging that the last part of Cudge's story is a bit implausible, Wilburn suggests that Old Charlie was likely referring to a nearby vein of white quartz of suitable quality for making arrowheads. Fragments and flakes of such arrowhead material have been found near the reputed site of Old Charlie's camp. References to Charlie Branch by Smoky Mountain bear hunters recorded by Joseph Hall in his *Preliminary Report on Hunting and Hunting Language in the Great Smoky Mountains* lend credibility to Wilburn's account.

The first white known to settle on Chasteen Creek was Joe Gunter, who in 1852 hauled his belongings by wagon to the upper end of the bottomland that is now occupied by Smokemont Campground. Gunter packed his belongings the last mile to Old Charlie's camp where he built a cabin. He later built and operated a small mill on Chasteen Branch just above its confluence with Bradley Fork.

Around 1867, Gess Stillwell, a mechanic and millwright, succeeded Gunter at the old camp site. He constructed a substantial log house and rebuilt the Gunter mill, cutting and installing new and larger millstones. In 1877, Stillwell also built a sash sawmill on nearby Bradley Fork. In the 1880s Chasteen Creek was sometimes referred to in title abstracts as Saw Mill Prong, evidently suggested by the proximity of the Stillwell sawmill.

Around 1885, Chastain Reagan and his wife Martha Ellison purchased the Stillwell property and built on it a frame house of hewn and sash sawmill timber. Reagan, who became one of the more prominent inhabitants on the upper Bradley Fork drainage, was known to be a skilled hunter and woodsman. His home later became a well-known rendezvous for hunting and mountaineering parties.

In Chastain Reagan's day, the stream near his home was known as Lower Big Creek. With the advent of the national park, the name was changed to Chasteen Creek in recognition of the colorful mountaineer who lived here. The spelling of Reagan's first name was evidently recorded incorrectly as Chasteen, and the error has remained a fixture in Smoky Mountain nomenclature.

The Chasteen Creek Trail is a lateral connector that links the Bradley Fork drainage with the crest of Hughes Ridge. It follows generally the course of an old logging road first cut by the Badgett and Latham Lumber Company in the 1920s. When it leaves the Bradley Fork Trail, the Chasteen Creek Trail follows a fine level track of loose stone for 130 yards before intersecting an access path on the right leading forty yards to the Lower Chasteen Backcountry Campsite (#50), one of the nicer campsites in the park. The campsite is a flat grassy space sparsely shaded by a few trees, secluded from the trail by hedges of rhododendron and bounded along the lower edge by Chasteen Creek. Residual effects from previous inhabitation betray the campsite's former occupation by Chastain Reagan's farm, and previous to that, perhaps even Joe Gunter's mill and Old Charlie's hunting camp. The campsite appears small and intimate, although the abundance of flat terrain yields several good-quality tent sites.

The trail continues beyond the campsite on its wide level track for 200 yards before crossing Chasteen Creek on a wooden bridge. At this juncture, the grade stiffens noticeably as the trail charts a course parallel to the stream. About a half-mile above the bridge, an access path drops down sharply from the left side of the trail twenty-five yards to a horse-hitching rack. The access then proceeds another 180 yards to Chasteen Creek Falls, a fifty-foot waterslide attractively sequestered in heavy thickets of woody undergrowth and large second-growth hemlocks and poplars. The rock surface over which the falls flow is not steeply pitched, and thus the stream does not display a forceful plunge.

Beyond the access to the falls, the Chasteen Creek Trail continues climbing while edging away from the main stream to follow an upstream course along a nameless tributary. The trail soon crosses the tributary at a switchback. On the right, water flowing down the slope has worn away the mantle of soil and vegetation, exposing the underlying rock and demonstrating in striking detail the thinness of the ground cover at the higher elevations. Beyond the crossing, the trail becomes considerably rockier and narrows appreciably. Following the tributary downstream, it returns to Chasteen Creek, turns, and resumes its upstream course.

For the next mile, the trail continues climbing steeply while maintaining a course high above Chasteen Creek. When the trail descends to the stream, it actually crosses a headwater tributary of Chasteen Creek and then immediately intersects an access path leading into the Upper Chasteen Backcountry Campsite (#48).

The Upper Chasteen Camp is situated on a long tapered gradient wedged between two headwater streams. The larger upper part of the camp is a rough galled spot pitched at an uncomfortably steep grade. At the lower end of the camp is a small nicely secluded plat that is a bit more accommodating. The nicest site in the camp is a level bench down along the edge of the stream. It is large enough for only a single tent though it enjoys a fine setting by the stream and shares little of the coarseness of the upper part of the camp. The food-storage cable is conveniently suspended across the middle of the camp.

During the summer of 1929, the *Asheville Times* sponsored a camping expedition into the Smokies as a promotional event publicizing the proposed new national park in the Smokies. On their trip, the expedition party stopped to rest at a bold spring in Sugar Orchard that was identified as being at the end of the logging railroad line on Chasteen Creek. The rail line ended at the campsite; thus there is some likelihood that the earlier settlers' name for the campsite here was Sugar Orchard. Prior to the logging railroad, Smoky Mountain bear hunters found the Sugar Orchard a good place for rousing bears.

Above the campsite, the steep climb resumes while the track degenerates into a bed of large loosely shifting stones that roll underfoot. After almost a half-mile, the trail diminishes to a single-file track and then begins negotiating at irregular intervals a series of switchbacks and feeder streams. Except for a couple of excursions through dry-ridge conditions, second-growth hardwoods remain the primary forest cover. A mile and a half above the campsite, the trail rolls up onto the crest of Hughes Ridge and terminates into the lower terminus of the Hughes Ridge Trail.

CABIN FLATS TRAIL

Bradley Fork Trail to the Cabin Flats Backcountry Campsite (#49)—0.9 mile.
POINT OF DEPARTURE: Hike 4.0 miles up the Bradley Fork Trail. The Cabin Flats Trail begins at the end of the road turnaround.
QUAD MAP: Smokemont 165-SE

0.0—Bradley Fork Trail. Jeep road turnaround.
0.1—Bradley Fork. Bridge.
0.2—Tennessee Branch. Footlog.
0.3—Dry Sluice Gap Trail exits left 4.2 miles to the Appalachian Trail at Dry Sluice Gap.
0.9—Cabin Flats Backcountry Campsite (#49).

The Cabin Flats Trail is one of the shorter trails in the park. It serves as a connector between the Bradley Fork Trail and the lower terminus of the Dry Sluice Gap Trail as well as the primary access to the Cabin Flats Backcountry Campsite (#49).

The trail begins at the upper end of the jeep road turnaround where the Bradley Fork Trail cuts sharply back to the right to enter the Taywa Creek drainage. The Cabin Flats Trail exits from the end of the turnaround, proceeds eighty-five yards to cross Bradley Fork on a metal truss bridge, and then immediately negotiates a tight switchback that directs the trail up the adjacent ridge. Three hundred yards above the bridge, the trail clears a short footlog over Tennessee Branch and then, forty yards farther, intersects the lower terminus of the Dry Sluice Gap Trail.

From this juncture, the trail proceeds on a fairly level course through woods that were only selectively cut by settlers. Great yellow poplars, white basswoods, yellow birches, yellow buckeyes, and cucumber trees shade open forests adorned in spring with foamflowers, Jack-in-the-pulpits, violets, and hepatica. After almost a half-mile, the trail enters a wide looping switchback that drops into a bottomland along Bradley Fork. As the trail enters the bottom, it passes on the left the first of four sites that constitute the Cabin Flats Backcountry Campsite (#49). Proceeding down and along the bottom, the trail passes in turn each of the three other sites, all on the left and along the stream. The trail terminates at the last campsite.

The Cabin Flats Camp is situated on a low, flat, weedy tract that is often damp. The ground, though quite level, is gritty soil mixed with small gravel. The setting among large trees and along the stream is uncommonly attractive; however, much of its charm is spoiled by its use as a horse camp. The last site downstream is the largest of the four. It is served by a nearby food-storage cable suspended across the trail from the campsite. The other three camps share a cable that is opposite the middle site.

Given the elevation and isolation of Cabin Flats, it is unlikely that it was ever permanently occupied by settlers, though there is anecdotal evidence that Wes Enloe maintained a ranger cabin in the flats for many years. During Enloe's tenure at Cabin Flats, a trail proceeded upstream along Bradley Fork for about a mile above the camp to the confluence of Bradley Fork and Washout Branch, a place known as Washout Camp. The name Washout was suggested by the occurrence of a cloudburst that sent a wall of water down the gulch, sweeping trees and rocks in its way. One of the earliest known camps here was a bark shelter built by Til Loven and used as a base for cattle ranging. Many years later, Charlie Conner, whose aching feet would play an instrumental role in the naming of Charlies Bunion, maintained a coon-hunting camp at Washout.

Sometime in the late summer or early fall of 1929, Charlie Conner accompanied Horace Kephart, George Masa, and others staying at his Washout Camp. Conner, acting as guide, took a party that included Masa to The Jumpoff (on what is now Mount Kephart), leaving Horace Kephart at the camp. In the late afternoon when the traveling party returned to camp, a lively discussion ensued about the terrain that had been covered that day. Conner removed his shoes and was attempting to ease his tired feet. While describing a certain knob that had been observed from The Jumpoff, Conner referred to it as being "about the size of this bunion on my foot." Kephart, who was a member of the North Carolina Nomenclature Committee, laughed heartily at the comparison and remarked that from now on the knob would be known as "Charlies Bunion." The name was quickly assimilated into general usage and later officially sanctioned by the National Geographic Board.

DRY SLUICE GAP TRAIL

Cabin Flats Trail to the Appalachian Trail at Dry Sluice Gap—4.2 miles.
POINT OF DEPARTURE: Hike 0.3 mile up the Cabin Flats Trail. The Dry Sluice Gap Trail begins on the left.
QUAD MAPS: Smokemont 165-SE
Mount Guyot 165-NE

0.0—Cabin Flats Trail.
0.1—Tennessee Branch. Footlog.
0.2—Tennessee Branch. Footlog.
0.6—Big poplar.
0.9—Tennessee Branch.
2.9—Grassy Branch Trail exits left 2.7 miles to the Kephart Prong Shelter.
4.2—Dry Sluice Gap. Appalachian Trail.

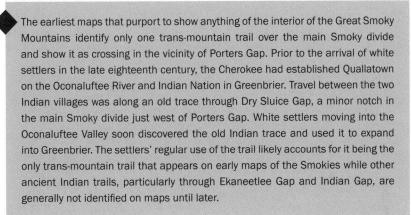

The earliest maps that purport to show anything of the interior of the Great Smoky Mountains identify only one trans-mountain trail over the main Smoky divide and show it as crossing in the vicinity of Porters Gap. Prior to the arrival of white settlers in the late eighteenth century, the Cherokee had established Quallatown on the Oconaluftee River and Indian Nation in Greenbrier. Travel between the two Indian villages was along an old trace through Dry Sluice Gap, a minor notch in the main Smoky divide just west of Porters Gap. White settlers moving into the Oconaluftee Valley soon discovered the old Indian trace and used it to expand into Greenbrier. The settlers' regular use of the trail likely accounts for it being the only trans-mountain trail that appears on early maps of the Smokies while other ancient Indian trails, particularly through Ekaneetlee Gap and Indian Gap, are generally not identified on maps until later.

The Dry Sluice Gap Trail begins in a rough washed-out intersection 340 yards above the lower terminus of the Cabin Flats Trail. A hundred and sixty yards above the intersection, the Dry Sluice Gap Trail crosses Tennessee Branch on a footlog and then begins climbing steeply through old-growth cove-hardwood forests that managed to escape the logger's axe. Here, large Carolina silverbells, white basswoods, yellow poplars, and yellow buckeyes preside over a thin understory.

Two feeder streams intervene before the trail advances another 270 yards to a second footlog over Tennessee Branch. At each stream crossing, the track becomes rocky and confined by over-reaching patches of pale jewel weeds, white wood asters, and stinging nettles. On the rocky flanks, Dutchman's-pipes and Jack-in-the-pulpits are prevalent. Above the second footlog, the trail executes three stream crossings in quick succession. The first is over Tennessee Branch. The other two clear tributaries.

Standing to the left of a switchback between the two tributary crossings is an enormous yellow poplar that rivals the largest trees in the Smokies.

The Dry Sluice Gap Trail crosses Tennessee Branch for the final time five hundred yards above the big poplar. It then leaves the stream drainage for a climb up the east flank of Richland Mountain. Here, the course deteriorates noticeably. Oaks and maples are prevalent with trailing arbutus, galax, and pink lady's-slipper noticeable in the groundcover. In the more moist places, particularly where seepages accumulate, white snakeroot, crimson bee-balm, Joe-pye-weed, black cohosh, pale and spotted jewel weed, and nettle are common.

Two miles above the last creek crossing, the trail reaches the crest of Richland Mountain and enters a level bench to intersect the upper terminus of the Grassy Branch Trail. A copse of tall, unusually straight rhododendron occupies the ground flanking the intersection.

From here, the trail eases out of the rhododendron and onto a slope that was burned in 1925 by wildfire ignited by a spark from a logging operation near Smokemont and propelled by wind up the mountainside. The watershed was incinerated down to bare rock, leaving only the blackened boles of old-growth trees. The burned-over area recovered to grassland, followed by thin stands of mountain ash, pin cherry, and yellow birch shading patches of blackberry and blueberry bushes. Where the forest remains sparse, it affords fine views into the Kephart Prong drainage and across to the main Smoky divide. Noticeable on the flank of Mount Kephart is the Icewater Spring Shelter, appearing tiny and insignificant against the vastness of the mountain slope.

The onset of small Fraser firs marks the transition from the once-burned grassland to a ridgeline course through stately balsams. At the end of the corridor, the Dry Sluice Gap Trail descends a hundred yards or so to terminate into the Appalachian Trail at Dry Sluice Gap. A few yards to the left, at the lowest point in the gap, a barely noticeable manway drops off the Appalachian Trail and descends into Porters Flat. The manway is exceedingly steep and obstructed by rock ledges. It is what remains of the ancient Indian trace which the Cherokee followed between Quallatown and Indian Nation and later appropriated by white settlers venturing from Oconaluftee into Greenbrier.

KEPHART PRONG TRAIL

Newfound Gap Road to the Sweat Heifer Creek Trail and Grassy Patch Trail at Kephart Prong Shelter—2.0 miles.

POINT OF DEPARTURE: From the Oconaluftee Visitor Center, drive north on Newfound Gap Road (US441) 8.2 miles to a pull-off along the side of the road. The Kephart Prong Trail begins on the wooden bridge over the Oconaluftee River.

QUAD MAP: Smokemont 165-SE

0.0—Newfound Gap Road. Oconaluftee River. Bridge.

0.3—Ruins of Civilian Conservation Corps camp.

0.4—Kephart Prong. Bridge.

0.7—Ruins of fish hatchery.

0.9—Kephart Prong. Footlog.

1.1—Kephart Prong. Footlog.

1.6—Kephart Prong. Footlog.

2.0—Kephart Prong Shelter. Sweat Heifer Creek Trail exits straight 3.7 miles to the Appalachian Trail. Grassy Branch Trail exits right 2.7 miles to the Dry Sluice Gap Trail.

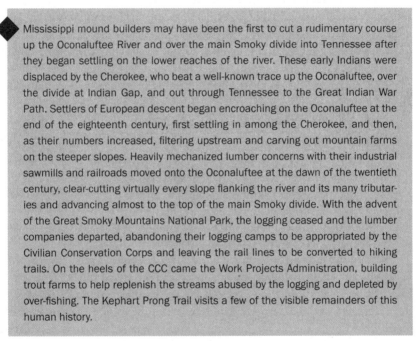

Mississippi mound builders may have been the first to cut a rudimentary course up the Oconaluftee River and over the main Smoky divide into Tennessee after they began settling on the lower reaches of the river. These early Indians were displaced by the Cherokee, who beat a well-known trace up the Oconaluftee, over the divide at Indian Gap, and out through Tennessee to the Great Indian War Path. Settlers of European descent began encroaching on the Oconaluftee at the end of the eighteenth century, first settling in among the Cherokee, and then, as their numbers increased, filtering upstream and carving out mountain farms on the steeper slopes. Heavily mechanized lumber concerns with their industrial sawmills and railroads moved onto the Oconaluftee at the dawn of the twentieth century, clear-cutting virtually every slope flanking the river and its many tributaries and advancing almost to the top of the main Smoky divide. With the advent of the Great Smoky Mountains National Park, the logging ceased and the lumber companies departed, abandoning their logging camps to be appropriated by the Civilian Conservation Corps and leaving the rail lines to be converted to hiking trails. On the heels of the CCC came the Work Projects Administration, building trout farms to help replenish the streams abused by the logging and depleted by over-fishing. The Kephart Prong Trail visits a few of the visible remainders of this human history.

The trail begins along Newfound Gap Road, immediately crosses the Oconaluftee River on a wooden bridge, and then begins following a wide level gravel track that was once a paved road. The trail leads into a narrow tract of bottomland that was a mountain farm before being occupied in 1933 by CCC Company 411. The most visible evidence of the old camp are the large boxwoods ranging along both sides of the trail about 500 yards above the bridge. On the left, a pair of two-foot-high stone uprights is flanked by low stone walls that marked the fronts of the camp barracks. The barracks, which housed two hundred corpsmen, extended perpendicularly to the stone walls. In addition to the barracks, the camp included officers' quarters, a mess hall, recreation and educational buildings, a latrine, and a wood-working shop.

A few yards up-trail and obscured by other boxwoods, a six-foot stone encasement built of river rocks and once used as a notice board for camp announcements stands on the right. A short distance farther, other remnants are visible—a six-foot-wide hearth, a well-preserved stone drinking fountain, a twenty-foot-high brick chimney, and, standing among a grove of hemlocks, a stone chimney with a fifteen-foot-wide hearth. Scattered about at the back of the camp is an assortment of rusting refuse—oil barrels, metal frames, and pieces of a metal stove. More conspicuous is an unexpected depression in the forest floor rimmed by a low hummock. The atypical nature of the hole suggests that it was a dug pit used either as a garbage dump or the camp latrine.

About 200 yards above the camp, the trail appears to fork, the old road track turning down left to Kephart Prong and a single-file track continuing a few yards to a narrow wooden footbridge over the stream. Once across the stream, the single-file track rejoins the roadbed near a remnant of stonework embedded with a pipe that once supplied water to the camp.

At this junction the grade becomes noticeably steeper and follows more closely along the stream. Five hundred yards above the footbridge in a steeply pitched niche just to the left of the trail a large cistern sealed with a flat concrete lid sits up in the slope of the mountain. Nearby is a smaller concrete tank with a central divider separating it into two basins. The structures were once part of a fish hatchery built on Kephart Prong by the WPA in 1936. Old photographs of the hatchery operation show several buildings and more than a dozen rock-rimmed fish ponds approximately ten feet in diameter. The adjacent slopes were completely cleared of trees. Very few vestiges of the buildings and rearing pools remain, the structures having succumbed to the wearing agents of time and nature.

Beyond the fish hatchery, the trail continues climbing along a pebbled-surfaced road track for about 300 yards before approaching the first of three footlogs over Kephart Prong. Again, the road drops down to the stream while a single-file track proceeds a few yards farther upstream in search of the footlog. Shortly beyond the footlog, the single-file track rejoins the wider road trace which is now climbing through stands of slender second-growth American beech trees. During the summer months, rue anemone and crimson bee-balm add color to the undergrowth.

A couple of railroad rails abandoned along the left 350 yards up-trail herald the approach to the second footlog. As before, the road plunges into the stream while a single-file track diverges to seek out the footlog.

At this elevation, the old jeep track ends, and the Kephart Prong Trail continues along the trace of a narrow-gauge rail line the Champion Lumber Company built to access red spruce stands near the Smoky main divide. The rail bed has deteriorated more than the old jeep road, and consequently the trail from this point on is somewhat less even. After a half-mile, the trail repeats its deft forking maneuver as it negotiates the third and final footlog crossing. Conditions moderate noticeably as the trail follows the winding rail bed for a final half-mile to reach a boulder-strewn bench where it terminates in a three-way intersection with the Sweat Heifer Creek Trail and the Grassy Branch Trail.

Commanding the center of the bench is the Kephart Prong Shelter with its back to Richland Mountain and facing Kephart Prong. The Grassy Branch Trail passes around to the back of the shelter on another rail grade running up the flank of Richland Mountain. The Sweat Heifer Creek Trail passes in front of the shelter and across Kephart Prong before climbing to the Appalachian Trail on the main Smoky divide.

GRASSY BRANCH TRAIL

Kephart Prong Trail to the Dry Sluice Gap Trail—2.7 miles.

POINT OF DEPARTURE: Hike 2.0 miles to the end of the Kephart Prong Trail. The Grassy Branch Trail begins on the right, circling behind the Kephart Prong Shelter.

QUAD MAPS: Smokemont 165-SE
Mount Guyot 165-NE

0.0—Kephart Prong Shelter. Kephart Prong Trail. Sweat Heifer Creek Trail.
1.1—Lower Grassy Branch.
2.3—Lower Grassy Branch.
2.7—Dry Sluice Gap Trail exits left 1.3 miles to the Appalachian Trail and right 2.9 miles to the Cabin Flats Trail.

The Grassy Branch Trail is a steep course that follows an old road that once linked the Champion Lumber Company Camp 6 with the crest of Richland Mountain. The trail is difficult to reach from either end. The upper end is anchored to the Dry Sluice Gap Trail far up Richland Mountain. Its lower end coincides with an intersection of the Sweat Heifer Creek Trail and the Kephart Prong Trail at the Kephart Prong Shelter.

From its lower terminus, the Grassy Branch Trail circles to the back of Kephart Prong Shelter and quickly executes a sharp switchback to the right. Until it was re-routed in 2010, the Grassy Branch trail proceeded to the left on a course roughly parallel to Kephart Prong. After being re-routed, it now turns south and follows another old roadbed for about a hundred yards before entering a series of tight switchbacks that position the trail higher up the mountain. At the last of the switchbacks the trail turns left, picks up an old road course, and begins angling across the flank of Richland Mountain.

A quarter-mile beyond the last switchback, the former course of the Grassy Branch Trail rises up on the left and merges almost unnoticed into the new re-routed course. A few yards beyond the merge junction, the trail morphs into a rocky grade and then proceeds 625 yards to a small stream at the back of a hollow. After it turns and exits the hollow, the trail circles right and enters the Lower Grassy Branch drainage. Five hundred and sixty yards beyond the feeder stream, the trail crosses Lower Grassy Branch, then shifts to a northerly course running parallel to Upper Grassy Branch visible down the mountain on the left.

A half-mile beyond the Lower Grassy Branch crossing, the trail executes a sharp switchback right and proceeds back toward the Lower Grassy Branch drainage. The forest cover here is primarily American beech, chestnut oak, red maple, and Fraser magnolia shading clusters of toothworts, goldenrods, mountain gentians, and white wood asters. Also noticeable are dense stands of large trees that resemble red spruce with low drooping limbs. These are Norway spruce, an exotic species planted by the Champion Lumber Company to replace the timber lost in a fire in 1925. There is concern by the Park Service that the non-native Norway spruce threatens to hybridize with the red spruce and alter the genetic integrity of the native species.

The trail eventually turns and proceeds on an upstream course high above Lower Grassy Branch. It soon crosses the stream and turns onto a western exposure of beech and birch stands shading thick turfs of rich grass and very little understory. The expanses of grass on this and adjourning slopes serve as the source for the name Grassy Branch.

The increasing occurrence of red spruce and a corridor of tall, leggy, remarkably straight rhododendron heralds the approach into a wide level bench on the crest of Richland Mountain. Here, the Grassy Branch Trail terminates in an intersection with the Dry Sluice Gap Trail.

SWEAT HEIFER CREEK TRAIL

Kephart Prong Trail to the Appalachian Trail—3.7 miles.
POINT OF DEPARTURE: Hike 2.0 miles to the end of the Kephart Prong Trail. The Sweat Heifer Creek Trail begins on the left, proceeding in front of the Kephart Prong Shelter.
QUAD MAPS: Smokemont 165-SE
Clingmans Dome 165-SW

0.0—Kephart Prong Trail. Grassy Branch Trail. Kephart Prong Shelter.
0.0—Kephart Prong. Footlog.
1.6—Sweat Heifer Creek.
1.8—Feeder stream.
3.0—Feeder stream.
3.7—Appalachian Trail.

During the final years of World War I, industrial suppliers of materiel required great quantities of light-weight red spruce for the production of warships and aircraft. Responding to the demand, the Champion Lumber Company began harvesting spruce timber on the upper reaches of the Oconaluftee River drainage. To transport the timber down-mountain, a network of rail lines was built on the face of the main Smoky divide almost up to the state line. To house the work crews, Champion established logging camps at strategic points along the rail lines. Champion's Camp 6 stood on the west side of Kephart Prong immediately across the stream from the Kephart Prong Shelter. Crews from Camp 6 could readily reach the spruce timber on spur lines that fanned out across the higher elevations. When Champion left the Smokies, sections of an abandoned line north of Kephart Prong were later upgraded and incorporated into the Sweat Heifer Creek Trail.

Kephart Prong Shelter is situated on a boulder-infested bench that extends from the flank of Richland Mountain to the stream. The lower corner of the bench is occupied by an intersection marking the upper terminus of the Kephart Prong Trail and the lower termini of the Sweat Heifer Creek and Grassy Branch trails. Beginning from this junction, the Sweat Heifer Creek Trail proceeds across the bench, passing immediately in front of the shelter, a three-sided stone structure recently remodeled with an added overhang extension. Seventy yards beyond the trail junction, the Sweat Heifer Creek Trail crosses Kephart Prong on a footlog and climbs quickly up and into the bottomland that once harbored Camp 6. Here, the trail narrows to a single-file track, soft underfoot, and follows an easy grade through a sparsely wooded ground that is slow in recovering from the effects of its industrial past.

Soon the trail leaves the bottom, crosses a small stream, completes a double-crossing of a minor stream, and then begins winding steeply up the contours of the adjacent slope, proceeding for about a half-mile before merging onto the bed of an abandoned rail line. The course along the rail grade remains fairly level, leading into the cool moist environment of the Sweat Heifer Creek drainage. Sweat Heifer Creek appears here as a long cascade over gently sloped ledges of stratified rock on which changes in sunlight reflect varying hues of red and yellow. Irregularly spaced pools break up the continuity of the cascade. The trail eases down through stands of tall yellow birches and clusters of boulders to cross Sweat Heifer Creek at the edge of a small pool.

At the pool, the trail turns to the left and proceeds about 300 yards to cross a feeder stream where it tumbles over a small rock face. Shortly the trail resumes its climb, entering the first of several well-constructed stone and log "steps" installed to arrest erosion and facilitate the climbing in steep places. While the Sweat Heifer Creek Trail is one of the least used in the park, it is also arguably one of the best maintained.

About a half-mile above the last stream crossing, the trail reaches a wide ridgeline and turns sharply right. On the left the ridgeline extends out to a fairly level gradient that is littered with miscellaneous pieces of industrial metal. Distance from water precludes suggesting that Champion Lumber Company maintained a logging camp on the site. More likely the company employed a small provisional outpost here while logging the higher elevations.

Soon after clearing the ridgeline, the trail enters a cooler environment where hemlocks and beeches began displacing the dry-ridge hardwoods. As elevation is gained, the occasional spruce and birch enter the mix. Almost a mile beyond the turn on the ridgeline, the trail clears the headwaters of Jack Bradley Branch and then enters a strenuous three-quarter-mile climb to the state-line divide. Immediately upon crossing the stream and to the right about ten yards off the trail stands a birch tree with a box resembling a bird house fastened to the tree's trunk about eight feet off the ground. There is no opening in the box for birds to enter. There are no other obvious indications of what the box may be, but only that it closely resembles a box fixed to a tree about 300 yards down the Fork Ridge Trail.

Higher up, the trail passes through the twilight of a dense spruce-fir stand and then into a thinner forest cover that offers occasional glimpses into North Carolina. A remarkably pure stand of thickset stunted beeches whose upper branches are sculpted into uniformly smooth contours by fierce winds sweeping up the Carolina slopes heralds the approach to the state-line divide and the Appalachian Trail. A short winding excursion through the beech thicket brings the trail to a small wooden bench on the left of the trail. Here the beeches subside, and the bench offers a nice place to sit and gaze out over the rolling sea of mountains upon mountains that extends deep into North Carolina.

Fifty yards beyond the bench, the Sweat Heifer Creek Trail terminates into the Appalachian Trail 1.7 miles above Newfound Gap.

KANATI FORK TRAIL

Newfound Gap Road to the Thomas Divide Trail—2.9 miles.

POINT OF DEPARTURE: From the Oconaluftee Visitor Center drive north on Newfound Gap Road (US441) 7.2 miles to a pull-off along the side of the road. The Kanati Fork Trail begins on the left side of the road.

QUAD MAPS: Smokemont 165-SE

Clingmans Dome 165-SW

0.0—Newfound Gap Road.

2.9—Thomas Divide Trail exits right 1.8 miles to Newfound Gap Road and left 11.9 miles to the park boundary at Galbraith Creek Road.

According to ancient Cherokee legend, there was once a cave on the north side of Black Mountain where all the game animals in the world were closely confined. Before that time the animals had never been known to roam over the mountains as they do now, all being in the keeping of an old Cherokee named Kanati.

Kanati, meaning "Lucky Hunter," often came home with a fine bear or deer, but would never tell anyone where he found such valuable game. Kanati had a mischievous son who was resentful of his father's hunting prowess. On one occasion when his father went hunting, the son hid among the trees and watched his father's movements. The son saw the old man go to the cave and push away a big stone at its entrance. Out ran a fine buck which the father killed with an arrow. Kanati then rolled the stone back in place.

When Kanati had gone with his deer, the boy went to the cave and thought he would try his luck in killing game. He rolled away the stone, and out jumped a wolf which so frightened the boy that he failed to replace the stone. Before he knew what was happening, all of the animals had made their escape and were fleeing down the mountain in every direction. When Kanati found out what foolishness his son had accomplished, he became very angry and then disappeared and was never heard from again.

The boy also became very unhappy and spent many days trying to find his father, but all his searching was in vain. As a last resort, he attempted an old Indian practice of shooting an arrow to determine which direction the old man had gone. He fired an arrow toward the north, but it returned and fell at his feet, and he knew that his father had not traveled in that direction. He fired arrows to the east and the south and the west, but they all also came back in the same manner. He then thought to fire one directly over his head. The arrow never returned. The boy knew then that his father had gone to the land of the spirits.

The Great Spirit was angry with the Cherokee nation for the boy's offense. To punish the Cherokee, he tore away the cave from the side of Black Mountain, leaving only a large cliff in its place. He then declared that the time would come when another race of men would possess the mountains where the Cherokee had flourished for many generations.

The Kanati legend did not take place in the Great Smoky Mountains, and thus it remains unclear how the name came to be associated with the Kanati Fork of the Oconaluftee River. Early settlers in the area often referred to the stream as the Left Fork, it being the left-most of three streams that converge to form the Oconaluftee.

The Kanati Fork Trail begins in a discreet opening along Newfound Gap Road where it enters immediately into a steep climb up the flank of Thomas Divide. The trail remains steep from beginning to end and affords no vantage point from which to survey the surrounding mountains; however, in springtime it offer access to a remarkably rich variety of wildflowers. Assorted violets and trilliums are found among rue anemone, trout lily, great chickweed, wood-betony, Dutchman's-britches and Dutchman's-pipe, crimson bee-balm, downy rattlesnake plantain, and false Solomon's-seal. At the lower and middle elevations, thickets of rosebay rhododendron and mountain laurel bloom profusely while higher up spiderwort, wild bergamot, Turk's-cap lily, Jack-in-the-pulpit, and witch-hobble are conspicuous.

When it leaves the road and enters the forest, the trail follow a course roughly parallel to the stream for which it is named. The trail never approaches the stream, always remaining a polite distance and separated by tangles of dog-hobble. A quarter-mile above the road and in the midst of a lush forest of yellow poplar, the trail encounters the first of several small feeder streams and seepages seeking outlets to Kanati Fork. The poplars soon yield to a wider mix of cove-hardwood species that include yellow birch, Fraser magnolia, eastern hemlock, red and sugar maple, white basswood, and Carolina silverbell interspersed with a few sourwoods and black gums.

Almost a mile above Newfound Gap Road, the trail crosses a feeder stream, executes a switchback, and then re-crosses the stream within an interval of 280 yards. A mile above the switchback, the grade eases considerably for a brief respite along a short ridge before resuming the steep climb. An acute switchback to the right heralds a sharply angled 300-yard approach to the crest of Thomas Divide, where the Kanati Fork Trail enters a ridgeline dell and terminates into the Thomas Divide Trail.

◆ DEEP CREEK ◆

The Deep Creek section is defined as the basin bounded on the east by the long curvature of Thomas Divide and on the west by Noland Divide and its lower appendage, Beaugard Ridge. The basin's rugged upper end reaches to the main Smoky divide near Mount Collins, and its lower end extends to a complex of bottomlands flanking Deep Creek. The drainage is subdivided haphazardly by a network of spurs, the largest of which is Sunkota Ridge, an appendage of Thomas Divide that separates Deep Creek from its primary tributary, Indian Creek.

The Deep Creek section features several long trails. The Noland Divide, Thomas Divide, and Deep Creek trails are all in excess of ten miles, and the Sunkota Ridge Trail is over eight. The Noland Divide and Thomas Divide trails trace the boundaries of the basin while the Deep Creek Trail forms the primary artery of a network of trails that probes into the recesses of the basin. The slopes west of Deep Creek are rugged and are accessed by two trails, the Pole Road Creek Trail climbing to Noland Divide at Upper Sassafras Gap and the Fork Ridge Trail reaching Clingmans Dome Road near Mount Collins. The primary trail east of Deep Creek is the Indian Creek Trail, which functions as the connecting artery for trails climbing the flanking ridges. One of these, the Deeplow Gap Trail, climbs to the spine of Thomas Divide and continues east to the Mingus Creek Trail in the Oconaluftee section.

The Deep Creek section affords ten backcountry campsites. Eight of the ten are on Deep Creek. The Bryson Place Camp (#57) and the Poke Patch Camp (#53) are old camps first maintained by hunters and fishermen who frequented the upper recesses of the basin. The remaining camps along Deep Creek are later additions, appropriated from old farm fields and settlers' improvements. The two campsites not on Deep Creek, the Estes Branch Camp (#46) on the Indian Creek Trail and the Georges Branch Camp (#51) on the Deeplow Gap Trail, were established early in the twenty-first century on sites once occupied by settlement farms.

To reach the Deep Creek section, drive on US441 south out of the park and continue through Cherokee, North Carolina. At the south end of Cherokee, turn right onto US19 and proceed ten miles to Bryson City, North Carolina. Turn right at the old Swain County Courthouse onto Everett Street. Follow Everett Street two blocks, crossing the Tuckasegee River and the railroad tracks. Turn right onto Depot Street. Depot Street leads out of town to Deep Creek Road. In approximately three miles, Deep Creek Road passes Deep Creek Campground and terminates in a turn-around at the head of the Deep Creek Trail.

The upper ends of the Thomas Divide Trail and the Deep Creek Trail can be reached from US441 just south of Newfound Gap. Except during the winter season when it is closed, Clingmans Dome Road offers access to the upper ends of the Fork Ridge Trail and the Noland Divide Trail.

DEEP CREEK TRAIL

Deep Creek Road to Newfound Gap Road—14.2 miles.

POINT OF DEPARTURE: From the Oconaluftee Visitor Center drive south on US441 through Cherokee, North Carolina, to US19. Turn right on US19 and drive ten miles to Bryson City. At the Swain County Courthouse, turn right onto Everett Street, cross the Tuckasegee River, and turn right onto Depot Street. Depot Street leads three miles to Deep Creek Road at the park boundary. Proceed on Deep Creek Road past Deep Creek Campground to the paved turnaround at the end of the road. The Deep Creek Trail begins at the end of the turnaround. Parking is available off Deep Creek Road just before reaching the turnaround.

QUAD MAPS: Bryson City 166-NW

Clingmans Dome 165-SW

0.0—Turnaround at the end of Deep Creek Road.

0.1—Juney Whank Falls Trail exits left 390 yards to Juney Whank Falls.

0.3—Tom Branch Falls.

0.4—Deep Creek. Bridge.

0.7—Indian Creek Trail exits right 3.6 miles to the Martins Gap Trail.

0.7—Indian Creek. Bridge.

0.8—Deep Creek. Bridge.

1.7—Deep Creek. Bridge.

1.7—Jenkins Place. Loop Trail exits right 1.2 miles to the Indian Creek Trail.

2.5—Bumgardner Branch. Footlog.

2.6—Bumgardner Branch Backcountry Campsite (#60).

5.0—McCracken Branch.

5.1—McCracken Branch Backcountry Campsite (#59).

5.4—Nicks Nest Branch.

5.5—Nicks Nest Branch Backcountry Campsite (#58).

6.0—Bryson Place Backcountry Campsite (#57). Martins Gap Trail exits right 3.0 miles to the Indian Creek Trail.

6.3—Elliot Cove Branch. Footlog.

6.5—Burnt Spruce Backcountry Campsite (#56).

6.7—Sassafras Ford. Pole Road Creek Trail exits left 3.3 miles to the Noland Divide Trail and the Noland Creek Trail.

6.8—Pole Road Backcountry Campsite (#55).

7.7—Nettle Creek Backcountry Campsite (#54).

7.7—Nettle Creek. Double-crossing.

9.0—Beetree Creek.

9.5—Cherry Creek.

10.3—Poke Patch Backcountry Campsite (#53). Fork Ridge Trail exits left 5.1 miles to Clingmans Dome Road.

12.8—Switchback.

14.2—Newfound Gap Road (US441).

In the June 1911 issue of *The Outing Magazine*, Horace Kephart published a curious article in which he advocated route sketching as a practical visual aid for augmenting written reports of excursions into uncharted wilderness. To illustrate his route-sketching techniques, Kephart included two examples. One depicted a wagon road and a trail up Deep Creek from the point of its confluence with Indian Creek to the Bryson Place, which Kephart identified as "the last house up Deep Creek." The wagon road forded the stream eighteen times over six miles. Kephart offered some warnings to those wishing to travel up Deep Creek. "Ford 10" is "the deep ford" where the stream "always wets a wagon bed," and "Ford 12" at Perrys Gap "is dangerous when there is ice." Between [William] "Hunnicutt's" and "McCracken's," a distance of two-and-a-half miles, there are ten fords and, Kephart adds, there are no inhabitants, implying that any would-be traveler up Deep Creek may be far from help.

The Deep Creek Trail was among the first to be re-routed and graded to National Park Service specifications after the federal government took possession of the land in the 1930s. R. P. White, an engineer retained by the Park Service to upgrade the trail, maintained the old wagon road used by the settlers as far up Deep Creek as the Jenkins Place (where the Loop Trail now intersects the Deep Creek Trail). A ford at the Jenkins Place was replaced by a wide concrete bridge and the remainder of the trail re-routed to stay to the east side of Deep Creek, thus eliminating the necessity of negotiating the eighteen fords Kephart had laboriously mapped.

The Deep Creek Trail begins just upstream from Deep Creek Campground along the end of the turnaround at the end of Deep Creek Road. From 1933 until 1936 the campground was the site of a Civilian Conservation Corps camp operated by Company 1216. The young men of Company 1216 were responsible for constructing the trail engineered by R. P. White. A short distance upstream of the campground and roughly adjacent to the turnaround was the site of the Thomas Wiggins Overshot Mill. The mill's flume extended up Deep Creek over a hundred yards almost to the base of Tom Branch Falls. The falls themselves were named for Tom Wiggins.

The mill was built in 1854 by Tom's father, James Holland Wiggins. In 1878, the elder Wiggins deeded the mill and thirty acres to Tom. The mill's dams, which spanned the stream just below the falls, were destroyed by a flood in 1862 and again in 1884. The mill itself was destroyed by a flood in 1892 and never rebuilt. The ruins were visible for several years afterward.

From the road turnaround, the Deep Creek Trail proceeds on an exceptionally wide roadbed following an easy grade along the stream for only 140 yards before encountering on the left the Juney Whank Falls Trail leading 390 yards to Juney Whank Falls.

At this low elevation, Deep Creek is quite wide and, as its name suggests, abounding in pools that are by Smoky Mountain standards uncommonly deep. Four hundred and forty yards up the trail, Toms Falls plunges into Deep Creek after cascading eighty feet down a near-vertical rock face. Wooden benches at the edge of the trail beckon the hiker to sit and enjoy the surpassing beauty of water falling gently down a bare scarp framed by lush woods and offset by a foreground of swiftly moving current.

Three hundred yards above Tom Branch Falls, the trail crosses Deep Creek for the first time, on a wide concrete bridge. The grade increases perceptibly, but the track remains wide and smooth with park benches at occasional intervals along trail's edge.

Noticeable about 300 yards above the bridge crossing is an unusually large boulder along the edge of Deep Creek. In 1911, large hemlocks were cut and lodged in against the boulder, forming a log dam to detain water for a power house that stood along the bank. The impounded water was channeled into a large tank and then into a turbine which turned a 140-horsepower generator. An ox was used to open and shut the dam's flood gates. At full pool, water impounded by the dam backed up to the base of Indian Creek Falls.

The small generator, capable of producing enough power to light 1,800 bulbs of 100-watt size, supplied electricity for Bryson City, mostly for its ice plant and roller mill. After eighteen years, a larger plant superseded the Deep Creek power plant and the old facility abandoned. When the Park Service took possession of Deep Creek in 1930, the log dam was still standing. Parts of the dam remained visible for several years afterward

Within 550 yards of the bridge, the Deep Creek Trail approaches the confluence of Indian Creek and Deep Creek, where it intersects the lower terminus of the Indian Creek Trail. The Indian Creek Trail follows its namesake east a hundred yards to Indian Creek Falls. Twenty yards beyond the junction, the Deep Creek Trail crosses Indian Creek on a wide concrete bridge and then proceeds an additional 145 yards to cross a bridge over Deep Creek, where Hammer Branch empties into the main stream.

Hammer Branch received its name from a pounding or hammer mill that was located at the mouth of the stream. The flats at the mouth of Hammer Branch were also the home of Samuel Hunnicutt, a well-known Smoky Mountain outdoorsman

who recorded many of his hunting and fishing expeditions in an awkwardly written narrative, *Twenty Years of Hunting and Fishing in the Great Smoky Mountains.* Sam Hunnicutt was a hunter's hunter. He had definite ideas about hunting and was not abashed about citing their virtues. "I claim to be the perfect hunter and fisherman for game and fish; I know the best kind of hunting outfit to use, I know the best kind of gun to use for killing game and also the best dogs to use for hunting." Along with Mark Cathey, Quill Rose, and Granville Calhoun, Sam Hunnicutt is recognized by Bob Plott, author of *A History of Hunting and Fishing in the Great Smoky Mountains*, as one of the four most skilled hunters ever to pursue game in the Smokies. Hunnicutt's book has some serious literary deficiencies; nevertheless, through its repetitive episodes the narrative offers the best accounts extant of the ridges, hollows, streams, gaps, and old hunters' camps in the Deep Creek backcountry.

Forty yards beyond the Hammer Branch crossing, the Deep Creek Horse Trail intersects from the left. The Deep Creek Trail continues its easy track along the stream for almost a mile before passing through George Washington Jenkins's old farm fields and negotiating the third and last crossing of Deep Creek. Like its predecessors, this crossing is on a concrete bridge. Where the trail reaches the bridge, a rough access track exits left on a very steep 160-yard climb to an eroded ridgeline occupied by an Indian cemetery. The cemetery harbors five graves, most marked with worn fieldstones. The access path continues on for well over a half-mile farther to the Hammer Branch Cemetery.

Visible on the left while looking down from the upstream side of the bridge is a spring that once served as the water supply for the Jenkins family, who lived just across the stream and farmed much of the land along this part of Deep Creek. The spring is fixed with a metal pipe that directs the flow into Deep Creek. On the far end of the bridge, the trail enters the old Jenkins Place, where it immediately intersects the western terminus of the Loop Trail.

 Jenkins purchased the 150-acre mountain farm in 1896 from W. P. Shuler and his wife, Narcissus. According to the deed, the farm was earlier known as the Corn Tassel Place, named for the Cherokee chief, Corn Tassel, who once lived here. Jenkins's two-story frame house stood along the upper side of the Loop Trail less than ten yards from its junction with the Deep Creek Trail. The old wagon road which Kephart sketched forded the stream just below the concrete bridge. It passed in front of the Jenkins house and then forded the stream again just above the bridge. To get to the spring, Jenkins maintained a footlog across Deep Creek where the concrete bridge now stands.

In his essay on route sketching, Kephart mentions that there were two ways into Bryson Place. The first followed the wagon road with the eighteen fords. The second was "across the mountain from [William] Hunnicutt's either from McCracken Gap or the Pullback." William Hunnicutt's home was on the far side of Deep Creek, but he maintained a stable near the turnaround above the Jenkins Place. The mountain Kephart refers to is Bumgardners Ridge. According to Kephart, "the trail at Hunnicutt's stable swerves sharply to the right, up a steep bank, and then through thick forests."

The trail "through thick forests" avoided most of the fords, but was not necessarily the more attractive option. An instance involving Mark Cathey, the famed fisherman from Indian Creek, illustrates the point. As a young man, Cathey was once retained to haul a wagon-load of fingerling trout up this trail. The trail was not only exceedingly steep but ranged high over Deep Creek. At a narrow place, a wheel slipped off the edge and the wagon overturned, taking it, the team, the fish, and all down the steep ridge and into Deep Creek far below.

At the turnaround, the modern Deep Creek Trail diminishes to a single-file track and climbs away from the stream on a course close to that followed by the unfortunate Cathey. The most noticeable feature along the climb is a pair of free-standing concrete posts down to the left of the trail. There is no other readily visible artificial structure nearby that might suggest what the original purpose of the twin posts might have been.

Seven hundred and fifty yards upstream of the road turnaround, the trail drops down to cross Bumgardner Branch and immediately enters the Bumgardner Branch Backcountry Campsite (#60), a large level camp attractively situated along Deep Creek and shaded by widely spaced eastern hemlocks and white pines. From the appearance of the immediate terrain, the campsite was evidently part of a farm clearing, perhaps belonging to William Hunnicutt, whose house stood across Deep Creek opposite the mouth of Bumgardner Branch. Notwithstanding its many fine features, the Bumgardner Branch Camp has something of a forlorn appearance. Because of its proximity to the trailhead, it is one of the most heavily used camps on Deep Creek.

At its confluence with Bumgardner Branch, Deep Creek enters a wide circumnavigation known as Bumgardner Bend, leaving the trail to seek its own course up and over an intervening ridge. For the next three-quarters of a mile, the trail follows closely the old wagon track sketched by Kephart. When the trail drops down again to Deep Creek, it reaches the point where the wagon road forded the stream. The trail, however, again turns away from the stream and begins another climb, soon rising high above the stream. Here, the adjacent mountain slopes are steep and closely spaced, rising like walls from the stream's edge and forcing Deep

Creek to run in a gorge. It is clear from this perspective why, as Kephart pointed out, there were no inhabitants on Deep Creek for the two miles above the William Hunnicutt place.

When the trail again drops down into bottomland, it enters a very pleasant excursion, wending for a short interval through tall lush hedges of dog-hobble and rhododendron. The trail once again climbs away from the stream only to drop to another small field of bottomland infested with rank entanglements of dog-hobble and rhododendron. Over those intervals where the trail courses through bottom-land, it traces the route of the old wagon road. When it is plying the slopes, it follows the redirected course engineered by R. P. White.

After one more climbing circumnavigation, the trail settles into a march across a creek bottom once known as the McCracken Improvement. The bottom was orig-inally cleared by Joseph McCracken, who settled here with his wife, Sarah Vaughn McCracken, sometime around 1800. Here the trail crosses McCracken Branch and 170 yards farther enters the McCracken Branch Backcountry Campsite (#59), one of the nicer campsites in the park. The camp is small and intimate, ranging along the left side of the trail and affording excellent tent sites tucked in among the thickets of rhododendron and dog-hobble. The ground is level, cushioned with thick layers of pine needles, and enjoys a pleasant proximity to Deep Creek. A food-storage cable is nearby on the right side of the trail.

From the McCracken Branch Camp, the trail climbs along a 700-yard section engineered by R. P. White before descending to cross Nicks Nest Branch and enter the Nicks Nest Branch Backcountry Campsite (#58). The Nicks Nest Camp is sim-ilar to the one at McCracken Branch. It is small, shaded by pines and tall leggy rho-dodendron, and situated close by the stream. The ground, though level, is somewhat compromised by the intrusion of roots from the shading trees. An attractive annex to the main campsite is found a few yards downstream. The annex is fairly free of ground roots, but branches from the partitioning rhododendron encroach a bit on the space overhead.

 When Horace Kephart died in 1931, he left among his papers an unpublished manuscript of a novel, *Smoky Mountain Magic*, which remained with Kephart's descendants until published in 2009. The novel, best described as a Victorian-style romance, is set on Deep Creek. In the story, Kephart makes frequent refer-ences to landmarks along the stream, most notably Bryson Place and Nicks Nest. The latter is referred to in a pejorative manner by the locals in the story as "Dog-eater Holler." The story's protagonist, John Cabarrus, builds a camp in Nicks Nest, a narrow draw which Kephart describes as "a terribly rough and devious gorge, hard to find a way into and worse to get out of."

From the Nicks Nest Camp, the trail passes the mouth of Dog-eater Holler on an easy half-mile excursion to Bryson Place, one of the best-known landmarks on Deep Creek.

On May 23, 1878, Col. Thaddeus Dillard Bryson, a Confederate war veteran and Assemblyman from Swain County purchased one thousand acres of mountain land on Deep Creek for 42 cents an acre. On the rough gradient now occupied by the Bryson Place Backcountry Campsite (#57), Colonel Bryson maintained a large pole cabin that served as a hunting lodge. Anecdotal accounts suggest that the pole cabin was built by Will Elliot, an early settler who had a clearing and cabin farther up Deep Creek. The pole cabin was later replaced by a forty-by-thirty-five-foot log hunting lodge that remained in use for almost a half-century until it was razed by the Park Service sometime in the 1940s. According to Sam Hunnicutt, Bryson Place was "where the hunters hunting in that section usually camped." The lodge at Bryson Place was strategically located below Sassafras Ford and near two trail junctions, affording hunters ready access to the many high ridges and hidden coves where bears were plentiful.

Much of the popular recognition accorded to Bryson Place derives from Horace Kephart having maintained a permanent camp here, spending his summers in refuge and writing. Kephart's camp was about fifty yards below the left side of the Deep Creek Trail, where it approaches a nameless stream along the south edge of the Bryson Place Camp. Kephart's old campsite is now completely obscured, submerged in thick entanglements of rhododendron, although it is marked by a millstone placed on the spot two months after his death on April 2, 1931. The millstone was hauled from nearby Elliot Cove Branch by a troop of Boy Scouts and affixed with a bronze plaque that reads: "On this spot Horace Kephart, Dean of American Campers and one of the principal founders of the Great Smoky Mountains National Park pitched his last permanent camp. Erected May 30, 1931 by Horace Kephart Troop, Boy Scouts of America, Bryson City, North Carolina."

According to early accounts, Bryson Place had a well-kept appearance, "like an English country park." Today the place is a gradient of hard-packed, sparsely shaded, heavily abused, bare ground used frequently as a horse camp. Whatever charm it may have had in Kephart's day has vanished. The place is vile and worn. A broken-down table and fire grates scattered across the camp yard lend an added dimension of despair. Some of the roughness of Bryson Place may be attributed to a Civilian Conservation Corps side camp that was located here from 1934 until 1935 to accommodate crews working on trails for the new national park. A number of barracks and an assortment of lean-tos, sheds, and rough buildings were set up on the slope now occupied by the camp. Today the most suitable tent sites are either at the far upper end of the camp or along the trail at the lower end, where the slope was built up to accommodate a building.

The small nameless stream that runs down to Kephart's old camp separates the campsite from a tethering rack and holding area for horses. At the point where the Deep Creek Trail crosses the feeder stream and enters the campsite, it intersects the western terminus of the Martins Gap Trail leading in from Indian Creek. At the intersection, the Deep Creek Trail turns and circles down and out along the lower end of the Bryson Place Camp.

Five hundred yards beyond Bryson Place, the trail crosses Elliot Cove Branch and enters an extensive stretch of bottomland once cleared by Will Elliot and subsequently known as the Elliot Improvement. Though once free of vegetation, the Elliot Improvement may not have been used much for farming, for it was reported by bear hunters as early as 1923 that the land Elliot cleared was already returning to wilderness.

Three hundred and fifty yards beyond the Elliot Cove Branch crossing, the trail reaches the Burnt Spruce Backcountry Campsite (#56). Spruce trees are conspicuously absent in the Elliot Improvement, and thus the camp likely received the name from its proximity to Burnt Spruce Ridge, which extends from Deep Creek to Noland Divide. The camp is situated on a small rectangular tract along the right side of the trail. The space is level and shaded by bordering pines that keep the site well blanketed with fallen needles. Except for some drainage problems during heavy rains, the site is one of the better camping places in the park. It is clean and affords proximity to the stream, but it is a bit too close to the trail and retains too much of the residue of the improvement to be an exceptionally attractive wilderness site.

Four hundred yards beyond the Burnt Spruce Camp, the Deep Creek Trail intersects the lower terminus of the Pole Road Creek Trail at Sassafras Ford. In Sam Hunnicutt's day, hunters and fishermen could gain access to Watson Cove by crossing Deep Creek at Sassafras Ford. From there they could either traverse the cove to Pole Road Creek or embark on a trail up Easy Ridge to Sassafras Knob on Noland Divide. Today, access to the Pole Road Creek Trail is by a footlog which spans Deep Creek at the old Sassafras Ford.

A hundred yards above the Pole Road Creek Trail junction, the Deep Creek Trail reaches a large rough plat that serves as the Pole Road Backcountry Campsite (#55). The camp is clearly in the heart of the old Elliot Improvement, as evidenced by the conspicuous traces of the former domestication of the bottomland flanking the camp. Much of the ground in the camp drains poorly and, where it is subjected to frequent visits by horse traffic, it is churned and uneven. The small section that is most suitable for camping is a bit drier but is not particularly level and is laced with protruding roots. The camp is worn and abused to the point that a rotting log table in the better part of the site appears as a welcome amenity. Food-storage cables are suspended conveniently near each end of the camp. Deep Creek, fifty yards away, affords a readily accessible source for water.

From the Pole Road Camp, the trail resumes its easy course through the upper end of the Elliot Improvement, where entanglements of rhododendron and dog-hobble encroach closely and water-slickened rocks and boles of fallen trees impede the way. Here, a remarkable variety of tree species shoulder one another. Eastern hemlocks and white pines grow close to yellow poplars and cucumber trees. American beeches and yellow birches are found near sugar maples and ash trees while sycamores can be seen in the vicinity of white basswoods and yellow buckeyes.

Five hundred yards above the Pole Road Camp, the trail crosses a large feeder stream near the point where Deep Creek is joined by its major tributary, the Left Fork. For many years the confluence of the two streams was considered the headwater of Deep Creek, and the two were referred to individually as the Left Fork and the Right Fork. The Left Fork has retained its name. The name Right Fork was superseded when surveyors began considering it as the main stream. Even though the trail passes close to the point where the two forks converge, it is easy to miss. Jim Casada explains in *Fly Fishing in the Great Smoky Mountains* that this is in part the case because the Left Fork empties into Deep Creek where the terrain is exceptionally flat and the stream breaks into what old-timers called "sluices."

According to a hand-drawn map by George Masa, the trail originally split at the confluence of the Left Fork and Deep Creek. The split going left crossed Deep Creek and followed up Left Fork to an old hunters' camp below Deep Creek Gap, and then proceeded through Deep Creek Gap to re-connect with its right-fork counterpart just above the Poke Patch. The split going right stayed along Deep Creek, crossing over and back on the stream a couple of time before crossing above the Poke Patch. From where the two forks re-connected above the Poke Patch, the trail remained on the west side of the Deep Creek.

After crossing the feeder stream, the Deep Creek Trail continues winding through a labyrinth of rhododendron for a little over a half-mile before entering an attractive campsite fitted nicely in the wide angle formed by the confluence of Nettle Creek and Deep Creek. The Nettle Creek Backcountry Campsite (#54), one of the more remote camps in the Smokies, is on fairly level ground and offers two or three discrete camping spots tucked in among high hedges of rhododendron. The camp is heavily shaded by virgin forest and completely surrounded by thickets of woody undergrowth. A food-storage cable is convenient, and water is readily available from nearby Nettle Creek.

The Deep Creek Trail passes through the middle of the campsite and then completes a double-crossing of Nettle Creek. The second, larger crossing is separated from the first by an island thirty yards across. Unless Nettle Creek is running low, neither of the two streams can be crossed by rock-hopping.

Beyond the Nettle Creek crossing, the terrain becomes exceptionally rugged, forcing the trail increasingly closer to Deep Creek. In places the track consists of upturned strata of rock, difficult to negotiate and treacherous when wet or slickened with decomposing leaves. At its most difficult point, the trail is pressed into a 100-yard gauntlet at the very edge of the surging stream. The surface of the strata is not only irregular but pitched steeply toward the stream. Half-way along, a feeder stream plunges across the trail and into Deep Creek. The frothing of the feeder is sufficient to make rock-hopping difficult. With Deep Creek roiling only inches away, the feeder crossing can be treacherous. Under conditions of a torrential rainstorm, the crossing may even be considered hazardous.

The trail negotiates a remaining fifty yards of strata before climbing quickly away to a position high and above the stream. The slopes on both sides of Deep Creek are steep and densely timbered down to the water's edge with tall trees of several species. Here, the gorge is severely constricted. In places the stream surges through narrow chasms, its turbulence setting up a roar that is audible even from this high vantage point.

The trail's sojourn along the high vantage is brief, ceasing when it descends to a half-mile excursion through a confining corridor of exceptionally high dog-hobble. Much of this area is low and boggy, particularly in the vicinity of Beetree Creek, and the trail in places is little more than a miry slough. Beetree Creek is a fairly shallow stream that is easily crossed. Cherry Creek, a half-mile above the Beetree Creek crossing, poses a greater difficultly. Cherry Creek is a wide stream with a deep channel down the middle. Even under the best of conditions it can rarely be crossed by rock-hopping.

Just less than a mile beyond the Cherry Creek crossing, the trail breaks out of the undergrowth and into a small circular clearing that harbors the Poke Patch Backcountry Campsite (#53). Poke Patch is an old camp, frequented by bear hunters from the time of the earliest settlements on Deep Creek. It is situated at the conjunction of Beetree, Shot Beech, and Fork Ridges with the campsite occupying the bottom of a bowl-shaped topography. Deep Creek appears momentarily in a tangent encounter with the upper edge of the camp, but otherwise remains hidden beneath thickets of surrounding undergrowth. A thin turf of grass carpets much of the level ground in the campsite, affording nice tent spots. When it rains, however, water collects in large puddles in the middle of the camp.

A food-storage cable is suspended from two of the very few trees that intrude on the interior of the camp. The most noticeable tree in the camp is a yellow birch standing up off the ground on its roots as though perched on stilts. Birch seedlings in the Smokies often germinate on fallen host logs and, as the tree grows, its roots extend downward through the host and eventually to the ground beneath. In time, when the host log rots away, the birch remains standing on the extended roots.

The Deep Creek Trail passes through the middle of the Poke Patch Camp, exits the upper end, and immediately intersects the lower terminus of the Fork Ridge Trail on the left. It is at this intersection that the old trail route sketched by George Masa crossed the stream and re-connected with the Left Fork counterpart descending from

Deep Creek Gap. It then turned upstream and remained on the west side of Deep Creek. The modern Deep Creek Trail stays to the east side of the stream and enters an earnest climb along the western flank of Shot Beech Ridge.

 According to an old legend recorded in *Meigs Line*, a historical novel by Dwight McCarter and Joe Kelly, there was a gold mine near Shot Beech Ridge where the Cherokee made rifle bullets. They fashioned the bullets out of the gold and shot them for practice at a beech tree, even having shooting matches to determine which of them could get closest to the center of the tree. A trader named Borus Felmet repeatedly attempted to persuade the Indians to show him the gold mine. One Indian finally relented and took Felmet to an old beech tree that had been shot many times, warning him that this tree was as close as he could get without being shot. The Indian left Felmet at the tree. Three hours later he returned with fresh chunks of gold to trade. While typical of the "lost" gold mine stories common to the Southern Appalachians, this one at least ties in nicely with the name Shot Beech Ridge.

As it gains elevation, the stream gorge becomes considerably steeper, and Deep Creek runs a swifter course attended by a retinue of small tributary streams. In several places the tributaries run in the trail, seeking a path of least resistance to the main stream. Lush stands of virgin northern hardwood forests are all around. In the more moist environments, yellow poplars, white basswoods, and giant eastern hemlocks are most prevalent. Where conditions are drier, yellow birch, American beech, and sprouts from American chestnut stumps are abundant.

Early hunters on the upper reaches of Deep Creek mentioned camping at Parris Cabin, a lean-to somewhere above the Poke Patch. The Parris Cabin likely stood in one of the small benches along the stream, the precise location now difficult to determine, its remnants having long been effaced by the agents of time or obscured by the fecundity of nature. Two-and-a-half miles above the Poke Patch, the trail enters a shallow cove that is a good candidate for the site of the former Parris Cabin. Here, the trail turns sharp right to leave Deep Creek and follows a course along a nameless tributary up the south flank of Thomas Ridge. Until sometime in the middle of the twentieth century, the trail did not turn here but continued on up Deep Creek and eventually to the state-line divide at Indian Gap.

Eighty yards beyond the sharp right turn, the trail turns sharply left and begins climbing the flank of Thomas Ridge. As elevation is gained, the yellow poplars are replaced by white and northern red oaks, and soon yellow birches become more numerous while red spruces, black cherries, and Fraser magnolias enter the mix. A lush environment of diverse ground-cover vegetation furnishes the primary understory. Seven hundred yards farther, the trail reaches a headwater crossing and then 500 yards farther, a second. A series of upper switchbacks heralds a long approach to trail's end at Newfound Gap Road (US441).

JUNEY WHANK FALLS TRAIL

Parking area at end of Deep Creek Road to Juney Whank Falls—0.3 mile.

POINT OF DEPARTURE: Follow directions to the Deep Creek Trail. The Juney Whank Falls Trail begins at the edge of the parking area for the Deep Creek Trail.

QUAD MAP: Bryson City 166-NW

0.0—Deep Creek Road parking area.
0.1—Deep Creek Horse Trail.
0.3—Access trail exits right 55 yards to Juney Whank Falls.
0.3—Deep Creek Horse Trail.
0.3—Juney Whank Falls Trail exits right 270 yards to the Deep Creek Trail.
0.5—Deep Creek Trail exits right 140 yards to the turnaround on Deep Creek Road.

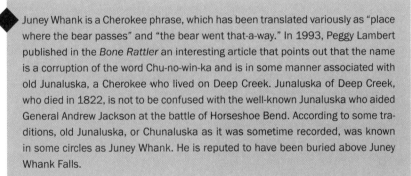

Juney Whank is a Cherokee phrase, which has been translated variously as "place where the bear passes" and "the bear went that-a-way." In 1993, Peggy Lambert published in the *Bone Rattler* an interesting article that points out that the name is a corruption of the word Chu-no-win-ka and is in some manner associated with old Junaluska, a Cherokee who lived on Deep Creek. Junaluska of Deep Creek, who died in 1822, is not to be confused with the well-known Junaluska who aided General Andrew Jackson at the battle of Horseshoe Bend. According to some traditions, old Junaluska, or Chunaluska as it was sometime recorded, was known in some circles as Juney Whank. He is reputed to have been buried above Juney Whank Falls.

The Juney Whank Falls Trail is actually a loop that visits Juney Whank Falls while sharing much of its course with the Deep Creek Horse Trail. The most readily available access to the falls begins along the far upper corner of the parking area at the end of Deep Creek Road. From the parking area, the Juney Whank Falls Trail climbs 155 yards to intersect the Deep Creek Horse Trail leading in from the Noland Divide Trail. Here, the Juney Whank Falls Trail turns right and proceeds jointly with the horse trail 265 yards before exiting on the right to descend fifty-five yards to a wooden platform spanning Juney Whank Branch at the waterfall. The platform is fitted with a nice bench on which to sit and observe the 125-foot cascade that flows down a rocky incline immediately at the front edge of the platform. Owing to its proximity to the platform, Juney Whank Falls affords a fine display of falling water, particularly after a rainstorm when the stream is running high.

At this point there are two options. The first is to turn and hike back to the parking area on the route taken in to the falls. This up-and-back excursion is just slightly more than half a mile. The second option is to continue north to the far end of the platform and follow the Juney Whank Falls Trail seventy yards out of the stream gorge to reunite with the horse trail which circles above the falls.

When the Juney Whank Falls Trail re-connects with the horse trail, the combined trails proceed only fifty feet before separating again. The Juney Whank Falls Trail splits off to the right and descends 270 yards through a shoulder-high rut leading to the Deep Creek Trail. It terminates into the Deep Creek Trail 140 yards above the turnaround at the end of Deep Creek Road, which is adjacent to the parking area at the trailhead. The round-trip loop back to the parking area following this route is about three-quarters of a mile.

Another option is to take the split to the left, remaining on the Deep Creek Horse Trail which winds through old farm settlements, clears a ridge, and then drops down and runs along Hammer Branch before intersecting the Deep Creek Trail about a mile above the parking area. The total distance of the horse trail loop is about two-and-a-half miles.

Because of its proximity to the park entrance and Deep Creek Campground, the Juney Whank Falls Trail is among the more frequently visited landmarks in the Smokies.

INDIAN CREEK TRAIL

Deep Creek Trail to the Martins Gap Trail—3.6 miles.
POINT OF DEPARTURE: Hike 0.7 mile up the Deep Creek Trail. The Indian
  Creek Trail begins on the right.
QUAD MAPS: Bryson City 166-NW
Clingmans Dome 165-SW

0.0—Deep Creek Trail.
0.1—Access path exits left to Indian Creek Falls.
0.1—Indian Creek. Bridge.
0.5—Stone Pile Gap Trail exits right 0.9 mile to the Thomas Divide Trail.
0.8—Loop Trail exits left 1.2 miles to the Deep Creek Trail.
1.4—Access path exits left 130 yards to the Laney Cemetery.
2.1—Indian Creek. Bridge.
2.6—Access path exits right 400 yards to the Queen Cemetery.
2.6—Indian Creek. Bridge.
2.9—Indian Creek. Georges Branch. Bridge.
2.9—Deeplow Gap Trail exits right 6.1 miles to the Mingus Creek Trail.
3.2—Indian Creek. Bridge.
3.5—Indian Creek. Bridge.
3.6—Estes Branch. Bridge.
3.6—Road turnaround.

3.6—Access path exits right 75 yards to the Estes Branch Backcountry Campsite (#46).

3.6—Martins Gap Trail exits left 3.0 miles to the Deep Creek Trail at Bryson Place.

When settlers of European descent first began venturing into the Great Smoky Mountains, they found that the Cherokee had established permanent homes along very few of the dozens of streams in the Smokies. Of these few, one was Indian Creek, the large tributary of Deep Creek that drains the narrow defile separating Sunkota Ridge and Thomas Divide. Indian Creek was easily accessed from the Cherokee villages on the Tuckasegee River, yet deep enough in the mountains to be considered a remote outpost. Settlers traveling up the Tuckasegee and Deep Creek soon found the old Cherokee clearings and began moving in. By the beginning of the twentieth century, the bottomland and lower slopes along Indian Creek were populated by mountain farms from the stream's mouth at Deep Creek almost to its headwaters on Thomas Divide.

The Indian Creek Trail affords one of the easiest and most pleasant streamside excursions in the park. From start to finish, it follows a smooth wide roadbed over a slight grade. It begins from a wide intersection with the Deep Creek Trail close to the confluence of Indian and Deep creeks and immediately alongside the concrete bridge where the Deep Creek Trail crosses Indian Creek.

A hundred yards above the trailhead, an access path on the left descends sharply twenty yards to the base of Indian Creek Falls, where the stream thunders over ledges arranged like steps of a colossal stairway before reaching a sharply pitched incline of smooth rock over which it races with hissing velocity into a deep pool. Here the water collects in an agitated boil before surging down through a channel to join Deep Creek. In spite of the inherent attractiveness of the display of cascading water, the falls are not an inviting place to linger. Heavy traffic from visitors has effaced the freshness of the natural setting, leaving a residue of fatigue and wear.

A hundred and twenty-five yards above the access to Indian Creek Falls, the trail crosses the stream on a wooden bridge and begins traversing what was once farmland belonging to Mark Cathey.

Uncle Mark, as he was affectionately addressed by those who knew him, was born in 1871 and spent most of his life on Indian Creek. By the beginning of the twentieth century he was regarded as an extraordinary fly fisherman. Jim Gasque, himself a highly skilled fly fisherman, devoted a special chapter to Cathey in his book *Hunting and Fishing in the Great Smoky Mountains*. Gasque proclaims "without fear of contradiction that from the nineties to the early forties Mark Cathey was the greatest dry-fly fisherman of the Smoky region." Cathey's fame rested on his unorthodox "dance of the dry fly," a technique which many fisherman carefully observed but none could successfully imitate. With an imperceptible movement of the wrist, Cathey could make the fly mimic a living insect, teasing a wary trout until the poor fish could no longer resist coming out to strike.

Uncle Mark was an eccentric mountaineer even by Smoky Mountain standards. He has been the subject of Smoky Mountain storytelling lore that has endured for over a hundred years. Several Uncle Mark episodes have been collected by George Ellison in a biographical profile, *The Heritage of Swain County, North Carolina* (1988), and in his well-written collection of essays *Mountain Passages: Natural and Cultural History of Western North Carolina and the Great Smoky Mountains* (2005). More recently, Jim Casada, a historian of fly-fishing and himself an accomplished fisherman, included several Uncle Mark stories in his fine treatise *Fly Fishing in the Great Smoky Mountains National Park* (2009).

Mark Cathey's fame as a fisherman only barely eclipses his reputation as a bear hunter. Samuel Hunnicutt, a resident on nearby Deep Creek and author of the peculiar little book *Twenty Years of Hunting and Fishing in the Great Smoky Mountains* (1926), who proclaimed himself "to be a perfect hunter," tacitly acknowledges that Mark Cathey was his equal as a bear hunter. Bob Plott, an avid hunter and author of *A History of Hunting in the Great Smoky Mountains*, recognizes Cathey along with Hunnicutt, Quill Rose, and Granville Calhoun as the four finest bear hunters ever on the North Carolina side of the mountain.

A friend of Jim Gasque's witnessed Mark Cathey catching his last fish. He described it as "one of Mark's greatest performances." For several minutes Cathey danced his dry-fly, teasing a sizable trout that remained hidden and wary. After what seemed an interminable interval, the trout darted from his rock toward the fly only to return to his hiding without taking. The fish repeated this darting action several times more. Finally, unable to resist, the creature abandoned all caution and took the fly. Two months later, in October 1944, Uncle Mark went squirrel hunting and did not return. He was found around midnight sitting under an oak tree, his arms across his lap, and his dog at his side. He had died of a heart seizure. A minister who was himself an avid outdoorsman wrote the epitaph engraved on Mark Cathey's tombstone. "Beloved Hunter and Fisherman / Was Himself caught by the Gospel Hook just / Before the season closed for good."

The Indian Creek Trail continues through Cathey's farm following the old wagon road that once served the mountain farms strung along the creek. Six hundred yards above Indian Creek Falls, the Stone Pile Gap Trail drops off the road to the right and climbs a mile to the Thomas Divide Trail.

Five hundred yards above the Stone Pile Gap junction, the Indian Creek Trail intersects the eastern terminus of the Loop Trail leading in from the old Jenkins

Place on Deep Creek. A little more than a half-mile beyond the Loop Trail junction, Queen Branch flows into Indian Creek just below the trail to the right. The stream was named for Joe T. Queen who maintained a large farm a half-mile up the branch. A rock wall to the left of the trail is part of the old Alfred Parris place. In 1886, Alf Parris built an overshot mill on Indian Creek near the rock wall. A flume extended over Indian Creek and channeled water from Queen Branch to power the mill's twelve-foot water wheel. Parris's blind grandson, John Chambers Kitchens, purchased the mill in 1919 and operated it until 1931.

 For three years, a young man named John Elander Davis lived on Alf Parris's property a short distance downstream. In 1898, Davis married Alf's daughter Lucretia (Creacy) Parris and purchased two tracts of land up Indian Creek on the side of Thomas Divide. In an interview with John Parris that was later recorded in *These Storied Mountains*, Davis explained that he "had to cut out trees to make a road into the place. It wasn't easy. Didn't have no help. Done all the tree-fellin' myself. And after I hacked my way into the place I'd picked out for my house, I started clearin' the land."

Davis chose chestnut logs for his house. Chestnut trees were fortuitously grouped closely in a copse on a bench of the mountain where Davis had decided to build. He "cut 'em on the spot and hewed 'em on the spot and raised 'em on the spot." It took him two years to complete the house. When finished, it was two stories high with two rooms and a kitchen downstairs and two rooms upstairs. The walls were constructed of "matched logs." In "matched" log construction, a log is split in half with the split faces hewn to a desired thickness; then one log is put in place in a wall, and the matching log is placed in the opposite wall at the same level.

Davis further explains that he "never used clay daubin' between the logs. Now, everybody else built houses by chinkin' the cracks. But I had me a idea of my own and I used it. Used rived boards between the hewed logs instead of clay. Made the tightest joints you ever saw. Kept the house all snug and warm in winter, no matter how hard the wind blowed, or how cold it got." Davis added a twenty-eight-foot stone chimney and a roof of riven oak shingles and then built all the furnishings for the house.

For seventeen years, John and Creacy Davis lived in their log house, farming the slopes of Thomas Divide and herding cattle on the head of Deep Creek before selling their home and farm to neighbor Joe Queen and moving out of the mountains. After the Park Service purchased land for the new national park, John and Creacy's old house stood for many years, empty and forlorn, way off on the back side of nowhere. In 1951, the house was dismantled and moved over the mountain to the Mountain Farm Museum near the Oconaluftee Visitor Center, where it remains on permanent display.

Just opposite the point where Queen Branch flows into Indian Creek, an access path exits left four hundred feet off the Indian Creek Trail to a cemetery known variously as the Lower Indian Creek, the Laney, and the Parris Cemetery. From this point the Indian Creek Trail passes along the upper side of an extended bottomland that once harbored several family farms. Log cabins, barns, corncribs, smokehouses, and various sheds and rough out-buildings ranged along the creek. Except for a few stone foundations, nothing remains of these structures. An occasional homesite can be approximated by the daffodils, boxwoods, or walnut trees, domesticated species that the inhabitants on Indian Creek often planted around their homes. Conspicuous along the left side of the trail is a cluster of fine boxwoods marking an old homesite. Behind the boxwoods are ruins of an old cabin and nearby a few stunted remains of an apple orchard. Scattered about are several discarded household items including, of course, the requisite rusting washtub.

Within a half-mile of the boxwoods, the Indian Creek Trail crosses the stream on a wooden bridge and enters into another stretch of former farm clearings before regaining the shade of forest cover. Eastern hemlocks and yellow buckeyes are prevalent with dog-hobble most conspicuous along the stream's edge.

The trail continues as a wide jeep track on a moderately easy grade for another half-mile until it reaches an access path on the right that leads 400 yards to the Upper Indian Creek Cemetery, also known as the Queen Cemetery. Immediately beyond its junction with the cemetery access path, the trail crosses Indian Creek on a wooden bridge and then continues a little over 500 yards to another wooden bridge situated immediately over the confluence of Georges Branch and Indian Creek. Sixty yards above the Georges Branch bridge is the western terminus of the Deeplow Gap Trail, a lateral connector that links the Indian Creek drainage with the Oconaluftee River Valley.

Here, the grade appreciates noticeably, rising steadily into a forest of yellow buckeye and white basswood. A quarter-mile above the Deeplow Gap Trail junction, the Indian Creek Trail crosses the stream again on a wooden bridge and then, a quarter-mile farther, crosses back on another wooden bridge. A hundred and twenty-five yards above this crossing, the jeep track moves away from Indian Creek to cross Estes Branch on a wooden bridge and then enters a wide turnaround that marks the trail's upper terminus.

Between the left-hand side of the turnaround and Indian Creek is a farm clearing once occupied by a cabin built by Ellis Parris. On the upper right-hand side of the turnaround an access path exits seventy-five yards to the recently established Estes Branch Backcountry Campsite (#46).

The Estes Branch Camp is divided into two distinct sites, the second another hundred yards up Estes Branch. Both sites are pitched on a bare gradient away from the stream and bear the marks of a recently cleared ground, rough and badly galled. The camp is spacious, but the sparseness of level ground limits the suitable tent sites. Estes

Branch runs a short distance below along the length of the camp, although intervening barriers of rhododendron make access to the stream difficult. Easier access to water is back down at the bridge where the Indian Creek Trail crosses Estes Branch.

The Indian Creek Trail terminates at the far end of the turnaround where it intersects the eastern terminus of the Martins Gap Trail leading over Sunkota Ridge from Bryson Place on Deep Creek.

STONE PILE GAP TRAIL

Indian Creek Trail to the Thomas Divide Trail at Stone Pile Gap—0.9 mile.
POINT OF DEPARTURE: Hike 0.5 mile up the Indian Creek Trail. The Stone Pile Gap Trail begins on the right.
QUAD MAP: Bryson City 166-NW

0.0—Indian Creek Trail.
0.1—Indian Creek. Footlog.
0.3—Switchback.
0.6—Old Stone Pile manway.
0.9—Stone Pile Gap. Thomas Divide Trail.

The Stone Pile Gap Trail is a lateral course that connects lower Indian Creek with the Thomas Divide Trail. Documents recording early transfers on Indian Creek occasionally refer to a Stone Pile Trail as a survey point or boundary, but early maps of the Smokies fail to show any trails in the immediate vicinity of the modern Stone Pile Gap Trail. Evidence indicates that the old Stone Pile Trail was farther upstream on Indian Creek. It apparently fell into disuse when superseded by the modern graded track which starts from a lower elevation.

When it leaves the Indian Creek Trail, the Stone Pile Gap Trail drops quickly into an upstream course between the creek and the Indian Creek Trail. Ninety yards up-trail it reaches a low split-log bench where the trail turns to cross the stream on a footlog. Immediately behind the log bench is characteristic evidence of visitation by beavers. Other signs of beaver activity in the area can be seen on gnawed trees just a few yards downstream.

Beyond Indian Creek, the trail continues thirty yards to cross a nameless feeder stream on a novel configuration of upended sections of logs arranged like stepping stones. A hundred yards farther up-trail, the stream is crossed a second time. Three more crossing occur at intervals of 200 yards, 40 yards, and 50 yards respectively. In several places the stream leaks out into the trail, making the course a changing mix of wetness, rockiness, and muddiness.

At the fifth crossing, the trail turns sharply left and leaves the drainage for a fairly easy climb on a well-graded track into a long, sweeping, five-hundred-foot, double-switchback that places it on the spine of a finger ridge. About a quarter-mile above the switchback, a manway exits on the left, leading back down the mountain to Indian Creek. The manway is likely part of the old Stone Pile Trail referenced in the early land transfer documents. It originates at what once was a crossroads in the more densely populated part of Indian Creek. The old trail likely turned at this point on the ridgeline and followed the route of the current trail to the Thomas Divide.

After passing the manway, the Stone Pile Gap Trail rolls off the finger ridge and follows the inside curvature of the slope up before rising into Stone Pile Gap and terminating into the Thomas Divide Trail. The gap harbors both the trail intersection and the park boundary. The Thomas Divide Trail continues down along the ridgeline 1.2 miles to terminate into Galbraith Creek Road at the park boundary.

DEEPLOW GAP TRAIL

Indian Creek Trail to the Mingus Creek Trail—6.1 miles.

POINT OF DEPARTURE: Hike 2.9 miles up the Indian Creek Trail. The Deeplow Gap Trail begins on the right.

QUAD MAPS: Clingmans Dome 165-SW
Smokemont 165-SE

0.0—Indian Creek Trail.
0.1—Georges Branch. Bridge.
0.4—Indian Creek Motor Trail exits right 1.8 miles to the Thomas Divide Trail.
0.5—Georges Branch Backcountry Campsite (#51).
2.2—Deeplow Gap. Thomas Divide Trail.
2.6—Switchback.
2.7—Little Creek. Footlog.
2.8—Little Creek.
2.9—Switchback.
3.0—Little Creek Falls. Footlog.
3.3—Switchback.
3.4—Little Creek. Footlog.
3.7—Cooper Creek Trail exits right 0.5 mile to the park boundary at Cooper Creek Road.
3.9—Cooper Creek. Footlog.
4.3—Cooper Creek.
4.5—Clearing. Chimney ruins.
4.9—Cooper Creek. Footlog.
5.4—Switchback. Trail leaves Cooper Creek.
6.1—Mingus Creek Trail exits right 2.9 miles to Mingus Mill on Newfound Gap Road and left 2.9 miles to the Newton Bald Trail.

The Deeplow Gap Trail is part of a lateral complex connecting the Deep Creek watershed with the lower Oconaluftee Valley and pieced together from old settlers' roads, rehabilitated manways, graded trails, and a modern jeep track.

Sixty yards above the confluence of Georges Branch and Indian Creek, the Deeplow Gap Trail exits the Indian Creek Trail on a wide jeep track leading up and into the Georges Branch drainage. A hundred and fifty yards above the trailhead, it crosses Georges Branch on a wooden bridge and then enters a bottomland that was once the Al Bumgarner farmstead. The jeep track is the remnant of a proposed automobile road that was to enter the park from the lower end of Thomas Divide, loop down and around by way of Georges Branch and Indian Creek, and then exit the park along Deep Creek. Although much of the road was graded, work ceased in 1974, and the project was never completed.

About a half-mile above the trailhead, the jeep track turns right and begins angling out of the bottomland and up the flank of Thomas Divide. At this juncture, the Deeplow Gap Trail turns left and follows an older narrower roadbed that probes deeper into the Georges Branch drainage. The jeep track, at this point, becomes the Indian Creek Motor Trail which exits the Deeplow Gap Trail and climbs 1.8 miles to the Thomas Divide Trail.

During the summer of 1919 while venturing near this part of Georges Branch, Horace Kephart's attention was attracted to a peculiar rhythmical sound coming from the vicinity of the stream's bank. Upon closer investigation, he discovered that the sound was being generated by a wooden contraption that he later described as "one of the most remarkable machines ever made by man." Kephart identified the machine as "a pounding mill or, facetiously, a 'lazy John' or 'tri-weekly'." It was built by Jim Bumgarner, a Smoky Mountaineer who lived near the mouth of Georges Branch. The thing that made the pounding mill so remarkable, Kephart noted, is that "it is the simplest possible application of power." Kephart was so fascinated by the pounding mill that he spent the remainder of that mid-summer day watching it operate.

Since the time he first came to the Smokies in 1904, Kephart had occasionally heard of references to "a mysterious machine whereby a pestle was worked up and down by water power." After stumbling upon the pounding mill on Georges Branch, he described the machine's inner workings in an article for *The Outing Magazine*. The mill consists of a post planted in the ground.

> To its upper part a horizontal pole about ten feet long is pivoted at the center, so that the ends are free to work up and down, like the walking-beam of an old-fashioned steamboat engine.
>
> At one end of the beam is similarly pivoted a pestle about five feet long and ten inches thick. The lower end of the pestle is shaved down to about two-inch diameter, where a narrow iron band keeps it from burring.

The mortar is nothing but a stump hollowed out to funnel-shape and boxed at the top to keep the grain from flying out. A hole is cut through to the bottom of the mortar, from which the meal is spooned out. The hole is closed by a little shutter at other times.

At the other end of the beam, and on top of it, is a box serving as the water bucket, which holds about six or seven gallons. This box is attached to the beam underneath by a wooden hinge, formed by a V-shaped withe on either side of the box, the lower part of which goes around a wooden pin stuck through the beam. Thus the bucket is pivoted and free to tilt when it descends. To keep it from tilting too far, another withe, like the bow of an ox-yoke, is attached to the end nearest the post, the U thus formed going down and around the beam.

To operate the mill, a trough from a stream carries water to the bucket. "When the pestle is down in the mortar, and the bucket is up under the spout, water is turned on. As the bucket fills, its weight overbalances that of the pestle. Down goes the bucket, up goes the pestle. The water being now mostly against the far end, the pivoted bucket has to tilt, and so all the water spills out. Then down goes the pestle with a hard thump."

When Kephart timed the machine, he found it pounded every five seconds. It has been estimated that the mill can "pound" about one gallon of corn a day to the degree of fineness suitable for making cornbread.

In 1927, Bumgarner's pounding mill was brought to the attention of W. J. Damtoft, a forester and property ranger for the Champion Fibre Company on whose land the Bumgarner home was located. Damtoft suggested to Reuben Robertson, president of Champion Fibre, that the pounding mill be preserved. Robertson bought the mill from Bumgarner for ten dollars and then had it dismantled, moved, and re-assembled at Timber Top, his summer lodge in Indian Gap on the main Smoky divide.

The pounding mill remained at Timber Top until 1936 when Robertson donated it to the Park Service to be put on display in a proposed museum of pioneer Smoky Mountain artifacts. The individual parts of the mill, properly numbered and tagged, were put in storage with hundreds of other artifacts, waiting for the museum to be built. In 1960, the park superintendent in charge ordered the pounding mill to be discarded, professing that "there is no value to it."

It is unfortunate that Jim Bumgarner's pounding mill had been lost, for there is, as Kephart pointed out, "a romantic simplicity about the little old mill and its business. There is, too, romance of another kind, furtive, mysterious, that clings to some of them. If it were not for them, the mountain moonshiners could not make blockade liquor."

A hundred and twenty yards above its intersection with the Indian Creek Motor Trail, the Deeplow Gap Trail intersects on the right an access path leading to the Georges Branch Backcountry Campsite (#51). The Georges Branch Camp is on a rolling gradient that was once part of the Sherrill Wiggins farmstead. The camp, established early in the 2000s, is little more than a galled gradient flanking either side of a slight rise. Fifty yards above the main site is a nice level annex capable of accommodating but a tent or two.

Notwithstanding the sparseness of level ground, the camp is, nonetheless, spacious and enjoys an attractive setting among large hardwoods. A food-storage cable is suspended along the edge of the camp nearest the entrance, and water is available from a small stream down the opposite slope.

Beyond the Georges Branch Camp, the trail remains on the roadbed, advancing deeper into the watershed. With increasing frequency, small feeder streams cross the trail, seeking refuge in nearby Georges Branch. The main stream remains out of sight, submerged beneath a welter of thick woody growth. In places, the feeders are little more than seepages spreading out across the trail and making the track wet and messy. About a half-mile above the Georges Branch Camp, the trail leaves the roadbed, turns up to the right and onto a narrow, steep, rocky, weed-infested course ascending the western flank of Thomas Divide. For much of the climb, the trail plays tag with a small stream. Where is does, the trail is often saturated.

One mile after exiting the roadbed, the Deeplow Gap Trail reaches Deeplow Gap, a distinct V-shaped notch in the crest of Thomas Divide, where it intersects the Thomas Divide Trail following along the spine of the divide. The Deeplow Gap Trail proceeds through the gap and begins descending the east side of the divide on a degree of steepness equal to that of the ascent.

On the downward course, the trail wanders through dry-ridge thickets of rhododendron and mountain laurel for a half-mile before settling into the Little Creek drainage. The first encounter with the stream is eighty yards below a switchback where the stream is crossed on a footlog. Two hundred and thirty-five yards farther, the trail reaches the top of Little Creek Falls and proceeds 200 yards to a sharp switchback that directs the trail back 150 yards to the base of the falls where the stream is crossed again on a footlog.

Little Creek Falls is a steeply pitched cascade that thoroughly scours a ninety-five-foot cliff face indented with dozens of small, closely spaced ledges. Little Creek enters the falls as a twenty-foot stream that widens to forty feet before it passes beneath the footlog spanning the base of the cascade. The dazzling whiteness of the cascading water is intensified by the contrasting dark greens and browns of the thick vegetation that encroaches on both sides.

Beyond Little Creek Falls the trail returns to its steep descent. Another switchback 500 yards below the falls redirects the course 120 yards back to Little Creek for another crossing on a footlog. Over the next 600 yards, the grade moderates as the trail negotiates two feeder streams and then enters a bottomland where it intersects the upper terminus of the Cooper Creek Trail.

Originally, the Deeplow Gap Trail terminated at this point. The Cooper Creek Trail then continued on upstream along Cooper Creek, turned, and climbed the adjacent ridge to meet the Mingus Creek Trail. A few years ago the Park Service annexed the upper part of the Cooper Creek Trail to the Deeplow Gap Trail, thus extending it to terminate at the Mingus Creek Trail. All that remains of the original Cooper Creek Trail is a half-mile rump that leads downstream to the park boundary near Cooper Creek Road.

From its junction with the Cooper Creek Trail, the Deeplow Gap Trail turns left onto a roadbed that follows closely along Cooper Creek. Though the stream is nearby, it is largely hidden from the road, buried beneath arbors of rhododendron, mountain laurel, and infestations of dog-hobble.

A footlog ushers the trail to the east side of Cooper Creek. Above this point the trail is frequently wet, saturated by seepages and runnels using the trail as a conduit to Cooper Creek. After a wet messy crossing back over the main stream, the trail soon enters a gentle terrain flanked by low weedy fields. Skeletal remains of two chimneys mark the site of an old farmhouse along the right side of the trail. Resting on the stone foundations of the farmhouse are rotting timbers from the house's wooden frame.

Upon passing the farm clearing, the course continues its gentle climb, negotiating a few more feeder streams and then easing onto a grassy track that is smooth and soft underfoot. About 700 yards above the clearing, Cooper Creek is crossed again on a footlog, and then, about a half-mile farther, the trail leaves the stream, executing a sharp switchback that redirects the course out of the creek bottom and up the steep flank of the adjacent ridge.

The final climb, about three-quarters of a mile, winds through dry-ridge pine-oaks stands that share space with hedges of mountain laurel. The Deeplow Gap Trail terminates at the crest of the ridge, where it intersects the Mingus Creek Trail descending from Newton Bald along the spine of the ridge. At the junction, the Mingus Creek Trail turns to descend the eastern flank of the ridge to Mingus Mill along Newfound Gap Road. Continuing along the ridgeline to the right of the junction is a faint unmaintained rump that leads to the park boundary at Adams Creek Road.

INDIAN CREEK MOTOR TRAIL

Deeplow Gap Trail to the Thomas Divide Trail—1.8 miles.
POINT OF DEPARTURE: Hike 0.4 mile up the Deeplow Gap Trail. The Indian Creek Motor Trail begins on the right.

QUAD MAPS: Clingmans Dome 165-SW
Bryson City 166-NW

0.0—Deeplow Gap Trail.
1.8—Thomas Divide Trail.

> Sometime during the early 1970s, construction was begun on a proposed automobile road that was designated to enter the park along the lower end of Thomas Divide, then drop down to Georges Branch before looping back along Indian Creek and exiting the park by Deep Creek. Most of the proposed road was to follow the course of pre-existing trails and settlers' old wagon roads, although a short section between the crest of Thomas Divide and Georges Branch was newly graded. Construction on the road ceased in 1974, and the project was soon abandoned. Later, the newly graded section was given the unbecoming name Indian Creek Motor Trail and incorporated into the park's hiking trail network.

The Indian Creek Motor Trail begins in a bottomland about 600 yards above the mouth of Georges Branch near the western end of the Deeplow Gap Trail. It starts quickly out of the bottom, setting a steeply angled course up the flank of Thomas Divide. Below, on the right, former farm fields are being reclaimed by a random mix of sourwood, dogwood, eastern hemlock, red maple, black oak, yellow birch, and white pine.

Higher up, straight-grained boles of fallen American chestnut trees lie scattered up and down the wooded slopes. Before their demise by a blight early in the twentieth century, the chestnuts with their spreading canopies were likely the prevalent species on these slopes. Old-timers have mentioned seeing slopes in the Smokies where the chestnuts comprised eighty percent of the forest cover. Unlike the oaks, whose output of acorns can vary widely in size from one year to the next, the chestnut masts were reliably abundant and an excellent fodder for foraging wildlife.

The prevalence of yellow poplar and pignut hickory trees in the forest cover is a signal that the trail is approaching the ridgeline of Thomas Divide. The trail never quite reaches the spine of the divide but levels out to terminate in a peculiar intersection with the Thomas Divide Trail just below the ridgeline. Here, the Thomas Divide Trail emerges as a narrow track rolling off the ridgeline and intersecting at a right angle to the roadbed. The roadbed continues straight ahead, but now under the auspices of the Thomas Divide Trail.

THOMAS DIVIDE TRAIL

Newfound Gap Road to Galbraith Creek Road—13.7 miles.

POINT OF DEPARTURE: From the Oconaluftee Visitor Center, drive on US441 north 12.1 miles to a small pull-over on the side of the road, or from Newfound Gap drive south 3.4 miles to the pull-over. The Thomas Divide Trail begins on the knoll adjacent to the pull-over.

QUAD MAPS: Clingmans Dome 165-SW

Smokemont 165-SE

Bryson City 166-NW

0.0—Newfound Gap Road (US441).

1.8—Kanati Fork Trail exits left 2.9 miles to Newfound Gap Road.

2.4—Nettle Creek Bald.

3.6—Tuskee Gap.

4.6—Sunkota Ridge Trail exits right 8.6 miles to the Loop Trail.

5.0—Newton Bald Trail exits left 5.5 miles to Newfound Gap Road at Smokemont.

8.1—Deeplow Gap. Deeplow Gap Trail exits right 2.2 miles to the Indian Creek Trail and left 3.9 miles to the Mingus Creek Trail.

10.5—Indian Creek Motor Trail exits right 1.8 miles to the Deeplow Gap Trail.

12.5—Stone Pile Gap. Stone Pile Gap Trail exits right 0.9 mile to the Indian Creek Trail.

13.7—Access path to Wiggins-Watson Cemetery. Park boundary. Galbraith Creek Road.

The Thomas Divide Trail is a long ridgeline course that begins along Newfound Gap Road and follows its namesake south to Galbraith Creek Road about a mile east of Deep Creek Campground. Largely because of its considerable length and change in elevation, the trail is home to an astonishing variety of wildflowers and a wide range of tree species.

Thomas Divide was named for William Holland Thomas, a land speculator who as a young man was adopted by the Cherokee Chief Yonaguska and given the name "Wil-usdi," "Little Will." When Yonaguska died in 1839, Little Will was elected chief by the remnant of Cherokee that remained in the Great Smoky Mountains following the Indian removal known as the Trail of Tears. During the Civil War, Thomas organized the Legion of Indian and Highlanders to defend the Smoky Mountain communities from attack by invading Union forces. Under his leadership, a party of six hundred Cherokee rehabilitated the ancient trace that crossed the Smoky divide at Indian Gap, making it serviceable as a road for the warring armies.

The Thomas Divide Trail begins in a nameless swag where Newfound Gap Road crosses over the divide. The trail starts up quickly and into an easy course along the ridgeline. From the outset, the track is even and soft underfoot, amply cushioned by layers of fallen leaves. It remains as such for most of the trail's course. Though not readily noticeable, the trail eases off Thomas Divide for a short diversion out and back along Beetree Ridge before settling into a gentle climb. Turfs of thick mountain grass flank the trail. At various irregular intervals, patches of squaw-root, panicles of Turk's-cap lily, wild bergamot, and fire pink, and carpets of galax and spring beauty are conspicuous. Red, sugar, and mountain maples are in the forest mix as well as white oaks, eastern hemlocks, American beeches, and yellow birches. Particularly noticeable are the low-growing sprouts of American chestnuts, identifiable by their coarsely serrated oblong leaves. The young chestnuts spring up from the root system of old chestnuts killed by a blight that was transported into the United States on nursery plants sometime during the early twentieth century. Large gray boles of fallen chestnut trees are plentiful on the higher slopes of Thomas Divide.

Almost two miles from the trailhead, the Thomas Divide Trail eases into a dell on the ridgeline where it intersects the upper terminus of the Kanati Fork Trail leading up from Newfound Gap Road. At this elevation, scarlet and chestnut oaks enter the forest mix as well as the occasional Allegheny serviceberry. Flame azaleas are interspersed among the understory while spiderwort, wood-betony, Indian cucumber root, and trailing arbutus are noticeable when in bloom.

From the Kanati Fork junction, the Thomas Divide Trail climbs moderately for a half-mile to the top of Nettle Creek Bald, a sparsely wooded knob once known by the local mountaineers as Collins Creek Bald and later identified on a few pre-park maps as Kanati Fork Bald. Irrespective of its name, Nettle Creek Bald is completely overgrown, though it affords limited views south along the spine of the divide to Newton Bald and east across the Oconaluftee watershed to Hughes Ridge. Newton Bald is visible as the prominent hump immediately along the left of the Thomas Divide ridgeline.

Nettle Creek Bald is separated from Newton Bald by Tuskee Gap. As the trail eases off Nettle Creek Bald it descends moderately for a little more than a mile to Tuskee Gap and then climbs on a corresponding grade for a half-mile before dropping into an intersection with the upper terminus of the Sunkota Ridge Trail entering from the right. From this junction, the Thomas Divide Trail continues on a slight climb for almost another mile to approach the western perimeter of Newton Bald, where it meets the upper terminus of the Newton Bald Trail.

The summit of Newton Bald is a half-mile east of the trail junction and, like its lesser sibling Nettle Creek Bald, it is completely overgrown. A hundred and sixty yards down the Newton Bald Trail is the Newton Bald Backcountry Campsite (#52), a fine camp situated on a narrow neck connecting the divide and the bald.

Beyond the Newton Bald junction, the Thomas Divide Trail offers a one-mile respite from the climbing before entering a very steep two-mile descent into Deeplow

Gap, a pronounced V-shaped notch in the ridgeline. Dry-ridge species, particularly sassafras, black locust, yellow poplar, and pignut hickory join the forest cover while pink lady's-slippers, white snakeroot, purple gerardia, and flowering spurge are prevalent in spring. In places, the trail is overgrown in weeds and in others cloistered within corridors of mountain laurel. About half-way down to Deeplow Gap, the trail deviates from the ridgeline where, in wintertime, the Cooper Creek watershed across to the perimeter of Cherokee, North Carolina, can be seen.

In Deeplow Gap, the Thomas Divide Trail intersects the Deeplow Gap Trail, a trans-mountain connector linking the Cooper Creek drainage on the east of the divide with that of Indian Creek on the west. When it leaves the gap, the Thomas Divide Trail enters an equally steep one-mile climb out and along the divide. At the top of the climb, the trail clears an insignificant knob and then starts into a steep descent that persists until trail's end at the park boundary.

Two-and-a-half miles out of Deeplow Gap, the trail turns off the ridgeline and drops onto a wide roadbed where it immediately enters a peculiar intersection with the upper terminus of the Indian Creek Motor Trail. In the early 1970s, work was started on a proposed automobile road that was to enter the park along the lower end of Thomas Divide, following it for about four miles before dropping down to Georges Branch and looping back along Indian Creek to exit the park by way of Deep Creek. Before the work was completed, the project was abandoned, leaving an unimproved roadbed along the west flank of Thomas Divide. That part of the roadbed descending to Georges Branch was later designated as the Indian Creek Motor Trail, and that part proceeding south along the divide was incorporated into the Thomas Divide Trail.

Here, at its intersection with the Indian Creek Motor Trail, the Thomas Divide Trail leaves its narrow cushioned track for the wider rougher course of the unimproved road. The steepness of the grade does not diminish, continuing for an additional two miles until the trail reaches Stone Pile Gap. Over this interval, lower-elevation species become prevalent, particularly dogwoods, yellow poplars, eastern hemlocks, white basswoods, black cherries, and white pines.

Prior to the proposed automobile road up the divide, the Thomas Divide Trail turned at Stone Pile Gap and descended directly to Indian Creek. With the reconfiguration that accompanied the Indian Creek Motor Trail, the Thomas Divide Trail was re-routed to continue on the road grade another mile to the park boundary at Galbraith Creek Road. The short remnant descending to Indian Creek was renamed the Stone Pile Gap Trail.

When the Thomas Divide Trail enters Stone Pile Gap, it levels out for a nice half-mile stretch and then descends steeply another half-mile through a cove of hardwoods and a belt of Virginia pines to terminate into the Galbraith Creek Road. A hundred and seventy yards prior to reaching the boundary, an access path exits on the right, leading to the Wiggins-Watson Cemetery. Deep Creek Campground lies a mile west along an unpaved section of Galbraith Creek Road.

COOPER CREEK TRAIL

Park boundary at Cooper Creek Road to the Deeplow Gap Trail—0.5 mile.

POINT OF DEPARTURE: From the Oconaluftee Visitor Center, drive on US441 south through Cherokee, North Carolina, to US19. Turn right on US19, and proceed in the direction of Bryson City 6 miles to Cooper Creek Road. On Cooper Creek Road drive 3 miles to the park boundary at the end of the road. The Cooper Creek Trail begins at the park boundary.

QUAD MAP: Whittier 166-NE

0.0—Park boundary.
0.5—Little Creek. Footlog.
0.5—Deeplow Gap Trail.

The Cooper Creek Trail is a short connector between the park boundary at Cooper Creek Road and the Deeplow Gap Trail. Access to the trailhead from Cooper Road, off US19, is 185 yards. It is best to secure permission from local residents before parking and hiking up the road to the boundary and the Cooper Creek Trail.

From the park boundary, the Cooper Creek Trail follows the roadbed upstream along Cooper Creek. Inside the park, the stream marks the park's boundary along the right. Three hundred and thirty yards into the park, a clear path exits to the right, leading to an unstable bridge over Cooper Creek and into a maintained clearing. The clearing is private property and not within the confines of the park. Above this juncture, an outlet stream of Cooper Creek flows down the roadbed, often leaving the course deep in water and difficult to hike. The best option is to exit the trail to the left and follow a well-worn path that circumvents the flooded section of the trail.

The outlet stream remains in the trail for an interval of 115 yards. Immediately above this point the road forks. The Cooper Creek Trail continues straight while the right fork turns off, fords the creek, and enters the upper end of the private property clearing. From here, the trail continues following upstream along Cooper Creek though the stream is submerged in heavy thickets of dog-hobble and rhododendron. At this elevation Cooper Creek is more characteristic of a cut-bank stream than a mountain torrent, and thus trees encroach closely on the banks.

A quarter-mile above the fork in the road, the trail enters the old Thomas Wiggins homesite, where it crosses a footlog spanning Little Creek. Forty yards beyond the footlog, the Cooper Creek Trail terminates into the Deeplow Gap Trail. At this junction, the Deeplow Gap Trail, descending from Thomas Divide, turns and follows the roadbed upstream along Cooper Creek.

LOOP TRAIL

Deep Creek Trail at the Jenkins Place to the Indian Creek Trail—1.2 miles.
POINT OF DEPARTURE: Hike 1.7 miles up the Deep Creek Trail. The Loop Trail
begins at the far end of the bridge over Deep Creek.
QUAD MAP: Bryson City 166-NW

0.0—Jenkins Place. Deep Creek Trail.
0.6—Sunkota Ridge Trail exits left 3.8 miles to the Martins Gap Trail and 8.6
miles to the Thomas Divide Trail.
1.2—Indian Creek Trail exits right 0.8 mile to the Deep Creek Trail and left
2.8 miles to the Martins Gap Trail.

At the foot of Sunkota Ridge, where Indian Creek empties into Deep Creek, the
Indian Creek Trail branches from the Deep Creek Trail and proceeds around the
east side of Sunkota Ridge, leaving the Deep Creek Trail to continue around the
west flank. A mile above this trail junction, the Loop Trail exits the Deep Creek
Trail, climbs the west flank of Sunkota Ridge, and then descends the east flank to
the Indian Creek Trail, thus forming a three-mile circuit, or loop, among the three
trails. Because of its proximity to Deep Creek Campground, the Loop Trail offers a
pleasant round-trip excursion that showcases the beauty of two large streams.

The Loop Trail begins in a bottomland along Deep Creek that was once settled
by the Cherokee chief Corn Tassel and subsequently known as the Corn Tassel Place.
The bottom was purchased in 1896 by G. W. Jenkins and his wife, Cora. They built
a large frame house near the intersection of the Loop Trail and Deep Creek Trail and
farmed several acres on both sides of the stream. A wagon road built by the early
settlers along Deep Creek passed through the Jenkins's farm, fording the stream
immediately below and above the house. The junction here came to be known locally
as the Jenkins Place, a name that has endured in Smoky Mountain nomenclature to
the present day.

When it leaves Deep Creek, the Loop Trail passes in front of the old Jenkins
homeplace. Nothing remains of the house or any of the attending outbuildings, but
signs of the place's former domestication are unmistakable. A hundred and forty
yards above Deep Creek, the Loop Trail leaves the creek bottom and crosses a nameless feeder stream to enter a half-mile climb up the flank of Sunkota Ridge. The
climb is moderately steep and follows the contours of the slope through a dry-ridge
mix of white pines, sourwoods, sugar maples, and eastern hemlocks.

The Loop Trail crests the ridge in a featureless intersection that harbors the
lower terminus of the Sunkota Ridge Trail. The lower part of the Sunkota Ridge
Trail, like the Loop Trail, is not an old mountaineers' trace. Both are graded courses
implemented by the Park Service to provide recreational access across the watershed.

Upon leaving the Sunkota Ridge junction, the Loop Trail begins a half-mile descent along the east flank of the ridge. Trail conditions here are similar to those on the west side of the ridge with the exception of a greater incidence of wildflowers on the downward side. Half-way down, the trail reaches a spring which forms the headwaters of a nameless feeder stream that accompanies the trail from here to its terminus. Near the spring is a stone wall that was, no doubt, associated in some way with the spring. With little change in grade, the trail wends down to terminate into the Indian Creek Trail about three-quarters of a mile above the intersection of the Indian Creek Trail and Deep Creek Trail.

SUNKOTA RIDGE TRAIL

Loop Trail to the Thomas Divide Trail—8.6 miles.
POINT OF DEPARTURE: Hike 0.6 miles up the Loop Trail. The Sunkota Ridge Trail begins on the left.
QUAD MAPS: Bryson City 166-NW
Clingmans Dome 165-SW

0.0—Loop Trail.
3.8—Martins Gap. Martins Gap Trail exits left 1.5 miles to the Deep Creek Trail at Bryson Place and right 1.5 miles to the Indian Creek Trail.
8.6—Thomas Divide Trail exits left 4.6 miles to Newfound Gap Road and right 0.4 mile to the Newton Bald Trail.

Sunkota Ridge is a long curved appendage that projects from the western flank of Thomas Divide and separates the Indian Creek drainage from that of lower Deep Creek. The upper end of Sunkota Ridge is anchored to the divide near Newton Bald, and its lower end grades into the bottomland that harbors the confluence of Indian and Deep creeks.

The Sunkota Ridge Trail is virtually synonymous with the spine of the ridge. The trail rarely strays far from the ridgeline, and from stem to stern the grade remains fairly uniform, affording a pleasant dry-ridge excursion through fine second-growth woodlands. The trail offers no outstanding features, and views are limited to occasional glimpses of the high contours of Noland Divide and Thomas Divide ranging across the watersheds.

The Sunkota Ridge Trail begins half-way along the Loop Trail, a short lateral connector between the Deep Creek Trail and the Indian Creek Trail. Initially the grade is level as the trail courses through a stand of white pine. It then begins to climb, moving out of the pines and into a dry-ridge association of several oak species mixed with maple, dogwood, sourwood, sassafras, pignut hickory, and yellow poplar.

Sunkota is believed to be a garbled rendition of the Cherokee word for apple, thus insinuating that apple trees once grew on the nearby slopes. If this was the case, the apple trees have long since disappeared.

The trail climbs a moderate grade for three miles and then descends about three-quarters of a mile to Martins Gap, where it intersects the Martins Gap Trail, a three-mile lateral connector between Bryson Place on Deep Creek and the upper terminus of the Indian Creek Trail. The lower part of the Sunkota Ridge Trail, between the Loop Trail and Martins Gap, was built by the Park Service shortly after 1970. The upper part, between Martins Gap and Thomas Divide, is older, having been built in the 1930s by the Civilian Conservation Corps.

There are no readily apparent differences in character or quality between the park trail and that graded by the CCC. Both are narrow tracks that are fairly free of obstructing roots and rocks and nicely cushioned by layers of leaves and pine needles. The upper section, though, enjoys a somewhat easier grade and affords more opportunities for surveying the adjacent mountain ranges.

As it moves out of Martins Gap, the Sunkota Ridge Trail enters a drier region where the forest cover remains mostly oaks. Galax, trailing arbutus, crested dwarf iris, and rue anemone are conspicuous among corridors of rhododendron and mountain laurel. A gentle grade through a park-like setting shaded by widely spaced spreading oaks heralds the approach to the crest of Thomas Divide, where the trail terminates into the Thomas Divide Trail. Slightly less than a half-mile down the divide is the upper terminus of the Newton Bald Trail.

MARTINS GAP TRAIL

Indian Creek Trail to the Deep Creek Trail at Bryson Place—3.0 miles.
POINT OF DEPARTURE: Hike 3.6 miles to the end of the Indian Creek Trail. The Martins Gap Trail begins at the end of the turnaround.
QUAD MAP: Clingmans Dome 165-SW

0.0—Indian Creek Trail. Road turnaround.
0.1—Indian Creek. Footlog.
0.1—Indian Creek. Footlog.
0.6—Indian Creek. Footlog.
1.5—Martins Gap. Sunkota Ridge Trail exits left 3.8 miles to the Loop Trail and right 4.8 miles to the Thomas Divide Trail.
2.7—Bridge.
3.0—Bryson Place Backcountry Campsite (#57). Deep Creek Trail.

Travelers on Deep Creek occasionally referred to a well-known notch in the crest of Sunkota Ridge as Pullback Gap and that part of the trail descending from Pullback Gap to Bryson Place as the Pullback Trail. The name Pullback survived well into the twentieth century and was referenced by Horace Kephart in his novel *Smoky Mountain Magic* as an alternate route into Bryson Place. The current name for the gap alludes to a Cherokee to whom the white settlers gave the name George Martin. The Indian apparently owned the land around Martins Gap, which he sold in 1887.

The Martins Gap Trail begins as a single-file track leading out of the road turn-around that marks the upper terminus of the Indian Creek Trail and then drops into a heavily shaded defile that harbors the course of Indian Creek. Eastern hemlock, white basswood, and red maple are prevalent in the tree cover while dense thickets of witch-hobble, dog-hobble, and rhododendron comprise the understory. In spring, showy orchis, false Solomon's-seal, wild geranium, crested dwarf iris, and trilliums are often conspicuous.

Two hundred yards up-trail, Indian Creek is crossed and then, thirty yards farther, crossed again. Both crossings are on footlogs. At this juncture, the stream gorge narrows considerably and the trail begins charting a much steeper course that edges up and away from the fast-moving Indian Creek.

A half-mile on, the trail enters a switchback to clear another footlog and cross Indian Creek for the final time. After proceeding downstream for about 300 yards, it switches back sharply to the right and begins climbing steeply up the flank of Sunkota Ridge through second-growth stands of scrub pine and mountain laurel. Galax, trailing arbutus, and pink lady's-slipper are common at the trailside. A small feeder stream seeking an outlet to Indian Creek runs a short way down the middle of the trail.

At the half-way point, the trail pulls into Martins Gap, the slight notch in Sunkota Ridge that was once known as Pullback Gap. Here, it intersects the Sunkota Ridge Trail following along the spine of the ridge.

In 1911 Horace Kephart published an article, "Route Sketching," which he later partly reproduced in his enlarged edition of *Camping and Woodcraft*. To illustrate his technique for route sketching, Kephart included a sketch of the old Pullback Trail. This old trail started in the vicinity of the turnaround on the Deep Creek Trail, followed up Bumgardner Branch, and then ascended the west flank of Sunkota Ridge to Martins Gap. It then descended to Bryson Place generally along the course of the current Martins Gap Trail.

When it leaves Martins Gap, the trail descends steeply along the west flank of Sunkota Ridge through a dry-ridge mix of eastern hemlock, white pine, sourwood, red maple, and several varieties of oaks. Three-quarters of a mile down, the grade moderates briefly at a wide circling switchback that clear a ridge point at the head of Nicks Nest Branch.

 Nicks Nest is some of the most forsaken terrain in the Deep Creek watershed. It figures prominently in Horace Kephart's novel, *Smoky Mountain Magic*, as the location of the protagonist's hidden camp. As Kephart describes it, "Nick Nest was a V-shaped trough, three to four hundred feet deep and about a half-mile long, from the swamp at its mouth to the cliffs below the Pullback trail. Throughout its course the wild waters of Nick's Run dashed and flashed, chattered and roared, over one cascade after another, between steep rocky banks covered with mosses and ferns and vines dripping in the spray." On one side of the Nicks Nest draw, "the mountain rose in a sheer wall, bristling with laurel and rhododendron. On the other side the slope was forty to fifty degrees, densely timbered with tall trees of many species, and the surface was broken with ledges and protruding rocks." Conditions in Nicks Nest have changed little since the time of Kephart's adventures, remaining "a terribly rough and devious gorge, hard to find a way into and worse to get out of."

Upon clearing the ridge point, the trail moves away from Nicks Nest and returns to a steeper course, soon reaching a wooden bridge over a nameless cascading stream. A switchback just beyond the bridge heralds a long gradual descent into Bryson Place, an old Smoky Mountain landmark now occupied by the Bryson Place Backcountry Campsite (#57). On the final approach, the trail passes through a stand of American holly trees before reaching the upper corner of the campsite and terminating into the Deep Creek Trail approaching the camp on the left.

POLE ROAD CREEK TRAIL

Deep Creek Trail at Sassafras Ford to the Noland Divide Trail at Upper Sassafras Gap—3.3 miles.
POINT OF DEPARTURE: Hike 6.7 miles up the Deep Creek Trail. The Pole Road Creek Trail begins on the left at the footlog over Deep Creek.
QUAD MAP: Clingmans Dome 165-SW

0.0—Deep Creek Trail. Sassafras Ford. Deep Creek. Footlog.
0.1—Pole Road Creek.
0.9—Pole Road Creek.

1.0—Pole Road Creek.

1.0—Pole Road Creek.

1.2—Pole Road Creek.

1.5—Pole Road Creek.

1.6—Pole Road Creek.

3.3—Upper Sassafras Gap. Noland Divide Trail exits right 3.8 miles to Clingmans Dome Road and left 7.8 miles to Deep Creek Road. The Noland Creek Trail exits straight 9.4 miles to Lakeview Drive.

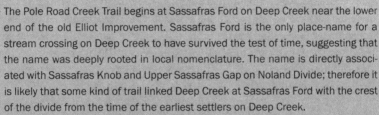

The Pole Road Creek Trail begins at Sassafras Ford on Deep Creek near the lower end of the old Elliot Improvement. Sassafras Ford is the only place-name for a stream crossing on Deep Creek to have survived the test of time, suggesting that the name was deeply rooted in local nomenclature. The name is directly associated with Sassafras Knob and Upper Sassafras Gap on Noland Divide; therefore it is likely that some kind of trail linked Deep Creek at Sassafras Ford with the crest of the divide from the time of the earliest settlers on Deep Creek.

The description "pole road" generally refers to the practice of aligning wooden poles like staves crosswise on an unimproved road to keep cattle and wagons from miring in the mud. At one time a pole road may have led to a splash dam that once stood just below the ford, thus giving rise to the name Pole Road Creek.

A footlog over Deep Creek at the ford now marks the trailhead to the Pole Road Creek Trail. From the footlog, the trail proceeds 170 yards across a bottomland at the mouth of Watson Cove to a difficult crossing of Pole Road Creek. Early hunters on Deep Creek occasionally mentioned a camp in the flats near the confluence of the two streams. Once across Pole Road Creek, the trail stays close to the smaller stream for fifty yards before inching away for a course higher on the adjacent slope. Along here, the grade is moderate and the track a narrow berm of hard-packed dirt relatively free of rocks and roots. White basswood and eastern hemlock are conspicuous in the tree cover with dog-hobble and Fraser magnolia sharing space along the stream.

Two hundred and seventy yards above the first crossing of Pole Road Creek, the trail meets the stream again in a difficult crossing at the lower end of a distinctive terrain which the early hunters called "the benches of Pole Road." One hundred and sixty yards farther is a third crossing, somewhat easier than the previous two. Here the grade stiffens noticeably, passing through a grove of large yellow poplars.

Thirty yards farther, the trail negotiates yet another difficult crossing, where yellow buckeyes enter the mix of the white basswoods, eastern hemlocks, and poplars. The fifth crossing of Pole Road Creek, 330 yards farther, is a bit easier than its predecessor, although by this juncture the trail has become considerably rougher. A sixth stream crossing follows 530 yards on, and then, 200 yards farther, a seventh crossing after which the trail turns sharply away from Pole Road Creek and begins climbing. As elevation is gained, occasional vantage points afford fines views of the surrounding topography, particularly Burnt Spruce Ridge and Sunkota Ridge. Within a span of less than 150 yards, the trail crosses four feeder streams before advancing around a ridge point and into drier conditions of a southern exposure where stands of hemlocks and Fraser magnolias are interspersed with the occasional striped maple. Where the forest cover permits, grand views of the lower extensions of Noland Divide and the wide basin of Deep Creek watershed can be surveyed.

The trail remains on the southern exposure for about a half-mile before turning to angle up and along the flank of Noland Divide for another half-mile to enter Upper Sassafras Gap. Dry-ridge conditions persist with black locust, chestnut oak, and red maple entering the mix of tree species and Turk's-cap lily, trailing arbutus, galax, may-apple, yellow fringed orchid, and wood-betony appearing at various intervals in the understory.

The Pole Road Creek Trail rises into Upper Sassafras Gap at a sharp angle and terminates in a crossroads intersection with the Noland Divide Trail and the Noland Creek Trail. The Noland Divide Trail passes through the gap along the spine of the divide while the Noland Creek Trail rises in from the opposite side to terminate in Upper Sassafras Gap.

FORK RIDGE TRAIL

Clingmans Dome Road to the Deep Creek Trail at the Poke Patch Backcountry Campsite (#53)—5.1 miles.

POINT OF DEPARTURE: From Newfound Gap drive 3.5 miles on Clingmans Dome Road to a pull-over on the left side of the road. The Fork Ridge Trail begins below the pull-over.

QUAD MAP: Clingmans Dome 165-SW

0.0—Clingmans Dome Road.
1.8—Switchback.
4.7—Deep Creek Gap.
5.1—Deep Creek. Deep Creek Trail exits left 3.9 miles to Newfound Gap Road (US441) and right 10.3 miles to Deep Creek Road.

From the time of the earliest settlers on Deep Creek until the arrival of the park, the human history of Fork Ridge has been mostly that of the Smoky Mountain bear hunter. Too remote to be inhabited and too rugged to be frequented by all but the hardiest traveler, Fork Ridge was assaulted only when hunters followed their dogs in pursuit of the bruin making an escape up the ridge and to safety across the main Smoky divide. Today, easy access to Fork Ridge from Clingmans Dome Road has greatly depreciated the nonpareil adventure of escaping into a *terra incognita* of unspoiled primeval wilderness. Nevertheless, an excursion onto the ridge is not without its charms, still affording a wealth of wonders of the high Smoky Mountain backcountry.

Fork Ridge is a long curvature that extends almost six miles from the main Smoky divide at Mount Collins to the confluence of Deep Creek and its primary tributary, Left Fork. As the name of the ridge implies, its topographic role is that of diverting the tributary where it "forks" from the main stream.

The Fork Ridge Trail begins from a small parking area on Clingmans Dome Road three-and-a-half miles above Newfound Gap. Immediately across the road is an access path leading fifty yards to the Appalachian Trail near Mount Collins.

When it leaves Clingmans Dome Road, the Fork Ridge Trail settles into a steady descent, quickly reaching a spring that spills out onto the path before entering a boreal stand of red spruce, Fraser fir, yellow birch, and mountain-ash. Formations of upthrust rock comprise much of the immediate terrain, making the trail itself rough and rocky in places.

One mile below the road, the trail turns onto an east-facing slope and begins angling down through the upper end of a fine copse of slender American beech trees, affording some fine views across the Deep Creek watershed and into a veritable sea of mountains ranging deep into North Carolina. Upon exiting the beech stands, the trail returns to the spruce association. Here, the trail completes a wide switchback and then re-enters the beech stand at a lower elevation. Midway through the switchback the trail approaches the headwaters of Keg Drive Branch, a major tributary of the Left Fork.

According to Smoky Mountain lore, the fastness of Keg Drive Branch was the site of a "cave" where the Cherokee Tsali allegedly hid out from federal troops during the Trail of Tears removal in 1838. George Ellison, in his fine book *Mountain Passages*, describes Tsali's cave as "a shelving rock high on a wooded slope above a dense rhododendron thicket along the main Left Fork." The rock shelter, as Ellison describes it, is in some of the roughest terrain in the Smokies, and even under the best of conditions is difficult to find. He speculates, however, that the rock overhang was used as a hunting camp by the Cherokee long before the fugitive Indian took refuge there.

There is some suggestion that the Keg Drive Branch received its name from the events associated with the surveying of the Pickens Line in 1797. Distance from the white settlements necessitated that the survey party transport provisions and supplies on mules, which they would drive over the rough mountain terrain. Among the provision loaded on the mules were wooden kegs filled with rum. The Pickens Line runs near Keg Drive Branch, an indication that the mules may have been driven down the stream. Hunters venturing into this vicinity recall seeing metal barrel rings in an old camp by the stream. They may well have known the source of the barrel rings and coined the name Keg Drive Branch.

Upon re-entering the beech stands, the trail executes a sharp switchback left to chart a northerly course that soon transitions out of the beeches and the last of the spruces and into a dry-ridge hardwood mix before regaining the spine of Fork Ridge. Along the ridge, the grade moderates nicely. Visible to the left is a short section of Newfound Gap Road running along the crest of Thomas Divide. On the right is the upper end of Noland Divide defining the south boundary of the Left Fork watershed.

The trail remains on the spine of Fork Ridge for only a quarter-mile before rolling off to the right into a long steady descent that roughly parallels the ridgeline. After a mile, the trail returns briefly to the ridgeline, running through a corridor of rhododendron, mountain laurel, and flame azalea before rolling off again to the right. Here, the rushing of Left Fork becomes clearly audible in the gorge below. As it continues descending, the trail circumnavigates a minor ridge point, circling to the left and quickly arriving at a narrow neck in Fork Ridge known as Deep Creek Gap. At this juncture, the roar of Deep Creek drowns out that of Left Fork.

In the day of the Smoky Mountain hunter, Deep Creek Gap was a major landmark, being the only convenient place of passage between the upper reaches of Deep Creek and Left Fork. At this point Deep Creek and Left Fork are only a quarter-mile apart, closer to each other than at any place except where they converge far down the mountain. Well-known camps were situated on both sides of the gap—one at the Poke Patch on Deep Creek and the other, called the Deep Gap Camp, on Left Fork. For many years a trail proceeding up Left Fork crossed through Deep Creek Gap and joined just above the Poke Patch a trail coming up Deep Creek.

At Deep Creek Gap, the Fork Ridge Trail becomes exceedingly steep, dropping 200 yards through a cove to Deep Creek. The forest cover here is sparse and open, mostly chestnut oak, yellow poplar, and white oak. In springtime, carpets of spring beauty and white fringed phacelia interspersed with trilliums blanket the slopes. As it approaches the stream, the trail wends through a small patch of nettle-infested boggy ground before reaching a slight hummock at the edge of the stream.

From the hummock, the trail proceeds across Deep Creek in a difficult crossing and then immediately terminates into the Deep Creek Trail. A footlog once spanned the creek at the point, but apparently it has been washed away by high water. Fifty yards downstream, the Deep Creek Trail enters the Poke Patch Backcountry Campsite (#53), one of the oldest camps in the Smoky backcountry.

NOLAND DIVIDE TRAIL

Deep Creek Road to Clingmans Dome Road—11.6 miles.

POINT OF DEPARTURE: Follow directions to the Deep Creek Trail. The Noland Divide Trail begins from the gravel parking area on Deep Creek Road across from the entrance to Deep Creek Campground.

QUAD MAPS: Bryson City 166-NW
Clingmans Dome 165-SW

0.0—Deep Creek Road.
0.1—Durham Branch. Footlog.
1.3—Switchback.
3.2—Switchback.
3.4—Vantage point.
3.5—Access path exits left 50 yards to Lonesome Pine Overlook.
4.9—Coburn Knob.
6.5—Lower Sassafras Gap.
7.8—Upper Sassafras Gap. Noland Creek Trail exits left 9.4 miles to Lakeview Drive. Pole Road Creek Trail exits right 3.3 miles to the Deep Creek Trail.
9.6—Roundtop Knob.
11.1—Jeep track.
11.2—Tower.
11.6—Clingmans Dome Road.

Noland Divide is a powerful ridge extending south from the main Smoky divide, separating the Deep Creek and Noland Creek watersheds, and distinguished by three prominent peaks—Roundtop Knob, Sassafras Knob, and Coburn Knob—spaced at irregular intervals along the divide. At Coburn Knob the divide splits. The westernmost ridge retains the name Noland Divide while the one that turns to the east is known as Beaugard Ridge.

The Noland Divide Trail generally traces the spine of the ridge, first following up Beaugard Ridge to Coburn Knob and then up Noland Divide to Clingmans Dome Road about a mile east of the dome. The trail is long and has the greatest net gain in elevation from beginning to end of any trail in the Smokies. The course is steepest at the lower end where it climbs Beaugard Ridge.

The trail begins along the upper side of a parking area on the left just inside Deep Creek Campground. It proceeds only 170 yards from the parking area before crossing slow-moving Durham Branch on a footlog. Initially the grade is easy, winding through second-growth stands of yellow poplar, red maple, and a variety of oaks.

Soon the hardwoods give way to stands of white pine, and the grade becomes noticeably steeper. It continues ascending through dry-ridge conditions for almost two miles until crossing a tributary of Juney Whank Branch, where the stream slithers slowly down a rock face. Above the stream crossing, the trail works its way into a narrow hollow shaded by pignut hickories and a variety of oaks and maples. The prevalence of grapevines hanging from the trees suggests that the soil conditions here are not particularly fertile. The trail soon completes a switchback and proceeds a half-mile back out of the hollow to reach the spine of Beaugard Ridge. At this juncture the trail returns to dry-ridge conditions as it turns for a northerly course along the east side of the ridge.

Beaugard Ridge is a rocky configuration that offers several vantage points for surveying the mountain terrain down the Lands Creek drainage and out over the Tuckasegee River basin to the western end of Bryson City. The grade and trail conditions remain unchanged for the next two miles until a very sharp switchback ushers the trail onto a narrow ridge of only a few feet's width where openings in the forest cover afford superb 360-degree views. On the left the mountain falls sharply away to the Lands Creek drainage. Beyond are the wide Tuckasegee basin and the upper reaches of Fontana Lake. In the distance are the Nantahalas. On the right the views are nothing less than astonishing. Here are unobstructed views into the immense gulf of the Deep Creek watershed. Thomas Divide commands the eastern edge of the gulf while Noland Divide forms the western counterpart. Between the two are countless overlapping ridges and spurs, all clad from base to spine in living green. In the fall the greens yield to a rich palette of Indian summer reds, yellows, oranges, russets, and scarlets.

The knife-edge spine on Beaugard Ridge extends for no more than a hundred yards, its upper end punctuated by Lonesome Pine Overlook, a rocky promontory jutting out on the south side of the ridge. The summit of the overlook is reached by a 50-yard access path that leads up from the back side of the promontory. At the top, vegetation gives way to a small rocky outcropping that offers another fine vantage point. Lonesome Pine Overlook is a superb place to sit, have a lunch or snack, and enjoy the views. Unfortunately the overlook is of such juxtaposition that a spur on the opposite side of Beaugard Ridge obstructs the view into much of the Deep Creek drainage, and thus the views here are not nearly as extensive as those from the knife-edge just below.

The name Lonesome Pine Overlook is ambiguous. Pines are certainly prevalent on Beaugard Ridge. Several are to be found on the slopes just below the promontory, but not one is to be found on the overlook. At one time perhaps a single pine may have strayed from the pack and was sufficiently conspicuous to have suggested the name.

A mile and a half above Lonesome Pine Overlook, the trail completes another sharp switchback and passes through a wet patch while circling east below the summit of Coburn Knob. The wet patch is run-off from a spring near the summit of Coburn Knob that marks the headwaters of Lands Creek, which then flows eventually into Bryson City.

Coburn Knob was known originally as Cold Spring Knob. The knob was renamed in 1932 in tribute to Jack Coburn, who was the first to donate land to the newly established Great Smoky Mountains National Park. Coburn was a native of Michigan who settled on Hazel Creek to work for a lumber company. He later operated a store on Hazel Creek and invested in timber land, eventually achieving, by Smoky Mountain standards, a fairly affluent standard of living. Coburn is best remembered for an altercation with a moonshiner in a story Horace Kephart recounted in *Our Southern Highlanders.*

James Andres Thompson, the mountaineer for whom Andrews Bald is named, was one of the earliest if not the first to build a home on Coburn Knob. In 1852, the same year he purchased the grassy bald that would later bear his name, Thompson built a cabin on Andrews Bald. During the summer, Thompson and his family would remain on the bald, farming and herding cattle. In the winter months when snow would often reach a depth of six feet, Thompson moved his family down to the lower elevation house on Coburn Knob.

After circling around Coburn Knob, the Noland Divide Trail begins an easy one-mile descent into Lower Sassafras Gap, coursing through stands of black cherry, black locust, and northern red oak interspersed with fallen American chestnut trees. For much of the way the divide is narrow and the trail stays to the crest of the ridge, affording occasional views into the Noland Creek and Deep Creek basins. At the gap, the trail veers to pass around the west side of Sassafras Knob.

According to notes collected by Pete Prince from interviews with local Smoky Mountaineers, there are two men buried on Sassafras Knob. One is a white man, the other a Cherokee. Both were found dead on the knob in 1929, but in separate instances. Hoy Lee Thomas Sr., later one of the first wardens for the Park Service in this area of the Smokies, helped bury the white man. He was interred about a quarter-mile east of the trail, which at that time skirted the east side of Sassafras Knob, where it intersected an old trail leading down East ridge to the Sassafras Ford and the old Elliot Improvement on Deep Creek.

As the trail works its way around the base of Sassafras Knob, Clingmans Dome comes into view, emerging as a rounded prominence at the upper end of Forney Ridge, the powerful spur immediately to the west. The base of Clingmans Dome is readily identified by the Forney Ridge parking area, which appears as a thin line of defacement on the mountainside.

A little more than a mile above Lower Sassafras Gap, the trail completes its circumnavigation of Sassafras Knob and drops into Upper Sassafras Gap, where it intersects the Noland Creek Trail entering the gap from the west and the Pole Road Creek

Trail entering from the east after ascending from Sassafras Ford on Deep Creek. Both trails terminate in the gap. The trail from Noland Creek is part of an old trace that once led up Bald Branch and into Andrews Bald. This is likely the route Andres Thompson and his family traveled when moving between the cabin on the bald and the home on Coburn Knob.

Upon leaving Upper Sassafras Gap, the Noland Divide Trail starts out steeply into dry-ridge conditions of a rhododendron-laurel tunnel sporting patches of galax and the occasional flame azalea along the trailside. The evergreen shrubs soon give way to stands of northern hardwood. A mile above Upper Sassafras Gap, the crest of the divide widens to a noticeable flat. Here, the trail enters a transition zone where the northern hardwoods begin yielding to the boreal species—Fraser fir, red spruce, American mountain-ash, and yellow birch interspersed with mountain winterberry and mountain maple. Indian-pipe, rosy twisted stalk, and Curtis' aster are prevalent in the understory.

The flat marks the upper end Roundtop Knob, a short stout spur that projects eastward from the side of Noland Divide. From the time settlers first moved onto Deep Creek, hunters maintained a camp in the flat on Roundtop Knob. The Roundtop site was not only suitable for camping but, according to old hunting tales recorded by Sam Hunnicutt in *Twenty Years of Hunting and Fishing in the Great Smoky Mountains,* it offered an excellent base from which to hunt along the upper reaches of Burnt Spruce, Bearpen, and Fork ridges.

Upon leaving the flat, the trail resumes its climb, soon entering into thick stands of fir trees where the hiking is quite pleasant. The grade is moderate, and the thick spongy humus of the boreal forest renders the track soft underfoot. Jewel weeds, crimson bee-balms, white wood asters, red elderberries, and blackberry bushes enter the understory mix, and turfs of rich mountain grass encroach on the sides. The sweet resinous scent of fir trees and the agreeable aroma of decaying boreal humus permeate the air. All around are a palpable silence and stillness that are distinctive of the boreal forests.

One-and-a-half miles above Roundtop Knob, the trail widens to a grassy jeep track. A metal frame tower equipped with instruments for monitoring acid rain appears on the left. The trail continues on the jeep track beyond the tower, remaining in the spruce-fir mix and maintaining a moderately easy grade for another half-mile to terminate on Clingmans Dome Road about a half-mile east of the dome.

◆ NOLAND AND FORNEY CREEKS ◆

The Noland and Forney Creeks section encompasses adjacent drainages separated by Forney Ridge, a powerful spur extending south from Clingmans Dome to Fontana Lake. The headwaters of both drainages form up high on the main Smoky divide, and the primary streams for each flow on parallel courses to separate embayments on the lake.

Noland Creek, the smaller of the two, is bounded on the east by Noland Divide. Only the Noland Creek Trail probes into the upper reaches of the drainage. The Springhouse Branch Trail, functioning as a lateral connector between the two streams, traverses the watershed separating Noland and Forney creeks. Six backcountry campsites are spaced at fairly close intervals along the Noland Creek Trail. The Lower Noland Creek Backcountry Campsite (#66) resides on the embayment at Fontana Lake while the remaining five occupy either abandoned logging camps or improvements from the former Rust estate.

The Forney Creek drainage, immediately west of Noland Creek, is bounded on the west by Welch Ridge, a long appendage that curls south from Silers Bald down to Fontana Lake. In addition to the Springhouse Branch Trail, only the Forney Ridge Trail, Forney Creek Trail, Bear Creek Trail, and Jonas Creek Trail venture into the upper reaches of the drainage. The Forney Creek Trail follows a streamside course that visits the high headwall of the main Smoky divide. The Bear Creek Trail and Jonas Creek Trail climb on westerly courses to the spine of Welch Ridge while the Forney Ridge Trail reaches to the base of Clingmans Dome near the state-line divide.

The Lower Forney Creek Camp (#74) resides at the head of the embayment where the Lakeshore Trail intersects the lower terminus of the Forney Creek Trail. Four other trails are spaced along Forney Creek and another on the Bear Creek Trail. The CCC Camp (#71) occupies a former Civilian Conservation Camp while the other four are situated in old logging camps.

The lower end of the Noland Creek Trail is crossed by a paved track, Lakeview Drive (popularly known as the Road to Nowhere), which itself terminates a mile west of the trail at the mouth of a tunnel. The tunnel marks the eastern locus of a small network of trails between the Noland Creek and Forney Creek embayments. The primary artery is the Lakeshore Trail, a 34.7-mile course that follows the north shore of the lake from the tunnel to the Appalachian Trail just above Fontana Dam. Because the Lakeshore Trail is long and traverses several watersheds, it is treated separately in its own section.

Also beginning near the tunnel are two short loops, the Tunnel Bypass Trail and the Goldmine Loop Trail. Two miles west is the Whiteoak Branch Trail, a short low-elevation connector between the Lakeshore Trail and the Forney Creek Trail. The Goldmine Branch Backcountry Campsite (#67) is found along the Goldmine Loop Trail.

To reach the Noland Creek Trail, drive on US441 south out of the park and continue through Cherokee, North Carolina. At the south end of Cherokee, turn right onto US19 and proceed ten miles to Bryson City, North Carolina. Turn right at the old Swain County Courthouse onto Everett Street. Follow Everett Street out of town, continuing three miles to the park boundary, where the road's name changes to Lakeview Drive. Remain on Lakeview Drive five miles to a parking area at the end of a viaduct over Noland Creek. A path to the Noland Creek Trail is along the upper end of the viaduct. Lakeview Drive continues a mile beyond the viaduct to the mouth of the tunnel that marks the eastern terminus of the Lakeshore Trail.

There is no direct access to the Forney Creek section except from the parking area at the end of Clingmans Dome Road. Otherwise, trails in this section can be reached only by hiking in or crossing Fontana Lake by boat. A commercial shuttle to the Forney Creek embayment is available from the Fontana Village Marina. Information on backcountry shuttle service from the marina is available at http://www.fontanavillage.com/marina/shuttle/ or by calling (428) 498-2129.

FORNEY RIDGE TRAIL

Clingmans Dome Road at the Forney Ridge parking area to the Springhouse Branch Trail at Board Camp Gap—5.6 miles.

POINT OF DEPARTURE: From Newfound Gap drive 7.1 miles to the large parking area at the end of Clingmans Dome Road. The Forney Ridge Trail begins at the west end of the parking area near the entrance to the paved access path to the Clingmans Dome Observation Tower.

QUAD MAPS: Clingmans Dome 165-SW
Silers Bald 157-SE

0.0—Clingmans Dome Road. Forney Ridge parking area.

0.2—Clingmans Dome Bypass Trail exits right 0.5 mile to the Appalachian Trail.

1.1—Forney Creek Trail exits right 11.4 miles to the Lakeshore Trail.

1.8—Andrews Bald.

5.6—Board Camp Gap. Springhouse Branch Trail exits left 2.8 miles to the Noland Creek Trail and right 4.3 miles to the Forney Creek Trail.

The Forney Ridge Trail is popularly known as "the trail to Andrews Bald." It begins at the west end of the Forney Ridge parking area in an opening along the stone retaining wall immediately adjacent to the half-mile paved track leading to the Clingmans Dome Observation Tower. Once through the opening, the trail descends the west flank of Forney Ridge on a steep rocky course 280 yards to intersect the lower terminus of the Clingmans Dome Bypass Trail. Here, the Forney Ridge Trail turns left and begins descending along low rocky bluffs shaded by mountain ash trees dispersed generously among the red spruce and Fraser fir encroaching on either side. Heavy seepages frequently gush from hidden outlets and collect in rivulets in the trail. Some of the natural unevenness of the trail along the bluffs is mitigated by steps fashioned from large stones.

A mile below the parking area, the rockiness subsides when the trail eases into a level bench where it intersects the Forney Creek Trail exiting on the right. Water collects on the sponge-like soil in the bench, making the trail a continuous track of muck and mire. Ten-inch-wide board cat-walks have been extended through the worst places to provide a hiking surface up out of the mire. The trail winds through the bench, climbs a low rocky knoll, and then exits from the balsam woods into the openness of Andrews Bald, a gentle gradient of grassland that straddles the ridgeline.

The origin of the name Andrews Bald has long been a subject of confusion. In 1852, Andres Thompson purchased a tract of land on Forney Ridge which included the bald. He built a small cabin near a spring down in the southwest corner of the bald and lived there with his family during the summer months while herding cattle on the high Smoky Mountain grazing ranges. During the winter months, Thompson moved his family to a lower-elevation home at Cold Spring Knob (now Coburn Knob) on Noland Divide.

Although there is no written instance of its occurrence, the mountaineers in this part of the Smokies during Thompson's time probably referred to the bald informally as "Andres's bald." In 1932, the U.S. Geological Survey officially named the place Andrews Bald, clearly a misspelling since there is no precedent for the bald being called Andrews. In 1973, the Sierra Club *Hiker's Guide to the Smokies* compounded the confusion by stating "the bald was the grazing pasture used by the Andres family." The U.S. Geological Survey acknowledged Andres Thompson a second time with the naming of a stream, which flows into Noland Creek from Coburn Knob as Andreas Branch. This, again, was a misspelling.

Well into the twentieth century, a cabin stood near the spring at the southwest corner of Andrews Bald. Whether this was the original cabin built by Andres Thompson or a later replacement is not known. From a picture taken in 1932 by Albert "Dutch" Roth, the cabin appears to be a primitive structure about fifteen by twenty-five feet, built on a slope, with a door, no windows, and a stone chimney affixed to the outside wall.

Andrews Bald is one of the finest examples of high-mountain grassy balds in the Southern Appalachians. Ecologists have determined that most of the bald is in a very old and mature stand of mountain oat grass. Judging from the depth of the sod, the bald may be several centuries old. It is known to have been here when white explorers first entered the Smokies.

The bald is surrounded by spruce-fir stands rising sharply on all sides. The origin of such a restricted grass area in the heart of a high-mountain balsam forest has engendered several theories. One of the more convincing is advanced by botanist B. W. Wells who contends that the balds are not the result of natural phenomena such as fire, climate, and soil conditions, but are the expansions of trails where the Indians established summer camps.

Balds in the Southern Appalachians are located on broadly rounded ridges or knob tops having warm south-facing slopes, and never on sharp ridges, which were not suitable for large camps. Usually a good spring is found in or near the lower margin of the bald. Wells postulates that these bald-camps were places where the Indians congregated during the warmer seasons and used as bases from which to conduct hunting forays. Because of their strategic position on high ridgelines, the balds furthermore may have been refuges for large numbers of Indians during time of war. Centuries of trampling feet compacted the soil such that the mountain oat grass has established stands that are resistant to the invasion of woody shrubs and the balsam species.

On a clear day the views from Andrews Bald are astonishing. To the east is the vast Noland Creek drainage bounded by Noland Divide sweeping down and away to Deep Creek. To the west is Welch Ridge, punctuated on its lower end by the sharp pinnacle High Rocks (5,190 feet). Below, inlets of Fontana Lake appear as giant puddles in among the overlapping lower ridges of the Smokies and the Nantahalas. Beyond the lake are layers upon layers of mountains rolling deep into North Carolina.

When the Norwood Lumber Company was logging the slopes of Forney south of Andrews Bald, the company maintained a dance hall near the bald for the entertainment of their crewmen. The dance hall was not within the perimeters of the bald, which at the time was about seventy-five acres. Accounts from old-timers indicate that the dance hall was in Flat Top Gap, a large level bench on a spur extending southeast between Andrews Bald and Jerry Bald.

The trail through Andrews Bald is a well-worn rut that proceeds to the southwest corner, then turns sharply back to the left, and re-enters the balsam forest. After proceeding only a short distance, the trail passes out of the balsam zone directly into a second-growth closed-oak association, essentially bypassing the northern hardwood stands that one would expect at this elevation. Along here, witch-hobble is found with trout lily, lousewort, blue bead lily, painted and Vasey's trillium, all of which bloom in early spring.

A mile and a half below Andrews Bald, the Forney Ridge Trail circumnavigates Buckhorn Bald, enters a slight gap, and then intersects an unmaintained manway on the right leading down Buckhorn Branch to Forney Creek. The manway may have once been the primary access to the dance hall from the logging camps on Forney Creek.

A mile below Buckhorn Bald, the grade eases onto a hard-packed dirt track where American beeches enter the forest mix. Umbrella-leaf, toothwort, crimson bee-balm, foamflower, and mountain gentian are found near the seepages from uphill springs.

About two miles below Buckhorn Bald, the Forney Ridge Trail terminates in Board Camp Gap at an intersection with the Springhouse Branch Trail. On the left, the Springhouse Branch Trail descends to Solola Valley on Noland Creek. On the right, it turns and follows the spine of Forney Ridge south for a half-mile before turning off and descending to Forney Creek. On the right side of Board Camp Gap, an unmaintained manway leads down to Forney Creek in the vicinity of the Huggins Backcountry Campsite (#69).

 The Forney Ridge Trail did not always terminate at Board Camp Gap. Until sometime in the late 1970s, the trail continued along the ridge an additional half-mile following the course of the current Springhouse Branch Trail and terminated into the Bee Gum Branch Trail. The Bee Gum Branch Trail was later wholly incorporated into the Springhouse Branch Trail. Prior to this, the Forney Ridge Trail did not even terminate at this point, but continued along the ridgeline for another two miles before ending in a three-way intersection with the Laurel Branch Trail and the Gray Wolf Creek Trail. The former descended to Noland Creek and the latter to Forney Creek. This lower nexus of trails was originally graded by crewmen under the direction of the Civilian Conservation Corps. None of it is now maintained.

CLINGMANS DOME BYPASS TRAIL

Forney Ridge Trail to the Appalachian Trail—0.5 mile.
POINT OF DEPARTURE: Hike 0.2 mile down the Forney Ridge Trail. The Clingmans Dome Bypass Trail begins on the right.
QUAD MAPS: Clingmans Dome 165-SW
Silers Bald 157-SE

0.0—Forney Ridge Trail.
0.5—Appalachian Trail.

The Clingmans Dome Bypass Trail is the shortest trail in the park. It provides an access between the Forney Ridge parking area and the Appalachian Trail that avoids the paved track to the observation tower on the summit of Clingmans Dome. The bypass trail is only a half-mile long, and thus can be combined with the paved track for a mile-and-a-half loop from the parking lot to the Appalachian Trail, then along the Appalachian Trail to the Clingmans Dome Observation Tower, then returning to the parking area.

The Clingmans Dome Bypass Trail begins below the parking lot, 280 yards down the Forney Ridge Trail. From here, it angles up and across the slope towards the spine of the main Smoky divide on a steep, rough, track of loosely shifting stones that is frequently saturated with heavy seepages percolating from the summit of the dome. The trail's most noticeable feature is the accompanying forest. Mountain ash, the most boreal of the deciduous species in the Smokies, is attractive with it striking red-orange clusters of fruit which mature in late summer. Farther up-trail, stands of densely growing Fraser firs—cold, gloomy, and forbidding—are a remnant of the subarctic wilderness that once prevailed on Clingmans Dome before the intrusion of artificial improvements and the invasion of the balsam woolly adelgid.

Balsam woolly adelgids are small wingless insects that infest and kill Fraser firs. They are an invasive species introduced to the United States from Europe around 1900, arriving in the Smokies sometime in the 1950s. Full-grown adelgids are microscopic, but their white, waxy, thread-like covering makes them appear as dots of "wool." These insects typically lay about a hundred eggs and produce three generations per year. The adelgid attacks the firs by feeding in the fissures that appear in the bark when the tree is about four feet high. As it feeds, the adelgid releases a toxin which retards the development of sapwood in the growing tree. The reduced sapwood induces water stress, which eventually kills the tree.

Because the balsam woolly adelgid is not native, the Fraser fir has not evolved any defenses against the insect's toxin. This predator has destroyed about ninety-five percent of the Fraser firs in the Smokies, creating large "ghost forests." The fir stands along the Clingmans Dome Bypass Trail are being chemically treated to resist the effects of the adelgid. An example of a "ghost forest" can be seen on the summit of Clingmans Dome.

Fir trees of all ages are attacked, but damage is usually minimal until the tree reaches maturity in about thirty years. Infected firs usually have an opportunity to produce one or two seeds before succumbing to severe decline and mortality. Openings in the tree canopy from the dead firs allow sunlight to reach the forest floor, causing the seedlings to be "released" and begin growing rapidly to fill the vacancy. The elimination of the large Fraser firs by the balsam woolly adelgid has triggered an explosion of young fir growth competing for space on the dome.

Formations of upturned rock strata impede the climb along much of the upper end of the trail. A transition from the gloom of the fir stands to the openness of a ragged semi-bald heralds a moderation in the grade and the approach to the spine of the main Smoky divide, where the Clingmans Dome Bypass Trail terminates into the Appalachian Trail. A right turn onto the Appalachian Trail leads back into the balsam stands and a half-mile to the Clingmans Dome Observation Tower.

NOLAND CREEK TRAIL

Fontana Lake at the Lower Noland Creek Backcountry Campsite (#66) to the Noland Divide Trail at Upper Sassafras Gap—10.3 miles.

POINT OF DEPARTURE: From the Oconaluftee Visitor Center drive on US441 south through Cherokee, North Carolina, to US19. Turn right on US19 and drive 10 miles to Bryson City. At the Swain County Courthouse, turn right onto Everett Street, cross the Tuckasegee River, and proceed north out of town. Three miles above town, the road crosses the park boundary and the name changes to Lakeview Drive. Five miles beyond the park boundary the Lakeview Drive reaches a parking area on the left at the head of a viaduct over Noland Creek. The Noland Creek Trail is reached from the upper end of the viaduct by way of a 190-yard access path.

QUAD MAPS: Noland Creek 158-NE

Bryson City 166-NW

Clingmans Dome 165-SW

Lakeshore Drive south to Fontana Lake—0.9 mile.

0.0—Access path exits 190 yards from Lakeshore Drive down to the Noland Creek Trail.

0.3—Paved access road to Lakeview Drive.

0.3—Noland Creek. Bridge.

0.4—Noland Creek. Bridge.

0.6—Noland Creek. Bridge.

0.6—Noland Creek. Bridge.

0.9—Lower Noland Creek Backcountry Campsite (#66). Embayment.

Lakeview Drive north to the Noland Divide Trail and Pole Road Creek Trail—9.4 miles.

0.0—Access path exits 190 yards from Lakeview Drive down to the Noland Creek Trail.

0.1—Noland Creek. Bridge.

1.3—Access path exits left to the Bearpen Branch Backcountry Campsite (#65).

2.0—Noland Creek. Bridge.

2.7—Noland Creek. Bridge. Access path exits left 250 yards to the Lower Noland Cemetery.

3.5—Lower end of Solola valley.

4.0—Noland Creek. Bridge.

4.1—Noland Creek. Bridge. Mill Creek Backcountry Campsite (#64). Springhouse Branch Trail exits left 7.1 miles to the Forney Creek Trail at the CCC Backcountry Campsite (#71).

4.2—Noland Creek. Footlog. Access path exits right 200 yards to the Upper Noland Cemetery.

5.0—Noland Creek. Footlog.

5.6—Jerry Flats Backcountry Campsite (#63). Access path exits left 330 yards to the Wiggins Cemetery.

6.0—Noland Creek. Footlog.

6.3—Noland Creek.

6.7—Upper Ripshin Backcountry Campsite (#62).

6.8—Upper Ripshin Branch. Footlog.

6.9—Noland Creek. Double-crossing.

8.2—Bald Creek Backcountry Campsite (#61).

9.4—Sassafras Gap. Noland Divide Trail exits left 3.8 miles to Clingmans Dome Road and right 7.8 miles to Deep Creek Campground. Pole Road Creek Trail exits straight 3.3 miles to the Deep Creek Trail.

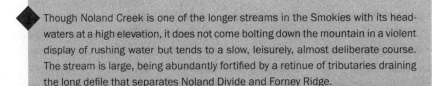

Though Noland Creek is one of the longer streams in the Smokies with its headwaters at a high elevation, it does not come bolting down the mountain in a violent display of rushing water but tends to a slow, leisurely, almost deliberate course. The stream is large, being abundantly fortified by a retinue of tributaries draining the long defile that separates Noland Divide and Forney Ridge.

Settlers began encroaching on the straitened creek bottoms along Noland Creek around the beginning of the nineteenth century. Andrew Noland, one of the earliest in the Smokies, first established residence near the confluence of Noland Creek and the Tuckasegee River where later the village of Noland, North Carolina, would be founded. Early twentieth-century historian John Preston Arthur claims that the stream was named for Andrew Noland, although a local village merchant offered an alternative origin with the remark that the bottoms along Noland Creek consisted of "no land, all rocks and no land."

By the close of the nineteenth century, the hamlet of Noland was rapidly becoming a logging community. In 1880, the Eversole Lumber Company established the first commercial operation to cut timber on Noland Creek, using steers to drag logs to its steam-powered mill on Bald Creek. In 1900, Eversole obtained permission from the Swain County Commission to build a road from the Tuckasegee River six miles north along the stream to Mill Creek in Solola Valley. Four years later the Eversole road was superseded by a pole road built by the J. J. Combs Lumber Company. This road proceeded along Noland Creek another two miles above Solola. In this same year, work was started by the M. T. Mason Lumber Company on the celebrated log flume that was noted for distinguishing the logging operations on Noland Creek from those on other streams in the Smokies.

The Smoky Mountain flumes, usually erected near points where two or three small streams converged, were constructed of two rows of logs spiked together with the insides hewed to form a V or trough-shaped runway set in a box that channeled water from the stream. There were generally two types of flume operations used in the Smokies, the "jiggering slide" and the "gravity slide." Jiggering slides were employed in places where logs would not slide of their own accord, but required pulling by teams of horses. Jiggering teams were occasionally used on gravity slides to start the logs, after which they slid on their own momentum. Sometimes it was necessary for lumbermen to affix sharp iron "check spikes" in the slide timbers in such a way as to dig into the logs and retard their progress, thus preventing the careening logs from escaping the flumes on sharp curves. Logs placed in the flumes on Noland Creek would be sent spinning down the water-slickened slides as far as eight miles to a railway siding in the village of Noland.

When the Noland Flume Company went into operation in 1907, it provided transport service for Eversole, Combs, and Mason, as well as the Harris-Woodbury Lumber Company, R. R. Hicks, Wolverine Lumber Company, and then later the Champion Lumber Company. In 1918, the flume was purchased by local Smoky Mountaineers who maintained it until operations ceased for good in 1922. After nearly a century, scars from the flume's track are still visible on the slopes along Noland Creek.

The lower end of the Noland Creek Trail cannot be accessed directly except by boat on Fontana Lake. One mile upstream where Lakeview Drive (more famously known as the Road to Nowhere) crosses on a viaduct, an access path leads 190 yards from the road down to the trail. For ease of understanding, the one-mile "rump" of the Noland Divide Trail between Lakeview Drive and Fontana Lake is treated here as if going south from the road to the lake. The remaining longer portion of the trail is treated as if going north from the road to Noland Divide.

At the bottom of the access path, the Noland Creek Trail proceeds south on an easy course following a wide level jeep track. On the left, 380 yards down-trail, a paved road intersects, leading down from the upper end of the parking area on Lakeview Drive. Thirty yards beyond the paved road, the trail crosses the first of four wooden bridges over Noland Creek. In quick succession the remaining three follow at intervals of 150 yards, 225 yards, and 95 yards. Down and to the right of the fourth crossing are traces of the ford used by the local mountaineers before the park upgraded the road and installed the bridges.

Beyond the last bridge, the trail continues meandering on a wide grassy track for about a quarter-mile before the ever-steepening terrain presses the course into closer proximity with the stream. Here, the roadbed narrows to a single-file track that is congested with accumulations of large pieces of driftwood deposited when the high water of Fontana Lake embayment recedes. When it breaks out into the openness of the embayment, the trail disappears, its track effaced by the wash of lake water.

Just upstream from the point where Noland Creek completes a ninety-degree bend and opens into Fontana Lake, a small gradient of sun-baked shoreline harbors the Lower Noland Creek Backcountry Campsite (#66). Except for a few small plots in the weedy grass along one corner of the campsite, there are no nice tent spots on the slope. Most of the area is too soft and sandy to be suitable for camping, and the higher ground is too wooded and rough. The camp is served by a food-storage cable suspended in the woods behind the upper downstream corner of the campsite.

The main part of the Noland Creek Trail proceeds north, beginning at the bottom of the access path leading down from the viaduct. The trail passes immediately under the viaduct and crosses Noland Creek on a wooden bridge. Here, the trail follows the old Eversole trace which is now graded to a jeep track, fairly level and easy to hike. About a mile above the bridge, a partially obscured access path intersects head-on at a point where the trail curves slightly to the right. The access leads up along Bearpen Branch 200 yards through a rhododendron tunnel to the Bearpen Branch Backcountry Campsite (#65).

The Bearpen Branch Camp is situated on a slender wedge-shaped gradient that was once occupied by a schoolhouse. Sparsely shading American beeches, white oaks, eastern hemlocks, the nearby stream, and the closeness of confining ridges make for a potentially attractive campsite. Unfortunately, the ground is badly galled and pitched a bit too steeply. The camp is spacious but offers only a few nice tent sites, and none that enjoy seclusion. Three badly worn picnic tables are spaced out along the camp, affording a nice amenity. A food-storage cable is suspended near the campsite's lower end.

Upon passing the access path to the Bearpen Branch Camp, the Noland Creek Trail continues a half-mile to an attractive copse of tall slender white pines interspersed with American beeches and American hollies. Beyond the pine grove the trail enters an old farm field to cross Noland Creek on another wide bridge. Visible to the right of the bridge at the stream's edge is a low stone wall that once served as an abutment for an earlier bridge over the stream. The abutment is likely a remnant from the old Eversole road which was later appropriated by the mountaineers who farmed along the creek.

Evidence of old farms and homesites is abundant beyond the bridge crossing. On the right a stone retaining wall forms up, but more noticeable are the remains of a low chimney fronted by large boxwoods and surrounded by a thin copse of struggling saplings. A little farther and at the edge of a small stream, Spanish bayonets and a road cut indicate the entrance to another homesite. A hundred yards farther on, a cluster of tall boxwoods at the edge of the trail marks a twenty-five-foot access path on the right leading to the remains of a house that was a part of the Rust estate. Pieces of pipe lying about are remainders of a plumbing system that once supplied water from a cistern on the slope behind the house. At the back of the house is the basin of what was once a shower.

The trail continues through old farm fields for another quarter-mile before crossing Noland Creek again on a bridge. Just beyond the bridge, the trail intersects an access path on the left that leads to the old I. K. Stearns homeplace. Stearns was a close friend of Horace Kephart, and after Kephart's death in an automobile accident, Stearns served as executor of Kephart's estate. The house at the Stearns place was used by the Park Service as a backcountry facility until sometime in the 1970s. Five hundred yards beyond the Stearns place is the Lower Noland Cemetery.

Beyond the access to the Stearns place, the trail continues on its easy grade for a mile to Solola Valley, the largest tract of bottomland along Noland Creek. The lower end of Solola is occupied by a meadow of great lobelias, wild golden-glows, crimson bee-balms, and elderberries shaded by a scattering of black walnut trees. Near the upper end of the meadow, the trail crosses another bridge and then proceeds 215 yards to yet another bridge crossing at the confluence of Mill and Noland creeks. Here the trail intersects the western terminus of the Springhouse Branch Trail, which also serves as the entrance to the Mill Creek Backcountry Campsite (#64).

 In 1852, William Holland Thomas, the white chief of the Cherokee, reported to the *Asheville News* that a Cherokee named Solola had captured a snake in the Great Smoky Mountains which he describes as being "of the usual size of Diamond Rattle Snakes found in the mountains of this country, of a dark color—on its tail it has ten rattles, on its head two forked horns of about three fourths of an inch long." The Cherokee claimed it to be a king among snakes of its species. Nothing of its kind had ever been seen by the oldest white inhabitants of the Smokies. Thomas's report was reprinted in *Scientific American*. Solola, a Cherokee word for "squirrel," was also known in the mountains as a metal worker noted for his ability to fashion rifles.

One of the first settlers in Solola was James Andres Thompson who lived here in the 1850s. For many years Thompson herded cattle on Andrews Bald, which he had purchased in 1852. Andrews Bald was later named for Thompson; however, in designating the name, the U.S. Geographic Board misspelled Thompson's given middle name. What was locally known as "Andres's bald" became officially fixed as Andrews Bald. Thompson's name was also incorrectly spelled in the case of Andreas Branch, a large tributary of lower Noland Creek.

The famed Noland Creek log flume operated through Solola Valley from 1904 until it was closed down in 1922. During the Great Depression, millionaire Philip G. Rust purchased over four thousand acres along Noland Creek, including Solola Valley, and built an estate on the Mill Creek confluence. Rust installed a power plant on the stream that provided electricity to the many houses and building on his estate. A wheel powered by the flow of Mill Creek operated the plant's generator. Remnants of the power plant's foundation are visible along the creek just downstream from the bridge.

The Mill Creek Backcountry Campsite is immediately adjacent to the intersection of the Springhouse Branch and Noland Creek trails, situated on an irregular plot aligned on a long slightly pitched gradient. The spacious upper part of the camp is rough, worn, and boasts no level ground. The middle part is a treeless grassy patch that affords a couple of flat spots. This part of the camp is somewhat spoiled by the Springhouse Branch Trail running through the level ground. The more attractive site is the smaller, lower part along the bank of Mill Creek. The ground here is quite level, but a bit gritty and always somewhat damp. While not as rough as the upper part, the lower site is heavily used and betrays the appearance of careless neglect. Two very small tent sites flank the lower part of the camp. The Mill Creek Camp boasts five picnic tables, two each in the upper and middle sections and one in the site by the stream. The upper section has a horse rack and a food-storage cable while the lower two sections share a cable.

One hundred and eighty yards beyond the entrance to the campsite, the Noland Creek Trail approaches a low bluff opposite a footlog over Noland Creek. At the far end of the footlog, an access path exits the trail to the right and passes through the foundation remains of a stone building that was once the summer home of Phillip Rust. The building appears to have been built of cast stone blocks. Fifty yards below the house are the remains of a fish hatchery. The path to the Rust house continues another 200 yards to the Upper Noland Cemetery.

Continuing upstream, the trail inches away from Noland Creek and enters a cove-hardwood association. A large white quartz boulder to the left is the most noticeable rarity along this part of the trail. Almost a half-mile farther, the stream is crossed again on a footlog and then, after another half-mile, reaches the Jerry Flats Backcountry Campsite (#63). On the left opposite the camp, an access path leads 330 yards to the Wiggins Cemetery.

Jerry Flats is a narrow creek bottom fitted between Jerry Bald and Jim Ute Ridge. Jerry is likely a corruption of "cherry," as in the wild cherry trees that were logged in this vicinity for the furniture industry. Jim Ute Ridge is named for Jim Uriah Wiggins, who operated a rugged farm high on Noland Creek. Jim Ute Branch, which drains into Jerry Flats, and the nearby Wiggins Cemetery likewise honor this early settler on Noland Creek.

The Jerry Flats Camp occupies an abandoned farm field shaded by a few slender American beeches, Fraser magnolias, a copse of struggling hemlocks, and a very sparse understory. The site is level but not particularly attractive, retaining too much of its domestic heritage as farm clearing. The camp straddles the trail and suffers from the coarseness of a horse camp. It is capable of accommodating several tents sites, and water is convenient from nearby Noland Creek.

A half-mile above the Jerry Flats Camp, the trail crosses the stream again on a long narrow footlog. Within the next quarter-mile, it approaches the stream at a wide spot that cannot be easily rock-hopped. After another half-mile, the trail reaches an access path to the Upper Ripshin Backcountry Campsite (#62), a wide galled spot about fifty yards below the trail on the right. The camp is spacious and lightly shaded with maples, but too severely sloped and worn by horse traffic to serve as an ideal site. Nevertheless, it does afford the amenity of a crude wooden table. Water is readily available from the stream running along the lower edge of the camp.

A second access path near the upstream end of the camp exits fifty yards to the main trail. Immediately, the trail negotiates a low crude bridge that spans Upper Ripshin Branch and then executes back-to-back wet crossings of a divided Noland Creek. From this juncture, the trail inches away from the stream and, for a short distance, offers a pleasant level excursion through rich cove-hardwood stands of red and sugar maples, Carolina silverbells, yellow buckeyes, white basswoods, yellow poplars, and eastern hemlocks. Soon, feeder streams intervene, the grade steepens, the track narrows, and the course becomes increasingly muddy and rough.

About a mile and a half above the Upper Ripshin Camp, the trail enters a small camping spot on the right. Down to the left and a little out of sight is a second smaller camp. These comprise the Bald Creek Backcountry Campsite (#61).

Both parts of the Bald Creek Camp are fairly level, but neither is large enough to support more than a couple of tents sites each. The lower camp is more attractive, cloistered by low woody undergrowth and thus sequestered a bit from the trail. Each camp has its own food-storage cable, and both are convenient to water.

 Until just before the turn of the twenty-first century, the Noland Creek Trail did not run through the campsite but turned east and proceeded up nearby Sassafras Branch to Upper Sassafras Gap. The camp then was reached by a 100-yard access path that exited the trail from the left. The combination of steep terrain, the close proximity of the stream, and the constant churning by horse traffic eventually rendered the trail up Sassafras Branch largely impassable. Consequently, the Noland Creek Trail was re-routed. The trail now turns down the old access path and through the middle of the Bald Creek Camp, then turns back east on a drier course into Upper Sassafras Gap. Prior to the trail being routed through it, the Bald Creek Camp was one of the nicer campsites in the Smokies.

The Bald Creek Camp is situated on the east side of Noland Creek and just to the north of Bald Creek. It was here that the Eversole Lumber Company operated an early steam mill. Later, the Harris-Woodbury Lumber Company logged the slopes along Bald Creek, where it then maintained a portable sawmill.

The distance from the Bald Creek Camp to the trail's end at Upper Sassafras Gap is a little over a mile. The grade here is much steeper than any other part of the trail, and the track is often filled with loose rock. In the gap, the trail terminates in a crossroads intersection with the Noland Divide Trail and the Pole Road Creek Trail. The Noland Divide Trail passes through Upper Sassafras Gap along the spine of Noland Divide while the Pole Creek Road Trail, leading up from Sassafras Ford on Deep Creek, rises into the gap from the opposite side.

TUNNEL BYPASS TRAIL

Lakeview Drive to the Lakeshore Trail—1.6 miles.

POINT OF DEPARTURE: Follow directions to the Noland Creek Trail, and remain on Lakeview Drive until it terminates at a tunnel. The Tunnel Bypass Trail begins on the left side of the road opposite the lower end of the parking area at the tunnel.

QUAD MAP: Noland Creek 158-NE

0.0—Parking area at the end of Lakeview Drive.
0.4—Goldmine Loop Trail exits left 2.0 miles to the Lakeshore Trail.
1.4—Hyatt Branch.
1.6—Lakeshore Trail exits right 440 yards to the tunnel at the end of Lakeview Drive.

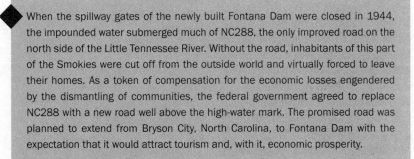

When the spillway gates of the newly built Fontana Dam were closed in 1944, the impounded water submerged much of NC288, the only improved road on the north side of the Little Tennessee River. Without the road, inhabitants of this part of the Smokies were cut off from the outside world and virtually forced to leave their homes. As a token of compensation for the economic losses engendered by the dismantling of communities, the federal government agreed to replace NC288 with a new road well above the high-water mark. The promised road was planned to extend from Bryson City, North Carolina, to Fontana Dam with the expectation that it would attract tourism and, with it, economic prosperity.

Construction on the proposed road, to be known as Lakeview Drive, was begun in 1960. Starting from Bryson City, work proceeded five miles into the park to Tunnel Ridge where a 365-yard tunnel was bored through the mountain. At this point all construction stopped. The road remained uncompleted. Over the course of the next several years, disagreement among parties opposing and favoring the road was often fierce. Many of those to whom the federal government had promised the road felt betrayed. From within the accumulating years of disgust and frustration, the five-mile rump of Lakeshore Drive came to be known as "the Road to Nowhere." The project was eventually abandoned in 2009.

The Road to Nowhere is now blocked 200 yards below the east entrance to the tunnel. Where the road is blocked the Lakeshore Trail begins. It follows the road track through the tunnel and then along the north shore of the lake 34.7 miles to terminate into the Appalachian Trail just above Fontana Dam. For horses and some hikers, the prospect of walking through the long unlit tunnel is a bit unsettling. As an alternative, the Park Service built the Tunnel Bypass Trail, a 1.6-mile detour that circles around the south end of Tunnel Ridge and approaches the Lakeshore Trail 440 yards beyond the west end of the tunnel.

The Tunnel Bypass Trail begins across the road from the lower end of the parking area at the end of the Road to Nowhere. It passes quickly through a band of eastern hemlocks and then into a dry-ridge hardwood mix. Four hundred and eighty yards above the road, it clears the low southern tip of Tunnel Ridge where the faint trace of a manway leads back up the ridgeline. Two hundred and forty yards farther, the trail intersects the eastern terminus of the Goldmine Loop Trail, which circles down to an embayment of Fontana Lake before climbing up and around to intersect the Lakeshore Trail 110 yards beyond the western terminus of the Tunnel Bypass Trail.

Upon leaving the Goldmine Loop junction, the Tunnel Bypass Trail remains in the dry-ridge hardwoods, proceeding a mile before crossing the headwaters of Hyatt Branch. From the creek crossing, the trail takes a course angling up to the Lakeshore Trail. It rises gradually over 350 yards to converge with the Lakeshore Trail 440 yards beyond the west end of the tunnel.

GOLDMINE LOOP TRAIL

Tunnel Bypass Trail to the Lakeshore Trail—2.0 miles.

POINT OF DEPARTURE: Hike 0.4 mile down the Tunnel Bypass Trail. The Goldmine Loop Trail begins on the left.

QUAD MAP: Noland Creek 158-NE

0.0—Tunnel Bypass Trail.
0.6—Switchback.

0.9—Embayment.

1.2—Access path exits right 330 yards to the Goldmine Branch Backcountry Campsite (#67).

1.8—Chimney ruins.

2.0—Lakeshore Trail.

According to early Smoky Mountain lore, Cherokee living in the vicinity of what is now Goldmine Branch maintained a tunnel or cave in the side of a nearby ridge in which they hid gold ore dug from the mountainside. When white settlers began drifting into the area in the early nineteenth century, they learned of the Cherokee's tunnel and likewise took up mining along the creek. Finding the ore to be of inferior quality, the settlers soon abandoned the undertaking. Even though the mining proved unprofitable and was soon forgotten, the legacy of the enterprise still survives in the names Goldmine Branch, Tunnel Ridge, and Tunnel Branch.

The Goldmine Loop Trail is a two-mile course that forms a deft loop on the eastern end of the Lakeshore Trail. The latter begins at the mouth of a 365-yard tunnel that marks the western end of the infamous Road to Nowhere. As a consideration for hikers and horses uncomfortable with the prospect of walking through a long unlit tunnel, the 1.6-mile Tunnel Bypass Trail is provided as an alternative that loops around to intersect the Lakeshore Trail on the far side of the tunnel.

In a similar manner, the Goldmine Loop Trail, after branching off from the Tunnel Bypass Trail, loops down and around to intersect the Lakeshore Trail at a point farther west of the tunnel. The tunnel which the Goldmine Loop and Tunnel Bypass trails circumnavigate is, oddly enough, bored through Tunnel Ridge. The circumstance, however, is totally coincidental as the name of the ridge predates the construction of the tunnel.

The Tunnel Bypass Trail begins across the Road to Nowhere from the lower end of the parking area just below the tunnel. It proceeds 700 yards to the crest of Tunnel Ridge, where it intersects the eastern terminus of the Goldmine Loop Trail. At this juncture the Tunnel Bypass trail turns right and proceeds up the ridgeline. The Goldmine Loop Trail begins here and follows south down the ridge.

The Goldmine Loop Trail eases out on a gentle grade, descending leisurely through a dry-ridge mix of sugar maple, pignut hickory, Fraser magnolia, American holly, and a variety of oaks. Soon the rate of descent begins to increase, progressing to a steep winding drop into a narrow hollow drained by Tunnel Branch. When the trail reaches the floor of the hollow, it switches back sharply right to pursue a more moderate course downstream along Tunnel Branch. Proximate ridgelines and overhanging rhododendron block out the direct sunlight, casting the hollow in a perpetual gloom.

The trail continues a quarter-mile until coming in sight of the Goldmine Branch embayment of Fontana Lake. Here it leaves Tunnel Branch, circles the end of the embayment, and turns right on an uphill course along Goldmine Branch. The course here is occasionally wet and muddy, and always shaded by leggy stands of rhododendron. A quarter-mile above the embayment, the trail crosses Hyatt Branch to intersect an access exiting right 330 yards to the Goldmine Branch Backcountry Campsite (#67).

The Goldmine Branch Camp, ranging along the edge of Hyatt Branch, occupies the lower part of an old farmyard that extended a considerable distance up the defile. The farmhouse stood across the stream and about twenty-five yards below the camp. A tall chimney marks the site of the house, and nearby stone walls outline the course of a road that once led to the house. The farm belonged to Elias Hyatt.

The camp is pitched in a quaint niche immediately by the stream. For the most part it is quite level but affords sites for only a few tents. Because it is in a remote location off an infrequently used trail, the camp shows little evidence of heavy use. Weeds encroach freely on every side, and the camp is shaded by the few trees that have managed to claim space on ground that was likely severely compacted by farm traffic.

Above the access path, the Goldmine Loop Trail continues its easy grade, often through muddy seepages and flanked by a mix of laurel, ferns, galax, rhododendron, and dog-hobble shaded by eastern hemlocks and chestnut oaks. On the left, 200 yards above the camp access, the former Cole Hyatt homeplace is marked by a few boxwoods surrounding a set of steps and a rock-lined cellar.

Conditions remain essentially unchanged until the trail coalesces into an old farm road. Almost a half-mile above the Cole Hyatt place, the trail skirts a large sedgy field that harbors the gaunt remains of the former Fred Fuller home. During the growing season the field is too heavily infested with weeds to make exploration a satisfactory exercise, but in the cooler seasons considerable refuse from former inhabitation can be seen scattered about the old farmyard.

A brisk climb from the field leads quickly through American holly and Fraser magnolia trees to a notch in the ridgeline where the trail turns sharply left and into a steep 200 yard climb to rendezvous with the Lakeshore Trail. The Goldmine Loop Trail intersects the Lakeshore Trail 440 yards west of the tunnel and 110 yards west of the upper terminus of the Tunnel Bypass Trail.

SPRINGHOUSE BRANCH TRAIL

Noland Creek Trail at Solola Valley to the Forney Creek Trail at the CCC Backcountry Campsite (#71)—7.1 miles.

POINT OF DEPARTURE: Hike 4.1 miles up the Noland Creek Trail to the Mill Creek Backcountry Campsite (#64). The Springhouse Branch Trail begins at the campsite.

QUAD MAPS: Noland Creek 158-NE
Silers Bald 157-SE

0.0—Solola Valley. Noland Creek Trail. Mill Creek Backcountry Campsite (#64).
0.1—Mill Creek.
0.6—Mill Creek. Footlog.
0.7—Stone wall.
1.3—Springhouse Branch.
2.8—Board Camp Gap. Forney Ridge Trail exits right 5.6 miles to the
   Clingmans Dome Parking area.
4.2—False gap.
7.0—Spring.
7.1—CCC Backcountry Campsite (#71). Forney Creek Trail exits right 8.6
   miles to the Forney Ridge Trail and left 2.8 miles to the Lakeshore Trail at
   the Lower Forney Creek Backcountry Campsite (#74).

The Springhouse Branch Trail begins at a campsite and ends at a campsite, its eastern
terminus anchored in the Mill Creek Backcountry Campsite (#64) and its western
at the CCC Backcountry Campsite (#71). Prior to the coming of the park, several
trails and manways traversed Forney Ridge, connecting communities and camps
on Noland Creek with those on Forney Creek. Of these traversing trails, only the
Springhouse Branch Trail is still usable.

During the Great Depression, millionaire Philip G. Rust purchased hundreds of
acres in Solola Valley on Noland Creek and built an estate at the confluence of
Mill and Noland creeks. Rust's estate included a great house, horse track, flower
gardens, pottery kilns, and a fish hatchery. Rust had a water-powered generator
installed on Mill Creek to supply electricity to the house and various outbuildings
on the property. The foundation of the power plant can be seen along Mill Creek,
and the remains of the main house are quite noticeable upstream across Noland
Creek. Otherwise, most vestiges of the Rust estate have been either removed or
effaced by the agents of time.

The Mill Creek Camp occupies what was then the center of the compound. The
camp is a wedge-shaped gradient whose lower end rests against Mill Creek, its
east side bounded by the Noland Creek Trail. It boasts five picnic tables and two
food-storage cables. Two of the tables are assigned to the rough, upper slope of
the camp; two are in an open grassy patch in the middle of the camp; and the
remaining one sits in a low flat space near the stream. Food-storage cables are
found in the upper and lower parts of the camp.

The site is heavily used as a horse camp and is frequently found littered with
debris. The upper part is sloped a bit too steeply, and the lower part is too worn
and over-used for either to be considered nice tent sites. The middle section is
suitably level and grassy but has the charm of a farmyard.

The Springhouse Branch Trail begins at an intersection with the Noland Creek Trail along the east side of the camp. It proceeds through the middle of the campsite and upstream along Mill Creek. Within the first hundred yards, it completes a wet, messy, double-crossing of Mill Creek and then continues with the stream on the left. The slopes along Mill Creek were once cleared and farmed, first by pioneering settlers and later by the Phillip Rust estate. Struggling hemlocks shade the once-galled farmyard while yellow birches, yellow poplars, sourwoods, black locusts, and sassafras now compete for space in the old farm fields. On the left, a former homesite is marked by a three-foot remnant of a house chimney. Farther upstream, skeletal remains of a ten-foot chimney on the right and several stone piles on the left are more testimonies to the mountain's farming heritage.

Three-quarters of a mile above the campsite, Mill Creek is crossed on a footlog near its confluence with Springhouse Branch. Here, the trail forsakes Mill Creek for a northwesterly course up the narrow Springhouse Branch hollow. On the right, immediately beyond the stream crossing, a stone wall ranges along the edge of another farm field that extends for a considerable distance up both sides of the trail. The Springhouse Branch drainage is shaded by eastern hemlocks and is considerably damper than the Mill Creek watershed.

A half-mile beyond the stone wall, the trail crosses Springhouse Branch and enters the lush environment of old-growth cove hardwoods. Wood-betony, black cohosh, Jack-in-the-pulpit, crimson bee-balm, trillium, foamflower, may-apple, blood-root, yellow mandarin, and rue anemone are a few of the flowering species that thrive in this moist shaded enclave. At this juncture, the grade becomes slightly steeper as the trail plies a southerly course along the flank of Forney Ridge. In places, the path is quite rocky and in others, visited by seepages.

After another half-mile, the trail turns right, the grade moderating considerably, and the track becoming soft underfoot, cushioned by leafy detritus from the shading oaks and maples. Mountain laurel flanks the trail at certain intervals and rhodo-dendron at others. Eventually the trail breaks out into an open deciduous forest before dropping into Board Camp Gap, a shallow swag on the spine of Forney Ridge where it intersects the lower terminus of the Forney Ridge Trail leading down from Andrews Bald. There is some evidence that Board Camp Gap was once occupied by a hunters' cabin. The gap is sufficiently level and wide enough to accommodate a modest structure.

Upon leaving Board Camp Gap, the Springhouse Branch Trail enters a steep modulating climb over a course cushioned by layers of fallen leaves. After a half-mile, it follows shortly along a level ridgeline before beginning a modulating descent to a false gap where it turns sharply right to descend the western flank of Forney Ridge. The false gap once harbored the intersection of three trails—an unnamed manway leading back down the eastern flank of Forney Ridge to the lower end of Solola Valley, the Bee Gum Branch Trail leading down the western flank of Forney Ridge to Forney Creek near the present CCC Backcountry Campsite (#71), and a now-disused segment of the Forney Ridge Trail that continued along the crest of the ridge for another two miles to an intersection with an old trail leading up Laurel Branch to Gray Wolf Creek. The manway to Solola and the continuation to Gray Wolf Creek were later abandoned. The old Bee Gum Branch Trail was incorporated into the present Springhouse Branch Trail.

From this juncture, the trail turns and descends on a northerly three-mile course over recovering slopes of a dry-ridge hardwood mix of chestnut oak, black locust, pignut hickory, ash, Fraser magnolia, cucumber tree, and red maple. After descending little more than a half-mile, it crosses the upper end of Bee Gum Branch and settles into a slow sinuous journey around the southern flank of Rough-hew Ridge and into the Bee Gum Branch drainage. In places the trail is saturated with seepages, and in others it follows stretches of dry ridge. A couple of minor feeder streams and an increase in seepages herald the approach to a wide shallow crossing of a tributary of Bee Gum Branch. On the right, immediately prior to the stream crossing, a deep spring confined within a deftly laid, U-shaped, rock wall flows under the trail and into a rock catch-basin on the other side. A fallen tree lying across the spring may make it difficult to spot.

At the stream crossing, the trail reaches a wide bottomland that once harbored Civilian Conservation Corps Camp NP-16. On the left, among a thicket of American holly trees, is the concrete foundation of an old camp building. Nearby is a large pit littered with bed springs, tin cans, wire fencing, pipes of various sizes, pieces of sheet metal, and an iron bathtub, all apparently refuse from the CCC outpost. On the right, a few yards down-trail, is the CCC Backcountry Campsite (#71). The trail skirts the lower side of the camp and terminates into the Forney Creek Trail near an imposing two-story chimney that once served a large lodge that was part of the CCC complex.

The CCC Backcountry Camp is one of the largest in the Park, situated in a spacious level plat sparsely shaded by pines and yellow poplars, and fitted nicely in the right angle formed by the intersection of the Springhouse Branch and the Forney Creek trails. The camp is available for horses, readily exposed to trails on two sides, and bears many vestiges of its heritage as an institutional camp. It lacks the streamside setting of nearby Forney Creek and enjoys little in the way of wilderness ambience. The site, nevertheless, remains a pleasant place to camp as it is suitably level, affords excellent tent sites, and is large enough to allow campers to spread out, thus affording virtual seclusion.

WHITEOAK BRANCH TRAIL

Lakeshore Trail to the Forney Creek Trail—1.8 miles.

POINT OF DEPARTURE: Follow directions to the Noland Creek Trail, and remain on Lakeview Drive until it terminates at a tunnel. Beginning at the tunnel, hike 1.9 miles along the Lakeshore Trail. The Whiteoak Branch Trail begins on the right.

QUAD MAP: Noland Creek 158-NE

0.0—Lakeshore Trail.
0.4—Gray Wolf Creek.
0.9—Chimney ruins.
1.7—Whiteoak Branch.
1.8—Forney Creek Trail.

The Whiteoak Branch Trail is a short connector that links the Lakeshore Trail with the Forney Creek Trail. Its junction with the Lakeshore Trail lies two miles west of the tunnel at the end of Lakeview Drive and is marked by a weedy clearing where clusters of daffodils betray the site of a settlement homestead. The Lakeshore Trail continues through the clearing before dropping into the bottomland along Gray Wolf Creek while the Whiteoak Branch Trail exits to the right and proceeds along the flank of the adjacent ridge on a hard-packed dirt track littered with loose stones kicked up by horse traffic.

The Whiteoak Branch Trail climbs easily along the ridge while making a transition from a cove-hardwood environment to a dry-ridge mix of pines and oaks. After a little less than a half-mile, an old roadbed veers off to the left just before the trail crosses Gray Wolf Creek and begins climbing away from the stream.

A half-mile above the stream crossing, the trail reaches a small clearing marked by a pile of chimney rocks. Nearby is a small spring. The trail continues climbing for another 300 yards before reaching a slight swag shaded by short-leaf, Table Mountain, and white pines. Here the trail leaves the Gray Wolf Creek drainage and begins descending to Forney Creek, soon easing in alongside Whiteoak Branch. In several places, runnels seeking the main stream cross the trail, making the track wet and muddy. Where horse traffic has churned the trail badly, the course is very rocky.

The trail soon crosses Whiteoak Branch and then, thirty yards farther, terminates into the Forney Creek Trail.

FORNEY CREEK TRAIL

Forney Ridge Trail to the Lakeshore Trail at the Lower Forney Creek Backcountry Campsite (#74)—11.4 miles.

POINT OF DEPARTURE: From the end of Clingmans Dome Road, hike 1.1 miles down the Forney Ridge Trail. The Forney Creek Trail begins on the right.

QUAD MAPS: Clingmans Dome 165-SW
Silers Bald 157-SE
Noland Creek 158-NE

0.0—Forney Ridge Trail.

0.9—Switchback.

1.4—Switchback.

1.9—Forney Creek. Rock Slab Falls.

2.0—Annex to the Steeltrap Branch Backcountry Campsite (#68).

2.4—Upper access to the Steeltrap Branch Backcountry Campsite (#68).

2.5—Lower access to the Steeltrap Branch Backcountry Campsite (#68).

2.7—Steeltrap Branch.

3.8—Switchback.

4.1—Little Steeltrap Creek.

4.3—Feeder stream. Footlog.

4.4—Little Steeltrap Creek. Footlog.

4.4—Forney Creek.

4.5—Buckhorn Branch. Footlog.

5.5—Switchback.

5.7—Switchback.

6.0—Feeder stream. Footlog.

6.0—Forney Creek.

6.0—Huggins Backcountry Campsite (#69).

6.1—Forney Creek.

6.3—Feeder stream. Footlog.

6.4—Forney Creek.

6.9—Feeder stream. Footlog.

7.2—Board Camp Creek. Footlog.

7.4—Jonas Creek Trail exits right 4.1 miles to the Welch Ridge Trail. Jonas Creek Backcountry Campsite (#70).

8.6—CCC Backcountry Campsite (#71). Springhouse Branch Trail exits left 7.1 miles to the Noland Creek Trail at the Mill Creek Backcountry Campsite (#64) in Solola Valley.

8.8—Bee Gum Branch.

10.0—Whiteoak Branch Trail exits left 1.8 miles to the Lakeshore Trail.

10.0—Whiteoak Branch.

11.1—Bear Creek Trail exits right 5.9 miles to the Welch Ridge Trail.

11.4—Lakeshore Trail. Lower Forney Creek Backcountry Campsite (#74).

 In 1903, outdoorsman W. L. Hicklin and two companions dropped off the main Smoky divide and descended into the Forney Creek watershed in what was then an untouched wilderness. Hicklin later wrote "the trees farther down in the cove were of enormous size. We measured a poplar and observed that the limbs were 125 feet from the ground. There was a holly tree of saw log size and its lower limbs were easily 70 feet from the ground. The hemlocks were the largest we had seen."

At the time of Hicklin's visit, the upper end of Forney Creek was a vast forested expanse unfamiliar to all but a few local hunters and fishermen. Near its lower end, where the stream emptied into the Little Tennessee River, a bustling mountain village stood at the center of a wider community known as Forneys Township. A few hardy settlers had established hardscrabble farms in the narrow rock-infested bottoms along the creeks, but they stayed mainly to the lower elevations.

By the second decade of the twentieth century, everything had changed. The Norwood Lumber Company had descended on Forney Creek and clear-cut the big trees Hicklin had so admired, leaving a trail of destruction and a landscape that Horace Kephart described as "wrecked, ruined, desecrated, turned into a thousand rubbish heaps, utterly vile and mean."

The Forney Creek Trail is largely a residue from the Norwood logging operation. The trail not only follows the trace of Norwood's old railroad grades, but the backcountry campsites along the way are themselves either former lumber camps or junctions for the rail lines. Foot-logs spanning Forney Creek at the upper elevations are often affixed to old substructures that once supported rail trestles over the stream.

The Forney Creek Trail begins along the Forney Ridge Trail about a mile below the Forney Ridge parking area (also known as the Clingmans Dome parking lot). The mile down the Forney Ridge Trail to the Forney Creek trailhead is fairly steep and rocky.

When it leaves the Forney Ridge Trail, the Forney Creek Trail angles across the mountain face following a narrow rut filled with loose rock and often saturated with water. At this elevation, the trail is in the boreal zone with yellow birch and mountain ash interspersed among the red spruce and Fraser fir. Much of the spruce here was harvested by the Norwood Lumber Company to supply light-weight wood for the building of airplanes and ships during World War I. To remove the timber, Norwood operated an incline railway that crossed the trail near Forney Creek. The rusting hulk of a boiler that once powered the incline remains in an opening several yards up the slope above the trail.

After almost a mile, the trail negotiates a switchback onto a single-file hard-packed dirt track that appears in places to be little more than a thin etching on the ground. It immediately crosses a feeder stream then descends a half-mile to another switchback before crossing the feeder a second time. From this juncture, the trail and stream diverge. The trail continues on a wide bench, becoming increasingly rocky to the point of being treacherous.

A half-mile farther, the trail crosses Forney Creek for the first time at the top of Rock Slab Falls. The falls are a spectacular cascade in which Forney Creek ripples down a wide, remarkably smooth, rock shield for fifty yards, collects momentarily in a shallow pool, and then continues, rippling down the shield. Seventy-five yards beyond the stream crossing, an access trail leads left sharply down to an annex of the Steeltrap Backcountry Campsite (#68). The access trail descends along the same shield washed by Rock Slab Falls. Embedded in the surface of the shield are thin bands of white quartz of varying widths and appearing as unevenly spaced stripes painted across the surface of the rock. During the geological upheavals that formed the Great Smoky Mountains, compressed strata of rock were broken and thrust upward, leaving these quartz veins tilted and exposed.

The annex site enjoys an attractive streamside setting by a pool at the base of Rock Slab Falls. It is situated on a tiny parcel of bare gritty ground fitted tightly between Forney Creek and the adjacent slope, and has space for perhaps two tents. For years this spot had been appropriated by hikers as a place to camp, although until recently it had not been sanctioned by the Park Service as an official campsite. At some point, workers mistakenly assumed this spot to be the Steeltrap Backcountry Campsite (#68), which is actually farther down-trail, when stringing up a food-storage cable. Rather than removing the cable, the decision was made to adopt the site as an upper extension of the original campsite near Steeltrap Branch.

The original Steeltrap Branch Backcountry Campsite is almost 600 yards down-trail near the confluence of Steeltrap Branch and Forney Creek. The interval between the two camps is steep, rocky, and often saturated with water. Crimson bee-balms and yellow golden-glows encroach on the path.

Though considerably larger, the lower site is similar to its upstream counterpart in that it is a level plat of gritty industrial ground cut into the mountain. The camp is uniformly round and enclosed by high weedy growth, partially turfed in tussocks of tough grass and, where bare, strewn with small rocks. It does not have the same intimacy with the stream that its upper counterpart enjoys, but like the upper camp, it has access trails entering from both ends. The Forney Creek Trail circumnavigates the camp in a double-switchback. However, the access trails into and out of the camp are more frequently used, leaving the main trail at this point to be somewhat of a superfluous weed-infested detour around the campsite.

Below the camp, the grade becomes fairly level over a 300-yard interval to Steel-trap Creek. After crossing the stream, the trail returns to its steady descent, albeit on a slightly easier grade.

Along here, remainders from the Norwood logging operation become increasingly noticeable. First is a sharp railroad switchback fitted around a stone retaining wall. At the next stream crossing are the remains of a stone corner section that once supported a wooden trestle over the stream gorge. Little Steeltrap Creek is then crossed at a steeply angled cliff where the stream ripples slowly down a smooth rock surface and out into the trail. Two hundred yards farther, another switchback forms up followed by a long rickety footlog whose ends rest upon wooden beams that once supported a rail trestle. Here, the stream gorge is quite deep, leaving the footlog suspended high above the ground and making it one of the more intimidating footlog crossings in the park.

Within another ninety yards, Little Steeltrap Creek is crossed a second time on a footlog and then, 135 yards farther, Forney Creek is crossed for the second time immediately adjacent to a stonework abutment that once supported a railroad bridge. The stream here is wide, but often shallow enough to be forded by rock-hopping.

Eighty yards beyond the Forney Creek crossing, the trail clears Buckhorn Branch on a short footlog and quickly enters a rugged boulder-infested terrain. At this elevation Forney Creek has dropped below the boreal zone and into a wide glen where a second-growth hardwood mix is vigorously reclaiming ground. Over the next mile the trail follows the former railroad trace, keeping a respectable distance from Forney Creek while descending on a remarkably uniform grade.

A long sharp switchback configured around an impressive stone retaining wall heralds the trail's return to the stream. On the approach, a second switchback and a footlog crossing of a feeder stream intervene. Thirty yards beyond the footlog is an easy crossing of Forney Creek and then, within 200 yards, the trail enters the Huggins Backcountry Campsite (#69).

 The Huggins Camp was preceded by the Monteith Camp built in 1929 and named for Samuel Westin Monteith, a timber cruiser for the lumber company. Prior to the Monteith Camp, the Norwood Lumber Company maintained a logging camp here known as the Junction Camp. The camp was situated near the confluences of Forney Creek, Huggins Creek, and Chokeberry Branch and harbored the junction of rail lines that proceeded up each of the streams. In addition to the rail junction, the camp had a large commissary, a schoolhouse, and portable housing.

The Huggins Camp is situated on a rough gradient near the mouth of Huggins Creek. Pieces of industrial refuse scattered about its gritty ground betray the camp's heritage as a rail yard. There is an assortment of suitable tent spots ranged beneath shading maples, oaks, and poplars. The site affords proximity to the stream and a remote setting of rocky ruggedness, making it an altogether pleasant camping place.

A hundred and twenty-five yards below the Huggins Camp, Forney Creek intervenes. This crossing, also at the edge of a stone abutment, frequently requires wading. From this juncture, the trail enters a pleasant 300-yard excursion that is interrupted only by a couple of passing feeder streams. The next crossing of Forney is difficult. Deep pools require patience and caution, particularly when the stream is running high and fast.

Here, the trail begins to distance itself from the stream, winding on an easy course through a delightful bottomland shaded with tall, slender, second-growth, cove hardwoods interspersed with sassafras, sourwood, American holly, and patches of rhododendron. After almost a half-mile, the trail returns to the stream for another difficult crossing and then remains along the stream on an easy course confined by encroaching dog-hobble and rhododendron. A footlog over Board Camp Creek heralds the approach to an intersection with the lower terminus of the Jonas Creek Trail.

The Jonas Creek Trail crosses Forney Creek on a footlog just above the mouth of Jonas Creek and enters immediately into the Jonas Creek Backcountry Campsite (#70). The campsite is a large triangular tract defined by the two streams and a steep-sided ridge. The trail runs through the campsite and then along the trace of a narrow gauge track that followed Jonas Creek deep into the watershed. When Norwood was cutting timber along Jonas Creek, logging crews were housed in portable boxcar dwellings set beside the narrow gauge. The boxcars were painted red and, accordingly, the camp was identified as the Red Ridge Camp. The adjacent ridge was occasionally referred to as Red Ridge. In 1932, the U.S. Geological Survey officially designated the ridge as Scarlett Ridge.

Before the Great Smoky Mountains National Park was formed and the U.S. Department of Interior took possession of the Smokies, the rail line along Forney Creek forded at several places along the stream. To avoid difficult stream crossings at the lower elevations, the Park Service re-routed the trail below the Jonas Creek junction, keeping it entirely on the east side of Forney Creek. In places where the trail was re-routed, its course deviates abruptly from the bottomland to engage in steep detours up the adjacent slopes. Where the trail remains by the stream, it follows the old railroad trace over an easy grade, though the course is sometimes a bit rough and uneven. In those instances where the trail deviates from the stream, it offers some of the most unpleasant hiking anywhere in the Smokies.

The first deviation occurs almost a half-mile below the Jonas Creek Trail junction. It starts sharply up on a coarse narrow track plying the contours of the slope. The steeper places are made worse by frequent plowing from horse traffic. The merest rain transforms the path to a sticky mire.

After three-quarters of a mile, the trail makes a steep descent to the old railroad trace and immediately enters the CCC Backcountry Campsite (#71), one of the largest campsites in the park. The camp is a level tract shaded by pines and poplars and fitted nicely into the right angle formed by the intersection of the Forney Creek Trail and the Springhouse Branch Trail. The site was once occupied by one of Norwood's largest logging camps. In May 1933, the federal government appropriated the old Norwood camp for the site of Civilian Conservation Corp Camp NP-16, the first CCC camp in the park. The camp accommodated two hundred men. In addition to grading many of the trails on the south side of the Smokies, men from this camp built the fire towers on Shuckstack and High Rocks.

Vestiges of the old CCC camp abound. Most noticeable is a two-story stone chimney with a brick-lined fireplace standing along the edge of the trail. The building that accompanied the chimney is gone, but the concrete floor and the boxwoods that festooned the yard give some indication of the layout of the facility. For many years an iron bathtub and a few miscellaneous fixtures lay scattered about the chimney. At the rear of the camp, along the nearby Springhouse Branch Trail, are foundation walls, a concrete platform and a cellar from other outbuildings. In a nearby open pit that once served either as a cellar or a trash dump, there are bedsprings, tin cans, wire fencing, pipes of various sizes, pieces of sheet metal, and an iron bathtub—perhaps the one that once resided by the chimney.

The backcountry camp that now occupies the old CCC site is an open, spacious, level allotment that offers a wide selection of excellent places to pitch a tent. The camp is too far from Forney Creek to be considered a streamside setting and reflects too much of its former domestication to possess a wilderness ambience; nevertheless it is not an unpleasant place to camp. Several fire rings are accompanied by two food-storage cables, and in one corner of the camp resides a crude wooden table.

The lower corner of the backcountry camp is marked by the intersection of the Forney Creek Trail and the western terminus of the Springhouse Branch Trail leading in from Solola Valley on Noland Creek. From this intersection, the Forney Creek Trail continues downstream, passing immediately on the left a small space strewn with old rails, large oil barrels, tin cans of various sizes, broken bottles, a metal stove hood, and an odd assortment of metal refuse—remains of a garbage dump that served the CCC camp. Immediately below the dump site, the trail completes a deft tangent encounter with Forney Creek, crosses Bee Gum Branch, then starts into its second deviation from the stream. Again the track becomes rough, rutted, and unpleasant to hike, though not as steep and considerably shorter than the previous detour.

When the trail returns to its streamside course, the track becomes level though a bit rough and uneven. Again, the big stream is nearby, but flowing discreetly behind screens of dog-hobble and rhododendron. A quarter-mile below the end of the second detour, the trail leaves the stream for the third time, climbing a hundred yards to an intersection with the Whiteoak Branch Trail and then, fourteen feet farther, to an easy crossing of Whiteoak Branch.

The climb to the intersection was formerly part of the Whiteoak Branch Trail. When the Forney Creek Trail was redirected away from the main stream, the hundred yards were incorporated into the re-route and the Whiteoak Branch Trail was truncated at the point where the Forney Creek Trail crosses Whiteoak Branch. The Whiteoak Branch Trail leads up its namesake and on into the Gray Wolf Creek drainage, eventually linking with the Lakeshore Trail.

Upon crossing Whiteoak Branch, the Forney Creek Trail proceeds 500 yards before dropping again to the streamside course. The trail beyond is straight, rigidly confined by dog-hobble and rhododendron, and shaded by sycamores, American beeches, red and sugar maples, and yellow poplars. The course remains level, alternating between a nice, smooth, pebbled track and places where it is washed out and rutted. The trail eventually widens to a jeep track just above the point it intersects the lower terminus of the Bear Creek Trail. The Bear Creek Trail exits to the right, crossing Forney Creek on a wide wooden bridge before climbing almost six miles to the Welch Ridge Trail near High Rocks.

From the Bear Creek intersection, the Forney Creek Trail follows the jeep track 620 yards until it terminates in the Lakeshore Trail at the upper end of the Lower Forney Creek Backcountry Campsite (#74). The hiking along this lower section is easy and pleasant, the track remaining wide, smooth, and along the big stream.

Before the stream was submerged by the rising waters of Fontana Lake, Forney Creek flowed another two miles to empty into the Little Tennessee River. The confluence of the two streams once marked the site of the principal community of the Forneys Creek Township. The township was established in 1873 and incorporated a wide swath of mountain land along lower Forney Creek. The origin of the name Forneys is not certain. A deed in 1849 refers to "Forneys Camp Site" on the Jesse Siler tract. There is some evidence that Thomas J. Forney purchased land on the creek in 1838. One Smoky Mountain tradition asserts that Thomas Forney was a surveyor who maintained a camp near the fork of the Tuckasegee and Little Tennessee rivers. Once, while surveying the mountain, he allegedly fell into a creek, prompting his co-worker, Jacob Siler, to yell "that's Forney's Creek!" In 1932 the U.S. Geographic Board changed the name from Forneys to Forney.

BEAR CREEK TRAIL

Forney Creek Trail to the Welch Ridge Trail—5.9 miles.
POINT OF DEPARTURE: Hike 11.1 miles down the Forney Creek Trail. The Bear Creek Trail begins on the bridge to the right.
QUAD MAPS: Noland Creek 158-NE
Silers Bald 157-SE

0.0—Forney Creek Trail. Forney Creek. Bridge.
0.2—Bear Creek. Bridge.
0.5—Access path exits right across Welch Branch on a bridge and then 0.8 miles to the Hoyle Cemetery. Switchback.
1.9—Bear Creek. Bridge.
2.0—Bear Creek. Bridge.
2.8—Poplar Flats Backcountry Campsite (#75).
3.2—Switchback.
5.9—Welch Ridge Trail exits right 6.4 miles to the Appalachian Trail at Silers Bald and left 0.9 mile to the Cold Spring Gap Trail.

One of the most desolate places in all the Smokies is High Rocks, a stout pinnacle of rock that punctuates the remote lower end of Welch Ridge. High Rocks is notable for its command of a panoramic view of the upper end of the Little Tennessee watershed. Trails approach High Rocks from three directions; nevertheless access remains difficult. The trails themselves are remote as well as being long and steep. One approach to High Rocks is along the Bear Creek Trail, which begins on the Forney Creek Trail a half-mile above the Forney Creek embayment on Fontana Lake. The trail follows the remnant of an old logging grade built by the Norwood Lumber Company.

When it leaves the Forney Creek Trail, the Bear Creek Trail proceeds only eighty feet before crossing Forney Creek on a wide wooden bridge, then skirts an unattractive patch of bare ground that was formerly the Bear Creek Backcountry Campsite. During Norwood's tenure in the Smokies, this campsite harbored a railroad junction that connected three spur lines, one that switched back and ascended Pilot Ridge, a second that turned and trailed up Bear Creek, and a third that stayed to the right, adhering to Forney Creek.

The Bear Creek Trail follows the latter course, tracing Forney Creek upstream on a wide, easy, light-gravel track. Two hundred yards beyond the old campsite, the trail crosses Bear Creek on a bridge at the point where the stream empties into Forney Creek. From this juncture, the trail continues on its course along the larger stream for another 200 yards before easing away for a course up Welch Branch.

Within the next 250 yards, the trail turns away from Welch Branch in a sharp switchback in the direction of Bear Creek. Just at the point when the trail turns, a short footbridge crosses the stream and onto an access path leading up into the extremely narrow Welch Branch drainage.

The access path follows the stream three-quarters of a mile to where the hollow opens out into a clearing that harbors the chimney ruins and foundation remains of a large cabin. Stones from the house are scattered on the gentle gradient below the cabin site. On the upper side terraced grounds bear the marks of having once been garden plots.

From the homesite, the access path continues another 200 yards, climbing very steeply to the crest of the adjacent ridge. At the apex of the ridge and completely enclosed by a tight thicket of laurel interspersed by a few stunted trees, a tiny clearing bears four graves—three adults and one child, all buried in the nineteenth century. This is the Hoyle Cemetery.

 Very few, if any, current landmarks in the Smokies testify more poignantly to the isolation and rugged subsistence of the early pioneer settlers than does this cemetery and homesite. The cabin occupies the only semblance of level ground. Steepness is all around. There is no easy way in or out. Traces of the old farm road can be seen below the access path, but it was likely not appreciably better than a rough mule track. When considering that the bottomland near the mouth of Forney Creek was sparsely settled until the mid- to late nineteenth century, the remoteness of the Hoyle cabin is an example of extreme isolation.

When the Bear Creek Trail switches away from Welch Branch, it begins following the contours of the lower end of Jumpup Ridge, soon working its way back to
Bear Creek. The trail quickly moves out from beneath a stand of eastern hemlock
and then proceeds through forest cover that alternates between pine-oak associations
and cove hardwoods. As the trail penetrates deeper into the drainage, it picks up a
wide easy track, soon maneuvering into a streamside course along Bear Creek. Here,
tall slender second-growth yellow poplars rise up like ship masts from arbors of rhododendron and dog-hobble that congest the bottom of the stream gorge.

A mile and a half above the switchback at Welch Branch, Bear Creek is crossed
on a wooden bridge. Three hundred yards farther, the stream is crossed again on
a bridge. The interval between the two crossings was used by Norwood for a rail
junction and logging outpost. A spur line to the left once ran up to the crest of Pilot
Ridge. For many years, an unmaintained graded trail followed the spur line, tracing
the crest of Pilot Ridge to Bee Knob and then to Cold Spring Gap. The most noticeable refuse from the Norwood operation are pieces of an old stove on the right just
below the first bridge and, just above and on the left, an abandoned washtub. Any
camp Norwood may have maintained here likely consisted of portable buildings
that were easily picked up and transported as the loggers moved deeper into the
watershed.

After the second crossing, the grade stiffens noticeably as the trail continues for
almost a mile to the Poplar Flats Backcountry Campsite (#75).

The Poplar Flats Camp, situated on a gently sloped badly eroded gradient,
appears rough and worn but nevertheless enjoys an attractive setting. The camp is
tucked into a hollow with the stream running down one side. The woods below the
camp are open and sparse.

Along the lower end, a few scattered pieces of metal and a couple of rails left
from the logging operation lie scattered about. In the flats, Norwood maintained a
rail junction and a portable sawmill operation. A spur line proceeded past the camp
and up Bear Creek. The main line, following a switchback through the camp, is now
incorporated into the Bear Creek Trail.

Above the Poplar Flats Camp, the trail narrows considerably, and the grade stiffens another few degrees. Over the next half-mile, it proceeds through second-growth
hardwood forests bearing remarkably little undergrowth and then negotiates a wide
S-shaped curve that conveys it onto the ill-defined crest of Jumpup Ridge. Following
the spine of Jumpup Ridge, the trail enters a pine-oak association and proceeds
through a laurel corridor before dropping into a slight swag. On the left the faint
trace of an unmaintained trail leads in from Ad-valorem Branch. Just above the swag,
openings in the forest cover offer some nice views of the upper reaches of Fontana
Lake.

The dry-ridge conditions soon give way to cove hardwoods as the trail resumes
its steep grade and begins tracing the contours of the steeply sloped flank of Jumpup

Ridge. A switchback circumnavigates the end of a ridge point marked by a grassy patch and the point where the trail leaves Jumpup Ridge for a course along Bald Ridge for the final mile. The crest of Bald Ridge is covered by mature open woodlands with low undergrowth. A moderate-to-easy stretch affords a pleasant, but short, respite from the steepness. Increasing rockiness signals the onset of the final steep pull onto the flank of Welch Ridge and into an intersection with the Welch Ridge Trail. Five hundred yards down the Welch Ridge Trail, an access trail exits right 560 yards to the summit of High Rocks.

JONAS CREEK TRAIL

Forney Creek Trail to the Welch Ridge Trail—4.1 miles.
POINT OF DEPARTURE: Hike 7.4 miles down the Forney Creek Trail. The Jonas Creek Trail begins on a footlog on the right.
QUAD MAP: Silers Bald 157-SE

0.0—Forney Creek. Footlog.
0.1—Jonas Creek Backcountry Campsite (#70).
0.4—Jonas Creek.
0.5—Jonas Creek.
1.0—Jonas Creek.
1.2—Jonas Creek.
1.3—Jonas Creek. Footlog.
1.8—Yanu Branch. Footlog.
4.1—Welch Ridge Trail exits right 2.4 miles to the Appalachian Trail at Silers Bald and left 4.9 miles to the Cold Spring Gap Trail.

When the Norwood Lumber Company first arrived on Forney Creek, the company was interested primarily in hardwood timber suitable for flooring. Much of the hardwood sought by Norwood was found in the Jonas Creek drainage. To transport the timber, a railroad line was laid along the lower reaches of Jonas Creek and up the eastern flank of Welch Ridge. The current Jonas Creek Trail follows the grade of the old rail line.

The Jonas Creek Trail begins along the Forney Creek Trail about four miles above the Forney Creek embayment of Fontana Lake. It immediately crosses Forney Creek on a footlog. Fifty yards above the crossing, the trail enters the Jonas Creek Backcountry Campsite (#70).

The Jonas Creek Camp is a long, level, three-sided tract wedged neatly into the angle formed by the confluence of Jonas and Forney creeks. The back of the camp is bounded by a steep slope. The interior of the camp is coarse ground largely bereft of trees. Water is convenient and two food-storage cables and a crude wooden table are welcome amenities; however, good tent sites are rather scarce. The site is heavily used and galled to the extent that it bears closer affinity to a barnyard than to unspoiled wilderness. The coarseness is exacerbated by the trail running through the middle of the camp.

During Norwood's tenure in the Smokies, Jonas Creek was known as Left Hand Prong, and the wedge of land at the confluence harbored the company's Red Ridge logging camp. The camp had a commissary and accommodations for thirty-six lumbermen and their families. The housing consisted of portable railroad boxcar dwellings painted red and set beside the narrow gauge track up along Jonas Creek. The long high ridge immediately west of the camp is known as Scarlett Ridge, suggesting that there may have been some connection between the name of the camp and the ridge.

Upon leaving the campsite, the Jonas Creek Trail enters a pleasant streamside excursion following the old logging grade. Just shy of a half-mile, the trail crosses the stream in a difficult rock-hop, proceeds 145 yards, then switches back across the stream in another rock-hop. At this juncture, the trail angles sharply to enter a narrow steep-sided cove. The fast-rushing stream, submerged in masses of rhododendron, occupies the bottom of the cove. Tall, slender, well-spaced American beeches, yellow birches, and yellow poplar, their lower boles hidden in a massy understory, resemble ship masts bearing upper branches forming a high canopy over the cove.

Soon, the trail assumes a course of close proximity to the stream. In places the stream appropriates the trail, making the hiking wet and messy. After a third crossing of Jonas Creek, the trail proceeds 410 yards to the fourth crossing which, like its predecessor, can be difficult when the stream is running high.

After another 215 yards, the trail crosses Jonas Creek for the fifth and final time, now on a footlog, and then turns away from the stream for a steep course along Little Jonas Creek up the eastern flank of Welch Ridge where red maples and chestnut oaks enter the mix with the American beeches and yellow poplars. A quarter-mile up Little Jonas Branch, the trail crosses the stream and begins following Yanu Branch. (Yanu is a Cherokee word meaning "bear.") Here the grade becomes noticeably steeper as the trail winds through a terrain of scattered boulders. Just beyond a footlog over Yanu Branch, the trail begins negotiating a series of grade-mitigating switchbacks, remnants of the logging railroad. Four switchbacks follow in quick succession and then, after a quarter-mile interval, another pair. A final switchback directs the trail away from Yanu Branch and into a climb up Yanu Ridge, a minor spur off Welch Ridge.

The cove hardwoods soon give way to the more open forests of the northern hardwoods, and the rocky course moderates to a hard-packed dirt track that is fairly free of obstacles. The trail follows generally the contours of the slope where, in places, yellow golden-glows, Curtis' asters, and an assortment of weeds encroach upon the trail and, in others, aisles of rhododendron and mountain laurel form up in tight corridors.

After a sharp turn, the trail enters the drier confines of a southern exposure. Oakes and laurel are the predominant tree species, with Curtis' asters, galax, yellow-bead lily, goldenrods, and sundrops at trail's edge. The last half-mile is marked by a short rhododendron tunnel and a final return to open woodland. The Jonas Creek Trail terminates in a nondescript intersection with the Welch Ridge Trail 2.4 miles below the Appalachian Trail at Silers Bald.

◆ LAKESHORE TRAIL ◆

The Lakeshore Trail is a relatively recent course designed by the Park Service to provide a continuous east-west inter-watershed connector along the north shore of Fontana Lake. The earliest precursor to the Lakeshore Trail is a toll road following down the Little Tennessee River from the mouth of the Tuckasegee River to Deals Gap, built in 1829 and known locally as the Joe Welch River Road. The Welch Road was later superseded by a modern county road, NC288, that followed a similar course, but on higher ground above the river. When the spillway gates of Fontana Dam were closed in 1944, the impounded water inundated much of NC288, leaving the Smokies bereft of a low-elevation east-west artery on the North Carolina side of the mountain.

The Lakeshore Trail was initially cobbled together from sections of NC288 that remained above the high-water line, old settlers' wagon roads, and long-established trails spliced together with sections of newly graded trail and directed to traverse the Noland Creek, Forney Creek, Chambers Creek, Pilkey Creek, Hazel Creek, and Eagle Creek watersheds. From its eastern terminus at the end of Lakeview Drive (popularly known as the Road to Nowhere) until it reached Fontana Dam Road at its western end, the Lakeshore Trail completed 43.3 miles. The trail's course expropriated 4.5 miles of the Hazel Creek Trail, the entirety of the Sugar Fork Trail and Pinnacle Creek Trail, the lower 1.2 miles of the Eagle Creek Trail, and the lower 0.4 mile of the Lost Creek Trail.

In 2001, the course of the Lakeshore Trail was changed. At Proctor, the reconfigured trail was directed away from the Hazel Creek Trail and up an old settlers' road following Shehan Branch into Possum Hollow. At the crest of Pinnacle Ridge, a newly graded track completed the connection to Eagle Creek. As a result, the 4.5 miles were deeded back to the Hazel Creek Trail, the Sugar Fork Trail was added to the Jenkins Ridge Trail, the Pinnacle Creek Trail was abandoned, and almost three-quarters of a mile returned to the Eagle Creek Trail. The current Lakeshore Trail is 34.7 miles long.

Fontana Lake limits access to the Lakeshore Trail. It remains one of the lesser used trails in the park, visiting what were once some of the more heavily settled hollows and creek bottoms in the Smokies, rich in ruins of old homesites, farms, and cemeteries. These hollows and bottoms now constitute some of the more remote backcountry in the park.

The Lakeshore Trail is served by eight backcountry campsites spaced at irregular intervals along the trail: Lower Forney Creek (#74), Chambers Creek (#98), Kirkland Branch (#76), Pilkey Creek (#77), North Shore (#81), Proctor (#86), Possum Hollow (#88), and Lost Cove (#90).

To reflect the general proclivities of hikers, the Lakeshore Trail is treated here as two separate trails. That part between the tunnel at the end of Lakeview Drive and Hazel Creek at Proctor, named here provisionally the "Lakeshore Trail–Eastern section," begins at the tunnel and proceeds west 24.2 miles to Proctor. That part from Fontana Dam Road to Hazel Creek at Proctor, designated the "Lakeshore Trail–Western section," begins at the end of Fontana Dam Road and proceeds east 10.5 miles to Proctor.

The trailhead for the Lakeshore Trail–Eastern section is reached by driving from the Oconaluftee Visitor Center south on US441 through Cherokee, North Carolina, to US19. Turn right on US19, and drive ten miles to Bryson City, North Carolina. At the Swain County Courthouse, turn right onto Everett Street, cross the Tuckasegee River, and continue north out of town. Three miles out of Bryson City the road crosses the park boundary, and the name changes to Lakeview Drive. Continue 5.7 miles on Lakeview Drive until it terminates at the mouth of a tunnel. The Lakeshore Trail begins at the tunnel.

The trailhead for the Lakeshore Trail–Western section is reached by driving NC28 or, from Tennessee, US129 to Fontana Dam. Cross the dam, and follow Fontana Dam Road 0.7 mile until it terminates at a small parking area adjacent to the Appalachian Trail. The Lakeshore Trail begins at the end of the road.

LAKESHORE TRAIL—EASTERN

End of Lakeview Drive to the Hazel Creek Trail at Proctor—24.2 miles.

POINT OF DEPARTURE: From the Oconaluftee Visitor Center drive south on US441 through Cherokee, North Carolina, to US19. Turn right on US19, and drive ten miles to Bryson City. At the Swain County Courthouse, turn right onto Everett Street, cross the Tuckasegee River, and proceed north out of town. Three miles above town, the road crosses the park boundary and the name changes to Lakeview Drive. Drive 5.7 miles to the tunnel at the end of Lakeview Drive. The east end of the Lakeshore Trail begins at the tunnel.

QUAD MAPS: Noland Creek 158-NE
Tuskeegee 158-NW

0.0—Lakeview Drive (the Road to Nowhere).

0.1—Entrance to tunnel.

0.4—End of paved track.

0.6—Tunnel Bypass Trail exits left and circles back 1.6 miles to Lakeview Drive.

0.6—Goldmine Loop Trail exits left 2.0 miles to the Tunnel Bypass Trail.

1.9—Whiteoak Branch Trail exits right 1.8 miles to the Forney Creek Trail.

2.1—Gray Wolf Creek. Bridge. Access path exits right 390 yards to the Woody Cemetery.

3.0—Forney Creek Trail exits right 11.4 miles to the Forney Ridge Trail. Lower Forney Creek Backcountry Campsite (#74).

3.1—Forney Creek. Bridge.

4.8—Glady Branch.

6.2—Jenny Branch.

7.0—Gunter Branch.

8.8—Roadbed.

9.0—Access path exits right 265 yards to the McClure Cemetery.

9.2—Chimney ruins.

9.6—Chambers Creek. Access path exits right 165 yards to the Chambers Creek Backcountry Campsite (#98).

11.5—Roadbed of old NC288.

11.9—Kirkland Branch Backcountry Campsite (#76).

12.0—Access path exits right to the Scott Anthony Cemetery and left to Fontana Lake.

15.5—Leaves old NC288 roadbed.

16.0—Pilkey Creek. Bridge. Access road exits upstream 700 yards to a fork; left fork climbs 220 yards to the Pilkey Cemetery, right fork proceeds 680 yards to the Posey Cemetery.

16.7—Clark Branch. Access path exits left 60 yards to the Pilkey Creek Backcountry Campsite (#77).

18.0—Chesquaw Branch. Access path exits right 550 yards to the Mitchell Cemetery and left to Fontana Lake.

19.9—Calhoun Branch.

20.5—Roadbed. Access path exits left 80 yards to the Cook Cemetery.

20.6—Mill Branch. Manway on right.

21.0—Access path exits left 125 yards to the North Shore Backcountry Campsite (#81).

21.1—Access path exits left 185 yards to the Noland Cemetery. Roadbed exits left 245 yards to a 60-yard access path to the Fairview Cemetery.

21.5—Whiteside Creek.

22.5—Welch Ridge.

23.5—Ollie Cove Trail exits 475 yards to Fontana Lake.

23.7—Western terminus of the Rowan Branch manway.

24.2—Hazel Creek. Access road exits left 290 yards to the Proctor Backcountry Campsite (#86). Bridge. Hazel Creek Trail exits right.

Ten years after the federal government established the Great Smoky Mountains National Park in 1934, the waters of the upper reaches of the Little Tennessee River were impounded by the newly constructed Fontana Dam, thus forming a lake along much of the park's southern boundary. Mountain communities along the river were either flooded or left stranded by the rising water. Roads connecting these communities were likewise inundated, leaving the former residents isolated from their old homeplaces and family cemeteries. The government, petitioned by the displaced to ameliorate the situation, agreed to build a new highway along the north shore of the lake from Bryson City, North Carolina, to Fontana Dam, a distance of more than forty miles.

Construction on the road began in the 1960s, proceeding three miles from Bryson City to the park boundary and then another six miles to a tunnel bored through the mountain. Because of budget constraints and environmental concerns, work ceased at the tunnel, and the road was never completed. This nine-mile rump, officially designated as Lakeview Drive, is now popularly known as "the Road to Nowhere."

The eastern end of the Lakeshore Trail begins from the parking area at the end of the Road to Nowhere, where the pavement continues another 200 yards into the mouth of the tunnel. Similar in construction to those on Newfound Gap Road, the Lakeshore tunnel extends 365 yards through the lower end of Tunnel Ridge. The name Tunnel Ridge, however, is totally coincidental to the location of the modern tunnel. The ridge derives its name from a legend among the mountaineers that the Cherokee were believed to have hidden gold ore in a tunnel or cave in the ridge near Goldmine Branch. The legend is reinforced by the fact that early settlers once dug gold in the vicinity.

For hikers uncomfortable with walking through the long dark tunnel, their fears can be allayed by way of the 1.6-mile Tunnel Bypass Trail, which begins across the road from the lower end of the parking area below the tunnel. The Bypass Trail circumnavigates the lower end of Tunnel Ridge and then loops back to intersect the Lakeshore Trail a quarter-mile beyond the tunnel's west end.

When it emerges from the far end of the tunnel, the Lakeshore Trail proceeds 150 yards to where the pavement gives way to a hard-packed dirt track. Two hundred and ninety yards beyond the end of the pavement, the trail intersects on the left the western terminus of the Tunnel Bypass Trail and then, 110 yards farther, intersects the upper terminus of the Goldmine Loop Trail. The Lakeshore Trail continues on the hard-packed track, climbing easily through a dry-ridge hardwood association for about three-quarters of a mile before beginning a half-mile descent into the Gray Wolf Creek drainage. The trail quickly picks a course along a tributary of Gray Wolf Creek, entering ever deeper into a cool moist environment of rhododendron before emerging into an old farm clearing. Along the upper end of the clearing, the trail intersects the lower terminus of the Whiteoak Branch Trail exiting right and proceeding 1.8 miles to the Forney Creek Trail.

The Lakeshore Trail skirts the southeast edge of the clearing, crossing a tributary, and then descending quickly to intersect a jeep track leading up from Fontana Lake. At this juncture, the trail turns right and follows the jeep track fifty-five yards to cross Gray Wolf Creek on a wide wooden bridge. Twenty feet beyond the bridge, the jeep track turns upstream and proceeds along the creek 400 yards to the Woody Cemetery. The Lakeshore Trail, however, turns left at the bridge and proceeds downstream on a single-file track that angles up the side of the adjacent slope. Prior to the coming of the park, the stream was known as Woody Branch, named for John Quincy Adams Woody, one of the earliest settlers on Forney Creek and a veteran of the Thomas Legion of the Confederate Army. Woody and his wife, Manerva Palestine Bradshaw Woody, gave land to build the first school on Forney Creek, a one-room structure that stood just downstream where Gray Wolf Creek once emptied into Forney Creek. The confluence of the two streams was submerged by the waters of Fontana Lake.

Rather than continuing downstream toward the old schoolhouse site, the Lakeshore Trail turns away to ascend the ridge separating Gray Wolf and Forney creeks. It quickly clears the ridgeline and begins a slow angling descent to Forney Creek. The big stream can be heard before it comes into view. Prior to reaching Forney Creek, the trail eases in along the upper side of the Lower Forney Creek Backcountry Campsite (#74), then circles down and around the end to intersect a jeep road leading up from Fontana Lake. The intersection marks the lower terminus of the Forney Creek Trail, which climbs 11.4 miles to the upper end of Forney Ridge near Andrews Bald. At the junction, the Lakeshore Trail turns left onto the jeep road and proceeds downstream along the western perimeter of Lower Forney Creek Camp 130 yards to the entrance of the camp. The road is all that separates the camp from Forney Creek.

The Lower Forney Creek Camp is one of the larger backcountry campsites in the Smokies. It is situated on a long slender plat that is uniformly level and enjoys an attractive setting near the stream. The camp is nicely shaded by tall maples and pines, and its lower end is open to the embayment. Unfortunately, the trail wraps tightly around on three sides, depriving the camp of seclusion. Easy access from the lake and the worn dusty appearance of the place suggest that the camp is heavily used.

The Forney Creek embayment affords the first instance in which Fontana Lake can be readily seen from the trail. Over the next half-dozen miles the lake will repeatedly come in and out of view, depending on the proximity of the trail to the low-water mark and the density of the intervening forest cover.

Three hundred yards below its intersection with the Forney Creek Trail and near the lower end of the camp, the Lakeshore Trail leaves the jeep road, turns right, crosses Forney Creek on a wooden bridge, and returns to a single-file track. Here it begins a long and arduous exercise of working around the countless ramifying finger ridges emanating from nearby Pilot Knob. The terrain is generally steep, and the trail is often little more than a narrow hard-packed berm etched into the slope. The trail follows the contours to clear the spine of one ridge, then drops down and circles to the back of the adjacent hollow only to repeat the cycle by proceeding up and over the next ridge. Whenever the trail is out on a ridge point, the forest cover varies from a hardwood mix of hickories, oaks, and maples to that of a pine-oak-laurel association. In the cooler shaded recesses of the hollows, yellow poplars, Fraser magnolias, and rhododendron blend into the maples and hickories. Rarely is the forest cover dense. Even in places where the trees are large, they are spaced well apart. Except for the occasional laurel and rhododendron thicket, the undergrowth is low and thin, and the openness is such that even in mid-summer one can see for considerable distances through the woods.

A mile and a half beyond the Forney Creek crossing, the cadence is interrupted briefly as the trail drops to cross Glady Branch. After crossing, the trail returns to plying the contours for another mile and a half before dropping to Jenny Branch. Conditions begin to change slightly as the trail passes beyond Pilot Knob and begins negotiating the lower extensions of Pilot Ridge. The somewhat drier environment is conducive to more frequent pine stands. The pine-bark beetle has wreaked havoc on many of the tall Table Mountain pines here whose boles are scattered across the mountainside. Rudimentary shelters formed by the fallen pines afford day beds for the wild boars that frequent this part of the Smokies.

Beyond Jenny Branch, the grade is easy in the sense that there are no long climbs or descents; nevertheless, there is a constant strenuousness in that the narrow hiking surface itself is often uneven, sloping badly from side to side. Otherwise, the trail continues as a long thin etch working its way across the terrain.

Three feeder streams intervene, and then Gunter Branch. Another feeder stream intervenes, and then a mile and a half beyond Gunter Branch the trail descends slightly to approach Welch Branch, where it enters a low flat-bottomed hollow drained by three slow-moving feeder streams. The interior of the hollow is dark, cool, and somewhat boggy. American hollies and infestations of spindly trees and woody scrub are the most conspicuous growth on the soft loamy soil. Terraces, scattered bricks, broken jars, pieces of a metal stove, and the requisite rusting washtub are residues from the homesteading activities that once transformed this isolated cove from wilderness to farmland.

On the east side of Welch Branch just above the high-water mark of Fontana Lake, an ancient Cherokee inscription is carved deeply into the surface of a rock. The inscription, known as a petroglyph, resembles a map. Historian Duane Oliver has determined that this petroglyph once indicated the location of certain Indian towns in the area and, more importantly, the direction of an old Cherokee trail going over the mountain into Tennessee. Before the creation of Fontana Lake, the mouth of Welch Branch was an important landmark for the Cherokee, being very near the confluence of the Tuckasegee and Little Tennessee rivers. The petroglyph is beside an old Cherokee trail that ran up from the Little Tennessee along Welch Branch, and then crossed through the flat-bottomed hollow to Chambers Creek. The Indian trail proceeded up Chambers Creek, crossed Welch Ridge, and descended to Hazel Creek whence it followed Forrester Ridge to the top of the main Smoky divide. It then traced the spine of old Smoky to Ekaneetlee Gap, where it intersected another old Indian trail that traversed the gap from Eagle Creek to Cades Cove.

The earliest settlers into the Smokies likely followed this old Cherokee trace into the mountains. They established an active town, Bushnell, at the confluence of the rivers which they reached by a long swinging bridge across the Little Tennessee.

Upon leaving the bottom along Welch Branch, the Lakeshore Trail climbs the adjacent ridge and quickly intersects a wide roadbed. To the right, the roadbed proceeds 265 yards to the McClure Cemetery, a rough eroded gradient of about twenty graves situated on the point of a flat ridgeline. Nearby is a row of sturdy picnic tables placed here for the annual decoration reunions by the Northshore Cemetery Association.

From its intersection with the cemetery access, the Lakeshore Trail follows the road going west to descend into the Chambers Creek drainage. In the interval, it passes a skeletal chimney just off to the right standing among a privet hedge and a scattering of household effects and broken crockery. The chimney is constructed of stacked stones and is otherwise unremarkable except for a decorative curved lintel of bricks held in place by a metal plate. Soon after passing the chimney, the trail descends to Chambers Creek, most likely along the track of the ancient Indian trace.

Chambers Creek, a moderately large stream, was named for John Chambers, who settled in the lower slopes of Welch Ridge in 1830. On early maps of the Smokies, this stream was identified as "Scotts Creek." It was widely thought to be named for General Winfield Scott, the commander responsible for the removal of the Indians on the infamous Trail of Tears in 1838. General Scott's forces maintained several forts along the Tuckasegee and the Little Tennessee, one which was near the mouth of the Chambers Creek. Historian John Preston Arthur later located a grant transfer of December 1795 conveying three hundred acres of land on Scotts Creek including property "which was said to be Scott's old lick blocks." Careful research by Arthur revealed that there were no grants to any Scott on that section of the mountains and thus concluded that the Scott who gave his name to this stream was "doubtless but a landless squatter who was grazing and salting his own cattle."

Upon descending to the stream, the Lakeshore Trail crosses Chambers Creek on a wooden bridge and immediately intersects an access path that winds 165 yards upstream to the Chambers Creek Backcountry Campsite (#98).

The Chambers Creek Camp is not heavily used, and thus during growing seasons thick patches of weeds encroach on the path and the camp. Halfway in, the path crosses Anthony Branch on a footlog. Along the left at the edge of Anthony Branch is a small galled spot with a fire ring and space for a tent or two. The larger part of the campsite is fifty yards farther along and near the base of a tall house chimney. The camp is clearly in the front yard of what was once a home, a level compact tract well-shaded by large yard trees and sequestered along Chambers Creek. Intervening weeds and rhododendron screen the creek from the camp, making it less a streamside and more a farmyard setting. The residue of former domestication is too evident for this to be considered an attractive campsite; nevertheless, it enjoys seclusion and the necessities of a fine camping spot. However, the proximity of the big chimney gives the camp a palpable eeriness.

Where the Lakeshore Trail crosses Chambers Creek, a jeep track leads downstream 250 yards to the embayment. The trail, however, does not descend to the lake. It veers right onto a single-file track a few yards below the bridge and then begins tracing the contours of the shoreline, sometime low and close to the water line and at others high and away, but seldom out of view of the lake.

Over the next couple of miles the trail passes several abandoned homesites, most of which are not readily noticeable. The occasional faint access path exiting from the trail alerts hikers to some of the old homesites scattered up the adjacent hollows. In one or two places a standing chimney may be spotted if the intervening vegetation permits.

Two miles beyond Chambers Creek, the trail merges into a wide graded track that was once the course of NC288. The road was built in 1926 to connect the small communities along the north side of the Little Tennessee River to the outside world. When the spill-way gates of Fontana Dam were closed, impounding the river's flow, much of NC288 was covered by the lake. Wherever the old highway remains above the high-water mark, its course has been appropriated by the Lakeshore Trail.

Four hundred yards along the old NC288 trace, the trail passes another standing chimney and homesite. Within 350 yards of the chimney, it enters the Kirkland Branch Backcountry Campsite (#76). The camp is on a small plot wedged between a bend in the trail and Kirkland Branch. Though completely exposed to the trail, the camp is sufficiently remote and far enough from the lake to be considered isolated. Nearby Kirkland Branch is secluded beneath engulfing rhododendron and woody scrub.

The Kirkland Branch Camp is situated at the mouth of a narrow draw. Fifty yards up the draw immediately back of the campsite and hidden in heavy undergrowth, a tall chimney presides over an extensive configuration of stone foundation walls. As expected, a rusting washtub is nearby. The camp occupies what was once the front yard of the large house that stood here. As a consequence, the camp enjoys what improvements were made on the terrain by the settlers but suffers from the incursions of the nettlesome early stages of reclamation.

 Kirkland Branch was named for Lt. John Jackson Kirkland, a veteran of the Third Tennessee Infantry during the Civil War and a landowner whose property included the campsite. A road built in 1829 on contract by Joe Welch passed through Kirkland's property near the campsite. There were toll gates on the road every ten or fifteen miles, one of which was located between Hazel Creek and Eagle Creek. The gate was operated by Kirkland, who received a percentage of the tolls in exchange for maintaining the road through his property. Later, Swain County floated bond issues to finance the construction of NC288 to replace the old Joe Welch river turnpike. The new road passed immediately in front of what is now the Kirkland Branch Campsite. Today, much of what survives as NC288 is incorporated into the Lakeshore Trail.

When it leaves the campsite, the trail enters one of the most pleasant stretches of hiking trail anywhere in the Smokies. The roadbed here is wide, smooth, and without impediments. The surrounding trees are tall and the undergrowth sparse, affording fine scenic views across the lake.

A hundred and fifty yards beyond the campsite, a noticeable access path on the left leads down to a small galled bench along the water line. From the campsite, this is the best point of access to the lake and is close enough for a refreshing dip after a long day of hiking. Just opposite the access path, a jeep track exits right and follows a feeder stream a quarter-mile to the Scott Anthony Cemetery. A small gradient of only fourteen graves, the cemetery is set on a slight ridge next to the site of a large house that belonged to Scott Anthony and Elizabeth McClure. All that remains are the stone foundation walls that outline the perimeter of the house and a nearby outbuilding.

For the next two miles, the trail continues its easy excursion following the old NC288 trace, staying mostly within sight of the lake and alternating between the dry exposures supporting a mix of Table Mountain pine, short-leaf pine, American holly, and laurel and the slightly more moist conditions where an oak-poplar-pine association is more prevalent. Eventually the trail crosses a small stream, then leaves NC288 for a single-file track that ascends the adjacent ridge. After clearing the ridge, the trail returns briefly to a lakeside course before turning up into a hollow and crossing Pilkey Creek on a wooden bridge.

 The area flanking the near end of the bridge was once occupied by the new Dorsey School, which ceased operation after only a couple of years due to the Fontana Dam project. The foundation walls are still standing, and bricks from the chimney are scattered about. The Posey Mill stood upstream from the schoolhouse on the same side of the creek. The mill was washed away by a flood sometime in the 1940s.

At the far end of the bridge, the trail intersects a jeep track running up along the west side of Pilkey Creek.

Seven hundred yards upstream from the bridge, the jeep track forks. The left prong proceeds a steep 220 yards to the Pilkey Cemetery. The most noticeable gravestone in the cemetery is a two-ton marble monument marking the final resting place of merchant and prosperous farmer William A. Herron and his wife Routhie C. Herron. The tombstone was first transported by rail to Hubbard at the mouth of Pilkey Creek. Without a road, it then took three days for a team of six oxen to haul the stone the final one-and-a-half miles up the mountain from Hubbard to the cemetery. Several of the gravestones around the Herron monument bear the name Pilkington. Some of the early Pilkingtons had their name legally changed to Pilkey, resulting in the prevalence of both names in the community.

The right fork of the jeep track proceeds another 335 yards into Coot Cove, named for John A. "Coot" Pilkington, where is makes a ninety-degree right turn and proceeds another 345 yards to the Posey Cemetery. The Posey Cemetery is situated on a dry sunny exposure and bears only five graves. At the ninety-degree turn, a manway continues straight north, proceeding through Deep Gap, turning west along Rowan Branch, and continuing to intersect the Lakeshore Trail just above Hazel Creek. The distance along the manway is a little more than four miles.

When the Lakeshore Trail intersects the jeep track at the bridge over Pilkey Creek, it turns downstream and follows the road, continuing 200 yards to an embayment. The shell of a vintage automobile lies off the road to the left and, farther on, a collection of picnic tables maintained for decoration-day events occupies a level bench along the stream.

Pilkey Creek was once known as Hubbard Mill Creek, the name suggested by a mill near the confluence of the stream and the Little Tennessee River. The name Hubbard Mill Creek appears on the 1906 U.S. Geological Survey maps and was still in use when TVA made the first land transactions in the 1940s. The 1906 maps, incidentally, identify Pilkey Creek as the stream now known as Kirkland Branch. In either case, the name Pilkey Creek was likely adopted in acknowledgment of Nathan Moses Pilkington, one of the earliest settlers in this part of the Smokies.

The Lakeshore Trail does not follow the jeep track to the abandoned automobile and the picnic tables. It turns right sixty-five yards below the bridge onto a single-file track leaving the roadbed and starting into a 215-yard climb to the crest of the adjacent ridge. On the ridge it turns and begins a descent of nearly a half-mile on an upstream course along Clark Branch. The trail crosses the stream in a tight hair-pin switchback and starts downstream. Forty feet below the stream crossing, an access path exits left sixty yards to a large gently sloped gradient that harbors the Pilkey Creek Backcountry Campsite (#77). Although the camp is on Clark Branch, it retains the name Pilkey in deference to the larger stream nearby and the prominence of the name in this part of the Smokies.

A pile of stones marks the home that once occupied this site. Today pines primarily shade the place and a nice blanket of needles carpets the ground. The camp is quite secluded and does not appear to be heavily used.

Beyond the Pilkey Camp the Lakeshore Trail returns to following the contours. In places the track is a bit rocky and in others a little more than a narrow abrasion excoriated into the slope. Generally the forest is open and the understory sparse. A mile and a quarter beyond the campsite, the trail passes at the foot of an attractive, thirty-five-foot, steeply pitched cascade as it crosses Chesquaw Branch. Just beyond the cascade, an extremely rough access path angles very steeply up almost a quarter-mile to the Mitchell Cemetery which is situated on a ridge slightly west of Chesquaw Branch. To the left of the access path, just where it leaves the Lakeshore Trail, the mountain slope has been leveled with a series of terraces, the individual quadrats held in place by stone retaining walls. The terraces were likely used as farm plots, but there is little else here to suggest that this area was ever very suitable for farming.

A half-mile beyond the Chesquaw Branch cascade, a lone chimney appears on the left, standing in a clearing being reclaimed by pines and oaks. A mile on, an embayment comes into view, and then shortly the trail drops sharply through rhododendron to Calhoun Branch and into a low-lying intervale that separates Calhoun Branch from a nearby tributary. The trail proceeds through the intervale, crossing a very small stream before passing more stonework terracing and a former homesite marked by daffodils, boxwoods, and a large chimney.

After another stream crossing, the trail climbs up and away from the Calhoun drainage, continuing for a half-mile along the spine of the adjacent ridge. Upon reaching a roadbed on the ridgeline, the trail travels seventy yards to a narrow access path leading left eighty yards to a tiny cemetery bearing two tombstones—that of Ellen Cook and an infant Cook. From the cemetery, the access path continues another 520 yards to terminate into Fontana Lake. Half-way down to the lake, it crosses Mill Branch.

From its junction with the access path to the Cook Cemetery, the Lakeshore Trail descends along a deeply rutted track for 230 yards, passing remnants of former inhabitation—rusted washtubs, boxwoods, stone piles, and a rock-wall lining the creek—to cross Mill Branch. After passing the skeletal remains of a chimney and root cellar, it proceeds sixty yards beyond the stream and encounters what appears to be an old wagon road intersecting a manway entering from the right. The Lakeshore Trail follows the wagon trace 420 yards to intersect an access path on the left that angles down along Mill Branch for 125 yards to the North Shore Backcountry Campsite (#81).

The North Shore Camp is situated on a level gradient in a secluded niche pitched in nicely along the stream. Thick layers of pine needles cushion what initially appears to be a small plot; however, on closer inspection, several fine tent sites can be found tucked discreetly among the pines along the perimeter. The setting is attractive and the camp lightly used. With a food-storage cable and access to water nearby, the site affords the amenities of a fine campsite.

Upon leaving the access to the North Shore Camp, the Lakeshore Trail stays to the old wagon rut, climbing 290 yards to an access path that leads left 190 yards to an exposed knob occupied by the Noland Cemetery. The cemetery contains only six graves, each marked with nothing more than irregularly shaped quartz stones placed at the head and foot of the burial plots.

From its junction with the cemetery access, the Lakeshore Trail continues on the wagon rut for 475 yards to intersect a level roadbed running along the spine of a ridge. On the left, the roadbed proceeds 245 yards to an access path leading sixty yards to the Fairview Cemetery. Like a few other of the cemeteries along the north shore, the Fairview is accompanied by picnic tables for decoration-day events.

Where the wagon rut meets the roadbed, the Lakeshore Trail turns right onto the road. After passing through a stand of pines, it descends 340 yards to cross White-side Creek, where a flattened bucket lying in the middle of the stream and a nearby gear from an old automobile are signs of another settlement. Here the trail widens, proceeding through what appears to be an old farmyard. At this juncture, the trail merges into what was once the main road from Hazel Creek to Wayside, North Carolina, before the construction of NC288. Wayside, now under Fontana Lake, was once a tiny hamlet on the banks of the Little Tennessee River. Lance Holland, a noted authority on Hazel Creek, has suggested that the name Whiteside Creek is derived from a corruption by some early residents referring to it as "Wayside Creek," since they followed the stream to the river on their way to Wayside.

Upon leaving Whiteside Creek, the Lakeshore Trail soon turns north and begins an arduous one-mile climb up Welch Ridge, or "River Mountain" as it was known by many early inhabitants. Stands of slender poplars in fields once tilled on the flanks of Welch Ridge betray the distinctive pattern of forest reclamation. After clearing the ridge, the trail begins an equally difficult half-mile descent past a standing chimney and into a muddy crossing of Laurel Branch. A rusting washtub, broken wheelbarrow, and another house site suggest that Laurel Branch may have been the nexus for several farms scattered up and down the hollow.

From Laurel Branch the trail climbs a finger ridge and drops to an intersection with the Ollie Cove Trail, an outlet road leading 475 yards down to Fontana Lake.

The Ollie Cove Trail is used primarily as an access for the Hazel Creek ferry service when the water level in the Hazel Creek embayment is too low.

After a brief climb over a final finger ridge, the Lakeshore Trail executes a U-shaped bend. At the midpoint of the bend, a noticeable path on the right marks the western terminus of the Rowan Branch manway leading in from Coot Cove near the Posey Cemetery. As the Lakeshore Trail eases out of the bend, it begins a long sinuous descent through a boulder-strewn terrain and into a wide bottomland flanking the southeast side of Hazel Creek.

Between 1917 and 1927 this bottomland was the site of Proctor, a mill town built by the W. M. Ritter Lumber Company to process timber logged on Hazel Creek. Struttin' Street was Proctor's main thoroughfare along this side of Hazel Creek. From interviews with former residents on Hazel Creek, Lance Holland has pieced together the artificial topography of Struttin' Street. The street fronted a row of neatly painted houses and was lined with a boardwalk, sugar maple trees, and picket fences. A rail line ran concurrent with the street to the nearby train depot. To the left, just at the point where the Lakeshore Trail eases into the level creek bottom, the remains of a concrete cold storage house are embedded in the side of a hill about thirty yards off the trail. Except for this concrete structure, few artifacts from Struttin' Street remain outside of a scattering of bed-frames, bottles, washtubs, and a few abandoned household effects.

The lower end of Struttin' Street is now marked by a wide wooden bridge spanning Hazel Creek. Along an access road 290 yards downstream from the bridge is the entrance to the Proctor Backcountry Campsite (#86). The Lakeshore Trail crosses the bridge to intersect the lower terminus of the Hazel Creek Trail, then continues on through Possum Hollow to Eagle Creek, and thence to its western terminus at an intersection with the Appalachian Trail just above Fontana Dam. The 10.5 miles of the Lakeshore Trail from Proctor to the Appalachian Trail are treated below.

LAKESHORE TRAIL–WESTERN

Fontana Dam Road to the Hazel Creek Trail at Proctor—10.5 miles.

POINT OF DEPARTURE: Cross Fontana Dam, and drive 0.7 mile to the end of the paved road. The west end of the Lakeshore Trail begins at the end of Fontana Dam Road.

QUAD MAPS: Fontana Dam 149-NE
Tuskeegee 158-NW

0.0—End of the Fontana Dam Road. Appalachian Trail.
0.3—Trail leaves old NC288 roadbed.
0.8—Payne Branch.
1.4—Trail returns to old NC288 roadbed.

2.5—Trail leaves old NC288 roadbed.

3.1—Birchfield Branch.

4.3—Snakeden Ridge.

5.2—Lost Cove Trail exits left 2.7 miles to the Appalachian Trail at Sassafras Gap on Twentymile Ridge.

5.6—Switchback. Eagle Creek Embayment. Access road exits right 360 yards to Fontana Lake.

5.7—Lost Cove Backcountry Campsite (#90). Lost Cove Creek. Footlog.

6.1—Eagle Creek. Bridge.

6.2—Eagle Creek Trail exits left 8.9 miles to the Appalachian Trail at Spence Field.

8.4—Pinnacle Ridge.

9.0—Chimney ruins.

9.1—Access path exits right 165 yards to the Possum Hollow Backcountry Campsite (#88).

9.2—Access path exits left 50 yards to chimney ruins.

9.4—Building ruins.

9.6—Gravel road turnaround. Access path exits left 400 yards to the Bradshaw Cemetery.

9.9—Access path exits left 50 yards to the Proctor Cemetery.

10.0—Chimney ruins.

10.4—Calhoun House.

10.5—Hazel Creek Trail exits left 14.7 miles to the Welch Ridge Trail at Mule Gap. Bridge. Across the bridge over Hazel Creek, access road exits right 290 yards to the Proctor Backcountry Campsite (#86).

From the west, the Appalachian Trail enters the Great Smoky Mountains National Park at Fontana Dam, crossing the dam on a paved road which it follows 0.7 mile before veering off to the left and climbing the west fork of Shuckstack Ridge. The Lakeshore Trail begins where the Appalachian Trail leaves the road, and the pavement degenerates to a wide, hard-packed roadbed that skirts the lower contours of Shuckstack Ridge. The slopes flanking the Lakeshore Trail are recovering nicely from clear-cutting by the Whiting Manufacturing Company in the early years of the twentieth century and now sport a healthy canopy of oaks, particularly northern red, southern red, chestnut, and white oak, but still sufficiently open to afford several glimpses of Fontana Lake.

Five hundred yards into the mountains, the Lakeshore Trail leaves the roadbed and curls into a short hollow drained by Payne Branch and shaded by eastern hemlocks and rhododendron. A half-mile into the hollow, the trail crosses Payne Branch, narrows to a single-file track, and then begins negotiating intervening fingers ridges for another half-mile before exiting and returning to the roadbed. At the mouth of the hollow, the remains of an abandoned automobile and a grove of black walnut trees mark an old homesite.

Three hundred yards farther, the hulk of another automobile can be seen leaning against a sycamore tree at the edge of a stream. Here, the Lakeshore Trail intersects a wide level trace that was once part of NC288 connecting Bryson City with Deals Gap. NC288 was abandoned and allowed to deteriorate when the flow of the Little Tennessee River impounded by Fontana Dam put sections of the highway under water. At this juncture, the Lakeshore Trail veers left to follow the trace of the old highway. Over the next quarter-mile, the remains of four more automobiles can be seen scattered along the edge of the road. These 1930s-era vehicles were likely parked here when their tires wore out and rationing during World War II made replacements difficult to obtain. They were later abandoned when rising water from the newly built Fontana Dam left them stranded on the north shore.

After following the highway trace for a mile, the Lakeshore Trail forsakes the roadbed for a narrower track that follows a stream for a short distance and then, as the grade stiffens slightly, begins negotiating a more severely undulating terrain. The trail establishes a pattern of climbing to a dry-ridge exposure, then dropping into the damper environment of a hollow before climbing again up and over the adjacent ridge. The trail continues this iteration for the next three miles until the sequence ends in Lost Cove. Generally hemlocks and rhododendron are prevalent in the hollows with rue anemones and trilliums dotting the trailside. Out on the ridgelines, a mix of oaks and pines are the primary forest cover.

A half-mile beyond the point where it leaves the old NC288 trace, the Lakeshore Trail enters a deep recess in the defile that separates Shuckstack Ridge from Snakeden Ridge and then crosses Birchfield Branch to begin negotiating the contours of the broad end of Snakeden Ridge. The grade remains moderately steep, the track fairly smooth, and the forest cover a uniform pine-oak mix. Except for a few brief glimpses of inlets on Fontana Lake, the trail varies very little from the established pattern until it clears the final finger ridge of Snakeden Ridge and descends steeply into Lost Cove, where it intersects the lower terminus of the Lost Cove Trail exiting left to climb to the Appalachian Trail at Sassafras Gap on Twentymile Ridge.

At this juncture, the Lakeshore Trail turns right to follow a wide track that proceeds down along Lost Cove Creek 700 yards to the Lost Cove Backcountry Campsite (#90) on the Eagle Creek embayment. Lost Cove is an exceedingly narrow hollow drained by a rapidly moving stream concealed in thickets of rhododendron and shaded by a high canopy of tall slender hardwoods. The amalgam of rushing stream, filtered sunlight, impending slope, and riot of forest vegetation compose a splendid tract of Smoky Mountain wilderness.

The trail down Lost Cove follows an old rail line graded by the Montvale Lumber Company while logging the cove during the early years of the twentieth century. As it approaches the campsite, the old rail grade curves right and away, and then downstream along the Eagle Creek embayment. The Lakeshore Trail, however, turns sharply back to the left and proceeds up the embayment ninety yards to the campsite. The road proceeding downstream is an outlet to a low-water boat landing 360 yards down the embayment.

The Lost Cove Camp is a large galled spot situated at the confluence of Lost Cove and Eagle creeks, where the two streams merge at the head of the embayment. The camp is more akin to the lake than to the stream. It has large coarse features and is worn bare of vegetation except for a few big trees. The wide lower end of the camp fronts on the embayment while the back tapers into the hollow of Lost Cove. The camp is level, but much of the ground is rough, heavily encumbered with rocks. The camp is served by two food-storage cables, and water is readily available from either of the streams. Though it is not suitable for camping, there is a fine grassy plot and a large fire ring in a meander of the Eagle Creek embayment immediately below the campsite.

The Lakeshore Trail cuts obliquely through the middle of the camp to cross Lost Cove Creek on a footlog and enter a small annex campsite. This annex is slightly more attractive than the larger camp and affords some measure of seclusion. Water is convenient, but the food-storage cables are in the main campsite.

Upon leaving the Lost Cove Camp, the trail remains on the level grade of a main rail line built by Montvale Lumber Company that traces a mile-long curve in Eagle Creek known as Horseshoe Bend. A quarter-mile into Horseshoe Bend, the trail crosses Eagle Creek on a metal frame bridge. Though it bears resemblance to an old railroad span that might have been left from the logging operation, the bridge was actually built in 1991. It was intentionally left unpainted to blend inconspicuously into the ambient woodlands.

Eighty-five yards beyond the bridge, the trail intersects the lower terminus of the Eagle Creek Trail. The intersection is unattractive, marked by a fresh rough cut. The Lakeshore Trail turns up to the right into the rough cut, leaving the Eagle Creek Trail to continue upstream on the level railroad grade.

Prior to 2001, the Lakeshore Trail advanced another three-quarters of a mile upstream to cross Eagle Creek and then proceed up Pinnacle Creek to Pickens Gap. From Pickens Gap it descended the old Sugar Fork Trail and then along the Hazel Creek Trail to Proctor. Because of multiple stream crossings and the deterioration of the Pinnacle Creek Trail, the Park Service re-routed the Lakeshore Trail away from Pinnacle Creek and onto a more direct course over Pinnacle Ridge and down Possum Hollow to Proctor. The Pinnacle Creek Trail is now an unmaintained manway.

When it leaves Eagle Creek, the Lakeshore Trail climbs up Pinnacle Ridge on a moderately steep grind along a southern exposure forested with red maples, black gums, Fraser magnolias, and a variety of oaks. On the drier slopes, pines prevail and several varieties of weeds encroach. A mile above the Eagle Creek junction, the trail clears a nameless ridge and then drops two hundred feet in elevation within the next half-mile. Within the following half-mile, it gains three hundred feet elevation to clear Pinnacle Ridge and begin a long descent into Possum Hollow.

The approach into Possum Hollow is an exercise in negotiating the fringe ridges of Pinnacle Ridge. Eventually the trail drops in alongside Shehan Branch to pick up an old wagon road and follow its course into a moist environment of eastern hemlocks and pignut hickory trees. Shehan is not the original name for this stream. It has been known at various times as Jim Branch, Jim Welch Branch, and Proctor Mill Branch. Its current name denotes a prominent family that lived near the stream's head at Shehan Gap. Along the wagon road, several feeder streams trickle into Shehan Branch, and in the wetter places Solomon's-seal, large-flowered bellwort, meadow parsnip, rue anemone, whorled loosestrife, pipsissewa, flame azalea, bloodroot, rattlesnake plantain, and black cohosh are conspicuous.

A feeder stream passing through a culvert beneath the road empties into Shehan Branch in a narrow over-grown field that was once occupied by a settlement home. Discarded household items are scattered about the creek bottom. A bed rail is noticeable leaning up against a tree, and a car axle lies abandoned in the bottom of the feeder stream. This homesite, the farthest up the stream and just below the Shehan Gap, was perhaps once occupied by the Shehan family for whom the stream is named.

A little farther downstream a tall brick chimney marking the site of the T. N. Bradshaw home stands in the bottomland along the upper side of Shehan Branch. The bottom is separated from the Shehan Branch by a stone retaining wall discretely lining the bank of the stream. The wall is more clearly visible two hundred feet downstream from the chimney where an access path exits right from the trail and crosses Shehan Branch to the Possum Hollow Backcountry Campsite (#88). As the access approaches the stream, it traverses a stone wall that once served as an abutment supporting a small bridge. This is a fine example of the remarkable stonework that confines the upper bank of this section of Shehan Branch.

From the Lakeshore Trail, the access into the Possum Hollow Camp is 165 yards. On the right and just below the campsite are the foundation remains of a stone building. From appearances, it is unlikely that the building was used as a home, but neither does it have the appearance of a conventional farm building. A few yards above the building site in a former farm field now thinly shaded by slender second-growth white pines and yellow poplars is the diminutive Possum Hollow Camp. The camp has more affinity with a commonplace hillside farm field than with a deep-woods wilderness; nevertheless it is sufficiently pleasant. The site is clean, fairly level, and suitably secluded. A food-storage cable is convenient, but the nearest water is Shehan Branch.

A hundred and twenty-five yards below the entrance to the Possum Hollow Camp, the Lakeshore Trail crosses another feeder stream where a faint path leads left up a short draw fifty yards to a standing chimney constructed of stacked stones on the exterior side and bricks lining the interior. The chimney is fairly low, indicating that it was attached to a single-story house. Discarded debris and household articles are scattered about the premises, and a large section of sheet metal which once served as the cabin's roof lies crumpled at the base of the chimney.

Back along the Lakeshore Trail and a few yards below the entrance to the home-site, more of the stone wall that channels Shehan Branch forms up. Beyond the wall, the creek bottom extends several hundred feet along the stream at the edge of which stands an odd-looking stone building littered with pieces of metal junk. Nearby are an unreadable sheet-metal commercial sign and the door of an automobile. The building shows no evidence of having had a chimney and, given the variety of mechanical scrap lying about, appears not to have been a home.

A hundred yards farther downstream, the trail widens slightly as it passes another old farm field conspicuous for the tall swamp-thistles growing there. The trail imme-diately enters a circular grassy clearing that marks the end of a well-maintained gravel road leading up from Hazel Creek. From the left side of the clearing, an access path leads up a very steep 400 yards to the Bradshaw Cemetery situated in a small flat tract at the top of the adjacent ridge. The cemetery is high over Possum Hollow, commanding a fine view of the surrounding mountains.

Below the grassy turnaround, the Lakeshore Trail follows a light-gravel road on an easy level course to reach another house site surrounded by a scattered assortment of domestic artifacts. Most noticeable are an axle and parts of an automobile chassis.

When the trail reaches the mouth of Possum Hollow, it veers left and away from Shehan Branch. Hazel Creek comes into view straight ahead. The trail continues with Hazel Creek appearing below and to the right. On the left, a well-marked access path with a wooden stairway climbs fifty yards to the Proctor Cemetery.

 In 1830, Moses and Patience Rustin Proctor came over the main Smoky divide from Cades Cove to become the first settlers on Hazel Creek. Their first home on Hazel Creek was a rudimentary cabin that stood on the ridge now occupied by the cemetery. The Proctors lived in this cabin for twenty years, raising all of their children here before moving to a second cabin built in 1850 farther up Pos-sum Hollow. When Moses and Patience died, they were buried in the cemetery, their final resting place marked by a large modern headstone. According to Smoky Mountain lore, the Proctors were buried in front of what was once the hearth of their first cabin.

Upon passing the cemetery, the trail descends slightly to approach a tall chimney that was once part of a fine house built for W. A. and Martha Franklin. The chimney is a blend of bricks and fieldstones. That part on the exterior facing the elements was made of stacked fieldstones while the trim at the top and that part facing into the interior of the house were of brick. Franklin operated a store and a warehouse that stood below the house in the wide bottom between the trail and Hazel Creek. The entire bottom was once cleared and settled with several homes and small businesses, and known then as Franklin Town. Franklin Town is now grown up in fields of tall weeds interspersed with sycamore trees.

 Immediately behind the Franklin house chimney, a small stream crosses the trail from the adjacent slope. A row of houses once stood across the trail and along the right side of the stream. On the left was the site of the first and second school-houses built on Hazel Creek. The first was a one-room log structure built in 1875. In 1908, The Ritter Lumber Company built a larger school across Hazel Creek near the Proctor Backcountry Campsite (#86).

The road along Franklin Town, then call the Possum Hollow Road, was first used as a sled run and did not follow the current gravel road upstream from the old Franklin house. Instead, it stayed to the top of the bluff overlooking the north side of Hazel Creek. The Lakeshore Trail traces a later wagon road that was built higher up on the mountainside. Consequently the current trail engages in a final steep climb away from Franklin Town to clear a bend in Hazel Creek before dropping down along the stream at the Calhoun House.

 The Calhoun House was built by George Higdon in 1928 and later purchased by Granville Calhoun from the lumber company. The house is a white frame structure erected on a foundation of river rocks overlooking a splendid streamside setting. A porch extends along the entire front of the house and serves as a ceiling for the outer part of a large cellar. At one time Calhoun operated the place as a boarding house. It may have been here that Grace Lumpkin, the novelist and communist intellectual, stayed during her sojourn to Hazel Creek in the summer of 1929. Her experiences and acquaintances made on Hazel Creek that summer provided background material for her best-known novel, *To Make My Bread*, written in 1932.

A hundred and fifty yards above the Calhoun House, the Lakeshore Trail intersects the lower terminus of the Hazel Creek Trail at the end of a wide wooden bridge spanning Hazel Creek. The Lakeshore Trail crosses the bridge and, at the far end, meets a well-maintained gravel road leading up from the Hazel Creek embayment. Three hundred yards down the gravel road is the Proctor Backcountry Campsite

(#86), a fine large camp situated in a wide bend in the stream on a tract formally occupied by the old Proctor School ball field. The school itself stood directly across the road from the camp.

Though the Proctor Camp is large, it is nicely broken up into smaller sites by several irregularly spaced thickets of trees. The site is remarkably level and affords a couple of attractive spots right along Hazel Creek. From a utilitarian perspective the camp occupies a superb site; nevertheless, time has yet to efface the effects of human improvement, and thus it lacks much of the distinctive deep-wilderness ethos that characterizes other campsites in the Smokies. Because of its proximity to Fontana Lake and its reputation as the gateway to Hazel Creek, the Proctor Camp is heavily used.

From the bridge spanning Hazel Creek, the Lakeshore Trail continues 24.2 miles to its eastern terminus at the tunnel that marks the end of Lakeview Drive. For the eastern part of the Lakeshore Trail, see page 448.

♦ HAZEL CREEK ♦

The Hazel Creek section is defined as the big basin bound on the east by the long crescent-shaped Welch Ridge extending from Silers Bald and curling down toward the Horseshoe, a minor mountain that flanks Hazel Creek. On the west, it is bound by Jenkins Trail Ridge extending south from Spence Field to join its lower appendage, the Horseshoe. From the headwall formed by the main Smoky divide between Silers Bald and Spence Field, hundreds of rills form up, collecting in streams that eventually coalesce into the large tributaries that empty into Hazel Creek, the principal stream draining the watershed.

The provisional center of the Hazel Creek section is Proctor, once a tiny mountain hamlet that was transformed into an industrial boomtown with the arrival of the W. M. Ritter Lumber Company in 1907. During its tenure as a mill town, Proctor was the most intensely populated industrial pocket within what is now the park. After the departure of the lumber company, Proctor became a noted attraction among sportsmen eager to fish Hazel Creek for its fine trout.

The Hazel Creek section harbors five trails in addition to the Lakeshore Trail, which makes only a passing trans-watershed appearance near the mouth of the stream. The Welch Ridge Trail and the Jenkins Ridge Trail trace generally the ridges that form the respective boundaries of the drainage. The Hazel Creek Trail, one of the longest in the park, follows the stream on an oblique course across the south flank of the Smoky divide, exhibiting little steepness of grade until the final climb up the flank of Welch Ridge. The shortest trails in this section are the Bone Valley Trail and Cold Spring Gap Trail. The former, with its level grade and sandy surface, ranks among the easiest in the park to hike. The latter, with a wide stream-crossing and degenerating trail surface, is among the most difficult.

The Hazel Creek section affords five backcountry campsites. All are along the Hazel Creek Trail. The Proctor Camp (#86) is situated at the mouth of the Hazel Creek embayment just below the point where the Lakeshore Trail crosses the stream. The Sawdust Pile Camp (#85) occupies what was once a sawmill yard, and the Sugar Fork Camp (#84), at the confluence of Haw Gap Branch and Hazel Creek, marks the former hamlet of Medlin. Farther upstream, the Bone Valley Camp (#83) and the Calhoun Camp (#82) occupy former homesites.

Access to the Hazel Creek section from any direction entails long hiking, unless approached from the embayment by boat on Fontana Lake. A commercial shuttle to the head of the Hazel Creek embayment is available from the Fontana Village Marina. Information on backcountry shuttle service from the marina is available at http://www.fontanavillage.com/marina/shuttle/ or by calling (428) 498-2129.

HAZEL CREEK TRAIL

Lakeshore Trail at Proctor to the Welch Ridge Trail at Mule Gap—14.7 miles.

POINT OF DEPARTURE: The lower end of the Hazel Creek Trail can be reached by hiking in from either the east or west along the Lakeshore Trail or by boat across Fontana Lake. A shuttle service to and from Hazel Creek is available from the Fontana Marina located 1.5 miles east of Fontana Village on NC28.

QUAD MAPS: Tuskeegee 158-NW

Thunderhead Mountain 157-SW

Silers Bald 157-SE

0.0—Proctor. Lakeshore Trail. Bridge. Across Hazel Creek, access road exits right 290 yards to the Proctor Backcountry Campsite (#86).

1.3—Hazel Creek. Bridge.

2.2—Hazel Creek. Bridge.

3.0—Sawdust Pile Backcountry Campsite (#85).

4.1—Hazel Creek. Bridge.

4.4—Hazel Creek. Bridge.

4.5—Medlin. Jenkins Ridge Trail exits left 8.9 miles to the Appalachian Trail at Spence Field.

4.6—Sugar Fork Backcountry Campsite (#84).

5.3—Access path exits left to the Bone Valley Cemetery.

5.4—Bone Valley Creek. Bridge. Bone Valley Trail exits left 1.8 miles to the Halls Cabin. Access path exits right to the Bone Valley Backcountry Campsite (#83).

6.0—Access path exits left 570 yards to the McCampbell Gap Cemetery.

6.6—Cold Spring Gap Trail exits right 3.5 miles to the Welch Ridge Trail at Cold Spring Gap.

7.9—Access path exits left 330 yards to the Calhoun Cemetery.

8.3—Calhoun Backcountry Campsite (#82).

9.1—Walker Creek. Access path exits left 310 yards to the Walker Cemetery.

9.3—Hazel Creek. Two crossings.

10.1—Access path exits left 420 yards to Wike Cemetery. Proctor Creek. Footlog.

12.8—Hazel Creek Cascades.

13.0—Last crossing of Hazel Creek.

14.7—Mule Gap. Welch Ridge Trail exits left 1.7 miles to the Appalachian Trail at Silers Bald and right 5.0 miles to High Rocks.

Officially, the Hazel Creek Trail begins at the west end of the bridge where the Lakeshore Trail crosses Hazel Creek. Conventionally, however, the Hazel Creek

Trail begins down along the Hazel Creek embayment where hikers crossing Fontana Lake by boat disembark at the end of a jeep road. The jeep road follows the Hazel Creek embayment upstream to reach the Lakeshore Trail at the east end of the bridge.

The distance along the jeep road from the embayment to the bridge depends on the water level of Fontana Lake. Somewhere in the neighborhood of a half-mile up along the embayment, the jeep road reaches the Proctor Backcountry Campsite (#86), a large, level tract situated between the road and Hazel Creek. The camp was once occupied by the Proctor School ball field. Children from the school played in the ball field as well as in a nearby deep pool in Hazel Creek known locally as "the baptizing hole." Today the former ball field harbors several nice camping spots shaded by stands of white pine planted by the Civilian Conservation Corps. The camp is heavily used and frequently visited, but surprisingly does not have a rough, worn appearance. Water is available both from the nearby stream and from a spring about a hundred yards back down the jeep road. An access path leads from the road down to the spring.

Directly across the road from the camp is the site of the former Proctor School house. The school, built by the Ritter Lumber Company in 1908, was a white frame building, 150 feet long and 36 feet wide, having eight classrooms and a lunchroom annex that was 36 feet square. In 1931, the school was accredited as Proctor High School, and thus became the only high school to be organized in what is now the Great Smoky Mountains National Park. In 1932, it was renamed Calhoun-Coburn High School, but the name was never popularly accepted.

Three hundred yards above the upper end of the Proctor Camp, the jeep road intersects the Lakeshore Trail at the point where a wide wooden bridge spans the stream. On the far end of the bridge, the Hazel Creek Trail begins, exiting from the Lakeshore Trail and proceeding upstream. The Lakeshore Trail turns and follows Hazel Creek downstream.

The earliest usable road proceeding up Hazel Creek was built by the Adams Mining Company to transport copper ore from mines on Little Fork to outlet roads along the Little Tennessee River. Later, the Ritter Lumber Company cut railroad grades along Hazel Creek and its tributaries to serve the logging camps and to haul timber down to its milling operation in Proctor. When Ritter pulled up stakes and left Hazel Creek in 1927, several of the railroad traces were appropriated by the mountaineers for local roads, and later, with the arrival of the national park, the mountaineer roads were reconditioned and utilized as trails. The Hazel Creek Trail is one such example. It is a wide gravel track adhering much to the old Ritter rail line. The old Adams road is also visible in several places, running in a parallel course above and to the left of the trail.

The bridge above the Proctor Campsite approximates the center of the former town of Proctor, North Carolina, named in 1886 for William Proctor, son of the first settlers on Hazel Creek, Moses and Patience Rustin Proctor. In 1907, when the Ritter Lumber Company established its milling operation at Proctor, the community expanded rapidly from a tiny hamlet of a few souls to a town of nearly fifteen hundred by the time Ritter departed the Smokies in 1927. Today several vestiges of the mill town are still visible and serve to provide some sense of the magnitude of the Ritter operation.

When it leaves the bridge, the Hazel Creek Trail begins following what was once Calico Street, one of the two main thoroughfares in "downtown" Proctor.

The other, Struttin Street, was immediately across the stream running a course parallel to Calico Street. Both streets were accoutered with boardwalks. According Lance Holland, an authority on Hazel Creek, a train depot, commissary, the offices of the Ritter Lumber Company, and a row of large frame houses stood between Struttin' Street and Hazel Creek. Distributed along the left side of Calico Street were another row of houses, the Ritter community building and theater, a café and ice cream shop, and the Primitive Baptist Church. Little remains of the frame buildings that stood in Proctor except for the Calhoun House (built in 1928), which is 150 yards downstream on the Lakeshore Trail and the concrete foundation of the church which is along the Hazel Creek Trail 300 yards above the bridge.

At the upper end of the old town of Proctor, Hazel Creek makes a wide U-shaped bend followed by the trail tracing the inside curvature of the bend.

Gaunt remnants of the lumber company's milling operation remain in the wide bottom circumscribed by the bend in the stream. Most conspicuous is the large concrete drying kiln looming up in the back of what was once the mill yard. An abandoned mill pond is noticeable as a shallow depression between the trail and the kiln. To the right of the mill pond are the remains of several stone and concrete valve houses. Running along the slope behind the drying kiln was Club House Hill Road, a spur that shorted the bend in Hazel Creek and provided quicker access to north Proctor. A boarding house, club house, and several frame houses fronted Club House Hill Road.

Much of the land that was once part of the lumber town and milling operation is now in the early stages of second-growth forest or grown up in fields of tall weedy flowers including wild golden-glow, crimson bee-balm, golden ragwort, Joe-pye-weed, filmy angelica, great lobelia, white wood aster, and grass-pink. One plant that is rarely noticed now is the hazelnut bush. When settlers first arrived on Hazel Creek, the lower part of the watershed apparently had an abundance of hazelnut bushes, and thus for years the stream itself was known as Hazelnut Creek. Early maps of the Smokies, particularly Nicholson's *Mountain Regions of North Carolina and Tennessee* (1864) and *Pearce's New Map of the State of North Carolina* (published in the 1870s), identify the stream as Hazelnut Creek. Beginning sometime in the mid-1800s the local custom was that only the qualifier "hazel" was being retained while the root word "nut" was allowed to fall into disuse, thus rendering the shortened name Hazel Creek. By the end of the nineteenth century, the use of Hazelnut had completely ceased.

When the trail leaves the mill yard, it starts into another wide bend in the stream known as the Horseshoe. The trail stays to the old rail grade along the bank of the stream. Although Hazel Creek is one of the loveliest streams in the Smokies and the trail one of the most pleasant to travel, the two do not share a common wilderness ethos. Commenting on his fishing adventures along Hazel Creek, writer Harry Middleton noted that "the relationship between the trail and creek is conventional, traditional, one of cordial, even-tempered tolerance rather than intimacy or some essential symbiosis." At the lower elevations, when the trail crosses the stream, it keeps a polite distance, always crossing on a sturdy bridge.

Within the space of a mile, the trail completes two bridge crossings of Hazel Creek. A mile above the second crossing, it enters the Sawdust Pile Backcountry Campsite (#85) situated on a wide tract that straddles the railroad trace. Three separate camping spots are aligned along the edge of Hazel Creek. On the stream side, each of the three has an obscured access to Hazel Creek, and on the opposite they are exposed to the trail. Across the trail in a spacious weedy tract are two additional, widely separated camping sites in addition to a horse rack and food-storage cable. Much of the camp is hard bare ground shaded by a thin copse of pine, yellow poplar, and red maple trees and clearly bears the scars of its former role in the logging industry. The origin of the name Sawdust Pile is rather obscure, although it is likely that the name is associated in some manner with a sawmill that was once in operation near the campsite.

One mile above the Sawdust Pile Camp, the trail crosses Hazel Creek on another wooden bridge and then, 150 yards beyond the bridge, a spring forms up on the right. The spring is conveniently accessorized with a pipe. Three hundred and fifty yards beyond the spring, a bridge at the fourth crossing of Hazel Creek heralds the approach to the former hamlet of Medlin, North Carolina. At the bridge, Hazel Creek and the trail part company with the stream diverging sharply right and the trail remaining on a straight course, though now along Haw Gap Branch. Sixty-five yards above the bridge, the trail intersects on the left the lower terminus of the Jenkins Ridge Trail, then turns right, and immediately crosses Haw Gap Branch on a short wooden bridge to enter the Sugar Fork Backcountry Campsite (#84).

Medlin became recognized as a place-name in 1887 when the U.S. Postal Service established a post office in Marion Medlin's store. When Horace Kephart first ventured into Medlin in 1904, he described the town itself as comprised of "two little stores of rough planks and bearing no signs, a corn mill, and four dwellings. A mile a half away was the log schoolhouse, which, once or twice a month, served also as a church. Scattered about the settlement were seven tiny tub-mills for grinding corn, some of them merely open sheds with a capacity of producing about a bushel of mill a day. Most of the dwellings were built of logs. Two or three, only were weather-boarded frame houses, and attained the dignity of a story and a half." All around was the forest primeval where sparse herds of cattle and hogs roamed among the wild native beasts. A few remnants of Medlin can be found along the faint roadbed leading up the right side of Haw Gap Branch.

More interesting, perhaps, is the garden plot once attended to by the William Calhoun family. Sugar Fork Camp, arguably one of the more attractive backcountry campsites in the Smokies, now occupies the garden. The camp is situated on two tiers of level ground that command an excellent setting over the confluence of Haw Gap Branch and Hazel Creek. The camp is well shaded by tall slender pines. It is sufficiently ample without being large, and its features are fine, having none of the coarseness of a horse camp.

When it leaves the Sugar Fork Camp, the trail returns to its course along Hazel Creek, proceeding almost three-quarters of a mile to a graded road that leads up the adjacent slope to the Bone Valley Cemetery. From the cemetery access, the trail drops down a hundred yards to a wooden bridge over Bone Valley Creek. At the south end of the bridge, a path exits right to the Bone Valley Backcountry Campsite (#83) situated on a large tract of creek bottom fitted loosely in the angle formed by the confluence of Bone Valley and Hazel creeks. The camp is wide and level with several niches that make excellent camping spots. Prior to the coming of the park, the bottom was occupied by the home of Jack Coburn, a native of Michigan who came to Hazel Creek with the Ritter Lumber Company and later became a prominent local businessman and an acquaintance of Horace Kephart.

On the north end of the bridge, the Hazel Creek Trail intersects the lower terminus of the Bone Valley Trail. The Bone Valley Trail proceeds left up the side of its namesake while the Hazel Creek Trail veers right and into a course that skirts a number of farm fields in bottomlands that are now growing up in new stands of cove hardwoods. Two hundred yards beyond the bridge and about twenty yards off to the right, the inhabitants of Hazel Creek gathered on Sundays at the Bone Valley Missionary Baptist Church for worship services. The church's "baptizing hole" was nearby at the confluence of Bone Valley Creek and Hazel Creek. Nothing remains of the church except a few shards of glass and an occasional brick foundation stone.

Just over a half-mile beyond the bridge, an access path exits left almost 600 yards to the top of a secluded knoll that bears the McCampbell Gap Cemetery. The cemetery harbors six graves, all marked with fieldstones, none readable.

> The finest house ever built on Hazel Creek stood in the bottom directly across the stream from the cemetery. The two-story frame structure, known as the Burlingame house, had fourteen rooms, six on the first floor and three bedrooms upstairs. The house included a laundry room, a room for canning, a sewing room, a large play room, and was serviced with hot and cold running water as well as a large furnace. Built in 1922 for Orson Burlingame, an engineer for the Ritter Lumber Company, the house was never quite finished.

Two hundred yards farther and along the left side of the trail, a short section of rock retaining wall marks the lower edge of the former Bone Valley School yard. Within the next half-mile, the trail enters a copse of thin pine trees and intersects the lower terminus of the Cold Spring Gap Trail exiting on the right to cross Hazel Creek and climb 3.5 miles to the Welch Ridge Trail at Cold Spring Gap. On the left opposite the Cold Spring Gap trailhead, a jeep road leads left to a bunkhouse for Park Service personnel.

About one-and-a-quarter miles above the Cold Spring Gap junction, the Hazel Creek Trail enters old farm fields that once belonged to Josh Calhoun. On the right between the trail and stream are the stone building foundations of the Calhouns' two-story frame house. Because Josh Calhoun's wife, Susan, was afraid of fire, the kitchen and dining room were built separately from the main house. On the left, an access path climbs 330 yards to a fieldstone marking the lone grave of the infant daughter of Josh and Susan Calhoun.

The upper end of the Calhoun place is now occupied by the Calhoun Backcountry Campsite (#82). The trail divides the Calhoun Camp in half. The lower half is situated on a narrow flat tract close along the bank of Hazel Creek and heavily shadowed by the near-vertical flank of Sawbrier Ridge rising immediately from the stream's edge. The lower camp is in an attractive, almost picturesque, mountain setting with a superb access to the stream and a rough, but suitable, picnic table as a welcome amenity. The upper half of the Calhoun Camp is a rough gradient liberally littered with boulders. It nevertheless affords several suitable camping spots and is considerably drier than the lower camp. A horse rack stands on the upper side of the camp, and at the lower corner is the rock foundation of a log cabin Josh

Calhoun built for a home when he first moved to Hazel Creek. Food-storage cables are suspended in both camps and water is readily available from the stream along the lower camp.

Above the Calhoun Camp, the trail remains level, but the surrounding terrain becomes more rugged and mountainous.

 It is along here, where the stream is pressed close against the adjacent slope, that the Taylor and Crate Lumber Company built a splash dam to hold water for floating logs down Hazel Creek. Release of the impounded water was timed to coincide with that of a similar dam on Bone Valley Creek so that the rush of water on the two streams would converge simultaneously at the confluence of Hazel and Bone Valley creeks, thus furnishing a spate capable of floating large boles of timber down Hazel Creek to the Little Tennessee River. The dam was about a half-mile above the Calhoun Camp, near the foundation remains of the Pink Martin house. Martin moved in and settled here on Hazel Creek soon after Taylor and Crate closed down their lumber operation in the Smokies.

Almost a mile above the Calhoun Camp, the Hazel Creek Trail enters an extensive level tract known as the Walker Fields, named for C. L. Walker, who obtained a grant for the land in 1855. Here, the trail crosses Walker Creek, a large stream flowing in from the left, then intersects a wide trail cutting sharply back to the left and leading 300 yards to the Walker Cemetery. The cemetery contains six graves and is situated on a knoll overlooking Walker Creek. Much of the area surrounding Walker Creek is remarkably level and once harbored a small community of several homes and a school.

Two hundred and twenty-five yards beyond the Walker Creek crossing, the trail fords Hazel Creek and then, eighty yards farther, fords it a second time. Both crossings are wide and difficult but can be circumvented by scrambling along a rudimentary path worn into the left bank above the stream. Within the next three-quarters of a mile and without further stream crossings, the trail eases into a patch of cleared ground just above the point where Proctor Creek empties into Hazel Creek. This grassy tract once harbored Ritter Camp 7, the uppermost of the Ritter logging camps on Hazel Creek. The camp consisted of several crude frame housing units called "red cars," a commissary, and a one-room schoolhouse with grades one through six and accommodating about three dozen students. After the arrival of the park, the old logging camp was occupied by the Proctor Creek Backcountry Camp until it was abandoned several years ago.

An access path exits the north side of the old camp and leads 400 yards to the Wike Cemetery. The cemetery contains six graves, all children of workers who lived in Camp 7. On the south side, the confluence of Proctor and Hazel creeks lies submerged in deep thickets of rhododendron and is not readily visible from the trail. The Hazel Creek Trail exits to the right at the upper end of the old camp on a footlog over Proctor Creek.

Up to this point the grade has been easy, with no steep climbs and always along a wide even railroad grade. On crossing Proctor Creek, the grade remains easy, but the track is reduced to a narrow path tracing the berm of an old rail line. Over the next three miles, the trail stays to the berm, crossing Hazel Creek and its tributaries more than a dozen times at intervals varying from slightly more than a half-mile to less than a hundred yards. None of the crossings is particularly difficult, but all require wading if the water level is up.

Immediately above the Proctor Creek crossing, the trail skirts a wide flat tract shaded by a high canopy of tall slender second-growth hardwood stands. Skeletal chimneys, sections of stone wall, piles of rock, and stands of withering old apple trees are remnants of the vanished settlements on this upstream section of Hazel Creek. Farther upstream, the trail enters into the gloom and moisture of a deep hollow where stream and trail often merge in an effort to share the restricted space allotted by the converging slopes. A lush field of ferns signals the onset of a general change in forest conditions. Botanists have noted that examples of nearly every flower, vine, shrub, and tree growing in the Smokies may be found in the Hazel Creek watershed. As the trail advances to the higher reaches, the cove hardwoods give way to the northern hardwood stands, a transition marked by the disappearance of the poplars and the prevalence of yellow birches and American beeches. This transition is further marked by the appearance of Turk's-cap lily, Michaux's saxifrage, pale and spotted jewel weed, yellow bead lily, monkshood, and grass-of-Parnassus, upland species not common in cove-hardwood conditions.

Only once during the first three miles above the Proctor Creek crossing does the trail venture more than a few yards from the stream. When it does, it completes a deft circling maneuver to finish out on the slope above the stream. As the trail proceeds along the slope, the stream below plunges through a narrow gorge and over a series of precipices known as the Hazel Creek Cascades. At the head of the gorge, the trail returns to the stream, crossing on a boulder at the uppermost falls of the cascades.

Two hundred yards above the Hazel Creek Cascades, the trail crosses the stream again and then enters an exquisitely charming little clearing that once harbored the now-abandoned Cascades Backcountry Campsite. A hundred yards beyond the old campsite, the trail crosses a headwater tributary of Hazel Creek, then starts steeply up the flank of Welch Ridge.

For the final mile and three-quarters, the Hazel Creek Trail leaves the stream and negotiates a series of switchbacks winding steeply to the crest of Welch Ridge. Originally the trail followed the stream for another quarter-mile before turning and ascending a ravine to the first gap on Welch Ridge below Silers Bald. Several years ago the trail was re-routed for the sake of a more gradual ascent. The older route, now an unmaintained manway, can be found at the first switchback where the trail makes its initial definitive cut away from Hazel Creek.

The appearance of the high-elevation species, most noticeably red spruce and mountain ash, heralds the approach to Mule Gap, a park-like setting in a wide swag along the crest of Welch Ridge. At Mule Gap the Hazel Creek Trail terminates into the Welch Ridge Trail leading in from the Appalachian Trail near Silers Bald. The Welch Ridge Trail continues five miles south to High Rocks.

JENKINS RIDGE TRAIL

Hazel Creek Trail at Medlin to the Appalachian Trail at Spence Field—8.9 miles.

POINT OF DEPARTURE: Hike 4.5 miles up the Hazel Creek Trail to the Sugar Fork Backcountry Campsite (#84). The Jenkins Ridge Trail begins on the left.

QUAD MAP: Tuskeegee 158-NW
Thunderhead Mountain 157-SW

0.0—Hazel Creek Trail near the Sugar Fork Backcountry Campsite (#84).

0.5—Access path exits left 200 yards to the Higdon Cemetery.

1.4—Little Fork. Access to the Adams mine.

2.4—Pickens Gap. Unmaintained Pinnacle Creek manway exits exits left 4.1 miles to the Eagle Creek Trail.

3.5—Woodward Knob.

4.8—Cherry Knob.

6.1—Haw Gap.

7.3—Meadow Gap.

8.9—Spence Field. Appalachian Trail.

Early one morning in 1904, Granville Calhoun, a lifelong resident on Hazel Creek, came down from the mountain to the railroad depot at Bushnell on the Little Tennessee River to meet a man whom he had never seen before. Calhoun had received word from a friend who was an official with a mining company that the man had come to the Great Smoky Mountains to get away by himself, as far away as he could. The mining official had asked Calhoun to show the man around Hazel Creek.

When Calhoun arrived at the depot, he found the man in a state of advanced alcoholism. In an account related to Michael Frome several years after the incident, Calhoun described the man as "puzzling both in appearance and behavior. He was medium in height—average flesh, medium all around—but pale and weak looking, like a very sick man, afflicted with tuberculosis, transfixed with some distant image." He was, as Granville Calhoun would later find out, "in flight away from himself and the world he knew before."

Calhoun mounted the stranger on a mule and transported him sixteen miles up the mountain to his home, a five-room house in Medlin, a tiny hamlet at the confluence of Haw Gap Branch and Hazel Creek. He carried the stranger into the house and offered him supper, but all he would eat was a cracker.

Under Calhoun's watchful eye the man emerged slowly from his intoxicated stupor and, three weeks later, moved into a miner's cabin on the Little Fork of Sugar Fork of Hazel Creek where, in Frome's words, "his life became the life of the mountain people and their chronicler as no one before or since." The stranger's name was Horace Kephart.

There is evidence that Calhoun's recollection of his first encounter with Kephart is largely inaccurate. Calhoun recounted this story when he was an old man, fifty years after the events took place. While the setting remains accurate, details of some of the events conflict with other known instances. It is doubtful that Kephart spent three weeks at Calhoun's recuperating from an illness. Nevertheless, Calhoun's account is an enduring part and parcel of the strange lore that masquerades as the life story of Horace Kephart.

Why Horace Kephart ever journeyed into the wilderness is a mystery. He wrote afterwards, "When I went south into the mountains I was seeking the Back of Beyond." Kephart remained permanently in the Smokies.

Kephart's affection for the Smoky Mountain wilderness and his affinity for its people produced two books that have stood up well against the passage of time. His *Camping and Woodcraft* remains a classic among a dull crowd of often unreadable outdoor field guides. *Our Southern Highlanders*, Kephart's personal account of the Back of Beyond, is the first and remains the foremost chronicle of the peculiar anachronisms of those pioneering mountaineers who subsisted anomalously well into the twentieth century in this isolated, forbidding, and mysterious niche of the southern highlands.

Several years prior to Kephart's arrival in the Great Smoky Mountains, the Adams Mining Company opened a copper mine along the Sugar Fork of Hazel Creek, far up under the lee of Thunderhead Mountain. A road was cut, leading from the mine along the Sugar Fork to Medlin. Litigation over ownership soon closed the mine, and Kephart got permission to occupy one of its abandoned cabins. To reach his new home, Kephart took the old Adams mining road, a path that would later become part of the Jenkins Ridge Trail.

The Jenkins Ridge Trail begins in Medlin, where the Hazel Creek Trail turns east to cross Haw Gap Branch and enter the Sugar Fork Backcountry Campsite (#84). In Kephart's day, the mountains surrounding Medlin were criss-crossed with settlers' paths and the creek bottoms cleared for farmland. The few buildings that marked the center of Medlin were huddled on the far side of Haw Gap Branch just above the trailhead.

As it leads out of Medlin, the Jenkins Ridge Trail follows a wide jeep road that turns away from Haw Gap Branch to follow Sugar Fork. A half-mile above the trailhead, a wide path cuts sharply back to the left, climbing 200 yards to a bare plot of ground known as the Higdon Cemetery.

Adjoining the twenty stark, upthrust gray stones that constitute the Higdon Cemetery there is a single marker standing outside the cemetery's perimeter and bearing the inscription "A Black Man." This lone stone serves both as an unintended testimony to the social distinctions prevalent in the Smoky Mountain communities and, more specifically, as a memorial to an unknown individual employed by the Ritter Lumber Company who died in the influenza epidemic of 1919. In 1987, a fence was extended to include the lone grave.

A half-mile above the cemetery, a smaller stream flows in from the left, marking the homesite of Marion Medlin, the preacher and postal clerk who maintained a store in the hamlet at the mouth of Haw Branch. The community bears Medlin's name in accordance with the U.S. Postal Service's practice of often identifying isolated mountain communities by the name of the store or building which housed the local post office.

About a mile above the cemetery access, the Sugar Fork is joined by its tributary, the Little Fork. Barely noticeable are two roads, one on each side of the Little Fork, that lead a quarter-mile to the old Adams mine. It is along the road on the left, the more modern of the two, that Horace Kephart traveled to his first home in the Smokies, a blacksmith's cabin situated in a small dell near the copper mines. It was here in the mountains, alone with the hooting of owls and screeching of bobcats, that Kephart began to chronicle the life of the Smoky Mountaineers. Kephart, however, left no written description of his first home in the Smokies. The only record is a photograph of the abandoned blacksmith's cabin which he included in *Our Southern Highlanders*.

The grade stiffens slightly as the trail advances higher into the mountains, eventually curling up into the east side of Pickens Gap at the foot of a crooked ridge that extends from the main Smoky divide at Spence Field. The ridge bears the odd name Jenkins Trail Ridge, implying that the Smoky Mountaineers identified the ridge by the local name of a trail that ran along its spine. Later, the official nomenclature committee simply named the trail the Jenkins Ridge Trail. So, beginning at Pickens Gap, the Jenkins Ridge Trail follows Jenkins Trail Ridge.

The west side of Pickens Gaps marks the upper terminus of a rough track that descends along Pinnacle Creek to its mouth at Eagle Creek. The trail was originally cut as part of a training exercise by U.S. military troops. When this part of the mountains was later incorporated into the park, the military road was officially adopted as the Pinnacle Creek Trail. In the 1980s the Pinnacle Creek Trail was incorporated into a linkage of trails that became known as the Lakeshore Trail and thus ceased to exist as an individual trail. In 2001, when the Lakeshore Trail was redirected up Shehan Branch, the Pinnacle Creek trace was dropped altogether as an official park trail, its status relegated to that of an unmaintained manway.

At Pickens Gap, the Jenkins Ridge Trail turns sharply right and enters a steep climb on a rough narrow track along the spine of Jenkins Trail Ridge.

There are conflicting traditions on the origins of the name Jenkins Trail Ridge. One contends that the ridge was named for Jonas Jenkins Jr., the son of a landowner from Soco Gap. The younger Jenkins was hired by the federal government in 1838 to aid in the removal of the Cherokee from North Carolina and was an eyewitness to the execution of Tsali. He later lived at Wayside on the Little Tennessee River above Bushnell. It is more likely that the ridge was named for John Jenkins, a native of Hazel Creek whose name is closely associated with the naming of Desolation and Defeat branches, tributaries of nearby Bone Valley Creek.

In Jenkins's day, the trail along this ridge was part of the primary access between Cades Cove and the middle section of Hazel Creek. During the nineteenth century when Tennessee and North Carolina were negotiating a road over the state-line divide through Spence Field, the North Carolina portion of the road was planned to follow along the upper part of Jenkins Trail Ridge. The Tennessee portion, following up Bote Mountain, was completed almost to Spence Field. North Carolina's half was never started.

After the initial steep climb out of Pickins Gap, the trail levels briefly and then returns to more steep climbing to reach Woodward Knob. Along this course the trail stays generally to the ridgeline. Woodward Knob was named for Henry G. Woodard, a man who had worked in the Adams copper mines in the 1890s and later lived in a miner's shack next door to Horace Kephart on the Little Fork. The variance in spelling is attributed to the U.S. Geological Survey inexplicably inserting an extra "w" in Henry Woodard's last name.

Beyond Woodward Knob, the trail descends considerably and then levels momentarily before launching a long steep climb to Cherry Knob. Along here, the trail advances through a dry-ridge hardwood association dominated by oaks that shade scattered pockets of white wood aster, galax, wild golden-glow, and laurel. After clearing Cherry Knob in a sharp right-handed turn, the trail drops into a slight gap that anchors the upper end of the Haw Gap Branch manway leading up from Medlin. About 200 yards beyond the intersection with the manway, the sparse remains of an old log structure once used by Will Meyer as a herders' cabin can be seen on the flat of the ridge. Meyer lived on Lost Cove Creek near Eagle Creek.

After another mile of steep climbing, the trail enters Haw Gap, a diminishing grassy bald now heavily infested with weeds, blackberry thickets, and red elderberry growth. During the summer months the trail through the gap can be difficult to discern because of tall weedy ground cover.

 Haw Gap became an early fixture in Smoky Mountain nomenclature, its name originating from the fact that travelers going up Jenkins Trail Ridge were instructed to go "haw," that is, turn left at this place to follow the best route over the main divide to Cades Cove. The landmark was cited in the *Bryson City Times* on February 21, 1896, in a story that reflects something of the raw wilderness of this part of the Smokies. The newspaper reported that "one day last week an unknown man was found in the Haw Gap on the divide, between Eagle Creek and Bone Valley. His eyes were picked out and the flesh of his face disfigured, supposed to have been done by Eagles and Buzzards and his shoes were gone. No definite information can be obtained that will in any way identify the body." Its remoteness notwithstanding, Haw Gap was for several years in the middle of the twentieth century used as a backcountry campsite.

When it exits the bald, the trail passes a weak stream 180 yards below Haw Gap and then enters a moderate descent over a course that is often quite rocky and, in places, exceedingly encumbered with blackberries, red elderberries, crimson beebalms, and other weedy infestations. As it descends, the trail offers several glimpses of the panorama of the high Smoky divide from Spence Field to Thunderhead presiding over the vast gulf of the Eagle Creek drainage. Two easy stream crossings herald the trail's drop into the moist environs of Meadow Gap, where the headwaters of Gunna Creek gather for a steep journey to their confluence with Eagle Creek. The occurrence of pale jewel weeds around the stream suggests that the trail is now in a transition zone between the dry-ridge oak association and northern hardwood stands.

The Gunna Creek crossing marks the beginning of a long moderate climb angling across the headwall of the Eagle Creek watershed. Here, the trail is on a southern exposure along the fringe of the great grassy bald that once extended far down the slopes between Spence Field and Thunderhead. The thick turfs of rich mountain grass are being invaded by non-grass species encroaching on the perimeter, inexorably eradicating the bald's place on the mountain. Species common to the northern hardwood forest—mountain maple, American beech, yellow birch, Allegheny serviceberry, and ferns—together with flame azalea, wild hydrangea, blackberry, white snake root, mountain laurel, and thickets of rhododendron are also major culprits contributing to the demise of the bald.

One-and-a-half miles above the Gunna Creek crossing, the Jenkins Ridge Trail emerges from a rhododendron thicket into the openness of Spence Field and immediately terminates into the Appalachian Trail near a fine vantage point. A small knob a hundred yards west of the intersection affords an excellent spot from which to view Thunderhead (5,527 feet), east along the main divide. Down to the south are Fontana Lake and Fontana Dam. Appearing just above Fontana Dam is Shuckstack (4,020 feet), the high point at the end of Twentymile Ridge. Faintly visible on Shuckstack is the Shuckstack fire tower. The grassy sward of Gregory Bald (4,494 feet) is visible along the divide farther to the right of Shuckstack.

Five hundred and eighty yards west of the Jenkins Ridge Trail junction, the Appalachian Trail intersects the upper terminus of the Bote Mountain Trail leading up from Laurel Creek Road in Tennessee. A hundred and ten yards farther west is the upper terminus of the Eagle Creek Trail.

BONE VALLEY TRAIL

Hazel Creek Trail at the Bone Valley Backcountry Campsite (#83) to the Halls Cabin—1.8 miles.

POINT OF DEPARTURE: Hike 5.4 miles up the Hazel Creek Trail to the Bone Valley Backcountry Campsite. The Bone Valley Trail begins on the left at the bridge over Bone Valley Creek.

QUAD MAPS: Tuskeegee 158-NW
Thunderhead Mountain 157-SW

0.0—Hazel Creek Trail. Access path to the Bone Valley Backcountry Campsite (#83).
0.5—Bone Valley Creek.
0.7—Bone Valley Creek.
1.2—Bone Valley Creek.
1.4—Mill Creek.
1.6—Bone Valley Creek.
1.8—Halls Cabin.

Bone Valley derives its name from an extraordinary blizzard that visited the area in 1880, bringing intense cold and snow that killed dozens of cattle grazing the balds on Thunderhead Mountain. The cattle, caught away from shelter, froze to death. For many years afterward, bleached bones could be seen scattered throughout the valley.

Bone Valley is a long narrow draw extending from the Hazel Creek to the lower southern slope of Thunderhead. Jesse Crayton (Crate) Hall and his wife, Mary Dills, were probably the first to settle in Bone Valley, making a home in what was then an undisturbed cove-hardwood forest of gigantic trees. Crate and Mary built a cabin, cleared and tilled the creek bottom, and grazed cattle on the high open grassland on the main Smoky Mountain divide. In 1892, the Crate and Taylor Lumber Company entered Bone Valley, selectively cutting the more valuable species of trees and floating the timber down Bone Valley Creek to Hazel Creek and then on out to the Little Tennessee River. Beginning in 1909, the Ritter Lumber Company moved into the Hazel Creek watershed, bringing heavy industrial logging equipment and laying railroad lines, then proceeded to clear-cut much of Bone Valley up to the main divide. And finally, after Ritter departed, the Stikeleather Lumber Company moved in to clear what timber Ritter had not taken. In the end, the pristine forest of Crate Hall's day was gone with little left than a desert of stumps and tangled debris. Horace Kephart afterward wrote, "Not long ago I went to that same place again. It was wrecked, ruined, desecrated, turned into a thousand rubbish heaps, utterly vile and mean."

The Bone Valley Trail begins opposite the access path leading to the Bone Valley Backcountry Campsite (#83) at the point where the Hazel Creek Trail crosses Bone Valley Creek on a wooden bridge. For its entire course, the Bone Valley Trail follows Bone Valley Creek on a wide jeep track that remains remarkably level for the duration and, if not for the four stream crossings, would rank among the easiest trails in all of the Smokies. The trail proceeds initially up the east side of the stream opposite a narrow stretch of creek bottom. According to an old sketch drawn by Horace Kephart, the bottom was once tilled by Walt Proctor, whose cabin stood at the stream's edge a hundred yards or so above the trailhead.

The trail first crosses Bone Valley Creek a half-mile above the trailhead and then crosses a second time 420 yards farther. Here the stream is about twenty feet wide and runs anywhere from six inches to two feet deep depending on the amount of rainfall. In Kephart's time, the trail up Bone Valley crossed the stream four times over this interval with the third and fourth crossings corresponding to the first two crossings today. Much of the bottomland between the two stream crossings was farmed by Kim Hall, a son of the first settlers in Bone Valley. Kim Hall maintained a store and home along the left side of the trail just a few yards above the first crossing. The old homesite is now occupied by a large patch of stonecrop which is so thick as to appear cultivated.

The trail continues on its easy course a half-mile before crossing the stream a third time. Here, just above the crossing, Crate and Taylor built a large splash dam to impound water for floating logs down the stream. The dam, made of timber, was 250 feet wide, 18 feet high, and had a spill-way gate that was 16 feet wide. When the spill-way was closed, backwash from the impounded water extended to within a few feet of Crate and Mary Dills Hall's cabin, a half-mile upstream.

Crate and Taylor were primarily in the market for yellow poplar, white ash, and cucumber trees, and they would not take a tree if there were two knots in it. They did their cutting along the creek and dumped the logs into the stream just below the splash dam. Two similar splash dams on Hazel Creek, one just above the Calhoun Backcountry Campsite (#82) and the other below the Proctor Backcountry Campsite (#86), worked in conjunction with the one in Bone Valley to maximize the flow of water. The two upper dams were timed so that, when the spill-way gates were opened, the released water would converge simultaneously at the confluence of Hazel and Bone Valley creeks, thus creating a flood sufficient to wash the logs on down Hazel Creek to the third dam at Proctor.

Timber cut in Bone Valley was floated out to the Little Tennessee and down to Chilhowee, where it was collected in log booms and floated downstream to mills in Chattanooga, Tennessee. The splash dam method of logging proved to be inefficient as the number of logs lost, damaged in transit, or hung up on the stream sides was too costly for business. Five years after coming to Bone Valley, Crate and Taylor encountered financial difficulties that forced them to pull up stakes and leave the Smoky Mountains. When the lumber company departed, they left unfinished another splash dam high on the upper reaches of Bone Valley Creek.

When it leaves the old dam site, the Bone Valley Trail continues 320 yards to cross Mill Branch near its confluence with Bone Valley Creek. About 200 yards up Mill Branch, a large beaver dam spans the stream. The bottomland along Mill Branch is fairly open and free of trees except for a few dead spars. A rough fisherman's trace works up the left side of Mill Creek toward the dam. In wintertime, when the weeds have died down, access to viewing the dam is easier across the open field along the right side of Mill Creek.

Four hundred yards above Mill Branch, the trail crosses Bone Valley Creek for the fourth time before completing a buttonhook turn that heralds the approach to the Hall family cabin. The trail enters the cabin yard on a wooden platform extended over a weed-infested seepage. Pale jewel weeds flank the entrance to the cabin yard.

The cabin currently resides in Mary Dills Hall's vegetable garden, where it was moved from its original location 200 feet away. Built around 1880, the cabin is twenty-four by seventeen feet, with a half loft, a six-foot front porch, and a gabled roof. The walls are split hewn logs with corner-dovetailed notches and no chinking between the cracks. Unlike most settlement cabins in the Smokies, this one has no chimney.

Partially hidden in the undergrowth thirty yards to the right of the Hall cabin are the foundation and chimney remains of the Kress Lodge, a large, ornately appointed house built by New York millionaire J. H. Kress, owner of the Kress dime stores. Kress leased the property from John Calhoun and, in March 1940, began building the hunting and fishing lodge as a retreat for entertaining friends and business associates. The lease was cancelled in 1944 when Fontana Dam was completed. Vandals later burned the lodge.

Crate Hall and his wife, Mary, farmed much of the bottomland on both sides of Bone Valley Creek as far down as Mill Branch. At one time Crate operated a tub mill in Bone Valley, probably near the mouth of Mill Branch, thus giving the stream its name. Sometime shortly after moving into the mountains, he began herding cattle on the rich grazing ranges along the high divide above Bone Valley and in 1882 began building a herders' cabin in a grassy field on the divide at a place now known as Derrick Knob. Crate Hall's herders' cabin became a widely known Smoky Mountain landmark identified by several travelers, most notably Horace Kephart. Well into the twentieth century this place was known as Hall Cabin.

Crate Hall died at the young age of fifty-four and was buried behind his home on Bone Valley Creek. A well-maintained path leads a quarter-mile from the upper corner of the cabin yard to a quiet, secluded, gently rolling ridge that harbors the Hall Cemetery.

COLD SPRING GAP TRAIL

Hazel Creek Trail to the Welch Ridge Trail at Cold Spring Gap—3.5 miles.

POINT OF DEPARTURE: Hike 6.6 miles up the Hazel Creek Trail. The Cold Spring Gap Trail begins on the right.

QUAD MAPS: Thunderhead Mountain 157-SW
Tuskeegee 158-NW
Noland Creek 158-NE

0.0—Hazel Creek Trail.
0.3—Hazel Creek.
1.2—Cold Spring Branch.
1.3—Switchback.
1.6—Cold Spring Branch. Corduroy bridge.
2.3—Cold Spring Branch.
2.6—Cold Spring Branch.

3.5—Cold Spring Gap. Welch Ridge Trail exits left 7.3 miles to the
Appalachian Trail at Silers Bald.

At the bottom of a narrow boulder-strewn defile wedged between High Rocks Ridge and the southern curvature of Welch Ridge, Cold Spring Branch and the Cold Spring Gap Trail compete for the path of least resistance through a wet, cramped, intensely rugged terrain. The stream makes the trail difficult to hike. The grade is steep, and the course is cluttered with loose glen stones and often saturated from runnels seeking suitable outlets to the nearby stream.

The lower stretch of the Cold Spring Gap Trail is a deceiving prelude to the rough conditions farther up. Beginning from its intersection with the Hazel Creek Trail, the Cold Spring Gap Trail follows an old wagon trace that once linked the bottom-land farms in the area with the main road leading down to Medlin and Proctor on Hazel Creek. The wagon trace descends gradually for 470 yards through stands of thin, struggling, old-field pines to encounter a difficult crossing of Hazel Creek. Hazel Creek at this point is well over ten yards wide and can easily be over three feet deep when the mountain streams are running high.

Upon crossing Hazel Creek, the Cold Spring Gap Trail climbs gradually away from the stream and wends through a scattering of old homesites tucked in among the lower contours of High Rocks Ridge. It soon merges into an old railroad grade abandoned by the Ritter Lumber Company. The fields here are heavily infested with rocks and were capable of supporting only the most stereotypical hards-crabble Smoky Mountain farming. Just over a mile above the Hazel Creek crossing, the trail clears Cold Spring Branch and then, 270 yards farther, completes a long sharp switchback left to begin its upstream course.

From this point, the grade becomes markedly steeper and the course wet and difficult where feeder streams, seepages, and runnels wash away the loamy detritus, leaving a rough track of exposed water-slickened rocks. As the trail progresses, the grade steepens. Flow from Cold Spring Gap occasionally escapes into the trail and, when combined with the loose shifting rocks, makes it difficult to gain purchase. Even the occasion of a corduroy footbridge in one of the wetter places is of little use as the wet wood is slicker than the wet rocks. Altogether, the trail here is an exceedingly difficult and exhausting climb.

Notwithstanding the arduous hiking conditions, the terrain flanking the trail is oddly attractive. Except along the stream bed where the rhododendron is thick and luxurious, there is very little woody undergrowth on the boulder-strewn slopes. Most of what thrives close to the ground are leafy plants and low browse, particularly stinging nettles and may-apples. Wild ginger, yellow lady's-slippers, wild geraniums, crested dwarf irises, pink turtleheads, purple wakerobins, and a variety of other trilliums are among the wildflowers that dot the slopes in the spring. The tree cover is mostly tall, slender, second-growth yellow poplars sparsely scattered across the landscape. Here the forest is not obscured by the trees, and there is an astonishing sense of depth of perception in being able to see clearly through the woods for a considerable distance in any direction.

A mile above the switchback, the trail crosses Cold Spring Branch and then a quarter-mile farther crosses it again. Adding to the difficulties of the steepness and the water-slickened rocks, the trail over this interval is often rutted and muddy. When it rains the track becomes an agglomeration of shifting stones and mire. As elevation is gained, conditions become a bit drier, but the steepness and ruts remain.

The boulder fields that clutter the Cold Spring Branch drainage are a result of the latest episode in the geological history of the Great Smoky Mountains that ended perhaps 20,000 years ago when the ice age retreated for the final time. The mountains were well south of the leading edge of the ice sheets and were never visited by glaciers, although the region did experience a more rigorous climate than now. The bare projecting rocks along the exposed High Rocks Ridge, riven by the intense cold and frost action, broke free and tumbled, producing boulder fields on the slopes flanking the stream. Over time, rain and water have worn the frost-fractured rock into the smooth glen stones that lie scattered throughout the hollow.

A perceptibly steeper final 300-yard climb heralds the approach into Cold Spring Gap. The trail over this stretch is wide, rocky, and leavened with ruts. On entering the gap, the trail intersects the lower terminus of the Welch Ridge Trail descending along the crest of Welch Ridge. A half-mile above the gap, an access path exits west from the Welch Ridge Trail 560 yards to High Rocks, a pinnacle bluff that affords exceptional views into the Tuckasegee and Little Tennessee river valleys. High Rocks is the residue that remained when the cold and ice of the last glacial age split off the boulders that now litter the flanks of Cold Spring Gap.

WELCH RIDGE TRAIL

Appalachian Trail at Silers Bald to the Cold Spring Gap Trail at Cold Spring Gap—7.3 miles.

POINT OF DEPARTURE: From Newfound Gap drive 7.1 miles to the large parking area at the end of Clingmans Dome Road. Hike 0.5 mile up the access to the Clingmans Dome Observation Tower, then 4.1 miles west on the Appalachian Trail to the base of Silers Bald. The Welch Ridge Trail begins on the left.

QUAD MAPS: Silers Bald 157-SE
Noland Creek 158-NE

0.0—Silers Bald. Appalachian Trail.

1.7—Mule Gap. Hazel Creek Trail exits right 14.7 miles to the Lakeshore Trail at Proctor.

2.4—Jonas Creek Trail exits left 4.1 miles to the Forney Creek Trail.

4.8—Mount Glory.

5.4—Spring headwaters of Hawk Ridge Branch.

5.7—Water Oak Gap.

6.0—Bearwallow Bald.

6.4—Bear Creek Trail exits left 5.9 miles to the Forney Creek Trail.

6.7—Access path exits right 560 yards to High Rocks.

7.3—Cold Spring Gap. Cold Spring Gap Trail exits right 3.5 miles to the Hazel Creek Trail.

Welch Ridge is a powerful spur anchored to the high Smoky divide at Silers Bald and extending south in a long sweeping arc down to the Little Tennessee River Valley. It is flanked on the east by the Forney Creek watershed and on the west by the vast Hazel Creek drainage. Silers Bald was once an open expanse of grassy meadow that extended a considerable distance down the mountain into North Carolina. During the early years of the twentieth century, herders drove cattle to the bald for summer grazing on the rich mountain grass that grew there. The Welch Ridge Trail, which generally traces the spine of Welch Ridge, likely follows the old cattle tracks that lead up to Silers from the valley farms below.

The upper terminus of the Welch Ridge Trail is affixed to the Appalachian Trail about 300 yards east of the highest point on Silers Bald. The Welch Ridge Trail is not heavily used, and where it leaves the Appalachian Trail the course is often overgrown in high thick weeds and blackberry brambles. Within a hundred yards the brambles subside, and the trail enters what is clearly a transitional zone with American beech and yellow birch encroaching upon the open grassy expanse that once defined the bald.

In 1904, W. Scott Adams purchased 1,683 acres of the bald from the estate of Jesse Richardson Siler for four dollars an acre. He subsequently established the Siler Meadow Mining and Lumber Company with the intent of mining copper on the bald. A few mine shafts were sunk, but the operation proved to be uneconomical as the ore had to be hauled by mules down the mountain for several miles. A remnant shaft can be found just to the left of the trail about 300 yards from the trailhead, but it is now little more than an overgrown pit and can be difficult to spot.

At that time, Siler Meadow extended down the mountain as far as a spring at the head of nearby Jonas Creek. West of the spring near the ridgeline and just below the edge of the meadow once stood the Monteith cabin, a well-known primitive shelter used by herders and bear hunters who frequented that part of the Smokies. The cabin had no windows, no chimney, and only an opening for a door, but it had a fireplace.

The trail itself reaches the spine of Welch Ridge for the first time about a half-mile below the main divide in a tiny clearing that once harbored the upper terminus of the Hazel Creek Trail. Several years ago the Hazel Creek Trail was re-routed to intersect the Welch Ridge Trail farther down the ridge at Mule Gap and thus left the disused upper rump to deteriorate to a manway.

From this juncture, the trail ambles along on an easy grade for about a mile before dropping into Mule Gap, a remarkably pleasant park-like setting in a wide gently sloped saddle on Welch Ridge. The origin of the name Mule Gap has vanished with the passage of time, but it is likely to have had some association with the mule teams used by the mining company for hauling cooper ore from the mines on Silers. Proximity to a fine spring and the short distance to the mines would have made Mule Gap a suitable staging place for working stock. The trees in Mule Gap are large and well spaced, and the patches of grass and wildflowers scattered among thick beds of ferns constitute the only understory. The trail passes along the eastern edge of the gap where it intersects the upper terminus of the Hazel Creek Trail ranging in from across the gap.

Below Mule Gap, forest conditions alternate between weedy infestations and open park-like woodlands as the trail begins negotiating a succession of knobs and gaps while switching back and forth across the spine of Welch Ridge. Three-quarters of a mile below Mule Gap, the trail descends through a weedy patch on the east side of a nameless knob to encounter a rather forlorn junction that marks the upper terminus of the Jonas Creek Trail leading up from Forney Creek. From here, the trail eases back across the ridgeline and into a three-mile exercise that first entails negotiating a slight knob, Scarlett Ridge, and then, after another mile, in quick succession, Mount Glory and the west flank of Hawk Knob. For much of the way the trail is soft underfoot and free of rocky obstructions, although in places, especially during the warmer seasons, it is choked with tall weeds and brambles. Except for the climb on the approach to Mount Glory, the grade remains fairly easy, shaded variously in widely spaced second-growth of pignut hickories, yellow buckeyes, and a variety of oaks, along with maples interspersed with yellow birches and an understory of rhododendron. The trail passes on the west flank just below the summit of Mount Glory and then rolls out to circumnavigate in less than a quarter-mile the summit of Hawk Knob.

Beyond Hawk Knob, the trail stays to the west side of the ridgeline, passing a weak spring protected by a dry-stack stone wall. Water from the spring dribbles out of a rusty pipe and onto the trail, forming the headwaters of Hawk Ridge Branch, a high-elevation tributary of Hazel Creek. Almost a half-mile beyond the spring, the trail returns to the ridgeline, descending first to Water Oak Gap and then climbing for a quarter-mile to skirt the west side of Bearwallow Bald.

The origin of the name Water Oak Gap is a mystery, especially since water oak trees are not found in the Smokies. Bearwallow Bald receives its name from the bathing habits of Smoky Mountain black bears. Unlike bears in the western United States, the Smoky Mountain bear is not fond of sitting in running water, preferring instead to claw a shallow hole in the ground that fills up with rainwater and provides a suitable tub in which to wallow. Characteristically, bears do not like being disturbed while in their tubs. Bearwallows, as these tubs are called, are often found on high, thinly forested, gently sloped knolls such as those on Welch Ridge. As the name suggests, Bearwallow Bald was likely locally recognized as a favorite haunt of the Smoky Mountain black bear.

Six hundred yards below Bearwallow Bald, the trail passes through weeds and blackberry brambles to intersect the upper terminus of the Bear Creek Trail leading up from Forney Creek. Five hundred yards beyond the Bear Creek junction, a narrow path exits right through heavy infestations of high weeds 560 yards to High Rocks, an outcropping that, at 5,180 feet, is higher than Gregory Bald (4,949 feet), Mount Cammerer (4,928 feet), and Newfound Gap (5,046 feet) and affords one of the finest vantage points on the North Carolina side of the mountains.

For most of the way, the trail to High Rocks follows a short spur that is often heavily congested with high weedy growth. Near its end, the trail negotiates a set of steps chiseled into the flank of a pronounced pinnacle that punctuates the end of the spur. The trail terminates abruptly on a small bare-rock exposure that falls sharply away to afford an astonishing view of the lower southern sweep of the Smokies and a panoply of mountain ranges in the Nantahala National Forest. In the gulf below, blue patches of Fontana Lake can be seen tucked in among the hollows where the lower extensions of the Great Smokies and the Nantahalas overlap.

Before it was dismantled several years ago, a fire tower stood on the pinnacle of High Rocks. From the tower, Andrews Bald (5,920 feet), Clingmans Dome (6,643 feet), Mount Le Conte (6,593 feet), Silers Bald (5,607 feet), Cold Spring Knob (5,200 feet), Thunderhead (5,527 feet), Gregory Bald (4,949 feet), Parson Bald (4,732 feet), and Shuckstack (4,020 feet) were observable to the north and west. A badly deteriorating warden's cabin that accompanied the fire tower still stands, perched precariously over a ledge fifty feet back of the old tower site. The cabin is a one-room log building with chestnut shake siding and accoutered with a storage lean-to and small porch. Natural light is afforded the cabin's interior through windows whose frames are painted green. It was heated by a wooden stove, and water was supplied from a cistern replenished by rainwater draining from the cabin's downspout. A vintage, but now completely collapsed, outhouse stood on the grassy slope a few yards behind the cabin. A loft above the main room of the cabin is now the home of a colony of bats.

At its junction with the access trail to High Rocks, the Welch Ridge Trail widens to a jeep track for a half-mile descent through boulders strewn across the slopes immediately below High Rocks. The descent is steep and in places quite rocky, but eases perceptibly at Cold Spring Gap. In the gap, the Welch Ridge Trail terminates into the upper end of the Cold Spring Gap Trail leading up from Hazel Creek. To the left, vestiges of an old trail can be seen where it exits the gap and proceeds down Pilot Ridge to the Bear Creek Trail.

◆ EAGLE CREEK AND TWENTYMILE ◆

Situated in the remote southwest corner of the park, the Eagle Creek and Twentymile drainages are adjacent watersheds separated by Twentymile Ridge and its southern appendage, Shuckstack. Eagle Creek is bound on the east by Jenkins Trail Ridge and drains the long headwall of the main Smoky divide between Spence Field and Doe Knob. The Twentymile section is bound on the west by the southern curvature of the Smoky divide and further subdivided by Wolf Ridge and Long Hungry Ridge.

Eagle Creek is visited by only three trails: the Eagle Creek Trail, the Lost Cove Trail, and the western end of the Lakeshore Trail. The Eagle Creek Trail, which probes the upper reaches of the headwall below Spence Field, entails eighteen stream crossings. When the stream is high, crossing can be difficult. When it is raging, crossing is hazardous. The Lost Cove Trail is a steep lateral course that exits to the Appalachian Trail at Sassafras Gap on Twentymile Ridge.

The Eagle Creek section harbors five backcountry campsites, four along Eagle Creek and one on Lost Cove Creek. The camp at the lowest elevation, Lost Cove Camp (#90) on Eagle Creek embayment, is along the Lakeshore Trail. Three others— the Lower Ekaneetlee Camp (#89), the Eagle Creek Island Camp (#96), and the Big Walnut Camp (#97)—are spaced out along the first five miles of the Eagle Creek Trail. All five campsites occupy former logging camps abandoned by the Montvale Lumber Company.

The Twentymile section sports four trails. The Long Hungry Ridge Trail and Wolf Ridge Trail climb to the main Smoky divide at Rich Gap and Sheep Pen Gap respectively. The Twentymile Creek Trail is an oblique lateral course that extends from the lower end of the watershed to the Appalachian Trail at Sassafras Gap on Twentymile Ridge. The only easy trail in this section is the Twentymile Loop Trail, a short lateral course linking the Wolf Ridge and Long Hungry Ridge trails.

Twentymile affords three backcountry campsites, one on the lower end of each of the major trails. The Sheep Pen Gap Camp (#13) anchors the upper end of the Wolf Ridge Trail but is treated as part of the Gregory Ridge Trail in the Cades Cove section.

Twentymile can be reached directly by automobile from the east along NC28 and the west by US129 ("The Dragon"). Access to Eagle Creek entails long hiking unless approached up the embayment by boat on Fontana Lake. A commercial shuttle to the Eagle Creek embayment is available from the Fontana Village Marina. Information on backcountry shuttle service from the marina is available at http://www.fontanavillage.com/marina/shuttle/ or by calling (428) 498-2129.

EAGLE CREEK TRAIL

Lakeshore Trail to the Appalachian Trail at Spence Field—8.9 miles.

POINT OF DEPARTURE: The lower end of the Eagle Creek Trail can be reached by hiking 6.2 miles from the west end of the Lakeshore Trail or by boat to the Eagle Creek embayment on Fontana Lake. A shuttle service to and from Eagle Creek is available from the Fontana Marina located 1.5 miles east of Fontana Village on NC28.

QUAD MAPS: Fontana Dam 149-NE

Cades Cove 148-SE

Thunderhead Mountain 157-SW

0.0—Lakeshore Trail.

0.2—Eagle Creek. Footlog.

0.7—Pinnacle Creek manway across Eagle Creek.

0.9—Eagle Creek.

1.1—Eagle Creek.

1.6—Lower Ekaneetlee Backcountry Campsite (#89).

1.6—Ekaneetlee Creek.

1.9—Eagle Creek.

2.1—Eagle Creek.

2.3—Eagle Creek (two crossings).

2.6—Eagle Creek.

2.6—Eagle Creek Island Backcountry Campsite (#96).

2.7—Eagle Creek (two crossings).

3.2—Eagle Creek.

3.6—Eagle Creek.

4.0—Eagle Creek.

4.1—Eagle Creek.

4.3—Eagle Creek.

4.6—Big Walnut Backcountry Campsite (#97).

4.7—Gunna Creek.

7.3—Gunna Creek.

7.4—Fodderstack Rock.

8.1—Spence Cabin Branch.

8.6—Spring.

8.7—Spence Field Shelter.

8.9—Spence Field. Appalachian Trail.

Because of the Eagle Creek Trail's rather convoluted history, its lower terminus has on occasions been shifted up and down the stream. Currently, it begins in an unconventional intersection a little more than a half-mile above the Lost Cove Backcountry Campsite (#90) on the Eagle Creek embayment.

During the early years of the twentieth century, the Montvale Lumber Company cut a railroad grade that proceeded from the mouth of Eagle Creek upstream to a logging camp tucked in the angle where Lost Cove Creek empties into Eagle Creek. The railroad line was then extended through the camp to follow Eagle Creek into the mountains. When the Great Smoky Mountains National Park was established in 1934, the Park Service appropriated the old Montvale grade as the course for the Eagle Creek Trail. Ten years later, when the waters of the Little Tennessee River were impounded by Fontana Dam and the lower end of Eagle Creek was flooded, the trailhead was moved from the mouth of Eagle Creek upstream to the head of the new embayment, which fortuitously coincided with the old logging camp at Lost Cove Creek. The logging camp was then appropriated as the Lost Cove Backcountry Campsite (#90). In the 1980s, the Park Service opened a new lateral connector, the Lakeshore Trail, that extended roughly forty-three miles along the north shore of Fontana Lake from the end of Lakeview Drive (popularly known as "the Road to Nowhere") to the Appalachian Trail above Fontana Dam. With this, a mile-and-a-quarter section of the Eagle Creek Trail immediately above the Lost Cove Camp was incorporated into the new Lakeshore Trail configuration, thus shifting the lower terminus of the Eagle Creek Trail upstream to the mouth of Pinnacle Creek. In 2001, the Lakeshore Trail was re-routed away from Hazel Creek, up Shehan Branch, through Possum Hollow, and then to Eagle Creek. As a consequence, three-quarters of a mile of the Lakeshore Trail was deeded back to the Eagle Creek Trail, thus shifting the head of the Eagle Creek Trail back downstream to within a half-mile of the Lost Cove Camp. The Eagle Creek Trail now begins in "mid-trail" at an aberrant junction where a rough, jarring cut of the re-routed Lakeshore Trail interrupts the unstudied continuity of the old established railroad trace along the stream.

Currently, the Eagle Creek Trail begins along the Lakeshore Trail a half-mile above the Lost Cove Backcountry Campsite (#90). It stays to the old Montvale rail grade, tracing a wide curvature of Eagle Creek known as Horseshoe Bend. Three hundred and fifty yards into the bend, the trail crosses Eagle Creek on a long slender footlog. This is the first of eighteen stream crossings that grace the Eagle Creek Trail. A half-mile above the first crossing, the trail passes the lower terminus of the old Pinnacle Creek Trail marked by stone supports that anchored a footlog over the stream. The Pinnacle Creek Trail once linked Eagle Creek with the Jenkins Ridge Trail at Pickens Gap. When the Lakeshore Trail was first established, the Pinnacle Creek Trail was wholly incorporated into the Lakeshore network. When the Lakeshore Trail was re-routed through Possum Hollow, the Pinnacle Trail was abandoned. It is now an unmaintained manway.

Three hundred and fifty yards above the Pinnacle Creek junction, the Eagle Creek Trail crosses the stream for the second time, and 450 yards farther it completes the third crossing. Both crossings can be difficult. After the third crossing, the trail remains on its easy course for another half-mile before entering the Lower Ekaneetlee Backcountry Campsite (#89), situated on the site of the former Montvale Logging Camp 9. The Lower Ekaneetlee Camp is one of the more attractive in the Smokies with the trail and Eagle Creek ranging along the lower side of the camp, Ekaneetlee Creek forming a discrete boundary on the upper end, and a steep slope commanding the back of the campsite. Tall leggy rhododendron form a soft perimeter around much of the camp, which itself is suitably level and nicely carpeted with pine needles and mats of partridge berry.

According to historian Duane Oliver, settlers on Eagle Creek never established a cemetery in the watershed, but chose to bury their dead elsewhere. However, the loggers in Montvale Camp 9 did maintain one small cemetery on Eagle Creek. It held the graves of one adult and two infants and is thought to be in the middle of the Lower Ekaneetlee Camp. At the time of the logging operations, the course of the main rail line approximated that of the trail. A spur from the main line exited through the upper end of the camp and proceeded up the far side of Ekaneetlee Creek. Abandoned sections of rail can be found along the edge of the campsite and in the bed of Ekaneetlee Creek.

 The site of the Lower Ekaneetlee Camp was once a staging point along an old Indian trace that connected the Cherokee villages in the Little Tennessee River Valley with hunting grounds in Cades Cove. The Indian trace followed Eagle Creek upstream to the site of the camp. Here, it turned up and followed Ekaneetlee Creek to its headwaters, where it then crossed the mountain at Ekaneetlee Gap, the lowest point on the western end of the main Smoky divide. The Ekaneetlee trace was one of the oldest trails into the Smokies and was later used by settlers coming into Cades Cove from South Carolina. It was still usable as a rudimentary manway until late into the twentieth century; however, it is now virtually impassable.

On leaving the campsite, the Eagle Creek Trail immediately crosses Ekaneetlee Creek just a few feet above the stream's confluence with Eagle Creek. To the left immediately beyond the stream crossing, Montvale Lumber Company maintained a schoolhouse for children of the loggers living in Camp 9.

Six hundred yards above the Lower Ekaneetlee Camp, the trail crosses Eagle Creek for the fourth time, putting the stream to the left side of the trail. The trail remains on the railroad bed near the stream and in the shade of pine-hardwood stands. After an interval of 325 yards it crosses the stream again and immediately enters a wide curve that skirts one of the few old farm fields on Eagle Creek. A tall barrier of rhododendron clearly delineates the edge of the trail, keeping it at a uniform distance from the stream. Just beyond the farm field, the trail drops to the stream to execute two crossings within an interval of fifty-five yards.

The trail returns to its easy comportment for another 600 yards before completing its ninth crossing and immediately entering the Eagle Creek Island Backcountry Campsite (#96). Eagle Creek Island was formed when Montvale built a logging sluice off the main stream. The island is about thirty yards at its widest point and a little longer than 200 yards. The camp consists of five small plats spaced out along both sides of the island with the trail running down the middle. Only one of the sites has an intimate streamside setting, the others being boxed out by rhododendron. The divided stream, the deep woods setting, and the remoteness of the place lend the Eagle Island Campsite a remarkable charm. Nevertheless, it suffers two defects. First, the camp is rather low in relation to the stream. During periods of heavy rain, water from Eagle Creek can seep into the camp. Second, most of the camping spots are almost in the trail, making them seem somewhat cramped.

In addition to the sluice, Montvale in 1908 established logging Camp 10 at the mouth of nearby Horse Cove Branch. Later, when the park was established, the Smoky Mountain Nomenclature Committee eliminated the name Horse Cove Branch, christening it Camp Ten Branch in acknowledgment of the history of the logging industry on Eagle Creek.

At the upper end of the island, the trail completes a wide shallow crossing that often appears as two separate streams. After this crossing the stream is to the right side of the trail. On the left is a fairly open flat area that was one of very few tracts on Eagle Creek tilled as farmland. After two more stream crossings, the trail skirts a small bottomland once settled by the legendary Smoky Mountain moonshiner Quill Rose.

Rose was described by those who knew him as a tall handsome man who was not afraid to kill another man for what he thought was just cause, but could always be trusted to be true to his word. Much of the aura of legend surrounding Quill Rose is attributable to his portrayal as an eccentric, but somewhat typical, Smoky Mountaineer in travel narratives widely distributed in the late nineteenth and early twentieth centuries. Rose was first introduced as an accomplished Smoky Mountain hunter and storyteller in Wilber Zeigler and Ben Grosscup's *The Heart of the Alleghanies: Or Western North Carolina* published in 1883. Quill was also one of the most memorable mountaineers portrayed in Horace Kephart's *Our Southern Highlanders* (1913) and was identified as a "picturesque blockader" by John Preston Arthur in his *Western North Carolina: A History* (1914). Each of these writers compiled a corpus of Quill Rose anecdotes which collectively have served to reinforce the popular stereotypical image of the Smoky Mountaineer.

Quill was born on May 4, 1841, in Cades Cove and christened Aquila Lian Rose, apparently in reference to a passage in Acts 18:2 and the Latin word for eagle. Quill married Levisa Emeline Hyde, who was part Cherokee and went by the name Vicie. Quill valued his privacy and did not want any suspicious "revenooeres" showing up unseen at his place of business. His home here on the upper reaches of Eagle Creek was, as Kephart noted, where "all roads and trails 'wiggled and winged around' so that some families were several miles from a neighbor. Fifteen homes had no wagon road and could be reached by no vehicle other than a narrow sled. Quill Rose had not even a sled path, but journeyed full five miles to the nearest wagon road." On an October day thirty years before Kephart recorded his observations of Quill Rose, a party led by outdoorsman Wilbur Zeigler ventured to meet the mountaineer at his cabin on Eagle Creek. They approached the cabin just after twilight: "Across our path, through the laurel appeared a vista of cleared land embosomed in a dark forest. The starlight revealed it. In the center stood a double-log house, with a mud-daubed stone chimney at each low gable, above which flying sparks made visible a column of smoke. The two doors were open, and through these streamed the lights from the fireplaces. No windows marred the structure; but chinks, through which one might easily stick his rifle to blaze away at a wild turkey in the cornfield, or at a revenue officer beyond the fence, made the exterior of the hut radiant with their filtration of light. Several low outbuildings were in the enclosure."

The inside of the cabin was no less rustic than its exterior. "On the scoured puncheon floor furtherest from the chimney, were three rough bed-steads, high with feather ticks and torn blankets. . . . No framed pictures adorned the smoky logs, but plastered all over the end where rose the chimney, was an assortment of startling illustrations cut from Harper's Weeklies, Police Gazettes, and almanacs, of date (if judged by their yellowness) before the war. A few cooking implements hung against the chimney."

Another visitor to Quill Rose's mountain farm noticed, "He operated the only blacksmith shop I ever saw where the fire was blown by a fan on a shaft driven by a water wheel." The air passed through a hollow gum log with a cast iron spindle from an old wagon axle placed on the end entering the fire.

Quill was noted for being an exceptional bear hunter and storyteller. He was especially adept at making moonshine and was able to do so here on Eagle Creek where land suitable for growing corn was scarce. The more remarkable achievement, however, was Quill's ability to evade the law. His lifelong motto was "don't get ketched." Not until he was a very old man did he once get too careless and found himself apprehended by revenuers. He was taken to Asheville, accompanied by Horace Kephart and Dr. Foster Sondley, to be tried before Judge James Edmund Boyd. According to a handwritten note by Sondley, they made a deal with Judge Boyd to have Quill go free in exchange for a promise that the mountaineer would never make moonshine again.

Beyond the old Quill Rose place, the Eagle Creek Trail completes three more stream crossings within the next half-mile and then proceeds an additional 500 yards to enter a narrow creek bottom that was once occupied by Montvale Camp 11. Various pieces of logging equipment and camp refuse can be found along the bottom to the right of the trail. More artifacts, including a circular sawmill blade, steel cables, logging hooks, washtubs, and other miscellaneous logging implements can be found on the left side of the trail where it enters the Big Walnut Backcountry Campsite (#97).

The Big Walnut Camp is situated on a small gently sloping gradient cloistered by rhododendron. It is shaded immediately by tall, slender, second-growth hardwoods and more generally by the adjacent near-vertical ridge which blocks out all but the noon-day sun. The camp itself is low with respect to the surrounding terrain. During heavy rain, water often drains across the lower part of the camp.

 Just below the Big Walnut Camp, Tub Mill Creek merges with Gunna Creek to form the headwaters of Eagle Creek. Tub Mill Creek was formerly known as Locust Creek but was re-named as a tribute to Jesse Crisp, who operated a tub mill at the confluence of the two streams. Local Smoky Mountaineers also knew the stream above the confluence with Tub Mill Creek as the upper part of Eagle Creek. This upper part was later deemed to be a tributary and given the name Gunna Creek. "Gunna," a Cherokee word for turkey, was selected because it was thought to be an Indian word that whites could pronounce.

Eighty yards above the campsite, the trail crosses Gunna Creek. On the far side a short section of handmade stone wall extends along a wide level bench that harbors an upper annex of the Big Walnut Camp. The annex is quite level, drier than the lower site, and situated in an open clearing. It has the disadvantages of being rather small and a bit far removed from the food-storage cables which are back across Gunna Creek in the main campsite. The bench occupied by the upper campsite was once part of a farm field tilled by Jesse Crisp.

On leaving the Big Walnut Camp, the trail follows Gunna Creek a short distance before easing into a switchback that places the trail on a narrow berm high over the stream. The grade stiffens slightly, the track becomes uneven, and the stream below is submerged in arbors of rhododendron. The trail remains on this higher trajectory for about 500 yards before returning to a streamside course. It then follows Gunna Creek for approximately a mile before completing two more crossings of the stream. A series of switchbacks over the next mile work the trail to a higher elevation where it crosses Gunna Creek for the fourth and final time. A noticeable flat area just beyond the stream crossing was once occupied by Montvale Camp 15, the last logging camp the lumber company built in the Eagle Creek drainage. Miscellaneous pieces of industrial equipment, bits of coal, and domestic camp refuse remain as testimonies to the lumber operations. Scattered about are several other larger pieces of logging equipment abandoned by the operation at Camp 15.

From this juncture, the trail edges away from Gunna Creek following the old railroad berm as it penetrates into a boulder-strewn terrain. Most noticeable is Fodderstack Rock, a large odd-shaped boulder resembling an upright pinnacle standing along the right side of the trail. Below, Gunna Creek thunders down a steep narrow gorge clogged with boulders and rhododendron.

Above Fodderstack Rock, the trail switches away from the Gunna Creek drainage to pursue a steep course along Spence Field Branch. Here the terrain is heavily congested with boulders and shaded by hardwood forest dominated by oaks. Doghobble fills the spaces between the boulders. Feeder streams and seepages percolating across the rocky grade make the trail wet and slick in many places. Wild golden-glow, meadow parsnip, heart-leafed aster, southern harebell, partridge-berry, Queen Anne's lace, hearts-a-bustin, jewel weed, umbrella-leaf, crimson bee-balm, stinging nettle, and white snakeroot are among the many flowering species encountered as the trail gains elevation. At the one point where the trail levels out momentarily, offering a brief respite from the climbing, it crosses Spence Field Branch. The stream here is wide and shallow, buried in a field of pale and yellow jewel weeds.

Thick grass appearing at trail's edge heralds the long final approach to Spence Field. The trail follows the stream for 300 yards before turning up into an exceedingly steep climb approaching a small spring that forms the headwaters of Spence Field Branch. The spring is the most convenient water source for the Spence Field Shelter, which stands 150 yards up-trail on the southwest corner of the bald.

The shelter is a recently remodeled three-sided wooden structure with a large overhanging roof. Twelve wooden platform bunks and a few benches and tables accommodate campers. A food-storage cable is suspended across the upper yard of the shelter, and an environmentally friendly composting toilet is down the slope to the right.

The Eagle Creek Trail passes in front of the shelter and out into the open bald of Spence Field, where clusters of Allegheny serviceberry and mountain maple are interspersed across the grassy sward. Two hundred and ninety yards above the shelter, the Eagle Creek Trail terminates in an intersection with the Appalachian Trail.

LOST COVE TRAIL

Lakeshore Trail to the Appalachian Trail on Twentymile Ridge at Sassafras Gap—2.7 miles.

POINT OF DEPARTURE: The Lost Cove Trail can be reached by hiking 5.2 miles in from the west end of the Lakeshore Trail or by boat to the Lost Cove Backcountry Campsite at the head of the Eagle Creek embayment. A shuttle service to and from Eagle Creek is available from the Fontana Marina located 1.5 miles east of Fontana Village on NC28.

QUAD MAP: Fontana Dam 149-NE

0.0—Lakeshore Trail.
0.1—Lost Cove Creek.
0.2—Lost Cove Creek.
0.4—Lost Cove Creek.
0.4—Lost Cove Creek.
0.5—Chimney ruins.
0.6—Lost Cove Creek.
0.6—Lost Cove Creek.
0.7—Upper Lost Cove Backcountry Campsite (#91).
1.4—Lost Cove Creek.
1.5—Lost Cove Creek.
1.6—Lost Cove Creek.
2.7—Sassafras Gap. Appalachian Trail. Twentymile Trail exits 5.0 miles to the Twentymile Ranger Station.

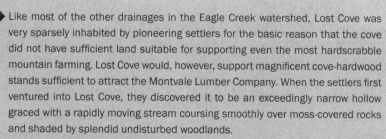

Like most of the other drainages in the Eagle Creek watershed, Lost Cove was very sparsely inhabited by pioneering settlers for the basic reason that the cove did not have sufficient land suitable for supporting even the most hardscrabble mountain farming. Lost Cove would, however, support magnificent cove-hardwood stands sufficient to attract the Montvale Lumber Company. When the settlers first ventured into Lost Cove, they discovered it to be an exceedingly narrow hollow graced with a rapidly moving stream coursing smoothly over moss-covered rocks and shaded by splendid undisturbed woodlands.

When Montvale finished logging Lost Cove, the company pulled up stakes and left behind a railroad grade that was later adapted as the course for the Lost Cove Trail. The grade up Lost Cove was a spur that exited the main line near what is today the Lost Cove Backcountry Campsite (#90) on the Eagle Creek embayment. The spur line followed a streamside course up Lost Cove Creek. Today the lower 700 yards of the old spur line has been apportioned to the Lakeshore Trail. The Lost Cove Trail, accordingly, begins where the Lakeshore Trail turns, leaves the old railroad grade, and begins climbing the flank of Snakeden Ridge and out of Lost Cove.

The Lost Cove Trail eases away from the Lakeshore Trail and into the draw on a wide level track marred only by its occasional unevenness. Within the first hundred yards, it encounters the first of ten stream crossings that occur within the span of two miles. In most instances Lost Cove Creek can be cleared by rock-hopping, however, some of the lower elevation crossings require wading when the stream is swollen from rain and snowmelt. After the first crossing, the trail maintains an exceedingly pleasant course, staying to the old railroad trace and fording the stream at intervals varying from slightly more than 350 yards to less than sixty yards.

After completing the fifth crossing, the trail enters a level tract that was once occupied by Montvale Camp 17, built in 1921. Prior to Montvale's arrival, a sawmill stood along the left bank of Lost Cove Creek. Will L. Meyer, one of the few settlers in Lost Cove, maintained a cabin on the right side of the stream. A partial chimney standing in the bench above the stream may be a remnant from Meyer's cabin. The chimney ruin is immediately adjacent to a small wooden bridge that spans a nearby feeder stream.

In 1899 Will Meyer built a newer house and a grist mill about 500 yards upstream near the confluence of Cold Spring Branch and Lost Cove Creek. Meyer's second homesite is now occupied by the Upper Lost Cove Backcountry Campsite (#91), a small, rough, bare plat that lies astride the trail. In the middle of the camp is a fine example of a birch tree standing up off the ground as though it were propped up on its roots. Birch trees in the Smokies often germinate on fallen host logs and, as the tree grows, its roots extend downward through the host and eventually to the ground beneath. In time, when the host log rots away, the birch remains standing stilt-like on the extended roots.

The left side of the Upper Lost Cove Camp is cloistered in rhododendron thickets, affording the camper some seclusion from the trail. The right side of the camp is exposed and hardly distinguishable from the course of the trail. Water is readily available from Lost Cove Creek just a few yards behind the camp.

Above the Upper Lost Cove Camp, the grade stiffens perceptibly and the cove narrows, pressing the trail and stream into closer proximity. Here, the terrain becomes noticeably rocky and the soil of poorer quality, although the abundance of moisture and intermittent shade makes this a splendid environment for spring wildflowers. Second-growth oaks are the dominant tree species, and grapevines are the most conspicuous of the woody growth. After three additional crossings of Lost Cove Creek, the trail leaves the drainage to begin a series of wide switchbacks that terminate a mile farther in Sassafras Gap on Twentymile Ridge. The course through the switchbacks is exceedingly steep, and the track is rough. The climb is arguably among the most difficult of any trail in the Smokies. At Sassafras Gap, the Lost Cove Trail terminates into the Appalachian Trail, following along the spine of Twentymile Ridge. Rising into the gap on the opposite side is the Twentymile Trail leading in five miles from the Twentymile Ranger Station. A half-mile south along the Appalachian Trail an access trail exits left 200 yards to the Shuckstack fire tower. The old fire tower is the only good vantage point in this part of the Smokies.

TWENTYMILE TRAIL

Twentymile Ranger Station to the Appalachian Trail at Sassafras Gap—5.0 miles.

POINT OF DEPARTURE: From Tennessee drive US129 ("The Dragon") to NC28. Turn left on NC28, and drive to the access road to the Twentymile Ranger Station. From North Carolina drive NC28 west to the access road to the Twentymile Ranger Station. The Twentymile Trail begins on the road above the ranger station.

QUAD MAPS: Tapoco 149-NW

Fontana Dam 149-NE

0.0—Twentymile Ranger Station.

0.5—Moore Spring Branch. Bridge. Wolf Ridge Trail exits left 6.3 miles to the Gregory Bald Trail at Sheep Pen Gap.

0.6—Access path exits right to Twentymile Creek Cascade.

1.5—Twentymile Creek. Bridge.

1.7—Twentymile Creek. Bridge.

1.8—Twentymile Creek Backcountry Campsite (#93).

1.8—Twentymile Creek. Bridge.

2.2—Feeder stream. Bridge.

2.4—Twentymile Creek. Bridge.

2.5—Twentymile Creek. Bridge.

3.1—Proctor Field Gap. Long Hungry Ridge Trail exits left 4.5 miles to the Gregory Bald Trail at Rich Gap. Twentymile Loop Trail exits left 2.9 miles to the Wolf Ridge Trail.

5.0—Sassafras Gap. Appalachian Trail. Lost Cove Creek Trail exits straight 2.7 miles to the Lakeshore Trail.

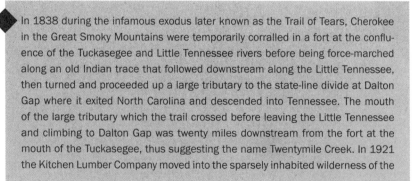

In 1838 during the infamous exodus later known as the Trail of Tears, Cherokee in the Great Smoky Mountains were temporarily corralled in a fort at the confluence of the Tuckasegee and Little Tennessee rivers before being force-marched along an old Indian trace that followed downstream along the Little Tennessee, then turned and proceeded up a large tributary to the state-line divide at Dalton Gap where it exited North Carolina and descended into Tennessee. The mouth of the large tributary which the trail crossed before leaving the Little Tennessee and climbing to Dalton Gap was twenty miles downstream from the fort at the mouth of the Tuckasegee, thus suggesting the name Twentymile Creek. In 1921 the Kitchen Lumber Company moved into the sparsely inhabited wilderness of the

Twentymile Creek drainage, grading a rail line that extended up the stream and then to the crest of Twentymile Ridge at Sassafras Gap. With the departure of the lumber company and the arrival of the park, the railroad trace was upgraded to a jeep road by the Civilian Conservation Corps to provide vehicle access to a newly built fire tower on Shuckstack, a pinnacle punctuating the south end of Twentymile Ridge. The jeep track was later officially designated by the Park Service as the Twentymile Trail.

The Twentymile Trail begins just above the Twentymile Ranger Station and follows the old CCC jeep course along the west side of the stream. The road is a wide, level, light-gravel track that proceeds an easy half-mile to cross Moore Spring Branch on a wooden bridge a few yards above the stream's confluence with Twentymile Creek. Moore Spring Branch was once known as Left Fork, identifying it as the major tributary of Twentymile Creek. The headwaters of Left Fork form up in a dell high under the lee of Gregory Bald, which harbors a bold spring and was once occupied by Moore Cabin, thus suggesting the name change from Left Fork to Moore Spring Branch.

Fifteen yards beyond the bridge, the Twentymile Trail intersects on the left the lower terminus of the Wolf Ridge Trail entering along Moore Spring Branch. From this juncture, the Twentymile Trail climbs ninety-five yards to an access path that descends on the right about a hundred yards to Twentymile Creek Cascade, where the stream spills over a series of uneven rock strata before sliding down a steeply pitched ledge.

The access path continues beyond the cascade to loop back to the Twentymile Trail about forty yards above the lower access. From here, the trail climbs briefly before resuming its easy course along the stream. In places Twentymile Creek is a maelstrom of crashing water roaring against solid boulders as it plunges down the steep gorges. The trail, however, refrains from any association with the ruggedness of the stream, remaining apart, adhering to the domestication of the jeep track. Even where the trail crosses the stream, it does so on a sturdy bridge, high and safe above the rushing water.

The trail crosses Twentymile Creek for the first time a mile above its junction with the Wolf Ridge Trail. It crosses a second time 370 yards farther, and then after another 400 yards it skirts a badly galled plat designated as the Twentymile Creek Backcountry Campsite (#93). The camp is fairly level and functional, but resembles the graded surface of a construction site, more akin to the jeep road than the ambient wilderness. A few yards upstream, a narrow annex site extends along the bank of Twentymile Creek. The annex is a bit nicer than the lower part of the camp, being level and more secluded, though its ground surface is somewhat marred by intervening roots. A food-storage cable is suspended in the main part of the campsite, and water is readily accessible from the nearby stream.

Near the entrance to the annex, the trail crosses Twentymile Creek for the third time and then continues on the jeep track for almost a half-mile before negotiating a bridge over a nameless feeder stream. From here, the trail enters an easy climb of 500 yards that ends with two crossings of Twentymile Creek within an interval of 150 yards. Within this interval, Twentymile Creek is joined by a large feeder stream entering from the east. Here the trail degenerates noticeably, becoming markedly steeper as it steers a course up the feeder stream drainage.

Slightly more than half a mile after leaving Twentymile Creek, the trail rolls up and onto a low ridgeline known as Proctor Field Gap, named for James and Milly Proctor, the only family that farmed in this part of the Twentymile watershed. In the gap, the Twentymile Trail enters a three-way intersection with the lower terminus of the Long Hungry Ridge Trail and the eastern terminus of the Twentymile Loop Trail. The Long Hungry Ridge Trail climbs to the state-line divide at Rich Gap. The Twentymile Loop Trail crosses Long Hungry Ridge to the Wolf Ridge Trail. The Twentymile Trail proceeds out of Proctor Field Gap on a fairly level course through old farm fields, soon entering the Proctor Branch drainage. The trail crosses the stream and immediately begins climbing the western flank of Twentymile Ridge. These slopes, first clear-cut by Kitchen Lumber Company in the 1920s and then burned by an unexplained fire in 1988, are recovering nicely in stands of dry-ridge hardwoods.

Two miles above Proctor Field Gap, the Twentymile Trail terminates into the Appalachian Trail at Sassafras Gap, where it also encounters the upper terminus of the Lost Cove Trail rising into the gap from Eagle Creek. A half-mile south along the Appalachian Trail, an access trail exits left 200 yards to the Shuckstack fire tower. The tower is the only good vantage point in the Smokies for surveying the entire Twentymile watershed.

WOLF RIDGE TRAIL

Twentymile Creek Trail to the Gregory Bald Trail at Sheep Pen Gap—6.3 miles.
POINT OF DEPARTURE: Hike the Twentymile Trail 0.5 mile to the bridge over Moore Spring Branch. The Wolf Ridge Trail begins at the end of the bridge.
QUAD MAPS: Fontana Dam 149-NE
Tapoco 149-NW
Calderwood 148-SW
Cades Cove 148-SE

0.0—Twentymile Creek Trail.
0.3—Moore Spring Branch. Footlog.
0.4—Moore Spring Branch. Footlog.
0.5—Moore Spring Branch. Footlog.
0.8—Moore Spring Branch. Footlog.

1.0—Moore Spring Branch. Footlog.

1.1—Twentymile Loop Trail exits right 2.9 miles to the Twentymile Trail and the Long Hungry Ridge Trail at Proctor Field Gap.

2.0—Access path exits left to the Dalton Branch Backcountry Campsite (#95).

3.3—Gap.

5.6—Parson Bald.

6.3—Sheep Pen Gap Backcountry Campsite (#13). Gregory Bald Trail exits right 0.4 mile to Gregory Bald.

Prior to the establishment of the Great Smoky Mountains National Park there were several streams in the Smokies known provisionally by the pioneer settlers as "Left Fork." The main tributary of Twentymile Creek was one such Left Fork. When it was later deemed necessary to distinguish the Left Fork of Twentymile Creek from the other Left Forks in the Smokies, the Park Nomenclature Committee recommended changing the name to Moore Spring Branch. The choice for this name originated with the fact that the headwaters of Left Fork form up at the well-known spring near the former Moore Cabin just below the summit of Gregory Bald.

Before the name was changed, the Kitchen Lumber Company built a railroad junction at the confluence of Twentymile Creek and Left Fork with the main line following upstream along Twentymile Creek and a spur line adhering closely to the tributary. Several years after Kitchen departed from the mountains, the Park Service appropriated the abandoned railroad grades for jeep roads and hiking trails. The trace following Twentymile Creek came to be known as the Twentymile Trail and that along Moore Spring Branch as the Wolf Ridge Trail. The old rail junction at the confluence of the streams is now occupied by an intersection that harbors the lower terminus of the Wolf Ridge Trail.

The initial lower course of the Wolf Ridge Trail is a wide easy grade that never deviates more than a few yards from Moore Spring Branch. Rhododendron remains dense along the stream. The adjacent slopes, clear-cut by the Kitchen logging crews, are recovering nicely in a mix of cove-hardwood species.

Five hundred and fifty yards above the old rail junction, the Wolf Ridge Trail crosses Moore Spring Branch on a footlog. Over the next three-quarters of a mile, the stream is crossed four more times, each time on a footlog and at intervals of 120 yards, 230 yards, 520 yards, and 390 yards. Throughout this exercise, the trail maintains a gentle grade, though occasionally becoming rough and rocky.

Twenty yards beyond the last stream crossing, the trail clears another footlog and then continues 145 yards to intersect the western terminus of the Twentymile Loop Trail leading in from Proctor Field Gap. At this juncture, the Wolf Ridge Trail turns left and enters a straitened hollow following a single-file berm along the slope above Dalton Branch. The grade remains unchanged, but the track becomes a hard-packed dirt course with occasional rocky patches.

Dalton Branch is associated with nearby Dalton Gap, named for John T. Dalton, a veteran of the War of 1812 who settled in the area shortly after his marriage to Mildred Metcalf in 1828. Dalton was retained by Joe Welch to maintain the western end of the so-called Welch River Road in exchange for a mountain farm and pasture land along the river. An old Indian trace through Dalton Gap was often remembered as the route by which the Cherokee were herded out of the mountains on the Trail of Tears.

About a mile above the Twentymile Loop intersection, the Wolf Ridge Trail enters a readily noticeable flat tract where it executes a sharp switchback to the right. At the point of the switchback, an access path exits to the left, immediately crosses a large feeder stream, and continues 250 yards to the Dalton Branch Backcountry Campsite (#95).

The Dalton Branch Camp is a rough galled gradient once occupied by a large logging camp maintained by the Kitchen Lumber Company. The site is badly sloped, yielding only a few level spots around the upper perimeter of the camp. Though well secluded, the site is generally unattractive, still bearing many rough scars from its service as a logging camp. A food-storage cable is suspended along the edge of the campsite, and water is accessible from Dalton Branch, reached by a steep path descending from the lower far corner of the campsite.

At the switchback, the Wolf Ridge Trail leaves the Dalton Branch drainage for a steep climb up the west flank of Wolf Ridge. After a little more than a mile, the trail reaches a gap on the crest of the ridge, where it intersects the faint trace of an older trail running along the spine of the ridge. The trace is the vestige of a trail that once followed the length of Wolf Ridge from Parson Bald to Moore Spring Branch. The current Wolf Ridge Trail crosses the old trace, passing through the gap and continuing its climb along the east flank of the ridge. Shortly, it turns back and crosses to the west flank where, with the assistance of switchbacks, it climbs steeply to reach the ridgeline again at a higher elevation. Here the trail merges imperceptibly onto the course of the old trace following down the ridgeline.

At this juncture the trail is advancing through a dry-ridge oak association that gradually diminishes in density as elevation is gained. The appearance of a fern understory alternating with weedy conditions heralds the approach into what was once the perimeter of Parson Bald. The grade lessens incrementally until leveling out as it nears the summit of the bald.

The summit of Parson Bald is marked by a small grassy plot that straddles both the trail and the state-line divide. During the earlier history of the mountains when cattle and sheep grazed along the higher peaks of the western Smokies, Parson Bald was a cleared expanse of several acres that afforded views into the Little Tennessee River Valley. With the advent of the park, livestock grazing ceased and the bald began the slow, but inexorable, process of returning to woodlands. In addition to the bald, the resurging forest also eradicated the former course of the Appalachian Trail, which passed south through the bald and down along the state-line divide to Deals Gap. The Appalachian Trail was re-routed in 1945 to follow the spine of Twentymile Ridge and exit the park at Fontana Dam.

Parson Bald was likely named for Joshua Parson, an early settler on Abrams Creek who was involved with the building of a road over the mountain from Cades Cove to North Carolina. The settler's name is also perpetuated in the instance of nearby Parson Branch Road. There is, however, another persistent strain of Smoky Mountain lore that claims the bald was occasionally used for religious camp meetings where a "parson" would hold forth with colorful preaching services. Nearby Bible Creek and Testament Branch are sometimes cited as corroborating evidence that the name Parson Bald is a reflection of a heritage of old-time gospel revivals.

Upon leaving Parson Bald, the Wolf Ridge Trail follows the old course of the Appalachian Trail north on a delightful excursion through a sylvan expanse that is more akin to a wooded park than a mountain fastness. Its large trees are widely spaced and shade an understory of little more than patches of white snakeroots. The trail, level and winding, eases along casually for a quarter-mile before edging into Sheep Pen Gap, a wide dell that straddles the Smoky divide.

The Tennessee side of the dell is occupied by the Sheep Pen Gap Backcountry Campsite (#13), the only backcountry campsite on the main Smoky divide. The Wolf Ridge Trail skirts the eastern edge of the camp and terminates into the Gregory Bald Trail precisely where the latter turns sharply to ascend to Gregory Bald.

LONG HUNGRY RIDGE TRAIL

Proctor Field Gap to the Gregory Bald Trail at Rich Gap—4.5 miles.

POINT OF DEPARTURE: Hike 3.1 miles up the Twentymile Trail to Proctor Field Gap. The Long Hungry Ridge Trail begins on the left.

QUAD MAPS: Fontana Dam 149-NE

Cades Cove 148-SE

0.0—Proctor Field Gap. Twentymile Trail. Twentymile Loop Trail.

0.1—Proctor Branch.

1.1—Feeder stream.

1.1—Upper Flats Backcountry Campsite (#92).

1.2—Greer Branch.

1.8—Twentymile Creek.

3.6—Rye Patch.

4.5—Rich Gap. Gregory Bald Trail exits left 0.7 mile to Gregory Bald.

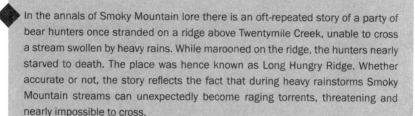

In the annals of Smoky Mountain lore there is an oft-repeated story of a party of bear hunters once stranded on a ridge above Twentymile Creek, unable to cross a stream swollen by heavy rains. While marooned on the ridge, the hunters nearly starved to death. The place was hence known as Long Hungry Ridge. Whether accurate or not, the story reflects the fact that during heavy rainstorms Smoky Mountain streams can unexpectedly become raging torrents, threatening and nearly impossible to cross.

The Long Hungry Ridge Trail begins in Proctor Field Gap three miles up the Twentymile Trail from the ranger station. Proctor Field Gap is a level bench straddling a minor ridge and bearing vestiges of stone fences, building foundations, and cleared fields remaining from a mountain farm once belonging to James and Milly Proctor. The gap is now marked by an intersection of the Twentymile Trail, the eastern terminus of the Twentymile Loop Trail, and the lower terminus of the Long Hungry Ridge Trail.

In the early 1920s the Kitchen Lumber Company built a railroad junction in Proctor Field Gap, directing one line into the Proctor Branch drainage and the other up the Twentymile Creek drainage. The Long Hungry Ridge Trail follows the latter, but after proceeding only 200 yards, encounters a rough rocky descent to an easy crossing of Proctor Branch. The trail climbs quickly from Proctor Branch and back onto the railroad trace. It remains on a level, albeit somewhat rocky, course that soon eases in alongside Twentymile Creek.

One mile above Proctor Field Gap, the trail crosses a small feeder stream and then enters a small basin known as Upper Flats where it executes a ninety-degree turn left. During Kitchen Lumber Company's tenure on Twentymile Creek, Upper Flats was occupied by a logging camp consisting of ten bunk shacks for housing loggers plus a kitchen and mess hall, a blacksmith shop, and barns for stabling teams of horses. The camp was built in 1921 and used until logging on Twentymile ceased in 1927.

Flanking both sides of the trail at the ninety-degree turn is the Upper Flats Backcountry Campsite (#92). The camp is large with excellent tent sites. To the right of the angle in the turn, a superb flat enclosure along the bank of a feeder stream harbors an excellent campsite. Immediately beyond the turn are other sites flanking both sides of the trail. The lower camp is an open-sloped gradient accompanied by a food-storage cable. The upper site is somewhat less sloped but more secluded and more heavily shaded. Water is accessible from Greer Branch, running along the west side of the campsite.

At the point of the turn, an access path leads straight ahead fifty yards to a large annex site that is shaded in a thin copse of poplar, maple, and cherry trees. The upper annex is considerably nicer than those clustered around the trail, affording seclusion plus opportunities to spread out on fairly level terrain. Access to Greer Branch is more immediate, and the campsite enjoys the convenience of its own food-storage cable.

Upon leaving the Upper Flats Camp, the trail crosses Greer Branch and then narrows to a single-file hard-packed dirt track that is frequently rough and rocky. The grade stiffens noticeably, proceeding first into the moist confines of a hollow before turning and crossing Twentymile Creek about three-quarters of a mile above the Upper Flats Camp.

Beyond Twentymile Creek, white snakeroot, mountain gentian, erect golden-rod, white wood aster, and ranks of weedy undergrowth encroach on the course until it emerges into the dry-woods conditions of an oak association. A switchback directs the trail west across the face of the mountain and through another stretch of weedy terrain. Almost two miles above the Twentymile Creek crossing, the trail eases up onto a flat ridgeline where it turns sharply right and proceeds into a shallow basin known as the Rye Patch where spiderworts are abundant among the bright red and yellow of fire pinks and sundrops.

The Rye Patch is a gently sloped gradient that extends from the ridge almost to the spine of the main Smoky divide. As its name suggests, the basin was once tilled as farmland. An old story of a fight between two bulls at the Rye Patch further suggests that the field was likewise used as pasture land.

According to a story recorded by Alberta and Carson Brewer in *Valley So Wild*, Russell Gregory built a two-story log house on the North Carolina side of the main divide near the Rye Patch. Gregory grew vegetables and maintained a rye field near the house, thus giving rise to the name Rye Patch. After Gregory's family left the Rye Patch, the second story of the house was removed, leaving the lower story as a herder's cabin.

In the eighty or so years since grazing and tillage in the Rye Patch ceased, the basin has reverted to a thinly forested enclave of low trees interspersed over a rather uniform undergrowth of flimsy weeds. The trail winds among the trees and weeds for the better part of a mile before rolling up onto the state-line divide and terminating into the Appalachian Trail on the east side of Rich Gap.

Prior to being known as Rich Gap, this wide swag in the state-line divide was called Gant Lot. When browsing stock roamed the Rye Patch and other grassy fields on the divide, herders rounded the cattle up and confined them to rudimentary split-rail pens at Gant Lot to be collected by their owners in the fall and driven down the mountain to the markets in Maryville and Knoxville. Owners late in retrieving their cattle often found them gaunt from being held for extended periods in the small enclosures. The mountaineers' corruption of the word gaunt resulted in the name Gant Lot.

TWENTYMILE LOOP TRAIL

Wolf Ridge Trail to the Twentymile Trail and the Long Hungry Ridge Trail at Proctor Field Gap—2.9 miles.

POINT OF DEPARTURE: Hike 1.1 miles up the Wolf Ridge Trail. The Twentymile Loop Trail begins on the right.

QUAD MAP: Fontana Dam 149-NE

0.0—Wolf Ridge Trail.
0.1—Moore Spring Branch. Footlog.
1.5—Long Hungry Ridge.
2.4—Feeder stream.
2.5—Twentymile Creek. Footlog.
2.8—Proctor Branch. Footlog.
2.9—Proctor Field Gap. Long Hungry Ridge Trail exits left 4.5 miles to the Gregory Bald Trail at Rich Gap. Twentymile Trail exits right 3.1 miles to the Twentymile Ranger Station and left 1.9 miles to the Appalachian Trail at Sassafras Gap.

Twentymile Creek is separated from its main tributary, Moore Spring Branch, by Long Hungry Ridge, a gently rounded spur that extends south from the main Smoky divide near Gregory Bald. Beginning in 1921, the Kitchen Lumber Company routed railroad lines up Twentymile Creek and Moore Spring Branch with a junction connecting the two rail lines near the confluence of the streams. With the departure of the lumber company in 1927 and the arrival of the park, the rail lines were converted to hiking trails and given the names Twentymile Trail and Wolf Ridge Trail.

Several years later, a trail linking the two older trails further up the mountain was built through a gap in Long Hungry Ridge. This connector, named the Twentymile Loop Trail, begins on its west end along the Wolf Ridge Trail at a vestigial junction that was once part of an old Indian trace that crossed the mountain at Dalton Gap.

It ends in Proctor Field Gap at the Twentymile Trail. The Twentymile Loop Trail affords a moderately easy round-trip course up Moore Spring Branch, across Long Hungry Ridge, and then returning by Twentymile Creek. Including the half-mile up and back from the Twentymile Ranger Station, the return trip by way of the Twentymile Loop is slightly less than eight miles.

From its western terminus, the Twentymile Loop Trail enters immediately onto a well-graded easy course up a rhododendron-cloistered hollow draining Moore Spring Branch. Two hundred and seventy yards upstream, the trail proceeds over Moore Spring Branch on a footlog and begins climbing up and out of the hollow. From here until reaching the crest of Long Hungry Ridge, the grade remains moderately steep and the course a superb track underfoot.

About a mile and a half above the Moore Spring Branch crossing, the grade moderates briefly while the trail winds through a minor gap in Long Hungry Ridge. Once through the gap, it begins descending on a moderately steep grade following a rather narrow berm for a mile before dropping into a hollow and crossing a nameless feeder stream. From this juncture, the grade levels out nicely, and the trail resumes its winding course, always cushioned by an abundance of needles shed by the shading pines.

Two hundred yards beyond the feeder crossing, the trail encounters a footlog over Twentymile Creek. After crossing, it turns up and into another hollow, continuing for 500 yards to clear a footlog over Proctor Branch. A final 220-yard climb through pines stands reaches a three-way intersection in Proctor Field Gap. Immediately on the left, the Long Hungry Ridge Trail exits to climb 4.5 miles to the Gregory Bald Trail at Rich Gap. Angling obliquely through the opposite side of Proctor Field Gap is the Twentymile Trail, climbing 5.0 miles from the Twentymile Ranger Station to the Appalachian Trail at Sassafras Gap on Twentymile Ridge. The Twentymile Loop Trail terminates in Proctor Field Gap.

I have never wanted to leave the top of a mountain.

—Harvey Broome